Collins
gem

D1585653

ENGLISH
DICTIONARY
& THESAURUS

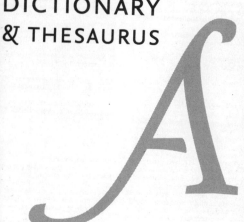

Published by Collins
An imprint of HarperCollins Publishers
Westerhill Road
Bishopbriggs
Glasgow G64 2QT

Sixth edition 2016

10 9 8 7 6 5

ISBN 978-0-00-814171-4

Collins® and Collins Gem® are registered trademarks of HarperCollins Publishers Limited

www.collinsdictionary.com
www.collins.co.uk/languagesupport

Typeset by Davidson Publishing Solutions, Glasgow

Printed in Italy by GRAFICA VENETA S.p.A.

The contents of this publication are believed correct at the time of printing. Nevertheless the Publisher can accept no responsibility for errors or omissions, changes in the detail given or for any expense or loss thereby caused.

HarperCollins does not warrant that any website mentioned in this title will be provided uninterrupted, that any website will be error free, that defects will be corrected, or that the website or the server that makes it available are free of viruses or bugs. For full terms and conditions please refer to the site terms provided on the website.

A catalogue record for this book is available from the British Library.

If you would like to comment on any aspect of this book, please contact us at the given address or online.
E-mail: dictionaries@harpercollins.co.uk
 facebook.com/collinsdictionary
 @collinsdict

Acknowledgements
We would like to thank those authors and publishers who kindly gave permission for copyright material to be used in the Collins Corpus. We would also like to thank Times Newspapers Ltd for providing valuable data.

Editors: Ian Brookes, Mary O'Neill
For the publisher: Gerry Breslin, Hannah Dove, Kerry Ferguson

Contents

iv
Abbreviations

1–631
Collins Gem Dictionary and Thesaurus

Supplement:
Punctuation and Spelling

How to use this Dictionary and Thesaurus

Main entry words from the Dictionary with a corresponding entry in the Thesaurus are marked with a ❶.

The thesaurus gives the main entry word in bold, followed by its part of speech and a list of synonyms. Key synonyms are preceded by an = symbol and highlighted in bold. Antonyms are preceded by a ≠ symbol and are highlighted in bold.

Synonyms belonging to different meanings of the word are separated by a semicolon, and a change in part of speech is indicated by an arrow, eg

> **account** *n* = **description**, report, story,
>   statement, version; = **importance**,
>   standing, concern/value, note
>   ▷ *v* = **consider**, rate, value, judge,
>   estimate

Abbreviations

abbrev	abbreviation	Lit	Literary
adj	adjective	masc	masculine
adv	adverb	Maths	Mathematics
Afr	African	Med	Medicine
Anat	Anatomy	Mil	Military
arch	Archaic	Mus	Music
Aust	Australian	Myth	Mythology
Bot	Botany	n	noun
Brit	Britain, British	N	North(ern)
Canad	Canadian	Naut	Nautical
cap.	capital	NZ	New Zealand
Chem	Chemistry	obs	Obsolete
comb.	combining	offens	Offensive
conj	conjuction	oft.	often
Comp	Computers	orig.	originally
dial	Dialect	Pathol	Pathology
E	East(ern)	pert.	pertaining
Eng	England, English	Photog	Photography
e.g.	for example	pl	plural
esp.	especially	Poet	Poetic
etc.	et cetera	prep	preposition
fem	feminine	pron	pronoun
fig	Figurative	S Afr	South African
foll.	followed	S	South(ern)
Fr	French	Scot	Scottish
Geog	Geography	sing.	singular
Hist	History	Sl	slang
Inf	Informal	US	United States
interj	interjection	usu.	usually
kg	kilogram(s)	v	verb
km	kilometre(s)	Vulg	Vulgar
Lat	Latin	W	West(ern)
lb(s)	pound(s)		

a

a, an adj **1** the indefinite article meaning one **2** an is used before vowels

AA 1 Alcoholics Anonymous **2** Automobile Association

aardvark n S Afr. anteater

aback adv **taken aback** startled

abandon ❶ v **1** desert **2** give up ▷ n **3** freedom from inhibitions etc. **abandoned** adj **1** deserted **2** uninhibited **3** wicked

abase v humiliate, degrade

abashed adj ashamed

abate v make or become less

abattoir n slaughterhouse

abbey ❶ n **1** community of monks or nuns **2** abbey church **abbot** n head of monastery

abbreviate v shorten **abbreviation** n shortened word or phrase

abdicate v give up (throne etc.)

abdomen n belly **abdominal** adj

abduct ❶ v carry off, kidnap

aberration n **1** deviation from normal **2** lapse

abet v **abetting, abetted** help, esp. in doing wrong

abeyance n **in abeyance** not in use

abhor v **-horring, -horred** loathe **abhorrence** n **abhorrent** adj

abide ❶ v **1** endure **2** (Obs) reside **abide by** obey

ability ❶ n, pl **-ties** competence, power

abject adj **1** wretched **2** servile

ablaze adj burning

able ❶ adj capable, competent, or talented **ably** adv

abnormal ❶ adj **1** not usual or typical **2** odd **abnormally** adv **abnormality** n

aboard adv on, onto ship, train, or aircraft

--- THESAURUS ---

abandon v = **leave**, strand, ditch, forsake, run out on; = **stop**, give up, halt, pack in (Brit Inf), discontinue **≠ continue** ▷ n = **recklessness**, wildness **≠ restraint**

abbey n = **monastery**, convent, priory, nunnery, friary

abduct v = **kidnap**, seize, carry off, snatch (Sl)

abide v = **tolerate**, suffer, accept, bear, endure

ability n = **capability**, potential, competence, proficiency **≠ inability**; = **skill**, talent, expertise, competence, aptitude

able adj = **capable**, qualified, efficient, accomplished, competent **≠ incapable**

abnormal adj = **unusual**, different, odd, strange, extraordinary **≠ normal**

abolish ⓥ *v* do away with
  abolition *n*

Aborigine *n* original inhabitant of Australia

abort ⓥ *v* **1** terminate (a pregnancy) prematurely **2** end prematurely and unsuccessfully
  abortion *n* **abortive** *adj* unsuccessful

abound ⓥ *v* be plentiful

about ⓥ *adv* **1** on all sides **2** nearly **3** astir ▷ *prep* **4** round **5** near **6** concerning **about-turn** *n* turn to the opposite direction

above ⓥ *adv* **1** higher up ▷ *prep* **2** over **3** higher than, more than **4** beyond

abrasion *n* **1** place scraped (e.g. on skin) **2** a wearing down
  abrasive *n* **1** substance for grinding, polishing etc. ▷ *adj* **2** causing abrasion **3** grating

abreast *adv* side by side

abridge *v* shorten

abroad ⓥ *adv* **1** to or in a foreign country **2** at large

abrupt ⓥ *adj* **1** sudden **2** blunt **3** steep **abruptly** *adv*

abscess *n* gathering of pus

abscond *v* leave secretly

absent ⓥ *adj* **1** away **2** missing ▷ *v* **3** keep away **absence** *n*
  absentee *n* one who stays away
  absently *adv*

absolute ⓥ *adj* **1** complete **2** unrestricted **3** pure **absolutely** *adv* **1** completely ▷ *interj* **2** certainly

absolve *v* free from, pardon

absorb ⓥ *v* **1** suck up **2** engross **3** take in **absorption** *n*
  absorbent *adj*

abstain *v* refrain **abstention** *n*
  abstinence *n*

THESAURUS

abolish *v* = **do away with**, end, destroy, eliminate, cancel ≠ **establish**

abort *v* = **terminate** (*a pregnancy*), miscarry; = **stop**, end, finish, check, arrest

abound *v* = **be plentiful**, thrive, flourish, be numerous, proliferate

about *prep* = **regarding**, on, concerning, dealing with, referring to; = **near**, around, close to, nearby, beside ▷ *adv* = **approximately**, around, almost, nearly, approaching

above *prep* = **over**, upon, beyond, on top of, exceeding ≠ **under**; = **senior to**, over, ahead of, in charge of, higher than

abroad *adv* = **overseas**, out of the country, in foreign lands, everywhere, here and there

abrupt *adj* = **sudden**, unexpected, rapid, surprising, quick ≠ **slow**; = **curt**, brief, short, rude, impatient ≠ **polite**

absent *adj* = **away**, missing, gone, elsewhere, unavailable ≠ **present**; = **absent-minded**, blank, vague, distracted, vacant ≠ **alert**

absolute *adj* = **complete**, total, perfect, pure, sheer; = **supreme**, sovereign, unlimited, ultimate, full

absorb *v* = **soak up**, suck up, receive, digest, imbibe; = **engross**, involve, engage, fascinate, rivet

abstemious *adj* sparing in eating and drinking

abstract ❶ *adj* 1 existing only in the mind 2 not concrete ▷ *n* 3 summary ▷ *v* 4 remove 5 summarize **abstracted** *adj* preoccupied **abstraction** *n*

abstruse *adj* hard to understand

absurd ❶ *adj* ridiculous **absurdity** *n*

abundant ❶ *adj* plentiful **abundantly** *adv* **abundance** *n* great amount

abuse ❶ *v* 1 misuse 2 address rudely. ▷ *n* 3 wrong treatment 4 insulting comments **abusive** *adj* **abusively** *adv*

abut *v* **abutting, abutted** adjoin

abysmal *adj* 1 immeasurable, very great 2 (*Inf*) extremely bad **abysmally** *adv*

abyss *n* very deep gulf or pit

AC alternating current

acacia *n* gum-yielding tree or shrub

academy *n, pl* **-mies** 1 society to advance arts or sciences 2 institution for specialized training 3 (*Scot*) secondary school

academic *adj* 1 of a place of learning 2 theoretical ▷ *n* 3 member of college or university

accede *v* 1 agree 2 attain (office etc.)

accelerate ❶ *v* (cause to) increase speed **acceleration** *n* **accelerator** *n* mechanism to increase speed

accent ❶ *n* 1 stress or pitch in speaking 2 mark to show this 3 style of pronunciation ▷ *v* 4 emphasize

accentuate *v* stress, emphasize

accept ❶ *v* 1 take, receive 2 admit, believe 3 agree to **acceptable** *adj* **acceptance** *n*

access ❶ *n* 1 right or means of entry ▷ *v* 2 (*Comp*) obtain (data) **accessible** *adj* easy to approach **accessibility** *n*

—— THESAURUS ——

abstract *adj* = **theoretical**, general, academic, speculative, indefinite ≠ **actual** ▷ *n* = **summary**, résumé, outline, digest, epitome ≠ **expansion** ▷ *v* = **extract**, draw, pull, remove, separate ≠ **add**

absurd *adj* = **ridiculous**, crazy (*Inf*), silly, foolish, ludicrous ≠ **sensible**

abundant *adj* = **plentiful**, full, rich, liberal, generous ≠ **scarce**

abuse *n* = **maltreatment**, damage, injury, hurt, harm; = **insults**, blame, slights,

put-downs, censure; = **misuse**, misapplication ▷ *v* = **ill-treat**, damage, hurt, injure, harm ≠ **care for**; = **insult**, offend, curse, put down, malign ≠ **praise**

accelerate *v* = **increase**, grow, advance, extend, expand ≠ **fall**

accent *n* = **pronunciation**, tone, articulation, inflection, brogue ▷ *v* = **emphasize**, stress, highlight, underline, underscore

accept *v* = **receive**, take, gain, pick up, secure

access *n* = **admission**, entry, passage

accession n 1 attaining of office, right etc. 2 addition

accessory ❶ n, pl -ries 1 supplementary part of car, woman's dress etc. 2 person assisting crime

accident ❶ n 1 event happening by chance 2 mishap, esp. causing injury **accidental** adj **accidentally** adv

acclaim ❶ v 1 applaud, praise ▷ n 2 applause **acclamation** n

acclimatize v accustom to new climate or environment

accolade n 1 public approval 2 honour 3 token of knighthood

accommodate ❶ v 1 supply, esp. with lodging 2 oblige 3 adapt **accommodating** adj obliging **accommodation** n lodgings

accompany ❶ v -nying, -nied 1 go with 2 supplement 3 occur with 4 play music to support a soloist **accompaniment** n

accomplice n one assisting another in crime

accomplish v 1 carry out 2 finish **accomplished** adj 1 complete 2 proficient

accord ❶ n 1 agreement, harmony ▷ v 2 (cause to) be in accord with 3 grant **according to** 1 as stated by 2 in conformity with **accordingly** adv 1 as the circumstances suggest 2 therefore

accordion n musical instrument with bellows and reeds

accost v approach and speak to

account ❶ n 1 report 2 importance 3 statement of moneys received, paid, or owed 4 person's money held in bank ▷ v 5 regard as 6 give reason, answer (for) **accountable** adj responsible **accountancy** n keeping, preparation of business accounts **accountant** n **accounting** n

accoutrements pl n 1 equipment, esp. military 2 trappings

accredited adj authorized, officially recognized

accessory n = **extra**, addition, supplement, attachment, adjunct; = **accomplice**, partner, ally, associate (in crime), assistant

accident n = **crash**, smash, wreck, collision; = **misfortune**, disaster, tragedy, setback, calamity

acclaim v = **praise**, celebrate, honour, cheer, admire ▷ n = **praise**, honour, celebration, approval, tribute ≠ **criticism**

accommodate v = **house**, put up, take in, lodge, shelter; = **help**, support, aid, assist, cooperate

with; = **adapt**, fit, settle, alter, adjust

accompany v = **go with**, lead, partner, guide, attend; = **occur with**, belong to, come with, supplement, go together with

accord n = **treaty**, contract, agreement, arrangement, settlement

account n = **description**, report, story, statement, version; = **importance**, standing, concern/ value, note ▷ v = **consider**, rate, value, judge, estimate

a

DICTIONARY

accrue v **-cruing, -crued 1** be added **2** result

accumulate ❶ v **1** gather **2** collect **accumulation** n

accurate ❶ adj exact, correct **accurately** adv **accuracy** n

accursed adj **1** under a curse **2** detestable

accuse ❶ v **1** charge with wrongdoing **2** blame **accusation** n

accustom ❶ v make used to, familiarize **accustomed** adj **1** usual **2** used (to) **3** in the habit (of)

ace ❶ n **1** one at dice, cards, dominoes **2** (Tennis) winning serve **3** (Inf) expert

acetylene n colourless, flammable gas

ache ❶ n **1** continuous pain ▷ v **2** to be in pain **aching** adj

achieve ❶ v accomplish, gain

achievement n

acid ❶ adj **1** sharp, sour ▷ n **2** (Chem) compound which combines with bases to form salts **acidic** adj **acidity** n

acknowledge ❶ v **1** admit, recognize **2** say one has received **acknowledgment, acknowledgement** n

acme n highest point

acne n pimply skin disease

acorn n fruit of the oak tree

acoustic adj of sound and hearing **acoustics** pl n **1** science of sounds **2** features of room or building as regards sounds heard in it

acquaint v make familiar, inform **acquaintance** n **1** person known **2** personal knowledge

acquiesce v agree, consent **acquiescence** n

acquire ❶ v gain, get **acquisition** n **1** act of getting **2** material gain

THESAURUS

accumulate v = **build up**, increase, be stored, collect, gather ≠ **disperse**

accurate adj = **precise**, close, correct, careful, strict ≠ **inaccurate**

accuse v = **charge with**, indict for, impeach for, censure with, incriminate for ≠ **absolve**

accustom v = **familiarize**, train, discipline, adapt, instruct

ace n (Cards, dice, etc.) = **one**, single point; (Inf) = **expert**, star, champion, authority, professional ▷ adj (Inf) = **great**, brilliant, fine, wonderful, excellent

ache v = **hurt**, suffer, burn, pain, smart ▷ n = **pain**, discomfort, suffering, hurt, throbbing (Inf)

achieve v = **accomplish**, fulfil, complete, gain, perform

acid adj = **sour**, tart, pungent, acerbic, acrid ≠ **sweet**; = **sharp**, cutting, biting, bitter, harsh ≠ **kindly**

acknowledge v = **admit**, own up, allow, accept, reveal ≠ **deny**; = **greet**, address, notice, recognize, salute ≠ **snub**; = **reply to**, answer, notice, recognize, respond to ≠ **ignore**

acquire v = **get**, win, buy, receive, gain ≠ **lose**

acquit ❶ v -quitting, -quitted
 1 declare innocent 2 settle (a debt)
 3 behave (oneself) **acquittal** n

acre n measure of land, 4840
 square yards

acrid adj pungent, sharp

acrobat n one skilled in gymnastic
 feats, esp. in circus etc. **acrobatic**
 adj **acrobatics** pl n

acronym n word formed from
 initial letters of other words

across adv/prep 1 crosswise
 2 from side to side 3 on or to the
 other side

acrylic n synthetic fibre

ACT Australian Capital Territory

act ❶ n 1 thing done, deed
 2 doing 3 law or decree 4 section
 of a play 5 performance, as in a
 play 6 exert force, work, as in
 mechanism 7 behave **acting**
 adj temporary **action** n
 1 operation 2 deed 3 gesture
 4 expenditure of energy 5 battle
 6 lawsuit **active** adj 1 in
 operation 2 busy, occupied
 3 brisk, energetic **activate** v
 actively adv **activity** n **actor,**

actress n one who acts in a play,
 film etc.

actual ❶ adj 1 existing in the
 present 2 real **actuality** n
 actually adv really, indeed

actuary n, pl -aries expert in
 insurance statistics

actuate v activate

acumen n keen discernment

acupuncture n medical
 treatment by insertion of needles
 into the body

acute ❶ adj 1 shrewd 2 sharp
 3 severe ▷ n 4 accent (´) over
 letter **acutely** adv

AD anno Domini

ad n abbrev. of ADVERTISEMENT

adage n proverb

adagio adj/n, pl -gios (Mus) slow
 (passage)

adamant ❶ adj unyielding

Adam's apple projecting part at
 front of throat

adapt ❶ v 1 alter for new use
 2 modify 3 change **adaptable** adj
 adaptation n **adaptor, -er** n
 device for connecting two electrical
 appliances to a single socket

—————————— THESAURUS ——————————

acquit v = **clear**, free, release,
 excuse, discharge **≠ find guilty**

act v = **do something**, perform,
 function, pretend to be,
 impersonate; = **perform**, mimic
 ▷ n = **deed**, action, performance,
 achievement, undertaking;
 = **pretence**, show, front,
 performance, display; = **law**, bill,
 measure, resolution, decree;
 = **performance**, show, turn,
 production, routine

actual adj = **real**, substantial,
 concrete, definite, tangible
 ≠ theoretical

acute adj = **serious**, important,
 dangerous, critical, crucial;
 = **sharp**, shooting, powerful,
 violent, severe

adamant adj = **determined**, firm,
 fixed, stubborn, uncompromising
 ≠ flexible

adapt v = **adjust**, change, alter,
 modify, accommodate

DICTIONARY

add ❶ v 1 join 2 increase by 3 say further **addition** n **additional** adj **additionally** adv **additive** n something added, esp. to foodstuffs

addendum n, pl **-da** thing to be added

adder n small poisonous snake

addict ❶ n one who has become dependent on something **addicted** adj **addiction** n

address ❶ n 1 direction on letter 2 place where one lives 3 speech ▷ v 4 mark destination 5 speak to 6 direct

adenoids pl n tissue at back of nose

adept ❶ adj 1 skilled ▷ n 2 expert

adequate ❶ adj 1 sufficient, suitable 2 not outstanding **adequacy** n **adequately** adv

adhere v 1 stick to 2 be firm in opinion etc. **adherence** n **adherent** n **adhesion** n **adhesive** adj/n

ad hoc adj/adv for a particular occasion only

adieu interj farewell

adjacent ❶ adj lying near, next (to)

adjective ❶ n word which qualifies a noun

adjoin ❶ v be next to 2 join

adjourn ❶ v 1 close (meeting etc.) temporarily 2 (Inf) move elsewhere **adjournment** n

adjudge v 1 declare 2 decide

adjudicate v 1 judge 2 sit in judgment **adjudication** n **adjudicator** n

adjunct n person or thing added or subordinate

adjure v earnestly entreat

adjust ❶ v 1 adapt 2 alter slightly, regulate **adjustable** adj **adjustment** n

adjutant n military officer who assists superiors

ad-lib v **-libbing, -libbed** 1 improvise ▷ n 2 improvised remark

administer ❶ v 1 manage 2 dispense, as justice etc.

THESAURUS

add v = **count up**, total, reckon, compute, add up ≠ **take away**; = **include**, attach, supplement, adjoin, augment

addict n = **junkie** (Inf), freak (Inf), fiend (Inf); = **fan**, lover, nut (Sl), follower, enthusiast

address n = **location**, home, place, house, point; = **speech**, talk, lecture, discourse, sermon ▷ v = **speak to**, talk to, greet, hail, approach

adept adj = **skilful**, able, skilled, expert, practised ≠ **unskilled** ▷ n = **expert**, master, genius, hotshot (Inf), dab hand (Brit Inf)

adequate adj = **sufficient**, enough ≠ **insufficient**

adjacent adj = **adjoining**, neighbouring, nearby ≠ **far away**

adjoin v = **connect with** or **to**, join, link with, touch on, border on

adjourn v = **postpone**, delay, suspend, interrupt, put off ≠ **continue**

adjust v = **adapt**, change, alter, accustom, regulate; = **change**, reform, alter, adapt, revise

administer v = **manage**, run, control, direct, handle; = **dispense**, give, share, provide, apply

administrate v manage (an organization) **administration** n **1** management, supervision **2** governing body **administrative** adj **administrator** n

admiral n naval officer of highest rank

admire ① v regard with approval, respect, or wonder **admirable** adj **admirably** adv **admiration** n **admirer** n **admiring** adj

admit ① v **-mitting, -mitted** **1** confess **2** accept as true **3** allow **4** let in **admissible** adj **admission** n **1** permission to enter **2** entrance fee **3** confession **admittance** n permission to enter **admittedly** adv

admonish v **1** reprove **2** exhort **admonition** n

ad nauseam (Lat) to a boring or disgusting extent

ado n fuss

adolescence ① n period of life just before maturity **adolescent** n/adj young (person)

adopt ① v **1** take as one's child **2** take up, as principle, resolution **adoption** n

adore ① v **1** love intensely **2** worship **adorable** adj **adoration** n **adoring** adj

adorn ① v decorate

adrenal adj near the kidney **adrenalin** n hormone secreted by adrenal glands

adrift ① adj/adv **1** drifting **2** (Inf) detached **3** (Inf) off course

adroit adj **1** skilful **2** clever **adroitly** adv

adulation n flattery

adult ① adj **1** grown-up **2** mature ▷ n **3** mature person, animal or plant

adulterate v make impure by addition **adulteration** n

adultery n, pl **-teries** sexual unfaithfulness of a husband or wife **adulterer** n **adulterous** adj

advance ① v **1** bring forward **2** suggest **3** lend (money) **4** go forward **5** improve in position or

—————— THESAURUS ——————

admire v = **respect**, value, prize, honoured, praise ≠ **despise**

admit v = **confess**, confide, own up, come clean (Inf); = **allow**, agree, accept, reveal, grant ≠ **deny**; = **let in**, allow, receive, accept, introduce ≠ **keep out**

adolescence n = **teens**, youth, minority, boyhood, girlhood

adopt v = **take in**, raise, nurse, mother, rear ≠ **abandon**

adore v = **love**, honour, admire, worship, esteem ≠ **hate**

adorn v = **decorate**, array,

embellish, festoon

adrift adj = **drifting**, afloat, unmoored, unanchored; = **aimless**, goalless, directionless, purposeless

adult n = **grown-up**, mature person, person of mature age, grown or grown-up person, man or woman ▷ adj = **fully grown**, mature, grown-up, of age, ripe

advance v = **progress**, proceed, come forward, make inroads, make headway ≠ **retreat**; = **accelerate**, speed, promote, hasten, bring forward; = **improve**, rise, develop, value ▷ *n* **6** progress **7** movement forward **8** improvement **9** a loan ▷ *adj* **10** ahead in time or position

advanced *adj* **1** at a late stage **2** not elementary **3** ahead of the times **advancement** *n*

advantage ❶ *n* more favourable position or state **advantageous** *adj*

advent *n* **1** arrival, coming **2** (with cap.) the four weeks before Christmas

adventure ❶ *n* exciting undertaking or happening **adventurous** *adj*

adverb *n* word added to verb etc. to modify meaning

adverse ❶ *adj* **1** hostile **2** unfavourable **adversary** *n* enemy **adversely** *adv* **adversity** *n* distress, misfortune

advert ❶ *n* (*Inf*) advertisement

advertise ❶ *v* **1** publicize **2** give notice of, esp. in newspapers etc.

3 make public request (for) **advertisement** *n* **advertising** *adj/n*

advice ❶ *n* **1** counsel **2** notification

advocate ❶ *n* **1** one who pleads the cause of another, esp. in court of law **2** (*Scot*) barrister ▷ *v* **3** recommend **advocacy** *n*

aeon *n* long period of time

aerate *v* **1** charge liquid with gas **2** expose to air

aerial *adj* **1** operating in the air **2** pertaining to aircraft ▷ *n* **3** part of radio etc. receiving or sending radio waves

aerobatics *pl n* stunt flying

aerobics *pl n* exercise system designed to increase oxygen in the blood **aerobic** *adj*

aerodrome *n* airfield

aerodynamics *pl n* study of air flow, esp. round moving solid bodies **aerodynamic** *adj*

THESAURUS

pick up, progress; **= suggest**, offer, present, propose, advocate **≠ withhold** ▷ *n* **= down payment**, credit, loan, fee, deposit; **= attack**, charge, strike, assault, raid; **= improvement**, development, gain, growth, breakthrough ▷ *adj* **= prior**, early, beforehand

advantage *n* **= benefit**, help, profit, favour **≠ disadvantage**; **= lead**, sway, dominance, precedence

adventure *n* **= venture**, experience, incident, enterprise, undertaking

adverse *adj* **= unfavourable**,

hostile, unlucky, opposing, hostile

advert *n* (*Brit Inf*) **= advertisement**, notice, commercial, ad (*Inf*), announcement

advertise *v* **= publicize**, promote, plug (*Inf*), announce, inform

advice *n* **= guidance**, help, opinion, direction, suggestion

advocate *v* **= recommend**, support, champion, encourage, propose **≠ oppose** ▷ *n* **= supporter**, spokesman, champion, defender, campaigner; (*Law*) **= lawyer**, attorney, solicitor, counsel, barrister

aeronautics pl n science of air navigation and flying in general **aeronautical** adj

aeroplane n heavier-than-air flying machine

aerosol n (substance dispensed from) pressurized can

aerospace n earth's atmosphere and space beyond

aesthetic adj relating to principles of beauty **aesthetics** pl n study of beauty **aesthetically** adv **aesthete** n

afar adv from, at, or to, a great distance

affable adj polite and friendly

affair ❶ n 1 thing done or attended to 2 business 3 happening 4 sexual liaison ▷ pl 5 personal or business interests 6 matters of public interest

affect ❶ v 1 act on 2 move feelings 3 make show of **affectation** n show, pretence **affected** adj 1 making a pretence

2 moved 3 acted upon **affection** n fondness, love **affectionate** adj **affectionately** adv

affidavit n written statement on oath

affiliate ❶ v/n (join as an) associate **affiliation** n

affinity ❶ n, pl **-ties** 1 natural liking 2 resemblance 3 chemical attraction

affirm ❶ v 1 assert positively 2 make solemn declaration **affirmation** n **affirmative** adj/n positive (statement)

affix v fasten (to)

afflict ❶ v cause to suffer **affliction** n

affluent ❶ adj wealthy **affluence** n

afford ❶ v 1 to be able to (buy, do) 2 provide **affordable** adj

affront v/n insult

afield adv **far afield** far away

aflame adv/adj burning

afloat adv 1 floating 2 at sea

afoot adv 1 astir 2 on foot

——————— THESAURUS ———————

affair n = **matter**, business, happening, event, activity; = **relationship**, romance, intrigue, fling, liaison

affect v = **influence**, concern, alter, change, manipulate; = **emotionally move**, touch, upset, overcome, stir

affiliate v = **associate**, unite, join, link, ally

affinity n = **attraction**, liking, leaning, sympathy, inclination ≠ **hostility**; = **similarity**, relationship, connection,

correspondence, analogy ≠ **difference**

affirm v = **declare**, state, maintain, swear, assert ≠ **deny**; = **confirm**, prove, endorse, ratify, verify ≠ **refute**

afflict v = **torment**, trouble, pain, hurt, distress

affluent adj = **wealthy**, rich, prosperous, loaded (Sl), well-off ≠ **poor**

afford v = **have the money for**, manage, bear/pay for, spare; = **bear**, stand, sustain, allow yourself

aforesaid, aforementioned
adj previously mentioned
afraid ❶ adj **1** frightened
2 regretful
afresh adv again, anew
African adj of Africa **African
violet** house plant with pink or
purple flowers
aft adv towards stern of ship
after ❶ adv **1** later **2** behind
▷ prep **3** behind **4** later than **5** on
the model of **6** pursuing ▷ conj
7 later than **afters** pl n dessert
afterbirth n membrane expelled
after a birth
aftermath ❶ n result, consequence
afternoon n time from noon to
evening
aftershave n lotion applied to
face after shaving
afterwards, afterward adv
later
again ❶ adv **1** once more **2** in

addition
against ❶ prep **1** in opposition to
2 in contact with **3** opposite
agape adj/adv open-mouthed
agate n semiprecious quartz
age ❶ n **1** length of time person or
thing has existed **2** time of life
3 period of history **4** long time
5 maturity, old age ▷ v **6** make or
grow old **aged** adj **1** old ▷ pl n
2 old people **ageing** n/adj
agenda ❶ pl n list of things to be
attended to
agent ❶ n **1** one authorized to act
for another **2** person or thing
producing effect **agency** n
1 organization providing service
2 business, premises of agent
aggrandize v make greater in
size, power, or rank
aggravate ❶ v **1** make worse or
more severe **2** (Inf) annoy
aggravation n

THESAURUS

afraid adj = **scared**, frightened,
nervous, terrified, shaken
≠ **unafraid**; = **reluctant**, frightened,
scared, unwilling, hesitant
after adv = **following**, later, next,
succeeding, afterwards
aftermath n = **effects**, results,
wake, consequences, outcome
again adv = **once more**, another
time, anew, afresh; = **also**, in
addition, moreover, besides,
furthermore
against prep = **beside**, on, up
against, in contact with, abutting;
= **opposed to**, anti (Inf), hostile to,
in opposition to, averse to; = **in
opposition to**, resisting, versus,

counter to, in the opposite direction
of
age n = **years**, days, generation,
lifetime, length of existence; = **old
age**, experience, maturity,
seniority, majority ≠ **youth**
agenda n = **programme**, list, plan,
schedule, diary
agent n = **representative**, rep
(Inf), negotiator, envoy, surrogate;
= **author**, worker, vehicle,
instrument, operator
aggravate v = **make worse**,
exaggerate, intensify, worsen,
exacerbate ≠ **improve**; (Inf) =
annoy, bother, provoke, irritate,
nettle ≠ **please**

aggregate ❶ v 1 gather into mass ▷ adj 2 gathered thus ▷ n 3 mass, sum total 4 gravel etc. for concrete

aggression ❶ n 1 unprovoked attack 2 hostile activity **aggressive** adj **aggressively** adv

aggrieved adj upset, angry

aghast adj appalled

agile adj 1 nimble 2 quick **agility** n

agitate ❶ v 1 stir, shake up 2 trouble 3 stir up public opinion (for or against) **agitation** n **agitator** n

aglow adj glowing

AGM Annual General Meeting

agnostic n one who believes that we cannot know whether God exists

ago adv in the past

agog adj/adv eager, astir

agony ❶ n, pl -nies extreme suffering **agonize** v suffer agony 2 worry greatly **agonizing** adj

agoraphobia n fear of open spaces **agoraphobic** adj/n

agree ❶ v agreeing, agreed 1 be of same opinion 2 consent 3 harmonize 4 approve **agreeable** adj 1 willing 2 pleasant **agreeably** adv **agreement** n

agriculture ❶ n (science of) farming **agricultural** adj

aground adv (of boat) touching bottom

ahead ❶ adv 1 in front 2 onwards

ahoy interj ship's hailing cry

aid ❶ v/n help, support

aide ❶ n assistant

AIDS n disease that destroys the body's immune system

ail v 1 trouble 2 be ill **ailing** adj **ailment** n illness

aim ❶ v 1 direct (weapon etc.) 2 intend ▷ n 3 aiming 4 intention **aimless** n without purpose **aimlessly** adv

ain't (Nonstandard) 1 am not

— THESAURUS —

aggregate n = **total**, body, whole, amount, collection ▷ v = **combine**, mix, collect, assemble, heap

aggression n = **hostility**, malice, antagonism, antipathy, aggressiveness; = **attack**, campaign, injury, assault, raid

agitate v = **stir**, beat, shake, disturb, toss; = **upset**, worry, trouble, excite, distract ≠ **calm**

agony n = **suffering**, pain, distress, misery, torture

agree v = **concur**, be as one, sympathize, assent, see eye to eye

≠ **disagree**; = **correspond**, match, coincide, tally, conform

agriculture n = **farming**, culture, cultivation, husbandry, tillage

ahead adv = **in front**, in advance, towards the front, frontwards

aid n = **help**, backing, support, benefit, favour ≠ **hindrance** ▷ v = **help**, support, serve, sustain, assist ≠ **hinder**

aide n = **assistant**, supporter, attendant, helper, right-hand man

aim v = **try for**, seek, work for, strive ▷ n = **intention**, point, plan, goal, design

2 is not **3** are not **4** has not **5** have not

air ◐ *n* **1** (gases of) earth's atmosphere **2** breeze **3** tune **4** manner ▷ *pl* **5** affected manners ▷ *v* **6** expose to air **7** communicate, make known **airless** *adj* stuffy **airy** *adj* **1** well-ventilated **2** jaunty, nonchalant **air bed** inflatable mattress **air conditioning** control of temperature and humidity in building **aircraft** *n* **1** flying machines generally **2** aeroplane **airfield** *n* landing and taking-off area for aircraft **air force** armed force using aircraft **air gun** gun discharged by compressed air **airline** *n* company operating aircraft **airliner** *n* large passenger aircraft **air mail** mail sent by aircraft **airman** *n* member of air force **airplay** *n* performances of a record on radio **airport** *n* station for civilian aircraft **air raid** attack by aircraft **airship** *n* lighter-than-air flying machine with means of propulsion **airstrip** *n* strip of ground where aircraft can take off and land **airtight** *adj* not allowing passage of air **airworthy** *adj* fit to fly

aisle ◐ *n* passage between rows of seats

ajar *adv* partly open

akimbo *adv* with hands on hips

akin *adj* **1** related by blood **2** alike

alabaster *n* white, decorative stone

à la carte (*Fr*) selected freely from the menu

alacrity *n* eager willingness

alarm ◐ *n* **1** fright **2** apprehension **3** danger signal ▷ *v* **4** frighten **5** alert **alarming** *adj*

alas *interj* cry of grief

albatross *n* large sea bird

albino *n*, *pl* **-nos** individual lacking pigmentation

album *n* **1** book for photographs, stamps etc. **2** collection of items in book or record form

alchemy *n* medieval form of chemistry **alchemist** *n*

alcohol *n* **1** intoxicating fermented liquor **2** class of organic chemical substances **alcoholic** *adj* **1** of alcohol ▷ *n* **2** person addicted to alcoholic drink **alcoholism** *n*

alcove *n* recess

alder *n* tree related to the birch

alderman *n* formerly, senior local councillor

ale *n* kind of beer

THESAURUS

air *n* = **wind**, breeze, draught, gust, zephyr; = **atmosphere**, sky, heavens, aerosphere; = **tune**, song, theme, melody, strain; = **manner**, appearance, look, aspect, atmosphere ▷ *v* = **publicize**, reveal, exhibit, voice, express; = **ventilate**, expose, freshen, aerate

aisle *n* = **passageway**, path, lane, passage, corridor

alarm *n* = **fear**, panic, anxiety, fright, apprehension ≠ **calmness**; = **danger signal**, warning, bell, alert, siren ▷ *v* = **frighten**, scare, panic, distress, startle ≠ **calm**

alert ❶ adj **1** watchful **2** brisk ▷ n **3** warning ▷ v **4** warn **5** draw attention to **alertness** n

alfresco adv/adj in the open air

algae pl n various water plants

algebra n method of calculating, using symbols to represent quantities

Algonquin, Algonkin n **1** a member of a North American Indian people formerly living along the St Lawrence and Ottawa Rivers in Canada **2** the language of this people, a dialect of Ojibwa

alias adv **1** otherwise ▷ n **2** assumed name

alibi n plea of being elsewhere at time of crime

alien ❶ adj **1** foreign **2** different in nature **3** repugnant (to) ▷ n **4** foreigner **alienate** v **1** estrange **2** transfer **alienation** n

alight¹ ❶ v **1** get down **2** land

alight² ❶ adj **1** burning **2** lit up

align ❶ v **1** bring into line or agreement **2** ally, side (with) **alignment** n

alike ❶ adj/adv similar(ly)

alimony n allowance paid to separated or divorced spouse

alive ❶ adj **1** living **2** active **3** aware **4** swarming

alkali n substance which combines with acid and neutralizes it, forming a salt **alkaline** adj

all ❶ adj **1** the whole of, every one of ▷ adv **2** entirely ▷ n **3** the whole **4** everything, everyone **all right** adj **1** adequate, satisfactory **2** unharmed ▷ interj **3** expression of approval

allay v relieve, soothe

allege ❶ v state without proof **allegation** n **allegedly** adv

alert adj = **attentive**, awake, vigilant, watchful, on the lookout ≠ **careless** ▷ n = **warning**, signal, alarm, siren ≠ **all clear** ▷ v = **warn**, signal, inform, alarm, notify ≠ **lull**

alien adj = **foreign**, strange, imported, unknown, exotic ▷ n = **foreigner**, incomer, immigrant, stranger, outsider ≠ **citizen**

alight¹ v = **get off**, descend, get down, disembark, dismount; = **land**, light, settle, come down, descend ≠ **take off**

alight² adj = **lit up**, bright, brilliant, shining, illuminated

align v = **ally**, side, join, associate,

affiliate; = **line up**, order, range, regulate, straighten

alike adj = **similar**, close, the same, parallel, resembling ≠ **different** ▷ adv = **similarly**, identically, equally, uniformly, correspondingly ≠ **differently**

alive adj = **living**, breathing, animate, subsisting, existing ≠ **dead**; = **in existence**, existing, functioning, active, operative ≠ **inoperative**

all adj = **complete**, greatest, full, total, perfect ▷ adv = **completely**, totally, fully, entirely, absolutely

allege v = **claim**, charge, challenge, state, maintain ≠ **deny**

allegiance ❶ n loyalty, esp. to one's country

allegory n, pl **-ries** symbolic story, poem **allegorical** adj

allegro adv/adj/n, pl **-gros** (Mus) fast (passage)

allergy ❶ n, pl **-gies** abnormal sensitivity to a specific substance **allergic** adj

alleviate ❶ v ease, lessen

alley ❶ n 1 narrow street 2 enclosure for skittles

alliance ❶ n union, e.g. by treaty, agreement, or marriage

alligator n animal of crocodile family found in America

alliteration n beginning of successive words with same sound

allocate ❶ v assign as a share **allocation** n

allot v **-lotting, -lotted** allocate **allotment** n 1 distribution 2 portion of land rented for cultivation 3 portion allotted

allow ❶ v 1 permit 2 set aside

3 acknowledge **allowable** adj **allowance** n

alloy n metallic mixture

allude v refer (to) **allusion** n

allure v 1 entice ▷ n 2 attractiveness **alluring** adj

ally ❶ v, pl **-lies** 1 join by treaty, friendship etc. ▷ n 2 friend **allied** adj

almanac n calendar of tides, events etc.

almighty adj 1 all-powerful 2 (Inf) very great

almond n 1 tree of peach family 2 its edible seed

almost adv very nearly

alms pl n gifts to the poor

aloft adv 1 on high 2 overhead

alone ❶ adj/adv 1 by oneself, by itself 2 without equal, unique

along adv 1 lengthwise 2 together (with) 3 forward ▷ prep 4 over the length of **alongside** adv/prep beside

aloof adj 1 indifferent 2 at a distance

— THESAURUS —

allegiance n = **loyalty**, devotion, fidelity, obedience, constancy ≠ **disloyalty**

allergy n = **sensitivity**, reaction, susceptibility, antipathy, hypersensitivity

alleviate v = **ease**, reduce, relieve, moderate, soothe

alley n = **passage**, walk, lane, pathway, alleyway

alliance n = **union**, league, association, agreement, marriage ≠ **division**

allocate v = **assign**, grant,

distribute, designate, set aside

allow v = **permit**, approve, enable, sanction, endure ≠ **prohibit**; = **let**, permit, sanction, authorize, license ≠ **forbid**; = **give**, provide, grant, spare, devote

ally n = **partner**, friend, colleague, associate, mate ≠ **opponent**

almost adv = **nearly**, about, close to, virtually, practically

alone adj = **solitary**, isolated, separate, apart, by yourself ≠ **accompanied**

aloud ❶ adv **1** loudly **2** audibly

alphabet n set of letters used in writing a language

already ❶ adv **1** previously **2** sooner than expected

Alsatian n large wolflike dog

also ❶ adv besides, moreover **also-ran** n loser in a contest

altar n **1** Communion table **2** sacrificial table

alter ❶ v change, make or become different **alterable** adj **alteration** n

altercation n quarrel

alternate ❶ v **1** (cause to) occur by turns ▷ adj **2** in turn **3** every second **alternately** adv **alternative** n **1** one of two choices ▷ adj **2** replacing **alternatively** adv

although ❶ conj despite the fact that

altitude n height, elevation

alto n, pl **-tos** (Mus) **1** male singing voice or instrument above tenor **2** contralto

altogether ❶ adv **1** entirely **2** in total

altruism n unselfish concern for others

aluminium n light nonrusting silvery metal

always ❶ adv **1** at all times **2** for ever

am first person sing. of BE

a.m. before noon

amalgamate v mix, (cause to) combine **amalgamation** n

amass ❶ v collect in quantity

amateur ❶ n **1** one who does something for interest not money **2** unskilled practitioner **amateurish** adj

amaut, amowt n (Canad) a hood on an Eskimo woman's parka for carrying a child

amaze ❶ v surprise greatly, astound **amazing** adj

————————— THESAURUS —————————

aloud adv = **out loud**, clearly, plainly, distinctly, audibly

already adv = **before now**, before, previously, at present, by now

also adv = **and**, too, further, in addition, as well

alter v = **modify**, change, reform, vary, transform

alternate v = **interchange**, change, fluctuate, take turns, oscillate ▷ adj = **alternating**, interchanging, every other, rotating, every second

although conj = **though**, while, even if, even though, whilst

altogether adv = **absolutely**, quite, completely, totally, perfectly; = **completely**, fully, entirely, thoroughly, wholly ≠ **partially**; = **on the whole**, generally, mostly, in general, collectively

always adv = **habitually**, regularly, every time, consistently, invariably ≠ **seldom**; = **forever**, for keeps, eternally, for all time, evermore

amass v = **collect**, gather, assemble, compile, accumulate

amateur n = **nonprofessional**, outsider, layman, dilettante, layperson

amaze v = **astonish**, surprise, shock, stun, alarm

a

amazement n

ambassador ❶ n senior diplomatic representative overseas

amber n yellow fossil resin

ambidextrous adj able to use both hands with equal ease

ambience n atmosphere of a place

ambiguous ❶ adj 1 having more than one meaning 2 obscure **ambiguity** n

ambition ❶ n 1 desire for success 2 goal, aim **ambitious** adj

ambivalence n simultaneous existence of conflicting emotions

amble v/n (move at an) easy pace

ambulance n conveyance for sick or injured people

ambush v/n attack from hiding

ameliorate v improve

amen interj so be it

amenable adj 1 easily controlled 2 answerable

amend ❶ v 1 correct 2 alter **amendment** n

amenity ❶ n, pl **-ties** (oft. pl) useful or pleasant facility or service

amiable adj friendly, kindly

amicable adj friendly **amicably** adv

amid, amidst ❶ prep among

amiss adj 1 wrong ▷ adv 2 faultily

ammonia n pungent alkaline gas

ammunition ❶ n 1 projectiles that can be discharged from weapon 2 facts that can be used in argument

amnesia n loss of memory

amnesty ❶ n, pl **-ties** general pardon

amoeba n, pl **-bae, -bas** microscopic single-celled animal

amok adv **run amok** run about in a violent frenzy

among, amongst ❶ prep 1 in the midst of 2 of the number of 3 between 4 with one another

amoral adj having no moral standards

amorous adj inclined to love

amorphous adj without distinct shape

THESAURUS

ambassador n = **representative**, minister, agent, deputy, diplomat

ambiguous adj = **unclear**, obscure, vague, dubious, enigmatic ≠ **clear**

ambition n = **goal**, hope, dream, target, aim; = **enterprise**, longing, drive, spirit, desire

ambush v = **trap**, attack, surprise, deceive, dupe ▷ n = **trap**, snare, lure, waylaying

amend v = **change**, improve, reform, fix, correct

amenity n = **facility**, service,

advantage, comfort, convenience

amid, amidst prep = **during**, among, at a time of, in an atmosphere of

ammunition n = **munitions**, rounds, shot, shells, powder

amnesty n = **general pardon**, mercy, pardoning, immunity, forgiveness

among, amongst prep = **in the midst of**, with, together with, in the middle of, amid; = **in the group of**, one of, part of, included in, in the company of; = **between**, to

amount ❶ v **1** come, be equal (to)
  ▷ n **2** quantity **3** sum total
amp n **1** ampere **2** (Inf) amplifier
ampere n unit of electric current
ampersand n sign (&) meaning
  and
amphetamine n synthetic
  medicinal stimulant
amphibian n **1** animal that lives
  first in water then on land
  2 vehicle, plane adapted to land
  and water **amphibious** adj
amphitheatre n arena
  surrounded by rising tiers of seats
ample ❶ adj **1** big enough **2** large,
  spacious **amply** adv
amplify v **-fying, -fied 1** increase
  2 make bigger, louder etc.
  amplification n **amplifier** n
amplitude n spaciousness, width
amputate v cut off (limb etc.)
  amputation n
amulet n thing worn as a charm
  against evil
amuse ❶ v **1** entertain **2** cause to
  laugh or smile **amusing** adj
  amusement n
an SEE A
anachronism n something put in
  wrong historical period

anaconda n large snake which
  kills by constriction
anaemia n deficiency of red blood
  cells **anaemic** adj pale, sickly
anaesthetic ❶ n/adj (drug)
  causing loss of sensation
  anaesthetist n **anaesthetize** v
anagram n word(s) whose letters
  can be rearranged to make new
  word(s)
anal SEE ANUS
analgesic adj/n (drug) relieving
  pain
analogy ❶ n, pl **-gies** likeness in
  certain respects **analogous** adj
  similar
analysis ❶ n, pl **-ses 1** separation
  into elements or components
  2 evaluation, study **analyse** v
  1 examine critically **2** determine
  constituent parts **analyst** n
  analytical adj
anarchy ❶ n **1** absence of
  government and law **2** disorder
  anarchic adj **anarchist** n one
  who opposes all forms of
  government
anathema n **1** anything detested
  2 curse of excommunication or
  denunciation

———————————— THESAURUS ————————————

amount n = **quantity**, measure,
  size, supply, mass
ample adj = **plenty of**, generous,
  lavish, abundant, plentiful
  ≠ **insufficient**
amuse v = **entertain**, please,
  delight, charm, cheer ≠ **bore**
anaesthetic n = **painkiller**,
  narcotic, sedative, opiate, anodyne
  ▷ adj = **pain-killing**, dulling,

numbing, sedative, deadening
analogy n = **similarity**, relation,
  comparison, parallel,
  correspondence
analysis n = **examination**, test,
  inquiry, investigation,
  interpretation
anarchy n = **lawlessness**,
  revolution, riot, disorder, confusion
  ≠ **order**

anatomy ❶ n, pl **-mies 1** (study of) bodily structure **2** detailed analysis **anatomical** adj **anatomist** n

ancestor ❶ n **1** person from whom another is descended **2** forerunner **ancestral** adj **ancestry** n

anchor n **1** heavy implement dropped to stop vessel drifting **2** any similar device ▷ v **3** secure with anchor **anchorage** n act, place of anchoring

anchovy n, pl **-vies** small savoury fish of herring family

ancient ❶ adj **1** belonging to former age **2** very old

ancillary adj subordinate, auxiliary

and ❶ conj word used to join words and sentences, introduce a consequence etc.

andante adv/adj/n (Mus) moderately slow (passage)

androgynous adj having male and female characteristics

android n robot resembling a human

anecdote ❶ n short account of a single incident **anecdotal** adj

anemone ❶ n flower related to buttercup

anew adv afresh, again

angel ❶ n **1** divine messenger **2** guardian spirit **3** very kind person **angelic** adj

anger ❶ n **1** extreme annoyance **2** wrath ▷ v **3** make angry **angry** adj **angrily** adv

angina n severe pain accompanying heart disease

angle ❶ n **1** meeting of two lines or surfaces **2** point of view ▷ v **3** bend at an angle **4** fish **angler** n one who fishes for sport **angling** n

Anglican adj/n (member) of the Church of England

Anglo- comb. form English or British, as in Anglo-Scottish, Anglo-American

angora n **1** goat with long white silky hair **2** cloth or wool of this

anguish ❶ n great mental or bodily pain **anguished** adj

——— THESAURUS ———

anatomy n = **structure**, build, make-up, frame, framework; = **examination**, study, division, inquiry, investigation

ancestor n = **forefather**, predecessor, precursor, forerunner, forebear ≠ **descendant**

ancient adj = **classical**, old, former, past, bygone

and conj = **also**, including, along with, together with, in addition to

anecdote n = **story**, tale, sketch, short story, yarn

angel n = **divine messenger**, cherub, archangel, seraph; (Inf) = **dear**, beauty, saint, treasure, darling

anger n = **rage**, outrage, temper, fury, resentment ≠ **calmness** ▷ v = **enrage**, outrage, annoy, infuriate, incense ≠ **soothe**

angle n = **gradient**, bank, slope, incline, inclination; = **intersection**, point, edge, corner, bend; = **point of view**, position, approach, direction, aspect

anguish n = **suffering**, pain, distress, grief, misery

angular *adj* 1 (of people) bony 2 having angles 3 measured by an angle

animal ❶ *n* 1 living creature that can move at will 2 beast ▷ *adj* 3 of animals 4 sensual

animate ❶ *v* 1 give life to 2 enliven 3 inspire 4 actuate 5 make cartoon film of **animated** *adj* **animation** *n* **animator** *n*

animosity *n, pl* **-ties** hostility, enmity

animus *n* 1 hatred 2 animosity

aniseed *n* liquorice-flavoured seed of plant

ankle *n* joint between leg and foot

annals *pl n* yearly records

annex *v* 1 append, attach 2 take possession of **annexation** *n*

annexe *n* 1 extension to a building 2 nearby building used as an extension

annihilate *v* reduce to nothing, destroy utterly **annihilation** *n*

anniversary *n, pl* **-ries** 1 yearly return of a date 2 celebration of this

anno Domini (*Lat*) in the year of our Lord

annotate *v* make notes upon **annotation** *n*

announce ❶ *v* make known, proclaim **announcement** *n* **announcer** *n*

annoy ❶ *v* 1 vex 2 irritate **annoyance** *n*

annual ❶ *adj* 1 yearly ▷ *n* 2 plant which completes its life cycle in a year 3 book published each year **annually** *adv*

annul *v* **-nulling, -nulled** make void, cancel **annulment** *n*

anodyne *n* 1 thing that relieves pain or distress ▷ *adj* 2 relieving pain or distress

anoint *v* 1 smear with oil or ointment 2 consecrate with oil

anomaly ❶ *n, pl* **-lies** irregular or abnormal thing **anomalous** *adj*

anon. anonymous

anonymous ❶ *adj* without (author's) name **anonymously** *adv* **anonymity** *n*

anorak *n* waterproof hooded jacket

anorexia *n* loss of appetite **anorexic** *adj/n*

———————— THESAURUS ————————

animal *n* = **creature**, beast, brute ▷ *adj* = **physical**, gross, bodily, sensual, carnal

animate *adj* = **living**, live, moving, alive, breathing ▷ *v* = **enliven**, excite, inspire, move, fire ≠ **inhibit**

announce *v* = **make known**, tell, report, reveal, declare, post, tweet ≠ **keep secret**

annoy *v* = **irritate**, trouble, anger, bother, disturb ≠ **soothe**

annual *adj* = **once a year**, yearly; = **yearlong**, yearly

anomaly *n* = **irregularity**, exception, abnormality, inconsistency, eccentricity

anonymous *adj* = **unnamed**, unknown, unidentified, nameless, unacknowledged ≠ **identified**; = **unsigned**, uncredited, unattributed ≠ **signed**; impersonal, faceless

another pron/adj 1 one other 2 a different one 3 one more

answer ❶ v 1 reply (to) 2 be accountable (for, to) 3 match 4 suit ▷ n 5 reply 6 solution **answerable** adj

ant n small social insect **anteater** n animal which feeds on ants

antagonist n opponent **antagonism** n **antagonistic** adj **antagonize** v arouse hostility in

Antarctic adj/n (of) south polar regions

ante- comb. form before, as in antechamber

antecedent adj/n (thing) going before

antelope n deerlike animal

antenatal adj of care etc. during pregnancy

antenna n 1 insect's feeler 2 aerial

anterior adj 1 to the front 2 before

anthem ❶ n 1 song of loyalty 2 sacred choral piece

anther n pollen sac of flower

anthology ❶ n, pl -gies collection of poems

anthracite n slow-burning coal

anthrax n infectious disease of cattle and sheep

anthropoid adj/n manlike (ape)

anthropology n study of origins, development of human race

anti- comb. form against, as in anti-aircraft

antibiotic n/adj (of) substance used against bacterial infection

antibody n, pl -**bodies** substance which counteracts bacteria

anticipate ❶ v 1 expect 2 look forward to 3 foresee **anticipation** n

anticlimax n sudden descent to the trivial or ludicrous

anticlockwise adv/adj in the opposite direction to the rotation of the hands of a clock

antics ❶ pl n absurd behaviour

anticyclone n high-pressure area and associated winds

antidote n counteracting remedy

antifreeze n liquid added to water to prevent freezing

antihistamine n drug used esp. to treat allergies

antimony n brittle, bluish-white metal

antipathy n dislike, aversion

antiperspirant n substance used to reduce sweating

—————— THESAURUS ——————

answer v = **reply**, explain, respond, resolve, react ≠ **ask** ▷ n = **reply**, response, reaction, explanation, comeback ≠ **question**; = **solution**, resolution, explanation; = **remedy**, solution

anthem n = **song of praise**, carol, chant, hymn, psalm

anthology n = **collection**, selection, treasury, compilation, compendium

anticipate v = **expect**, predict, prepare for, hope for, envisage; = **await**, look forward to, count the hours until

antics pl n = **clowning**, tricks, mischief, pranks, escapades

antipodes pl n regions on opposite side of the globe **antipodean** adj

antique ❶ n 1 object valued because of its age ▷ adj 2 ancient 3 old-fashioned **antiquarian** n collector of antiques **antiquated** adj out-of-date **antiquity** n 1 great age 2 former times

antiseptic n/adj 1 (substance) preventing infection ▷ adj 2 free from infection

antisocial adj 1 avoiding company 2 (of behaviour) harmful to society

antithesis n, pl -ses 1 direct opposite 2 contrast

antler n branching horn of certain deer

antonym n word of opposite meaning to another

anus n open end of rectum **anal** adj

anvil n heavy iron block on which a smith hammers metal

anxious ❶ adj 1 uneasy 2 concerned **anxiety** n **anxiously** adv

any adj/pron 1 one indefinitely 2 some 3 every **anybody** n **anyhow** adv **anyone** n **anything** n **anyway** adv **anywhere** adv

aorta n main artery carrying blood from the heart

apace adv swiftly

apart ❶ adv 1 separately, aside 2 in pieces

apartheid n (esp. formerly in S Africa) official policy of segregation

apartment ❶ n 1 room 2 flat

apathy ❶ n 1 indifference 2 lack of emotion **apathetic** adj

ape n 1 tailless monkey 2 imitator ▷ v 3 imitate

aperitif n alcoholic appetizer

aperture n opening, hole

apex n 1 top, peak 2 vertex

aphid, aphis n small insect which sucks the sap from plants

aphorism n maxim, clever saying

aphrodisiac adj/n (substance) exciting sexual desire

apiece ❶ adv for each

aplomb n assurance

apocalypse n prophetic

--- THESAURUS ---

antique n = **period piece**, relic, bygone, heirloom, collector's item ▷ adj = **vintage**, classic, antiquarian, olden; = **old-fashioned**, outdated, obsolete, archaic

anxious adj = **eager**, keen, intent, yearning, impatient ≠ **reluctant**; = **uneasy**, concerned, worried, troubled, nervous ≠ **confident**

apart adv = **to pieces**, to bits, asunder; = **away from each other**, distant from each other

apartment n (US) = **flat**, room, suite, penthouse, crib; = **rooms**, quarters, accommodation, living quarters

apathy n = **lack of interest**, indifference, inertia, coolness, passivity ≠ **interest**

apiece adv = **each**, individually, separately, for each, to each ≠ **all together**

revelation, esp. of the end of the world **apocalyptic** adj

apocryphal adj of questionable authenticity

apology ❶ n, pl **-gies** 1 expression of regret for a fault 2 poor substitute (for) **apologetic** adj **apologetically** adv **apologize** v

apoplexy n paralysis caused by broken or blocked blood vessel in the brain **apoplectic** adj 1 of apoplexy 2 (Inf) furious

Apostle n 1 one of the first disciples of Jesus 2 (without cap.) enthusiastic supporter of a cause

apostrophe n mark (') showing omission of letter(s)

app n computer program designed for a particular purpose

appal ❶ v **-palling, -palled** dismay, terrify **appalling** adj (Inf) terrible

apparatus ❶ n equipment for performing experiment, operation etc.

apparel n clothing

apparent ❶ adj 1 seeming 2 obvious 3 acknowledged **apparently** adv

apparition n ghost

appeal ❶ v 1 make earnest request 2 be attractive 3 apply to higher court ▷ n 4 request 5 attractiveness **appealing** adj

appear ❶ v 1 become visible or present 2 seem, be plain 3 be seen in public 4 perform **appearance** n 1 an appearing 2 aspect 3 pretence

appease ❶ v pacify, satisfy **appeasement** n

append v join on, add

appendicitis n inflammation of the appendix

appendix ❶ n, pl **-dices, -dixes** 1 supplement 2 (Anat) small worm-shaped part of the intestine

appertain v belong, relate to

appetite ❶ n desire, inclination, esp. for food **appetizer** n

—— THESAURUS ——

apology n = **regret**, explanation, excuse, confession; = **mockery of**, excuse for, imitation of, caricature of, travesty of

appal v = **horrify**, shock, alarm, frighten, outrage

apparatus n = **organization**, system, network, structure, bureaucracy

apparent adj = **seeming**, outward, superficial, ostensible ≠ **actual**; = **obvious**, marked, visible, distinct ≠ **unclear**

appeal v = **plead**, ask, request, pray, beg ≠ **refuse** ▷ n = **plea**, call, application, request, prayer

≠ **refusal**; = **attraction**, charm, fascination, beauty, allure ≠ **repulsiveness**

appear v = **look** (like or as if), seem, occur, look to be, come across as; = **come into view**, emerge, occur, surface, come out ≠ **disappear**

appease v = **pacify**, satisfy, calm, soothe, quiet ≠ **anger**; = **ease**, calm, relieve, soothe, alleviate

appendix n = **supplement**, postscript, adjunct, appendage, addendum

appetite n = **desire**, liking, longing, demand, taste ≠ **distaste**

something stimulating appetite
appetizing adj

applaud ❶ v 1 praise by clapping
2 praise loudly **applause** n

apple n 1 round, firm fleshy fruit
2 tree bearing it

appliance ❶ n piece of
equipment, esp. electrical

apply ❶ v -plying, -plied 1 utilize
2 lay or place on 3 devote 4 have
reference (to) 5 make request (to)
applicable adj relevant **applicant**
n **application** n 1 request for a
job etc. 2 diligence 3 use, function
applied adj put to practical use

appoint ❶ v 1 assign to a job or
position 2 fix, equip
appointment n 1 engagement to
meet 2 (selection for a) job

apportion v divide out in shares

apposite adj appropriate

appraise v estimate value of
appraisal n

appreciate ❶ v 1 value at true
worth 2 be grateful for
3 understand 4 rise in value
appreciable adj noticeable
appreciably adv **appreciation** n
appreciative adj

apprehend v 1 arrest
2 understand 3 dread
apprehension n anxiety
apprehensive adj

apprentice ❶ n 1 person learning
a trade 2 novice
apprise v inform

approach ❶ v 1 draw near (to)
2 set about 3 address request to
4 approximate to ▷ n 5 a drawing
near 6 means of reaching or doing
7 approximation **approachable**
adj

approbation n approval

appropriate ❶ adj 1 suitable,
fitting ▷ v 2 take for oneself
3 allocate **appropriately** adv

——————— THESAURUS ———————

applaud v = **clap**, encourage,
praise, cheer, acclaim ≠ **boo**;
= **praise**, celebrate, approve,
acclaim, compliment ≠ **criticize**

appliance n = **device**, machine,
tool, instrument, implement

apply v = **request**, appeal, put in,
petition, inquire; = **be relevant**,
relate, refer, be fitting, be
appropriate; = **use**, exercise, carry
out, employ, implement; = **put on**,
work in, cover with, lay on, paint on

appoint v = **assign**, name, choose,
commission, select ≠ **fire**;
= **decide**, set, choose, establish, fix
≠ **cancel**

appreciate v = **enjoy**, like, value,

respect, prize ≠ **scorn**; = **be aware
of**, understand, realize, recognize,
perceive ≠ **be unaware of**; = **be
grateful**, be obliged, be thankful,
give thanks, be indebted ≠ **be
ungrateful** for; = **increase**, rise,
grow, gain, improve ≠ **fall**

apprentice n = **trainee**, student,
pupil, novice, beginner ≠ **master**

approach v = **move towards**,
reach, near, come close, come near;
= **make a proposal to**, speak to,
apply to, appeal to, proposition;
= **set about**, tackle, undertake,
embark on, get down to ▷ n
= **advance**, coming, nearing,
appearance, arrival; = **access**, way,

approve ❶ v 1 think well of, commend 2 authorize **approval** n

approx. approximate(ly)

approximate adj 1 nearly correct 2 inexact ▷ v 3 come or bring close 4 be almost the same as **approximately** adv **approximation** n

Apr. April

après-ski n social activities after skiing

apricot n orange-coloured fruit related to plum

April n fourth month

apron n 1 covering worn in front to protect clothes 2 in theatre, strip of stage before curtain 3 on airfield, tarmac area where aircraft stand, are loaded etc.

apropos adv 1 with reference to ▷ adj 2 appropriate

apt ❶ adj 1 suitable 2 likely 3 quick-witted **aptitude** n **aptly** adv

aqualung n breathing apparatus used in underwater swimming

aquamarine n 1 precious stone ▷ adj 2 greenish-blue

aquarium n, pl **aquariums**, **aquaria** tank for water animals or plants

aquatic adj living, growing, done in or on water

aqueduct n artificial channel for water, esp. one like a bridge

aquiline adj like an eagle

arable adj suitable for growing crops

arbiter n judge, umpire **arbitrary** adj 1 despotic 2 random **arbitrate** v settle (dispute) impartially **arbitration** n **arbitrator** n

arboreal adj of or living in trees

arc ❶ n part of circumference of circle or similar curve

arcade ❶ n 1 row of arches on pillars 2 covered walk or avenue

arcane adj secret

arch¹ ❶ n 1 curved structure spanning an opening 2 a curved shape 3 curved part of the sole of the foot ▷ v 4 form, make into, an arch

— THESAURUS —

drive, road, passage; often plural
= **proposal**, offer, appeal, advance, application

appropriate adj = **suitable**, fitting, relevant, to the point, apt ≠ **unsuitable** ▷ v = **seize**, claim, acquire, confiscate, usurp ≠ **relinquish**; = **allocate**, allow, budget, devote, assign ≠ **withhold**

approve v = **agree to**, allow, pass, recommend, permit ≠ **veto**

apt adj = **appropriate**, fitting,

suitable, relevant, to the point
≠ **inappropriate**; = **inclined**, likely, ready, disposed, prone; = **gifted**, skilled, quick, talented, sharp
≠ **slow**

arc n = **curve**, bend, bow, arch, crescent

arcade n = **gallery**, cloister, portico, colonnade

arch¹ n = **archway**, curve, dome, span/vault; = **curve**, bend, bow, crook, arc ▷ v = **curve**, bridge, bend, bow, span

arch² ➊ *adj* knowingly playful
arch- *comb. form* chief, as in *archangel, archenemy*
archaeology *n* study of ancient times from remains **archaeologist** *n*
archaic *adj* old, primitive **archaism** *n* word no longer in use
archbishop *n* chief bishop
archetype *n* 1 prototype 2 perfect specimen **archetypal** *adj*
archipelago *n, pl* **-gos** group of islands
architect ➊ *n* 1 person qualified to design buildings 2 contriver **architecture** *n*
Arctic ➊ *adj* 1 of north polar region 2 (*without cap.*) very cold ▷ *n* 3 north polar region
ardent ➊ *adj* 1 intensely enthusiastic 2 passionate **ardently** *adv*
arduous *adj* hard to accomplish
are *pres. tense of* BE (*used with you, we and they*)
area ➊ *n* 1 surface extent

2 two-dimensional expanse enclosed by boundary 3 region 4 part 5 field of activity
arena ➊ *n* 1 space in middle of amphitheatre or stadium 2 sphere, territory
argon *n* gas found in the air
argue ➊ *v* **-guing, -gued** 1 quarrel, offer reasons (for) 2 debate **arguable** *adj* **arguably** *adv* argument **n** **argumentative** *adj*
aria *n* song in opera etc.
arid *adj* 1 dry 2 dull
arise ➊ *v* **arising, arose, arisen** 1 get up 2 rise (up) 3 come about
aristocracy *n, pl* **-cies** upper classes **aristocrat** *n* **aristocratic** *adj*
arithmetic *n* science of numbers
ark *n* Noah's vessel
arm¹ ➊ *n* 1 upper limb from shoulder to wrist 2 anything similar, as branch of sea, supporting rail of chair etc. 3 sleeve **armful** *n* **armhole** *n* **armpit** *n* hollow under arm at shoulder

————————— THESAURUS —————————

arch² *adj* = **playful**, sly, mischievous, saucy, pert
architect *n* = **designer**, planner, draughtsman, master builder, father
Arctic *adj* = **polar**, far-northern, hyperborean
ardent *adj* = **enthusiastic**, keen, eager, avid, zealous ≠ **indifferent**; = **passionate**, intense, impassioned, lusty, amorous ≠ **cold**
area *n* = **region**, quarter, district, zone, neighbourhood; = **part**,

section, sector, portion, reach
arena *n* = **ring**, ground, field, theatre, bowl
argue *v* = **quarrel**, fight, row, clash, dispute; = **discuss**, debate, dispute; = **claim**, reason, challenge, insist, maintain
arise *v* = **happen**, start, begin, follow, result; (*Old-fashioned*) = **get to your feet**, get up, rise, stand up, spring up
arm¹ *n* = **upper limb**, limb, appendage, part, office

arm² ❶ v 1 supply with weapons
2 take up arms ▷ pl n 3 weapons
4 war 5 heraldic emblem

armada n large fleet

armadillo n, pl -los S.Amer.
animal protected by bony plates

armistice n truce

armour ❶ n 1 defensive covering
2 plating of tanks, warships etc.
3 armoured fighting vehicles
armoury n

army ❶ n, pl **armies** 1 military
land force 2 great number

aroma ❶ n sweet smell **aromatic**
adj

around ❶ prep/adv 1 on all sides
(of) 2 somewhere in or near
3 approximately 4 in a circle

5 here and there

arouse ❶ v awaken, stimulate

arraign v accuse, indict

arrange ❶ v 1 set in proper
order 2 make agreement
3 plan 4 adapt music
arrangement n

array ❶ n 1 order, esp. military
2 dress 3 imposing show ▷ v 4 set
out 5 dress richly

arrears pl n money owed

arrest ❶ v 1 detain by legal
authority 2 stop 3 catch attention
▷ n 4 seizure by warrant
arresting adj striking

arrive ❶ v 1 reach destination
2 reach, attain 3 (Inf) succeed
arrival n

--- **THESAURUS** ---

arm² v = **equip**, provide, supply,
array, furnish

armour n = **protection**, covering,
shield, sheathing, armour plate

army n = **soldiers**, military, troops,
armed force, legions; = **vast
number**, host, gang, mob, flock

aroma n = **scent**, smell, perfume,
fragrance, bouquet

around prep = **surrounding**,
about, enclosing, encompassing,
framing; = **approximately**, about,
nearly, close to, roughly ▷ adv
= **everywhere**, about, throughout,
all over, here and there; = **near**,
close, nearby, at hand, close at hand

arouse v = **stimulate**, encourage,
inspire, prompt, spur ≠ **quell**;
= **awaken**, wake up, rouse, waken

arrange v = **plan**, agree, prepare,
determine, organize; = **put in
order**, group, order, sort, position

≠ **disorganize**; = **adapt**, score,
orchestrate, harmonize, instrument

array n = **arrangement**, show,
supply, display, collection; (Poet)
= **clothing**, dress, clothes,
garments, apparel ▷ v = **arrange**,
show, group, present, range;
= **dress**, clothe, deck, decorate,
adorn

arrest v = **capture**, catch, nick (Sl,
chiefly Brit), seize, detain ≠ **release**;
= **stop**, end, limit, block, slow
≠ **speed up**; = **fascinate**, hold,
occupy, engage, grip ▷ n
= **capture**, bust (Inf), detention,
seizure ≠ **release**; = **stoppage**,
suppression, obstruction, blockage,
hindrance ≠ **acceleration**

arrive v = **come**, appear, turn up,
show up (Inf), draw near ≠ **depart**;
(Inf) = **succeed**, make it (Inf),
triumph, do well, thrive

arrow ❶ n shaft shot from bow
arsenal ❶ n stores for guns etc.
arsenic n soft, grey, very poisonous
metallic element
arson n crime of intentionally
setting property on fire
art ❶ n 1 human skill as opposed to
nature 2 creative skill in painting,
poetry, music etc. 3 any of the
works produced thus 4 craft
5 knack ▷ pl 6 branches of
learning other than science 7 wiles
artful adj wily **artfully** adv
artist n one who practises fine art,
esp. painting **artiste** n
professional entertainer **artistic**
adj **artistry** n **artless** adj
natural, frank **arty** adj **artier,
artiest** ostentatiously artistic
artefact n something made by
man
artery n, pl **-teries** 1 tube carrying
blood from heart 2 any main
channel of communications
arthritis n painful inflammation of
joint(s) **arthritic** adj/n
artichoke n thistle-like plant with

edible flower
article ❶ n 1 item, object 2 short
written piece 3 (Grammar) words
the, a, an 4 clause in a contract
articled adj bound as an
apprentice
articulate ❶ adj 1 fluent 2 clear,
distinct ▷ v 3 utter distinctly
articulated adj jointed
artifice n contrivance, trick
artificial adj 1 synthetic
2 insincere **artificially** adv
artillery ❶ n 1 large guns on
wheels 2 troops who use them
artisan n craftsman
as ❶ adv/conj 1 denoting:
comparison 2 similarity 3 equality
4 identity 5 concurrence 6 reason
asbestos n fibrous mineral which
does not burn
ascend v 1 go, come up 2 climb
ascendancy n dominance
ascent n
ascertain v find out
ascetic n/adj (person) practising
severe self-denial
ascribe v attribute, assign

——— THESAURUS ———

arrow n = **dart**, flight, bolt, shaft
(Archaic), quarrel; = **pointer**,
indicator, marker
arsenal n = **armoury**, supply,
store, stockpile, storehouse
art n = **artwork**, style of art, fine
art, creativity
article n = **feature**, story, paper,
piece, item; = **thing**, piece, unit,
item, object; = **clause**, point, part,
section, item
articulate adj = **expressive**, clear,
coherent, fluent, eloquent

≠ incoherent ▷ v = **express**, say,
state, word, declare
artillery n = **big guns**, battery,
cannon, ordnance, gunnery
as conj = **when**, while, just as, at
the time that, during the time
that ▷ prep = **in the role of**,
being, under the name of, in the
character of ▷ conj = **in the way
that**, like, in the manner that;
= **since**, because, seeing that,
considering that, on account
of the fact that

asexual *adj* without sex

ash¹ *n* remains of anything burnt
ashen *adj* pale

ash² *n* **1** deciduous timber tree **2** its wood

ashamed ❶ *adj* feeling shame

ashore ❶ *adv* on shore

aside ❶ *adv* **1** to, on one side **2** privately ▷ *n* **3** words spoken so as not to be heard by all

asinine *adj* stupid, silly

ask ❶ *v* **1** make request or inquiry **2** invite **3** require

askance *adv* with mistrust

askew *adv* awry

asleep ❶ *adj/adv* sleeping

asp *n* small poisonous snake

asparagus *n* plant with edible young shoots

aspect ❶ *n* **1** appearance **2** outlook **3** side

aspen *n* type of poplar tree

aspersion *n* (*usu. pl*) malicious remark

asphalt *n* covering for road surfaces etc.

aspic *n* jelly used to coat meat, eggs, fish etc.

aspidistra *n* plant with long tapered leaves

aspire *v* have great ambition **aspiration** *n* **aspiring** *adj*

aspirin *n* (tablet of) drug used to relieve pain and fever

ass ❶ *n* **1** donkey **2** fool

assail *v* **1** attack, assault **2** criticize **assailable** *adj* **assailant** *n*

assassin ❶ *n* one who kills for money or political reasons **assassinate** *v* **assassination** *n*

assault ❶ *n/v* attack

assemble ❶ *v* **1** meet, bring together **2** put together **assembly** *n*

assent *v* **1** agree ▷ *n* **2** agreement

ashamed *adj* = **embarrassed**, sorry, guilty, distressed, humiliated ≠ **proud**

ashore *adv* = **on land**, on the beach, on the shore, aground, to the shore

aside *adv* = **to one side**, separately, apart, beside, out of the way ▷ *n* = **interpolation**, parenthesis

ask *v* = **inquire**, question, quiz, query, interrogate ≠ **answer**; = **request**, appeal to, plead with, demand, beg; = **invite**, bid, summon

asleep *adj* = **sleeping**, napping, dormant, dozing, slumbering

aspect *n* = **feature**, side, factor, angle, characteristic; = **position/ view**, situation, scene, prospect; = **appearance**, look, air, condition, quality

ass *n* = **donkey**, moke (*Sl*); = **fool**, idiot, twit (*Inf, chiefly Brit*), oaf, jackass

assassin *n* = **murderer**, killer, slayer, liquidator, executioner

assault *n* = **attack**, raid, invasion, charge, offensive ≠ **defence** ▷ *v* = **strike**, attack, beat, knock, bang

assemble *v* = **gather**, meet, collect, rally, bring together ≠ **scatter**; = **bring together**, collect, gather, rally, come together

assert ❶ v declare strongly, insist upon **assertion** n **assertive** adj **assertively** adv

assess ❶ v 1 fix value or amount of 2 evaluate **assessment** n **assessor** n

asset ❶ n 1 valuable or useful person, thing ▷ pl 2 things that can be used to raise money

assiduous adj persevering **assiduously** adv

assign ❶ v 1 appoint 2 allot 3 transfer **assignation** n secret meeting **assignment** n

assimilate v 1 take in 2 incorporate 3 (cause to) become similar **assimilation** n

assist ❶ v give help to **assistance** n **assistant** n

associate ❶ v 1 link, connect 2 join 3 keep company 4 combine, unite ▷ n 5 partner 6 friend 7 subordinate member ▷ adj

8 affiliated **association** n

assonance n rhyming of vowel sounds but not consonants

assorted ❶ adj mixed **assortment** n mixture

assume ❶ v 1 take for granted 2 pretend 3 take on **assumption** n

assure ❶ v 1 tell positively, promise 2 make sure 3 insure against loss, esp. of life **assurance** n **assured** adj 1 sure 2 confident, self-possessed

aster n plant with starlike flowers

asterisk n star (*) used in printing

astern adv 1 in, behind the stern 2 backwards

asteroid n small planet

asthma n illness in which one has difficulty breathing **asthmatic** adj/n

astigmatism n inability of lens (esp. of eye) to focus properly

astir adv on the move

————— THESAURUS —————

assert v = **state**, argue, maintain, declare, swear ≠ **deny**; = **insist upon**, stress, defend, uphold, put forward ≠ **retract**

assess v = **judge**, estimate, analyse, evaluate, rate; = **evaluate**, rate, tax, value, estimate

asset n = **benefit**, help, service, aid, advantage ≠ **disadvantage**

assign v = **give**, set, grant, allocate, give out; = **select for**, post, commission, elect, appoint; = **attribute**, credit, put down, set down, ascribe

assist v = **help**, support, aid, cooperate with, abet

associate v = **connect**, link, ally,

identify, join ≠ **separate**; = **socialize**, mix, accompany, mingle, consort ≠ **avoid** ▷ n = **partner**, friend, ally, colleague, mate (Inf)

assorted adj = **various**, different, mixed, varied, diverse ≠ **similar**

assume v = **presume**, think, believe, expect, suppose ≠ **know**; = **take on**, accept, shoulder, take over, put on; = **simulate**, affect, adopt, put on, imitate

assure v = **convince**, encourage, persuade, satisfy, comfort; = **make certain**, ensure, confirm, guarantee, secure; = **promise to**, pledge to, vow to, guarantee to, swear to

astonish ❶ v amaze, surprise, stun **astonishment** n

astound v astonish greatly **astounding** adj

astral adj of the stars

astray adv/adj 1 off the right path 2 into error or sin

astride adv with legs apart

astringent adj 1 sharp 2 stopping bleeding ▷ n 3 astringent substance

astrology n foretelling of events by stars **astrologer** n **astrological** adj

astronaut n one trained for travel in space

astronomy n scientific study of heavenly bodies **astronomer** n **astronomical** adj 1 very large 2 of astronomy **astronomically** adv

astute ❶ adj perceptive, shrewd **astutely** adv

asunder adv 1 apart 2 in pieces

asylum ❶ n 1 refuge, place of safety 2 (Obs) psychiatric hospital

asymmetry n lack of symmetry **asymmetrical** adj

at prep/adv 1 denoting: location in space or time 2 rate 3 condition or state 4 amount 5 direction 6 cause

atheism n belief that there is no God **atheist** n

athlete n person trained in or good at track and field sports

atlas n book of maps

atmosphere ❶ n 1 gases surrounding earth etc. 2 prevailing mood **atmospheric** adj **atmospherics** pl n radio interference

atoll n ring-shaped coral island enclosing lagoon

atom ❶ n 1 smallest unit of matter which can enter into chemical combination 2 any very small particle **atomic** adj **atomizer** n instrument for discharging liquids in a fine spray **atomic bomb** bomb with immense power derived from nuclear fission or fusion **atomic energy** nuclear energy

atonal adj (of music) not in an established key

atone v make amends (for) **atonement** n

atop prep on top of

atrocious adj 1 extremely cruel 2 horrifying 3 (Inf) very bad **atrociously** adv **atrocity** n

atrophy n, pl **-phies** 1 wasting away ▷ v 2 waste away

attach ❶ v 1 join, fasten 2 attribute **attached** adj (with to) fond of **attachment** n

— THESAURUS —

astonish v = **amaze**, surprise, stun, stagger, bewilder

astute adj = **intelligent**, sharp, clever, subtle, shrewd ≠ **stupid**

asylum n (Old-fashioned) = **psychiatric hospital**, hospital, institution, mental hospital, madhouse (Inf); = **refuge**, haven, safety, protection, preserve

atmosphere n = **air**, sky, heavens, aerosphere; = **feeling**, character, environment, spirit, surroundings

atom n = **particle**, bit, spot, trace, molecule

attach v = **ascribe**, connect, attribute, assign, associate

attaché n specialist attached to diplomatic mission **attaché case** flat rectangular briefcase

attack ❶ v 1 take action against 2 criticize 3 set about with vigour 4 affect adversely ▷ n 5 attacking action 6 bout **attacker** n

attain ❶ v 1 arrive at 2 achieve **attainable** adj **attainment** n

attempt ❶ v/n try

attend ❶ v 1 be present at 2 accompany 3 (with to) take care of 4 pay attention to **attendance** n 1 an attending 2 persons attending **attendant** n/adj **attention** n 1 notice 2 heed 3 care 4 courtesy **attentive** adj 1 giving attention 2 considerately helpful

attest v bear witness to

attic ❶ n space within roof

attire v/n dress, array

attitude ❶ n 1 mental view, opinion 2 posture, pose 3 disposition, behaviour

attorney n person legally appointed to act for another, esp. a lawyer

attract ❶ v 1 draw (attention etc.) 2 arouse interest of 3 cause to come closer (as magnet etc.) **attraction** n **attractive** adj

attribute ❶ v 1 regard as belonging to or produced by ▷ n 2 quality or characteristic **attributable** adj **attribution** n

attrition n wearing away

attune v 1 tune 2 adjust

atypical adj not typical

aubergine n purple fruit eaten as vegetable

auburn adj/n reddish brown

auction n 1 public sale in which goods are sold to the highest bidder ▷ v 2 sell by auction **auctioneer** n

audacious adj 1 bold 2 impudent **audaciously** adv **audacity** n

audible adj able to be heard **audibly** adv

— THESAURUS —

attack v = assault, strike (at), mug, ambush, tear into ≠ defend; = invade, occupy, raid, infringe, storm ▷ n = assault, charge, campaign, strike, raid ≠ defence; = criticism, censure, disapproval, abuse, bad press; = bout, fit, stroke, seizure, spasm

attain v = obtain, get, reach, complete, gain

attempt v = try, seek, aim, struggle, venture ▷ n = try, go (Inf), shot (Inf), effort, trial

attend v = be present, go to, visit,

frequent, haunt ≠ be absent; = pay attention, listen, hear, mark, note ≠ ignore

attic n = loft, garret, roof space

attitude n = opinion/view, position, approach, mood; = position, bearing, pose, stance, carriage

attract v = allure, draw, persuade, charm, appeal to ≠ repel; = pull, draw, magnetize

attribute v = ascribe, credit, refer, trace, assign ▷ n = quality, feature, property, character, element

audience ❶ n 1 people assembled to listen or watch 2 formal interview

audit n 1 formal examination of accounts ▷ v 2 examine accounts **auditor** n

audition n 1 test of prospective performer ▷ v 2 set, perform such a test **auditorium** n place where audience sits

Aug. August

augment v increase, enlarge

augur v foretell

August n eighth month

auk n northern sea bird

aunt n 1 father's or mother's sister 2 wife of parent's sibling **auntie** n (Inf) aunt

au pair n young foreigner who receives board and lodging in return for housework etc.

aura ❶ n atmosphere considered distinctive of person or thing

aural adj of, by ear

auricle n 1 outside ear 2 an upper cavity of heart

aurora n, pl -ras, -rae 1 lights in the sky radiating from polar regions 2 dawn

auspices pl n patronage **auspicious** adj giving hope of future success **auspiciously** adv

austere adj 1 severe 2 without luxury **austerity** n

authentic ❶ adj genuine **authentically** adv **authenticate** v make valid **authenticity** n

author ❶ n 1 writer 2 originator

authority ❶ n, pl -ties 1 legal power or right 2 delegated power 3 influence 4 permission 5 expert 6 board in control **authoritarian** n/adj (person) insisting on strict obedience **authoritative** adj **authorize** v 1 empower 2 permit **authorization** n

autism n developmental condition characterized by limited ability to communicate **autistic** adj

auto- comb. form self, as in autosuggestion

autobiography n, pl -phies life of person written by himself **autobiographical** adj

autocrat ❶ n 1 absolute ruler 2 despotic person **autocratic** adj **autocracy** n

Autocue® n electronic television device displaying speaker's script unseen by audience

autogiro, autogyro n, pl -ros self-propelled aircraft with unpowered rotor

---

— THESAURUS —

audience n = **spectators**, company, crowd, gathering, gallery; = **interview**, meeting, hearing, exchange, reception

aura n = **air**, feeling, quality, atmosphere, tone

authentic adj = **real**, pure, genuine, valid, undisputed ≠ **fake**

author n = **writer**, composer, novelist, hack, creator; = **creator**, father, producer, designer, founder

authority n usually plural = **powers that be**, government, police, officials, the state; = **expert**, specialist, professional, master, guru; = **command**, power, control, rule, management (Inf)

autograph n **1** signature ▷ v **2** sign

automatic ❶ adj **1** operated or controlled mechanically or without conscious thought ▷ adj/n **3** self-loading (weapon) **automatically** adv **automation** n introduction of automatic devices in industry **automaton** n **1** robot **2** person who acts mechanically

automobile n motorcar

autonomy ❶ n self-government **autonomous** adj

autopsy n, pl **-sies** postmortem

autumn n season after summer **autumnal** adj

auxiliary adj/n (person) helping, subsidiary

avail v **1** be of use, advantage ▷ n **2** benefit **available** adj **1** obtainable **2** accessible **availability** n

avalanche ❶ n **1** mass of snow, ice, sliding down mountain **2** any great quantity

avant-garde ❶ adj innovative and progressive

avarice n greed for wealth **avaricious** adj

avatar n **1** (Hinduism) appearance of a god in animal or human form **2** (Computers) graphical representation of a person in a virtual environment, such as an online role-playing game

avenge v take vengeance for

avenue ❶ n **1** wide street **2** approach **3** double row of trees

aver v **averring, averred** affirm, assert

average ❶ n **1** middle or usual value ▷ adj **2** ordinary ▷ v **3** calculate an average **4** form an average

averse adj disinclined **aversion** n (object of) dislike

avert ❶ v **1** turn away **2** ward off

aviary n, pl **aviaries** enclosure for birds

━━━━━━━━━━━ THESAURUS ━━━━━━━━━━━

automatic adj = **mechanical**, automated, mechanized, push-button, self-propelling ≠ **done by hand**; = **involuntary**, natural, unconscious, mechanical, spontaneous ≠ **conscious**

autonomy n = **independence**, freedom, sovereignty, self-determination, self-government ≠ **dependency**

avalanche n = **snow-slide**, landslide, landslip; = **large amount**, barrage, torrent, deluge, inundation

avant-garde adj = **progressive**, pioneering, experimental, innovative, unconventional ≠ **conservative**

avenue n = **street**, way, course, drive, road

average n = **standard**, normal, usual, par ▷ adj = **usual**, standard, general, normal, regular ≠ **unusual**; = **mean**, middle, medium, intermediate, median ≠ **minimum** ▷ v = **make on average**, be on average, even out to, do on average, balance out to

avert v = **ward off**, avoid, prevent, frustrate, fend off; = **turn away**, turn aside

aviation n art of flying aircraft **aviator** n

avid adj 1 keen 2 greedy (for) **avidly** adv

avocado n, pl **-dos** tropical pear-shaped fruit

avoid ① v 1 keep away from 2 refrain from 3 not allow to happen **avoidable** adj **avoidance** n

avow v 1 declare 2 admit **avowal** n **avowed** adj

await ① v 1 wait or stay for 2 be in store for

awake ① v awaking, awoke, awoken 1 emerge or rouse from sleep 2 (cause to) become alert ▷ adj 3 not sleeping **awaken** v awake **awakening** n

award ① v 1 give formally ▷ n 2 thing awarded

aware ① adj informed, conscious **awareness** n

awash adv covered by water

away ① adv 1 absent, apart, at a distance, out of the way ▷ adj 2 not present

awe ① n 1 dread mingled with reverence ▷ v 2 astonish, frighten **awesome** adj

awful ① adj 1 dreadful (Inf) very great **awfully** adv 1 in an unpleasant way 2 (Inf) very much

awhile adv for a time

awkward ① adj 1 clumsy 2 difficult 3 inconvenient 4 embarrassed **awkwardly** adv **awkwardness** n

— THESAURUS —

avoid v = **prevent**, stop, frustrate, hamper, foil; = **refrain from**, bypass, dodge, eschew, escape; = **keep away from**, dodge, shun, evade, steer clear of

await v = **wait for**, expect, look for, look forward to, anticipate; = **be in store for**, wait for, be ready for, lie in wait for, be in readiness for

awake adj = **not sleeping**, sleepless, wide-awake, aware, conscious ≠ **asleep** ▷ v = **wake up**, come to, wake, stir, awaken; = **alert**, stimulate, provoke, revive, arouse

award n = **prize**, gift, trophy, decoration, grant ▷ v = **present with**, give, grant, hand out, confer

aware adj = **informed**, enlightened, knowledgeable, learned, expert ≠ **ignorant**

away adj = **absent**, out, gone, elsewhere, abroad ▷ adv = **off**, elsewhere, abroad, hence, from here; = **aside**, out of the way, to one side; = **at a distance**, far, apart, remote, isolated

awe n = **wonder**, fear, respect, reverence, horror ≠ **contempt** ▷ v = **impress**, amaze, stun, frighten, terrify

awful adj = **bad**, poor, terrible, appalling, foul ≠ **wonderful**; = **unwell**, poorly (Inf), ill, terrible, sick

awkward adj = **embarrassing**, difficult, sensitive, delicate, uncomfortable ≠ **comfortable**; = **inconvenient**, difficult, troublesome, cumbersome, unwieldy ≠ **convenient**; = **clumsy**, lumbering, bumbling, unwieldy, ponderous ≠ **graceful**

awl n tool for boring wood etc.

awning n (canvas) roof to protect from weather

AWOL adj (Mil) absent without leave

awry adv 1 crookedly 2 amiss ▷ adj 3 crooked 4 wrong

axe ❶ n 1 tool for chopping 2 (Inf) dismissal from employment ▷ v 3 (Inf) dismiss from employment

axiom n accepted principle

axiomatic adj

axis ❶ n, pl **axes** (imaginary) line round which body spins

axle n shaft on which wheels turn

aye, ay interj 1 yes ▷ n 2 affirmative answer or vote

azalea n genus of shrubby flowering plants

azure adj sky-blue

————————————— THESAURUS —————————————

axe n = **hatchet**, chopper, tomahawk, cleaver, adze ▷ v (Inf) = **abandon**, end, eliminate, cancel, scrap

axis n = **pivot**, shaft, axle, spindle, centre line

b

BA Bachelor of Arts

baas n (S Afr) boss

babble v/n (make) foolish, incoherent speech

babe n baby

babiche n (Canad) thongs or lacings of rawhide

baboon n large monkey

baby ① n, pl **-bies** infant **baby-sitter** n one who cares for children when parents are out **baby-sit** v

bach n (NZ) small holiday cottage

bachelor n unmarried man

bacillus n, pl **-li** minute organism sometimes causing disease

back ① n **1** hind part of anything, e.g. human body **2** part opposite front **3** part further away or less used **4** (position of) player in ball games ▷ adj **5** situated behind **6** earlier ▷ adv **7** at, to the back **8** in, into the past **9** in return ▷ v **10** move backwards **11** support **12** put wager on **13** provide with back **14** provide with musical accompaniment **backer** n **backward** adj towards the rear **backwardness** n **backwards** adv to rear, past, worse state **backbite** v slander absent person **backbone** n **1** spinal column **2** strength of character **backcloth, backdrop** n painted cloth at back of stage **backdate** v make effective from earlier date **backfire** v **1** (of plan, scheme, etc.) fail to work **2** ignite wrongly **backgammon** n game played with draughtsmen and dice **background** n **1** space behind chief figures of picture etc. **2** past history of person **backhand** n stroke made with hand turned backwards **backlash** n sudden adverse reaction **backside** n rump **backpack** n **1** large pack carried on the back ▷ v **2** go travelling or hiking with a backpack **bacon** n cured pig's flesh

bacteria ① n pl n, sing **-rium** microscopic organisms **bacterial** adj **bacteriology** n

bad ① adj **worse, worst 1** faulty

baby n = **child**, infant, babe, bairn (Scot.), newborn child ▷ adj = **small**, little, minute, tiny, mini

back n = **spine**, backbone, vertebrae, spinal column/vertebral column ▷ adj = **rearmost**, hind, hindmost ▷ v = **support**, help, aid, champion, defend ≠ **oppose**

bacteria pl n = **microorganisms**, viruses, bugs (SI), germs, microbes

bad adj = **harmful**, damaging, dangerous, destructive, unhealthy

b

2 harmful 3 evil 4 severe 5 rotten
6 (Sl) very good **badly** adv
badge ❶ n distinguishing emblem
badger ❶ n 1 burrowing night
animal ▷ v 2 pester, worry
badminton n game played with
rackets and shuttlecocks
baffle ❶ v 1 check, frustrate,
bewilder ▷ n 2 device to regulate
flow of liquid etc.
bag ❶ n 1 sack 2 measure of
quantity 3 woman's handbag ▷ v
4 bulge 5 sag 6 put in bag 7 kill
as game, etc. **baggy** adj loose
bagatelle n 1 trifle 2 game like
pinball
baggage ❶ n suitcases, luggage
bagpipes pl n musical wind
instrument
bail¹ ❶ n (Law) 1 security given for
person's reappearance in court ▷ v
2 (obtain) release on security

bail² n (Cricket) crosspiece on
wicket
bail³, bale v empty water from
boat **bail out** parachute
bailiff n land steward, agent
bait ❶ n 1 food to entice fish 2 any
lure ▷ v 3 lure 4 persecute
baize n smooth woollen cloth
bake v 1 cook or harden by dry heat
▷ v 2 make bread, cakes etc.
baker n **bakery** n, pl **-eries**
baking powder raising agent used
in cooking
bakeapple n cloudberry
bakkie n (SAfr) small truck
balalaika n Russian musical
instrument, like guitar
balance ❶ n 1 pair of scales
2 equilibrium 3 surplus 4 sum due
on an account 5 difference
between two sums ▷ v 6 weigh
7 bring to equilibrium

THESAURUS

≠ **beneficial**; = **unfavourable**,
distressing, unfortunate, grim,
unpleasant; = **inferior**, poor,
inadequate, faulty, unsatisfactory
≠ **satisfactory**; = **incompetent**,
poor, useless, incapable, unfit;
= **grim**, severe, hard, tough;
= **wicked**, criminal, evil, corrupt,
immoral ≠ **virtuous**
badge n = **image**, brand, stamp,
identification, crest
badger v = **pester**, harry, bother,
bug (Inf), bully
baffle v = **puzzle**, confuse, stump,
bewilder, confound ≠ **explain**
bag n = **sack**, container, sac,
receptacle, land ▷ v = **catch**, kill,
shoot, capture, acquire

baggage n = **luggage**, things,
cases, bags, equipment
bail¹ n (Law) = **security**, bond,
guarantee, pledge, warranty
bait n = **lure**, attraction, incentive,
carrot (Inf), temptation ▷ v = **tease**,
annoy, irritate, bother, mock
balance ❶ v = **stabilize**, level, steady
≠ **overbalance**; = **offset**, match,
square, even up; = **weigh**, consider,
compare, estimate, contrast;
(Accounting) = **calculate**, total,
determine, estimate, settle ▷ n
= **equilibrium**, stability, steadiness,
evenness ≠ **instability**; = **stability**,
equanimity, steadiness; = **parity**,
equity, fairness, impartiality,
equality

b

balcony ⓷ n, pl **-nies 1** platform outside window **2** upper seats in theatre

bald ⓷ adj **1** hairless **2** plain **3** bare **balding** adj

bale n, v bundle or package

baleful adj menacing

balk, baulk v **1** swerve, pull up **2** thwart **3** shirk ▷ n **4** hindrance

ball¹ ⓷ n **1** anything round **2** globe, sphere, esp. as used in games ▷ v **3** gather into a mass **ball bearings** steel balls used to lessen friction

ball² n **1** assembly for dancing **ballroom** n

ballad n **1** narrative poem **2** simple song

ballast n heavy material put in ship to steady it

ballet n theatrical presentation of dancing and miming **ballerina** n

ballistics pl n scientific study of motion of projectiles

balloon ⓷ n **1** large bag filled with air or gas ▷ v **2** puff out

ballot ⓷ n **1** voting, usually by paper ▷ v **2** vote

balm n healing or soothing

(ointment)

balmy adj **balmier, balmiest** (of weather) mild and pleasant

balsa n Amer. tree with light but strong wood

balsam n resinous aromatic substance

bamboo n large tropical treelike reed

bamboozle v mystify, hoax

ban ⓷ v **banning, banned 1** prohibit, forbid, outlaw ▷ n **2** prohibition **3** proclamation

banal adj commonplace, trite **banality** n

banana n **1** tropical treelike plant **2** its fruit

band¹ ⓷ n **1** strip used to bind **2** range of frequencies **bandage** n, v (apply) strip of cloth for binding wound

band² ⓷ n **1** company **2** company of musicians ▷ v **3** bind together

bandanna, bandana n handkerchief

B & B bed and breakfast

bandit ⓷ n **1** outlaw **2** robber

bandwagon n **jump on the bandwagon** join something that

balcony n = **terrace**, veranda; = **upper circle**, gods, gallery

bald adj = **hairless**, depilated, baldheaded; = **plain**, direct, frank, straightforward, blunt

ball¹ n = **sphere**, drop, globe, pellet, orb

balloon v = **expand**, rise, increase, swell, blow up

ballot n = **vote**, election/voting, poll, polling

ban v = **prohibit**, bar, block, veto, forbid ≠ **permit** ▷ n = **prohibition**, restriction/veto, boycott, embargo ≠ **permission**

band¹ n = **headband**, strip, ribbon, strip, belt

band² n = **ensemble**, group, orchestra, combo; = **gang**, company, group, party, team

bandit n = **robber**, outlaw, raider, plunderer, mugger (Inf) seems assured of success

bandy v -dies, -diest toss from one to another **bandy-legged** adj curving outwards

bane n person or thing causing misery or distress **baneful** adj

bang ❶ n 1 sudden loud noise 2 heavy blow ▷ v 3 make loud noise 4 beat 5 slam

banger n (Sl) 1 sausage 2 (Inf) old car 3 loud firework

bangle n ring worn on arm or leg

banish ❶ v 1 exile 2 drive away

banisters pl n railing on staircase

banjo n, pl -jos, -joes musical instrument like guitar

bank¹ ❶ n 1 mound of earth 2 edge of river etc. ▷ v 3 enclose with ridge 4 pile up

bank² ❶ n 1 establishment for keeping, lending, exchanging etc. money ▷ v 2 put in bank 3 keep with bank **banker** n **banking** n **banknote** n written promise of payment **bank on** rely on

bankrupt ❶ n 1 one who fails in business, insolvent debtor ▷ adj 2 financially ruined ▷ v 3 make bankrupt **bankruptcy** n

banner ❶ n 1 placard 2 flag

banns pl n public declaration of intended marriage

banquet ❶ n/v feast

banshee n spirit whose wailing warns of death

bantam n 1 small chicken 2 very light boxing weight

banter v 1 make fun of ▷ n 2 light, teasing language

bar ❶ n 1 rod or block of any substance 2 obstacle 3 rail in law court 4 body of lawyers 5 counter where drinks are served 6 unit of music 7 bank 8 obstruct 9 exclude ▷ prep 10 except **barman** n

barachois n (in the Atlantic Provinces of Canada) a shallow lagoon formed by a sand bar

barb n 1 sharp point curving backwards 2 cutting remark **barbed** adj

---

THESAURUS

bang n = **explosion**, pop, clash, crack, blast; = **blow**, knock, stroke, punch, bump ▷ v = **resound**, boom, explode, thunder, thump ▷ adv = **exactly**, straight, square, squarely, precisely

banish v = **expel**, exile, outlaw, deport ≠ admit; = **get rid of**, remove

bank¹ n = **side**, edge, margin, shore, brink; = **mound**, banking, rise, hill, mass ▷ v = **tilt**, tip, pitch, heel, slope

bank² n = **financial institution**, repository, depository; = **store**,

fund, stock, source, supply ▷ v = **deposit**, keep, save

bankrupt adj = **insolvent**, broke (Inf), ruined, wiped out (Inf), impoverished ≠ solvent

banner n = **flag**, standard, colours, placard, pennant

banquet n = **feast**, spread (Inf), dinner, meal, revel

bar n = **public house**, pub (Inf, chiefly Brit), counter, inn, saloon; = **rod**, staff, stick, stake, rail; = **obstacle**, block, barrier, hurdle, hitch ≠ aid ▷ v = **lock**, block, secure, attach,

barbecue n 1 meal cooked outdoors over open fire ▷ v 2 cook thus

barber n person who shaves beards and cuts hair

barbiturate n derivative of barbituric acid used as drug

bard n poet

bare ❶ adj 1 uncovered 2 naked 3 plain 4 scanty ▷ v 5 make bare **barely** adv only just **barefaced** adj shameless

bargain ❶ n 1 something bought at favourable price 2 agreement ▷ v 3 haggle, negotiate

barge ❶ n 1 flat-bottomed freight boat ▷ v 2 (Inf) bump (into), push

baritone n 1 (singer with) second lowest adult male voice ▷ adj 2 of, for this voice

barium n white metallic element

bark¹ ❶ n/v (utter) sharp loud cry of dog etc.

bark² ❶ n outer layer of tree

barley n grain used for food and making malt

barmy adj **-mier, -miest** (Sl) insane

barn n building to store grain, hay etc. **barnyard** n

barnacle n shellfish which sticks to rocks and ships

barometer n instrument to measure pressure of atmosphere **barometric** adj

baron n 1 member of lowest rank of peerage 2 powerful businessman **baronial** adj

baronet n lowest British hereditary title

baroque adj extravagantly ornamented

barque n sailing ship

barracks ❶ pl n building for lodging soldiers

barrage ❶ n 1 heavy artillery fire 2 continuous heavy delivery of questions etc. 3 dam across river

barrel n 1 round wooden vessel 2 tube of gun etc.

barren ❶ adj 1 sterile 2 unprofitable

— THESAURUS —

bolt; **= block**, restrict, restrain, hamper, thwart; **= exclude**, ban, forbid, prohibit, keep out of ≠ admit

bare adj **= naked**, nude, stripped, uncovered, undressed ≠ dressed; **= simple**, spare, stark, austere, spartan ≠ adorned

bargain n **= good buy**, discount purchase, good deal, steal (Inf), snip (Inf); **= agreement**, deal (Inf), promise, contract, arrangement ▷ v **= negotiate**, deal, contract, mediate, covenant

barge n **= canal boat**, lighter, narrow boat, flatboat

bark¹ v **= yap**, bay, howl, snarl, growl ▷ n **= yap**, bay, howl, snarl, growl

bark² n **= covering**, casing, cover, skin, layer

barracks pl n **= camp**, quarters, garrison, encampment, billet

barrage n **= bombardment**, attack, bombing, assault, shelling; **= torrent**, mass, burst, stream, hail

barren adj **= desolate**, empty, desert, waste; **= unproductive**, dry, arid, unfruitful ≠ fertile

b

barricade ❶ n **1** improvised barrier ▷ v **2** block

barrier ❶ n fence, obstruction

barrister n advocate in the higher law courts

barrow n **1** small wheeled handcart **2** wheelbarrow

barter v/n (trade by) exchange of goods

base¹ ❶ n **1** bottom, foundation **2** starting point **3** centre of operations ▷ v **4** found, establish **baseless** adj **basement** n lowest storey of building

base² ❶ adj **1** low, mean **2** despicable

baseball n game played with bat and ball

bash ❶ (Inf) ▷ v **1** strike violently ▷ n **2** blow **3** attempt

bashful adj shy, modest

basic ❶ adj **1** relating to, serving as base **2** fundamental **3** necessary **basically** adv **basics** pl n fundamental principles, facts etc.

basil n aromatic herb

basin n **1** deep circular dish **2** harbour **3** land drained by river

basis ❶ n, pl **-ses 1** foundation **2** principal constituent

bask ❶ v lie in warmth and sunshine

basket n vessel made of woven cane, straw etc. **basketball** n ball game played by two teams

bass¹ ❶ n **1** lowest part in music **2** bass singer or voice ▷ adj **3** of bass

bass² n sea fish

bassoon n woodwind instrument of low tone

bastard n **1** child born of unmarried parents **2** (Inf) unpleasant person ▷ adj **3** illegitimate **4** spurious

bastion n **1** projecting part of fortification **2** defence

bat¹ n **1** club used to hit ball in cricket etc. ▷ v **2** strike with bat

bat² n nocturnal mouselike flying animal

batch ❶ n group or set of similar objects

──────── THESAURUS ────────

barricade n = **barrier**, wall, fence, blockade, obstruction ▷ v = **bar**, block, defend, secure, lock

barrier n = **barricade**, wall, bar, fence, boundary

base¹ n = **bottom**, floor, lowest part ≠ **top**; = **support**, stand, foot, rest, bed; = **foundation**, institution, organization, establishment ▷ v = **ground**, found, build, establish, depend; = **place**, set, post, station, establish

base² adj = **dishonourable**, evil, disgraceful, shameful, immoral ≠ **honourable**

bash v (Inf); = **hit**, beat, strike, knock, smash

basic adj = **fundamental**, main, essential, primary, vital; = **vital**, needed, important, key, necessary

basis n = **arrangement**, way, system, footing, agreement

bask v = **lie**, relax, lounge, sprawl, loaf

bass¹ adj = **deep**, low, resonant, sonorous, low-pitched

batch n = **group**, set, lot, crowd, pack

bated adj **with bated breath** anxiously

bath ❶ n 1 vessel or place to bathe in 2 water for bathing 3 act of bathing ▷ v 4 wash **bathroom** n

bathe ❶ v 1 swim 2 apply liquid 3 wash 4 immerse in water ▷ n 5 swim 6 wash **bather** n

baton ❶ n stick, esp. of policeman, conductor, marshal

battalion n military unit of three companies

batten n 1 strip of wood ▷ v 2 fasten

batter ❶ v 1 strike continuously ▷ n 2 mixture of flour, eggs, milk, used in cooking

battery ❶ n, pl **-teries** 1 connected group of electrical cells 2 accumulator 3 number of similar things occurring together 4 (Law) assault by beating 5 number of guns

battle ❶ n 1 fight between armies ▷ v 2 fight **battle-axe** n 1 large

heavy axe 2 (Inf) domineering woman

battlement n wall with openings for shooting

battleship n heavily armed and armoured fighting ship

batty ❶ adj **-tier, -tiest** (Inf) crazy, silly

bauble n showy trinket

bawdy adj **bawdier, bawdiest** obscene, lewd

bawl v/n 1 cry 2 shout

bay¹ ❶ n wide inlet of sea

bay² ❶ n 1 space between two columns 2 recess

bay³ ❶ n/v bark **at bay** 1 cornered 2 at a distance

bayonet n 1 stabbing weapon fixed to rifle ▷ v 2 stab with this

bazaar ❶ n 1 market (esp. in the East) 2 sale for charity

bazooka n powerful rocket launcher

BBC British Broadcasting Corporation

BC before Christ

— THESAURUS —

bath n = **wash**, cleaning, shower, soak, cleansing ▷ v = **clean**, wash, shower, soak, cleanse

bathe v = **wash**, clean, bath, shower, soak; = **cleanse**, clean, wash, soak, rinse

baton n = **stick**, club, staff, pole, rod

batter v = **beat**, hit, strike, knock, bang

battery n = **artillery**, ordnance, gunnery, gun emplacement, cannonry

battle n = **fight**, attack, action, struggle, conflict ≠ **peace**;

= **conflict**, campaign, struggle, dispute, contest ▷ v = **wrestle**, war, fight, argue, dispute

batty adj = **crazy**, odd, mad, eccentric, peculiar

bay¹ n = **inlet**, sound, gulf, creek, cove

bay² n = **recess**, opening, corner, niche, compartment

bay³ v = **howl**, cry, roar, bark, wail ▷ n = **cry**, roar, bark, howl, wail

bazaar n = **market**, exchange, fair, marketplace; = **fair**, fête, gala, bring-and-buy

be ❶ v, present sing 1st person **am**
2nd person **are** 3rd person **is**
present pl **are** past sing 1st person
was 2nd person **were** 3rd person
was past pl **were** present
participle **being** past participle
been 1 live 2 exist 3 have a state
or quality

beach ❶ n 1 shore of sea ▷ v
2 run boat on shore

beacon ❶ n 1 fire used to give
signal 2 lighthouse, buoy

bead ❶ n 1 little ball pierced for
threading 2 drop of liquid
beaded adj **beady** adj small
and glittering

beagle n small hound

beak n 1 projecting horny jaws of
bird 2 anything similar 3 (Sl)
magistrate

beaker n 1 large drinking cup
2 glass vessel used by chemists

beam ❶ n 1 long thick piece of
wood 2 ray of light etc. ▷ v 3 aim
light, radio waves etc. (to) 4 shine
5 smile broadly

bean n edible seed of various
leguminous plants

beanie n (Brit, Aust & NZ)
close-fitting woolen hat

bear¹ ❶ v **bearing, bore, borne**
1 carry 2 support 3 produce
4 endure 5 press (upon)
bearer n

bear² n heavy carnivorous
animal

beard n 1 hair on chin ▷ v
2 oppose boldly

bearing ❶ n 1 support for
mechanical part 2 relevance
3 behaviour 4 direction 5 relative
position

beast ❶ n 1 four-footed animal
2 brutal man **beastly** adj

beat ❶ v **beating, beat, beaten**
1 strike repeatedly 2 overcome
3 surpass 4 stir vigorously 5 flap
(wings) 6 make, wear (path)
7 throb ▷ n 8 stroke 9 pulsation
10 appointed course 11 basic
rhythmic unit of music ▷ adj 12 (Sl)
exhausted **beater** n

THESAURUS

be v = **be alive**, live, exist, survive,
breathe

beach n = **shore**, coast, sands,
seaside, water's edge

beacon n = **signal**, sign, beam,
flare, lighthouse

bead n = **drop**, tear, bubble, pearl,
dot

beam v = **smile**, grin; = **transmit**,
show, air, broadcast, cable ▷ n
= **ray**, flash, stream, glow, streak;
= **rafter**, support, timber, spar,
plank; = **smile**, grin

bear¹ v = **carry**, take, move, bring,

transfer ≠ **put down**; = **support**,
shoulder, sustain, endure, uphold
≠ **give up**, have, show, hold, carry; = **suffer**, experience, go
through, sustain, stomach

bearing n usually with **on** or **upon**
= **relevance**, relation, application,
connection, import ≠ **irrelevance**;
= **manner**, attitude, conduct,
aspect, behaviour

beast n = **animal**, creature, brute;
= **brute**, monster, savage,
barbarian, fiend

beat v = **batter**, hit, strike, knock,

beau *n, pl* **beaux, beaus** suitor
beauty ❶ *n, pl* **-ties** **1** loveliness, grace **2** beautiful person or thing **beautiful** *adj* **beautifully** *adv* **beautician** *n* person who gives beauty treatments
beaver *n* **1** amphibious rodent **2** its fur ▷ *v* **3** work industriously
becalmed *adj* (of ship) motionless through lack of wind
because ❶ *adv/conj* by reason of, since
beckon ❶ *v* summon by signal
become ❶ *v* **-coming, -came, -come** **1** come to be **2** suit **becoming** *adj* suitable
bed ❶ *n* **1** piece of furniture for sleeping on **2** garden plot **3** bottom of river **4** layer, stratum ▷ *v* **5** lay in a bed **6** plant **bedding** *n* **bedpan** *n* container used as a lavatory by bedridden people **bedridden** *adj* confined to bed **bedroom** *n* **bedsit** *n* one-roomed flat **bedstead** *n* framework of a bed

bedevil *v* **-illing, -illed** harass or torment
bedlam *n* noisy confused scene
bedraggled *adj* messy and wet
bee *n* insect that makes honey
beech *n* European tree with smooth greyish bark and small nuts
beef *n* **1** flesh of cattle for eating **2** (*Inf*) complaint ▷ *v* **3** (*Inf*) complain **beefy** *adj* muscular **beefburger** *n* flat grilled or fried cake of minced beef
beer *n* fermented alcoholic drink made from hops and malt **beer parlour** (*Canad*) licensed place where beer is sold to the public
beet *n* any of various plants with root used for food **beetroot** *n* type of beet plant with a dark red root
beetle *n* class of insect with hard upper-wing cases
befall *v* happen (to)
befit *v* be suitable to
before ❶ *prep* **1** in front of **2** in presence of **3** in preference to **4** earlier than ▷ *adv* **5** earlier **6** in

b

— THESAURUS —

pound (*Inf*); = **pound**, strike, hammer, batter, thrash; = **throb**, thump, pound, quake, vibrate; = **hit**, strike, bang ▷ *n* = **throb**, pounding, pulse, thumping, vibration; = **route**, way, course, rounds, path
beauty *n* = **attractiveness**, charm, grace, glamour, elegance ≠ **ugliness**; = **good-looker**, lovely (*Sl*), belle, stunner (*Inf*)
because *conj* = **since**, as, in that
beckon *v* = **gesture**, sign, wave, indicate, signal

become *v* = **come to be**, develop into, be transformed into, grow into, change into; = **suit**, fit, enhance, flatter, embellish
bed *n* = **bedstead**, couch, berth, cot, bunk; = **plot**, area, row, strip, patch; = **bottom**, ground, floor
before *prep* = **earlier than**, ahead of, prior to, in advance of ≠ **after**; = **in front of**, ahead of, in advance of ▷ *adv* = **previously**, earlier, sooner, in advance, formerly ≠ **after**; = **in the past**, earlier, once, previously, formerly

front ▷ conj **7** sooner than

beforehand adv previously

befriend v become a friend to

beg ❶ v **begging, begged 1** ask earnestly **2** ask for money or food **beggar** n

begin ❶ v **-ginning, -gan, -gun** (cause to) start **beginner** n **beginning** n

begonia n tropical plant

begrudge v grudge, envy anyone the possession of

beguile v **1** charm, fascinate **2** amuse **3** deceive

behalf n **on behalf of** in the interest of

behave ❶ v **1** act in particular way **2** act properly **behaviour** n conduct

behead v cut off the head of

behest n charge, command

behind ❶ prep **1** further back or earlier than ▷ adv **2** in the rear

behold v **-holding, -held** watch, see

beholden adj bound in gratitude

beige n **1** undyed woollen cloth **2** its colour

being ❶ n **1** existence **2** that which exists **3** creature: present participle of BE

belated adj **1** late **2** too late

belch v **1** expel wind by mouth **2** eject violently ▷ n **3** this act

beleaguered ❶ adj **1** besieged **2** surrounded or beset

belfry n, pl **-fries** bell tower

belie v show to be untrue

believe v **1** regard as true or real **2** have faith **belief** n **believable** adj **believer** n

belittle v regard, speak of, as having little worth

bell n **1** hollow metal instrument giving ringing sound when struck **2** electrical device emitting ring

belle n beautiful woman

bellicose adj warlike

——————— THESAURUS ———————

beg v = **implore**, plead with, beseech, request, petition; = **scrounge**, bum (Inf), touch (someone) for (Sl), cadge, sponge on (someone) for ≠ **give**

begin v = **start**, commence, proceed ≠ **stop**; = **commence**, start, initiate, embark on, set about

behave v often reflexive = **be well-behaved**, mind your manners, keep your nose clean, act correctly, conduct yourself properly ≠ **misbehave**

behind prep = **at the rear of**, at the back of, at the heels of; = **after**,

following ▷ adv = **after**, next, following, afterwards, subsequently ≠ **in advance of**; = **behind schedule**, delayed, running late, behind time ≠ **ahead**

being n = **individual**, creature, human being, living thing; = **life**, reality ≠ **nonexistence**; = **soul**, spirit, substance, creature, essence

beleaguered adj = **harassed**, troubled, plagued, hassled (Inf), badgered; = **besieged**, surrounded, blockaded, beset, encircled

bellow v = **shout**, cry (out),

belligerent *adj* 1 hostile, aggressive 2 making war **belligerence** *n*

bellow *v/n* 1 roar 2 shout

bellows *pl n* instrument for creating stream of air

belly ❶ *n, pl* **-lies** 1 stomach ▷ *v* 2 swell out

belong *v* 1 be property of 2 be member of 3 have an allotted place 4 pertain to **belongings** *pl n* personal possessions

beloved ❶ *adj* 1 much loved ▷ *n* 2 dear one

below ❶ *adv* 1 beneath ▷ *prep* 2 lower than

belt ❶ *n* 1 band 2 girdle 3 zone ▷ *v* 4 (*Inf*) thrash

bemoan *v* grieve over

bench ❶ *n* 1 long seat 2 seat or body of judges etc.

bend ❶ *v* bending, bent (cause to) form a curve

beneath ❶ *prep* 1 under, lower than ▷ *adv* 2 below

benefit ❶ *n* 1 advantage, profit 2 money paid to unemployed etc. ▷ *v* 3 do good to 4 receive good **benefactor** *n* 1 one who helps or does good to others 2 patron **beneficial** *adj*

benign ❶ *adj* kindly, favourable

bent ❶ *adj* 1 curved 2 resolved (on) 3 (*Inf*) corrupt 4 (*Inf*) deviant ▷ *n* 5 inclination

benzene *n* one of group of flammable liquids used as solvents etc.

bequeath *v* leave property etc. by will **bequest** *n* 1 bequeathing 2 legacy

berate *v* scold harshly

scream, roar, yell ▷ *n* = **shout**, cry, scream, roar, yell

belly *n* = **stomach**, insides (*Inf*), gut, abdomen, tummy

beloved *adj* = **dear**, loved, valued, prized, admired

below *prep* = **under**, underneath, lower than ▷ *adv* = **lower**, down, under, beneath, underneath

belt *n* = **waistband**, band, sash, girdle, girth; = **conveyor belt**, band, loop, fan belt, drive belt

bench *n* = **seat**, stall, pew; = **worktable**, stand, table, counter, trestle table

bend *v* = **twist**, turn, wind, lean, hook ▷ *n* = **curve**, turn, corner, twist, angle

beneath *prep* = **under**, below, underneath, lower than ≠ **over**; = **inferior to**, below ▷ *adv* = **underneath**, below, in a lower place

benefit *n* = **good**, help, profit, favour ≠ **harm** ▷ *v* = **profit from**, make the most of, gain from, do well out of, reap benefits from

benign *adj* = **benevolent**, kind, kindly, warm, friendly ≠ **unkind**; (*Medical*) = **harmless**, innocent, innocuous, curable, inoffensive ≠ **malignant**

bent *adj* = **misshapen**, twisted, angled, bowed, curved ≠ **straight** ▷ *n* = **inclination**, ability, leaning, tendency, preference

beret n round, close-fitting hat

berg[1] n (S Afr) mountain

berg[2] n iceberg

berry n, pl **-ries** small juicy stoneless fruit

berm n (NZ) narrow grass strip between the road and the footpath in a residential area

berserk adj **go berserk** become violent or destructive

berth ❶ n 1 ship's mooring place 2 place to sleep in ship ▷ v 3 moor

beryl n variety of crystalline mineral, e.g. aquamarine, emerald

beseech v **-seeching, -sought** entreat, implore

beset v surround with danger, problems

beside ❶ prep 1 by the side of, near 2 distinct from **besides** adv/prep in addition (to)

besiege ❶ v surround

besotted adj 1 drunk 2 foolish 3 infatuated

best ❶ adj/adv 1 superlative of GOOD and WELL ▷ v 2 defeat **best man** groom's attendant at wedding **bestseller** n book sold in great numbers

bestial adj like a beast, brutish

bestir v rouse to activity

bestow ❶ v give, confer

bet ❶ v 1 agree to pay money if wrong in guessing result of contest ▷ n 2 money so risked

bête noire n particular dislike

betray ❶ v 1 be disloyal to 2 reveal, divulge 3 show signs of **betrayal** n

better ❶ adj/adv 1 comparative of GOOD and WELL ▷ v 2 improve

between ❶ prep/adv 1 in the intermediate part, in space or time 2 indicating reciprocal relation or

— THESAURUS —

berth n = **bunk**, bed, hammock, billet; = **anchorage**, haven, port, harbour, dock ▷ v = **anchor**, land, dock, moor, tie up

beside prep = **next to**, near, close to, neighbouring, alongside

besiege v = **harass**, harry, plague, hound, hassle (Inf); = **surround**, enclose, blockade, encircle, hem in

best adj = **finest**, leading, supreme, principal, foremost ▷ adv = **most highly**, mostly fully, most deeply

bestow v = **present**, give, award, grant, commit ≠ **obtain**

bet v = **gamble**, chance, stake, venture, hazard ▷ n = **gamble**, risk, stake, venture, speculation

betray v = **be disloyal to**, double-cross (Inf), stab in the back, be unfaithful to, inform on or against; = **give away**, reveal, expose, disclose, uncover

better ❶ adv = **to a greater degree**, more completely, more thoroughly; = **in a more excellent manner**, more effectively, more attractively, more advantageously, more competently ≠ **worse** ▷ adj = **well**, stronger, recovering, cured, fully recovered ≠ **worse**; = **superior**, finer, higher-quality, surpassing, preferable ≠ **inferior**

between prep = **amidst**, among, mid, in the middle of, betwixt comparison

bevel n 1 angled surface ▷ v 2 slope, slant

beverage ❶ n drink

beverage room n (Canad) tavern

bevy n, pl **bevies** flock or group

bewail v lament

beware ❶ v be on one's guard

bewilder ❶ v puzzle, confuse

bewitch v charm, fascinate

beyond ❶ adv 1 farther away ▷ prep 2 on the farther side of 3 out of reach of

bias ❶ n 1 slant 2 inclination ▷ v 3 influence, affect **biased** adj prejudiced

bib n 1 cloth put under child's chin when eating 2 top of apron

Bible n sacred writings of the Christian religion **biblical** adj

bibliography n, pl **-phies** list of books on a subject

bicentenary n 200th anniversary

biceps n two-headed muscle, esp. of upper arm

bicker v/n quarrel over petty things

bicycle n vehicle with two wheels **bicyclist** n

bid ❶ v **bidding, bade, bidden** 1 offer 2 say 3 command 4 invite ▷ n 5 offer, esp. of price 6 try 7 (Card games) call **bidder** n **bidding** n command

bide v 1 remain 2 dwell 3 await

bier n frame for coffin

big ❶ adj **bigger, biggest** of great size, height, number, power etc. **bighead** n (Inf) conceited person **big-headed** adj

bigamy n crime of marrying a person while one is still legally married to someone else **bigamist** n

bigot n person intolerant of ideas of others **bigoted** adj **bigotry** n

bike n short for BICYCLE or MOTORBIKE

bikini n woman's two-piece swimming costume

bilberry n small moorland plant with edible blue berries

bile n 1 fluid secreted by the liver

b

— THESAURUS —

beverage n = **drink**, liquid, liquor, refreshment

beware v = **be careful**, look out, watch out, be wary, be cautious

bewilder v = **confound**, confuse, puzzle, baffle, perplex

beyond prep = **after**, over, past, above

bias n = **prejudice**, leaning, tendency, inclination, favouritism ≠ **impartiality** ▷ v = **influence**, colour, weight, prejudice, distort

bid n = **attempt**, try, effort, go (Inf),

shot (Inf); = **offer**, price, amount, advance, proposal ▷ v = **make an offer**, offer, propose, submit, tender; = **wish**, say, call, tell, greet; = **tell**, ask, order, require, direct

big adj = **large**, great, huge, massive, vast ≠ **small**; = **important**, significant, urgent, far-reaching ≠ **unimportant**; = **powerful**, important, prominent, dominant, influential; = **grown-up**, adult, grown, mature, elder ≠ **young**

b

2 ill temper **bilious** adj nauseous, nauseating

bilge n 1 bottom of ship's hull 2 dirty water collecting there 3 (Inf) nonsense

bilingual adj speaking, or written in, two languages

bill¹ ❶ n 1 written account of charges 2 draft of Act of Parliament 3 poster 4 commercial document 5 (US & Canad) banknote ▷ v 6 present account of charges 7 announce by advertisement

bill² ❷ n bird's beak

billet n/v **-leting, -leted** (provide) civilian quarters for troops

billiards n game played on table with balls and cues

billion n 1 thousand million, 10^9 2 (Obs) million million, 10^{12}

billow n 1 swelling wave ▷ v 2 swell

biltong n (S Afr) strips of dried meat

bin n receptacle for corn, refuse etc.

binary adj 1 composed of, characterized by, two 2 dual

bind ❸ v **binding, bound** 1 tie fast 2 tie round 3 oblige 4 seal 5 constrain 6 bandage 7 cohere

8 put (book) into cover **binder** n **binding** n 1 cover of book 2 tape for hem etc.

binge ❹ n (Inf) spree

bingo n game of chance in which numbers drawn are matched with those on a card

binoculars pl n telescope made for both eyes

bio- comb. form life, living, as in biochemistry

biodegradable adj capable of decomposition by natural means

biofuel n fuel derived from renewable biological resources

biography ❺ n, pl **-phies** story of one person's life **biographer** n **biographical** adj

biology n study of living organisms **biological** adj **biologist** n

bionic adj having physical functions aided by electronic equipment

biopsy n, pl **-sies** examination of tissue from a living body

biped n two-footed animal

birch n 1 tree with silvery bark 2 rod for punishment ▷ v 3 flog

bird n feathered animal

bill¹ n = **charges**, rate, costs, score, account; = **act of parliament**, measure, proposal, piece of legislation, projected law; = **list**, listing, programme, card, schedule; = **advertisement**, notice, poster, leaflet, bulletin ▷ v = **charge**, debit, invoice, send a statement to, send an invoice to; = **advertise**, post, announce, promote, plug

(Inf)

bill² n = **beak**, nib, neb (archaic or dialect), mandible

bind v = **oblige**, make, force, require, engage; = **tie**, join, stick, secure, wrap ≠ **untie**

binge n (Inf) = **bout**, spell, fling, feast, stint

biography n = **life story**, life, record, account, profile

birdie n (Golf) score of one stroke under par

Biro® n Trademark ballpoint pen

birth ❶ n **1** bearing, or the being born, of offspring **2** parentage, origin **birthday** n **birthmark** n blemish on the skin

biscuit n dry, small, thin variety of cake

bisect v divide into two equal parts

bisexual adj sexually attracted to both men and women

bishop n **1** clergyman governing diocese **2** chess piece

bison n, pl **-son 1** large wild ox **2** Amer. buffalo

bistro n, pl **-tros** small restaurant

bit¹ ❶ n fragment, piece

bit² n **1** biting, cutting part of tool **2** mouthpiece of horse's bridle

bit³ n (Comp) smallest part of information

bitch n **1** female dog, fox, or wolf **2** (Offens) spiteful woman **bitchy** adj

bite ❶ v biting, bit, bitten **1** cut into, esp. with teeth **2** grip **3** rise to the bait **4** corrode ▷ n

5 act of biting **6** wound so made **7** mouthful **biting** adj **1** piercing or keen **2** sarcastic

bitter ❶ adj **1** sour tasting **2** (of person) resentful **3** sarcastic **bitterly** adv **bitterness** n

bittern n wading bird

bitumen n viscous substance occurring in asphalt, tar etc.

bivouac n **1** temporary encampment of soldiers, hikers etc. ▷ v **2** camp

bizarre ❶ adj unusual, weird

blab v blabbing, blabbed **1** reveal secrets **2** chatter idly

black ❶ adj **1** of the darkest colour **2** without light **3** dark **4** evil ▷ n **5** darkest colour **6** black dye, clothing etc. **7** (with cap.) person of dark-skinned race ▷ v **8** boycott in industrial dispute **blacken** v **1** make black **2** defame **blackball** v vote against, exclude **blackberry** n plant with dark juicy berries, bramble **blackbird** n common European songbird **blackboard** n dark surface for writing on with chalk **black box** Inf. name for FLIGHT RECORDER **blackhead** n

---

THESAURUS

birth n = **childbirth**, delivery, nativity, parturition ≠ **death**; = **ancestry**, stock, blood, background, breeding

bit¹ n = **piece**, scrap

bite v = **nip**, cut, tear, wound, snap ▷ n = **snack**, food, piece, taste, refreshment; = **wound**, sting, pinch, nip, prick

bitter adj = **resentful**, angry, offended, sour, sore ≠ **happy**;

= **freezing**, biting, severe, intense, raw ≠ **mild**; = **sour**, sharp, acid, harsh, tart ≠ **sweet**

bizarre adj = **strange**, unusual, extraordinary, fantastic, weird ≠ **normal**

black adj = **dark**, raven, ebony, sable, jet ≠ **light**; = **gloomy**, sad, depressing, grim, bleak ≠ **happy**; = **terrible**, bad, devastating, tragic, fatal

b

small dark spot on skin **blackleg** n strikebreaker **blacklist** n **1** list of people considered suspicious ▷ v **2** put on such a list **black market** illegal buying and selling of goods **black spot** dangerous place, esp. on a road

blackguard n scoundrel

blackmail ❶ v **1** extort money by threats ▷ n **2** extortion **blackmailer** n

blackout n **1** complete failure of electricity supply **2** state of temporary unconsciousness **3** obscuring of lights as precaution against night air attack

blacksmith n person who works in iron

bladder n membranous bag to contain liquid

blade n **1** edge, cutting part of knife or tool **2** leaf of grass etc. **3** sword

blame ❶ n **1** censure **2** culpability ▷ v **3** find fault with **4** censure **blameless** adj **blameworthy** adj

blanch v **1** whiten, bleach **2** turn pale

blancmange n pudding made from milk

bland ❶ adj **1** devoid of distinctive characteristics **2** smooth in manner **blandly** adv

blank ❶ adj **1** without marks or writing **2** empty **3** vacant, confused ▷ n **4** empty space **5** cartridge containing no bullet **blankly** adv

blanket ❶ n **1** thick bed cover **2** concealing cover ▷ v **3** cover, stifle

blare v **1** sound loudly and harshly ▷ n **2** such sound

blarney n flattering talk

blasé adj **1** indifferent through familiarity **2** bored

blaspheme v show contempt for God, esp. in speech **blasphemous** adj **blasphemy** n

blast ❶ n **1** explosion **2** shock wave **3** gust of wind **4** loud sound ▷ v **5** blow up **6** blight

THESAURUS

blackmail n = **threat**, intimidation, ransom, extortion, hush money (SI) ▷ v = **threaten**, squeeze, compel, intimidate, coerce

blame v = **hold responsible**, accuse, denounce, indict, impeach ≠ **absolve** (used in negative constructions) ▷ n = **responsibility**, liability, accountability, onus, culpability ≠ **praise**

bland adj = **dull**, boring, plain, flat, dreary ≠ **exciting**

blank adj = **unmarked**, white, clear, clean, empty ≠ **marked**; = **expressionless**, empty, vague, vacant, deadpan ≠ **expressive** ▷ n = **empty space**, space, gap

blanket n = **cover**, rug, coverlet; = **covering**, sheet, coat, layer, carpet ▷ v = **coat**, cover, hide, mask, conceal

blast n = **explosion**, crash, burst, discharge, eruption; = **gust**, rush, storm, breeze, puff; = **blare**, blow, scream, trumpet, wail ▷ v = **blow up**, bomb, destroy, burst, ruin

blatant ❶ *adj* obvious **blatantly** *adv*

blaze¹ ❶ *n* 1 strong fire or flame 2 brightness 3 outburst ▷ *v* 4 burn strongly 5 be very angry

blaze² *v* 1 establish trail ▷ *n* 2 white mark on horse's face

blazer *n* type of jacket worn esp. for sports

bleach ❶ *v* 1 make or become white ▷ *n* 2 bleaching substance

bleak ❶ *adj* 1 cold, exposed 2 dismal **bleakness** *n*

bleary *adj* **-rier, -riest** with eyes dimmed, as with tears, sleep

bleat *v* 1 cry, as sheep 2 say plaintively ▷ *n* 3 sheep's cry

bleed ❶ *v* **bleeding, bled** 1 lose blood 2 draw blood from

bleep *n* short high-pitched sound **bleeper** *n*

blemish *n* 1 defect ▷ *v* 2 make defective **blemished** *adj*

blend ❶ *v* 1 mix ▷ *n* 2 mixture **blender** *n* electrical appliance for mixing food

bless ❶ *v* 1 consecrate 2 ask God's favour for 3 make happy **blessed** *adj* **blessing** *n*

blether *v* 1 speak at length, esp. foolishly ▷ *n* 2 foolish or babbling talk

blight ❶ *n* 1 plant disease 2 harmful influence ▷ *v* 3 injure

blighter *n* (*Inf*) irritating person

blind ❶ *adj* 1 unable to see 2 heedless 3 closed at one end ▷ *v* 4 deprive of sight ▷ *n* 5 window screen 6 pretext **blindly** *adv* **blindness** *n* **blindfold** *v/n* (cloth used to) cover the eyes

——— THESAURUS ———

blatant *adj* = **obvious**, clear, plain, evident, glaring ≠ **subtle**

blaze¹ *v* = **burn**, glow, flare, be on fire, go up in flames ▷ *n* = **inferno**, fire, flames, bonfire, combustion; = **flash**, glow, glitter, flare, glare

bleach *v* = **lighten**, wash out, blanch, whiten

bleak *adj* = **dismal**, dark, depressing, grim, discouraging ≠ **cheerful**; = **exposed**, empty, bare, barren, desolate ≠ **sheltered**

bleed *v* = **lose blood**, flow, gush, spurt, shed blood; (*Inf*) = **extort**, milk, squeeze, drain, exhaust

blend *v* = **mix**, join, combine, compound, merge; = **go well**, match, fit, suit, go with ▷ *n* = **mixture**, mix, combination, compound, brew

bless *v* = **sanctify**, dedicate, ordain, exalt, anoint ≠ **curse**; = **endow**, give to, provide for, grant for, favour ≠ **afflict**

blight *n* = **curse**, suffering, evil, corruption, pollution ≠ **blessing**; = **disease**, pest, fungus, mildew, infestation ▷ *v* = **frustrate**, destroy, ruin, crush, mar

blind *adj* = **sightless**, unsighted, unseeing, eyeless, visionless ≠ **sighted**; (*often with to*) = **unaware of**, unconscious of, ignorant of, indifferent to, insensitive to ≠ **aware**; = **unquestioning**, prejudiced, wholesale, indiscriminate, uncritical

blink ❶ v **1** wink **2** twinkle ▷ n **3** gleam **blink at** ignore **on the blink** (Inf) not working

blip n repetitive sound or visible pulse, e.g. on radar screen

bliss ❶ n perfect happiness **blissful** adj **blissfully** adv

blister ❶ n **1** bubble on skin **2** surface swelling ▷ v **3** form blisters (on) **blistering** adj **1** very hot **2** extremely harsh

blithe adj happy **blithely** adv

blitz ❶ n concentrated attack

blizzard n blinding storm of wind and snow

blob n soft mass or drop

block ❶ n **1** solid (rectangular) piece of wood, stone etc. **2** obstacle **3** pulley with frame **4** large building of offices, flats etc. ▷ v **5** obstruct, stop up **6** shape **blockage** n **blockhead** n stupid person **block letter** plain capital letter

blockade ❶ n **1** physical prevention of access, esp. to port ▷ v **2** prevent access

bloke ❶ n (Inf) fellow, chap

blood ❶ n **1** red fluid in veins **2** kindred ▷ v **3** initiate (into hunting, war etc.) **bloodless** adj **bloody** adj **1** covered in blood **2** savage **3** extreme ▷ adv **4** (Sl) extremely ▷ v **5** make bloody **blood bath** massacre **bloodhound** n large dog used for tracking **bloodshed** n slaughter **bloodshot** adj (of eyes) inflamed **bloodthirsty** adj cruel **bloody-minded** adj deliberately unhelpful

bloom ❶ n **1** flower **2** prime **3** glow ▷ v **4** be in flower **5** flourish

bloomer n (Inf) mistake

bloomers pl n wide, baggy knickers

blossom ❶ n **1** flower ▷ v

——————— THESAURUS ———————

blink v = **flutter**, wink, bat; = **flash**, flicker, wink, shimmer, twinkle **on the blink** (Inf) = **not working (properly)**, faulty, defective, playing up, out of action

bliss n = **joy**, ecstasy, euphoria, rapture, nirvana ≠ **misery**

blister n = **sore**, boil, swelling, cyst, pimple

blitz n = **attack**, strike, assault, raid, offensive

block n = **piece**, bar, mass, brick, lump; = **obstruction**, bar, barrier, obstacle, impediment ▷ v = **obstruct**, close, stop, plug, choke ≠ **clear**

blockade n = **stoppage**, block, barrier, restriction, obstacle

bloke n (Inf) = **man**, person, individual, character (Inf), guy (Inf)

blood n = **lifeblood**, gore, vital fluid; = **family**, relations, birth, descent, extraction

bloom n = **flower**, bud, blossom; = **prime**, flower, beauty, height, peak; = **glow**, freshness, lustre, radiance ≠ **pallor** ▷ v = **flower**, blossom, open, bud ≠ **wither**; = **grow**, develop, wax

blossom n = **flower**, bloom, bud, efflorescence, floret ▷ v = **bloom**, grow, develop, mature; = **succeed**,

DICTIONARY

2 flower **3** flourish

blot n **1** spot, stain ▷ v **2** spot, stain **3** obliterate **4** soak up ink
blotter n

blotch n **1** dark spot ▷ v **2** make spotted

blouse n light, loose upper garment

blow¹ ❶ v **blowing, blew, blown 1** make a current of air **2** pant **3** drive air upon or into **4** drive by current of air **5** make sound **6** (Sl) squander ▷ n **7** blast **8** gale
blower n **blowfly** n fly which infects food etc. **blowlamp** n small burner with hot flame
blowout n **1** sudden puncture in tyre **2** uncontrolled escape of oil, gas, from well **3** (Sl) large meal
blow up 1 explode **2** fill with air **3** (Inf) enlarge photograph **4** (Inf) lose one's temper

blow² ❶ n **1** stroke, knock **2** sudden misfortune

blubber v **1** weep ▷ n **2** whale fat

bludge v **1** (Aust & NZ, Inf) evade work **2** scrounge **bludger** n person who scrounges

bludgeon n **1** short thick club ▷ v **2** strike with one **3** coerce

blue ❶ adj **1** of the colour of sky **2** depressed **3** indecent ▷ n **4** colour of sky **5** dye or pigment ▷ pl **6** (Inf) depression **7** form of jazz music ▷ v **8** make blue **bluish** adj **bluebell** n wild spring flower **bluebottle** n blowfly **blueprint** n **1** copy of drawing **2** original plan

bluff¹ ❶ n **1** cliff, steep bank **2** (Canad) clump of trees ▷ adj **3** hearty **4** blunt

bluff² ❶ v/n (deceive by) pretence

blunder ❶ n/v (make) clumsy mistake

blunt ❶ adj **1** not sharp **2** (of speech) abrupt ▷ v **3** make blunt **bluntly** adv

blur ❶ v **blurring, blurred 1** make, become less distinct ▷ n **2** something indistinct

THESAURUS

progress, thrive, flourish, prosper

blow¹ v = **move**, carry, drive, sweep, fling; = **be carried**, flutter; = **exhale**, breathe, pant, puff

blow² n = **knock**, stroke, punch, bang, sock (Sl); = **setback**, shock, disaster, reverse, disappointment

blue adj = **depressed**, low, sad, unhappy, melancholy ≠ **happy**; = **smutty**, obscene, indecent, lewd, risqué ≠ **respectable**

bluff¹ n = **precipice**, bank, peak, cliff, ridge ▷ adj = **hearty**, open, blunt, outspoken, genial ≠ **tactful**

bluff² n = **deception**, fraud, sham,

pretence, deceit ▷ v = **deceive**, trick, fool, pretend, cheat

blunder n = **mistake**, slip, fault, error, oversight ≠ **correctness** ▷ v = **make a mistake**, blow it (Sl), err, slip up (Inf), foul up ≠ **be correct**; = **stumble**, fall, reel, stagger, lurch

blunt adj = **frank**, forthright, straightforward, rude, outspoken ≠ **tactful**; = **dull**, rounded, dulled, edgeless, unsharpened ≠ **sharp** ▷ v = **dull**, weaken, soften, numb, dampen ≠ **stimulate**

blur n = **haze**, confusion, fog, obscurity, indistinctness ▷ v

blurb n statement recommending book etc.

blurt v utter suddenly

blush ❶ v 1 become red in face 2 be ashamed ▷ n 3 this effect **blusher** n cosmetic to give rosy colour to face

bluster v/n (indulge in) noisy, aggressive behaviour **blustery** adj (of wind) gusty

BO (Inf) body odour

boa n 1 large, nonpoisonous snake 2 long scarf of fur or feathers

boar n 1 male pig 2 wild pig

board ❶ n 1 broad, flat piece of wood, card etc. 2 table 3 meals 4 group of people who administer company ▷ v 5 cover with planks 6 supply food daily 7 enter ship etc. 8 take daily meals **boarder** n **boardroom** n

boast ❶ v 1 speak too much in praise of oneself 2 brag of 3 have to show ▷ n 4 thing boasted (of) **boastful** adj

boat n 1 small open vessel 2 ship ▷ v 3 sail about in boat **boater** n flat straw hat **boatswain** n ship's

officer in charge of equipment

bob ❶ v **bobbing, bobbed** 1 move up and down 2 move jerkily 3 cut (women's) hair short ▷ n 4 jerking motion 5 short hairstyle 6 weight on pendulum etc.

bobbin n reel for thread

bobble n small, tufted ball

bobby n, pl **-bies** (Inf) police officer

bobotie n (S Afr) dish of curried mince

bobsleigh n 1 sledge for racing ▷ v 2 ride on this

bode v be an omen of

bodice n upper part of woman's dress

bodkin n large blunt needle

body ❶ n, pl **bodies** 1 whole frame of man or animal 2 corpse 3 main part 4 substance 5 group regarded as single entity **bodily** adj/adv **bodyguard** n escort to protect important person **body mass index** measure used to gauge whether a person is overweight: a person's weight in kilograms divided by the square of his or her height in

= **become indistinct**, become vague, become hazy, become fuzzy

blush v = **turn red**, colour, glow, flush, redden ≠ **turn pale** ▷ n = **reddening**, colour, glow, flush, pink tinge

board n = **plank**, panel, timber, slat, piece of timber; = **council**, directors, committee, congress, advisers; = **meals**, provisions, victuals, daily meals ▷ v = **get on**, enter, mount, embark ≠ **get off**

boast v = **brag**, crow, vaunt, talk big (Sl), blow your own trumpet ≠ **cover up**; = **possess**, exhibit

bob v = **bounce**, duck, hop, wobble, oscillate

body n = **physique**, build, form, figure, shape; = **torso**, trunk; = **corpse**, dead body, remains, stiff (Sl), carcass; = **organization**, company, group, society, association; = **main part**, matter, material, mass, substance metres **bodywork** n outer shell of motor vehicle

boffin n (Inf) scientist

bog ⊕ n 1 wet, soft ground **boggy** adj **bog down bogging, bogged** stick as in a bog

bogan n (Aust dated & NZ, Sl) youth who dresses and behaves rebelliously

bogey, bogy ⊕ n 1 thing that causes fear 2 (Golf) score of one stroke over par

boggle v stare, be surprised

bogus ⊕ adj sham, false

bohemian n/adj (person) leading unconventional life

boil¹ ⊕ v 1 (cause to) change from liquid to gas, esp. by heating 2 cook or become cooked by boiling 3 (Inf) be hot 4 (Inf) be angry ⊳ n 5 boiling state **boiler** n equipment providing hot water

boil² ⊕ n inflamed swelling on skin

boisterous adj 1 wild 2 noisy

bold ⊕ adj 1 daring, presumptuous 2 prominent **boldly** adv **boldness** n

bole n tree trunk

bolero n, pl -ros 1 Spanish dance 2 short loose jacket

bollard n 1 post to secure mooring lines 2 post in road as barrier

bolster ⊕ v 1 support, uphold ⊳ n 2 long pillow 3 pad, support

bolt ⊕ n 1 bar or pin (esp. with thread for nut) 2 rush 3 lightning 4 roll of cloth ⊳ v 5 fasten 6 swallow hastily 7 rush away

bomb ⊕ n 1 explosive projectile 2 any explosive device ⊳ v 3 attack with bombs **bomber** n 1 aircraft that drops bombs 2 person who throws or plants a bomb **bombard** v 1 shell 2 attack (verbally) **bombshell** n shocking surprise

bona fide (Lat) genuine

bonanza n sudden wealth

bond ⊕ n 1 thing which binds 2 link 3 written promise ⊳ v 4 bind

bondage n slavery

bone n 1 hard substance forming

bog n = **marsh**, swamp, slough, wetlands, fen

bogey n = **bugbear**, bête noire, horror, nightmare, bugaboo

bogus adj = **fake**, false, artificial, forged, imitation ≠ **genuine**

boil¹ v = **simmer**, bubble, foam, seethe, fizz

boil² n = **pustule**, gathering, swelling, blister, carbuncle

bold adj = **fearless**, enterprising, brave, daring, heroic ≠ **timid**; = **impudent**, forward, confident, rude, cheeky ≠ **shy**

bolster v = **support**, help, boost, strengthen, reinforce

bolt n = **pin**, rod, peg, rivet; = **bar**, catch, lock, latch, fastener ⊳ v = **lock**, close, bar, secure, fasten; = **dash**, fly; = **gobble**, stuff, wolf, cram, gorge

bomb n = **explosive**, mine, shell, missile, device ⊳ v = **blow up**, attack, destroy, assault, shell

bond n = **tie**, union, coupling, link, association; = **fastening**, tie, chain, cord, shackle; = **agreement**, word, skeleton **2** piece of this ▷ v **3** take out bone **bony** adj **bone-idle** adj extremely lazy

bonfire n large outdoor fire

bongo n, pl **-gos, -goes** small drum played with fingers

bonk v (Inf) **1** hit **2** have sexual intercourse (with)

bonnet n **1** hat with strings **2** cap **3** cover of motor vehicle engine

bonny adj **-nier, -niest** beautiful, handsome

bonsai n, pl **-sai** (art of growing) dwarf trees, shrubs

bonus ❶ n **1** extra (unexpected) payment or gift

boo interj **1** expression of disapproval **2** exclamation to surprise esp. child ▷ v **3** make this sound

boob n (Sl) **1** foolish mistake **2** female breast

boogie v (Inf) dance quickly to pop music

book ❶ n **1** sheets of paper bound together **2** literary work ▷ v **3** reserve room, ticket etc. **4** charge with legal offence **5** enter name in book **booklet** n **book-keeping** n systematic

recording of business transactions **bookmaker** n one who takes bets **bookworm** n person devoted to reading

boom[1] ❶ n **1** sudden commercial activity **2** prosperity ▷ v **3** prosper

boom[2] v/n (make) deep sound

boom[3] n long spar for bottom of sail

boomerang n curved wooden missile of Aust. Aborigines, which returns to the thrower

boon ❶ n something helpful, favour

boor n rude person **boorish** adj

boost ❶ n **1** encouragement **2** upward push **3** increase ▷ v **4** encourage **5** push **booster** n

boot ❶ n **1** covering for the foot and ankle **2** luggage space in car **3** (Inf) kick ▷ v **4** (Inf) kick

booth n **1** stall **2** cubicle

bootleg v **1** make, carry, sell illicit goods, esp. alcohol ▷ adj **2** produced, sold illicitly **bootlegger** n

booty n, pl **-ties** plunder, spoil

booze n/v (Inf) (consume) alcoholic drink

— THESAURUS —

promise, contract, guarantee ▷ v **= form friendships**, connect

bonus n = **extra**, prize, gift, reward, premium

book n = **work**, title, volume, publication, tract; = **notebook**, album, journal, diary, pad ▷ v **= reserve**, schedule, engage, organize, charter

boom[1] n = **expansion**, increase,

development, growth, jump ≠ **decline**

boon n = **benefit**, blessing, godsend, gift

boost v = **increase**, develop, raise, expand, add to ≠ **decrease** ▷ n **= rise**, increase, jump, addition, improvement ≠ **fall**; **= encouragement**, help

boot v = **kick**, punt, put the boot

b

border ❶ n 1 margin 2 frontier 3 limit 4 strip of garden ▷ v 5 provide with border 6 adjoin

bore¹ ❶ v 1 pierce hole ▷ n 2 hole 3 calibre of gun

bore² ❶ v 1 make weary by repetition ▷ n 2 tiresome person or thing **boredom** n **boring** adj

boron n chemical element used in hardening steel etc.

borough n town

borrow ❶ v 1 obtain on loan 2 copy, steal **borrower** n

borstal n formerly, prison for young criminals

borzoi n tall dog with long, silky coat

bosom n human breast

boss ❶ n 1 person in charge of or employing others ▷ v 2 be in charge of 3 be domineering over **bossy** adj **bossier, bossiest** overbearing

botany n study of plants **botanical** adj **botanist** n

botch v 1 spoil by clumsiness ▷ n

2 blunder

both adj/pron the two

bother ❶ v 1 pester 2 perplex 3 trouble ▷ n 4 fuss, trouble

Botox® n 1 drug used to treat muscle spasms and to reduce wrinkles ▷ v 2 apply Botox to (a person or a body part)

bottle n 1 vessel for holding liquid 2 its contents ▷ v 3 put into bottle 4 restrain **bottleneck** n narrow outlet which impedes smooth flow

bottom ❶ n 1 lowest part 2 bed of sea etc. 3 buttocks ▷ adj 4 lowest ▷ v 5 put bottom to 6 base (upon) 7 get to bottom of **bottomless** adj

bough n branch of tree

boulder n large rock

boulevard n broad street or promenade

bounce ❶ v 1 (cause to) rebound on impact ▷ n 2 rebounding 3 quality causing this 4 (Inf) vitality **bouncer** n person who removes unwanted people from

---

THESAURUS

---

in(to) (Sl), drop-kick

border n = **frontier**, line, limit, bounds, boundary; = **edge**, margin/ verge, rim ▷ v = **edge**, bound, decorate, trim, fringe

bore¹ v = **drill**, mine, sink, tunnel, pierce

bore² v = **tire**, fatigue, weary, wear out, jade ≠ **excite** ▷ n = **nuisance**, pain (Inf), yawn (Inf), anorak (Inf)

borrow v = **take on loan**, touch (someone) for (Sl), scrounge (Inf), cadge, use temporarily ≠ **lend**; = **steal**, take, copy, adopt, pinch (Inf)

boss n = **manager**, head, leader, director, chief

bother v = **trouble**, concern, worry, alarm, disturb ▷ n = **trouble**, problem, worry, difficulty, fuss ≠ **help**

bottom n = **lowest part**, base, foot, bed, floor ≠ **top**; = **underside**, sole, underneath, lower side ▷ adj = **lowest**, last ≠ **higher**

bounce v = **rebound**, recoil, ricochet ▷ n = **springiness**, give, spring, resilience, elasticity; (Inf) = **life**, go (Inf), energy, zip (Inf), nightclub etc. **bouncing** *adj* vigorous

bound¹ ❶ *n* 1 (*usu. pl*) limit ▷ *v* 2 restrict **boundary** *n* **boundless** *adj*

bound² *v/n* spring, leap

bound³ *adj* on a specified course

bound⁴ *adj* 1 committed 2 certain 3 tied

bounty *n*, *pl* **-ties** 1 liberality 2 gift 3 premium **bounteous, bountiful** *adj*

bouquet ❶ *n* 1 bunch of flowers 2 aroma 3 compliment

bourbon *n* (US) whisky made from maize

bourgeois ❶ *n/adj* middle class

bout ❶ *n* 1 period of time spent doing something 2 contest, fight

boutique *n* small shop, esp. one selling clothes

bow¹ ❶ *v* 1 bend body in respect, assent etc. 2 submit 3 bend downwards 4 crush ▷ *n* 5 bowing

bow² *n* 1 weapon for shooting arrows 2 implement for playing

violin etc. 3 ornamental knot 4 bend ▷ *v* 5 bend

bow³ ❶ *n* fore end of ship

bowel *n* 1 part of intestine 2 (*oft. pl*) inside of anything

bowl¹ ❶ *n* 1 round vessel, deep basin 2 drinking cup 3 hollow

bowl² ❶ *n* 1 wooden ball ▷ *pl* 2 game played with such balls ▷ *v* 3 roll or throw ball in various ways **bowler** *n* **bowling** *n*

bowler *n* man's low-crowned stiff felt hat

box¹ ❶ *n* 1 (wooden) container, usu. rectangular 2 its contents 3 any boxlike cubicle or receptacle ▷ *v* 4 put in box 5 confine **box office** place where tickets are sold

box² ❶ *v* 1 fight with fists, esp. with padded gloves on 2 strike ▷ *n* 3 blow **boxer** *n* 1 one who boxes 2 large dog resembling bulldog **boxing** *n*

box³ ❶ *n* evergreen shrub used for hedges

THESAURUS

vigour

bound¹ *v* = **surround**, confine, enclose, encircle, hem in; = **limit**, restrict, confine, restrain, circumscribe

bound² *n* = **leap**, bob, spring, jump, bounce

bouquet *n* = **bunch of flowers**, spray, garland, wreath, posy; = **aroma**, smell, scent, perfume, fragrance

bourgeois *adj* = **middle-class**, traditional, conventional, materialistic, hidebound

bout *n* = **period**, term, fit, spell, turn; = **fight**, match, competition, struggle, contest

bow¹ *v* = **bend**, bob, nod, stoop, droop ▷ *n* = **bending**, bob, nod, obeisance, kowtow

bowl¹ *n* = **basin**, plate, dish, vessel

bowl² *v* = **throw**, hurl, launch, cast, pitch

box¹ *n* = **container**, case, chest, trunk, pack ▷ *v* = **pack**, package, wrap, encase, bundle up

box² *v* = **fight**, spar, exchange blows

boy ❶ n 1 male child 2 young man **boyish** adj **boyfriend** n woman's male companion

boycott ❶ v 1 refuse to deal with or participate in ▷ n 2 such refusal

bra n woman's undergarment, supporting breasts

braaivlies, braai (S Afr) n 1 2 grill on which food is cooked over hot charcoal, usu. outdoors ▷ v 3 4 cook (food) in this way

brace ❶ n 1 tool for boring 2 clamp 3 pair 4 support ▷ pl 5 straps to hold up trousers ▷ v 6 steady (oneself) as before a blow 7 support **bracelet** n ornament for the arm **bracing** adj invigorating

bracken n large fern

bracket n 1 support for shelf etc. 2 group ▷ pl 3 marks, ( ) used to enclose words etc. ▷ v 4 enclose in brackets 5 connect

brackish adj (of water) slightly salty

brag v **bragging, bragged** 1 boast ▷ n 2 boastful talk **braggart** n

braid v 1 interweave 2 trim with braid ▷ n 3 anything plaited 4 ornamental tape

Braille n system of printing for blind, with raised dots

brain n 1 mass of nerve tissue in head 2 intellect ▷ v 3 kill by hitting on head **brainy** adj **brainchild** n creative idea of a person **brainwash** v force someone to change beliefs **brainwave** n sudden, clever idea

braise v stew in covered pan

brake ❶ n 1 instrument for slowing motion of wheel on vehicle ▷ v 2 apply brake to

bramble n prickly shrub

bran n sifted husks of corn

branch ❶ n 1 limb of tree 2 local office ▷ v 3 bear branches 4 diverge 5 spread

brand ❶ n 1 trademark 2 class of goods 3 particular kind 4 mark made by hot iron 5 burning piece of wood ▷ v 6 burn with iron 7 mark 8 stigmatize **brand-new** adj absolutely new

brandish v flourish, wave

brandy n, pl **-dies** spirit distilled from wine

brash ❶ adj bold, impudent

brass n 1 alloy of copper and zinc 2 group of brass wind instruments

boy n = **lad**, kid (Inf), youth, fellow, youngster

boycott v = **embargo**, reject, snub, black ≠ **support**

brace v = **steady**, support, secure, stabilize ▷ n = **support**, stay, prop, bolster, bracket

brake n = **control**, check, curb, restraint, constraint ▷ v = **slow**, decelerate, reduce speed

branch n = **bough**, shoot, arm, spray, limb; = **office**, department, unit, wing, chapter

brand n = **label**, mark, sign, stamp, symbol ▷ v = **stigmatize**, mark, expose, denounce, disgrace; = **mark**, burn, label, stamp, scar

brash adj = **bold**, rude, cocky, pushy (Inf), brazen ≠ **timid**

3 (Inf) money **4** (Inf) (army) officers ▷ adj **5** made of brass
brassiere n bra
brat n unruly child
bravado n showy display of boldness
brave ❶ adj **1** courageous **2** splendid ▷ n **3** warrior ▷ v **4** defy, meet boldly **bravery** n
bravo interj well done!
brawl ❶ v/n (take part in) noisy fight
brawn n **1** muscle **2** strength **3** pickled pork **brawny** adj
bray n/v (make) donkey's cry
brazen adj **1** of, like brass **2** shameless ▷ v **3** face, carry through with impudence
brazier n pan for burning coals
breach n **1** opening **2** breaking of rule etc. ▷ v **3** make a gap in
bread ❶ n **1** food made of flour baked **2** food **3** (Sl) money **breadwinner** n main earner in family
breadth ❶ n **1** extent across,

width **2** largeness of view, mind
break ❶ v **breaking, broke, broken 1** part by force **2** shatter **3** burst, destroy **4** become broken **5** fail to observe **6** disclose **7** interrupt **8** surpass **9** weaken **10** accustom (horse) to being ridden **11** decipher (code) **12** open, appear **13** come suddenly ▷ n **14** fracture **15** gap **16** opening **17** separation **18** interruption **19** respite **20** interval **21** (Inf) opportunity **breakable** adj **breakage** n **breaker** n **1** one that breaks **2** wave beating on shore **breakdown** n **1** collapse **2** failure to function **3** analysis **breakfast** n first meal of the day **break-in** n illegal entering of building **breakneck** adj fast and dangerous **breakthrough** n important advance **breakwater** n barrier to break force of waves
bream n broad, thin fish
breast n **1** human chest

—————————————— THESAURUS ——————————————

brave adj = **courageous**, daring, bold, heroic, adventurous ≠ **timid** ▷ v = **confront**, face, suffer, tackle, endure ≠ **give in to**
brawl n = **fight**, clash, fray, skirmish, scuffle ▷ v = **fight**, scrap (Inf), wrestle, tussle, scuffle
breach n = **nonobservance**, abuse, violation, infringement, trespass ≠ **compliance**; = **opening**, crack, split, gap, rift
bread n = **food**, fare, nourishment, sustenance

breadth n = **width**, spread, span, latitude, broadness; = **extent**, range, scale, scope, compass
break v = **shatter**, separate, destroy, crack, snap ≠ **repair**; = **fracture**, crack, smash; = **burst**, tear, split; = **disobey**, breach, defy, violate, disregard ≠ **obey**; = **stop**, cut, suspend, interrupt, cut short; = **disturb**, interrupt ▷ n = **fracture**, opening, tear, hole, split; = **interval**, pause, interlude, intermission; = **holiday**, leave, vacation, time off, recess

b

2 milk-secreting gland on woman's chest 3 seat of the affections ▷ v 4 face, oppose 5 reach summit of **breaststroke** n stroke in swimming

breath ❶ n 1 air used by lungs 2 life 3 respiration 4 slight breeze **breathe** v 1 inhale and exhale (air) 2 live 3 rest 4 whisper **breather** n short rest **breathing** n **breathless** adj **breathtaking** adj causing awe or excitement

Breathalyser® n Trademark device that estimates amount of alcohol in breath **breathalyse** v

breech n 1 buttocks 2 hind part of anything **breeches** pl n trousers

breed ❶ v **breeding, bred** 1 generate 2 rear 3 be produced 4 be with young 5 offspring produced 6 race, kind **breeder** n **breeding** n result of good upbringing

breeze ❶ n gentle wind **breezy** adj 1 windy 2 lively

brethren pl n brothers

brevity n 1 conciseness of expression 2 short duration

brew ❶ v 1 prepare liquor, as beer 2 make drink, as tea 3 plot 4 be in preparation ▷ n 5 beverage produced by brewing **brewer** n **brewery** n, pl -eries

brier, briar n wild rose with long thorny stems

bribe ❶ n 1 anything offered or given to gain favour ▷ v 2 influence by bribe **bribery** n

bric-a-brac n small ornamental objects

brick n 1 oblong mass of hardened clay used in building ▷ v 2 build, block etc. with bricks **bricklayer** n

bride n woman about to be, or just, married **bridal** adj **bridesmaid** n

bridge¹ ❶ n 1 structure for crossing river etc. 2 something joining or supporting other parts 3 raised narrow platform on ship 4 upper part of nose ▷ v 5 make bridge over, span

bridge² n card game

bridle n 1 headgear of horse 2 curb ▷ v 3 put on bridle 4 restrain 5 show resentment

breath n = **inhalation**, breathing, pant, gasp, gulp

breed n = **variety**, race, stock, type, species; = **kind**, sort, type, variety, brand ▷ v = **rear**, tend, keep, raise, maintain; = **reproduce**, multiply, propagate, procreate, produce offspring; = **produce**, cause, create, generate, bring about

breeze n = **light wind**, air, draught, gust, waft

brew v = **boil**, make, soak, steep, stew; = **make**, ferment ▷ n = **drink**, preparation, mixture, blend, liquor

bribe n = **inducement**, pay-off (Inf), sweetener (Sl), kickback (US), backhander (Sl) ▷ v = **buy off**, reward, pay off (Inf), corrupt, suborn

bridge¹ n = **arch**, span/viaduct, flyover, overpass

brief ① ▷ adj 1 short in duration **2** concise **3** scanty ▷ *n* **4** document containing facts of legal case **5** summary ▷ *pl* **6** underpants **7** panties ▷ *v* **8** give instructions **briefly** *adv* **briefcase** *n* flat case for carrying papers, books etc.

brier, briar SEE BRIAR

brigade ① ▷ n 1 subdivision of army **2** organized band **brigadier** *n* high-ranking army officer

brigand *n* bandit

bright ① ▷ adj 1 shining **2** full of light **3** cheerful **4** clever **brighten** *v* **brightly** *adv* **brightness** *n*

brilliant ① ▷ adj 1 shining **2** sparkling **3** splendid **4** very clever **5** distinguished **brilliance, brilliancy** *n*

brim ① ▷ n margin, edge, esp. of river, cup, hat **brimful** *adj*

brine *n* **1** salt water **2** pickle

bring ① ▷ v bringing, brought **1** fetch **2** carry with one **3** cause to happen

brinjal *n* (*S Afr*) dark purple tropical fruit, cooked and eaten as a vegetable

brink ① ▷ n edge of steep place

brisk ① ▷ adj active, vigorous **briskly** *adv*

brisket *n* meat from breast

bristle ① ▷ n 1 short stiff hair ▷ *v* **2** stand erect **3** show temper **bristly** *adj*

brittle ① ▷ adj 1 easily broken **2** curt

broach *v* **1** introduce (subject) **2** open

broad ① ▷ adj 1 wide, spacious, open **2** obvious **3** coarse **4** general **broaden** *v* **broadly** *adv* **broadcast** *v* **1** transmit by

———————— THESAURUS ————————

brief *adj* = **short**, quick, fleeting, swift, short-lived ≠ **long** ▷ *v* = **inform**, prime, prepare, advise, fill in (*Inf*) ▷ *n* = **summary**, résumé, outline, sketch, abstract

brigade *n* = **corps**, company, force, unit, division

bright *adj* = **vivid**, rich, brilliant, glowing, colourful; = **shining**, glowing, dazzling, gleaming, shimmering

brilliant *adj* = **intelligent**, sharp, intellectual, clever, profound ≠ **stupid**; = **expert**, masterly, talented, gifted, accomplished ≠ **untalented**; = **splendid**, famous, celebrated, outstanding, superb

brim *n* = **rim**, edge, border, lip,

margin ▷ *v* = **be full**, spill, well over, run over

bring *v* = **fetch**, take, carry, bear, transfer; = **take**, guide, conduct, escort

brink *n* = **edge**, limit, border, lip, margin

brisk *adj* = **quick**, lively, energetic, active, vigorous ≠ **slow**

bristle *n* = **hair**, spine, thorn, whisker, barb ▷ *v* = **stand up**, rise, stand on end; = **be angry**, rage, seethe, flare up, bridle

brittle *adj* = **fragile**, delicate, crisp, crumbling, frail ≠ **tough**

broad *adj* = **wide**, large, ample, generous, expansive; = **large**, huge, vast, extensive, ample ≠ **narrow**

radio or television **2** make widely known ▷ n **3** radio or television programme **broadcaster** n **broadcasting** n **broad-minded** adj tolerant **broadside** n **1** discharge of guns **2** strong (verbal) attack

brocade n rich woven fabric with raised design

broccoli n type of cabbage

brochure ❶ n pamphlet

broekies pl n (S Afr, Inf) underpants

brogue n **1** stout shoe **2** dialect, esp. Irish accent

broil v (US & Canad) grill

broke ❶ adj (Inf) having no money

broker ❶ n one employed to buy and sell for others

bromide n chemical compound used in medicine and photography

bromine n liquid element used in production of chemicals

bronco n, pl **-cos** (US) wild pony

brontosaurus n large plant-eating dinosaur

bronze ❶ n **1** alloy of copper and tin ▷ adj **2** made of, or coloured like, bronze ▷ v **3** give appearance

of bronze to

brooch n ornamental pin

brood ❶ n **1** family of young, esp. of birds ▷ v **2** sit, as hen on eggs **3** fret over **broody** adj

brook¹ ❶ n small stream

brook² ❶ v put up with

broom n **1** brush for sweeping **2** yellow-flowered shrub **broomstick** n handle of broom

broth n thick soup

brothel n house of prostitution

brother ❶ n **1** son of same parents **2** one closely united with another **brotherly** adj **brotherhood** n **1** fellowship **2** association **brother-in-law** n, pl **brothers-in-law 1** brother of husband or wife **2** husband of sibling

brow n **1** ridge over eyes **2** forehead **3** eyebrow **4** edge of hill **browbeat** v frighten with threats

brown ❶ adj **1** of dark colour inclining to red or yellow ▷ n **2** the colour ▷ v **3** make, become brown

browse ❶ v **1** look through (book etc.) in a casual manner **2** feed on shoots and leaves

---

— THESAURUS —

brochure n = **booklet**, advertisement, leaflet, hand-out, circular

broke adj (Inf) = **penniless**, short, ruined, bust (Inf), bankrupt ≠ **rich**

broker n = **dealer**, agent, trader, supplier, merchant

bronze adj = **reddish-brown**, copper, tan, rust, chestnut

brood n = **offspring**, issue, clutch, litter, progeny ▷ v = **think**, obsess,

muse, ponder, agonize

brook¹ n = **stream**, burn (Scot. & Northern English), rivulet, beck, watercourse

brother n = **sibling**, blood brother, kin, kinsman, relation, relative

brown adj = **brunette**, bay, coffee, chocolate, chestnut ▷ v = **fry**, cook, grill, sear, sauté

browse v = **skim**, scan, glance at, survey, look through; = **graze**, eat,

bruise ❶ v **1** injure without breaking skin ▷ n **2** contusion, discoloration caused by blow **bruiser** n tough person

brumby n (Aust) **1** wild horse **2** unruly person

brunch n breakfast and lunch combined

brunette n **1** woman of dark complexion and hair ▷ adj **2** dark brown

brunt n chief shock of attack

brush¹ ❶ n **1** device with bristles, hairs etc. used for cleaning, painting etc. **2** act of brushing **3** brief contact **4** skirmish **5** bushy tail ▷ v **6** apply, remove, clean, with brush **7** touch lightly

brush² n thick shrubbery

brusque adj curt

Brussels sprout vegetable like a tiny cabbage

brute ❶ n **1** any animal except man **2** crude, vicious person ▷ adj **3** animal **4** sensual **5** stupid **6** physical **brutal** adj **brutality** n **brutally** adv

BSc Bachelor of Science

BST British Summer Time

bubble ❶ n **1** hollow globe of liquid, blown out with air **2** something insubstantial ▷ v **3** rise in bubbles **bubbly** adj

bubonic plague acute infectious disease characterized by swellings

buccaneer n pirate

buck ❶ n **1** male deer, or other male animal **2** act of bucking **3** (US & Aust, Sl) dollar ▷ v **4** (of horse) attempt to throw rider **buckshot** n lead shot in shotgun shell

bucket n vessel, round with arched handle, for water etc. **bucketful** n

buckle ❶ n **1** metal clasp for fastening belt, strap etc. ▷ v **2** fasten with buckle **3** warp, bend

bud ❶ n **1** shoot containing unopened leaf, flower etc. ▷ v **2** begin to grow

budge ❶ v move, stir

budgerigar, budgie n small Aust. parakeet

budget ❶ n **1** annual financial statement **2** plan of systematic

— THESAURUS —

feed, nibble

bruise n = **discoloration**, mark, injury, blemish, black mark ▷ v = **hurt**, injure, mark

brush¹ n = **broom**, sweeper, besom; = **conflict**, clash, confrontation, skirmish, tussle; = **encounter**, meeting, confrontation, rendezvous ▷ v = **clean**, wash, polish, buff; = **touch**, sweep, kiss, stroke, glance

bubble n = **air ball**, drop, bead,

blister, blob ▷ v = **boil**, seethe; = **foam**, fizz, froth, percolate, effervesce

buckle n = **fastener**, catch, clip, clasp, hasp ▷ v = **fasten**, close, secure, hook, clasp; = **distort**, bend, warp, crumple, contort

bud n = **shoot**, branch, sprout, sprig, offshoot ▷ v = **develop**, grow, shoot, sprout, burgeon

budge v = **move**, stir

budget n = **allowance**, means, funds, income, finances ▷ v spending ▷ v **3** make financial plan

buff[1] ❶ n **1** leather from buffalo hide **2** light yellow colour **3** polishing pad ▷ v **4** polish

buff[2] ❶ n expert

buffalo n type of cattle

buffer ❶ n device to lessen impact

buffet[1] ❶ n **1** refreshment bar **2** meal at which guests serve themselves **3** sideboard

buffet[2] n **1** blow, slap ▷ v **2** strike with blows **3** contend against

buffoon n **1** clown **2** fool

bug ❶ n **1** any small insect **2** (Inf) disease, infection **3** concealed listening device ▷ v **4** annoy **5** listen secretly

bugbear n **1** object of needless terror **2** nuisance

bugger n (Sl) unpleasant person or thing

bugle n instrument like trumpet

build ❶ v building, built **1** construct by putting together

parts **2** develop ▷ n **3** make, form **builder** n **building** n **building society** organization where money can be borrowed or invested

bulb n **1** modified leaf bud emitting roots from base, e.g. onion **2** globe surrounding filament of electric light **bulbous** adj

bulge ❶ n **1** swelling **2** temporary increase ▷ v **3** swell

bulk ❶ n **1** size **2** volume **3** greater part **4** cargo ▷ v **5** be of weight or importance **bulky** adj

bull n **1** male of cattle **2** male of various other animals **bulldog** n thickset breed of dog **bulldozer** n powerful tractor for excavating etc. **bullfight** n public show in which bull is killed **bullock** n castrated bull **bull's-eye** n centre of target

bullet ❶ n projectile discharged from rifle, pistol etc.

bulletin ❶ n official report

= **plan**, estimate, allocate, cost, ration

buff[1] v = **polish**, smooth, brush, shine, rub

buff[2] n (Inf) = **expert**, fan, addict, enthusiast, admirer

buffer n = **safeguard**, screen, shield, cushion, intermediary

buffet[1] n = **snack bar**, café, cafeteria, brasserie, refreshment counter

bug n (Inf) = **illness**, disease, virus, infection, disorder ▷ v = **tap**, eavesdrop, listen in on; (Inf) = **annoy**, bother, disturb, irritate, hassle (Inf)

build v = **construct**, make, raise, put up, assemble ≠ **demolish** ▷ n = **physique**, form, body, figure, shape

bulge v = **swell out**, project, expand, stick out, protrude ▷ n = **lump**, swelling, bump, projection, hump ≠ **hollow** = **increase**, rise, boost, surge, intensification

bulk n = **size**, volume, dimensions, magnitude, substance; = **weight**, size, mass, heaviness, poundage

bullet n = **projectile**, ball, shot, missile, slug

bulletin n = **report**, account,

bullion n gold or silver in mass

bully ❶ n, pl **-lies** one who hurts or intimidates weaker people ▷ v

bulrush n tall reedlike marsh plant

bulwark n 1 rampart 2 any defence

bum n (Sl) buttocks, anus

bumble v perform clumsily

bumblebee n large hairy bee

bumf, bumph n (Inf) official papers

bump ❶ n 1 knock 2 thud 3 swelling ▷ v 4 strike or push against **bumper** n 1 horizontal bar on motor vehicle to protect against damage ▷ adj 2 abundant

bumpkin n simple country person

bumptious adj self-assertive

bun n 1 small, round cake 2 round knot of hair

bunch ❶ n 1 number of things tied or growing together 2 group, party ▷ v 3 gather together

bundle ❶ n 1 package 2 number of things tied together ▷ v 3 tie in bundle 4 send (off) without

ceremony

bung n 1 stopper for cask ▷ v 2 stop up 3 (Sl) sling

bungalow n one-storeyed house

bungle ❶ v/n botch

bunion n inflamed swelling on foot or toe

bunk n narrow shelflike bed

bunker n 1 large storage container for coal etc. 2 sandy hollow on golf course 3 underground defensive position

bunny n, pl **-nies** (Inf) rabbit

bunting n material for flags

bunyip n (Aust) legendary monster said to live in swamps and lakes

buoy ❶ n 1 floating marker anchored in sea ▷ v 2 prevent from sinking **buoyancy** n **buoyant** adj

burden ❶ n 1 load 2 weight, cargo 3 anything difficult to bear ▷ v 4 load, encumber **burdensome** adj

bureau ❶ n, pl **-reaus, -reaux** 1 writing desk 2 office

---

statement, message, communication

bully n = **persecutor**, tough, oppressor, tormentor, bully boy ▷ v = **persecute**, intimidate, torment, oppress, pick on

bump v = **knock**, hit, strike, crash, smash; = **jerk**, shake, bounce, rattle, jog ▷ n = **knock**, blow, impact, collision, thump; = **thud**, crash, knock, bang, smack

bunch n = **group**, band, crowd, party, team; = **cluster**, clump

bundle n = **bunch**, group, collection, mass, pile ▷ v = **push**, thrust, shove, throw, rush

bungle v = **mess up**, blow (Sl), ruin, spoil, blunder ≠ **accomplish**

buoy n = **float**, guide, signal, marker, beacon

burden n = **trouble**, worry, weight, responsibility, strain; = **load**, weight, cargo, freight, consignment ▷ v = **weigh down**, worry, load, tax, bother

bureau n = **office**, department, section, branch, station

b

3 government department
bureaucracy n **1** government by officials **2** body of officials **bureau de change** place where foreign currencies can be exchanged **bureaucrat** n

burgeon v **1** bud **2** flourish

burglar ⓐ n one who enters building to commit crime esp. theft **burglary** n **burgle** v

burgundy n name of various wines, white and red

burlesque n/v caricature

burly adj **-lier, -liest** sturdy, stout, robust

burn ⓐ v **burning, burnt** **1** destroy or injure by fire **2** be on fire **3** be consumed by fire ▷ n **4** injury, mark caused by fire **burning** adj **1** intense **2** urgent

burnish v, n polish

burp v, n (Inf) belch

burrow ⓐ n **1** hole dug by rabbit etc. ▷ v **2** dig

bursar n official managing finances of college etc. **bursary** n

scholarship

burst ⓐ v **bursting, burst** **1** break into pieces **2** break suddenly into some expression of feeling **3** shatter, break violently ▷ n **4** bursting **5** explosion **6** outbreak **7** spurt

bury ⓐ v **burying, buried** **1** put underground **2** inter **3** conceal **burial** n/adj

bus n large motor vehicle for passengers

bush ⓐ n **1** shrub **2** uncleared country **bushy** adj shaggy **bushbaby** n tree-living, nocturnal Afr. animal

bushel n dry measure of eight gallons

business ⓐ n **1** occupation **2** commercial or industrial establishment **3** trade **4** responsibility **5** work **businesslike** adj **businessman** n **businesswoman** n

busker n street entertainer **busk** v

— THESAURUS —

burglar n = **housebreaker**, thief, robber, pilferer, filcher

burn v = **be on fire**, blaze, be ablaze, smoke, flame; = **set on fire**, light, ignite, kindle, incinerate; = **scorch**, toast, sear, char, singe

burrow n = **hole**, shelter, tunnel, den, lair ▷ v = **dig**, tunnel, excavate

burst v = **explode**, blow up, break, split, crack; = **rush**, run, break, break out, erupt ▷ n = **rush**, surge, outbreak, outburst, spate; = **explosion**, crack, blast, bang, discharge

bury v = **inter**, lay to rest, entomb, consign to the grave, inhume ≠ **dig up**; = **hide**, cover, conceal, stash (Inf), secrete ≠ **uncover**

bush n = **shrub**, plant, hedge, thicket, shrubbery

business n = **trade**, selling, industry, manufacturing, commerce; = **establishment**, company, firm, concern, organization; = **profession**, work, job, line, trade; = **concern**, affair

bust¹ ❶ n 1 sculpture of head and shoulders 2 woman's breasts

bust ❶² (Inf) ▷ v 1 burst 2 make, become bankrupt 3 raid 4 arrest ▷ adj 5 broken 6 bankrupt

bustle ❶ v 1 be noisily busy ▷ n 2 fuss, commotion

busy ❶ adj **busier, busiest** 1 actively employed 2 full of activity ▷ v 3 occupy **busily** adv **busybody** n nosy person

but ❶ conj 1 without 2 except 3 yet 4 still 5 besides ▷ adv 6 only

butane n gas used for fuel

butch adj (Inf) aggressively masculine

butcher ❶ n 1 one who kills animals for food, or sells meat 2 savage man ▷ v 3 slaughter **butchery** n

butler n chief male servant

butt¹ ❶ n 1 thick end 2 unused end

butt² ❶ n 1 target 2 object of ridicule

butt³ ❶ v 1 strike with head 2 interrupt ▷ n 3 blow made with head

butter n 1 fatty substance got from cream by churning ▷ v 2 spread with butter 3 flatter

buttercup n plant with glossy, yellow flowers

butterfly n insect with large wings

butterscotch n kind of hard, brittle toffee

buttock n (usu. pl) rump, protruding hind part

button n 1 knob, stud for fastening dress 2 knob that operates doorbell, machine etc. ▷ v 3 fasten with buttons **buttonhole** n 1 slit in garment to pass button through 2 flower worn on lapel etc. ▷ v 3 detain (unwilling) person in conversation

buttress n 1 structure to support wall 2 prop ▷ v 3 support

buxom adj full of health, plump

— THESAURUS —

bust¹ n = **bosom**, breasts, chest, front

bust² (Inf) ▷ v = **break**, smash, split, burst, shatter; = **arrest**, catch, raid

bustle v = **hurry**, rush, fuss, hasten, scuttle ≠ **idle** ▷ n = **activity**, to-do, stir, excitement, fuss ≠ **inactivity**

busy adj = **active**, industrious, rushed off your feet ≠ **idle**; = **occupied with**, working, engaged in, on duty, employed in ≠ **unoccupied**

but conj = **however**, still, yet, nevertheless ▷ adv = **only**, just, simply, merely

butcher n = **murderer**, killer, slaughterer, slayer, destroyer ▷ v = **slaughter**, prepare, carve, cut up, dress; = **kill**, slaughter, massacre, destroy, cut down

butt¹ n = **end**, handle, shaft, stock, shank; = **stub**, tip, leftover, fag end (Inf)

butt² n = **target**, victim, dupe, laughing stock, Aunt Sally

butt³ v = **knock**, push, bump, thrust, ram

buy ❶ *v* **buying, bought 1** get by payment, purchase **2** bribe ▷ *n* **3** thing purchased **buyer** *n*

buzz *v/n* (make) humming sound **buzzer** *n* **buzzword** *n* fashionable word

buzzard *n* bird of prey

by ❶ *prep* **1** near **2** along **3** past **4** during **5** not later than **6** through use or agency of **7** in units of ▷ *adv* **8** near **9** aside **10** past **by and by** soon **by and large** on the whole

bye, bye-bye *n (Sport)* situation where player or team wins by default of opponent

by-election *n* election to fill vacant seat

bygone *adj* **1** past, former ▷ *n* **2** *(oft. pl)* past occurrence **3** small antique

bylaw, bye-law *n* law, regulation made by local authority

bypass ❶ *n* **1** road for diversion of traffic from overcrowded centres ▷ *v* **2** make detour round

byre *n* cowshed

byte *n (Comp)* sequence of bits processed as single unit of information

byway *n* secondary or side road

byword *n* well-known name or saying

—— THESAURUS ——

buy *v* = **purchase**, get, pay for, obtain, acquire ≠ **sell** ▷ *n* = **purchase**, deal, bargain, acquisition, steal (*Inf*)

by *prep* = **through**, through the agency of; = **via**, over, by way of; = **near**, past, along, close to, closest to ▷ *adv* = **nearby**, close, handy, at hand, within reach

bypass *v* = **get round**, avoid

C

C 1 (*Chem*) carbon **2** Celsius **3** Centigrade

c. circa

cab ❶ n **1** taxi **2** driver's compartment on lorry etc.

cabal n **1** small group of intriguers **2** secret plot

cabaret n floor show at a nightclub

cabbage n green vegetable

cabin ❶ n **1** hut, shed **2** small room, esp. in ship

cabinet ❶ n **1** piece of furniture with drawers or shelves **2** outer case of television, radio etc. **3** committee of politicians

cable n **1** strong rope **2** wires conveying electric power, television signals etc. **3** telegraph ▷ v **4** telegraph by cable **cable car** vehicle pulled up slope on cable

cache n **1** secret hiding place **2** store of food etc.

cackle v/n (make) chattering noise, as of hen

cacophony n **1** disagreeable sound **2** discord of sounds

cactus n, pl **-tuses, -ti** spiny succulent plant

cad n unchivalrous person

cadaver n corpse **cadaverous** adj

caddie, caddy n, pl **-dies** golfer's attendant

caddy n, pl **-dies** small box for tea

cadence n fall or modulation of voice in music or verse

cadenza n (*Mus*) elaborate solo passage

cadet n youth in training, esp. for armed forces

cadge v get (food, money etc.) by begging

cadmium n metallic element

caecum n, pl **-ca** part of large intestine

Caesar n title of Roman emperors **Caesar salad** n salad of lettuce, cheese, and croutons, with olive oil, garlic, and lemon juice

Caesarean section n surgical operation to deliver a baby

caesium n metallic element

café n small restaurant serving light refreshments **cafeteria** n self-service restaurant

caffeine n stimulating chemical found in tea and coffee

— THESAURUS —

cab n = **taxi**, minicab, taxicab, hackney carriage

cabin n = **room**, berth, quarters, compartment; = **hut**, shed, cottage, lodge, shack

cabinet n = **cupboard**, case, locker, dresser, closet; (*often cap.*) = **council**, committee, administration, ministry, assembly

café n = **snack bar**, restaurant,

caftan n see KAFTAN

cage ❶ n 1 enclosure, box with bars or wires, esp. for keeping animals or birds ▷ v 2 put in cage, confine **cagey** adj wary

cagoule n lightweight anorak

cairn n heap of stones, esp. as monument or landmark

cajole v persuade by flattery, wheedle

cake ❶ n 1 baked, sweet, bread-like food 2 compact mass ▷ v 3 harden (as of mud)

calamine n soothing ointment

calamity n, pl -ties disaster **calamitous** adj

calcium n metallic element, the basis of lime

calculate ❶ v 1 estimate 2 compute 3 make reckonings **calculable** adj **calculating** adj 1 shrewd 2 scheming **calculation** n **calculator** n electronic device for making calculations

calendar n 1 table of months and days in the year 2 list of events

calf¹ n, pl **calves** n 1 young of cow and other animals 2 leather of calf's skin

calf² n fleshy back of leg below knee

calibre, US **caliber ❶** n 1 size of bore of gun 2 capacity, character **calibrate** v

calico n, pl **-coes** cotton cloth

call ❶ v 1 speak loudly to attract attention 2 summon 3 telephone 4 name 5 shout 6 pay visit ▷ n 7 shout 8 animal's cry 9 visit 10 inner urge 11 demand **caller** n **calling** n vocation, profession **call up** 1 summon to serve in army 2 imagine

calligraphy n handwriting

callous adj hardened, unfeeling

callow adj inexperienced

callus n, pl **-luses** area of hardened skin

calm ❶ adj, v 1 (make, become) still, tranquil 2 (make) composed ▷ n 3 absence of wind **calmly** adv **calmness** n

calorie n 1 unit of heat 2 unit of

cafeteria, coffee shop, brasserie

cage n = **enclosure**, pen, coop, hutch, pound

cake n = **block**, bar, slab, lump, cube

calculate v = **work out**, determine, estimate, count, reckon; = **plan**, design, aim, intend, arrange

calibre, US **caliber** n = **worth**, quality, ability, talent, capacity; = **standard**, level, quality, grade

call v = **name**, entitle, dub,

designate, term; = **cry**, shout, scream, yell, whoop ≠ **whisper**; = **phone**, telephone, ring (up) (Inf, chiefly Brit); summon; = **summon**, gather, rally, assemble, muster ≠ **dismiss**; = **waken**, arouse, rouse ▷ n = **request**, order, demand, appeal, notice; (usually used in a negative construction) = **need**, cause, reason, grounds, occasion

calm adj = **cool**, relaxed, composed, sedate, collected ≠ **excited**; = **still**, quiet, smooth, mild, serene ≠ **rough** ▷ n = **peacefulness**, energy from foods

calypso n, pl **-sos** (West Indies) improvised song

cam n device to change rotary to reciprocating motion

camaraderie n spirit of comradeship, trust

camber n curve on road surface

cambric n fine white linen or cotton cloth

camcorder n portable video camera and recorder

camel n animal of Asia and Africa, with humped back

camellia n ornamental shrub

cameo n, pl **-meos 1** medallion, brooch etc. with design in relief **2** small part in film etc.

camera n apparatus used to make photographs **cameraman** n

camisole n underbodice

camouflage ❶ n **1** disguise, means of avoiding enemy observation ▷ v **2** disguise

camp¹ ❶ n **1** (place for) tents of hikers, army etc. ▷ v **3** form or lodge in camp

camp² ❶ adj (Inf) **1** homosexual **2** consciously artificial

campaign ❶ n/v (organize) series of coordinated activities for some

purpose, e.g. political, military

camphor n solid essential oil with aromatic taste and smell

campus n, pl **-puses** grounds of university

can¹ v past **could 1** be able **2** have the power **3** be allowed

can² n **1** container, usu. metal, for liquids, foods ▷ v **2** put in can **canned** adj **1** preserved in can **2** (of music) previously recorded

Canada Day n July 1, the anniversary of the day when Canada became the first British colony to receive dominion status

Canada goose n large greyish-brown N American goose with a black neck and head and a white throat patch

Canada jay n a large common jay of North America with a grey body, and a white-and-black crestless head

canal ❶ n **1** artificial watercourse **2** duct in body

canary n, pl **-ries** yellow singing bird

canasta n card game played with two packs

cancan n high-kicking dance

— THESAURUS —

peace, serenity ▷ v = **soothe**, quiet, relax, appease, still ≠ **excite**

camouflage n = **disguise**, cover, screen, blind, mask ▷ v = **disguise**, cover, screen, hide, mask ≠ **reveal**

camp¹ n = **camp site**, tents, encampment, bivouac, camping

ground

camp² adj (Inf) = **affected**, mannered, artificial, posturing, ostentatious

campaign n = **drive**, appeal, movement, push (Inf), offensive; = **operation**, drive, attack, movement, push

cancel ❶ v **-celling, -celled**
1 cross out **2** annul **3** call off
cancellation n

cancer ❶ n malignant growth or
tumour **cancerous** adj

candid adj frank, impartial
candour n

candidate ❶ n **1** one who seeks
office etc. **2** person taking
examination **candidacy,
candidature** n

candle n **1** stick of wax with wick
2 light **candelabrum** n large,
branched candle holder
candlestick n

candy n, pl **-dies 1** crystallized
sugar **2** (US) confectionery in
general ▷ v **3** preserve with sugar
candyfloss n fluffy mass of spun
sugar

cane n **1** stem of small palm or
large grass **2** walking stick ▷ v
3 beat with cane

canine adj **1** of or like a dog ▷ n
2 sharp pointed tooth

canister n container, usu. of
metal, for storing dry food

canker n **1** eating sore **2** thing
that destroys, corrupts

cannabis n **1** hemp plant **2** drug
derived from this

cannelloni pl n tubular pieces of

pasta filled with meat etc.

cannibal n one who eats human
flesh **cannibalism** n

cannon¹ ❶ n large gun
cannonball n heavy metal ball

cannon² n **1** billiard stroke ▷ v
2 make this stroke **3** rebound,
collide

cannot negative form of CAN¹

canny adj **-nier, -niest 1** shrewd
2 cautious

canoe n **1** very light boat propelled
with paddle ▷ v **2** travel by canoe

canon ❶ n **1** law or rule, esp. of
church **2** standard **3** list of saints
canonize v enrol in list of saints

canopy ❶ n, pl **-pies 1** covering
over throne, bed etc. ▷ v **2** cover
with canopy

cant n **1** hypocritical speech
2 technical jargon **3** slang, esp. of
thieves ▷ v **4** use cant

cantankerous adj quarrelsome

cantata n choral work

canteen n place in factory, school
etc. where meals are served

canter n/v (move at) easy gallop

cantilever n beam, girder etc.
fixed at one end only

Canuck n/adj (Inf) Canadian

canvas n coarse cloth used for
sails, painting etc.

canal n = **waterway**, channel,
passage, conduit, duct

cancel v = **call off**, drop, forget
about

cancer n = **growth**, tumour,
malignancy, corruption, sickness

candidate n = **contender**,
competitor, applicant, nominee,

entrant

cannon¹ n = **gun**, big gun, field
gun, mortar

canon n = **rule**, standard, principle,
regulation, formula; = **list**, index,
catalogue, roll

canopy n = **awning**, covering,
shade, sunshade

canvass v 1 solicit votes, contributions etc. 2 discuss

canyon n deep gorge

cap ❶ n 1 covering for head 2 lid, top ▷ v 3 put a cap on 4 outdo

capable ❶ adj 1 able 2 competent 3 having the power **capability** n

capacity ❶ n, pl **-ties** 1 power of holding 2 room 3 volume 4 function, role 5 ability

cape¹ ❶ n headland

cape² n covering for shoulders

caper n 1 skip 2 frolic 3 escapade ▷ v 4 skip, dance

capillary n, pl **-laries** small blood vessel

capital ❶ n 1 chief town 2 money 3 large-sized letter ▷ adj 4 involving or punishable by death 5 chief 6 excellent **capitalism** n economic system based on private ownership of industry **capitalist** n/adj **capitalize** v 1 convert into capital 2 turn to advantage

capitulate v surrender

capon n castrated cock fowl fattened for eating

cappuccino n, pl **-nos** coffee with steamed milk

caprice n whim, freak **capricious** adj

capsize v (of boat) overturn accidentally

capstan n machine to wind cable

capsule ❶ n case for dose of medicine

captain ❶ n 1 commander of vessel or company of soldiers 2 leader ▷ v 3 be captain of **captaincy** n

caption n heading, title of article, picture etc.

captive ❶ n 1 prisoner ▷ adj 2 taken, imprisoned **captivate** v fascinate **captivity** n

capture ❶ v 1 seize, make prisoner ▷ n 2 seizure, taking **captor** n

car ❶ n 1 road vehicle 2 passenger

— THESAURUS —

cap v (Inf) = **beat**, top, better, exceed, eclipse

capable adj = **accomplished**, qualified, talented, gifted, efficient ≠ **incompetent**

capacity n = **ability**, facility, gift, genius, capability; = **size**, room, range, space, volume; = **function**, position, role, post, province

cape¹ n = **headland**, point, head, peninsula, promontory

capital n = **money**, funds, investment(s), cash, finances ▷ adj (Old-fashioned) = **first-rate**, fine,

excellent, superb, sterling

capsule n = **pill**, tablet, lozenge; (Botany) = **pod**, case, shell, vessel, sheath

captain n = **leader**, boss, master, skipper, head

captive adj = **confined**, caged, imprisoned, locked up, enslaved ▷ n = **prisoner**, hostage, convict, prisoner of war, detainee

capture v = **catch**, arrest, take, bag, secure ≠ **release** ▷ n = **arrest**, catching, trapping, imprisonment, seizure

car n = **vehicle**, motor, wheels (Inf),

compartment of a vehicle

carafe n glass water bottle for the table, decanter

caramel n 1 burnt sugar for cooking 2 chewy sweet

carat n 1 weight used for gold, diamonds etc. 2 measure used to state fineness of gold

caravan n 1 large vehicle for living in, pulled by car etc. 2 company of merchants travelling together

caraway n plant with spicy seeds used in cakes etc.

carbohydrate n any compound containing carbon, hydrogen and oxygen, esp. sugars and starches

carbon n nonmetallic element, substance of pure charcoal, found in all organic matter **carbonate** n salt of carbonic acid **carbon copy** 1 copy made with carbon paper 2 very similar person or thing **carbon dioxide** colourless gas exhaled in respiration

carbon-neutral adj not affecting the overall volume of carbon dioxide in the atmosphere

carbuncle n inflamed ulcer, boil or tumour

carburettor n device for mixing petrol with air in engine

carcass, carcase n dead animal

body

card n 1 thick, stiff paper 2 piece of this giving identification etc. 3 illustrated card sending greetings etc. 4 playing card ▷ pl 5 any card game **cardboard** n thin, stiff board made of paper pulp

cardsharp n cheating card player

cardiac adj pert. to the heart **cardiograph** n instrument which records movements of the heart **cardiology** n study of heart diseases

cardigan n knitted jacket

cardinal ❶ adj 1 chief, principal ▷ n 2 rank next to the Pope in R.C. church **cardinal numbers** 1,2,3 etc.

care ❶ v 1 be anxious 2 have regard or liking (for) 3 look after 4 be disposed to ▷ n 5 attention 6 protection 7 anxiety 8 caution **careful** adj **careless** adj **carefree** adj **caretaker** n person in charge of premises

career ❶ n 1 course through life 2 profession 3 rapid motion ▷ v 4 run or move at full speed

caress v 1 fondle, embrace, treat with affection ▷ n 2 affectionate embrace or touch

caret n mark (∧) showing where to

— THESAURUS —

auto (US), automobile; (US & Canad) = **(railway) carriage**, coach, cable car, dining car, sleeping car

ardinal adj = **principal**, first, leading, chief, main ≠ secondary

are v = **be concerned**, mind, bother, be interested, be bothered ▷ n = **custody**, keeping, control,

charge, management; = **caution**, attention, pains, consideration, heed ≠ carelessness; = **worry**, concern, pressure, trouble, responsibility ≠ pleasure

career n = **occupation**, calling, employment, pursuit, vocation ▷ v = **rush**, race, speed, tear, dash insert word etc.

cargo ❶ *n, pl* **-goes** load, freight, carried by ship, plane etc.

caribou *n, pl* **-bou** N American reindeer

caricature ❶ *n* **1** likeness exaggerated to appear ridiculous ▷ *v* **2** portray in this way

cark *v* (*Aust & NZ, Sl*) die

carnage ❶ *n* slaughter

carnal *adj* fleshly, sensual

carnation *n* cultivated flower

carnival ❶ *n* **1** festive occasion **2** travelling fair

carol ❶ *n/v* (sing) song or hymn of joy

carouse *v* have merry drinking spree **carousal** *n*

carousel *n* **1** (*US*) merry-go-round **2** rotating device for holding slides

carp¹ ❶ *v* **1** find fault **2** nag

carp² *n* freshwater fish

carpenter ❶ *n* worker in timber **carpentry** *n*

carpet *n* heavy fabric for covering floor

carriage ❶ *n* **1** railway coach **2** bearing **3** horse-drawn vehicle

carriageway *n* part of road along which traffic passes in a single line

carrion *n* rotting dead flesh

carrot *n* **1** plant with orange-red edible root **2** inducement

carry ❶ *v* **-rying, -ried 1** convey, transport **2** capture, win **3** effect **4** behave **5** (of projectile, sound) reach **carrier** *n*

cart *n* **1** open (two-wheeled) vehicle ▷ *v* **2** carry in cart **3** carry with effort **carthorse** *n* heavily built horse **cartwheel** *n* sideways somersault

carte blanche (*Fr*) complete authority

cartel *n* industrial alliance for fixing prices etc.

cartilage *n* **1** firm elastic tissue in the body **2** gristle

cartography *n* map making

carton ❶ *n* cardboard or plastic container

cartoon ❶ *n* **1** drawing, esp.

━━━━━━━━━━━━━━━ THESAURUS ━━━━━━━━━━━━━━━

cargo *n* = **load**, goods, contents, shipment, freight

caricature *n* = **parody**, cartoon, distortion, satire, send-up (*Brit inf*) ▷ *v* = **parody**, take off (*Inf*), mock, distort, ridicule

carnage *n* = **slaughter**, murder, massacre, holocaust, havoc

carnival *n* = **festival**, fair, fête, celebration, gala

carol *n* = **song**, hymn, Christmas song

carp¹ *v* = **find fault**, complain, criticize, reproach, quibble

≠ **praise**

carpenter *n* = **joiner**, cabinet-maker, woodworker

carriage *n* = **vehicle**, coach, trap, gig, cab; = **bearing**, posture, gait, deportment, air

carry *v* = **convey**, take, move, bring, bear; = **transport**, take, transfer

carton *n* = **box**, case, pack, package, container

cartoon *n* = **drawing**, parody, satire, caricature, comic strip; = **animation**, animated film, humorous or satirical **2** sequence of drawings telling story **cartoonist** n

cartridge n **1** case containing charge for gun **2** container for film etc.

carve ❶ v **1** cut **2** hew **3** sculpture **4** engrave **5** cut (meat) in pieces or slices **carving** n

cascade ❶ n waterfall

case¹ ❶ n **1** instance **2** circumstance **3** question at issue **4** arguments supporting particular action etc. **5** (Med) patient **6** lawsuit **in case** so as to allow for eventualities

case² ❶ n **1** box, sheath, covering **2** receptacle **3** box and contents ▷ v **4** put in a case

cash ❶ n **1** money, banknotes and coins ▷ v **2** turn into or exchange for money **cashier** n one in charge of receiving and paying of money

cashier v dismiss from office

cashmere n fine soft fabric made from goat's wool

casino n, pl **-nos** building,

institution for gambling

cask n barrel

casket n small case for jewels etc.

casserole n **1** fireproof cooking dish **2** stew

cassette n plastic container for film, magnetic tape etc.

cassock n clergyman's long tunic

cast ❶ v **1** throw or fling **2** shed **3** deposit (a vote) **4** allot, as parts in play **5** mould ▷ n **6** throw **7** squint **8** mould **9** that which is shed or ejected **10** set of actors **11** type or quality **castaway** n shipwrecked person **cast-iron** adj **1** made of hard, brittle type of iron **2** rigid or unchallengeable **cast-off** adj/n discarded (garment)

castanets pl n two small curved pieces of wood clicked together in hand

caste ❶ n **1** section of society in India **2** social rank

caster sugar, castor sugar n finely powdered sugar

castigate v rebuke severely

castle ❶ n fortress

—————— THESAURUS ——————

animated cartoon

carve v = **sculpt**, cut, chip, whittle, chisel; = **etch**, engrave

cascade n = **waterfall**, falls, torrent, flood, shower

case¹ n = **situation**, event, circumstance(s), state, position; = **instance**, example, occasion, specimen, occurrence; (Law) = **lawsuit**, trial, suit, proceedings, dispute

case² n = **cabinet**, box, chest, holder

cash n = **money**, funds, notes,

currency, silver

cast n = **actors**, company, players, characters, troupe; = **type**, sort, kind, style, stamp ▷ v = **choose**, name, pick, select, appoint; = **bestow**, give, level, direct; = **give out**, spread, deposit, shed, distribute; = **throw**, launch, pitch, toss, thrust

caste n = **class**, order, rank, status, stratum

castle n = **fortress**, keep, palace, tower, chateau

castor n **1** bottle with perforated top **2** small swivelled wheel on table leg etc.

castor oil n vegetable medicinal oil

castrate v remove testicles **castration** n

casual ❶ adj **1** accidental **2** unforeseen **3** occasional **4** unconcerned **5** informal **casually** adv **casualty** n person killed or injured in accident, war etc.

cat ❶ n any of various feline animals, esp. small domesticated furred animal **catty** adj spiteful **catcall** n derisive cry **catkin** n drooping flower spike **catnap** v/n doze **Catseye** n glass reflector set in road to indicate traffic lanes **catwalk** n narrow platform

cataclysm n **1** (disastrous) upheaval **2** deluge

catalogue, US **catalog ❶** n **1** descriptive list ▷ v **2** make such list of

catalyst n substance causing or assisting a chemical reaction without taking part in it

catamaran n type of sailing boat with twin hulls

catapult n **1** small forked stick with sling for throwing stones **2** launching device ▷ v **3** launch with force

cataract n **1** waterfall **2** downpour **3** disease of eye

catarrh n inflammation of mucous membrane

catastrophe ❶ n great disaster **catastrophic** adj

catch ❶ v **catching, caught 1** take hold of **2** hear **3** contract disease **4** be in time for **5** detect **6** be contagious **7** get entangled **8** begin to burn ▷ n **9** seizure **10** thing that holds, stops etc. **11** what is caught **12** (Inf) snag, disadvantage **catcher** n **catching** adj **catchy** adj (of tune) easily remembered

catechism n instruction by questions and answers

category ❶ n, pl **-ries** class, order **categorize** v **categorical** adj positive

cater v provide, esp. food **caterer** n

casual adj = **careless**, relaxed, unconcerned, blasé, offhand ≠ **serious**; = **chance**, unexpected, random, accidental, incidental ≠ **planned**; = **informal**, leisure, sporty, non-dressy ≠ **formal**

cat n = **feline**, pussy (Inf), moggy (Sl), puss (Inf), tabby

catalogue, US **catalog** n = **list**, record, schedule, index, register ▷ v = **list**, file, index, register, classify

catastrophe n = **disaster**, tragedy, calamity, cataclysm, trouble

catch v = **capture**, arrest, trap, seize, snare ≠ **free**; = **trap**, capture, snare, ensnare, entrap; = **seize**, get, grab, snatch; = **grab**, take, grip, seize, grasp ≠ **release** ▷ n = **fastener**, clip, bolt, latch, clasp; (Inf) = **drawback**, trick, trap, disadvantage, hitch ≠ **advantage**

category n = **class**, grouping,

caterpillar n hairy grub of moth or butterfly

catharsis n, pl **-ses** relief of strong suppressed emotions **cathartic** adj

cathedral n principal church of diocese

Catherine wheel n rotating firework producing sparks

catholic adj 1 universal 2 including whole body of Christians 3 (with cap.) relating to R.C. church ▷ n 4 (with cap.) adherent of R.C. church **Catholicism** n

cattle ① pl n pasture animals, esp. oxen, cows **cattleman** n

cauldron n large pot used for boiling

cauliflower n variety of cabbage with edible white flowering head

cause ① n 1 that which produces an effect 2 reason 3 motive 4 charity, movement 5 lawsuit ▷ v 6 bring about, make happen

causeway n raised path over marsh etc.

caustic adj 1 burning 2 bitter ▷ n 3 corrosive substance

cauterize v burn with caustic or hot iron

caution ① n 1 heedfulness, care 2 warning ▷ v 3 warn **cautionary** adj **cautious** adj

cavalcade n procession

cavalier adj 1 careless, disdainful ▷ n 2 courtly gentleman 3 (Obs) horseman 4 (with cap.) supporter of Charles I

cavalry ① n, pl **-ries** mounted troops

cave ① n 1 hollow place in the earth 2 den **cavern** n deep cave **cavernous** adj **cavity** n hollow **caveman** n prehistoric cave dweller

caviar, caviare n salted sturgeon roe

cavil v **-illing, -illed** make trifling objections

cavort v prance, frisk

CBE Commander of the British Empire

CC cubic centimetre

CD compact disc **CD-ROM** compact disc storing written information, displayed on VDU

cease ① v bring or come to an end

THESAURUS

heading, sort, department
cattle pl n = **cows**, stock, beasts, livestock, bovines
cause n = **origin**, source, spring, agent, maker ≠ **result**; = **reason**, call, need, grounds, basis; = **aim**, movement, principle, ideal, enterprise ▷ v = **produce**, create, lead to, result in, generate ≠ **prevent**
caution n = **care**, discretion, heed,

prudence, vigilance ≠ **carelessness**; = **reprimand**, warning, injunction, admonition ▷ v = **warn**, urge, advise, alert, tip off
cavalry n = **horsemen**, horse, mounted troops ≠ **infantrymen**
cave n = **hollow**, cavern, grotto, den, cavity
cease v = **stop**, end, finish, come to an end ≠ **start**

ceaseless adj **ceasefire** n temporary truce

cedar n large evergreen tree

cede v yield, give up, transfer

cedilla n accent (,) below letter

ceilidh n informal social gathering for dancing

ceiling n inner, upper surface of a room

celebrate ❶ v **1** have festivities to mark (happy day, event etc.) **2** observe (birthday etc.) **3** perform (religious ceremony etc.) **4** praise publicly **celebrated** adj famous **celebration** n **celebrity** n, pl **-rities 1** famous person **2** fame

celery n vegetable with long juicy edible stalks

celestial adj heavenly, divine

cell ❶ n **1** small room in prison **2** small cavity **3** minute, basic unit of living matter **4** device converting chemical into electrical energy **cellular** adj

cellar n **1** underground room for storage **2** stock of wine

cello n, pl **-los** stringed instrument of violin family

Cellophane® n transparent wrapping

cellulose n fibrous carbohydrate

Celsius adj/n (of) scale of temperature from 0° to 100°

cement ❶ n **1** fine mortar **2** glue ▷ v **3** unite as with cement

cemetery ❶ n, pl **-teries** burial ground

cenotaph n monument to one buried elsewhere

censor ❶ n **1** one authorized to examine films, books etc. and suppress parts considered unacceptable ▷ v **2** suppress **censorious** adj fault-finding **censorship** n

censure ❶ n/v blame

census n, pl **-suses** official counting of people, things etc.

cent n hundredth part of dollar etc.

centaur n mythical creature, half man, half horse

centenary n, pl **-naries 1** 100 years **2** celebration of hundredth anniversary ▷ adj **3** pert. to a hundred

centigrade adj/n another name for CELSIUS

centimetre n hundredth part of metre

centipede n small segmented

———— THESAURUS ————

celebrate v = **rejoice**, party, enjoy yourself, carouse, live it up (Inf); = **commemorate**, honour, observe, toast, drink to

cell n = **room**, chamber, lock-up, compartment, cavity; = **unit**, group, section, core, nucleus

cement n = **mortar**, plaster, paste; = **sealant**, glue, gum, adhesive ▷ v = **stick**, join, bond, attach, seal

cemetery n = **graveyard**, churchyard, burial ground, necropolis, God's acre

censor v = **expurgate**, cut, blue-pencil, bowdlerize

censure v = **criticize**, blame, condemn, denounce, rebuke ≠ **applaud** ▷ n = **disapproval**, criticism, blame, condemnation, rebuke ≠ **approval**

animal with many legs

centre ❶ n 1 midpoint 2 pivot 3 place for specific organization or activity **central** adj **centralize** v **centrally** adv

centurion n Roman commander of 100 men

century n, pl **-ries** 1 100 years 2 any set of 100

cereal n 1 any edible grain 2 (breakfast) food

cerebral adj pert. to brain

ceremony ❶ n, pl **-nies** 1 formal observance 2 sacred rite 3 courteous act **ceremonial** adj/n

certain ❶ adj 1 sure 2 inevitable 3 some, one 4 moderate (in quantity, degree etc.) **certainly** adv **certainty** n

certify ❶ v **-fying, -fied** 1 declare formally 2 guarantee **certificate** n written declaration

cervix n, pl **cervixes, cervices** neck, esp. of womb **cervical** adj

cessation n stop, pause

chafe v 1 make sore or worn by rubbing 2 warm 3 vex

chaff n 1 husks of corn 2 worthless matter ▷ v 3 tease

chaffinch n small songbird

chagrin n 1 vexation, disappointment ▷ v 2 embarrass

chain ❶ n 1 series of connected rings 2 thing that binds 3 connected series of things or events 4 surveyor's measure ▷ v 5 fasten with a chain 6 restrain

chair n 1 movable seat, with back, for one person 2 seat of authority ▷ v 3 preside over 4 carry in triumph **chairman** n one who presides over meeting **chairperson** n **chairwoman** n

chalet n Swiss wooden house

chalice n (Poet) cup

chalk n 1 white substance, carbonate of lime 2 crayon ▷ v 3 mark with chalk **chalky** adj

challenge ❶ v 1 call to fight or account 2 dispute 3 stimulate ▷ n 4 challenging **challenger** n

chamber ❶ n 1 (room for)

centre n = middle, heart, focus, core, nucleus ≠ edge

ceremony n = ritual, service, rite, observance, commemoration; = formality, ceremonial, propriety, decorum

certain adj = sure, convinced, positive, confident, satisfied ≠ unsure; = bound, sure, fated, destined ≠ unlikely

certify v = confirm, declare, guarantee, assure, testify

chain n = tether, coupling, link,

bond, shackle; = series, set, train, string, sequence ▷ v = bind, confine, handcuff, shackle

challenge n = dare, provocation; = test, trial, opposition, confrontation, ultimatum ▷ v = dispute, question, tackle, confront, defy

chamber n = hall, room; = council, assembly, legislature, legislative body; = room, bedroom, apartment, enclosure, cubicle

assembly **2** compartment **3** cavity
▷ *pl* **4** office or apartment of
barrister **chambermaid** *n*
woman who cleans bedrooms
chameleon *n* lizard with power of
changing colour
chamois *n, pl* **-ois 1** goatlike
mountain antelope **2** soft pliable
leather
champ 1 munch noisily **2** be
impatient
champagne *n* light, sparkling
white wine
champion ❶ *n* **1** one that excels
all others **2** defender of a cause ▷ *v*
3 fight for **championship** *n*
chance ❶ *n* **1** unpredictable
course of events **2** luck
3 opportunity **4** possibility **5** risk
6 probability ▷ *v* **7** risk **8** happen
▷ *adj* **9** casual, unexpected
chancy *adj*
chancel *n* part of a church where
altar is

chancellor *n* **1** high officer of
state **2** head of university
chandelier *n* hanging frame with
branches for lights
change ❶ *v* **1** alter, make or
become different **2** put on
(different clothes, fresh coverings)
3 put or give for another
4 exchange ▷ *n* **5** alteration
6 variety **7** coins **8** balance
received on payment **changeable**
adj
channel ❶ *n* **1** bed of stream
2 strait **3** deeper part of strait
4 groove **5** means of conveying
6 band of radio frequencies
7 television broadcasting station
▷ *v* **8** groove **9** guide
chant ❶ *n* **1** simple song or
melody **2** rhythmic slogan ▷ *v*
3 utter chant **4** speak
monotonously
chaos ❶ *n* disorder, confusion
chaotic *adj*

——————— THESAURUS ———————

champion *n* = **winner**, hero,
victor, conqueror, title holder;
= **defender**, guardian, patron,
backer, protector ▷ *v* = **support**,
back, defend, promote, advocate
chance *n* = **probability**, odds,
possibility, prospect, likelihood
≠ **certainty**; = **opportunity**,
opening, occasion, time;
= **accident**, fortune, luck, fate,
destiny ≠ **design**; = **risk**,
speculation, gamble, hazard ▷ *v*
= **risk**, try, stake, venture, gamble
change *n* = **alteration**,
innovation, transformation,
modification, mutation; = **variety**,

break (*Inf*), departure, variation,
novelty ≠ **monotony** ▷ *v* = **alter**,
reform, transform, adjust, revise
≠ **keep**; = **shift**, vary, transform,
alter, modify ≠ **stay**
channel *n* = **means**, way, course,
approach, medium; = **strait**, sound,
route, passage, canal; = **duct**, artery,
groove, gutter, furrow ▷ *v* = **direct**,
guide, conduct, transmit, convey
chant *n* = **song**, carol, chorus,
melody, psalm ▷ *v* = **sing**, chorus,
recite, intone, carol
chaos *n* = **disorder**, confusion,
mayhem, anarchy, lawlessness
≠ **orderliness**

chap¹ ❶ n (Inf) fellow, man

chap² v (of skin) become raw and cracked

chapati, chapatti n thin unleavened bread used in Indian cookery

chapel n 1 place of worship 2 division of church with its own altar

chaplain n clergyman attached to prison, college etc.

chapter ❶ n 1 division of book 2 assembly of clergy 3 organized branch of society

char v charring, charred scorch

character ❶ n 1 nature 2 qualities making up individuality 3 moral qualities 4 eccentric person 5 fictional person
characteristic adj 1 typical ▷ n 2 distinguishing feature
characterize v 1 mark out 2 describe

charade n 1 absurd act ▷ pl 2 word-guessing game

charcoal n charred wood

charge ❶ v 1 ask as price 2 bring accusation against 3 lay task on 4 attack 5 fill (with electricity) 6 make onrush, attack ▷ n 7 price 8 accusation 9 attack 10 command 11 accumulation of electricity **chargeable** adj
charger n 1 that which charges, esp. electrically 2 warhorse

chargé d'affaires pl **chargés d'affaires** head of small diplomatic mission

chariot n 1 two-wheeled vehicle used in ancient fighting 2 state carriage **charioteer** n

charisma ❶ n special power of individual to inspire fascination, loyalty etc. **charismatic** adj

charity ❶ n, pl -ties 1 giving of help, money to needy

─────── THESAURUS ───────

chap¹ n (Inf) = **fellow**, man, person, individual, character

chapter n = **section**, part, stage, division, episode; = **period**, time, stage, phase

character n = **personality**, nature, attributes, temperament, complexion; = **nature**, kind, quality, calibre; = **reputation**, honour, integrity, good name, rectitude; = **role**, part, persona; = **eccentric**, card (Inf), original, oddball (Inf)

charge v = **accuse**, indict, impeach, incriminate, arraign ≠ **acquit**; = **attack**, assault, assail ≠ **retreat**; = **rush**, storm, stampede; = **fill**, load ▷ n = **price**, rate, cost, amount, payment; = **accusation**, allegation, indictment, imputation ≠ **acquittal**; = **care**, trust, responsibility, custody, safekeeping; = **attack**, rush, assault, onset, onslaught ≠ **retreat**

charisma n = **charm**, appeal, personality, attraction, lure

charity n = **charitable organization**, fund, movement, trust, endowment; = **donations**, help, relief, gift, contributions ≠ **meanness**; = **kindness**, humanity, goodwill, compassion, generosity ≠ **ill will**

2 organization for this **3** love, kindness **charitable** adj

charlatan ❶ n impostor

charm ❶ n **1** attractiveness **2** anything that fascinates **3** amulet **4** magic spell ▷ v **5** bewitch **6** delight **charmer** n **charming** adj

chart ❶ n **1** map of sea **2** tabulated statement ▷ v **3** map

charter ❶ n **1** document granting privileges etc. ▷ v **2** let or hire **3** establish by charter **chartered** adj officially qualified

charwoman n woman paid to clean office, house etc.

chary adj **-rier, -riest** cautious, sparing

chase ❶ v **1** hunt, pursue **2** drive from, away, into etc. ▷ n **3** pursuit, hunting

chasm n deep cleft

chassis n, pl **-sis** framework of motor vehicle

chaste adj **1** virginal **2** pure **3** modest **4** virtuous **chastity** n

chasten v **1** correct by punishment **2** subdue **chastise** v inflict punishment on

chat ❶ v **1** talk idly or familiarly ▷ n **2** such talk **chatty** adj

chateau n, pl **-teaux, -teaus** (esp. in France) castle, country house

chauffeur n paid driver of motorcar

chauvinism n irrational feeling of superiority **chauvinist** n/adj

cheap ❶ adj **1** low in price **2** of little value **3** inferior **cheaply** adv **cheapen** v **cheapskate** n (Inf) miserly person

cheat ❶ v **1** deceive **2** practise deceit to gain advantage ▷ n

— THESAURUS —

charm n = **attraction**, appeal, fascination, allure, magnetism ≠ **repulsiveness**; = **talisman**, trinket, amulet, fetish; = **spell**, magic, enchantment, sorcery ▷ v = **attract**, delight, fascinate, entrance, win over ≠ **repel**; = **persuade**, seduce, coax, beguile, sweet-talk (Inf)

chart n = **table**, diagram, blueprint, graph, plan ▷ v = **plot**, map out, delineate, sketch, draft; = **monitor**, follow, record, note, document

charter n = **document**, contract, permit, licence, deed ▷ v = **hire**, commission, employ, rent, lease; = **authorize**, permit, sanction, entitle, license

chase v = **pursue**, follow, track, hunt, run after ▷ n = **pursuit**, race, hunt, hunting

chat v = **talk**, gossip, jaw (Sl), natter, blather ▷ n = **talk**, tête-à-tête, conversation, gossip, heart-to-heart

cheap adj = **inexpensive**, reduced, keen, reasonable, bargain ≠ **expensive**; = **inferior**, poor, worthless, second-rate, shoddy ≠ **good**; (Inf) = **despicable**, mean, contemptible ≠ **decent**

cheat v = **deceive**, trick, fool, con (Inf), mislead ▷ n = **deceiver**, sharper, shark, charlatan, trickster

3 fraud

check ⓥ v **1** stop **2** control **3** examine ▷ n **4** stoppage **5** restraint **6** brief examination **7** pattern of squares **8** threat to king at chess **checkmate** n/v (make) final winning move **checkout** n counter in supermarket where customers pay **check-up** n examination (esp. medical) to see if all is in order

Cheddar n smooth hard cheese

cheek ⓝ n **1** side of face below eye **2** (Inf) impudence **cheeky** adj

cheep v/n (utter) high-pitched cry, as of young bird

cheer ⓥ v **1** comfort **2** gladden **3** encourage by shouts **4** shout applause ▷ n **5** shout of approval **6** happiness **7** mood **cheerful** adj **cheerless** adj **cheery** adj

cheerio interj (Inf) goodbye

cheese n food made from solidified curd of milk **cheesy** adj **cheesecake** n dessert made from biscuits and cream cheese

cheetah n large, swift, spotted feline animal

chef n head cook

chemistry n science concerned with properties of substances and their combinations and reactions **chemical** n/adj **chemically** adv

chemist n **1** dispenser of medicines **2** shop that sells medicines etc. **3** one trained in chemistry

chemotherapy n treatment of disease by chemicals

chenille n soft cord, fabric of silk or worsted

cheque n **1** written order to banker to pay money from one's account **2** printed slip of paper used for this **chequebook** n **cheque card** banker's card

chequer n **1** marking as on chessboard **2** marble, peg etc. used in games ▷ v **3** mark in squares **4** variegate **chequered** adj

cherish ⓥ v treat tenderly

cherry n, pl **-ries 1** small red fruit with stone **2** tree bearing it

cherub n, pl **-ubs, -ubim 1** winged creature with human face **2** angel **cherubic** adj

chess n game played on chequered board **chessman** n piece used in chess

chest ⓝ n **1** upper part of trunk of body **2** large, strong box **chest of drawers** piece of furniture

— THESAURUS —

check v (often with **out**) = **examine**, test, study, look at, research ≠ **overlook**; = **stop**, limit, delay, halt, restrain ≠ **further** ▷ n = **examination**, test, research, investigation, inspection

cheek n (Inf) = **impudence**, nerve, disrespect, audacity, lip (Sl)

cheer v = **applaud**, hail, acclaim,

clap ≠ **boo**; = **hearten**, encourage, comfort, uplift, brighten ≠ **dishearten** ▷ n = **applause**, ovation, plaudits, acclamation

cherish v = **care for**, love, support, comfort, look after ≠ **neglect**

chest n = **breast**, front

containing drawers

chestnut n **1** tree bearing large nut in prickly husk **2** (Inf) old joke ▷ adj **3** reddish-brown

chevron n (Mil) V-shaped braid designating rank

chew ❶ v **1** grind with teeth ▷ n **2** chewing **chewy** adj **chewing gum** flavoured gum

chianti n red Italian wine

chic ❶ adj **1** stylish ▷ n **2** stylishness

chicane n obstacle on racing circuit **chicanery** n trickery

chick n **1** young of birds, esp. of hen **2** (Sl) girl, young woman **chickpea** n edible pealike seed

chicken n **1** domestic fowl **2** (Sl) coward ▷ adj **3** cowardly **chickenpox** n infectious disease

chicory n, pl **-ries** salad plant whose root is used instead of coffee

chide v **chiding, chided** scold

chief ❶ n **1** head or principal person ▷ adj **2** principal, foremost **chiefly** adv **chieftain** n leader of tribe

chiffon n gauzy material

chilblain n inflamed sore on

hands, legs etc. due to cold

child ❶ n, pl **children 1** young human being **2** offspring **childish** adj silly **childlike** adj **1** of or like a child **2** innocent **childhood** n

chill ❶ n **1** coldness **2** cold with shivering **3** anything that discourages ▷ v **4** make, become cold **chilly** adj **1** cold **2** unfriendly

chilli, chili n small red hot-tasting seed pod

chime n **1** sound of bell ▷ v **2** ring harmoniously **3** agree **4** strike (bells)

chimney n vertical passage for smoke

chimpanzee n ape of Africa

chin n part of face below mouth **chinwag** n (Inf) chat

china ❶ n **1** fine earthenware, porcelain **2** cups, saucers etc.

chinchilla n S Amer. rodent with soft, grey fur

chink n cleft, crack

chintz n cotton cloth printed in coloured designs

chip ❶ n **1** splinter **2** place where piece has been broken off **3** thin strip of potato, fried **4** tiny wafer of

━━━━━━ THESAURUS ━━━━━━

chew v = **munch**, bite, grind, champ, crunch

chic adj = **stylish**, smart, elegant, fashionable, trendy (Brit Inf) ≠ **unfashionable**

chief n = **head**, leader, director, manager, boss (Inf) ≠ **subordinate** ▷ adj = **primary**, highest, leading, main, prime ≠ **minor**

child n = **youngster**, baby, kid (Inf), infant, babe

chill v = **cool**, refrigerate, freeze; = **dishearten**, depress, discourage, dismay, dampen ▷ n = **coldness**, bite, nip, sharpness, coolness ▷ adj = **chilly**, biting, sharp, freezing, raw

china n = **pottery**, ceramics, ware, porcelain, crockery

chip n = **fragment**, shaving, wafer, sliver, shard ▷ v = **nick**, damage, gash

silicon forming integrated circuit ▷ v
5 chop into small pieces **6** break
small pieces from **7** break off **chip
in 1** interrupt **2** contribute

chipmunk n small, striped N
Amer. squirrel

chiropodist n one who treats
disorders of feet **chiropody** n

chirp n/v (make) short, sharp cry
chirpy adj (Inf) happy

chisel n **1** cutting tool ▷ v **2** cut
with chisel **3** (Sl) cheat

chit n informal note

chitchat n gossip

chivalry n **1** bravery and courtesy
2 medieval system of knighthood
chivalrous adj

chlorine n nonmetallic element,
yellowish-green poison gas
chloride n bleaching agent
chlorinate v disinfect

chloroform n volatile liquid
formerly used as anaesthetic

chlorophyll n green colouring
matter in plants

chock n block or wedge

chocolate n confectionery, drink
made from ground cacao seeds

choice n **1** act or power of
choosing **2** alternative **3** thing or
person chosen ▷ adj **4** select, fine

choir n band of singers

choke ❶ v **1** hinder, stop the
breathing of **2** smother, stifle

3 obstruct **4** suffer choking ▷ n
5 act, noise of choking **6** device to
increase richness of petrol-air
mixture **choker** n tight-fitting
necklace

cholera n deadly infectious disease

choleric adj bad-tempered

cholesterol n substance found in
animal tissue and fat

chook n (Aust & NZ) hen or chicken

choose ❶ v **choosing, chose,
chosen 1** pick out, select **2** take
by preference **3** decide, think fit
choosy adj

chop ❶ v **chopping, chopped**
1 cut with blow **2** hack ▷ n
3 cutting blow **4** cut of meat with
bone **chopper** n **1** short axe
2 (Inf) helicopter **choppy** adj
-pier, -piest (of sea) having short,
broken waves

chopsticks pl n implements used
by Chinese for eating food

choral adj of, for a choir

chorale n slow, stately hymn tune

chord n simultaneous sounding of
musical notes

chore ❶ n (unpleasant) task

choreography n art of arranging
dances, esp. ballet **choreographer**
n

chorister n singer in choir

chortle v/n (make) happy
chuckling sound

THESAURUS

choice n = **range**, variety,
selection, assortment; = **selection**,
preference, pick ▷ adj = **best**,
prime, select, excellent, exclusive

choke v = **suffocate**, stifle,
smother, overpower, asphyxiate;

= **strangle**, throttle, asphyxiate

choose v = **pick**, prefer, select,
elect, adopt ≠ **reject**

chop v = **cut**, fell, hack, sever,
cleave

chore n = **task**, job, duty, burden,

chorus ❶ n, pl **-ruses 1** (music for) band of singers **2** refrain ▷ v **3** sing or say together

chow¹ n (Inf) food

chow² n thick-coated dog with curled tail, orig. from China

Christian n/adj (person) following, believing in Christ **christen** v baptize, give name to **christening** n **Christianity** n

Christmas ❶ n festival of birth of Christ

chromosome n microscopic gene-carrying body in the tissue of a cell

chronic adj **1** lasting a long time **2** habitual **3** (Inf) serious **4** (Inf) of bad quality

chronicle ❶ n/v (write) record of historical events

chrysalis n **1** resting state of insect **2** case enclosing it

chrysanthemum n garden flower of various colours

chub n freshwater fish

chubby adj **-bier, -biest** plump

chuck ❶ v (Inf) **1** throw **2** pat affectionately (under chin) **3** give up

chuckle ❶ v/n (make) soft laugh

chuffed adj (Inf) pleased, delighted

chum ❶ n (Inf) close friend **chummy** adj

chunk ❶ n thick, solid piece **chunky** adj

church ❶ n **1** building for Christian worship **2** (with cap.) whole body or sect of Christians **3** clergy

churlish adj rude or surly

churn ❶ n **1** large container for milk **2** vessel for making butter ▷ v **3** shake up, stir **4** (with out) produce rapidly

chute n slide for sending down parcels, coal etc.

chutney n pickle of fruit, spices etc.

CIA (US) Central Intelligence Agency

CID Criminal Investigation Department

cider n fermented drink made from apples

cigar n roll of tobacco leaves for smoking **cigarette** n finely-cut tobacco rolled in paper for smoking

cinch n (Inf) easy task

cinder n remains of burned coal

cinema ❶ n **1** building used for

─────────── THESAURUS ───────────

hassle (Inf)

chorus n = **refrain**, response, strain, burden; = **choir**, singers, ensemble, vocalists, choristers

Christmas n = **festive season**, Noël, Xmas (Inf), Yule (Archaic), Yuletide (Archaic)

chronicle v = **record**, tell, report, enter, relate ▷ n = **record**, story, history, account, register

chuck v (Inf) = **throw**, cast, pitch,

toss, hurl

chuckle v = **laugh**, giggle, snigger, chortle, titter

chum n (Inf) = **friend**, mate (Inf), pal (Inf), companion, comrade

chunk n = **piece**, block, mass, portion, lump

churn v = **stir up**, beat, disturb, swirl, agitate

cinema n = **pictures**, movies, picture-house, flicks (Sl); = **films**, showing of films **2** films generally

cinnamon n spice from bark of Asian tree

cipher n **1** secret writing **2** arithmetical symbol **3** person of no importance

circa (Lat) about, approximately

circle ❶ n **1** perfectly round figure **2** ring **3** (Theatre) section of seats above main level of auditorium **4** group, society with common interest ▷ v **5** surround **6** move round **circular** adj **1** round ▷ n **2** letter sent to several persons **circulate** v **1** move round **2** pass round **3** send round **circulation** n **1** flow of blood **2** act of moving round **3** extent of sale of newspaper etc.

circuit ❶ n **1** complete round or course **2** area **3** path of electric current **4** round of visitation **circuitous** adj indirect

circumcise v cut off foreskin of **circumcision** n

circumference n boundary line, esp. of circle

circumflex n accent (^) over a letter

circumnavigate v sail right round

circumscribe v confine, bound, limit

circumspect adj cautious

circumstance ❶ n **1** detail **2** event ▷ pl **3** state of affairs **4** condition in life, esp. financial **5** surroundings or things accompanying an action **circumstantial** adj

circumvent v outwit, evade, get round

circus n, pl **-cuses** (performance of) acrobats, clowns, performing animals etc.

cirrhosis n disease of liver

cirrus n, pl **-ri** high wispy cloud

cistern n water tank

citadel n city fortress

cite ❶ v **1** quote **2** bring forward as proof **citation** n **1** quoting **2** commendation for bravery etc.

citizen ❶ n **1** member of state, nation etc. **2** inhabitant of city **citizenship** n

citrus fruit lemons, oranges etc.

city ❶ n, pl **-ties** large town

civic ❶ adj pert. to city or citizen

pictures, movies, big screen (Inf), motion pictures

circle n = **ring**, disc, hoop, halo; = **group**, company, set, club, society ▷ v = **go round**, ring, surround, enclose, envelop; = **wheel**, spiral

circuit n = **course**, tour, track, route, journey

circumstance n usually plural = **situation**, condition,

contingency, state of affairs, lie of the land

cite v = **quote**, name, advance, mention, extract

citizen n = **inhabitant**, resident, dweller, denizen, subject

city n = **town**, metropolis, municipality, conurbation

civic adj = **public**, municipal, communal, local

civil ● adj 1 relating to citizens 2 not military 3 refined, polite 4 (*Law*) not criminal **civilian** *n* nonmilitary person **civility** *n*

civilize ● *v* 1 bring out of barbarism 2 refine **civilization** *n* 1 refinement 2 cultured society **civilized** *adj*

claim ● *v* 1 demand as right 2 assert 3 call for ▷ *n* 4 demand for thing supposed due 5 right 6 thing claimed **claimant** *n*

clairvoyance *n* power of seeing things not present to senses **clairvoyant** *n/adj*

clam *n* edible mollusc

clamber *v* to climb awkwardly

clammy *adj* **-mier, -miest** moist and sticky

clamour ● *n/v* (make) loud outcry **clamorous** *adj*

clamp ● *n* 1 tool for holding ▷ *v* 2 fasten with or as with clamp

3 (with *down*) become stricter

clan ● *n* 1 collection of families of common ancestry 2 group

clandestine *adj* 1 secret 2 sly

clang *v* 1 (cause to) make loud ringing sound ▷ *n* 2 this sound

clap ● *v* **clapping, clapped** 1 (cause to) strike with noise 2 strike (hands) together 3 applaud 4 pat 5 place or put quickly ▷ *n* 6 hard, explosive sound 7 slap

claret *n* dry red wine

clarify ● *v* **-fying, -fied** make or become clear **clarification** *n* **clarity** *n*

clarinet *n* woodwind instrument

clash ● *n* 1 loud noise 2 conflict, collision ▷ *v* 3 make clash 4 come into conflict 5 strike together

clasp ● *n* 1 hook or fastening 2 embrace ▷ *v* 3 fasten 4 embrace, grasp

class ● *n* 1 any division, order,

— THESAURUS —

civil *adj* = **civic**, political, domestic, municipal ≠ **state**; = **polite**, obliging, courteous, considerate, affable ≠ **rude**

civilize *v* = **cultivate**, educate, refine, tame, enlighten

claim *v* = **assert**, insist, maintain, allege, uphold; = **demand**, call for, ask for, insist on ▷ *n* = **assertion**, statement, allegation, declaration, pretension; = **demand**, application, request, petition, call

clamour *n* = **noise**, shouting, racket, outcry, din

clamp *n* = **vice**, press, grip, bracket, fastener ▷ *v* = **fasten**, fix, secure, brace, make fast

clan *n* = **family**, group, society, tribe, fraternity; = **group**, set, circle, gang, faction

clap *v* = **applaud**, cheer, acclaim ≠ **boo**

clarify *v* = **explain**, interpret, illuminate, clear up, simplify

clash *v* = **conflict**, grapple, wrangle, lock horns, cross swords; = **disagree**, conflict, vary, counter, differ ▷ *n* = **conflict**, fight, brush, confrontation, collision

clasp *v* = **grasp**, hold, press, grip, seize ▷ *n* = **grasp**, hold, grip, embrace, hug; = **fastening**, catch, grip, hook, pin

class *n* = **group**, set, division, rank

DICTIONARY

kind, sort **2** rank **3** group of school pupils **4** division by merit **5** quality ▷ v **6** assign to proper division
classy adj (Inf) stylish, elegant
classify v arrange methodically in classes **classification** n
classic ❶ adj **1** of highest rank, esp. of art **2** typical **3** famous ▷ n **4** (literary) work of recognized excellence ▷ pl **5** ancient Greek and Latin literature **classical** adj **1** refined, elegant **2** of ancient Greek and Latin culture
clatter n **1** rattling noise ▷ v **2** (cause to) make clatter
clause ❶ n **1** part of sentence **2** article in formal document
claustrophobia n abnormal fear of confined spaces **claustrophobic** adj
clavicle n collarbone
claw ❶ n **1** sharp hooked nail of animal ▷ v **2** tear with claws
clay n **1** fine-grained earth, plastic when wet, hardening when baked **2** earth **clayey** adj

clean ❶ adj **1** free from dirt **2** pure **3** guiltless **4** trim ▷ adv **5** so as to leave no dirt **6** entirely ▷ v **7** free from dirt **cleaner** n **cleanliness** n **cleanly** adv **cleanse** v make clean
clear ❶ adj **1** pure, bright **2** free from cloud **3** transparent **4** plain, distinct **5** without defect **6** unimpeded ▷ adv **7** brightly **8** wholly, quite ▷ v **9** make clear **10** acquit **11** pass over **12** make as profit **13** free from obstruction, difficulty **14** become clear, bright, free, transparent **clearly** adv **clearance** n **clearing** n land cleared of trees
cleave¹ v cleaving, cleft, cleaved (cause to) split **cleavage** n **cleaver** n short chopper
cleave² v **1** stick, adhere **2** be loyal
clef n (Mus) mark to show pitch
cleft n crack, fissure, chasm
clematis n climbing plant
clement adj **1** merciful **2** gentle **3** mild **clemency** n

THESAURUS

▷ v = **classify**, group, rate, rank, brand
classic adj = **typical**, standard, model, regular, usual; = **masterly**, best, finest, world-class, consummate ≠ **second-rate** ▷ n = **standard**, masterpiece, prototype, paradigm, exemplar
clause n = **section**, condition, article, chapter, passage
claw n = **nail**, talon ▷ v = **scratch**, tear, dig, rip, scrape
clean adj = **hygienic**, fresh, sterile, pure, purified ≠ **contaminated**;

= **spotless**, fresh, immaculate, impeccable, flawless ≠ **dirty**;
= **moral**, good, pure, decent, innocent ≠ **immoral** ▷ v
= **cleanse**, wash, scrub, rinse, launder ≠ **dirty**
clear adj = **comprehensible**, explicit, understandable ≠ **confused**; = **obvious**, plain, apparent, evident, distinct ≠ **ambiguous**; = **certain**, sure, convinced, positive, satisfied ≠ **confused**; = **transparent**, see-through, translucent,

clench v 1 set firmly together
2 grasp, close (fist)

clergy ❶ n body of ministers of
Christian church **clergyman** n

clerical adj 1 of clergy 2 of office
work **cleric** n clergyman

clerk n 1 subordinate who keeps
files etc. 2 officer in charge of
records, correspondence etc.

clever ❶ adj 1 intelligent 2 able,
skilful, adroit **cleverly** adv

cliché ❶ n stereotyped hackneyed
phrase

click n/v (make) short, sharp sound

client ❶ n customer **clientele** n
clients

cliff ❶ n steep rock face
cliffhanger n thing which is
exciting and full of suspense

climate ❶ n condition of country
with regard to weather

climatic adj

climax ❶ n highest point,
culmination **climactic** adj

climb ❶ v go up or ascend **climber**
n

clinch ❶ v conclude (agreement)

cling ❶ v **clinging, clung**
1 adhere 2 be firmly attached to
clingfilm n thin polythene
wrapping material

clinic n place for medical
examination, advice or treatment
clinical adj

clink n 1 sharp metallic sound ▷ v
2 (cause to) make this sound

clip¹ ❶ v **clipping, clipped** 1 cut
with scissors 2 cut short ▷ n
3 (Inf) sharp blow **clipping** n thing
cut out, esp. newspaper article

clip² ❶ v (attach with) gripping
device

————— THESAURUS —————

crystalline, glassy ≠ **opaque**;
= **unobstructed**, open, free, empty,
unhindered ≠ **blocked** ▷ v
= **unblock**, free, loosen, extricate,
open; = **remove**, clean, wipe,
cleanse, tidy (up); = **brighten**,
break up, lighten; = **pass over**,
jump, leap, vault, miss

clergy n = **priesthood**, ministry,
clerics, clergymen, churchmen

clever adj = **intelligent**, bright,
talented, gifted, smart ≠ **stupid**;
= **shrewd**, bright, ingenious,
resourceful, canny
≠ **unimaginative**

cliché n = **platitude**, stereotype,
commonplace, banality, truism

client n = **customer**, consumer,
buyer, patron, shopper

cliff n = **rock face**, overhang, crag,
precipice, escarpment

climate n = **weather**,
temperature, environment, spirit,
surroundings

climax n = **culmination**, top,
summit, height, highlight

climb v = **ascend**, scale, mount, go
up, clamber

clinch v = **secure**, close, confirm,
conclude, seal

cling v = **clutch**, grip, embrace,
grasp, hug

clip¹ v = **trim**, cut, crop, prune,
shorten; (Inf) = **smack**, strike,
knock, punch, thump ▷ n (Inf)
= **smack**, strike, knock, punch,
thump

clip² v = **attach**, fix, secure,

clipper *n* fast sailing ship

clique *n* **1** small exclusive set **2** faction, group of people

clitoris *n* part of female genitals **clitoral** *adj*

cloak ❶ *n/v* **1** (cover with) loose outer garment **2** disguise **cloakroom** *n*

clobber *v* (*Inf*) beat, batter

clock *n* instrument for measuring time **clockwise** *adv/adj* in the direction that the hands of a clock rotate **clockwork** *n* wind-up mechanism for clocks, toys etc.

clod *n* lump of earth

clog ❶ *v* clogging, clogged **1** hamper, impede, choke up ▷ *n* **2** wooden-soled shoe

cloister *n* **1** covered pillared arcade **2** monastery or convent **cloistered** *adj* secluded

clone *n* **1** cells of same genetic constitution as another, derived by asexual reproduction **2** (*Inf*) lookalike ▷ *v* **3** replicate

close¹ ❶ *v* **1** shut **2** stop up

3 prevent access to **4** finish **5** come together **6** grapple ▷ *n* **7** end **8** shut-in place **9** precinct of cathedral **closure** *n*

close² ❶ *adj* **1** near **2** compact **3** crowded **4** intimate **5** almost equal **6** careful, searching **7** confined **8** secret **9** unventilated **10** niggardly **11** restricted ▷ *adv* **12** nearly **13** tightly **closely** *adv* **close-up** *n* close view

closet *n* **1** small private room **2** (*US*) cupboard ▷ *adj* **3** secret ▷ *v* **4** shut away in private

clot *n* **1** mass or lump (of blood) **2** (*Inf*) fool ▷ *v* **3** (cause to) form into lumps

cloth ❶ *n* woven fabric **clothe** *v* put clothes on **clothes** *pl n* **1** dress **2** bed coverings **clothing** *n*

cloud ❶ *n* **1** vapour floating in air **2** state of gloom ▷ *v* **3** darken **4** become cloudy **cloudy** *adj*

clout ❶ *n* (*Inf*) **1** blow **2** influence, power ▷ *v* **3** strike

---

THESAURUS

---

connect, pin

cloak *n* = **cape**, coat, wrap, mantle ▷ *v* = **cover**, coat, wrap, blanket, shroud

clog *v* = **obstruct**, block, jam, hinder, impede

close¹ *v* = **shut**, lock, fasten, secure ≠ **open**; = **shut down**, finish, cease; = **wind up**, finish, shut down, terminate ▷ *n* = **end**, ending, finish, conclusion, completion

close² *adj* = **near**, neighbouring, nearby, handy, adjacent ≠ **far**;

= **intimate**, loving, familiar, thick (*Inf*), attached ≠ **distant**; = **careful**, detailed, intense, minute, thorough; = **even**, level, neck and neck, fifty-fifty (*Inf*), evenly matched; = **imminent**, near, impending, at hand, nigh ≠ **far away**

cloth *n* = **fabric**, material, textiles

cloud *n* = **mist**, haze, vapour, murk, gloom ▷ *v* = **darken**, dim, be overshadowed

clout (*Inf*) ▷ *v* = **hit**, strike, punch, slap, sock (*Sl*) ▷ *n* = **thump**, blow,

clove n pungent spice

clover n forage plant

clown ❶ n circus comic

club ❶ n **1** thick stick **2** bat **3** association **4** suit at cards ▷ v **5** strike **6** join

cluck v/n (make) noise of hen

clue ❶ n indication, esp. of solution of mystery or puzzle **clueless** adj stupid

clump¹ n cluster of plants

clump² ❶ v/n (move with) heavy tread

clumsy ❶ adj **-sier, -siest** awkward **clumsily** adv **clumsiness** n

cluster ❶ n/v group, bunch

clutch ❶ v **1** grasp eagerly **2** snatch (at) ▷ n **3** grasp, tight grip **4** device enabling two revolving shafts to be

(dis)connected at will

clutter ❶ v **1** cause obstruction, disorder ▷ n **2** disordered mass

cm centimetre

Co. 1 Company **2** County

co- comb. form together, jointly, as in coproduction

c/o 1 care of **2** carried over

coach ❶ n **1** long-distance bus **2** large four-wheeled carriage **3** railway carriage **4** tutor, instructor ▷ v **5** instruct

coagulate v curdle, clot

coal n **1** mineral used as fuel **2** glowing ember

coalesce v unite

coalition ❶ n alliance

coarse ❶ adj **1** rough **2** unrefined **3** indecent **coarsely** adv **coarseness** n

——————— THESAURUS ———————

punch, slap, sock (Sl)

clown n = **comedian**, fool, comic, harlequin, joker ▷ v (usually with **around**) = **play the fool**, mess about, jest, act the fool

club n = **association**, company, group, union, society; = **stick**, bat, bludgeon, truncheon, cosh (Brit) ▷ v = **beat**, strike, hammer, batter, bash

clue n = **indication**, lead, sign, evidence, suggestion

clump¹ n = **cluster**, group, bunch, bundle

clump² v = **stomp**, thump, lumber, tramp, plod

clumsy adj = **awkward**, lumbering, bumbling, ponderous, ungainly ≠ **skilful**

cluster n = **gathering**, group, collection, bunch, knot ▷ v = **gather**, group, collect, bunch, assemble

clutch v = **hold**, grip, embrace, grasp, cling to

clutter n = **untidiness**, mess, disorder, confusion, litter ≠ **order** ▷ v = **litter**, scatter, strew, mess up ≠ **tidy**

coach n = **instructor**, teacher, trainer, tutor, handler; = **bus**, charabanc ▷ v = **instruct**, train, prepare, exercise, drill

coalition n = **alliance**, union, association, combination, merger

coarse adj = **rough**, crude, unfinished, homespun, impure

coast ❶ n 1 sea shore ▷ v 2 move under momentum **coastal** adj **coaster** n 1 small ship 2 small mat

coat ❶ n 1 sleeved outer garment 2 animal's fur 3 covering layer ▷ v 4 cover **coating** n covering layer

coax ❶ v persuade

cob n 1 short-legged stout horse 2 male swan 3 head of corn

cobalt n 1 metallic element 2 blue pigment from it

cobber n (Aust or NZ, Inf) friend

cobble v 1 patch roughly 2 mend shoes ▷ n 3 round stone **cobbler** n

cobra n poisonous, hooded snake

cobweb n spider's web

cocaine n addictive narcotic drug used medicinally

cochineal n scarlet dye

cock n 1 male bird, esp. of domestic fowl 2 tap 3 hammer of gun ▷ v 4 draw back to firing position 5 raise, turn **cockerel** n young cock

cockatoo n crested parrot

cockie, cocky n, pl **-kies** (Aust & NZ, Inf) farmer

cockle n shellfish

cockpit n pilot's seat, compartment in small aircraft

cockroach n insect pest

cocktail n 1 mixed drink of spirits 2 appetizer

cocky adj **cockier, cockiest** conceited, pert

cocoa n 1 powdered seed of cacao tree 2 drink made from this

coconut n large, hard nut

cocoon n sheath of insect in chrysalis stage

COD cash on delivery

cod n large sea fish

coda n (Mus) final part of musical composition

code ❶ n 1 system of letters, symbols to transmit messages secretly 2 scheme of conduct 3 collection of laws 4 instructions in a computer program **codify** v

codeine n pain-killing drug

coerce v compel, force **coercion** n

coexist v exist together **coexistence** n

C of E Church of England

coffee n 1 seeds of tropical shrub 2 drink made from these

coffer n chest for valuables

coffin n box for corpse

cog n one of series of teeth on rim of wheel **cogwheel** n

cogent adj convincing

cogitate v think, reflect, ponder **cogitation** n

cognac n French brandy

≠ smooth; = **vulgar**, rude, indecent, improper, earthy

coast n = **shore**, border, beach, seaside, coastline ▷ v = **cruise**, sail, drift, taxi, glide

coat n = **fur**, hair, skin, hide, wool; = **layer**, covering, coating, overlay

▷ v = **cover**, spread, plaster, smear

coax v = **persuade**, cajole, talk into, wheedle, sweet-talk (Inf) ≠ **bully**

code n = **principles**, rules, manners, custom, convention; = **cipher**, cryptograph

cognizance n knowledge
  cognizant adj
cohabit v live together as a couple
  without being married
cohere v stick together, be
  consistent **coherent** adj
  1 capable of logical speech, thought
  2 connected, making sense
  cohesion n tendency to unite
  cohesive adj
cohort n 1 troop 2 associate
coiffure n hairstyle
coil ❶ v 1 twist into winding shape
  ▷ n 2 series of rings 3 anything
  coiled
coin ❶ n 1 piece of money
  2 money ▷ v 3 stamp 4 invent
  coinage n
coincide ❶ v happen together
  coincidence n chance happening
  coincidental adj
coke¹ n residue left from distillation
  of coal, used as fuel
coke² n 1 Coca-Cola 2 (Sl) cocaine
cola n flavoured soft drink
colander n strainer for food

cold ❶ adj 1 lacking heat
  2 indifferent, unmoved
  3 unfriendly ▷ n 4 lack of heat
  5 illness, marked by runny nose etc.
  coldly adv **cold-blooded** adj
  lacking pity
coleslaw n cabbage salad
colic n severe pains in the
  intestines
collaborate ❶ v work with
  another **collaboration** n
  collaborator n
collage n (artistic) composition of
  bits and pieces stuck together on
  background
collapse ❶ v 1 fall 2 fail ▷ n
  3 act of collapsing 4 breakdown
  collapsible adj
collar ❶ n 1 band, part of
  garment, worn round neck ▷ v
  2 seize **collarbone** n bone joining
  shoulder blade to breast bone
collate v compare carefully
collateral n security pledged for
  loan
colleague ❶ n fellow worker

———————————— THESAURUS ————————————

coil v = **wind**, twist, curl, loop,
  spiral
coin n = **money**, change, cash,
  silver, copper ▷ v = **invent**, create,
  make up, forge, originate
coincide v = **occur
  simultaneously**, coexist,
  synchronize, be concurrent
cold adj = **chilly**, freezing, bleak,
  arctic, icy **≠ hot**; = **distant**,
  reserved, indifferent, aloof, frigid
  ≠ emotional ▷ n = **coldness**, chill,
  frigidity, frostiness, iciness
collaborate v = **work together**,

team up, join forces, cooperate,
  play ball (Inf); = **conspire**,
  cooperate, collude, fraternize
collapse v = **fall down**, fall, give
  way, subside, cave in; = **fail**, fold,
  founder, break down, fall through
  ▷ n = **falling down**, falling
  apart, cave-in, disintegration;
  = **failure**, slump, breakdown, flop,
  downfall
collar v (Inf) = **seize**, catch, arrest,
  grab, capture
colleague n = **fellow worker**,
  partner, ally, associate, assistant

DICTIONARY

collect ❶ v gather, bring, come together **collected** adj calm
collection n **collective** adj
1 factory, farm etc. owned by its workers ▷ adj **2** shared
collectively adv **collector** n
college n place of higher education **collegiate** adj
collide ❶ v crash together **collision** n
collie n breed of sheepdog
colliery n, pl **-lieries** coal mine
colloquial adj pert. to, or used in, informal conversation
colloquialism n
collusion n secret agreement for a fraudulent purpose **collude** v
cologne n perfumed liquid
colon¹ n mark (:) indicating break in a sentence
colon² n part of large intestine
colonel n commander of regiment or battalion
colonnade n row of columns
colony ❶ n, pl **-nies 1** body of people who settle in new country **2** country so settled **colonial** adj

colonist n **colonize** v
colonization n
colossal adj huge, gigantic
colour, US **color** ❶ n **1** hue, tint **2** complexion **3** paint **4** pigment **5** (Fig) semblance, pretext **6** timbre, quality ▷ pl **7** flag **8** (Sport) distinguishing badge, symbol ▷ v **9** stain, paint **10** disguise **11** influence or distort **12** blush **colourful** adj **1** bright **2** interesting **colourless** adj
colour-blind adj unable to distinguish between certain colours
colt n young male horse
columbine n garden flower
column ❶ n **1** long vertical pillar **2** division of page **3** body of troops **columnist** n journalist writing regular feature
coma ❶ n unconsciousness **comatose** adj
comb ❶ n **1** toothed instrument for tidying hair **2** cock's crest **3** mass of honey cells ▷ v **4** use comb on **5** search
combat ❶ v/n **-bating, -bated**

THESAURUS

collect v = **gather**, save, assemble, heap, accumulate ≠ **scatter**; = **assemble**, rally, cluster, come together ≠ **disperse**
collide v = **crash**, clash, meet head-on, come into collision; = **conflict**, clash, be incompatible, be at variance
colony n = **settlement**, territory, province, possession, dependency
colour, US **color** n = **hue**, tone, shade, tint, colourway; = **paint**,

stain, dye, tint, pigment ▷ v = **blush**, flush, redden
column n = **pillar**, support, post, shaft, upright; = **line**, row, file, rank, procession
coma n = **unconsciousness**, trance, oblivion, stupor
comb v = **untangle**, arrange, groom, dress; = **search**, hunt through, rake, sift, scour
combat n = **fight**, war, action, battle, conflict ≠ **peace** ▷ v = **fight**, oppose, resist, defy,

fight, contest **combatant** n
combative adj
combine ❶ v **1** join together ▷ n
2 syndicate, esp. of businesses
combination n **combine**
harvester machine to harvest and
thresh grain
combustion n process of burning
combustible adj
come ❶ v **coming, came, come**
1 approach, arrive, move towards
2 reach **3** occur **4** originate (from)
5 become **comeback** n **1** (Inf)
return to active life **2** retort
comedown n **1** decline in status
2 disappointment **comeuppance**
n (Inf) deserved punishment
comedy ❶ n, pl **-dies 1** light,
amusing play **2** humour
comedian n entertainer who tells
jokes
comely adj **-lier, -liest**
good-looking

comet n luminous heavenly body
comfort ❶ n **1** ease **2** (means of)
consolation ▷ v **3** soothe
4 console **comfortable** adj
1 giving comfort **2** well-off
comfortably adv **comforter** n
comic ❶ adj **1** relating to comedy
2 funny ▷ n **3** comedian
4 magazine of strip cartoons
comical adj
comma n punctuation mark (,)
command ❶ v **1** order **2** rule
3 compel **4** have in one's power
▷ n **5** order **6** power of controlling
7 mastery **8** post of one
commanding **9** jurisdiction
commandant n **commandeer** v
seize for military use **commander**
n **commandment** n
commando n, pl **-dos, -does**
(member of) special military unit
commemorate ❶ v keep in
memory by ceremony

— THESAURUS —

withstand ≠ support
combine v = **amalgamate**, mix,
blend, integrate, merge ≠ separate
come v = **approach**, near, advance,
move towards, draw near; = **reach**,
extend, come up to, come as far as;
= **happen**, fall, occur, take place,
come about
comedy n = **light entertainment**
≠ tragedy; = **humour**, fun,
joking, farce, jesting
≠ seriousness
comfort n = **ease**, luxury,
wellbeing, opulence;
= **consolation**, succour, help,
support, relief ≠ annoyance ▷ v
= **console**, reassure, soothe,

hearten, commiserate with
≠ distress
comic adj = **funny**, amusing, witty,
humorous, farcical ≠ sad ▷ n
= **comedian**, funny man, humorist,
wit, clown
command v = **order**, tell, charge,
demand, require ≠ beg; = **have**
authority over, lead, head,
control, rule ≠ be subordinate to
▷ n = **order**, demand, instruction,
requirement, decree;
= **domination**, control, rule,
mastery, power
commemorate v = **celebrate**,
remember, honour, recognize,
salute ≠ ignore

commemoration n
commemorative adj
commence ❶ v begin
commend ❶ v 1 praise 2 entrust
commendable adj
commendation n
commensurate adj 1 equal 2 in proportion
comment ❶ n/v 1 remark 2 gossip 3 note **commentary** n, pl **-taries** 1 explanatory notes 2 spoken accompaniment to film etc. **commentate** v
commentator n
commerce n trade **commercial** adj 1 of business, trade etc. ▷ n 2 advertisement, esp. on radio or television
commiserate v sympathize with **commiseration** n
commission ❶ n 1 authority 2 (body entrusted with) some special duty 3 agent's payment by percentage 4 document appointing to officer's rank

5 committing ▷ v 6 charge with duty 7 (Mil) confer a rank 8 give order for **commissioner** n
commissionaire n uniformed doorman
commit ❶ v -mitting, -mitted 1 give in charge 2 be guilty of 3 pledge 4 send for trial **commitment** n **committal** n
committee n body appointed, elected for special business
commode n 1 chest of drawers 2 stool containing chamber pot
commodity n, pl -ities article of trade
commodore n 1 senior naval or air officer 2 president of yacht club
common ❶ adj 1 shared by all 2 public 3 ordinary 4 inferior ▷ n 5 land belonging to community ▷ pl 6 ordinary people 7 (with cap.) House of Commons **commoner** n one not of the nobility **commonly** adv **commonplace** adj 1 ordinary ▷ n 2 trite remark

commence v = **embark on**, start, open, begin, initiate ≠ **stop**
commend v = **praise**, acclaim, applaud, compliment, extol ≠ **criticize**; = **recommend**, suggest, approve, advocate, endorse
comment v = **remark**, say, note, mention, point out ▷ n = **remark**, statement, observation; = **note**, explanation, illustration, commentary, exposition
commission v = **appoint**, order, contract, select, engage ▷ n = **duty**, task, mission, mandate,

errand; = **fee**, cut, percentage, royalties, rake-off (Sl); = **committee**, board, representatives, commissioners, delegation
commit v = **do**, perform, carry out, execute, enact; = **put in custody**, confine, imprison ≠ **release**
common adj = **usual**, standard, regular, ordinary, familiar ≠ **rare**; = **popular**, general, accepted, standard, routine; = **shared**, collective; = **ordinary**, average, typical ≠ **important**

c

commonwealth n 1 republic 2 (with cap.) federation of self-governing states

commotion n stir, disturbance

commune¹ v converse intimately

communion n 1 sharing of thoughts, feelings etc. 2 (with cap.) (participation in) sacrament of the Lord's Supper

commune² ❶ n group living together and sharing property, responsibility etc. **communal** adj for common use

communicate ❶ v 1 impart, convey 2 reveal ▷ v 3 give or exchange information 4 have connecting door **communicable** adj **communication** n 1 giving information 2 message 3 (usu. pl) means of exchanging messages **communicative** adj willing to talk

communiqué n official announcement

communism ❶ n doctrine that all means of production etc. should

be property of community **communist** n/adj

community ❶ n, pl -ties 1 body of people living in one district 2 the public 3 joint ownership 4 similarity

commute v 1 travel daily some distance to work 2 exchange 3 reduce (punishment) **commuter** n

compact¹ ❶ adj 1 closely packed 2 solid 3 terse ▷ v 4 make, become compact **compact disc** small audio disc played by laser

compact² ❶ n agreement

compact³ ❶ n small case to hold face powder etc.

companion ❶ n comrade

company ❶ n, pl -nies 1 gathering of persons 2 companionship 3 guests 4 business firm 5 division of regiment

compare ❶ v 1 notice likenesses and differences 2 liken 3 be like

━━━━━━━ THESAURUS ━━━━━━━

commune² n = **community**, collective, cooperative, kibbutz

communicate v = **contact**, talk, speak, make contact, get in contact

communism n = **socialism**, Marxism, collectivism, Bolshevism, state socialism

community n = **society**, people, public, residents, commonwealth

compact¹ adj = **closely packed**, solid, thick, dense, compressed ≠ **loose**; = **concise**, brief, to the point, succinct, terse ≠ **lengthy** ▷ v = **pack closely**, stuff, cram, compress, condense ≠ **loosen**

compact² n = **agreement**, deal, understanding, contract, bond

companion n = **friend**, partner, ally, colleague, associate; = **assistant**, aide, escort, attendant

company n = **business**, firm, association, corporation, partnership; = **group**, set, community, band, crowd; = **troop**, unit, squad, team; = **companionship**, society, presence, fellowship

compare v = **contrast**, balance, weigh, set against, juxtapose

4 compete with **comparability** n
comparable adj **comparative**
adj 1 relative 2 (Grammar)
denoting form of adjective, adverb
meaning *more* **comparison** n act
of comparing

compartment ❶ n part divided
off

compass ❶ n 1 instrument for
showing north 2 (usu. pl)
instrument for drawing circles
3 scope ▷ v 4 surround
5 comprehend 6 attain

compassion ❶ n pity, sympathy
compassionate adj

compatible ❶ adj agreeing with
compatibility n

compatriot n fellow countryman

compel ❶ v -pelling, -pelled
force

compendium n, pl -diums, -dia
1 collection of different games
2 summary **compendious** adj

brief but inclusive

compensate ❶ v 1 make up for
2 recompense **compensation** n

compere n 1 one who introduces
cabaret, television shows etc. ▷ v
2 act as compere

compete ❶ v strive in rivalry,
contend for **competition** n
1 rivalry 2 contest **competitive**
adj **competitor** n

competent ❶ adj 1 able
2 properly qualified 3 sufficient
competence n

compile ❶ v make up from various
sources **compilation** n

complacent ❶ adj self-satisfied
complacency n

complain ❶ v 1 grumble 2 make
known a grievance 3 (with of) make
known that one is suffering from
complaint n 1 grievance 2 illness

complement ❶ n 1 something
making up a whole 2 complete

compartment n = **section**,
carriage, berth; = **bay**, booth,
locker, niche, cubicle

compass n = **range**, field, area,
reach, scope

compassion n = **sympathy**,
understanding, pity, humanity,
mercy ≠ **indifference**

compatible adj = **consistent**, in
keeping, congruous
≠ **inappropriate**

compel v = **force**, make, railroad
(Inf), oblige, constrain

compensate v = **recompense**,
repay, refund, reimburse,
remunerate; = **make amends**,
make up for, atone, make it up to

someone, pay for

compete v = **contend**, fight, vie,
challenge, struggle

competent adj = **able**, skilled,
capable, proficient ≠ **incompetent**

compile v = **put together**, collect,
gather, organize, accumulate

complacent adj = **smug**,
self-satisfied, pleased with yourself,
resting on your laurels, contented
≠ **insecure**

complain v = **find fault**, moan,
grumble, whinge (Inf), carp

complement v = **enhance**,
complete, improve, boost, crown
▷ n = **accompaniment**,
companion, accessory, completion,

amount ▷ v **3** add to, make
complete **complementary** adj
complete **①** adj **1** perfect
2 ended **3** entire **4** thorough ▷ v
5 make whole **6** finish
completely adv **completion** n

complex **①** adj **1** intricate,
compound, involved ▷ n **2** group
of related buildings **3** obsession
complexity n

complexion **①** n **1** look, colour of
skin, esp. of face **2** aspect,
character

complicate **①** v make involved,
difficult **complication** n

complicity n partnership in
wrongdoing

compliment **①** n/v praise
complimentary adj **1** expressing

praise **2** free of charge

comply **①** v **-plying, -plied** do as
asked **compliance** n **compliant**
adj

component **①** n part,
constituent of whole

compose **①** v **1** put in order
2 write, invent **3** make up
4 calm **composer** n one who
composes, esp. music **composite**
adj made up of distinct parts
composition n **composure**
n calmness

compos mentis (Lat) sane

compost n decayed vegetable
matter for fertilizing soil

compound¹ **①** n **1** substance,
word, made up of parts ▷ adj **2** not
simple **3** composite ▷ v **4** mix,

——————— THESAURUS ———————

finishing touch; = **total**, capacity,
quota, aggregate, contingent
complete adj = **total**, perfect,
absolute, utter, outright; = **whole**,
full, entire ≠ **partial**; = **entire**, full,
whole, intact, unbroken
≠ **incomplete** ▷ v = **finish**,
conclude, end, close, settle ≠ **start**
complex adj = **compound**,
multiple, composite, manifold,
heterogeneous; = **complicated**,
difficult, involved, elaborate,
tangled ≠ **simple** ▷ n = **structure**,
system, scheme, network,
organization; (Inf) = **obsession**,
preoccupation, phobia, fixation,
fixed idea
complexion n = **skin**, colour,
colouring, hue, skin tone; = **nature**,
character, make-up
complicate v = **make difficult**,

confuse, muddle, entangle, involve
≠ **simplify**
compliment n = **praise**, honour,
tribute, bouquet, flattery
≠ **criticism** ▷ v = **praise**, flatter,
salute, congratulate, pay tribute to
≠ **criticize**
comply v = **obey**, follow, observe,
submit to, conform to ≠ **defy**
component n = **part**, piece, unit,
item, element
compose v = **put together**, make
up, constitute, comprise, make
≠ **destroy**; = **create**, write,
produce, invent, devise; = **arrange**,
make up, construct, put together,
order
compound¹ n = **combination**,
mixture, blend, composite, fusion
≠ **element** ▷ v = **intensify**, add to,
complicate, worsen, heighten

make up **5** make worse
6 compromise
compound² n enclosure
containing houses etc.
comprehend ❶ v **1** understand
2 include **comprehensible** adj
comprehension n
comprehensive adj **1** taking in
much **2** pert. to education of
children of all abilities
compress ❶ v **1** squeeze together
2 make smaller ▷ n **3** pad of lint
applied to wound, inflamed part
etc. **compressible** adj
compression n **compressor** n
comprise ❶ v include, contain
compromise ❶ n **1** coming to
terms by giving up part of claim ▷ v
2 settle by making concessions
3 expose to suspicion

compulsion n **1** act of compelling
2 urge **compulsive** adj
compulsory adj not optional
compunction n regret
compute ❶ v calculate
computation n **computer** n
electronic machine for processing
information **computerize** v
comrade ❶ n friend
con¹ ❶ v (Inf) swindle
con² n vote against
concave adj rounded inwards
conceal ❶ v hide **concealment**
n
concede ❶ v **1** admit truth of
2 give up
conceit n vanity **conceited** adj
conceive ❶ v **1** believe **2** become
pregnant **3** devise **conceivable**
adj

— THESAURUS —

≠ **lessen**; = **combine**, unite, mix,
blend, synthesize ≠ **divide**
comprehend v = **understand**,
see, take in, perceive, grasp
≠ **misunderstand**
compress v = **squeeze**, crush,
squash, press; = **condense**,
contract, concentrate, shorten,
abbreviate
comprise v = **be composed of**,
include, contain, consist of, take in
compromise n = **give-and-take**,
agreement, settlement,
accommodation, concession
≠ **disagreement** ▷ v = **meet
halfway**, concede, make
concessions, give and take, strike a
balance ≠ **disagree**; = **undermine**,
expose, embarrass, weaken,
prejudice ≠ **support**

compute v = **calculate**, total,
count, reckon, figure out
comrade n = **companion**, friend,
partner, ally, colleague
con¹ (Inf) ▷ v = **swindle**, trick,
cheat, rip off (Sl), deceive ▷ n
= **swindle**, trick, fraud, deception,
scam (Sl)
conceal v = **hide**, bury, cover,
screen, disguise ≠ **reveal**
concede v = **admit**, allow, accept,
acknowledge, own ≠ **deny**; = **give
up**, yield, hand over, surrender,
relinquish ≠ **conquer**
conceive v = **imagine**, envisage,
visualize, think; = **think up**, create, design, devise,
formulate; = **become pregnant**,
get pregnant, become
impregnated

concentrate ❶ v 1 focus (one's efforts etc.) 2 increase in strength 3 devote all attention ▷ n 4 concentrated substance **concentration** n

concentric adj having the same centre

concept ❶ n abstract idea **conceptual** adj

conception ❶ n 1 idea, notion 2 act of conceiving

concern ❶ v 1 relate to 2 worry 3 involve (oneself) ▷ n 4 affair 5 worry 6 business, enterprise **concerned** adj 1 worried 2 involved **concerning** prep about

concert n 1 musical entertainment 2 agreement **concerted** adj mutually planned **concertina** n musical instrument with bellows **concerto** n composition for solo instrument and orchestra

concession ❶ n 1 act of conceding 2 thing conceded **concession road** n (Canad) (esp. in Ontario) one of a series of roads separating concessions in a township

conch n seashell

conciliate v win over from hostility **conciliation** n **conciliatory** adj

concise adj brief, terse

conclave n private meeting

conclude ❶ v 1 finish 2 deduce 3 settle 4 decide **conclusion** n **conclusive** adj decisive

concoct v 1 make mixture 2 contrive **concoction** n

concord n 1 agreement 2 harmony

concourse n 1 crowd 2 large, open place in public area

concrete ❶ n 1 mixture of sand, cement etc. ▷ adj 2 specific 3 actual 4 solid

—— THESAURUS ——

concentrate v = **focus your attention on**, focus on, pay attention to, be engrossed in, put your mind to ≠ **pay no attention to**; = **focus**, centre, converge, bring to bear

concept n = **idea**, view, image, theory, notion

conception n = **idea**, plan, design, image, concept; = **impregnation**, insemination, fertilization, germination

concern n = **anxiety**, fear, worry, distress, unease; = **worry**, care, anxiety; = **affair**, issue, matter, consideration ▷ v = **worry**, trouble,

bother, disturb, distress; = **be about**, cover, deal with, go into, relate to

concession n = **compromise**, agreement, settlement, accommodation/adjustment; = **privilege**, right, permit, licence, entitlement

conclude v = **decide**, judge, assume, gather, work out; = **come to an end**, end, close, finish, wind up ≠ **begin**; = **bring to an end**, end, close, finish, complete ≠ **begin**

concrete adj = **specific**, precise, explicit, definite, clear-cut ≠ **vague**; = **real**, material, actual, substantial, sensible ≠ **abstract**

DICTIONARY

concubine n 1 woman cohabiting with man 2 secondary wife

concur v -curring, -curred 1 agree 2 happen together **concurrent** adj **concurrently** adv

concussion n brain injury

condemn ❶ v 1 blame 2 find guilty 3 doom 4 declare unfit **condemnation** n

condense v 1 concentrate 2 turn from gas to liquid **condensation** n

condescend v 1 treat graciously one regarded as inferior 2 stoop **condescension** n

condiment n seasoning for food

condition ❶ n 1 state or circumstances 2 thing on which something else depends 3 prerequisite 4 physical fitness ▷ v 5 accustom 6 regulate 7 make fit **conditional** adj dependent on events **conditioner** n liquid to make hair or clothes feel softer

condolence n sympathy

condom n sheathlike rubber contraceptive worn by man

condone ❶ v overlook, forgive

conducive adj leading (to)

conduct ❶ n 1 behaviour 2 management ▷ v 3 guide 4 direct 5 manage 6 transmit (heat etc.) **conduction** n **conductor** n 1 person in charge of bus etc. 2 director of orchestra 3 substance capable of transmitting heat etc.

conduit n channel or pipe for water, cables etc.

cone n 1 tapering figure with circular base 2 fruit of pine, fir etc. **conical** adj

confederate n 1 ally 2 accomplice ▷ v 3 unite **confederation** n alliance of political units

confer ❶ v -ferring, -ferred 1 grant 2 talk with **conference** n meeting for consultation

confess ❶ v 1 admit 2 declare one's sins orally to priest

THESAURUS

condemn v = **denounce**, damn, criticize, disapprove, censure ≠ **approve**; = **sentence**, convict, damn, doom, pass sentence on ≠ **acquit**

condition n = **state**, order, shape, nick (Brit Inf), trim; = **situation**, state, position, status, circumstances; = **requirement**, terms, rider, restriction, qualification; = **health**, shape, fitness, trim, form ▷ v = **train**, teach, adapt, accustom

condone v = **overlook**, excuse,

forgive, pardon, turn a blind eye to ≠ **condemn**

conduct v = **carry out**, run, control, manage, direct; = **accompany**, lead, escort, guide, steer ▷ n = **management**, running, control, handling, administration; = **behaviour**, ways, bearing, attitude, manners

confer v = **discuss**, talk, consult, deliberate, discourse; = **grant**, give, present, accord, award

confess v = **admit**, acknowledge, disclose, confide, own up ≠ **cover**

confession n **confessional** n
confessor's box **confessor** n priest
who hears confessions

confetti pl n bits of coloured paper
thrown at weddings

confide ❶ v **1** tell secrets
2 entrust **confidence** n **1** trust
2 assurance **3** intimacy **4** secret
confident adj **1** certain
2 self-assured **confidential** adj
1 private **2** secret

configuration n shape

confine ❶ v **1** keep within bounds
2 shut up **confines** pl n limits
confinement n **1** being confined
2 childbirth

confirm ❶ v **1** make sure
2 strengthen **3** make valid
4 admit as member of church
confirmation n **confirmed** adj
long-established

confiscate ❶ v seize by authority
confiscation n

conflict ❶ n **1** struggle
2 disagreement ▷ v **3** be at odds

with **4** clash

conform ❶ v **1** comply with
accepted standards etc. **2** adapt to
rule, pattern, custom etc.
conformist n **conformity** n

confound ❶ v **1** perplex
2 confuse **confounded** adj (Inf)
damned

confront ❶ v **1** face **2** bring face
to face with **confrontation** n

confuse ❶ v **1** bewilder **2** jumble
3 make unclear **4** mistake
confusion n

conga n **1** dance by people in single
file **2** large drum

congeal v solidify

congenial adj pleasant

congenital adj **1** existing at birth
2 dating from birth

conger n sea eel

conglomerate adj **1** substance
composed of smaller elements
2 business organization
comprising many companies
conglomeration n

_____ THESAURUS _____

up; = **declare**, allow, reveal,
confirm, concede
confide v = **tell**, admit, reveal,
confess, whisper
confine v = **imprison**, enclose,
shut up, intern, incarcerate;
= **restrict**, limit
confirm v = **prove**, support,
establish, back up, verify; = **ratify**,
establish, sanction, endorse,
authorize
confiscate v = **seize**, appropriate,
impound, commandeer, sequester
≠ **give back**
conflict n = **dispute**, difference,

opposition, hostility, disagreement
≠ **agreement**; = **struggle**, battle,
clash, strife ▷ v = **be
incompatible**, clash, differ,
disagree, collide ≠ **agree**
conform v = **fit in**, follow, adjust,
adapt, comply; = **fulfil**, meet,
match, suit, satisfy
confound v = **bewilder**, baffle,
confuse, astound, perplex
confront v = **tackle**, deal with,
cope with, meet head-on
confuse v = **mix up with**, take for,
muddle with; = **bewilder**, puzzle,
baffle, perplex, mystify

DICTIONARY

congratulate ❶ v express pleasure at good fortune, success etc. **congratulations** pl n

congregate v 1 assemble 2 flock together **congregation** n assembly, esp. for worship

congress ❶ n 1 formal assembly 2 legislative body

conifer n cone-bearing tree **coniferous** adj

conjecture n/v guess **conjectural** adj

conjugal adj of marriage

conjugate v (Grammar) inflect verb in its various forms **conjugation** n

conjunction n 1 union 2 simultaneous happening 3 part of speech joining words, phrases etc. **conjunctive** adj

conjunctivitis n inflammation of membrane of eye

conjure ❶ v 1 produce magic effects 2 perform tricks **conjuror, -er** n

conker n (Inf) horse chestnut

connect ❶ v 1 join together, unite 2 associate in the mind **connection, connexion** n 1 association 2 connecting thing 3 relation

connive v conspire

connoisseur n expert in fine arts

conquer ❶ v 1 overcome 2 defeat 3 be victorious **conqueror** n **conquest** n

conscience ❶ n sense of right or wrong **conscientious** adj

conscious ❶ adj 1 aware 2 awake 3 intentional **consciousness** n

conscript n 1 one compulsorily enlisted for military service ▷ v 2 enlist thus **conscription** n

consecrate v make sacred **consecration** n

consecutive ❶ adj in unbroken succession **consecutively** adv

consensus ❶ n widespread agreement

consent ❶ v 1 agree to ▷ n

C

THESAURUS

congratulate v = **compliment**, pat on the back, wish joy to

congress n = **meeting**, council, conference, assembly, convention

conjure v = **produce**, generate, bring about, give rise to, make

connect v = **link**, join, couple, attach, fasten ≠ **separate**

conquer v = **seize**, obtain, acquire, occupy, overrun; = **defeat**, overcome, overthrow, beat, master ≠ **lose to**

conscience n = **principles**, scruples, moral sense, sense of right and wrong, still small voice

conscious adj (often with **of**) = **aware of**, alert to, responsive to, sensible of ≠ **unaware**; = **deliberate**, knowing, studied, calculated, self-conscious ≠ **unintentional**; = **awake**, wide-awake, sentient, alive ≠ **asleep**

consecutive adj = **successive**, running, succeeding, in turn, uninterrupted

consensus n = **agreement**, general agreement, unanimity, common consent, unity

consent n = **agreement**, sanction,

c

2 permission 3 agreement

consequence ❶ n 1 result, outcome 2 importance **consequent** adj **consequential** adj important **consequently** adv therefore

conserve ❶ v 1 keep from change etc. 2 preserve ▷ n 3 jam **conservation** n protection of environment **conservationist** n **conservative** adj/n 1 (person) tending to avoid change 2 moderate (person) **conservatory** n greenhouse

consider ❶ v 1 think over 2 examine 3 make allowance for 4 be of opinion that **considerable** adj 1 important 2 large **considerably** adv **considerate** adj thoughtful towards others **consideration** n 1 act of considering 2 recompense **considering** prep taking into account

consign v 1 hand over 2 entrust **consignment** n goods consigned

consignor n

consist v be composed of **consistency** n 1 agreement 2 degree of firmness **consistent** adj **consistently** adv

console¹ ❶ v comfort, cheer in distress **consolation** n

console² n 1 bracket 2 keyboard etc. of organ 3 cabinet for television, radio etc.

consolidate ❶ v 1 combine 2 make firm **consolidation** n

consommé n clear meat soup

consonant n 1 sound, letter other than a vowel ▷ adj 2 agreeing with, in accord **consonance** n

consort v 1 associate ▷ n 2 husband, wife, esp. of ruler **consortium** n association of banks, companies etc.

conspicuous ❶ adj noticeable

conspire ❶ v plot together **conspiracy** n **conspirator** n

constable n policeman **constabulary** n, pl **-laries** police force

—— THESAURUS ——

approval, go-ahead (Inf), permission ≠ **refusal** ▷ v = **agree**, approve, permit, concur, assent ≠ **refuse**

consequence n = **result**, effect, outcome, repercussion, issue; = **importance**, concern, moment, value, account

conserve v = **save**, husband, take care of, hoard, store up ≠ **waste**

consider v = **think**, see, believe, rate, judge; = **think about**, reflect on, weigh, contemplate, deliberate;

= **bear in mind**, remember, respect, think about, take into account

console¹ v = **comfort**, cheer, soothe, support, encourage ≠ **distress**

consolidate v = **strengthen**, secure, reinforce, fortify, stabilize; = **combine**, unite, join, merge, unify

conspicuous adj = **obvious**, clear, patent, evident, noticeable ≠ **inconspicuous**

conspire v = **plot**, scheme, intrigue, manoeuvre, contrive

constant ❶ adj 1 unchanging
2 steadfast 3 continual ▷ n
4 quantity that does not vary
constancy n loyalty **constantly**
adv

constellation n group of stars

consternation n alarm, dismay

constipation n difficulty in
emptying bowels **constipated** adj

constituent ❶ adj 1 making up
whole ▷ n 2 component part
3 elector **constituency** n, pl -cies
1 body of electors 2 parliamentary
division

constitute ❶ v 1 form 2 found
constitution n 1 composition
2 health 3 principles on which
state is governed **constitutional**
adj 1 inborn 2 statutory ▷ n
3 walk for good of health

constrain ❶ v force **constraint**
n 1 compulsion 2 restriction

construct ❶ v 1 build 2 put
together **construction** n
constructive adj positive

construe v -struing, -strued
interpret

consul n government
representative in a foreign country
consulate n consul's office

consult ❶ v seek advice,
information from **consultancy** n,
pl -cies **consultant** n specialist,
expert **consultation** n
consultative adj

consume ❶ v 1 eat or drink
2 engross 3 use up 4 destroy
consumer n **consumption** n

consummate v/adj 1 perfect
2 complete **consummation** n

cont. continued

contact ❶ n 1 touching 2 being
in touch 3 useful acquaintance ▷ v
4 get in touch with **contact lens**

—————— THESAURUS ——————

constant adj = **continuous**,
sustained, perpetual, interminable,
unrelenting ≠ **occasional**;
= **unchanging**, even, fixed,
permanent, stable ≠ **changing**;
= **faithful**, true, devoted, loyal,
stalwart ≠ **undependable**

constituent n = **voter**, elector,
member of the electorate;
= **component**, element, ingredient,
part, unit ▷ adj = **component**,
basic, essential, integral, elemental

constitute v = **represent**, be,
consist of, embody, exemplify

constrain v = **force**, bind, compel,
oblige, necessitate

construct v = **build**, make, form,
create, fashion ≠ **demolish**

consult v = **ask**, refer to, turn to,
take counsel, pick (someone's)
brains

consume v = **eat**, swallow,
devour, put away, gobble (up);
= **use up**, spend, waste, absorb,
exhaust; = **destroy**, devastate,
demolish, ravage, annihilate; often
passive = **obsess**, dominate, absorb,
preoccupy, eat up

contact n = **communication**, link,
association, connection,
correspondence; = **touch**,
contiguity; = **connection**,
colleague, associate, liaison,
acquaintance ▷ v = **get** or **be in
touch with**, call, reach, approach,
write to

lens fitting over the eyeball

contain ❶ v 1 hold 2 have room for 3 comprise 4 restrain **container** n

contaminate ❶ v pollute **contamination** n

contemplate ❶ v 1 meditate on 2 gaze upon 3 intend **contemplation** n

contemporary ❶ adj 1 existing at same time 2 modern ▷ n 3 one of same age **contemporaneous** adj

contempt ❶ n 1 scorn, disgrace 2 wilful disrespect of authority **contemptible** adj **contemptuous** adj showing contempt

contend ❶ v 1 strive, dispute 2 maintain (that) **contender** n

competitor **contention** n **contentious** adj

content¹ ❶ adj 1 satisfied 2 willing (to) ▷ v 3 satisfy ▷ n 4 satisfaction **contented** adj **contentment** n

content² ❶ n 1 thing contained ▷ pl 2 index of topics

contest ❶ n 1 competition ▷ v 2 dispute 3 compete for **contestant** n

context ❶ n words coming before and after a word or passage

continent¹ n large continuous mass of land **continental** adj

continent² adj in control of bodily functions

contingent adj 1 depending (on) ▷ n 2 group part of larger group **contingency** n, pl **-cies**

contain v = **hold**, incorporate, accommodate, enclose, have capacity for; = **include**, consist of, embrace, comprise, embody; = **restrain**, control, hold in, curb, suppress

contaminate v = **pollute**, infect, stain, corrupt, taint ≠ **purify**

contemplate v = **consider**, plan, think of, intend, envisage; = **think about**, consider, ponder, reflect upon, ruminate (upon); = **look at**, examine, inspect, gaze at, eye up

contemporary adj = **modern**, recent, current, up-to-date, present-day ≠ **old-fashioned**; = **coexisting**, concurrent, contemporaneous ▷ n = **peer**, fellow, equal

contempt n = **scorn**, disdain, mockery, derision, disrespect ≠ **respect**

contend v = **argue**, hold, maintain, allege, assert; = **compete**, fight, struggle, clash, contest

content¹ adj = **satisfied**, happy, pleased, contented, comfortable

content² n = **subject matter**, material, theme, substance, essence; = **amount**, measure, size, load, volume

contest n = **competition**, game, match, trial, tournament ▷ v = **compete in**, take part in, fight in, go in for, contend for; = **oppose**, question, challenge, argue, debate

context n = **circumstances**,

continue ❶ v -tinuing, -tined
1 remain 2 carry on 3 resume
4 prolong **continual** adj
continually adv **continuation** n
continuity n, pl logical sequence
continuous adj

contort v twist out of normal
shape **contortion** n
contortionist n

contour n outline, shape, esp.
mountains, coast etc.

contra- comb. form against

contraband n/adj smuggled
(goods)

contraception n prevention of
conception **contraceptive** adj/n

contract ❶ v 1 make or become
smaller 2 enter into agreement
3 incur ▷ n 4 agreement
contraction n **contractor** n one
making contract, esp. builder
contractual adj

contradict ❶ v 1 deny 2 be
inconsistent with **contradiction**
n **contradictory** adj

contraflow n flow of traffic in
opposite direction

contralto n, pl **-tos** lowest
female voice

contraption n 1 gadget 2 device

contrary ❶ adj 1 opposed
2 perverse ▷ n 3 the exact
opposite ▷ adv 4 in opposition

contrast ❶ v 1 bring out, show
difference ▷ n 2 striking difference

contravene v infringe

contribute ❶ v 1 give, pay to
common fund 2 help to occur
3 write for the press **contribution**
n **contributor** n

contrite adj remorseful
contrition n

contrive ❶ v 1 arrange 2 devise,
invent **contrivance** n

conditions, situation, ambience
continue v = **keep on**, go on,
maintain, sustain, carry on ≠ **stop**;
= **go on**, progress, proceed, carry
on, keep going; = **resume**, return
to, take up again, proceed, carry on
≠ **stop**
contract n = **agreement**,
commitment, arrangement,
settlement, bargain ▷ v = **agree**,
negotiate, pledge, bargain,
undertake ≠ **refuse**; = **constrict**,
confine, tighten, shorten,
compress; = **tighten**, narrow,
shorten ≠ **stretch**
contradict v = **deny**, challenge,
belie, fly in the face of, be at
variance with; = **deny**, negate,

rebut, controvert ≠ **confirm**
contrary adj = **opposite**, different,
opposed, clashing, counter ≠ **in
agreement**; = **perverse**, difficult,
awkward, intractable, obstinate
≠ **cooperative** ▷ n = **opposite**,
reverse, converse, antithesis
contrast n = **difference**,
opposition, comparison,
distinction, foil ▷ v
= **differentiate**, compare, oppose,
distinguish, set in opposition;
= **differ**, be contrary, be at variance,
be dissimilar
contribute v = **give**, provide,
supply, donate, subscribe
contrive v = **devise**, plan,
fabricate, create, design;

control ❶ v 1 command
2 regulate 3 direct, check ▷ n
4 power to direct or determine
5 curb, check ▷ pl 6 instruments
to control car, aircraft etc.
controller n

controversy ❼ n, pl -sies
debate **controversial** adj

contusion n bruise

conundrum n riddle

conurbation n large built-up area

convalesce v recover health after
illness, operation etc.
convalescence n **convalescent**
adj/n

convection n transmission of
heat by currents

convene ❶ v call together,
assemble **convenor, -er** n
convention n 1 assembly
2 treaty 3 accepted usage
conventional adj 1 (slavishly)
observing customs of society
2 customary 3 (of weapons, war
etc.) not nuclear

convenient ❶ adj 1 handy
2 favourable to needs, comfort
convenience n 1 ease, comfort,
suitability 2 public toilet ▷ adj
3 (of food) quick to prepare
conveniently adv

convent n religious community,
esp. of nuns

convention ❶ see CONVENE

converge ❶ v tend to meet

conversant adj familiar (with),
versed in

converse[1] v 1 talk (with) ▷ n
2 talk **conversation** n
conversational adj

converse[2] adj 1 opposite,
reversed ▷ n 2 the opposite
conversely adv

convert ❶ v 1 apply to another
purpose 2 change 3 transform
4 cause to adopt (another) religion,
opinion ▷ n 5 converted person
conversion n **convertible** n
1 car with folding roof ▷ adj
2 capable of being converted

———————————— THESAURUS ————————————

= **manage**, succeed, arrange,
manoeuvre
control n = **power**, authority,
management, command,
guidance; = **restraint**, check,
regulation, brake, limitation ▷ v
= **have power over**, manage,
direct, handle, command; = **limit**,
restrict, curb
controversy n = **argument**,
debate, row, dispute, quarrel
convene v = **call**, gather,
assemble, summon, bring together
convenient adj = **suitable**, fit,
handy, satisfactory; = **useful**,

practical, handy, serviceable,
labour-saving ≠ **useless**; = **nearby**,
available, accessible, handy, at
hand ≠ **inaccessible**
convention n = **custom**, practice,
tradition, code, usage;
= **agreement**, contract, treaty,
bargain, pact; = **assembly**,
meeting, council, conference,
congress
converge v = **come together**,
meet, join, combine, gather
convert v = **change**, turn,
transform, alter, transpose;
= **adapt**, modify, remodel,

convex adj curved outwards
convey 1 v 1 transport 2 impart
3 (Law) transfer **conveyance** n
conveyancer n one skilled in legal
forms of transferring property
conveyancing n **conveyor belt**
continuous moving belt
convict 1 v 1 prove or declare
guilty ▷ n 2 criminal serving prison
sentence **conviction** n 1 verdict
of guilty 2 being convinced, firm
belief
convince v persuade by evidence
or argument **convincing** adj
convivial adj sociable
convoluted adj 1 involved
2 coiled **convolution** n
convoy n 1 party (of ships etc.)
travelling together for protection
▷ v 2 escort
convulse v 1 shake violently
2 affect with spasms
convulsion n
coo n/v **cooing, cooed** (make) cry
of doves
cook v 1 prepare food, esp. by heat
2 undergo cooking ▷ n 3 one who

prepares food **cooker** n apparatus
for cooking **cookery** n **cookie** n
1 (US) biscuit 2 data allowing user of
website to be identified on future visits
cool 1 adj 1 moderately cold
2 calm 3 lacking friendliness ▷ v
4 make, become cool **coolly** adv
coop¹ n/v (shut up in) cage
coop², **co-op** n cooperative
society or shop run by one
cooperate 1 v work together
cooperation n **cooperative** adj
1 willing to cooperate 2 (of an
enterprise) owned collectively ▷ n
3 collectively owned enterprise
coordinate v 1 bring into order,
harmony ▷ adj 2 equal in degree,
status etc. **coordination** n
coordinator n
coot n small black water bird
cop n (SI) policeman
cope 1 v 1 deal successfully (with)
2 manage
coping n sloping top course of wall
copious adj abundant
copper¹ n 1 reddish-brown metal
2 coin

reorganize, customize ▷ n
= **neophyte**, disciple, proselyte
convey v = **communicate**,
impart, reveal, relate, disclose;
= **carry**, transport, move, bring,
bear
convict v = **find guilty**, sentence,
condemn, imprison, pronounce
guilty ▷ n = **prisoner**, criminal, lag
(SI), felon, jailbird
convince v = **assure**, persuade,
satisfy, reassure
cool adj = **cold**, chilled, refreshing,

chilly, nippy ≠ **warm**;
= **calm**, collected, relaxed,
composed, sedate ≠ **agitated**;
= **unfriendly**, distant,
indifferent, aloof, lukewarm
≠ **friendly** ▷ v = **lose heat**, cool
off ≠ **warm (up)**
cooperate v = **work together**,
collaborate, coordinate, join forces,
conspire ≠ **conflict**
cope v = **manage**, get by (Inf),
struggle through, survive,
carry on

copper² n (Inf) policeman

coppice, copse n small wood

copulate v unite sexually **copulation** n

copy ❶ n, pl **copies 1** imitation **2** single specimen of book ▷ v **3** make copy of, imitate **copyright** n **1** legal exclusive right to print and publish book, work of art etc. ▷ v **2** protect by copyright

coquette n flirt

coracle n small round boat

coral n hard substance made by sea polyps

cord ❶ n **1** thin rope or thick string **2** ribbed fabric

cordial adj **1** sincere, warm ▷ n **2** fruit-flavoured drink

cordon ❶ n **1** chain of troops or police ▷ v **2** form barrier round **cordon bleu** (of cookery) of the highest standard

corduroy n cotton fabric with velvety, ribbed surface

core ❶ n **1** seed case of apple **2** innermost part ▷ v **3** take out core

corgi n small Welsh dog

coriander n herb

cork n **1** bark of an evergreen Mediterranean oak tree **2** stopper for bottle etc. ▷ v **3** stop up with

cork corkscrew n tool for pulling out corks

corm n underground stem like a bulb

cormorant n large voracious sea bird

corn¹ n grain, fruit of cereals **corny** adj (Inf) trite, oversentimental **corned beef** beef preserved in salt **cornflakes** pl n breakfast cereal **cornflour** n finely ground maize **cornflower** n blue flower growing in cornfields

corn² n horny growth on foot

cornea n, pl **-neas, -neae** transparent membrane covering front of eye

corner ❶ n **1** part where two sides meet **2** remote or humble place **3** (Business) monopoly ▷ v **4** drive into position of no escape **5** establish monopoly **6** move round corner **cornerstone** n indispensable part

cornet n **1** trumpet with valves **2** cone-shaped ice cream wafer

cornice n moulding below ceiling

cornucopia n horn overflowing with fruit and flowers

corollary n, pl **-laries 1** inference from a preceding statement **2** deduction

copy n = **reproduction**, duplicate, replica, imitation, forgery **≠ original** ▷ v = **reproduce**, replicate, duplicate, transcribe, counterfeit **≠ create**; = **imitate**, act like, emulate, behave like, follow

cord n = **rope**, line, string, twine

cordon n = **chain**, line, ring, barrier, picket line

core n = **heart**, essence, nucleus, kernel, crux

corner n = **angle**, joint, crook; = **bend**, curve ▷ v = **trap**, catch, run to earth; = **monopolize**, take over, dominate, control, hog (Sl)

DICTIONARY

coronary adj **1** of blood vessels surrounding heart ▷ n **2** coronary thrombosis **coronary thrombosis** disease of the heart

coronation n ceremony of crowning a sovereign

coroner n officer who holds inquests on unnatural deaths

coronet n small crown

corporal¹ adj of the body

corporal² n noncommissioned officer below sergeant

corporation ❶ n body of persons legally authorized to act as an individual **corporate** adj

corps ❶ n, pl **corps 1** military force **2** any organized body of persons

corpse ❶ n dead body

corpulent adj fat **corpulence** n

corpus n, pl **corpora** main part or body of something

corpuscle n minute particle, esp. of blood

corral n (US) enclosure for cattle

correct ❶ v **1** set right **2** indicate

errors in **3** punish ▷ adj **4** right, accurate **correctly** adv

correction n **corrective** n/adj

correlate v bring into reciprocal relation **correlation** n

correspond ❶ v **1** be similar (to) **2** exchange letters **correspondence** n **correspondent** n **1** writer of letters **2** one employed by newspaper etc. to report on particular topic

corridor ❶ n passage

corroborate v confirm

corroboree n (Aust) Aboriginal gathering or dance

corrode v eat into **corrosion** n **corrosive** adj

corrupt ❶ adj **1** lacking integrity **2** involving bribery **3** wicked ▷ v **4** make evil **5** bribe **6** make rotten **corruption** n

corsage n (flower worn on) bodice of woman's dress

corset n close-fitting undergarment to support the body

THESAURUS

corporation n = **business**, company, concern, firm, society; = **town council**, council, municipal authorities, civic authorities

corps n = **team**, unit, regiment, detachment, company

corpse n = **body**, remains, carcass, cadaver, stiff (SI)

correct adj = **accurate**, right, true, exact, precise **≠ inaccurate**; = **right**, standard, appropriate, acceptable, proper ▷ v = **rectify**, remedy, redress, right, reform

≠ spoil; = **rebuke**, discipline, reprimand, chide, admonish **≠ praise**

correspond v = **be consistent**, match, agree, accord, fit **≠ differ**; = **communicate**, write, keep in touch, exchange letters

corridor n = **passage**, alley, aisle, hallway, passageway

corrupt adj = **bent** (SI), crooked (Inf), fraudulent, unscrupulous; = **depraved**, vicious, degenerate, debased, profligate; = **distorted**, doctored, altered, falsified

cortege n formal (funeral) procession

cortex n, pl **-tices** outer layer of brain etc.

cortisone n synthetic hormone used medically

cosh n 1 blunt weapon ▷ v 2 strike with one

cosine n in a right-angled triangle, ratio of adjacent side to hypotenuse

cosmetic ❶ n/adj (preparation) to improve appearance only

cosmic ❶ adj 1 relating to the universe 2 vast

cosmopolitan ❶ adj/n (person) familiar with many countries

cosmos n the universe considered as an ordered system

cosset v **cosseting, cosseted** pamper, pet

cost ❶ n 1 price 2 expenditure of time, labour etc. 3 damage ▷ v 4 have as price 5 entail payment, or loss of **costly** adj 1 valuable 2 expensive

costume ❶ n style of dress of particular place or time

cosy ❶ adj **-sier, -siest** snug, comfortable

cot n child's bed

cote n shelter for animals or birds

coterie n social clique

cottage ❶ n small house **cottage cheese** mild, soft cheese **cottage pie** dish of minced meat and potato

cotton n 1 plant with white downy fibres 2 cloth of this

couch n 1 piece of furniture for reclining on ▷ v 2 put into (words)

cougar n puma

cough ❶ v 1 expel air from lungs with sudden effort and noise ▷ n 2 act of coughing

could past tense of CAN¹

coulomb n unit of electric charge

council ❶ n 1 deliberative or administrative body 2 local governing authority of town etc. **councillor** n

— THESAURUS —

▷ v = **bribe**, fix (Inf), buy off, suborn, grease (someone's) palm (Sl); = **deprave**, pervert, subvert, debauch ≠ **reform**

cosmetic adj = **superficial**, surface, nonessential

cosmic adj = **extraterrestrial**, stellar

cosmopolitan adj = **sophisticated**, cultured, refined, cultivated, urbane ≠ **unsophisticated**

cost n = **price**, worth, expense, charge, damage (Inf) ▷ v = **sell at**, come to, set (someone) back (Inf), be priced at, command a price of; = **lose**, deprive of, cheat of

costume n = **outfit**, dress, clothing, uniform, ensemble

cosy adj = **comfortable**, homely, warm, intimate, snug, sheltered, comfy (Inf)

cottage n = **cabin**, lodge, hut, shack, chalet

cough v = **clear your throat**, bark, hack ▷ n = **frog** or **tickle in your throat**, bark, hack

council n = **committee**, governing body, board

counsel ❶ n 1 advice
2 barrister(s) ▷ v 3 advise,
recommend **counsellor** n
count¹ ❶ v 1 reckon, number
2 consider to be 3 be reckoned in
4 depend (on) 5 be of importance
▷ n 6 reckoning 7 total number
8 act of counting **countless** adj
too many to be counted
countdown n counting of the
seconds before an event
count² n nobleman **countess** n
noblewoman
countenance n 1 face, its
expression ▷ v 2 support, approve
counter¹ n 1 horizontal surface in
bank, shop etc., on which business
is transacted
counter² ❶ adv 1 in opposite
direction ▷ v 2 oppose
counter- comb. form reversed,
opposite, rival, retaliatory, as in
counterclaim, counterproductive
counteract v neutralize
counterattack v/n attack in
response to attack

counterbalance n 1 weight
balancing another ▷ v 2 act as
balance
counterfeit adj 1 sham, forged
▷ n 2 imitation, forgery ▷ v
3 imitate with intent to deceive
4 forge
counterfoil n part of cheque,
receipt etc. kept as record
countermand v cancel (previous
order)
counterpane n bed covering
counterpart ❶ n something
complementary to another
counterpoint n melody added as
accompaniment to existing melody
countersign v sign document
already signed by another
countersink v enlarge top of hole
to take head of screw, bolt etc.
below surface
countertenor n male alto
country ❶ n, pl -tries 1 region
2 nation 3 people of nation 4 land
of birth 5 rural districts
countryman n **countryside** n

———— THESAURUS ————

counsel n = **advice**, information,
warning, direction, suggestion;
= **legal adviser**, lawyer, attorney,
solicitor, advocate ▷ v = **advise**,
recommend, advocate, warn, urge
count¹ v (often with up) = **add (up)**,
total, reckon (up), tot up, calculate;
= **matter**, be important, carry
weight, tell, rate; = **consider**,
judge, regard, deem, think of;
= **include**, number among, take
into account or consideration ▷ n
= **calculation**, poll, reckoning,
sum, tally

counter² v = **oppose**, meet, block,
resist, parry ▷ adv = **opposite to**,
against, versus, conversely, in
defiance of ≠ **in accordance with**
counterpart n = **opposite
number**, equal, twin, equivalent,
match
country n = **nation**, state, land,
commonwealth, kingdom;
= **people**, community, nation,
society, citizens; = **countryside**,
provinces, sticks (Inf), farmland,
outback (Aust & NZ) ≠ **town**;
= **territory**, land, region, terrain

county ❶ n, pl **-ties** division of country

coup ❶ n **1** successful stroke **2** sudden/violent seizure of government

coup de grace (Fr) decisive action

coupé n sporty style of motorcar

couple ❶ n **1** two, pair **2** husband and wife ▷ v **3** connect, fasten together **4** join, associate **couplet** n two lines of verse **coupling** n connecting device

coupon ❶ n ticket entitling holder to discount, gift etc.

courage ❶ n bravery, boldness **courageous** adj **courageously** adv

courgette n type of small vegetable marrow

courier ❶ n **1** messenger **2** person who guides travellers

course ❶ n **1** movement in space or time **2** direction **3** sequence

4 line of action **5** series of lectures etc. **6** any of successive parts of meal **7** area where golf is played **8** racetrack ▷ v **9** hunt **10** run swiftly **11** (of blood) circulate

court ❶ n **1** space enclosed by buildings, yard **2** area for playing various games **3** royal household **4** body with judicial powers, place where it meets, one of its sittings ▷ v **5** woo **6** seek, invite **courtier** n one who frequents royal court **courtly** adj **1** ceremoniously polite **2** characteristic of a court **court card** king, queen or jack at cards **court martial** pl **courts martial** court for trying naval or military offences **courtship** n wooing **courtyard** n enclosed paved area

courtesy ❶ n politeness **courteous** adj

cousin n son or daughter of uncle or aunt

— THESAURUS —

county n = **province**, district, shire

coup n = **masterstroke**, feat, stunt, action, exploit

couple n = **pair**, two, brace, duo, twosome

coupon n = **slip**, ticket, certificate, token/voucher

courage n = **bravery**, nerve, resolution, daring, pluck ≠ **cowardice**

courier n = **messenger**, runner, carrier, bearer, envoy; = representative, escort, conductor

course n = **route**, way, line, road, track; = **procedure**, plan, policy, programme, method; = **progression**, order, unfolding,

development, movement; = **classes**, programme, schedule, lectures, curriculum; = **racecourse**, circuit, cinder track; = **period**, duration, term, passing ▷ v = **run**, flow, stream, gush, race; = **hunt**, follow, chase, pursue

court n = **law court**, bar, bench, tribunal; = **palace**, hall, castle, manor; = **royal household**, train, suite, attendants, entourage ▷ v = **cultivate**, seek, flatter, solicit, pander to; = **invite**, seek, attract, prompt, provoke; = **woo**, go (out) with, date, take out, run after

courtesy n = **politeness**, good

cove ❶ n small inlet of coast

coven n gathering of witches

covenant ❶ n 1 agreement
2 compact ▷ v 3 agree to a
covenant

cover ❶ v 1 place over 2 extend,
spread 3 bring upon (oneself)
4 protect 5 travel over 6 include
7 be sufficient 8 report ▷ n
9 covering thing 10 shelter
11 insurance **coverage** n

coverlet n top covering of bed

covert adj secret, sly

covet ❶ v coveting, coveted
long to possess, esp. what belongs
to another **covetous** adj

cow¹ n female of bovine and other
animals **cowboy** n 1 ranch
worker who herds cattle 2 (Inf)
irresponsible worker

cow² v frighten, overawe

coward ❶ n one who lacks
courage **cowardice** n **cowardly**
adj

cower v crouch in fear

cowl n 1 monk's hooded cloak
2 hooded top for chimney

cowslip n wild primrose

coxswain n steersman of boat

coy adj (pretending to be) shy,
modest **coyly** adv

coyote n prairie wolf

coypu n aquatic rodent

crab n edible crustacean **crabbed**
adj (of handwriting) hard to read
crabby adj bad-tempered

crab apple wild sour apple

crack ❶ v 1 split partially 2 break
with sharp noise 3 break down,
yield 4 (Inf) tell (joke) 5 solve,
decipher 6 make sharp noise ▷ n
7 sharp explosive noise 8 split
9 flaw 10 (Inf) joke 11 chat 12 (Sl)
highly addictive form of cocaine
▷ adj 13 (Inf) very skilful **cracker** n
1 decorated paper tube, pulled
apart with a bang, containing toy
etc. 2 explosive firework 3 thin
dry biscuit **crackers** adj (Sl) crazy
cracking adj very good **crackle**
n/v (make) sound of repeated small
cracks **crackpot** n (Inf) eccentric

— THESAURUS —

manners, civility, gallantry,
graciousness

cove n = **bay**, sound, inlet,
anchorage

covenant n = **promise**, contract,
agreement, commitment,
arrangement

cover v = **conceal**, hide, mask,
disguise, obscure ≠ **reveal**;
= **clothe**, dress, wrap, envelop
≠ **uncover**; = **overlay**, blanket;
= **coat**, cake, plaster, smear,
envelop ▷ n = **protection**, shelter,
shield, defence, guard;

= **insurance**, protection,
compensation, indemnity,
reimbursement; = **covering**, case,
top, coating, envelope;
= **bedclothes**, bedding, sheets,
blankets, quilt

covet v = **long for**, desire, envy,
crave, aspire to

coward n = **wimp**, chicken (Sl),
scaredy-cat (Inf), yellow-belly (Sl)

crack v = **break**, split, burst, snap,
fracture; = **snap**, ring, crash, burst,
explode; (Inf); = **hit**, clip (Inf), slap,
smack, clout (Inf); = **break**, cleave;

person; crank

cradle ❶ n 1 infant's bed ▷ v
2 hold or rock as in a cradle
3 cherish

craft[1] ❶ n 1 skilled trade 2 skill,
ability 3 cunning **crafty** adj
cunning **craftsman** n
craftsmanship n

craft[2] ❶ n 1 vessel 2 ship

crag n steep rugged rock

cram ❶ v **cramming, crammed**
1 stuff 2 prepare quickly for
examination

cramp[1] ❶ n painful muscular
contraction

cramp[2] ❶ v hinder

cranberry n edible red berry

crane n 1 wading bird with long
legs 2 machine for moving heavy
weights ▷ v 3 stretch neck **crane
fly** long-legged insect

cranium n, pl **-niums, -nia** skull

cranial adj

crank n 1 arm at right angles to
axis for turning main shaft 2 (Inf)
eccentric person ▷ v 3 start
(engine) by turning crank **cranky**
adj eccentric

cranny n, pl **-nies** small opening

crash ❶ v 1 (cause to) make loud
noise 2 (cause to) fall with crash
3 smash 4 collapse 5 cause
(aircraft) to hit land or water
6 collide with 7 move noisily ▷ n
8 loud, violent fall or impact
9 collision 10 uncontrolled descent
of aircraft 11 sudden collapse
12 bankruptcy **crash helmet**
protective helmet

crass adj grossly stupid

crate ❶ n large (usu. wooden)
container for packing goods

crater ❶ n 1 mouth of volcano
2 bowl-shaped cavity

— THESAURUS —

= **solve**, work out, resolve, clear up,
fathom ▷ n = **break**, chink, gap,
fracture, rift; = **split**, break,
fracture; = **snap**, pop, crash, burst,
explosion; (Inf); = **blow**, slap,
smack, clout (Inf), cuff ▷ adj (SI)
= **first-class**, choice, excellent, ace,
elite

cradle n = **crib**, cot, Moses basket,
bassinet ▷ v = **hold**, support, rock,
nurse, nestle

craft[1] n = **occupation**, work,
business, trade, employment;
= **skill**, art, ability, technique,
know-how (Inf)

craft[2] n = **vessel**, boat, ship, plane,
aircraft

cram v = **stuff**, force, jam, shove,

compress; = **pack**, fill, stuff

cramp[1] n = **spasm**, pain, ache,
contraction, pang

cramp[2] v = **restrict**, hamper,
inhibit, hinder, handicap

crash n = **collision**, accident,
smash, wreck, prang (Inf);
= **smash**, clash, boom, bang,
thunder; = **collapse**, failure,
depression, ruin, downfall
▷ v = **fall**, plunge, topple, lurch,
hurtle; = **plunge**, hurtle;
= **collapse**, fail, go under, be
ruined, go bust (Inf)

crate n = **container**, case, box,
packing case, tea chest

crater n = **hollow**, hole,
depression, dip, cavity

cravat n man's neckcloth

crave ⊕ v 1 have very strong desire for 2 beg **craving** n

craven adj cowardly

crawl ⊕ v 1 move on hands and knees 2 move very slowly 3 ingratiate oneself 4 swim with crawl stroke 5 be overrun (with) ▷ n 6 crawling motion 7 racing stroke at swimming

crayfish n edible freshwater crustacean

crayon n stick or pencil of coloured wax etc.

craze ⊕ n 1 short-lived fashion 2 strong desire 3 madness **crazed** adj **crazy** adj 1 insane 2 very foolish 3 madly eager (for)

creak n/v (make) grating noise

cream ⊕ n 1 fatty part of milk 2 food like this 3 cosmetic like this 4 yellowish-white colour 5 best part ▷ v 6 take cream from 7 take best part from 8 beat to creamy

consistency **creamy** adj

crease ⊕ n 1 line made by folding 2 wrinkle ▷ v 3 make, develop creases

create ⊕ v 1 bring into being 2 make 3 (Inf) make a fuss **creation** n **creative** adj imaginative, inventive **creativity** n **creator** n

creature ⊕ n living being

crèche n day nursery for very young children

credentials ⊕ pl n 1 testimonials 2 letters of introduction

credible ⊕ adj worthy of belief **credibility** n

credit ⊕ n 1 commendation 2 source of honour 3 trust 4 good name 5 system of allowing customers to pay later 6 money at one's disposal in bank etc. ▷ v 7 attribute, believe 8 put on credit side of account **creditable** adj bringing honour **creditor** n one to

— THESAURUS —

crave v = **long for**, yearn for, hanker after, want, desire; (Inf) = **beg**, ask for, seek, petition, pray for

crawl v = **creep**, slither, inch, wriggle, writhe ≠ **run** be crawling with something = **be full of**, teem with, be alive with, swarm with, be overrun with

craze n = **fad**, fashion, trend, rage, enthusiasm

cream n = **lotion**, ointment, oil, essence, cosmetic; = **best**, elite, prime, pick, flower ▷ adj = **off-white**, ivory, yellowish-white

crease n = **fold**, line, ridge, groove,

corrugation ▷ v = **crumple**, rumple, fold, double up, corrugate

create v = **cause**, lead to, occasion, bring about; = **make**, produce, invent, compose, devise ≠ **destroy**

creature n = **living thing**, being, animal, beast, brute

credentials pl n = **qualifications**, ability, skill, fitness, attribute

credible adj = **believable**, possible, likely, reasonable, probable ≠ **unbelievable**; = **reliable**, honest, dependable, trustworthy, sincere ≠ **unreliable**

credit n = **praise**, honour, recognition, approval, tribute;

whom debt is due **credit crunch**
period during which there is a
sudden reduction in the availability
of credit from banks, mortgage
lenders, etc

credulous adj too easy of belief,
gullible **credulity** n

creed ❶ n statement of belief

creek ❶ n narrow inlet on coast

creep ❶ v **creeping, crept**
1 move slowly, stealthily **2** crawl
3 act in servile way **4** (of flesh) feel
shrinking sensation ▷ n **5** creeping
6 (Sl) repulsive person ▷ pl
7 feeling of fear or repugnance
creeper n creeping or climbing
plant **creepy** adj

creole n language developed from
mixture of languages

creosote n oily liquid used for
preserving wood

crepe n fabric with crimped surface

crescendo n, pl **-dos** (Mus)
gradual increase of loudness

crescent ❶ n (shape of) moon
seen in first or last quarter

cress n various plants with edible
pungent leaves

crest ❶ n **1** tuft on bird's or
animal's head **2** top of mountain,
wave etc. **3** badge above shield of
coat of arms **crestfallen** adj
disheartened

cretin n **1** (Obs) person with disability
caused by thyroid deficiency **2** (Inf)
stupid person **cretinous** adj

crevasse n deep open chasm

crevice n cleft, fissure

crew ❶ n **1** ship's, aircraft's
company **2** (Inf) gang

crib n **1** child's cot **2** rack for fodder
3 plagiarism ▷ v **4** copy
dishonestly

cribbage n card game

crick n cramp esp. in neck

cricket¹ n chirping insect

cricket² n game played with bats,
ball and wickets **cricketer** n

crime ❶ n **1** violation of law
2 wicked act **criminal** adj/n

crimson adj/n (of) rich deep red

cringe v **1** shrink, cower **2** behave

THESAURUS

= **source of satisfaction** or **pride**,
asset, honour, feather in your cap;
= **prestige**, reputation, standing,
position, influence; = **belief**, trust,
confidence, faith, reliance ▷ v
= **believe**, rely on, have faith in,
trust, accept

creed n = **belief**, principles,
doctrine, dogma, credo

creek n = **inlet**, bay, cove, bight,
firth or frith (Scot, US, Canad, Aust, &
NZ); = **stream**, brook, tributary,
bayou, rivulet

creep v = **sneak**, steal, tiptoe, slink,

skulk ▷ n (Sl) = **bootlicker** (Inf),
sneak, sycophant, crawler (Sl),
toady

crescent n = **meniscus**, sickle,
new moon

crest n = **top**, summit, peak, ridge,
highest point; = **tuft**, crown, comb,
plume, mane; = **emblem**, badge,
symbol, insignia, bearings

crew n = **(ship's) company**, hands,
(ship's) complement; = **team**, squad,
gang, corps, posse; (Inf) = **crowd**,
set, bunch (Inf), band, pack

crime n = **offence**, violation,

obsequiously

crinkle v/n wrinkle

crinoline n hooped petticoat or skirt

cripple ⊕ n 1 (Offens) disabled person ▷ v 2 disable

crisis ⊕ n, pl **-ses** 1 turning point 2 time of acute danger

crisp ⊕ adj 1 brittle 2 brisk 3 clear-cut 4 fresh ▷ n 5 very thin, fried slice of potato **crispy** adj **crispbread** n thin dry biscuit

crisscross v 1 go in crosswise pattern ▷ adj 2 crossing in different directions

criterion ⊕ n, pl **-ria** standard of judgment

critic ⊕ n 1 professional judge of any of the arts 2 person who finds fault

critical adj 1 fault-finding 2 discerning 3 skilled in judging

croak v/n (utter) deep hoarse cry

crochet n/v **-cheting, -cheted** (do) handicraft like knitting

crock n earthenware pot **crockery** n earthenware dishes etc.

crocodile n large amphibious reptile

crocus n, pl **-cuses** small bulbous plant

croft n small farm

croissant n crescent-shaped bread roll

crone n witchlike old woman

crony n, pl **-nies** intimate friend

crook ⊕ n 1 hooked staff 2 (Inf) swindler, criminal **crooked** adj 1 twisted 2 deformed 3 dishonest

croon v sing in soft tone

crop ⊕ n 1 produce of cultivated plants 2 harvest 3 pouch in bird's gullet 4 whip 5 short haircut ▷ v 6 cut short 7 produce crop 8 (of animals) bite, eat down **cropper** n 1 (Inf) heavy fall 2 disastrous failure **crop up** (Inf) happen unexpectedly

croquet n lawn game played with balls and hoops

croquette n fried ball of minced meat, fish etc.

cross ⊕ n 1 structure or symbol of two intersecting lines or pieces

---

trespass, felony, misdemeanour; **= lawbreaking**, corruption, illegality, vice, misconduct

cripple v **= disable**, paralyse, lame, maim, incapacitate; **= damage**, destroy, ruin, spoil, impair ≠ **help**

crisis n **= emergency**, plight, predicament, trouble, deep water; **= critical point**, climax, height, crunch (Inf), turning point

crisp adj **= firm**, crunchy, crispy, crumbly, fresh ≠ **soft**; **= bracing**, fresh, refreshing, brisk, invigorating

≠ **warm**; **= clean**, smart, trim, neat, tidy

criterion n **= standard**, test, rule, measure, principle

critic n **= judge**, authority, expert, analyst, commentator

crook n (Inf) **= criminal**, rogue, cheat, thief, shark

crop n **= yield**, produce, gathering, fruits, harvest ▷ v **= graze**, eat, browse, feed on, nibble; **= cut**, trim, clip, prune, shear

cross v **= go across**, pass over,

2 such a structure as means of execution **3** symbol of Christian faith **4** any thing in shape of cross **5** affliction **6** hybrid ▷ v **7** move or go across (something) **8** intersect **9** meet and pass **10** mark with lines across **11** (with *out*) delete **12** place in form of cross **13** make sign of cross **14** breed by intermixture **15** thwart ▷ *adj* **16** angry **17** transverse **18** contrary

crossing n **1** intersection of roads, rails etc. **2** part of street where pedestrians are expected to cross

cross-country *adj/adv* by way of open fields **cross-examine** v examine witness already examined by other side **cross-examination** n **cross-eyed** *adj* having eyes turning inward **cross-ply** *adj* (of tyre) having fabric cords in outer casing running diagonally **cross-reference** n reference within text to another part of text **crossroads** n **crossword puzzle** puzzle built up of intersecting words, indicated by clues **The Cross** cross on which Jesus Christ was executed

crosswalk n (Canad) place marked where pedestrians may cross a road

crotch n angle between legs

crotchet n musical note

crotchety *adj* (Inf) bad-tempered

crouch ❶ v **1** bend low **2** huddle down close to ground **3** stoop

croupier n person dealing cards, collecting money etc. at gambling table

crouton n piece of toasted bread served in soup

crow¹ n large black carrion-eating bird

crow² ❶ v **1** utter cock's cry **2** boast ▷ n **3** cock's cry

crowbar n iron bar

crowd ❶ n **1** throng, mass ▷ v **2** flock together **3** cram, pack **4** fill with people

crown ❶ n **1** monarch's headdress **2** royal power **3** various coins **4** top of head **5** summit, top

traverse, cut across, move across; = **span**, bridge, go across, extend over; = **intersect**, intertwine, crisscross; = **oppose**, interfere with, obstruct, block, resist; = **interbreed**, mix, blend, cross-pollinate, crossbreed ▷ n = **trouble**, worry, trial, load, burden; = **mixture**, combination, blend, amalgam, amalgamation ▷ *adj* = **angry**, annoyed, put out, grumpy, short ≠ **good-humoured**

crouch v = **bend down**, kneel, squat, stoop, bow

crow² v = **gloat**, triumph, boast, swagger, brag

crowd ❶ n = **multitude**, mass, throng, army, host; = **group**, set, lot, circle, gang ▷ v = **flock**, mass, collect, gather, stream; = **squeeze**, pack, pile, bundle, cram

crown n = **coronet**, tiara, diadem, circlet; = **laurel wreath**, trophy, prize, honour, garland; = **high point**, top, tip, summit, crest ▷ v = **top**, cap, be on top of, surmount; = **cap**, finish, complete, perfect, round off; (Sl) = **strike**, belt (Inf),

6 perfection of thing ▷ v **7** put crown on **8** occur as culmination **9** (Inf) hit on head

crucial ❶ adj **1** decisive, critical **2** (Inf) very important **crucially** adv

crucible n small melting pot

crude ❶ adj **1** vulgar **2** in natural or raw state **3** rough **crudely** adv **crudity** n

cruel ❶ adj causing pain or suffering **cruelly** adv **cruelty** n

cruet n small container for salt, pepper etc.

cruise ❶ v **1** travel about in a ship ▷ n **2** voyage **cruiser** n **1** ship that cruises **2** warship

crumb ❶ n fragment of bread

crumble ❶ v **1** break into small fragments **2** collapse **crumbly** adj

crumpet n **1** flat, soft cake eaten with butter **2** (Sl) sexually desirable woman or women

crumple ❶ v **1** (cause to) collapse **2** make or become creased

crunch ❶ v **1** sound made by chewing crisp food, treading on gravel etc. **2** (Inf) critical situation ▷ v **3** make crunching sound **crunchy** adj

crusade ❶ n **1** medieval Christian war **2** concerted action to further a cause ▷ v **3** take part in crusade **crusader** n

crush ❶ v **1** compress so as to break **2** break to small pieces **3** defeat utterly ▷ n **4** act of crushing **5** crowd of people etc.

crust ❶ n **1** hard outer part of bread **2** similar casing **crusty** adj **1** having crust **2** bad-tempered

crustacean n hard-shelled

THESAURUS

---

bash, hit over the head, box

crucial adj (Inf) = **vital**, important, pressing, essential, urgent

crude adj = **rough**, basic, makeshift; = **simple**, rudimentary, basic, primitive, coarse; = **vulgar**, dirty, rude, obscene, coarse ≠ **tasteful**

cruel adj = **brutal**, ruthless, callous, sadistic, inhumane ≠ **kind**

cruise n = **sail**, voyage, boat trip, sea trip ▷ v = **sail**, coast, voyage; = **travel along**, coast, drift, keep a steady pace

crumb n = **bit**, grain, fragment, shred, morsel

crumble v = **disintegrate**, collapse, deteriorate, decay, fall apart; = **crush**, fragment, pulverize,

pound, grind

crumple v = **crush**, squash, screw up, scrumple; = **crease**, wrinkle, rumple, ruffle, pucker

crunch v = **chomp**, champ, munch, chew noisily, grind ▷ n (Inf) = **critical point**, test, crisis, emergency, crux

crusade n = **campaign**, drive, movement, cause, push

crush v = **squash**, break, squeeze, compress, press; = **overcome**, overwhelm, put down, subdue, overpower; = **demoralize**, depress, devastate, discourage, humble ▷ n = **crowd**, mob, horde, throng, pack

crust n = **layer**, covering, coating, skin, surface

animal, e.g. crab, lobster

crutch n 1 staff with crosspiece to go under armpit of lame person 2 support 3 crotch

crux n, pl **cruxes** that on which a decision turns

cry ❶ v **crying, cried** 1 weep 2 utter call 3 shout 4 beg (for) 5 proclaim ▷ n 6 loud utterance 7 call of animal 8 fit of weeping

crypt n vault, esp. under church **cryptic** adj secret, mysterious

crystal n 1 transparent mineral 2 very clear glass 3 cut-glass ware 4 form with symmetrically arranged plane surfaces **crystalline** adj **crystallize** v 1 form into crystals 2 become definite

cu. cubic

cub ❶ n 1 young of fox and other animals 2 (with cap.) junior Scout

cubbyhole n small enclosed space

cube n 1 solid figure with six equal square sides 2 cube-shaped block 3 product obtained by multiplying number by itself twice ▷ v 4 multiply thus **cubic** adj

cubicle n enclosed section of room

cuckoo n 1 migratory bird 2 its call

cucumber n long fleshy green fruit used in salad

cud n food which ruminant animal brings back into mouth to chew again

cuddle ❶ v 1 hug 2 lie close and snug, nestle ▷ n 3 hug **cuddly** adj

cudgel n 1 short thick stick ▷ v 2 beat with cudgel

cue¹ ❶ n 1 signal to act or speak 2 hint

cue² n long tapering rod used in billiards

cuff¹ n ending of sleeve

cuff² v 1 strike with open hand ▷ n 2 blow with hand

cuisine n 1 style of cooking 2 food cooked

cul-de-sac n street open only at one end

culinary adj of, for, suitable for, cooking or kitchen

cull v 1 select 2 take out animals from herd

culminate ❶ v 1 reach highest point 2 come to a head **culmination** n

culottes pl n women's trousers flared like skirt

culpable adj blameworthy

culprit ❶ n one guilty of offence

cult ❶ n 1 system of worship 2 devotion to some person, thing

cry v = **weep**, sob, shed tears, blubber, snivel ≠ **laugh**; = **shout**, scream, roar, yell, howl ≠ **whisper** ▷ n = **shout**, call, scream, roar, yell; = **appeal**, plea

cub n = **young**, baby, offspring, whelp

cuddle v = **hug**, embrace, fondle, cosset

cue¹ n = **signal**, sign, hint, prompt, reminder

culminate v = **end up**, close, finish, conclude, wind up

culprit n = **offender**, criminal, felon, guilty party, wrongdoer

cult n = **sect**, faction, school,

cultivate ❶ v 1 till and prepare (ground) 2 develop, improve 3 devote attention to **cultivated** adj cultured **cultivation** n

culture ❶ n 1 state of manners, taste and intellectual development 2 cultivating **cultural** adj **cultured** adj

culvert n drain under road

cumbersome adj unwieldy

cummerbund n sash worn round waist

cumulative adj becoming greater by successive additions

cumulus n, pl **-li** round billowing cloud

cunning ❶ adj 1 crafty, sly ▷ n 2 skill in deceit or evasion

cup ❶ n 1 small drinking vessel with handle 2 various cup-shaped formations 3 cup-shaped trophy as prize ▷ v 4 shape as cup (hands etc.) **cupful** n **cupboard** n piece of furniture with door, for storage

cur n 1 dog of mixed breed 2 contemptible person

curate n parish priest's appointed assistant

curator n custodian, esp. of museum

curb ❶ n 1 check, restraint ▷ v 2 restrain 3 apply curb to

curd n coagulated milk **curdle** v turn into curd, coagulate

cure ❶ v 1 heal, restore to health 2 remedy 3 preserve (fish, skins etc.) ▷ n 4 remedy 5 course of medical treatment 6 restoration to health **curable** adj

curfew n 1 official regulation prohibiting movement of people, esp. at night 2 deadline for this

curio n, pl **-rios** rare or curious thing sought for collections

curious ❶ adj 1 eager to know, inquisitive 2 puzzling, odd **curiosity** n **curiously** adv

— THESAURUS —

religion, clique; = **craze**, fashion, trend, fad

cultivate v = **farm**, work, plant, tend, till; = **develop**, establish, foster; = **court**, seek out, run after, dance attendance upon

culture n = **civilization**, society, customs, way of life; = **lifestyle**, habit, way of life, mores

cunning adj = **crafty**, sly, devious, artful, sharp ≠ **frank**; = **ingenious**, imaginative, sly, devious, artful ▷ n = **craftiness**, guile, trickery, deviousness, artfulness ≠ **candour**; = **skill**, subtlety, ingenuity, artifice, cleverness ≠ **clumsiness**

cup n = **mug**, goblet, chalice, teacup, beaker

curb v = **restrain**, control, check, restrict, suppress ▷ n = **restraint**, control, check, brake, limitation

cure v = **make better**, correct, heal, relieve, remedy; = **preserve**, smoke, dry, salt, pickle ▷ n = **remedy**, treatment, antidote, panacea, nostrum

curious adj = **inquisitive**, interested, questioning, searching, inquiring ≠ **uninterested**; = **strange**, unusual, bizarre, odd, novel ≠ **ordinary**

curl ❶ v 1 take, bend into spiral or curved shape ▷ n 2 spiral lock of hair 3 spiral **curly** adj

curlew n large long-billed wading bird

curmudgeon n bad-tempered person

currant n 1 dried type of grape 2 fruit of various plants allied to gooseberry

current ❶ adj 1 of immediate present 2 in general use ▷ n 3 body of water or air in motion 4 transmission of electricity **currently** adv **currency** n, pl **-cies** 1 money in use 2 state of being in use

curriculum n, pl **-la, -lums** specified course of study **curriculum vitae** outline of career

curry n, pl **-ries** 1 highly-flavoured, pungent condiment 2 dish flavoured with it ▷ v 3 prepare, flavour dish with curry

curse ❶ n 1 profane or obscene expression of anger etc. 2 magic

spell 3 affliction ▷ v 4 utter curse, swear (at) 5 afflict

cursor n movable point showing position on computer screen

cursory adj hasty, superficial

curt adj rudely brief, abrupt

curtail ❶ v cut short

curtain ❶ n 1 hanging drapery at window etc. ▷ v 2 provide, cover with curtain

curtsy, curtsey v/n, pl **-sies, -seys** (perform) woman's bow

curve ❶ n 1 line of which no part is straight ▷ v 2 bend into curve

cushion ❶ n 1 bag filled with soft stuffing or air, to support or ease body ▷ v 2 provide, protect with cushion 3 lessen effects of

cushy adj **cushier, cushiest** (Inf) easy

custard n 1 dish made of eggs and milk 2 sweet sauce of milk and cornflour

custody ❶ n guardianship, imprisonment **custodian** n keeper, curator

THESAURUS

curl n = ringlet, lock ▷ v = twirl, turn, bend, twist, curve

current n = flow, course, undertow, jet, stream; = draught, flow, breeze, puff ▷ adj = present, fashionable, up-to-date, contemporary, trendy (Brit Inf) ≠ out-of-date; = prevalent, common, accepted, popular, widespread

curse v = swear, cuss (Inf), blaspheme, take the Lord's name in vain; = abuse, damn, scold, vilify ▷ n = oath, obscenity, blasphemy, expletive, profanity; = malediction,

anathema, jinx, hoodoo (Inf), excommunication; = affliction, plague, scourge, trouble, torment

curtail v = reduce, diminish, decrease, dock, cut back

curtain n = hanging, drape (chiefly US), portière

curve n = bend, turn, loop, arc, curvature ▷ v = bend, turn, wind, twist, arch

cushion n = pillow, pad, bolster, headrest, beanbag ▷ v = soften, dampen, muffle, mitigate, deaden

custody n = care, charge,

custom ❶ n 1 habit 2 practice 3 usage 4 business patronage ▷ pl 5 taxes levied on imports
customary adj usual, habitual
customer n 1 one who enters shop to buy, esp. regularly 2 purchaser
cut ❶ v **cutting, cut** 1 sever, wound, divide 2 pare, detach, trim 3 intersect 4 reduce, decrease 5 abridge 6 (Inf) ignore (person) ▷ n 7 act of cutting 8 stroke 9 blow, wound 10 reduction 11 fashion, shape 12 (Inf) share
cutter n **cutting** n 1 piece cut from plant 2 article from newspaper 3 passage for railway ▷ adj 4 keen, piercing 5 hurtful
cutthroat n 1 killer ▷ adj 2 murderous 3 fiercely competitive
cute ❶ adj appealing, pretty
cuticle n dead skin, esp. at base of fingernail
cutlass n curved sword
cutlery n knives, forks etc.
cutlet n small piece of meat
cuttlefish n sea mollusc like squid
CV curriculum vitae

cyanide n extremely poisonous chemical compound
cybernetics pl n comparative study of control mechanisms of electronic and biological systems
cyclamen n plant with flowers having turned-back petals
cycle ❶ n 1 recurrent, complete series or period 2 bicycle ▷ v 3 ride bicycle **cyclical** adj **cyclist** n bicycle rider
cyclone n circular storm
cygnet n young swan
cylinder n roller-shaped body, of uniform diameter **cylindrical** adj
cymbal n one of two brass plates struck together to produce clashing sound
cynic ❶ n one who believes the worst about people or outcome of events **cynical** adj **cynicism** n being cynical
cypress n coniferous tree with very dark foliage
cyst n sac containing liquid secretion or pus **cystitis** n inflammation of bladder

— THESAURUS —

protection, supervision, safekeeping; = **imprisonment**, detention, confinement, incarceration
custom n = **tradition**, practice, convention, ritual, policy; = **habit**, way, practice, procedure, routine; = **customers**, business, trade, patronage
cut v = **slit**, score, slice, slash, pierce; = **chop**, split, slice, dissect; = **carve**, slice; = **sever**, cut in two; = **shape**, carve, engrave, chisel, form; = **slash**, wound; = **clip**, mow,

trim, prune, snip ▷ n = **incision**, nick, stroke, slash, slit; = **gash**, nick, wound, slash, laceration; = **reduction**, fall, lowering, slash, decrease; (Inf) = **share**, piece, slice, percentage, portion
cute adj = **appealing**, sweet, attractive, engaging, charming
cycle n = **series of events**, circle, revolution, rotation
cynic n = **sceptic**, doubter, pessimist, misanthrope, misanthropist

d

dab ❶ v **dabbing, dabbed** 1 apply with momentary pressure ▷ n 2 small mass

dabble v 1 splash about 2 be amateur (in)

dachshund n short-legged long-bodied dog

dad, daddy n (Inf) father **daddy-longlegs** n (Inf) fly with long thin legs

daffodil n yellow spring flower

daft ❶ adj foolish, crazy

dagga n (S Afr, Inf) cannabis

dagger n short stabbing weapon

dahlia n garden plant of various colours

daily ❶ adj/adv 1 (done) every day ▷ n 2 daily newspaper 3 charwoman

dainty adj **-tier, -tiest** 1 delicate 2 choice 3 fastidious ▷ n 4 delicacy **daintiness** n

dairy n, pl **dairies** place for processing milk and its products

dais n raised platform

daisy n, pl **-sies** flower with yellow centre and white petals

dale n valley

dally v **-lying, -lied** 1 trifle 2 loiter

Dalmatian n white dog with black spots

dam ❶ n/v (barrier to) hold back flow of waters

damage ❶ n 1 injury, harm ▷ pl 2 compensation for injury ▷ v 3 harm

damask n 1 patterned woven material 2 velvety red

dame ❶ n (Obs) 1 lady 2 (with cap.) title of lady in Order of the British Empire 3 (Sl) woman

damn ❶ v 1 condemn 2 curse ▷ interj 3 expression of annoyance etc. **damnable** adj **damnation** n

---

dab v = **pat**, touch, tap; = **apply**, daub, stipple ▷ n = **spot**, bit, drop, pat, smudge; = **touch**, stroke, flick

daft adj (Inf, chiefly Brit) = **stupid**, crazy, silly, absurd, foolish

daily adv = **every day**, day by day, once a day ▷ adj = **everyday**, diurnal, quotidian

dam n = **barrier**, wall, barrage, obstruction, embankment ▷ v = **block up**, restrict, hold back,

barricade, obstruct

damage v = **spoil**, hurt, injure, harm, ruin ≠ **fix** ▷ n = **destruction**, harm, loss, injury, suffering ≠ **improvement**; (Inf) = **cost**, price, charge, bill, amount

dame n = **lady**, baroness, dowager, grande dame (Fr), noblewoman

damn v = **criticize**, condemn, blast, denounce, put down ≠ **praise**

DICTIONARY

damp ❶ adj 1 moist ▷ n
2 moisture ▷ v 3 make damp
4 deaden **dampen** v damp
damper n 1 anything that
discourages 2 plate in flue

damson n small dark-purple plum

dance ❶ v 1 move with rhythmic
steps, to music 2 bob up and down
3 perform (dance) ▷ n
4 rhythmical movement 5 social
gathering **dancer** n

dandelion n yellow-flowered wild
plant

dandruff n dead skin in small
scales among the hair

dandy n, pl **-dies 1** man
excessively concerned with
smartness of dress ▷ adj 2 (Inf)
excellent

danger ❶ n 1 exposure to harm
2 peril **dangerous** adj
dangerously adv

dangle ❶ v hang loosely

dank adj damp and chilly

dapper adj neat, spruce

dappled adj marked with spots

dare ❶ v 1 have courage (to)
2 challenge ▷ n 3 challenge
daring adj/n **daredevil** adj/n
reckless (person)

dark ❶ adj 1 without light
2 gloomy 3 deep in tint
4 unenlightened ▷ n 5 absence of
light **darken** v **darkly** adv
darkness n **dark horse** person,
thing about whom little is known

darling ❶ adj/n beloved (person)

darn v mend (hole) by sewing

dart ❶ n 1 small pointed missile
2 darting motion 3 small seam
▷ pl 4 indoor game played with
numbered target ▷ v 5 throw, go
rapidly

dash ❶ v 1 move hastily 2 throw,
strike violently 3 frustrate ▷ n
4 rush 5 small amount

THESAURUS

damp adj = **moist**, wet, soggy,
humid, dank ≠ **dry** ▷ n
= **moisture**, liquid, drizzle,
dampness, wetness ≠ **dryness** ▷ v
= **moisten**, wet, soak, dampen,
moisturize

dance v = **prance**, trip, hop, skip,
sway; = **caper**, trip, spring, jump,
bound ▷ n = **ball**, social, hop (Inf),
disco, knees-up (Brit Inf)

danger n = **jeopardy**, vulnerability

dangle v = **hang**, swing, trail,
sway, flap

dare v = **risk doing**, venture,
presume, make bold, hazard doing;
= **challenge**, provoke, defy, taunt,
goad

dark adj = **dim**, murky, shady,
shadowy, grey; = **black**, brunette,
ebony, dark-skinned, sable ≠ **fair**;
= **evil**, foul, sinister, vile, wicked;
= **secret**, hidden, mysterious,
concealed; = **gloomy**, sad, grim,
miserable, bleak ≠ **cheerful** ▷ n
= **darkness**, shadows, gloom, dusk,
obscurity; = **night**, twilight,
evening, dusk, night-time

darling n = **beloved**, love, dear,
dearest, angel ▷ adj = **beloved**,
dear, treasured, precious, adored

dart v = **dash**, run, race, shoot, fly

dash v = **rush**, run, race, shoot, fly
≠ **dawdle**; = **throw**, cast, pitch,
slam, toss; = **crash**, break, smash,

6 smartness **7** punctuation mark (–) showing change of subject
dashing adj lively, stylish
dashboard n instrument panel
dastardly adj mean
data ❶ pl n **1** (oft. with sing v) series of facts **2** information **database** n store of information
date¹ ❶ n **1** day of the month **2** time of occurrence **3** appointment ▷ v **4** mark with date **5** reveal age of **6** exist (from) **7** become old-fashioned **dated** adj
date² n fruit of palm
daub v paint roughly
daughter n one's female child **daughter-in-law** n, pl **daughters-in-law** wife of one's child
dawdle v idle, loiter
dawn ❶ n **1** daybreak **2** beginning ▷ v **3** begin to grow light **4** (begin to) be understood
day ❶ n **1** period of 24 hours **2** time when sun is above horizon

3 time period **daybreak** n dawn
daydream n **1** idle fancy ▷ v **2** have such fancies **daydreamer** n **daylight** n **1** natural light **2** dawn
daze ❶ v **1** stun, bewilder ▷ n **2** bewildered state **dazed** adj
dazzle ❶ v **1** blind, confuse with brightness **2** impress greatly **dazzling** adj
DC direct current
de- comb. form removal of, from, reversal of, as in delouse, desegregate
deacon n one who assists in a church
dead ❶ adj **1** no longer alive **2** obsolete **3** numb **4** lacking vigour **5** complete ▷ n **6** dead person(s) ▷ adv **7** utterly **deaden** v **deadly** adj **1** fatal **2** deathlike ▷ adv **3** as if dead **4** extremely **deadline** n limit of time allowed **deadlock** n standstill **deadpan** adj expressionless

━━━━━━━ THESAURUS ━━━━━━━

shatter, splinter ▷ n = **rush**, run, race, sprint, dart; = **drop**, little, bit, shot (Inf), touch ≠ **lot**; = **style**, spirit, flair, flourish, verve
data n = **information**, facts, figures, details, intelligence
date n = **time**, stage, period; = **appointment**, meeting, arrangement, commitment, engagement ▷ v = **put a date on**, assign a date to, fix the period of; = **become dated**, become old-fashioned
dawn n = **daybreak**, morning, sunrise, daylight, aurora (Poet); (Lit)

= **beginning**, start, birth, rise, origin ▷ v = **begin**, start, rise, develop, emerge; = **grow light**, break, brighten, lighten
day n = **daytime**, daylight
daze v = **stun**, shock, paralyse, numb, stupefy ▷ n = **shock**, confusion, distraction, trance, bewilderment
dazzle v = **impress**, amaze, overwhelm, astonish, overpower; = **blind**, confuse, daze, bedazzle
dead adj = **deceased**, departed, late, perished, extinct ≠ **alive**; = **boring**, dull, dreary, flat, plain;

deaf ❶ adj **1** without hearing
2 unwilling to listen **deafen** v
make deaf **deafness** n

deal¹ ❶ v **1** distribute **2** act
3 treat **4** do business (with, in) ▷ n
5 agreement **6** treatment **7** share
dealer n

deal² n (plank of) pine wood

dean n **1** university official **2** head
of cathedral chapter

dear ❶ adj **1** beloved **2** precious
3 expensive ▷ n **4** beloved one
dearly adv

dearth n scarcity

death ❶ n **1** dying **2** end of life
3 end **deathly** adj/adv

debacle, débâcle ❶ n utter
collapse, rout, disaster

debase v lower in value

debate ❶ v **1** argue, esp. formally
▷ n **2** formal discussion
debatable adj **debater** n

debilitate v weaken

debit (Finance) ▷ n **1** entry in
account of sum owed ▷ v **2** enter
as due

debonair adj suave, genial

debrief v report result of mission

debris ❶ n rubbish

debt ❶ n **1** what is owed **2** state
of owing **debtor** n

debunk v expose falseness of, esp.
by ridicule

debut ❶ n first appearance in
public **debutante** n girl making
society debut

—————— THESAURUS ——————

= **not working**, useless, inactive,
inoperative ≠ **working**; = **numb**,
frozen, paralysed, insensitive, inert;
= **total**, complete, absolute, utter,
outright; (Inf) = **exhausted**, tired,
worn out, spent, done in (Inf) ▷ n
= **middle**, heart, depth, midst
▷ adv (Inf) = **exactly**, completely,
totally, directly, fully

deaf adj = **hard of hearing**,
without hearing, stone deaf;
= **oblivious**, indifferent,
unmoved, unconcerned,
unsympathetic

deal¹ n (Inf) = **agreement**,
understanding, contract,
arrangement, bargain;
= **amount**, quantity, measure,
degree, mass

dear adj = **beloved**, close, valued,
favourite, prized ≠ **hated**; (Brit Inf)
= **expensive**, costly, high-priced,

pricey (Inf), at a premium ≠ **cheap**
▷ n = **darling**, love, dearest, angel,
treasure

death n = **dying**, demise, end,
passing, departure ≠ **birth**;
= **destruction**, finish, ruin,
undoing, extinction
≠ **beginning**

debacle, débâcle n = **disaster**,
catastrophe, fiasco

debate n = **discussion**, talk,
argument, dispute, analysis ▷ v
= **discuss**, question, talk about,
argue about, dispute; = **consider**,
reflect, think about, weigh,
contemplate

debris n = **remains**, bits, waste,
ruins, fragments

debt n = **debit**, commitment,
obligation, liability

debut n = **entrance**, beginning,
launch, coming out, introduction

Dec. December

decade n period of ten years

decaffeinated adj (of tea, coffee) with caffeine removed

decant v pour off (wine) **decanter** n stoppered bottle

decapitate v behead

decathlon n athletic contest with ten events

decay ❶ v 1 rot 2 decline ▷ n 3 rotting

decease n 1 death ▷ v 2 die **deceased** adj/n dead (person)

deceive ❶ v mislead, delude **deceit** n 1 fraud 2 duplicity **deceitful** adj

decelerate v slow down

December n twelfth month

decent ❶ adj 1 respectable 2 fitting 3 adequate 4 (Inf) kind **decency** n

deception ❶ n 1 deceiving 2 trick **deceptive** adj misleading

decibel n unit for measuring intensity of sound

decide ❶ v 1 (cause to) reach a

decision 2 settle (a contest or question) **decision** n judgment, conclusion or resolution

deciduous adj (of trees) losing leaves annually

decimal adj 1 relating to tenths ▷ n 2 decimal fraction

decimalization n **decimal point** dot between unit and fraction

decimate v destroy or kill a tenth of, large contingent

decipher v 1 make out meaning of 2 decode

deck n 1 floor, esp. one covering ship's hull 2 turntable of record player ▷ v 3 decorate **deck chair** folding canvas chair

declaim v speak rhetorically

declare ❶ v 1 announce formally 2 state emphatically **declaration** n

decline ❶ v 1 refuse 2 slope downwards 3 deteriorate 4 diminish ▷ n 5 deterioration 6 diminution 7 downward slope

decode v convert from code into

─────────── THESAURUS ───────────

decay v = **rot**, spoil, crumble, deteriorate, perish; = **decline**, diminish, crumble, deteriorate, fall off ≠ **grow** ▷ n = **rot**, corruption, mould, blight, decomposition; = **decline**, collapse, deterioration, failing, fading ≠ **growth**

deceive v = **take in**, trick, fool (Inf), cheat, con (Inf)

decent adj = **satisfactory**, fair, all right, reasonable, sufficient ≠ **unsatisfactory**; = **proper**, becoming, seemly, fitting, appropriate ≠ **improper** (Inf);

= **respectable**, pure, proper, modest, chaste

deception n = **trickery**, fraud, deceit, cunning, treachery ≠ **honesty**; = **trick**, lie, bluff, hoax, decoy

decide v = **resolve**, answer, determine, conclude, clear up; = **settle**, determine, resolve

declare v = **state**, claim, announce, voice, express

decline v = **deteriorate**, weaken, pine, decay, worsen ≠ **improve**; = **refuse**, reject, turn down, avoid,

ordinary language **decoder** n
decompose v rot
decongestant adj/n (drug)
relieving (esp. nasal) congestion
decontaminate v render
harmless
decor n decorative scheme
decorate ❶ v 1 beautify 2 paint
room etc. 3 invest (with medal
etc.) **decoration** n **decorative**
adj **decorator** n
decorum n propriety, decency
decorous adj
decoy n 1 bait, lure ▷ v 2 lure, be
lured as with decoy
decrease ❶ v 1 diminish, lessen
▷ n 2 diminishing
decree ❶ n/v (give) order having
the force of law
decrepit adj 1 old 2 worn out
decry v -crying, -cried disparage
dedicate ❶ v 1 commit wholly to

special purpose 2 inscribe or
address 3 devote **dedicated** adj
dedication n
deduce v draw as conclusion
deduct ❶ v subtract **deductible**
adj **deduction** n 1 deducting
2 amount subtracted 3 conclusion
deed ❶ n 1 action 2 exploit
3 legal document
deem v judge, consider, regard
deep ❶ adj 1 extending far down
2 at, given depth 3 profound
4 hard to fathom 5 (of colour) dark
6 (of sound) low ▷ n 7 deep place
8 the sea ▷ adv 9 far down etc.
deeply adv **deepen** v
deer n, pl **deer** ruminant animal
typically with antlers in male
deface v spoil or mar surface
defame v speak ill of **defamation**
n **defamatory** adj
default ❶ n 1 failure to act,

d

---

spurn ≠ **accept** ▷ n = **depression**,
recession, slump, falling off,
downturn ≠ **rise**
decorate v = **adorn**, trim,
embroider, ornament, embellish;
= **do up**, paper, paint, wallpaper,
renovate; = **pin a medal on**, cite,
confer an honour on or upon
decrease v = **drop**, decline, lessen,
lower, shrink ▷ n = **lessening**,
decline, reduction, loss, falling off
≠ **growth**
decree n = **law**, order, ruling, act,
command ▷ v = **order**, rule,
command, demand, proclaim
dedicate v = **devote**, give, apply,
commit, pledge; = **offer**, address,
inscribe

deduct v = **subtract**, remove,
take off, take away, reduce by
≠ **add**
deed n = **action**, act, performance,
achievement, exploit; (Law)
= **document**, title, contract
deep adj = **big**, wide, broad,
profound, yawning ≠ **shallow**;
= **intense**, great, serious (Inf),
acute, extreme ≠ **superficial**;
= **sound**, profound, unbroken,
undisturbed, untroubled;
= **dark**, strong, rich, intense,
vivid ≠ **light**; = **low**, booming,
bass, resonant, sonorous
≠ **high** ▷ n = **middle**, heart,
midst, dead
default v = **fail to pay**, dodge,

appear or pay ▷ v **2** fail (to pay)
defeat ❶ v **1** vanquish **2** thwart
▷ v **3** overthrow
defecate v empty the bowels
defect ❶ n **1** lack, blemish ▷ v
2 desert **defection** n **defective**
adj **defector** n
defend ❶ v **1** protect, ward off
attack **2** support by argument
defence n **1** protection
2 justification **3** statement by
accused person in court
defenceless adj **defendant** n
person accused in court **defender**
n **defensible** adj **defensive** adj
1 serving for defence ▷ n
2 attitude of defence
defer[1] ❶ v postpone
defer[2] v **-ferring, -ferred** submit
to opinion or judgement of another
deference n **1** obedience
2 respect **deferential** adj
deficient adj lacking in
something **deficiency** n **deficit**
n amount by which sum of money
is too small
defile ❶ v **1** soil **2** sully
define ❶ v **1** state meaning of

2 mark out **definite** adj **1** exact
2 clear **3** certain **definitely** adv
definition n **definitive** adj
conclusive
deflate v (cause to) collapse by
release of gas from **deflation** n
(Economics) reduction of economic
and industrial activity
deflect ❶ v (cause to) turn from
straight course **deflection** n
deform v **1** spoil shape of
2 disfigure **deformity** n
defraud v cheat, swindle
defrost v **1** make, become free of
frost, ice **2** thaw
deft adj skilful, adroit
defunct adj dead, obsolete
defuse v **1** remove fuse of bomb
etc. **2** remove tension
defy ❶ v **-fying, -fied** challenge,
resist successfully **defiance** n
resistance **defiant** adj openly and
aggressively hostile
degenerate ❶ v **1** deteriorate to
lower level ▷ adj **2** fallen away in
quality ▷ n **3** degenerate person
degeneration n **degenerative**
adj

— THESAURUS —

evade, neglect ▷ n = **failure**,
neglect, deficiency, lapse, omission
defeat v = **beat**, crush, overwhelm,
conquer, master ≠ **surrender**;
= **frustrate**, foil, thwart, ruin,
baffle ▷ n = **conquest**, beating,
overthrow, rout ≠ **victory**
defect n failing ▷ v = **desert**,
rebel, quit, revolt, change sides
defend v = **protect**, cover, guard,
screen, preserve; = **support**,
champion, justify, endorse, uphold

defer[1] v = **postpone**, delay, put off,
suspend, shelve
define v = **mark out**, outline, limit,
bound, delineate; = **describe**,
interpret, characterize, explain,
spell out
deflect v = **turn aside**, bend
defy v = **resist**, oppose, confront,
brave, disregard
degenerate v = **decline**, slip, sink,
decrease, deteriorate ▷ adj
= **depraved**, corrupt, low,

degrade ⊙ v 1 dishonour
2 debase 3 reduce 4 decompose
chemically **degradable** adj
degradation n

degree n 1 step, stage in process
2 university rank 3 unit of
measurement

dehydrate v remove moisture
from

deify v **-fying, -fied** make a god of
deity n god

deign v condescend

déjà vu (Fr) feeling of having
experienced something before

dejected adj miserable
dejection n

delay ⊙ v 1 postpone 2 linger ▷ n
3 delaying

delectable adj delightful

delegate ⊙ n 1 representative
▷ v 2 send as deputy 3 entrust
delegation n

delete ⊙ v remove, erase
deletion n

deliberate ⊙ adj 1 intentional
2 well-considered 3 slow ▷ v
4 consider **deliberately** adv
deliberation n

delicate ⊙ adj 1 exquisite
2 fragile 3 requiring tact **delicacy**
n 1 elegance 2 delicious food

delicatessen n shop selling esp.
imported or unusual foods

delicious ⊙ adj delightful,
pleasing to taste

delight ⊙ v 1 please greatly
2 take great pleasure (in) ▷ n
3 great pleasure **delightful** adj
charming

delinquent n/adj (one) guilty of
delinquency **delinquency** n
(minor) offence or misdeed

delirium n 1 disorder of mind, esp.
in feverish illness 2 violent

—————— THESAURUS ——————

perverted, immoral

degrade v = **demean**, disgrace,
humiliate, shame, humble
≠ **ennoble**; = **demote**, lower,
downgrade ≠ **promote**

delay v = **put off**, suspend,
postpone, shelve, defer; = **hold up**,
detain, hold back, hinder, obstruct
≠ **speed (up)** ▷ n = **hold-up**, wait,
setback, interruption, stoppage

delegate n = **representative**,
agent, deputy, ambassador,
commissioner ▷ v = **entrust**,
transfer, hand over, give, pass on;
= **appoint**, commission, select,
contract, engage

delete v = **remove**, cancel, erase,
strike out, obliterate

deliberate adj = **intentional**,
meant, planned, intended,
conscious ≠ **accidental**; = **careful**,
measured, slow, cautious,
thoughtful ≠ **hurried** ▷ v
= **consider**, think, ponder, discuss,
debate

delicate adj = **fine**, elegant,
exquisite, graceful; = **subtle**, fine,
delicious, faint, refined ≠ **bright**;
= **fragile**, weak, frail, brittle,
tender; = **skilled**, precise, deft,
Victorian, proper (Inf, Inf)

delicious adj = **delectable**, tasty,
choice, savoury, dainty
≠ **unpleasant**

delight n = **pleasure**, joy,
satisfaction, happiness, ecstasy

excitement **delirious** adj

deliver ❶ v 1 carry to destination
2 hand over 3 release 4 give birth
or assist in birth (of) 5 utter

deliverance n rescue **delivery** n,
pl **-eries**

dell n wooded hollow

delta n alluvial tract at river mouth

delude v 1 deceive 2 mislead
delusion n

deluge n 1 flood, downpour ▷ v
2 flood, overwhelm

de luxe 1 rich, sumptuous
2 superior in quality

delve v 1 search intensively 2 dig

demagogue n mob leader or
agitator

demand ❶ v 1 ask as giving an
order 2 call for as due, necessary
▷ n 3 urgent request 4 call for
demanding adj requiring effort

demean v degrade, lower

demeanour n conduct, bearing

demented adj mad, crazy

dementia n mental deterioration

demerit n undesirable quality

demi- comb. form half, as in
demigod

demijohn n large bottle

demilitarize v prohibit military
presence

demise ❶ n 1 death
2 conveyance by will or lease

demobilize v 1 disband (troops)
2 discharge (soldier)

democracy ❶ n, pl **-cies**
1 government by the people or their
elected representatives 2 state so
governed **democrat** n advocate
of democracy **democratic** adj

demolish ❶ v 1 knock to pieces
2 destroy utterly **demolition** n

demon ❶ n devil, evil spirit

demonstrate ❶ v 1 show by
reasoning, prove 2 describe,
explain 3 make exhibition of
support, protest etc.
demonstrable adj

THESAURUS

≠ **displeasure** ▷ v = **please**,
satisfy, thrill, charm, cheer
≠ **displease**

deliver v = **bring**, carry, bear,
transport, distribute; (sometimes
with **up**) = **hand over**, commit, give
up, yield, surrender; = **give**, read,
present, announce, declare;
= **strike**, give, deal, launch, direct;
(Dated) = **release**, free, save,
rescue, loose

demand v = **request**, ask (for),
order, expect, claim; = **challenge**,
ask, question, inquire; = **require**,
want, need, involve, call for
≠ **provide** ▷ n = **request**, order;

= **need**, want, call, market, claim

demise n = **failure**, end, fall,
defeat, collapse; (Euphemistic)
= **death**, end, dying, passing,
departure

democracy n = **self-
government**, republic,
commonwealth

demolish v = **knock down**, level,
destroy, dismantle, flatten ≠ **build**

demon n = **evil spirit**, devil, fiend,
goblin, ghoul; = **wizard**, master,
ace (Inf), fiend, beast

demonstrate v = **prove**, show,
indicate, make clear, manifest;
= **show**, express, display, indicate,

DICTIONARY

demonstration n

demonstrative adj 1 expressing feelings 2 pointing out 3 conclusive **demonstrator** n 1 one who takes part in a public demonstration 2 assistant in laboratory etc.

demoralize v 1 deprive of courage 2 undermine morally

demote v reduce in rank **demotion** n

demur v -murring, -murred 1 make difficulties, object ▷ n 2 demurring

demure adj reserved

den ❶ n 1 hole of wild beast 2 small room, esp. study

denigrate v belittle

denim n strong cotton fabric

denizen n inhabitant

denote v 1 stand for 2 show

denouement n unravelling of plot

denounce ❷ v 1 speak violently

against 2 accuse **denunciation** n

dense ❶ adj 1 thick, compact 2 stupid **density** n, pl -ties

dent ❶ n/v (make) hollow or mark by blow or pressure

dental adj of teeth or dentistry **dentist** n surgeon who attends to teeth **dentistry** n art of dentist **denture** n set of false teeth

denude v strip, make bare

deny ❶ v -nying, -nied 1 declare untrue 2 contradict 3 reject 4 refuse to give **denial** n

depart ❶ v 1 go away 2 start out 3 vary 4 die **departure** n

department n 1 division 2 branch **departmental** adj

depend ❶ v 1 (usu. with on) rely entirely 2 live 3 be contingent **dependable** adj reliable **dependant** n one who relies on another **dependent** adj depending on **dependence, dependency** n

THESAURUS

exhibit; = **march**, protest, rally, object, parade

den n = **lair**, hole, shelter, cave, haunt; = **study**, retreat, sanctuary, hideaway, sanctum

denounce v = **condemn**, attack, censure, revile, vilify

dense adj = **thick**, heavy, solid, compact, condensed ≠ **thin**; = **heavy**, thick, opaque, impenetrable; = **stupid** (Inf), thick, dull, dumb (Inf), dozy (Brit Inf) ≠ **bright**

dent v = **make a dent in**, press in, gouge, hollow, push in ▷ n = **hollow**, chip, indentation,

depression, impression

deny v = **contradict**, disagree with, rebuff, negate, rebut ≠ **admit**; = **renounce**, reject, retract, repudiate, disown; = **refuse**, forbid, reject, rule out, turn down ≠ **permit**

depart v = **leave**, go, withdraw, retire, disappear ≠ **arrive**; = **deviate**, vary, differ, stray, veer

department n = **section**, office, unit, station, division

depend v = **be determined by**, be based on, be subject to, hang on, rest on; = **count on**, turn to, trust in, bank on, lean on

depict ⓥ v 1 give picture of 2 describe **depiction** n

deplete ⓥ v 1 empty 2 reduce **depletion** n

deplore ⓥ v 1 lament, regret 2 denounce **deplorable** adj

deploy ⓥ v organize (troops) in battle formation **deployment** n

depopulate v (cause to) be reduced in population **depopulation** n

deport ⓥ v expel, banish **deportation** n

deportment n behaviour

depose ⓥ v 1 remove from office 2 make statement on oath

deposit ⓥ v 1 set down 2 give into safe keeping 3 let fall ▷ n 4 thing deposited 5 money given in part payment 6 sediment **deposition** n 1 statement written and attested 2 act of deposing or depositing **depositor** n **depository** n

depot ⓥ n storehouse

deprecate v express disapproval of

depreciate v 1 (cause to) fall in value, price 2 belittle **depreciation** n

depress ⓥ v 1 affect with low spirits 2 lower **depression** n 1 hollow 2 low spirits 3 low state of trade

deprive v dispossess **deprivation** n **deprived** adj lacking adequate food, care, amenities etc.

depth ⓝ n 1 (degree of) deepness 2 deep place 3 intensity

deregulate v remove regulations or controls from

derelict ⓥ adj 1 abandoned 2 falling into ruins **dereliction** n 1 neglect of duty 2 abandonment

deride v treat with contempt, ridicule **derision** n **derisive** adj **derisory** adj

derive v get, come from **derivation** n **derivative** adj

— THESAURUS —

depict v = illustrate, portray, picture, paint, outline; = describe, present, represent, outline, characterize

deplete v = use up, reduce, drain, exhaust, consume ≠ increase

deplore v = disapprove of, condemn, object to, denounce, censure

deploy v = use, station, position, arrange, set out

deport v = expel, exile, throw out, oust, banish

depose v = oust, dismiss, displace, demote, dethrone

deposit n = down payment,

security, stake, pledge, instalment; = accumulation, mass, build-up, layer ▷ v = put, place, lay, drop; = store, keep, put, bank, lodge

depot n = storehouse, depository, warehouse

depress v = sadden, upset, distress, discourage, grieve ≠ cheer; = lower, cut, reduce, diminish, decrease ≠ raise; = devalue, depreciate, cheapen

depth n = deepness, drop, measure, extent; = insight, wisdom, penetration, profundity, discernment ≠ superficiality

derelict adj = abandoned,

dermatitis n inflammation of skin

derogatory adj belittling

derv n diesel oil for road vehicles

descant n (Mus) decorative variation to basic melody

descend ① ① v 1 come or go down 2 spring from 3 be transmitted 4 attack **descendant** n person descended from an ancestor **descent** n

describe ① v give detailed account of **description** n **descriptive** adj

desecrate v 1 violate sanctity of 2 profane

desert¹ ① n uninhabited and barren region

desert² ① v 1 abandon, leave 2 run away from service **deserter** n **desertion** n

desert³ n (usu. pl) what is due as reward or punishment

deserve ① v show oneself worthy of

design ① v 1 sketch 2 plan 3 intend ▷ n 4 sketch 5 plan 6 decorative pattern 7 project **designer** n/adj

designate ① v 1 name, appoint ▷ adj 2 appointed but not yet installed

desire ① v 1 wish, long for 2 ask for ▷ n 3 longing 4 expressed wish 5 sexual appetite **desirable** n 1 worth having 2 attractive **desirability** n **desirous** adj

desist v cease, stop

desk n writing table

desolate adj 1 uninhabited 2 neglected 3 solitary 4 forlorn ▷ v 5 lay waste 6 overwhelm with grief **desolation** n

despair ① v 1 lose hope ▷ n 2 loss of all hope 3 cause of this

---

THESAURUS

deserted, ruined, neglected, discarded

descend v = **fall**, drop, sink, go down, plunge ≠ **rise**; = **go down**, come down, walk down, move down, climb down; = **slope**, dip, incline, slant

describe v = **relate**, tell, report, explain, express; = **portray**, depict

desert¹ n = **wilderness**, waste, wilds, wasteland, dry

desert² v = **abandon**, leave, quit, forsake

deserve v = **merit**, warrant, be entitled to, have a right to, rate

design v = **plan**, draw, draft, trace, outline; = **create**, plan, fashion,

propose, invent; = **intend**, mean, plan, aim, purpose ▷ n = **pattern**, form, style, shape, organization; = **plan**, drawing, model, scheme, draft; = **intention**, end, aim, goal, target

designate v = **name**, call, term, style, label; = **choose**, reserve, select, label, flag

desire n = **wish**, want, longing, hope, urge; = **lust**, passion, libido, appetite, lasciviousness ▷ v = **want**, long for, crave, hope for, ache for

despair n = **despondency**, depression, misery, gloom, desperation ▷ v = **lose hope**, give

desperate ❶ adj 1 reckless from despair 2 hopelessly bad **desperately** adv **desperation** n **desperado** n reckless, lawless person

despise ❷ v look down on as inferior **despicable** adj base, contemptible, vile

despite ❸ prep in spite of

despoil v plunder, rob

despondent adj dejected, depressed

despot n tyrant, oppressor **despotic** adj **despotism** n

dessert n sweet course, or fruit, served at end of meal

destination ❹ n place one is bound for

destitute adj in absolute want

destroy ❺ v 1 ruin 2 put an end to 3 demolish **destroyer** n small, swift warship **destructible** adj **destruction** n ruin **destructive** adj

desultory adj 1 aimless 2 unmethodical

detach ❻ v unfasten, separate **detachable** adj **detached** adj 1 standing apart 2 disinterested **detachment** n 1 aloofness 2 detaching 3 body of troops on special duty

detail ❼ n 1 particular 2 small or unimportant part 3 treatment of anything item by item 4 soldier assigned for duty ▷ v 5 relate in full 6 appoint

detain ❽ v 1 keep under restraint 2 keep waiting **detention** n

detect ❾ v find out or discover **detection** n **detective** n policeman detecting crime **detector** n

deter ❿ v -terring, -terred 1 discourage 2 prevent **deterrent** adj/n

detergent n/adj cleaning (substance)

— THESAURUS —

up, lose heart

desperate adj = **grave**, pressing, serious, severe, extreme; = **last-ditch**, daring, furious, risky, frantic

despise v = **look down on**, loathe, scorn, detest, revile ≠ **admire**

despite prep = **in spite of**, in the face of, regardless of, even with, notwithstanding

destination n = **stop**, station, haven, resting-place, terminus

destroy v = **ruin**, crush, devastate, wreck, shatter

detach v = **separate**, remove, divide, cut off, sever ≠ **attach**

detail n = **point**, fact, feature, particular, respect; = **fine point**, particular, nicety, triviality; (Mil) = **party**, force, body, duty, squad ▷ v = **list**, relate, catalogue, recount, rehearse; = **appoint**, name, choose, commission, select

detain v = **hold**, arrest, confine, restrain, imprison; = **delay**, hold up, hamper, hinder, retard

detect v = **discover**, find, uncover, track down, unmask; = **notice**, see, spot, note, identify

deter v = **discourage**, inhibit, put off, frighten, intimidate

deteriorate ❶ v become or make worse **deterioration** n

determine ❶ v 1 decide 2 fix 3 be deciding factor in 4 come to an end 5 come to a decision **determination** n 1 determining 2 resolute conduct 3 resolve **determined** adj resolute

detest v hate, loathe **detestable** adj

dethrone v remove from position of authority

detonate v (cause to) explode **detonation** n **detonator** n

detour n roundabout way

detract v take away (a part) from, diminish **detractor** n

detriment n harm done, loss, damage **detrimental** adj

deuce n 1 card with two spots 2 (Tennis) forty all 3 in exclamatory phrases, the devil

devalue v **-valuing, -valued** reduce in value **devaluation** n

devastate ❶ v 1 lay waste 2 ravage **devastated** adj

extremely shocked **devastation** n

develop ❶ v 1 bring to maturity 2 elaborate 3 evolve 4 treat photographic film to bring out image 5 improve or change use of (land) 6 grow to maturer state **developer** n **development** n

deviate v diverge **deviant** n/adj (person) deviating from normal, esp. in sexual practices **deviation** n **devious** adj 1 deceitful 2 roundabout **deviousness** n

device ❶ n 1 contrivance 2 scheme

devil ❶ n 1 personified spirit of evil 2 person of great wickedness, cruelty etc. 3 (Inf) fellow 4 (Inf) something difficult or annoying **devilish** adj **devilment** n **devilry** n **devil-may-care** adj happy-go-lucky

devise ❶ v plan

devoid ❶ adj (usu. with of) empty

devolve v (cause to) pass on to another **devolution** n **devolving**

devote ❶ v give up exclusively (to

—— THESAURUS ——

deteriorate v = **decline**, worsen, degenerate, slump, go downhill (Inf) ≠ **improve**

determine v = **settle**, learn, establish, discover, find out; = **decide on**, choose, elect, resolve; = **decide**, conclude, resolve, make up your mind

devastate v = **destroy**, ruin, sack, wreck, demolish

develop v = **grow**, advance, progress, mature, evolve; = **establish**, set up, promote, generate, undertake

device n = **gadget**, machine, tool, instrument, implement; = **ploy**, scheme, plan, trick, manoeuvre

devil n = **evil spirit**, demon, fiend; = **brute**, monster, beast, barbarian, fiend; = **person**, individual, soul, creature, thing; = **scamp**, rogue, rascal, scoundrel, scallywag (Inf)

devise v = **work out**, design, construct, invent, conceive

devoid adj (with of) = **lacking in**, without, free from, wanting in, bereft of

devote v = **dedicate**, give,

person, purpose etc.) **devoted** adj
loving **devotee** n ardent
enthusiast **devotion** n **1** deep
affection **2** dedication ▷ pl
3 prayers

devour ❶ v eat greedily

devout ❶ adj deeply religious

dew n moisture from air deposited
as small drops at night

dexterity n manual skill
dexterous adj

diabetes n various disorders
characterized by excretion of
abnormal amount of urine
diabetic n/adj

diabolic adj devilish **diabolical**
adj (Inf) extremely bad

diadem n crown

diagnosis ❶ n, pl -ses
identification of disease from
symptoms **diagnose** v

diagonal adj/n (line) from corner
to corner

diagram ❶ n drawing, figure, to
illustrate something

dial n **1** face of clock etc. **2** plate
marked with graduations on which
pointer moves **3** numbered disc in
front of telephone ▷ v **4** operate
telephone

dialect n characteristic speech of
district

dialogue ❶ n conversation

dialysis n (Med) filtering of blood
through membrane to remove
waste products

diameter n (length of) straight
line through centre of circle
diametrically adv completely

diamond n **1** very hard and
brilliant precious stone **2** rhomboid
figure **3** suit at cards

diaper n (US & Canad) n towelling
cloth to absorb baby's excrement

diaphragm n muscle between
abdomen and chest

diarrhoea n excessive looseness
of the bowels

diary ❶ n, pl -ries **1** daily record of
events **2** book for this

diatribe n violently bitter verbal
attack, denunciation

dice n, pl **dice 1** cube with six sides
marked one to six for games of
chance ▷ v **2** gamble with dice
3 (Cookery) cut vegetables into small
cubes

dichotomy n, pl -mies division
into two parts

dictate ❶ v **1** say or read for

_____ THESAURUS _____

commit, apply, reserve

devour v = **eat**, consume, swallow,
wolf, gulp

devout adj = **religious**, godly,
pious, pure, holy ≠ **irreverent**

diagnosis n = **identification**,
discovery, recognition, detection

diagram n = **plan**, figure, drawing,
chart, representation

dialogue n = **discussion**,

conference, exchange,
debate; = **conversation**,
discussion, communication,
discourse

diary n = **journal**, chronicle

dictate v = **speak**, say, utter, read
out ▷ n = **command**, order,
decree, demand, direction;
= **principle**, law, rule, standard,
code

another to transcribe **2** prescribe **3** impose ▷ n **4** bidding **dictation** n **dictator** n absolute ruler **dictatorial** adj **dictatorship** n

diction n **1** choice and use of words **2** enunciation

dictionary ❶ n, pl **-aries** book listing, alphabetically, words with meanings etc.

did past tense of DO

die¹ ❶ v **dying, died 1** cease to live **2** end **3** (Inf) look forward (to) **die-hard** n/adj (person) resisting change

die² n shaped block to form metal in forge, press etc.

diesel adj pert. to internal-combustion engine using oil as fuel ▷ n **2** this engine **3** the fuel

diet ❶ n **1** restricted or regulated course of feeding **2** kind of food lived on ▷ v **3** follow a diet, as to lose weight **dietary** adj

differ ❶ v **1** be unlike **2** disagree **difference** n **1** unlikeness **2** point

of unlikeness **3** disagreement **4** remainder left after subtraction **different** adj **differently** adv

differential adj **1** varying with circumstances ▷ n **2** mechanism in car etc. allowing back wheels to revolve at different speeds **3** difference between two rates of pay **differentiate** v serve to distinguish between, make different **2** discriminate

difficult ❶ adj **1** requiring effort, skill etc. **2** not easy **3** obscure **difficulty** n **1** difficult task, problem **2** embarrassment **3** hindrance **4** trouble

diffident adj lacking confidence

diffuse v **1** spread slowly ▷ adj **2** widely spread **3** loose, wordy **diffusion** n

dig ❶ v **digging, dug 1** work with spade **2** turn up with spade **3** excavate **4** thrust into ▷ n **5** piece of digging **6** thrust **7** jibe ▷ pl **8** (Inf) lodgings

dictionary n = **wordbook**, vocabulary, glossary, lexicon

die¹ v = **pass away**, expire, perish, croak (Sl), give up the ghost ≠ **live**; = **stop**, fail, halt, break down, run down; = **dwindle**, decline, sink, fade, diminish ≠ **increase**

diet n = **food**, provisions, fare, rations, nourishment; = **fast**, regime, abstinence, regimen ▷ v = **slim**, fast, lose weight, abstain, eat sparingly ≠ **overindulge**

differ v = **be dissimilar**, contradict, contrast with, vary, belie ≠ **accord**; = **disagree**, clash, dispute, dissent

≠ **agree**

difficult adj = **hard**, tough, taxing, demanding, challenging ≠ **easy**; = **problematical**, involved, complex, complicated, obscure ≠ **simple**; = **troublesome**, demanding, perverse, fussy, fastidious ≠ **cooperative**

dig v = **hollow out**, mine, quarry, excavate, scoop out; = **delve**, tunnel, burrow; = **search**, hunt, root, delve, forage ▷ n = **cutting remark**, crack (Sl), insult, taunt, sneer; = **poke**, thrust, nudge, prod, jab

digest ❶ v 1 prepare (food) in stomach etc. for assimilation 2 bring into handy form by summarizing ▷ n 3 methodical summary **digestible** adj **digestion** n **digestive** adj

digit n 1 finger or toe 2 numeral **digital** adj

dignity ❶ n, pl **-ties** 1 stateliness, gravity 2 worthiness **dignify** v give dignity to **dignitary** n holder of high office

digress v deviate from subject **digression** n

dike n see DYKE

dilapidated adj in ruins

dilate v widen, expand **dilation** n

dilemma ❶ n position offering choice only between unwelcome alternatives

dilettante n, pl **-tantes, -tanti** 1 person who enjoys fine arts as pastime 2 dabbler

diligent adj hard-working

diligently adv **diligence** n

dill n herb with medicinal seeds

dilute ❶ v reduce (liquid) in strength, esp. by adding water **dilution** n

dim ❶ adj **dimmer, dimmest** 1 faint, not bright 2 mentally dull 3 unfavourable ▷ v 4 make, grow dim **dimly** adv

dime n (US) 10-cent piece

dimension ❶ n measurement, size

diminish ❶ v lessen **diminutive** adj very small

diminuendo adj/adv (Mus) (of sound) dying away

dimple n small hollow in surface of skin, esp. of cheek

din ❶ n 1 continuous roar of confused noises ▷ v 2 ram (fact, opinion etc.) into

dine ❶ v eat dinner **diner** n

dinghy n, pl **-ghies** 1 small open boat 2 collapsible rubber boat

— THESAURUS —

digest v = **ingest**, absorb, incorporate, dissolve, assimilate; = **take in**, absorb, grasp, soak up ▷ n = **summary**, résumé, abstract, epitome, synopsis

dignity n = **decorum**, gravity, majesty, grandeur, respectability; = **self-importance**, pride, self-esteem, self-respect

dilemma n = **predicament**, problem, difficulty, spot (Inf), mess

dilute v = **water down**, thin (out), weaken, adulterate, make thinner ≠ **condense**; = **reduce**, weaken, diminish, temper, decrease ≠ **intensify**

dim adj = **poorly lit**, dark, gloomy, murky, shady; = **cloudy**, grey, gloomy, dismal, overcast ≠ **bright**; = **unclear**, obscured, faint, blurred, fuzzy ≠ **distinct** ▷ v = **turn down**, fade, dull; = **grow or become faint**, fade, dull, grow or become dim

dimension n = **aspect**, side, feature, angle, facet

diminish v = **decrease**, decline, lessen, shrink, dwindle ≠ **grow**

din n = **noise**, row, racket, crash, clamour ≠ **silence**

dine v = **eat**, lunch, feast, sup

dingo n, pl **-goes** Aust. wild dog

dingy adj **-gier, -giest** dirty-looking, dull

dinner ❶ n **1** chief meal of the day **2** official banquet

dinosaur n extinct reptile, often of gigantic size

dint n **by dint of** by means of

diocese n district, jurisdiction of bishop

diode n (Electronics) device for converting alternating current to direct current

dip ❶ v **dipping, dipped 1** plunge or be plunged partly or for a moment into liquid **2** take up in ladle, bucket etc. **3** direct headlights of vehicle downwards **4** go down **5** slope downwards ▷ n **6** act of dipping **7** bathe **8** downward slope **9** hollow

diphtheria n infectious disease causing breathing difficulties

diphthong n union of two vowel sounds

diploma n document vouching for person's proficiency

diplomacy ❶ n **1** management of international relations **2** tactful dealing **diplomat** n **diplomatic** adj

dipper n **1** ladle, scoop **2** bird (water ouzel)

dipsomania n uncontrollable craving for alcohol **dipsomaniac** n/adj

dire ❶ adj **1** terrible **2** urgent

direct ❶ v **1** control, manage, order **2** point out the way **3** aim ▷ adj **4** frank **5** straight **6** immediate **7** lineal **direction** n **1** directing **2** aim **3** instruction **directive** adj/n **directly** adv **directness** n **director** n **1** one who directs, esp. a film **2** member of board managing company **directorial** adj **directorship** n **directory** n book of names, addresses, streets etc.

dirge n song of mourning

dirk n short dagger

—————— THESAURUS ——————

dinner n = **meal**, main meal, spread (Inf), repast

dip v = **plunge**, immerse, bathe, duck, douse; = **drop (down)**, fall, lower, sink, descend ▷ n = **plunge**, ducking, soaking, drenching, immersion; = **nod**, drop, lowering, slump, sag; = **hollow**, hole, depression, pit, basin

diplomacy n = **statesmanship**, statecraft, international negotiation; = **tact**, skill, sensitivity, craft, discretion ≠ **tactlessness**

dire adj = **desperate**, pressing, critical, terrible, crucial

direct adj = **quickest**, shortest; = **first-hand**, personal, immediate ≠ **indirect** ▷ v = **aim**, point, level, train, focus; = **guide**, show, lead, point the way, point in the direction of; = **control**, run, manage, lead, guide; = **order**, command, instruct, charge, demand

direction n = **way**, course, line, road, track; = **management**, control, charge, administration,

dirt ① n 1 filth **2** soil **3** obscene material **dirty** adj **1** unclean **2** obscene **3** unfair **4** dishonest

dis- comb. form 1 negation, opposition, deprivation **2** in many verbs indicates undoing of the action of simple verb

disable ① v 1 make unable **2** cripple, maim **disabled** adj **disability** n, pl **-ties**

disabuse v **1** undeceive, disillusion **2** free from error

disadvantage ① n 1 drawback **2** hindrance ▷ v **3** handicap **disadvantaged** adj deprived, discriminated against **disadvantageous** adj

disaffected adj ill-disposed **disaffection** n

disagree ① v -greeing, -greed 1 be at variance **2** conflict **3** (of food etc.) have bad effect on **disagreeable** adj **disagreement** n

disallow v reject as invalid

disappear ① v 1 cease to be visible **2** cease to exist **disappearance** n

disappoint ① v fail to fulfil (hope) **disappointment** n

disarm ① v 1 deprive of weapons **2** win over **disarming** adj removing hostility, suspicion **disarmament** n

disarray ① n 1 throw into disorder ▷ n **2** disorderliness

disaster ① n sudden or great misfortune **disastrous** adj

disband v (cause to) cease to function as a group

disbelieve v reject as false

disburse v pay out money

disc n **1** thin, flat, circular object **2** record **disc jockey** announcer playing records

discard ① v 1 reject **2** cast off

discern v **1** make out **2** distinguish **discernible** adj **discerning** adj discriminating

——————————————————— THESAURUS ———————————————————

leadership

dirt n = **filth**, muck, grime, dust, mud; = **soil**, ground, earth, clay, turf

disable v = **handicap**, cripple, damage, paralyse, impair

disadvantage n = **drawback**, trouble, handicap, nuisance, snag ≠ **advantage**

disagree v = **differ (in opinion)**, argue, clash, dispute, dissent ≠ **agree**; = **make ill**, upset, sicken, trouble, hurt

disappear v = **vanish**, recede, evanesce ≠ **appear**; = **pass**, fade

away, bolt, run away, take off (Inf)

disappoint v = **let down**, dismay, fail, disillusion, dishearten

disarm v = **demilitarize**, disband, demobilize, deactivate; = **win over**, persuade

disarray n = **confusion**, disorder, indiscipline, disunity, disorganization ≠ **order**; = **untidiness**, mess, chaos, muddle, clutter ≠ **tidiness**

disaster n = **catastrophe**, trouble, tragedy, ruin, misfortune

discard v = **get rid of**, drop, throw

DICTIONARY

discharge ❶ v 1 release
2 dismiss 3 emit 4 perform
(duties), fulfil (obligations) 5 fire
off 6 unload 7 pay ▷ n
8 discharging 9 being discharged

disciple n follower of a teacher

discipline ❶ n 1 training that
produces orderliness, obedience,
self-control 2 system of rules etc.
3 punishment ▷ v 4 train
5 punish **disciplinarian** n person
practising strict discipline
disciplinary adj

disclaim v deny, renounce
disclaimer n

disclose ❶ v make known
disclosure n

disco n, pl **-cos** club etc. for
dancing to recorded music

discolour v stain

discomfit v embarrass

discomfort ❶ n inconvenience

disconcert v ruffle, upset

disconnect v 1 break connection
2 stop supply of electricity, gas etc.

disconsolate adj very unhappy

discontent ❶ n lack of
contentment

discontinue v bring to an end

discord n 1 strife 2 disagreement
of sounds **discordant** adj

discount ❶ v 1 reject as
unsuitable 2 deduct from usual
price ▷ n 3 amount deducted from
cost

discourse ❶ n 1 conversation
2 speech ▷ v 3 speak, converse

discourteous adj showing bad

THESAURUS

away or out, reject, abandon
≠ **keep**

discharge v = **release**, free, clear,
liberate, pardon; = **dismiss**, sack
(Inf), fire (Inf), remove, expel;
= **carry out**, perform, fulfil,
accomplish, do; = **pay**, meet, clear,
settle, square (up); = **pour forth**,
release, leak, emit, dispense; = **fire**,
shoot, set off, explode, let off ▷ n
= **release**, liberation, clearance,
pardon, acquittal; = **dismissal**,
notice, removal, the boot (Sl),
expulsion; = **emission**, ooze,
secretion, excretion, pus; = **firing**,
report, shot, blast, burst

discipline n = **control**, authority,
regulation, supervision, orderliness;
= **punishment**, penalty, correction,
chastening, chastisement ▷ v
= **punish**, correct, reprimand,

castigate, chastise; = **train**,
educate

disclose v = **make known**,
reveal, publish, relate, broadcast
≠ **keep secret**; = **show**,
reveal, expose, unveil, uncover
≠ **hide**

discomfort n ≠ **comfort**;
= **uneasiness**, worry, anxiety,
doubt, distress ≠ **reassurance**

discontent n = **dissatisfaction**,
unhappiness, displeasure, regret,
envy

discount n = **deduction**, cut,
reduction, concession, rebate ▷ v
= **mark down**, reduce, lower;
= **disregard**, reject, ignore,
overlook, discard

discourse n = **conversation**, talk,
discussion, speech,
communication; = **speech**, essay,

manners; impolite

discover ❶ v **1** (be the first to) find **2** learn about for first time **discovery** n, pl **-eries**

discredit ❶ v **1** damage reputation of **2** cast doubt on **3** reject as untrue ▷ n **4** disgrace **5** doubt

discreet ❶ adj prudent, circumspect

discrepancy ❶ n, pl **-cies** variation, as between figures

discrete adj separate, distinct

discretion ❶ n **1** quality of being discreet **2** freedom to act as one chooses **discretionary** adj

discriminate ❶ v **1** show prejudice **2** distinguish between **discriminating** adj showing good taste **discrimination** n

discursive adj rambling

discus n disc-shaped object thrown in athletic competition

discuss ❶ v **1** exchange opinions about **2** debate **discussion** n

disdain ❶ n/v scorn **disdainful** adj

disease ❶ n illness

disembark v land from ship etc.

disembodied adj (of spirit) released from bodily form

disembowel v **-elling, -elled** remove the entrails of

disenchanted adj disillusioned **disenchantment** n

disengage v release

disfavour n disapproval

disfigure v mar appearance of

disgrace ❶ n **1** shame, dishonour ▷ v **2** bring shame upon **disgraceful** adj **disgracefully** adv

——————— THESAURUS ———————

lecture, sermon, treatise

discover v = **find out**, learn, notice, realize, recognize; = **find**, come across, uncover, unearth, turn up

discredit v = **disgrace**, shame, smear, humiliate, taint ≠ **honour**; = **dispute**, question, challenge, deny, reject ▷ n = **disgrace**, scandal, shame, disrepute, stigma ≠ **honour**

discreet adj = **tactful**, diplomatic, guarded, careful, cautious ≠ **tactless**

discrepancy n = **disagreement**, difference, variation, conflict, contradiction

discretion n = **tact**, consideration, caution, diplomacy,

prudence ≠ **tactlessness**; = **choice**, will, pleasure, preference, inclination

discriminate v = **differentiate**, distinguish, separate, tell the difference, draw a distinction

discuss v = **talk about**, consider, debate, examine, argue about

disdain n = **contempt**, scorn, arrogance, derision, haughtiness ▷ v = **scorn**, reject, slight, disregard, spurn

disease n = **illness**, condition, complaint, infection, disorder

disgrace n = **shame**, degradation, disrepute, ignominy, dishonour ≠ **honour**; = **scandal**, stain, stigma, blot, blemish ▷ v = **shame**,

disgruntled ① *adj* 1 vexed 2 put out

disguise ① *v* 1 change appearance of, make unrecognizable 2 conceal ▷ *n* 3 device to conceal identity

disgust ① *n/v* (affect with) violent distaste, loathing

dish ① *n* 1 shallow vessel for food 2 portion or variety of food ▷ *v* 3 serve (up)

dishearten *v* weaken hope, enthusiasm etc.

dishevelled *adj* untidy

dishonest *adj* not honest or fair **dishonesty** *n*

dishonour *v* 1 treat with disrespect ▷ *n* 2 lack of respect 3 shame, disgrace **dishonourable** *adj*

disillusion *v* 1 destroy ideals of ▷ *n* 2 disenchantment

disinformation *n* false information intended to mislead

disingenuous *adj* not sincere

disinherit *v* deprive of inheritance

disintegrate ① *v* fall to pieces

disinterested *adj* free from bias or partiality

disk *n* computer storage device

dislike ① *v* 1 consider unpleasant or disagreeable ▷ *n* 2 feeling of not liking

dislocate *v* put out of joint **dislocation** *n*

dislodge *v* drive out from previous position

disloyal *adj* deserting one's allegiance **disloyalty** *n*

dismal ① *adj* depressing

dismantle ① *v* take apart

dismay ① *v* 1 dishearten, daunt ▷ *n* 2 consternation

dismember *v* tear limb from limb

dismiss ① *v* 1 discharge from employment 2 send away 3 reject **dismissal** *n* **dismissive** *adj* scornful

— THESAURUS —

humiliate, discredit, degrade, taint ≠ **honour**

disgruntled *adj* = **discontented**, dissatisfied, annoyed, irritated, put out

disguise *n* = **costume**, mask, camouflage ▷ *v* = **hide**, cover, conceal, screen, mask

disgust *n* = **loathing**, revulsion, hatred, dislike, nausea ≠ **liking** ▷ *v* = **sicken**, offend, revolt, put off, repel ≠ **delight**

dish *n* = **bowl**, plate, platter, salver; = **food**, fare, recipe

disintegrate *v* = **break up**, crumble, fall apart, separate, shatter

dislike *v* = **hate**, object to, loathe, despise, disapprove of ≠ **like**

dismal *adj* = **bad**, awful, dreadful, rotten (*Inf*), terrible

dismantle *v* = **take apart**, strip, demolish, disassemble, take to pieces *or* bits

dismay *n* = **alarm**, fear, horror, anxiety, dread ▷ *v* = **alarm**, frighten, scare, panic, distress

dismiss *v* = **reject**, disregard; = **banish**, dispel, discard, set aside, cast out; = **sack**, fire (*Inf*), remove (*Inf*), axe (*Inf*), discharge

dismount v get off horse, bicycle

disobey v refuse or fail to obey
disobedience n **disobedient** adj

disorder ❶ n 1 confusion
2 ailment **disorderly** adj
1 disorganized 2 unruly

disorientate, disorient v
cause (someone) to lose his
bearings, confuse
disorientation n

disown v refuse to acknowledge

disparage v belittle

dispassionate adj impartial

dispatch, despatch ❶ v 1 send
off promptly 2 finish off ▷ n
3 speed 4 official message

dispel ❶ v -pelling, -pelled drive
away

dispense ❶ v 1 deal out 2 make
up (medicine) 3 administer
(justice) **dispensable** adj

dispensary n, pl **-saries** place
where medicine is made up

dispensation n **dispense with**
1 do away with 2 manage
without

disperse ❶ v scatter **dispersal** n

displace ❶ v 1 move from its
place 2 take place of
displacement n

display ❶ v/n show

displease v 1 offend 2 annoy
displeasure n

dispose ❶ v 1 arrange
2 distribute 3 deal with
disposable adj designed to be
thrown away after use **disposal** n
disposition n 1 temperament
2 arrangement **dispose of** sell,
get rid of

disprove v show to be incorrect

dispute ❶ v 1 debate, discuss

THESAURUS

disorder n = **illness**, disease,
complaint, condition, sickness;
= **untidiness**, mess, confusion,
chaos, muddle; = **disturbance**, riot,
turmoil, unrest, uproar

dispatch, despatch v = **send**,
consign; = **kill**, murder, destroy,
execute, slaughter; = **carry out**,
perform, fulfil, effect, finish ▷ n
= **message**, news, report, story,
account

dispel v = **drive away**, dismiss,
eliminate, expel, disperse

dispense v = **distribute**, assign,
allocate, allot, dole out; = **prepare**,
measure, supply, mix;
= **administer**, operate, carry out,
implement, enforce

disperse v = **scatter**, spread,

distribute, strew, diffuse; = **break
up**, separate, scatter, dissolve,
disband ≠ gather

displace v = **replace**, succeed,
supersede, oust, usurp (Inf);
= **move**, shift, disturb, budge,
misplace

display v = **show**, present, exhibit,
put on view ≠ **conceal** ▷ n
= **proof**, exhibition, demonstration,
evidence, expression; = **exhibition**,
show, demonstration,
presentation, array

dispose v = **arrange**, put, place,
group, order

dispute n = **disagreement**,
conflict, argument, dissent,
altercation ▷ v = **contest**,
question, challenge, deny, doubt;

2 call into question **3** contest ▷ n
4 disagreement **disputable** adj

disqualify ❶ v make ineligible
disqualification n

disquiet n anxiety, uneasiness

disregard ❶ v **1** ignore ▷ n **2** lack
of attention, respect

disrepair n state of bad repair,
neglect

disrepute n bad reputation
disreputable adj

disrespect n lack of respect
disrespectful adj

disrupt ❶ v throw into disorder
disruption n **disruptive** adj

dissatisfied ❶ adj not pleased,
disappointed **dissatisfaction** n

dissect v cut up (body) for detailed
examination

dissemble v pretend, disguise

disseminate v spread abroad

dissent ❶ v **1** differ in opinion ▷ n
2 such difference **dissension** n

dissertation n written thesis

disservice n ill turn, wrong

dissident ❶ n/adj (one) not in
agreement, esp. with government

dissimilar adj not alike,
different

dissipate v **1** scatter **2** waste,
squander **dissipated** adj
dissipation n

dissociate v separate, sever

dissolute adj lax in morals

dissolution n **1** break up
2 termination

dissolve ❶ v **1** absorb or melt in
fluid **2** annul **3** disappear
4 scatter **dissolvable, dissoluble**
adj

dissuade v advise to refrain,
persuade not to

distance ❶ n **1** amount of space
between two things **2** remoteness
3 aloofness **distant** adj

distaste n dislike **distasteful** adj

distemper n **1** disease of dogs
2 paint

distend v swell out **distension** n

distil ❶ v **-tilling, -tilled** **1** vaporize
and recondense a liquid **2** purify
distillation n **distiller** n maker of
alcoholic drinks **distillery** n, pl
-leries

= **argue**, fight, clash, disagree, fall
out (Inf)

disqualify v = **ban**, rule out,
prohibit, preclude, debar

disregard v = **ignore**, discount,
overlook, neglect, pass over ≠ **pay
attention to**

disrupt v = **interrupt**, stop, upset,
hold up, interfere with

dissatisfied adj = **discontented**,
frustrated, unhappy, disappointed,
fed up ≠ **satisfied**

dissent n = **disagreement**,

opposition, protest, resistance,
refusal ≠ **assent**

dissident n = **protester**, rebel,
dissenter, demonstrator, agitator
▷ adj = **dissenting**, disagreeing,
nonconformist, heterodox

dissolve v = **melt**, soften, thaw,
liquefy, deliquesce; = **end**, suspend,
break up, wind up, terminate

distance n = **space**, length,
extent, range, stretch; = **aloofness**,
reserve, detachment, restraint,
stiffness

distinct ❶ adj 1 easily seen
2 definite 3 separate **distinctly**
adv **distinction** n 1 point of
difference 2 act of distinguishing
3 repute, high honour **distinctive**
adj characteristic

distinguish ❶ v 1 make
difference in 2 recognize 3 honour
4 (usu. with between) draw
distinction, grasp difference
distinguishable adj
distinguished adj

distort ❶ v 1 put out of shape
2 misrepresent **distortion** n

distract ❶ v 1 draw attention
away 2 divert 3 perplex, drive mad
distraction n 1 agitation
2 amusement

distraught ❶ adj frantic,
distracted

distress ❶ n 1 trouble, pain ▷ v
2 afflict

distribute ❶ v 1 deal out
2 spread **distribution** n
distributor n

district ❶ n 1 region, locality
2 portion of territory

distrust ❶ v 1 regard as
untrustworthy ▷ n 2 suspicion,
doubt

disturb ❶ v 1 intrude on
2 trouble, agitate, unsettle
disturbance n

disuse n state of being no longer
used **disused** adj

ditch ❶ n 1 long narrow hollow
dug in ground for drainage etc. ▷ v
2 (Inf) abandon

dither v 1 be uncertain or
indecisive ▷ n 2 this state

THESAURUS

distinct adj = **different**, individual,
separate, discrete, unconnected
≠ **similar**; = **striking**, dramatic,
outstanding, noticeable,
well-defined

distinguish v = **differentiate**,
determine, separate, discriminate,
decide; = **characterize**, mark,
separate, single out, set apart;
= **make out**, recognize, perceive,
know, see

distort v = **misrepresent**, twist,
bias, disguise, pervert; = **deform**,
bend, twist, warp, buckle

distract v = **divert**, sidetrack,
draw away, turn aside, lead astray;
= **amuse**, occupy, entertain,
beguile, engross

distraught adj = **frantic**,
desperate, distressed, distracted,

worked-up

distress n = **suffering**, pain,
worry, grief, misery; = **need**,
trouble, difficulties, poverty, hard
times ▷ v = **upset**, worry, trouble,
disturb, grieve

distribute v = **hand out**, pass
round; = **circulate**, deliver, convey

district n = **area**, region, sector,
quarter, parish

distrust v = **suspect**, doubt, be
wary of, mistrust, disbelieve
≠ **trust** ▷ n = **suspicion**, question,
doubt, disbelief, scepticism ≠ **trust**

disturb v = **interrupt**, trouble,
bother, plague, disrupt; = **upset**,
concern, worry, trouble, alarm
≠ **calm**; = **muddle**, disorder, mix
up, mess up, jumble up

ditch n = **channel**, drain, trench,

ditto *n, pl* **-tos** the same

ditty *n, pl* **-ties** simple song

divan *n* bed, couch without back or head

dive ❶ *v* diving, dived **1** plunge under surface of water **2** descend suddenly **3** go deep down into ▷ *n* **4** act of diving **5** (*Sl*) disreputable bar or club **diver** *n*

diverge *v* **1** get farther apart **2** separate

diverse ❶ *adj* different, varied **diversify** *v* **-fying, -fied** make varied **diversity** *n, pl* **-ties**

divert ❶ *v* **1** turn aside **2** amuse **diversion** *n*

divide ❶ *v* **1** make into parts, split up **2** distribute, share **3** become separated ▷ *n* **4** watershed **dividend** *n* share of profits

divine ❶ *adj* **1** of, pert. to God

2 sacred ▷ *v* **3** guess **4** predict

divinity *n* **1** being divine **2** study of theology

division ❶ *n* **1** act of dividing **2** part of whole **3** barrier **4** section **5** difference in opinion etc. **6** (*Maths*) method of finding how many times one number is contained in another **7** army **divisible** *adj* **divisive** *adj* causing disagreement

divorce ❶ *n/v* **1** (make) legal dissolution of marriage **2** split **divorcée** *n* divorced person

divulge *v* reveal

DIY do-it-yourself

dizzy ❶ *adj* **-zier, -ziest** feeling dazed, unsteady **dizziness** *n*

DJ disc jockey

DNA *n abbrev. for* deoxyribonucleic acid, main constituent of the chromosomes of all organisms

---- THESAURUS ----

dyke, furrow ▷ *v* (*Sl*) **= get rid of**, dump (*Inf*), scrap, discard, dispose of

dive *v* **= plunge**, drop, duck, dip, descend ▷ *n* **= plunge**, spring, jump, leap, lunge

diverse *adj* **= various**, mixed, varied, assorted, miscellaneous; **= different**, unlike, varying, separate, distinct

divert *v* **= redirect**, switch, avert, deflect, deviate; **= distract**, sidetrack, lead astray, draw or lead away from; **= entertain**, delight, amuse, please, charm

divide *v* (sometimes with **up**) **= share**, distribute, allocate, dispense, allot; **= split**, break up, come between, estrange, cause to disagree

divine *adj* **= heavenly**, spiritual, holy, immortal, supernatural; **= sacred**, religious, holy, spiritual, blessed ▷ *v* **= guess**, suppose, perceive, discern, infer

division *n* **= separation**, dividing, splitting up, partition, cutting up; **= sharing**, distribution, assignment, rationing; **= disagreement**, split, rift, rupture, abyss ≠ **unity**; **= department**, group, branch

divorce *n* **= separation**, split, break-up, parting, split-up ▷ *v* **= separate**, split up, part company, dissolve your marriage

dizzy *adj* **= giddy**, faint, light-headed, swimming, reeling; **= confused**, dazzled, at sea,

do v **does, doing, did, done**
1 perform, effect, finish **2** work at
3 solve **4** suit **5** provide **6** (Sl)
cheat **7** act **8** fare **9** suffice
10 makes negative and
interrogative sentences and
expresses emphasis ▷ n **11** (Inf)
celebration **do away with**
destroy **do up 1** fasten
2 renovate

dob in v **dobbing, dobbed** (Aust &
NZ, Inf) **1** inform against
2 contribute to a fund

Doberman pinscher,
Doberman large black-and-tan
dog

docile adj willing to obey,
submissive **docility** n

dock¹ ❶ n **1** artificial enclosure for
loading or repairing ships ▷ v **2** put
or go into dock **docker** n
dockyard n

dock² ❶ n **1** solid part of tail
2 stump ▷ v **3** cut short **4** deduct
(an amount) from

dock³ n enclosure in criminal court
for prisoner

dock⁴ n coarse weed

docket n piece of paper sent with
package etc.

doctor ❶ n **1** medical practitioner
2 one holding university's highest
degree ▷ v **3** treat medically
4 repair **5** falsify (accounts etc.)

doctrine ❶ n **1** what is taught
2 belief, dogma **doctrinaire** adj
stubbornly insistent about applying
theories

document ❶ n **1** piece of paper
etc. providing information ▷ v
2 furnish with proofs

documentary adj/n, pl **-ries** (of)
type of film dealing with real life

dodder v totter, as with age

dodge ❶ v **1** (attempt to) avoid by
moving quickly **2** evade ▷ n
3 trick, act of dodging **dodgy** adj
dodgier, dodgiest (Inf)
untrustworthy

Dodgem® n car used for bumping
other cars in rink at funfair

dodo n, pl **dodos, dodoes** large
extinct bird

doe n female of deer, hare, rabbit

does third person sing. of DO

doff v take off

━━━━━━━━━ THESAURUS ━━━━━━━━━

bewildered, muddled

dock¹ n = **port**, haven, harbour,
pier, wharf ▷ v = **moor**, land,
anchor, put in, tie up; (of spacecraft)
= **link up**, unite, join, couple,
rendezvous

dock² v = **cut**, reduce, decrease,
diminish, lessen ≠ **increase**;
= **deduct**, subtract

doctor n = **physician**, medic (Inf),
general practitioner, medical
practitioner, G.P. ▷ v = **change**,

alter, interfere with, disguise,
pervert; = **add to**, spike, cut, mix
something with something, dilute

doctrine n = **teaching**, principle,
belief, opinion, conviction

document n = **paper**, form,
certificate, report, record ▷ v
= **support**, certify, verify, detail,
validate

dodge v = **duck**, dart, swerve,
sidestep, shoot; = **evade**, avoid,
escape, get away from, elude

dog ❶ n 1 domesticated
carnivorous four-legged mammal
2 male of wolf, fox and other
animals 3 person (in contempt,
abuse or playfully) ▷ v 4 follow
closely **dogged** adj persistent,
tenacious **dog-ear** n
turned-down corner of page in
book **dog-end** n 1 (Inf) cigarette
end 2 rejected piece of anything
dogfight n 1 close combat
between fighter aircraft 2 rough
fight **dogleg** n sharp bend
dogsbody n (Inf) one carrying out
menial tasks

doggerel n trivial verse

dogma n article of belief
dogmatic adj asserting opinions
with arrogance

doily n, pl **-lies** small lacy mat to
place under cake, dish etc.

doldrums pl n 1 state of
depression 2 region of light winds
and calms near the equator

dole n (Inf) 1 payment made to
unemployed ▷ v 2 (usu. with out)
distribute

doleful adj dreary, mournful

doll n child's toy image of human
being

dollar n standard monetary unit of
many countries, esp. USA

dollop n (Inf) semisolid lump

dolly n, pl **-lies** 1 doll 2 wheeled
support for film, TV camera

dolphin n sea mammal with
beaklike snout

domain n 1 lands held or ruled
over 2 sphere of influence

dome n 1 rounded roof
2 something of this shape

domestic ❶ adj 1 of, in the home
2 home-loving 3 (of animals)
tamed 4 of, in one's own country
▷ n 5 house servant **domesticate**
v tame

domicile n person's regular place
of abode

dominate ❶ v 1 rule, control
2 (of heights) overlook 3 be most
influential **dominance** n
dominant adj **domination** n
domineering adj imperious

dominion n 1 sovereignty 2 rule
3 territory of government

don¹ ❶ v donning, donned put
on (clothes)

don² n 1 fellow or tutor of college

——— THESAURUS ———

▷ n = **trick**, scheme, ploy, trap,
device

dog n = **hound**, canine, pooch (Sl),
cur, man's best friend ▷ v
= **plague**, follow, trouble, haunt,
hound; = **pursue**, follow, track,
chase, trail

domestic adj = **home**, internal,
native, indigenous; = **household**,
home, family, private;
= **home-loving**, homely,

housewifely, stay-at-home,
domesticated; = **domesticated**,
trained, tame, pet, house-trained
▷ n = **servant**, help, maid, daily,
char (Inf)

dominate v = **control**, rule, direct,
govern, monopolize; = **tower
above**, overlook, survey, stand
over, loom over

don¹ v = **put on**, get into, dress in,
pull on, change into

2 Spanish title, Sir

donate ❶ v give **donation** n
donor n

done past participle of DO

donkey n ass

doodle v/n scribble

doom ❶ n 1 fate 2 ruin 3 judicial
sentence ▷ v 4 condemn
5 destine **doomsday** n 1 day of
Last Judgment 2 dreaded day

door ❶ n hinged barrier to close
entrance **doorway** n

dope ❶ n 1 narcotic drug 2 (Inf)
stupid person ▷ v 3 drug **dopey**,
dopy adj

dormant adj 1 not active
2 sleeping

dormitory n, pl -ries sleeping
room with many beds

dormouse n, pl -mice small
hibernating mouselike rodent

dorp n (S Afr) small town

dorsal adj of, on back

dose ❶ n 1 amount (of drug etc.)
▷ v 2 give doses to **dosage** n

dossier n set of papers on
particular subject

dot ❶ n 1 small spot, mark ▷ v
2 mark with dots 3 sprinkle

dote v **dote on** love to an
excessive degree **dotage** n
senility

double ❶ adj 1 of two parts, layers
etc. 2 twice as much or many
3 designed for two users ▷ adv
4 twice 5 to twice the amount or
extent 6 in a pair ▷ n 7 person or
thing exactly like another
8 quantity twice as much as
another 9 sharp turn 10 running
pace ▷ v 11 make, become double
12 increase twofold 13 fold in two
14 turn sharply **doubly** adv
double bass lowest member of
violin family **double-cross** v
betray

doubt ❶ v 1 suspect 2 hesitate to
believe 3 call in question ▷ n
4 (state of) uncertainty **doubtful**
adj **doubtless** adv 1 certainly
2 presumably

dough n 1 flour or meal kneaded
with water 2 (Sl) money
doughnut n sweetened and fried

— THESAURUS —

donate v = give, present,
contribute, grant, subscribe

doom n = destruction, ruin,
catastrophe, downfall ▷ v
= condemn, sentence, consign,
destine

door n = opening, entry, entrance,
exit, doorway

dope n (Sl) = drugs, narcotics,
opiates; (Inf) = idiot, fool, twit (Inf,
chiefly Brit), dunce, simpleton (Inf)
▷ v = drug, knock out, sedate,
stupefy, anaesthetize

dose n = measure, amount,
allowance, portion,
prescription

dot n = spot, point, mark, fleck, jot
▷ v = spot, stud, fleck, speckle

double adj = dual, enigmatic,
twofold ▷ v = multiply by two,
duplicate, increase twofold,
enlarge, increase twofold ▷ n
= twin, lookalike, spitting image,
clone, replica (Inf)

doubt n = uncertainty, confusion,
hesitation, suspense, indecision

piece of dough

doughty adj **-tier, -tiest** hardy, resolute

dour adj grim, severe

douse v 1 thrust into water 2 extinguish (light)

dove n bird of pigeon family

dovetail v fit closely, neatly together

dowager n widow with title or property from husband

dowdy adj **-dier, -diest** shabbily dressed

dowel n wooden, metal peg

dowry n, pl **-ries** property wife brings to husband

down¹ ❶ adv 1 to, in, or towards, lower position 2 (of payment) on the spot ▷ prep 3 from higher to lower part of 4 along ▷ adj 5 depressed ▷ v 6 knock, pull, push down 7 (Inf) drink
 downward adj/adv **downwards** adv **downbeat** adj (Inf) gloomy **downcast** adj 1 dejected 2 looking down **downfall** n sudden loss of position **downpour** n heavy fall of rain **downright** adj 1 straightforward ▷ adv 2 quite, thoroughly **down-and-out** adj/n destitute, homeless (person)

down² n 1 soft underfeathers, hair 2 fluff **downy** adj

downs pl n open high land

downtown (US, Canad and NZ) n 1 the central or lower part of a city, especially the main commercial area ▷ adv 2 towards, to, or into this area

doyen n senior, respected member of group

doze v/n sleep, nap **dozy** adj **dozier, doziest**

dozen n (set of) twelve

drab adj **drabber, drabbest** dull, monotonous

draconian adj very harsh, cruel

draft ❶ n 1 sketch 2 rough copy of document 3 order for money 4 detachment of troops ▷ v 5 make sketch of 6 make rough copy of 7 send detached party

draft² v (US) select for compulsory military service

drag ❶ v **dragging, dragged** 1 pull along with difficulty 2 trail 3 sweep with net 4 protract 5 lag, trail 6 be tediously protracted ▷ n 7 check on progress 8 checked motion

dragon n mythical fire-breathing monster **dragonfly** n long-bodied insect with gauzy wings

---

THESAURUS

≠ **certainty** ▷ v = **be uncertain**, be sceptical, be dubious; = **waver**, hesitate, vacillate, fluctuate

down¹ adj = **depressed**, low, sad, unhappy, discouraged ▷ v (of water) = **swallow**, drink (down), drain, gulp (down), put away

draft¹ n = **outline**, plan, sketch, version, rough; = **money order**, bill (of exchange), cheque, postal order ▷ v = **outline**, write, plan, produce, create

drag v = **pull**, draw, haul, trail, tow ▷ n (Sl) = **nuisance**, pain (Inf), bore, bother, pest

dragoon n 1 cavalryman ▷ v 2 coerce

drain ❶ v 1 draw off (liquid) by pipes, ditches etc. 2 dry 3 empty, exhaust 4 flow off or away ▷ n 5 channel 6 sewer 7 depletion 8 strain **drainage** n

drake n male duck

dram n small draught of strong drink

drama ❶ n 1 stage play 2 art or literature of plays 3 playlike series of events **dramatic** adj 1 of drama 2 striking or effective **dramatist** n writer of plays **dramatize** v adapt for acting **drape** ❶ v cover, adorn with cloth **draper** n dealer in cloth, linen etc. **drapery** n, pl -peries

drastic ❶ adj 1 extreme 2 severe

draught ❶ n 1 current of air 2 act of drawing 3 act of drinking 4 quantity drunk at once ▷ pl 5 game played on chessboard with flat round pieces ▷ adj 6 for drawing 7 drawn **draughty** adj

full of air currents **draughtsman** n one who makes drawings, plans etc. **draughtsmanship** n

draw ❶ v drawing, drew, drawn 1 portray with pencil etc. 2 pull, haul 3 attract 4 come (near) 5 entice 6 take from (well, barrel etc.) 7 receive (money) 8 get by lot 9 make, admit current of air 10 (of game) tie ▷ n 11 act of drawing 12 casting of lots 13 tie **drawer** n 1 one who or that which draws 2 sliding box in table or chest **drawing** n 1 art of depicting in line 2 sketch so done **drawback** n snag **drawbridge** n hinged bridge to pull up **drawing room** living room, sitting room **draw up** 1 arrange in order 2 stop **drawl** v 1 speak slowly ▷ n 2 such speech

drawn ❶ adj haggard

dread ❶ v 1 fear greatly ▷ n 2 awe, terror 3 adj 3 feared, awful **dreadful** adj disagreeable, shocking or bad **dreadfully** adv

— THESAURUS —

drain v = **remove**, draw, empty, withdraw, tap; = **flow out**, leak, trickle, ooze, seep; = **drink up**, swallow, finish, put away, quaff ▷ n = **sewer**, channel, pipe, sink, ditch; = **reduction**, strain, drag, exhaustion, sapping

drama n = **play**, show, stage show, dramatization; = **theatre**, acting, stagecraft, dramaturgy; = **excitement**, crisis, spectacle, turmoil, histrionics

drape v = **cover**, wrap, fold, swathe

drastic adj = **extreme**, strong, radical, desperate, severe

draught n = **breeze**, current, movement, flow, puff

draw v = **sketch**, design, outline, trace, portray; = **pull**, drag, haul, tow, tug; = **extract**, take, remove; = **deduce**, make, take, derive, infer ▷ n = **tie**, deadlock, stalemate, impasse, dead heat; (Inf) = **appeal**, pull (Inf), charm, attraction, lure

drawn adj = **tense**, worn, stressed, tired, pinched

dread v = **fear**, shrink from, cringe

DICTIONARY

dream ❶ n 1 vision during sleep 2 fancy, reverie, aspiration ▷ v 3 have dreams 4 see, imagine in dreams 5 think of as possible **dreamer** n **dreamy** adj

dreary ❶ adj **drearier, dreariest** dismal, dull **drearily** adv

dredge v 1 bring up mud etc. from sea bottom ▷ n 2 scoop **dredger** n boat with machinery for dredging

dregs pl n sediment, grounds

drench ❶ v wet thoroughly, soak

dress ❶ v 1 put on clothes 2 array for show 3 prepare 4 put dressing on (wound) ▷ n 5 one-piece garment for woman 6 clothing 7 evening wear **dresser** n 1 one who dresses 2 kitchen sideboard **dressing** n put on something applied, as sauce to food, ointment to wound etc. **dressing-down** n (Inf) severe scolding **dressing gown** robe worn before dressing **dressy** adj

(of persons) stylish

dressage n method of training horse

drey n squirrel's nest

dribble ❶ v 1 flow in drops, trickle 2 run at the mouth ▷ n 3 trickle, drop

drift ❶ v 1 be carried as by current of air, water ▷ n 2 process of being driven by current 3 tendency 4 meaning 5 wind-heaped mass of snow, sand etc. **drifter** n **driftwood** n wood washed ashore by sea

drill¹ ❶ n 1 boring tool 2 exercise of soldiers 3 routine teaching ▷ v 4 bore hole 5 exercise in routine 6 practise routine

drill² ❶ v/n (machine to) sow seed in furrows

drink ❶ v **drinking, drank, drunk** 1 swallow liquid ▷ n 2 liquid for drinking 3 intoxicating liquor

d

THESAURUS

at the thought of, quail from, shudder to think about ▷ n = **fear**, alarm, horror, terror, dismay

dream n = **vision**, illusion, delusion, hallucination; = **ambition**, wish, fantasy, desire, pipe dream; = **delight**, pleasure, joy, beauty, treasure ▷ v = **have dreams**, hallucinate

dreary adj = **dull**, boring, tedious, drab, tiresome ≠ **exciting**

drench v = **soak**, flood, wet, drown, steep

dress n = **frock**, gown, robe; = **clothing**, clothes, costume, garments, apparel ▷ v = **put on clothes**, don clothes, slip on or into

something ≠ **undress**; = **bandage**, treat, plaster, bind up

dribble v = **run**, drip, trickle, drop, leak; = **drool**, drivel, slaver, slobber

drift v = **float**, go (aimlessly), bob, coast, slip; = **wander**, stroll, stray, roam, meander ▷ n = **pile**, bank, mass, heap, mound; = **meaning**, point, gist, direction, import

drill n = **bit**, borer, gimlet, boring tool; = **training**, exercise, discipline, instruction, preparation ▷ v = **bore**, pierce, penetrate, sink in, puncture; = **train**, coach, teach, exercise, discipline

drink v = **swallow**, sip, suck, gulp, sup; = **booze** (Inf), tipple, tope, hit

drinkable adj **drinker** n

drip ❶ v **dripping, dripped 1** fall or let fall in drops ▷ n **2** (Med) intravenous administration of solution **3** (Inf) insipid person

dripping n **1** melted fat from roasting meat ▷ adj **2** very wet

drip-dry adj (of fabric) drying free of creases if hung up while wet

drive ❶ v **driving, drove, driven 1** urge in some direction **2** make move and steer (vehicle, animal etc.) **3** be conveyed in vehicle **4** hit with force ▷ n **5** act, action of driving **6** journey in vehicle **7** united effort, campaign **8** energy **9** forceful stroke **driver** n

drivel v **1** run at the mouth **2** talk nonsense ▷ n **3** silly nonsense

drizzle v/n rain in fine drops

droll adj funny, odd

dromedary n, pl **-daries** one-humped camel

3 deep humming ▷ v **4** hum **5** talk in monotonous tone

drool v slaver, drivel

droop v **1** hang down **2** wilt, flag ▷ adj **droopy** adj

drop ❶ n **dropping, dropped 1** globule of liquid **2** very small quantity **3** fall, descent **4** distance to fall ▷ v **5** (let) fall **6** utter casually **7** set down **8** discontinue **9** come or go casually **droplet** n

dropout n person who fails to complete course of study or one who rejects conventional society

droppings pl n dung of rabbits, sheep, birds etc.

dropsy n disease causing watery fluid to collect in the body

dross n **1** scum of molten metal **2** impurity, refuse

drought ❶ n long spell of dry weather

drove ❶ n herd, flock, esp. in motion **drover** n driver of cattle etc.

--- THESAURUS ---

the bottle (Inf) ▷ n = **glass**, cup, draught; = **beverage**, refreshment, potion, liquid, hooch or hootch (Inf, chiefly US & Canad)

drip v = **drop**, splash, sprinkle, trickle, dribble ▷ n = **drop**, bead, trickle, dribble, droplet; (Inf) = **weakling**, wet (Brit Inf), weed (Inf), softie (Inf), mummy's boy (Inf)

drive v = **operate**, manage, direct, guide, handle; = **push**, propel; = **thrust**, push, hammer, ram; = **herd**, urge, impel ▷ n = **run**, ride, trip, journey, spin (Inf); = **initiative**, energy, enterprise,

ambition, motivation; = **campaign**, push (Inf), crusade, action, effort

drop v = **fall**, decline, diminish; (often with **away**) = **decline**, fall, sink; = **plunge**, fall, tumble, descend, plummet ▷ n = **decrease**, fall, cut, lowering, decline; = **droplet**, bead, globule, bubble, pearl; = **dash**, shot (Inf), spot, trace, sip; = **fall**, plunge, descent

drought n = **water shortage**, dryness, dry spell, aridity ≠ **flood**

drove n often plural = **herd**,

—— DICTIONARY ——

drown ❶ v **1** die or be killed by immersion in liquid **2** make sound inaudible by louder sound

drudge v **1** work at menial or distasteful tasks ▷ n **2** one who drudges **drudgery** n

drug ❶ n **1** medical substance **2** narcotic ▷ v **3** mix drugs with **4** administer drug to

drum ❶ n **1** percussion instrument of skin stretched over round hollow frame **2** thing shaped like drum ▷ v **3** play drum **4** tap, thump continuously **drummer** n **drum major** leader of military band **drumstick** n **1** stick for beating drum **2** lower joint of cooked fowl's leg

drunk ❶ adj/n (person) overcome by strong drink **drunkard** n **drunken** adj **drunkenness** n

dry ❶ adj **drier, driest 1** without moisture **2** not yielding liquid

3 unfriendly **4** caustically witty **5** uninteresting **6** lacking sweetness ▷ v **7** remove water, moisture **8** become dry **9** evaporate **dryer, drier** n **1** person or thing that dries **2** apparatus for removing moisture **dryly, drily** adv **dry-clean** v clean clothes with solvent **dry-cleaner** n **dry-cleaning** n

dual ❶ adj twofold

dub v **dubbing, dubbed 1** confer knighthood on **2** give title to **3** provide film with soundtrack

dubious ❶ adj causing doubt

duchess n duke's wife or widow

duck ❶ n **1** common swimming bird ▷ v **2** plunge (someone) under water **3** bob down **4** (Inf) avoid **duckling** n young duck

duct n channel, tube

dud n **1** futile, worthless person or thing ▷ adj **2** worthless

—— THESAURUS ——

company, crowds, collection, mob

drown v = **drench**, flood, soak, steep, swamp; = **overwhelm**, overcome, wipe out, overpower, obliterate

drug n = **medication**, medicine, remedy, physic, medicament; = **dope** (Sl), narcotic (Sl), stimulant, opiate ▷ v = **knock out**, dope (Sl), numb, deaden, stupefy

drum v = **pound**, beat, tap, rap, thrash

drunk adj = **intoxicated**, plastered (Sl), drunken, merry (Brit Inf), under the influence (Inf) ▷ n = **drunkard**, alcoholic, lush (Sl), boozer (Inf),

wino (Inf)

dry adj = **dehydrated**, dried-up, arid, parched, desiccated ≠ **wet**; = **thirsty**, parched; = **sarcastic**, cynical, low-key, sly, sardonic ▷ v = **drain**, make dry

dual adj = **twofold**, double, twin, matched, paired

dubious adj = **suspect**, suspicious, crooked, dodgy (Brit, Aust, & NZ Inf), questionable ≠ **trustworthy**; = **unsure**, uncertain, suspicious, hesitating, doubtful ≠ **sure**

duck v = **bob**, drop, lower, bend, bow; (Inf) = **dodge**, avoid, escape, evade, elude; = **dunk**, wet, plunge, dip, submerge

d

due ❶ *adj* **1** owing **2** proper, expected **3** timed for ▷ *adv* **4** (with points of compass) exactly ▷ *n* **5** person's right **6** (*usu. pl*) charge, fee etc. **duly** *adj* **1** properly **2** punctually **due to 1** attributable to **2** caused by

duel ❶ *n* **1** arranged fight with deadly weapons, between two persons ▷ *v* **2** fight in duel

duet *n* piece of music for two performers

duffel, duffle *n* **1** coarse woollen cloth **2** coat of this

duffer *n* stupid inefficient person

dugout *n* **1** covered excavation to provide shelter **2** canoe of hollowed-out tree **3** (*Sport*) covered bench for players when not on the field

duke *n* peer of rank below prince **dukedom** *n*

dulcet *adj* (of sounds) sweet, melodious

dulcimer *n* stringed instrument played with hammers

dull ❶ *adj* **1** stupid **2** sluggish **3** tedious **4** overcast ▷ *v* **5** make or become dull **dullard** *n* **dully** *adj*

dumb ❶ *adj* **1** (*Offens*) incapable of speech **2** silent **3** (*Inf*) stupid **dumbbell** *n* weight for exercises **dumbfound** *v* confound into silence

dummy ❶ *n, pl* **-mies 1** tailor's or dressmaker's model **2** imitation object **3** baby's dummy teat ▷ *adj* **4** sham, bogus

dump ❶ *v* **1** throw down in mass **2** deposit **3** unload ▷ *n* **4** rubbish heap **5** temporary depot of stores **6** (*Inf*) squalid place ▷ *pl* **7** low spirits **dumpling** *n* small round pudding of dough **dumpy** *adj* short, stout

dunce *n* stupid pupil

dune *n* sandhill

dung *n* excrement of animals

due *adj* = **expected**, scheduled; = **fitting**, deserved, appropriate, justified, suitable; = **payable**, outstanding, owed, owing, unpaid ▷ *adv* = **directly**, dead, straight, exactly, undeviatingly ▷ *n* = **right(s)**, privilege, deserts, merits, comeuppance (*Inf*)

duel *n* = **single combat**, affair of honour ▷ *v* = **fight**, struggle, clash, compete, contest

dull *adj* = **boring**, tedious, dreary, flat, plain ≠ **exciting**; = **lifeless**, indifferent, apathetic, listless, unresponsive ≠ **lively**; = **cloudy**, dim, gloomy, dismal, overcast

≠ **bright**; = **blunt**, blunted, unsharpened ≠ **sharp** ▷ *v* = **relieve**, blunt, lessen, moderate, soften

dumb *adj* = **silent**, mute, speechless, tongue-tied, wordless, unable to speak ≠ **articulate**

dummy *n* = **model**, figure, mannequin, form, manikin; = **imitation**, copy, duplicate, sham, counterfeit ▷ *adj* = **imitation**, false, fake, artificial, mock

dump *v* = **drop**, deposit, throw down, let fall, fling down; = **get rid of**, tip, dispose of, unload, jettison

dungarees pl n overalls made of coarse cotton fabric

dungeon n underground cell for prisoners

dunk v dip bread etc. into liquid before eating it

duo n, pl **duos** pair of performers

duodenum n, pl **-na -nums** upper part of small intestine **duodenal** adj

dupe n **1** victim of delusion or sharp practice ▷ v **2** deceive

duplex n (US & Canad) an apartment on two floors

duplicate ❶ v **1** make exact copy of ▷ adj **2** double ▷ n **3** exact copy **duplication** n **duplicator** n **duplicity** n deceitfulness, double-dealing

durable ❶ adj lasting, resisting wear **durability** n

duration ❶ n time things last

duress n compulsion

during prep throughout, in the time of, in the course of

dusk ❶ n darker stage of twilight

dusky adj

dust ❶ n **1** fine particles, powder of earth or other matter **2** ashes of the dead ▷ v **3** sprinkle with powder **4** rid of dust **duster** n cloth for removing dust **dusty** adj covered with dust **dustbin** n container for household rubbish

Dutch adj pert. to the Netherlands, its inhabitants, its language

duty ❶ n, pl **-ties 1** moral or legal obligation **2** that which is due **3** tax on goods **duteous** adj **dutiful** adj

duvet n quilt filled with down or artificial fibre

dwarf ❶ n, pl **dwarfs, dwarves 1** very undersized person **2** mythological, small, manlike creature ▷ adj **3** unusually small ▷ v **4** make seem small **5** make stunted

dwell ❶ v **dwelling, dwelt 1** live, make one's home (in) **2** think, speak at length (on) **dwelling** n house

d

--- **THESAURUS** ---

▷ n = **rubbish tip**, tip, junkyard, rubbish heap, refuse heap; (Inf) = **pigsty**, hole (Inf), slum, hovel

duplicate v = **repeat**, reproduce, copy, clone, replicate ▷ adj = **identical**, matched, matching, twin, corresponding ▷ n = **copy**, facsimile

durable adj = **hard-wearing**, strong, tough, reliable, resistant ≠ fragile

duration n = **length**, time, period, term, stretch

dusk n = **twilight**, evening, nightfall, sunset, dark ≠ dawn

dust n = **grime**, grit, powder ▷ v = **sprinkle**, cover, powder, spread, spray

duty n = **responsibility**, job, task, work, role; = **tax**, toll, levy, tariff, excise

dwarf v = **tower above** or over, dominate, overlook, stand over, loom over ▷ adj = **miniature**, small, baby, tiny, diminutive

dwell v (Formal, Lit) = **live**, reside, lodge, abide

dwindle ❶ v waste away

dye ❶ v 1 impregnate (cloth etc.) with colouring matter 2 colour thus ▷ n 3 colouring matter in solution

dyke, dike n 1 embankment to prevent flooding 2 ditch

dynamic ❶ adj full of energy, ambition, and new ideas

dynamics pl n branch of physics dealing with force as producing or affecting motion **dynamic** adj energetic and forceful

dynamite n 1 high-explosive mixture ▷ v 2 blow up with this

dynamo n, pl **-mos** machine to convert mechanical into electrical energy, generator of electricity

dynasty ❶ n, pl **-ties** line, family of hereditary rulers

dysentery n infection of intestine causing severe diarrhoea

dysfunction n abnormal, impaired functioning

dyslexia n impaired ability to read **dyslexic** adj

dyspepsia n indigestion **dyspeptic** adj/n

dystrophy n wasting of bodily tissues, esp. muscles

——————— THESAURUS ———————

dwindle v = **lessen**, decline, fade, shrink, diminish ≠ increase

dye v = **colour**, stain, tint, tinge, pigment ▷ n = **colouring**, colour, pigment, stain, tint

dynamic adj = **energetic**, powerful, vital, go-ahead, lively ≠ apathetic

dynasty n = **empire**, house, rule, regime, sovereignty

e

E 1 East **2** Eastern **3** English

each ❶ *adj, pron* every one taken separately

eager ❶ *adj* **1** having a strong wish **2** keen, impatient

eagle *n* large bird of prey

ear¹ ❶ *n* **1** organ of hearing **2** sense of hearing **3** sensitiveness to sounds **4** attention **earache** *n* pain in ear **eardrum** *n* thin piece of skin inside the ear **earmark** *v* assign for definite purpose **earphone** *n* receiver for radio etc.

held or put in ear **earring** *n* ornament for lobe of the ear **earshot** *n* hearing distance **earwig** *n* small insect with pincer-like tail

ear² ❶ *n* spike, head of corn

earl *n* British nobleman

early ❶ *adj/adv* **-lier, -liest** **1** before expected or usual time **2** in first part, near beginning

earn ❶ *v* **1** obtain by work or merit **2** gain **earnings** *p, n*

earnest ❶ *adj* serious, sincere

earth ❶ *n* **1** planet we live on **2** ground **3** soil **4** electrical connection to earth ▷ *v* cover, connect with earth **earthly** *adj* possible **earthy** *adj* **1** of earth **2** uninhibited **earthenware** *n* (vessels of) baked clay **earthquake** *n* convulsion of earth's surface **earthworm** *n*

ease ❶ *n* **1** comfort **2** freedom from constraint, awkwardness or trouble **3** idleness ▷ *v* **4** reduce burden **5** give ease to **6** slacken

THESAURUS

each *pron* **= every one**, all, each one, each and every one, one and all

eager *adj* **= anxious**, keen, hungry, impatient, itching ≠ **unenthusiastic**

ear *n* **= sensitivity**, taste, discrimination, appreciation, observation

early *adv* **= in good time**, beforehand, ahead of schedule, in advance, with time to spare ≠ **late** ▷ *adj* **= first**, opening, initial, introductory; **= premature**, forward, advanced, untimely,

unseasonable ≠ **belated**

earn *v* **= be paid**, make, get, receive, gain; **= deserve**, win, gain, attain, justify

earnest *adj* **= serious**, grave, intense, dedicated, sincere ≠ **frivolous**; **= determined**, dogged, intent, persistent, persevering

earth *n* **= world**, planet, globe, sphere, orb; **= ground**, land, dry land, terra firma

ease *n* **= straightforwardness**, simplicity, readiness; **= comfort**, luxury, leisure, relaxation,

7 (cause to) move carefully **easily** adv **easy** adj **1** not difficult **2** free from pain, care, or anxiety **3** compliant **4** comfortable

easy-going adj **1** not fussy **2** indolent

easel n frame to support picture etc.

east n **1** part of horizon where sun rises **2** eastern lands, orient ▷ adj **3** on, in, or near, east **4** coming from east ▷ adv **5** from, or to, east **easterly** adj/adv **eastern** adj **eastward** adj/adv **eastwards** adv

Easter n festival of the Resurrection of Christ

easy ❶ adj **easier, easiest** see EASE

eat ❶ v **eating, ate, eaten 1** chew and swallow **2** destroy **3** gnaw **4** wear away **eatable** adj

eau de Cologne (Fr) light perfume

eaves pl n overhanging edges of roof **eavesdrop** v listen secretly

ebb ❶ v **1** flow back **2** decay ▷ n **3** flowing back of tide **4** decline, decay

ebony adj/n, pl **-onies** (made of) hard black wood

ebullient adj exuberant **ebullience** n

eccentric ❶ adj **1** odd, unconventional **2** irregular **3** not placed centrally ▷ n **4** odd, unconventional person **eccentricity** n

echo ❶ n, pl **-oes 1** repetition of sounds by reflection **2** imitation ▷ v **3** repeat as echo **4** imitate **5** resound **6** be repeated

éclair n finger-shaped iced cake filled with cream

eclectic adj selecting from various sources

eclipse ❶ n **1** blotting out of sun, moon etc. by another heavenly

———————— THESAURUS ————————

prosperity ≠ hardship; = **peace of mind**, peace, content, quiet, comfort ≠ **agitation** ▷ v = **relieve**, calm, soothe, lessen, alleviate ≠ **aggravate**; = **reduce**, diminish, lessen, slacken; = **move carefully**, edge, slip, inch, slide

easy adj = **simple**, straightforward, no trouble, not difficult, effortless ≠ **hard**; = **untroubled**, relaxed, peaceful, serene, tranquil; = **carefree**, comfortable, leisurely, trouble-free, untroubled ≠ **difficult**

eat v = **consume**, swallow, chew, scoff (Sl), devour; = **have a meal**, lunch, breakfast, dine, snack

ebb v = **flow back**, go out, withdraw, retreat, wane; = **decline**, flag, diminish, decrease, dwindle ▷ n = **flowing back**, going out, withdrawal, retreat, wane

eccentric adj = **odd**, strange, peculiar, irregular, quirky ≠ **normal** ▷ n = **crank** (Inf), character (Inf), oddball (Inf), nonconformist, weirdo or weirdie (Inf)

echo n = **reverberation**, ringing, repetition, answer, resonance; = **copy**, reflection, clone, reproduction, imitation ▷ v = **reverberate**, repeat, resound, ring, resonate; = **recall**, reflect, copy, mirror, resemble

body 2 obscurity ▷ v 3 obscure
4 surpass

economy ❶ n, pl **-mies 1** careful
management of resources to avoid
unnecessary expenditure **2** system
of interrelationship of money,
industry and employment
economic adj **economical** adj
frugal **economics** pl n **1** study of
economies of nations **2** (used as pl)
financial aspects **economist** n
economize v

ecstasy ❶ n exalted state of
feeling **ecstatic** adj

eczema n skin disease

eddy n, pl **eddies 1** small whirl in
water, smoke etc. ▷ v **2** move in
whirls

edge ❶ n **1** border, boundary
2 cutting side of blade **3** sharpness
4 advantage ▷ v **5** sharpen **6** give
edge or border to **7** move gradually
edgy adj irritable **on edge**
1 nervy **2** excited

edible adj eatable

edict n order, decree

edifice n building

edify v **-fying, -fied** improve
morally, instruct

edit ❶ v prepare book, film, tape
etc. **edition** n **1** form in which
something is published **2** number
of copies **editor** n **editorial** adj/n
article stating opinion of
newspaper etc.

educate ❶ v **1** provide schooling
for, teach **2** train **education** n
educational adj

eel n snakelike fish

eerie ❶ adj **eerier, eeriest** weird,
uncanny

efface v wipe or rub out

effect ❶ n **1** result **2** impression
3 condition of being operative ▷ pl
4 property **5** lighting, sounds etc.
▷ v **6** bring about **effective** adj
1 useful **2** in force **effectual** adj

effeminate adj womanish,
unmanly

efficient ❶ adj capable,
competent **efficiency** n

effigy n, pl **-gies** image, likeness

---

eclipse n = **obscuring**, covering,
blocking, shading, dimming ▷ v
= **surpass**, exceed, overshadow,
excel, transcend

economy n = **financial system**,
financial state

ecstasy n = **rapture**, delight, joy,
bliss, euphoria ≠ **agony**

edge n = **border**, side, limit,
outline, boundary ▷ v = **inch**, ease,
creep, slink, steal; = **border**, fringe,
hem, pipe

edit v = **revise**, improve, correct,
polish, adapt

educate v = **teach**, school, train,
develop, improve

eerie adj = **uncanny**, strange,
frightening, ghostly, weird

effect n = **result**, consequence,
conclusion, outcome, event;
= **impression**, feeling, impact,
influence; = **purpose**, impression,
sense, intent, essence ▷ v = **bring
about**, produce, complete, achieve,
perform

efficient adj = **effective**,
successful, structured, productive,
systematic ≠ **inefficient**

effluent n liquid discharged as waste

effort ❶ n exertion, endeavour, attempt or something achieved **effortless** adj

effrontery n impudence

e.g. for example

egalitarian adj believing that all people should be equal

egg¹ n oval or round object from which young emerge

egg² v **egg on** urge

ego n, pl **egos** the self **egotism, egoism** n 1 selfishness 2 self-conceit **egotist, egoist** n **egotistic, -ical** adj **egocentric** adj self-centred

egregious adj blatant

eider n Arctic duck **eiderdown** n 1 its breast feathers 2 quilt

eight adj/n cardinal number one above seven **eighteen** adj/n eight more than ten **eighteenth** adj/n **eighth** adj/n **eightieth** adj/n **eighty** adj/n ten times eight

either adj/n 1 one or the other 2 one of two 3 each ▷ adv/conj 4 bringing in first of alternatives

ejaculate v 1 eject (semen) 2 exclaim **ejaculation** n

eject ❶ v 1 throw out 2 expel

ejection n **ejector** n

eke out make (supply) last

elaborate ❶ adj 1 detailed 2 complicated ▷ v 3 expand (upon) 4 work out in detail **elaboration** n

élan n style and vigour

elapse v (of time) pass

elastic ❶ adj 1 springy 2 flexible ▷ n 3 tape containing strands of rubber **elasticity** n

elbow ❶ n 1 joint between fore and upper parts of arm 2 part of sleeve covering this ▷ v 3 shove with elbow **elbowroom** n room to move

elder¹ ❶ adj 1 older, senior ▷ n 2 person of greater age 3 official of certain churches **elderly** adj **eldest** adj oldest

elder² ❶ n tree with black berries

elect ❶ v 1 choose by vote 2 choose ▷ adj 3 appointed but not yet in office 4 chosen **election** n **elective** adj appointed by election **elector** n **electoral** adj **electorate** n body of electors

electricity ❶ n 1 form of energy 2 electric current **electric** adj of, transmitting or powered by electricity **electrical** adj

— THESAURUS —

effort n = **attempt**, try, endeavour, shot (Inf), bid; = **exertion**, work, trouble, energy, struggle

eject v = **throw out**, remove, turn out, expel, oust

elaborate adj = **complicated**, detailed, studied, complex, precise ▷ v = **develop**, flesh out

elastic adj = **flexible**, supple, rubbery, pliable, plastic ≠ **rigid**; = **adaptable**, yielding, variable, flexible, accommodating ≠ **inflexible**

elbow n = **joint**, angle, curve

elder adj = **older**, first, senior, first-born ▷ n = **older person**, senior, leader

elect v = **vote for**, choose, pick,

electrician n one trained in installation etc. of electrical devices **electrify** v **electrification** n

electro- comb. form by, caused by electricity, as in electrotherapy

electrocute v kill by electricity **electrocution** n

electrode n conductor of electric current

electron n one of fundamental components of atom, charged with negative electricity **electronics** pl n technology of electronic devices and circuits

electronic adj 1 (of a device) dependent on the action of electrons 2 (of a process) using electronic devices

elegant ❶ adj 1 graceful, tasteful 2 refined **elegance** n

elegy n, pl **-egies** lament for the dead in poem **elegiac** adj

element ❶ n 1 substance which cannot be separated by ordinary chemical techniques 2 component part 3 trace 4 heating wire in electric kettle etc. 5 proper sphere ▷ pl 6 powers of atmosphere 7 rudiments **elemental** adj

elementary adj rudimentary, simple

elephant n huge animal with ivory tusks and long trunk

elevate ❶ v raise, exalt **elevation** n 1 raising 2 height, esp. above sea level 3 drawing of one side of building etc. **elevator** n (US) lift

eleven adj/n number next above 10 **eleventh** adj

elf n, pl **elves** fairy **elfin**, **elvish** adj

elicit ❶ v draw out

eligible ❶ adj 1 qualified 2 desirable **eligibility** n

eliminate ❶ v remove, get rid of, set aside **elimination** n

elite ❶ n the pick or best part of society

elixir n remedy

elk n large deer

ellipse n oval **elliptical** adj

elm n tree with serrated leaves

elocution n art of public speaking

elongate v lengthen

elope v run away from home with lover **elopement** n

eloquence n fluent, powerful use of language **eloquent** adj **eloquently** adv

determine, select

elegant adj = **stylish**, fine, sophisticated, delicate, handsome ≠ **inelegant**

element n = **component**, part, unit, section, factor

elevate v = **promote**, raise, advance, upgrade, exalt; = **increase**, lift, raise, step up, intensify

elicit v = **bring about**, cause, derive, bring out, evoke; = **obtain**, extract, exact, evoke, wrest

eligible adj = **entitled**, fit, qualified, suitable ≠ **ineligible**

eliminate v = **remove**, end, stop, withdraw, get rid of (Sl)

elite n = **aristocracy**, best, pick, cream, upper class ≠ **rabble**

else adv 1 besides, instead 2 otherwise **elsewhere** adv in or to some other place

elucidate v explain

elude ❶ v 1 escape 2 baffle **elusive** adj difficult to catch

emaciated adj abnormally thin

emanate ❶ v issue, proceed from **emanation** n

emancipate v set free **emancipation** n

emasculate v 1 castrate 2 enfeeble, weaken **emasculation** n

embalm v preserve corpse

embankment n artificial mound carrying road, railway, or to dam water

embargo ❶ n, pl **-goes** 1 order stopping movement of ships 2 ban ▷ v 3 put under embargo 4 requisition

embark ❶ v 1 board ship, aircraft etc. 2 (with on) commence new project etc.

embarrass ❶ v 1 disconcert 2 abash 3 confuse **embarrassment** n

embassy n, pl **-sies** office or official residence of ambassador

embattled adj having many difficulties

embed v **-bedding, -bedded** fix fast (in)

embellish v adorn, enrich **embellishment** n

ember n glowing cinder

embezzle v misappropriate (money in trust etc.) **embezzlement** n **embezzler** n

emblem n 1 symbol 2 badge **emblematic** adj

embody ❶ v **-bodying, -bodied** represent, include, be expression of **embodiment** n

embolism n (Med) obstruction of artery

embrace ❶ v 1 clasp in arms, hug 2 accept 3 comprise ▷ n 4 hug

embrocation n lotion for rubbing limbs etc. to relieve pain

embroider v ornament with needlework **embroidery** n

embroil ❶ v involve (someone) in problems

─────────────── THESAURUS ───────────────

elude v = **evade**, escape, lose, avoid, flee; = **baffle**, frustrate, puzzle, stump

emanate v = **flow**, emerge, spring, proceed, arise

embargo v = **ban**, bar, restriction, boycott, restraint ▷ v = **block**, stop, bar, ban, restrict

embark v = **go aboard**, climb aboard, board ship, step aboard, go on board ≠ **get off**

embarrass v = **shame**, distress,

show up (Inf), humiliate, disconcert

embody v = **personify**, represent, stand for, manifest, exemplify; = **incorporate**, include, contain, combine, collect

embrace v = **hug**, hold, cuddle, seize, squeeze; = **accept**, support, welcome, adopt, take up; = **include**, involve, cover, contain, take in ▷ n = **hug**, hold, cuddle, squeeze, clinch (Sl)

embroil v = **involve**, mix up,

embryo ❶ *n, pl* **-bryos**
undeveloped offspring, germ
embryonic *adj*

emend *v* to remove errors from,
correct **emendation** *n*

emerald *n* bright green gem

emerge ❶ *v* **1** come up, out **2** rise
to notice **emergence** *n*

emergency ❶ *n, pl* **-cies** sudden
unforeseen event needing prompt
action

emery *n* hard mineral used for
polishing

emigrate ❶ *v* go and settle in
another country **emigrant** *n*
emigration *n*

eminent ❶ *adj* distinguished
eminently *adv* **eminence** *n*

emissary *n, pl* **-saries** agent,
representative sent on mission

emit ❶ *v* **emitting, emitted** give
out, put forth **emission** *n*

emoji *n* image used in electronic
messages

emollient *adj* **1** softening,
soothing ▷ *n* **2** ointment

emotion ❶ *n* excited state of
feeling, as joy, fear etc. **emotional**
adj **emotive** *adj* arousing emotion

empathy *n* understanding of
another's feelings

emperor *n* ruler of an empire

emphasis ❶ *n, pl* **-ses**
1 importance attached **2** stress on
words **emphasize** *v* **emphatic** *adj*
forceful

emphysema *n* disease of lungs,
causing breathlessness

empire ❶ *n* group of states under
supreme leader

empirical, empiric ❶ *adj* relying
on experiment or experience

emplacement *n* position for gun

employ ❶ *v* **1** provide work for in
return for money **2** keep busy
3 use **employee** *n* **employer** *n*
employment *n* **1** employing,
being employed **2** work

e

THESAURUS
---

implicate, entangle, mire
embryo *n* = **foetus**, unborn child,
fertilized egg

emerge *v* = **come out**, appear,
surface, rise, arise ≠ **withdraw**;
= **become apparent**, come out,
become known, come to light, crop
up

emergency *n* = **crisis**, danger,
difficulty, accident, disaster

emigrate *v* = **move abroad**,
move, relocate, migrate, resettle

eminent *adj* = **prominent**, noted,
respected, famous, celebrated
≠ **unknown**

emit *v* = **give off**, release, leak,

transmit, discharge ≠ **absorb**

emotion *n* = **feeling**, spirit, soul,
passion, excitement

emphasis *n* = **importance**,
attention, weight, significance,
stress; = **stress**, accent, force,
weight

empire *n* = **kingdom**, territory,
province, federation, commonwealth

empirical, empiric *adj*
= **first-hand**, direct, observed,
practical, actual ≠ **hypothetical**

employ *v* = **hire**, commission,
appoint, take on, retain; = **use**,
apply, exercise, exert, make use of;
= **spend**, fill, occupy, involve, engage

3 occupation; job
empower ❶ v authorize
empty ❶ adj **-tier, -tiest**
1 containing nothing **2** unoccupied
3 senseless ▷ v **4** make, become
devoid of content **5** discharge
(contents) into **empties** pl n
empty bottles etc. **emptiness** n
emu n large Aust. flightless bird
emulate ❶ v **1** strive to equal or
excel **2** imitate **emulation** n
emulsion n **1** light-sensitive
coating of film **2** liquid with oily
particles in suspension **3** paint in
this form **emulsifier** n
enable ❶ v make able
enact ❶ v **1** make law **2** act part
enamel n **1** glasslike coating
applied to metal etc. **2** coating of
teeth **3** any hard coating ▷ v
4 cover with this

encapsulate v **1** summarize
2 enclose
enchant ❶ v bewitch, delight
enchantment n
encircle v **1** surround **2** enfold
enclave n part of country entirely
surrounded by foreign territory
enclose, inclose ❶ v **1** shut in
2 surround **3** place in with letter
enclosure n
encompass ❶ v surround,
contain
encore interj **1** again ▷ n **2** (call
for) repetition of song etc.
encounter ❶ v meet
unexpectedly **2** meet in conflict
▷ n **3** encountering
encourage ❶ v **1** inspire with
hope **2** embolden
encouragement n
encroach v intrude (on)

——————————— THESAURUS ———————————

empower v = **authorize**, allow,
commission, qualify, permit
empty adj = **bare**, clear,
abandoned, deserted, vacant
≠ **full**; = **meaningless**, cheap,
hollow, vain, idle; = **worthless**,
meaningless, hollow, pointless,
futile ≠ **meaningful** ▷ v = **clear**,
drain/void, unload, pour out ≠ **fill**
emulate v = **imitate**, follow, copy,
mirror, echo
enable v = **allow**, permit,
empower, give someone the
opportunity, give someone the
means ≠ **prevent**
enact v = **establish**, order,
command, approve, sanction;
= **perform**, play, present, stage,
represent

enchant v = **fascinate**, delight,
charm, entrance, dazzle
enclose, inclose v = **surround**,
circle, bound, fence, confine;
= **send with**, include, put in,
insert
encompass v = **include**, hold,
cover, admit, deal with;
= **surround**, circle, enclose, close
in, envelop
encounter v = **experience**, meet,
face, suffer, have; = **meet**,
come across, bump into (Inf), run
across ▷ n = **meeting**, brush,
confrontation, rendezvous, chance
meeting; = **battle**, conflict, clash,
contest, run-in (Inf)
encourage v = **inspire**, comfort,
cheer, reassure, console

encroachment *n*

encrust *v* cover with layer

encumber *v* 1 hamper 2 burden
encumbrance *n*

encyclopedia, encyclopaedia
n book, set of books of information
on one or all subjects
encyclopedic, -paedic *adj*

end ❶ *n* 1 limit 2 extremity
3 conclusion 4 fragment 5 latter
part 6 death 7 event 8 aim ▷ *v*
9 put an end to 10 come to an end,
finish ending *n* endless *adj*

endanger ❶ *v* put in danger

endear *v* make beloved
endearment *n* loving word

endeavour ❶ *v* 1 try, strive after
▷ *n* 2 attempt

endorse ❶ *v* 1 sanction
2 confirm 3 sign back of 4 record
conviction on driving licence
endorsement *n*

endow ❶ *v* 1 provide permanent

income for 2 furnish (with)
endowment *n*

endure ❶ *v* 1 undergo 2 tolerate,
bear 3 last endurable *adj*
endurance *n*

enema *n* medicine, liquid injected
into rectum

enemy ❶ *n*, *pl* -mies 1 hostile
person 2 opponent 3 armed foe

energy ❶ *n*, *pl* -gies 1 vigour,
force, activity 2 source of power, as
oil, coal etc. 3 capacity of machine,
battery etc. for work energetic
adj energize *v*

enervate *v* weaken

enfeeble *v* weaken

enfold *v* cover by wrapping
something around

enforce ❶ *v* 1 compel obedience
to 2 impose (action) upon
enforceable *adj* enforcement *n*

enfranchise *v* 1 give right of
voting to 2 give parliamentary

— THESAURUS —

≠ **discourage**; = **urge**, persuade,
prompt, spur, coax ≠ **dissuade**

end *n* = **close**, ending, finish, expiry,
expiration ≠ **beginning**;
= **conclusion**, ending, climax,
completion, finale ≠ **start**;
= **finish**, close, stop, resolution,
conclusion; = **extremity**, limit,
edge, border, extent; = **tip**, point,
head, peak, extremity ▷ *v*
= **stop**, finish, halt, cease, wind up
≠ **start**

endanger *v* = **put at risk**, risk,
threaten, compromise, jeopardize
≠ **save**

endeavour *v* = **try**, labour,
attempt, aim, struggle ▷ *n*

= **attempt**, try, effort, trial, bid

endorse *v* = **approve**, back,
support, champion, promote;
= **sign**, initial, countersign, sign on
the back of

endow *v* = **provide**, favour, grace,
bless, supply

endure *v* = **experience**, suffer,
bear, meet, encounter; = **last**,
continue, remain, stay, stand

enemy *n* = **foe**, rival, opponent,
the opposition, competitor
≠ **friend**

energy *n* = **strength**, might,
stamina, forcefulness

enforce *v* = **carry out**, apply,
implement, fulfil, execute

representation to **3** set free
engage ❶ v **1** participate
2 involve **3** employ **4** bring into
operation **5** begin conflict
engaged adj **1** pledged to be
married **2** in use **engagement** n
1 appointment **2** pledge of
marriage **engaging** adj charming
engender ❶ v give rise to
engine ❶ n **1** any machine to
convert energy into mechanical
work **2** railway locomotive
engineer n **1** one who is in charge
of engines, machinery etc. **2** one
who originates, organizes ▷ v
3 construct as engineer **4** contrive
engineering n
engrave v **1** cut in lines on metal
for printing **2** carve, incise
3 impress deeply **engraving** n
engross v **1** absorb (attention)
2 occupy wholly

engulf ❶ v swallow up
enhance ❶ v intensify value or
attractiveness of
enhancement n
enigma n puzzling thing or person
enigmatic adj
enjoy ❶ v **1** delight in **2** have
benefit of **enjoy oneself** be happy
enjoyable adj **enjoyment** n
enlarge ❶ v **1** make bigger
2 grow bigger **3** talk in greater
detail **enlargement** n
enlighten ❶ v give information to
enlightenment n
enlist ❶ v engage as soldier or
helper
enliven v animate
enmity n, pl **-ties** ill will, hostility
enormous ❶ adj very big, vast
enormity n, pl **-ties** gross offence
enough ❶ adj/n/adv as much as
need be

—————————— THESAURUS ——————————

engage v (with **in**) = **participate
in**, join in, take part in, undertake,
embark on; = **captivate**, catch,
arrest, fix, capture; = **occupy**,
involve, draw, grip, absorb;
= **employ**, appoint, take on, hire,
retain ≠ **dismiss**; = **set going**,
apply, trigger, activate,
switch on
engine n = **machine**, motor,
mechanism, generator, dynamo
engineer v = **design**, plan, create,
construct, devise
engulf v = **immerse**, swamp,
submerge, overrun, inundate
enhance v = **improve**, better,
increase, lift, boost ≠ **reduce**
enjoy v = **take pleasure in** or

from, like, love, appreciate, relish
≠ **hate**; = **have**, use, own,
experience, possess
enlarge v = **expand**, increase,
extend, add to, build up ≠ **reduce**;
= **grow**, increase, extend, expand,
swell
enlighten v = **inform**, tell, teach,
advise, counsel
enlist v = **join up**, join, enter (into),
register, volunteer; = **recruit**, take
on, hire, sign up, call up
enormous adj = **huge**, massive,
vast, extensive, tremendous
≠ **tiny**
enough adv = **sufficiently**, amply,
reasonably, adequately,
satisfactorily

DICTIONARY

enquire see INQUIRE
enrich ⓥ v 1 make rich 2 add to
enrol ⓥ v -rolling, -rolled 1 write
name of on roll 2 enlist 3 become
member
en route ⓕ (Fr) on the way
ensemble ⓝ n 1 all parts taken
together 2 woman's complete
outfit 3 (Mus) group of soloists
performing together
enshrine v preserve with sacred
affection
ensign n 1 naval or military flag
2 badge
enslave v make into slave
ensnare v 1 trap 2 entangle
ensue ⓥ v follow, happen after
ensure ⓥ v make certain

entail ⓥ v necessitate
entangle v 1 ensnare 2 perplex
entente n friendly understanding
between nations
enter ⓥ v 1 go, come into
2 penetrate 3 join 4 write in
5 begin **entrance** n 1 going,
coming in 2 door, passage 3 right
to enter 4 fee **entrant** n one who
enters **entry** n, pl -tries
enterprise ⓝ n 1 bold
undertaking 2 bold spirit
3 business **enterprising** adj
entertain ⓥ v 1 amuse, receive as
guest 2 consider **entertainer** n
entertainment n
enthral v -thralling, -thralled
captivate

e

THESAURUS

enrich v = enhance, develop,
improve, boost, supplement;
= make rich, make wealthy, make
affluent, make prosperous, make
well-off
enrol v = enlist, register, be
accepted, be admitted, join up
en route adv = on or along the
way, travelling, on the road, in
transit, on the journey
ensemble n = group, company,
band, troupe, cast; = collection,
set, body, whole, total; = outfit,
suit, get-up (Inf), costume
ensue v = follow, result, develop,
proceed, arise ≠ come first
ensure v = make certain,
guarantee, make sure, make
confirm; = protect, defend, secure,
safeguard, guard
entail v = involve, require,
produce, demand, call for

enter v = come or go in or into,
arrive, set foot in somewhere, cross
the threshold of somewhere, make
an entrance ≠ exit; = penetrate,
get in, pierce, pass into, perforate;
= join, start work at, begin work at,
enrol in, enlist in ≠ leave;
= participate in, join (in), be
involved in, get involved in, play a
part in
enterprise n = firm, company,
business, concern, operation;
= venture, operation, project,
adventure, undertaking;
= initiative, energy, daring,
enthusiasm, imagination
entertain v = amuse, interest,
please, delight, charm; = show
hospitality to, receive,
accommodate, treat, put up;
= consider, imagine, think about,
contemplate, conceive of

enthusiasm ❶ n ardent
eagerness **enthuse** v **enthusiast**
n **enthusiastic** adj
entice ❶ v allure, attract
entire ❶ adj whole, complete
entirely adv **entirety** n
entitle ❶ v 1 qualify 2 name
entitlement n
entity ❶ n, pl **-ties** 1 thing's being
or existence 2 reality
entomology n study of insects
entourage n group of people
assisting important person
entrails pl n intestines
entrance¹ n SEE ENTER
entrance² ❶ v delight
entreat v 1 ask earnestly 2 beg,
implore **entreaty** n, pl **-ties**
entrench v establish firmly
entrepreneur ❶ n businessman

who attempts to profit by risk and
initiative
entrust, intrust ❶ v commit,
charge with
entwine v plait, interweave
enumerate v mention one by one
enunciate v state clearly
envelop v enveloping,
enveloped wrap up, surround
envelope ❶ n cover of letter
environment ❶ n
1 surroundings 2 conditions of life
or growth **environmental** adj
environs pl n outskirts
envisage ❶ v visualize
envoy ❶ n diplomat
envy ❶ v 1 grudge another's good
fortune ▷ n 2 (object of) this
feeling **enviable** adj **envious** adj
enzyme n any of group of proteins

— THESAURUS —

enthusiasm n = **keenness**,
interest, passion, motivation, relish

put a spell on, cast a spell on
entrepreneur n = **businessman**
or **businesswoman**, tycoon,
executive, industrialist, speculator
entrust, intrust v = **give
custody of**, deliver, commit,
delegate, hand over
envelope n = **wrapping**, casing,
case, covering, cover
environment n = **surroundings**,
setting, conditions, situation,
medium
envisage v = **imagine**,
contemplate, conceive (of),
visualize, picture
envoy n = **ambassador**, diplomat,
emissary, **= messenger**, agent,
representative, delegate, courier
envy n = **covetousness**,
resentment, jealousy, bitterness,

entice v = **lure**, attract, invite,
persuade, tempt
entire adj = **whole**, full, complete,
total, gross
entitle v = **give the right to**,
allow, enable, permit, sanction;
= call, name, title, term, label
entity n = **thing**, being, individual,
object, substance
entrance¹ n = **way in**, opening,
door, approach, access ≠ **exit**;
= appearance, coming in, entry,
arrival, introduction ≠ **exit**;
= admission, access, entry, entrée,
admittance
entrance² v = **enchant**, delight,
charm, fascinate, dazzle ≠ **bore**;
= mesmerize, bewitch, hypnotize,

produced by living cells and acting as catalysts

epaulette n shoulder ornament on uniform

ephemeral adj short-lived

epic n **1** long poem telling of achievements of hero ▷ adj **2** on grand scale

epicentre n point immediately above origin of earthquake

epicure n one delighting in eating and drinking **epicurean** adj/n

epidemic ❶ adj **1** (esp. of disease) prevalent and spreading rapidly ▷ n **2** serious outbreak

epidermis n outer skin

epidural n spinal anaesthetic

epigram n witty saying

epigraph n **1** quotation at start of book **2** inscription

epilepsy n disorder of nervous system causing fits **epileptic** n/adj

epilogue n closing speech

episcopal adj of, ruled by bishop

episode ❶ n **1** incident **2** section of (serialized) book etc.

episodic adj

epistle n letter

epitaph n inscription on tomb

epithet n descriptive word

epitome n typical example **epitomize** v

epoch n period, era

equable adj even-tempered, placid

equal ❶ adj **1** the same in number, size, merit etc. **2** fit ▷ n **3** one equal to another ▷ v **4** be equal to **equally** adv **equality** n **equalize** v

equanimity n composure

equate ❶ v make equal **equation** n equating of two mathematical expressions

equator n imaginary circle round earth equidistant from the poles

equestrian adj of horse-riding

equilateral adj having equal sides

equilibrium ❶ n, pl **-ria** state of steadiness

equinox n time when sun crosses equator and day and night are equal

equip ❶ v **equipping, equipped** supply, fit out **equipment** n

————— THESAURUS —————

resentfulness ▷ v = **be jealous (of)**, resent, begrudge, be envious (of)

epidemic n = **outbreak**, plague, growth, spread, scourge; = **spate**, plague, outbreak, wave, rash

episode n = **event**, experience, happening, matter, affair; = **instalment**, part, act, scene, section

equal adj = **identical**, the same, matching, equivalent, uniform ≠ **unequal** = **fair**, just, impartial, egalitarian, unbiased ≠ **unfair**;

= **even**, balanced, fifty-fifty, (Inf), evenly matched ≠ **uneven** ▷ n = **match**, equivalent, twin, counterpart ▷ v = **amount to**, make, come to, total, level ≠ **be unequal to**

equate v = **identify**, associate, connect, compare, relate

equilibrium n = **stability**, balance, symmetry, steadiness, evenness

equip v = **supply**, provide for, stock, arm, array

equivalent ❶ *adj* equal in value
equivocal *adj* of double or doubtful meaning **equivocate** *v*
era ❶ *n* period of time
eradicate ❶ *v* wipe out
erase ❶ *v* 1 rub out 2 remove
ere *prep/conj* (Poet) before
erect ❶ *adj* 1 upright ▷ *v* 2 set up 3 build **erection** *n*
ermine *n* stoat in northern regions
erode ❶ *v* 1 wear away 2 eat into **erosion** *n*
erotic ❶ *adj* of sexual pleasure
err *v* 1 make mistakes 2 be wrong 3 sin **erratic** *adj* irregular **erratum** *n, pl* **-ta** error, esp. in printing **erroneous** *adj* wrong **error** *n* mistake
errand *n* short journey for simple business
errant *adj* wandering
erstwhile *adj* former

erudite *adj* learned
erupt ❶ *v* burst out **eruption** *n*
escalate ❶ *v* increase, be increased, in extent, intensity etc. **escalation** *n*
escalator *n* moving staircase
escape ❶ *v* 1 get free 2 get off safely 3 find way out 4 elude 5 leak ▷ *n* 6 escaping **escapade** *n* wild adventure **escapism** *n* taking refuge in fantasy
escarpment *n* steep hillside
eschew *v* avoid, shun
escort ❶ *n* 1 person accompanying another to guard, guide etc. ▷ *v* 2 accompany
Eskimo *n* (Offens) 1 a member of a group of peoples inhabiting N Canada, Greenland, Alaska, and E Siberia, having a material culture adapted to an extremely cold climate 2 the language of these peoples

————————— THESAURUS —————————

equivalent *adj* = **equal**, same, comparable, parallel, identical ≠ **different**
era *n* = **age**, time, period, date, generation
eradicate *v* = **wipe out**, eliminate, remove, destroy, get rid of
erase *v* = **delete**, cancel out, wipe out, remove, eradicate; = **rub out**, remove, wipe out, delete
erect *v* = **build**, raise, set up, construct, put up ≠ **demolish**; = **found**, establish, form, create, set up ▷ *adj* = **upright**, straight, stiff, vertical, elevated ≠ **bent**
erode *v* = **disintegrate**, crumble, deteriorate, corrode, break up
erotic *adj* = **sexual**, sexy (Inf),

crude, explicit, sensual
erupt *v* = **explode**, blow up, emit lava; = **discharge**, expel, emit, eject, spout
escalate *v* = **grow**, increase, extend, intensify, expand ≠ **decrease**
escape *v* = **get away**, flee, take off, fly, bolt; = **avoid**, miss, evade, dodge, shun; = **leak out**, flow out, gush out, emanate, seep out ▷ *n* = **getaway**, break, flight, break-out; = **avoidance**, evasion, circumvention
escort *n* = **guard**, bodyguard, train, convoy, entourage; = **companion**, partner, attendant, guide, beau ▷ *v*

esoteric adj obscure

ESP extrasensory perception

especial adj 1 pre-eminent
2 particular **especially** adv

espionage ⊙ n spying

esplanade n promenade

espouse v 1 support 2 (Obs)
marry **espousal** n

espy v espying, espied catch
sight of

Esq. Esquire, title used on letters

essay ⊙ n 1 prose composition
2 attempt ▷ v 3 try

essence ⊙ n 1 all that makes
thing what it is 2 extract got by
distillation **essential** adj 1 vitally
important 2 basic ▷ n 3 essential
thing

establish ⊙ v 1 set up 2 settle
3 prove **establishment** n

estate ⊙ n 1 landed property

2 person's property 3 area of
property development **estate
agent** one who values, leases and
sells property

esteem v/n regard, respect

ester n (Chem) organic compound

estimate ⊙ v/n (form)
approximate idea of (amounts,
measurements etc.) **estimable**
adj worthy of regard **estimation**
n opinion

estranged adj no longer living
with one's spouse

estuary ⊙ n, pl -aries mouth of
river

etc. et cetera

et cetera (Lat) and the rest, and
others, and so on

etch ⊙ v make engraving on metal
plate with acids etc. **etching** n

eternal ⊙ adj everlasting

THESAURUS

= **accompany**, lead, partner,
conduct, guide

espionage n = **spying**, intelligence,
surveillance, counter-intelligence,
undercover work

essay n = **composition**, study,
paper, article, piece ▷ v (Formal)
= **attempt**, try, undertake,
endeavour

essence n = **fundamental
nature**, nature, being, heart,
spirit; = **concentrate**, spirits,
extract, tincture, distillate

establish v = **set up**, found,
create, institute, constitute;
= **prove**, confirm, demonstrate,
certify, verify

estate n = **lands**, property, area,
grounds, domain; = **area**, centre,

park, development, site

esteem n = **respect**, regard,
honour, admiration, reverence ▷ v
= **respect**, admire, think highly of,
love, value

estimate v = **calculate roughly**,
value, guess, judge, reckon;
= **think**, believe, consider, rate,
judge ▷ n = **approximate
calculation**, guess, assessment,
judgment, valuation;
= **assessment**, opinion, belief,
appraisal, evaluation

estuary n = **inlet**, mouth, creek,
firth, fjord

etch v = **engrave**, cut, impress,
stamp, carve

eternal adj = **interminable**,
endless, infinite, continual,

eternity n

ether n 1 colourless liquid used as anaesthetic 2 clear sky **ethereal** adj 1 airy 2 heavenly

ethnic, ethnical ❶ adj of race or relating to classification of humans into different groups

ethos n distinctive spirit of people, culture etc.

etiquette n conventional code of conduct

étude n short musical composition, exercise

etymology n, pl **-gies** tracing, account of word's origin, development

eucalyptus, eucalypt n Aust. tree, providing timber and gum

Eucharist n Christian sacrament of the Lord's Supper

eugenics pl n science of improving the human race by selective breeding

eulogy n, pl **-gies** praise **eulogize** v

eunuch n castrated man

euphemism n substitution of mild term for offensive one **euphemistic** adj

euphoria ❶ n sense of elation **euphoric** adj

eureka interj exclamation of triumph

euthanasia n painless putting to death to relieve suffering

evacuate ❶ v 1 empty 2 withdraw from **evacuation** n **evacuee** n

evade ❶ v 1 avoid 2 elude **evasion** n **evasive** adj

evaluate ❶ v find or judge value of **evaluation** n

evangelical adj of, or according to, gospel teaching **evangelism** n **evangelist** n

evaporate ❶ v turn into vapour **evaporation** n

eve ❶ n 1 evening before 2 time just before **evensong** n evening service

even ❶ adj 1 flat, smooth 2 uniform, equal 3 divisible by two

───── THESAURUS ─────

immortal ≠ occasional

ethnic, ethnical adj = cultural, national, traditional, native, folk

euphoria n = elation, joy, ecstasy, rapture, exhilaration ≠ despondency

evacuate v = remove, clear, withdraw, expel, move out

evade v = avoid, escape, dodge, get away from, elude ≠ face; = avoid answering, parry, fend off, fudge, hedge

evaluate v = assess, rate, judge, estimate, reckon

evaporate v = disappear, vaporize, dematerialize, vanish, dissolve; = dry up, dry, dehydrate, vaporize, desiccate

eve n = night before, day before, vigil; = brink, point, edge, verge, threshold

even adj = regular, stable, constant, steady, smooth ≠ variable; = level, straight, flat, smooth, true ≠ uneven; = equal, like, matching, similar, identical ≠ unequal; = equally matched, level, tied, on a par, neck and neck

4 impartial ▷ v 5 smooth
6 equalize ▷ adv 7 equally
8 simply 9 notwithstanding
evening ❶ n close of day
event ❶ n 1 happening 2 notable occurrence 3 result 4 any one contest in sporting programme
eventful adj full of exciting events
eventual adj resulting in the end
eventuality n possible event
ever ❶ adv 1 always 2 at any time
evergreen n/adj (tree or shrub) bearing foliage throughout the year
evermore adv for all time to come
every adj 1 each of all 2 all possible **everybody** n **everyday** adj usual, ordinary **everyone** n **everything** n **everywhere** adv in all places
evict v expel by legal process, turn out **eviction** n
evidence ❶ n 1 ground of belief 2 sign 3 testimony ▷ v 4 indicate,

prove **evident** adj plain, obvious
evil ❶ adj/n (what is) bad or harmful
evoke ❶ v 1 call to mind 2 bring about **evocation** n
evocative adj
evolve ❶ v 1 (cause to) develop gradually 2 undergo slow changes
evolution n development of species from earlier forms
ewe n female sheep
ex- comb. form 1 out from, from, out of, formerly, as in exclaim, exodus
exacerbate v aggravate, make worse
exact ❶ adj 1 precise, strictly correct ▷ v 2 demand, extort
exacting adj making rigorous demands **exactly** adv
exaggerate ❶ v magnify beyond truth, overstate **exaggeration** n
exalt v 1 raise up 2 praise
exam n examination

e

--- THESAURUS ---

≠ ill-matched
evening n = dusk, night, sunset, twilight, sundown
event n = incident, happening, experience, affair, occasion; = competition, game, tournament, contest, bout
ever adv = at any time, at all, in any case, at any point, by any chance; = always, for ever, at all times, evermore
evidence n = proof, grounds, demonstration, confirmation/ verification; = sign(s), suggestion, trace, indication ▷ v = show, prove, reveal, display, indicate
evil n = wickedness, bad, vice, sin,

wrongdoing; = harm, suffering, hurt, woe ▷ adj = wicked, bad, malicious, immoral, sinful; = harmful, disastrous, destructive, dire, catastrophic; = demonic, satanic, diabolical, hellish, devilish
evoke v = arouse, cause, induce, awaken, give rise to ≠ suppress
evolve v = develop, metamorphose, adapt yourself
exact adj = accurate, correct, true, right, specific ≠ approximate ▷ v = demand, claim, force, command, extract
exaggerate v = overstate, enlarge, embroider, amplify, embellish

examine ❶ v 1 investigate 2 look at closely 3 ask questions of 4 test knowledge of **examination** n **examiner** n

example ❶ n 1 specimen 2 model

exasperate v irritate **exasperation** n

excavate v 1 hollow out 2 dig 3 unearth **excavator** n

exceed ❶ v 1 be greater than 2 go beyond **exceedingly** adv very

excel ❶ v -celling, -celled 1 surpass 2 be very good **excellence** n **excellent** adj very good

except, except for ❶ prep 1 not including ▷ v 2 exclude **exception** n 1 thing not included in a rule 2 objection **exceptional** adj above average

excerpt ❶ n passage from book etc.

excess ❶ n 1 too great amount

2 intemperance **excessive** adj

exchange ❶ v 1 give (something) in return for something else 2 barter ▷ n 3 giving one thing and receiving another 4 thing given 5 building where merchants meet for business 6 central telephone office **exchangeable** adj

excise¹ n duty charged on home goods

excise² v cut away

excite ❶ v 1 arouse to strong emotion, stimulate 2 set in motion **excitable** adj **excitement** n **exciting** adj

exclaim ❶ v speak suddenly, cry out **exclamation** n **exclamation mark** punctuation mark (!), used after exclamations

exclude ❶ v 1 shut out 2 debar from 3 reject, not consider **exclusion** n **exclusive** adj 1 excluding 2 select

——————— THESAURUS ———————

examine v = **inspect**, study, survey, investigate, explore; = **test**, question, assess, quiz, evaluate; = **question**, quiz, interrogate, cross-examine, grill (Inf)

example n = **instance**, specimen, case, sample, illustration

exceed v = **surpass**, better, pass, eclipse, beat; = **go over the limit of**, go beyond, overstep

excel v = **be superior**, eclipse, beat, surpass, transcend

except, except for prep = **apart from**, but for, saving, barring, excepting ▷ v = **exclude**, leave out, omit, disregard, pass over

excerpt n = **extract**, part, piece,

section, selection

excess n = **surfeit**, surplus, overload, glut, superabundance ≠ **shortage**; = **overindulgence**, extravagance, profligacy, debauchery, dissipation ≠ moderation

exchange v = **interchange**, change, trade, switch, swap ▷ n = **conversation**, talk, word, discussion, chat

excite v = **thrill**, inspire, stir, provoke, animate; = **arouse**, provoke, rouse, stir up

exclaim v = **cry out**, declare, shout, proclaim, yell

exclude v = **keep out**, bar, ban,

exclusiveness, exclusivity n

excommunicate v cut off from sacraments of the Church **excommunication** n

excrement n waste matter from bowels **excrete** v discharge from the system **excretion** n **excretory** adj

excruciating adj unbearably painful

excursion ① n trip for pleasure

excuse ① v 1 overlook 2 try to clear from blame 3 gain exemption 4 set free ▷ n 5 that which serves to excuse 6 apology **excusable** adj

execrable adj hatefully bad

execute ① v 1 inflict capital punishment on, kill 2 carry out, perform 3 make **execution** n **executioner** n **executive** n/adj 1 (of) person in administrative

position 2 (of) branch of government enforcing laws **executor** n person appointed to carry out provisions of a will

exemplify ① v -fying, -fied serve as example of

exempt ① v 1 free from 2 excuse ▷ adj 3 freed from, not liable for **exemption** n

exercise ① n 1 use of limbs for health 2 practice 3 task 4 use ▷ v 5 use 6 carry out 7 take exercise

exert ① v make effort **exertion** n

exhale v breathe out

exhaust ① v 1 tire out 2 use up 3 empty ▷ n 4 waste gases from engine 5 passage for this **exhausting** adj **exhaustion** n state of extreme fatigue **exhaustive** adj comprehensive

exhibit ① v 1 show, display ▷ n

refuse, forbid ≠ **let in**; = **omit**, reject, eliminate, rule out, miss out ≠ **include**

excursion n = **trip**, tour, journey, outing, expedition

excuse n = **justification**, reason, explanation, defence, grounds ≠ **accusation** ▷ v = **justify**, explain, defend, vindicate, mitigate ≠ **blame**; = **forgive**, pardon, overlook, tolerate, acquit; = **free**, relieve, exempt, release, spare ≠ **convict**

execute v = **put to death**, kill, shoot, hang, behead; = **carry out**, effect, implement, accomplish, discharge

exemplify v = **show**, represent,

display, demonstrate, illustrate

exempt adj = **immune**, free, excepted, excused, released ≠ **liable** ▷ v = **grant immunity**, free, excuse, release, spare

exercise v = **put to use**, use, apply, employ, exert; = **train**, work out, practise, keep fit, do exercises ▷ n = **use**, practice, application, operation, discharge; = **exertion**, training, activity, work, labour

exert v = **apply**, use, exercise, employ, wield

exhaust v = **tire out**, fatigue, drain, weaken, weary; = **use up**, spend, consume, waste, go through

exhibit v = **show**, reveal, display, demonstrate, express; = **display**,

2 thing shown **exhibition** n
1 display 2 public show
exhibitionist n one with
compulsive desire to attract
attention **exhibitor** n
exhilarate v enliven, gladden
exhilaration n
exhort v urge
exhume v dig up (corpse etc.)
exigency n, pl **-cies** urgent need
exile ⊕ n 1 banishment, expulsion
from one's own country 2 one
banished ▷ v 3 banish
exist ⊕ v be, have being, live
existence n **existent** adj
exit ⊕ n 1 way out 2 going out ▷ v
3 go out
exodus ⊕ n departure
exonerate v free, declare free,
from blame
exorbitant adj excessive
exorcize v cast out (evil spirits) by

invocation **exorcism** n **exorcist** n
exotic ⊕ adj 1 foreign 2 unusual
expand ⊕ v increase, spread out
expandable adj **expanse** n wide
space **expansion** n **expansive**
adj 1 extensive 2 friendly
expatiate v speak or write at
great length (on)
expatriate ⊕ adj/n (one) living in
exile
expect ⊕ v 1 regard as probable
2 look forward to **expectant** adj
expectation n
expedient adj 1 fitting 2 politic
3 convenient ▷ n 4 something
suitable, useful **expediency** n
expedite v help on, hasten
expedition n 1 journey for
definite purpose 2 people,
equipment comprising
expel ⊕ v **-pelling, -pelled** 1 drive

—————————— THESAURUS ——————————

show, set out, parade, unveil
exile n = **banishment**, expulsion,
deportation, eviction, expatriation;
= **expatriate**, refugee, outcast,
émigré, deportee ▷ v = **banish**,
expel, throw out, deport, drive out
exist v = **live**, be present, survive,
endure, be in existence; = **occur**, be
present; = **survive**, stay alive, make
ends meet, subsist, eke out a living
exit n = **way out**, door, gate, outlet,
doorway ≠ **entry**; = **departure**,
withdrawal, retreat, farewell, going
▷ v = **depart**, leave, go out,
withdraw, retire ≠ **enter**
exodus n = **departure**,
withdrawal, retreat, leaving, flight
exotic adj = **unusual**, striking,

strange, fascinating, mysterious
≠ **ordinary**; = **foreign**, alien,
tropical, external, naturalized
expand v = **get bigger**, increase,
grow, extend, swell ≠ **contract**;
= **make bigger**, increase, develop,
extend, widen ≠ **reduce**; = **spread
(out)**, stretch (out), unfold, unravel,
diffuse
expatriate n = **exile**, refugee,
emigrant, émigré ▷ adj = **exiled**,
refugee, banished, emigrant,
émigré
expect v = **think**, believe, suppose,
assume, trust; = **anticipate**, look
forward to, predict, envisage, await
expel v = **throw out**, exclude, ban,
dismiss, kick out (Inf) ≠ **let in**;

out **2** exclude **expulsion** n
expend v **1** spend, pay out **2** use
up **expendable** adj likely to be
used up **expenditure** n **expense**
n **1** cost ▷ pl **2** charges incurred
expensive adj
experience ❶ n **1** observation of
facts as source of knowledge
2 being affected by event **3** the
event **4** knowledge, skill gained
▷ v **5** undergo, suffer, meet with
experienced adj
experiment ❶ n/v test to
discover or prove something
experimental adj
expert ❶ n/adj (one) skilful,
knowledgeable, in something
expertise n
expiate v make amends for
expire ❶ v **1** come to an end **2** die

3 breathe out **expiry** n end
explain ❶ v **1** make clear,
intelligible **2** account for
explanation n **explanatory** adj
expletive n **1** exclamation
2 oath
explicable adj explainable
explicit ❶ adj clearly stated
explode ❶ v **1** (make) burst
violently **2** (of population) increase
rapidly **3** discredit **explosion** n
explosive adj/n
exploit ❶ n **1** brilliant feat, deed
▷ v **2** turn to advantage **3** make
use of for one's own ends
exploitation n
explore ❶ v **1** investigate
2 examine (country etc.) by going
through it **exploration** n
exploratory adj **explorer** n

—————— THESAURUS ——————

= **banish**, exile, deport, evict, force
to leave ≠ **take in**
experience n = **knowledge**,
practice, skill, contact, expertise;
= **event**, affair, incident, happening,
encounter ▷ v = **undergo**, feel,
face, taste, go through
experiment n = **test**, trial,
investigation, examination,
procedure; = **research**,
investigation, analysis,
observation, research and
development ▷ v = **test**,
investigate, trial, research, try
expert n = **specialist**, authority,
professional, master, genius
≠ **amateur** ▷ adj = **skilful**,
experienced, professional, masterly,
qualified ≠ **unskilled**
expire v = **become invalid**, end,

finish, conclude, close; = **die**,
depart, perish, kick the bucket (Inf),
depart this life
explain v = **make clear** or **plain**,
describe, teach, define, resolve;
= **account for**, excuse, justify, give
a reason for
explicit adj = **clear**, obvious,
specific, direct, precise ≠ **vague**
explode v = **blow up**, erupt, burst,
go off, shatter; = **detonate**, set off,
discharge, let off
exploit v = **take advantage of**,
abuse, use, manipulate, milk;
= **make the best use of**, use, make
use of, utilize, cash in on (Inf) ▷ n
= **feat**, act, achievement,
enterprise, adventure
explore v = **travel around**, tour,
survey, scout, reconnoitre;

exponent see EXPOUND

export v 1 send (goods) out of the country ▷ n 2 exporting 3 product sold abroad

expose ❶ v 1 display 2 reveal (scandalous) truth 3 leave unprotected **exposure** n

exposé n bringing of scandal, crime etc, to public notice

expound v explain, interpret **exponent** n 1 one who expounds or promotes (idea, cause etc.) 2 performer **exposition** n 1 explanation 2 exhibition of goods etc.

express ❶ v 1 put into words 2 make known or understood ▷ adj 3 definitely stated 4 specially designed 5 speedy ▷ adv 6 with speed ▷ n 7 express train 8 rapid parcel delivery service **expression** n 1 expressing 2 word, phrase 3 look **expressive** adj

expropriate v dispossess

expunge v delete, blot out

expurgate v remove objectionable parts (from book etc.)

exquisite ❶ adj of extreme beauty or delicacy

extend ❶ v 1 stretch out 2 prolong 3 widen 4 accord, grant 5 reach 6 cover area 7 have range or scope **extension** n 1 extending 2 additional part **extensive** adj wide **extent** n 1 space 2 scope 3 size

extenuate v 1 make less blameworthy 2 lessen 3 mitigate

exterior ❶ n 1 outside ▷ adj 2 outer, external

exterminate v destroy completely **extermination** n

external ❶ adj outside, outward **externally** adv

extinct ❶ adj 1 having died out 2 quenched **extinction** n

extinguish ❶ v 1 put out, quench

─────── THESAURUS ───────

= **investigate**, consider, research, survey, search

expose v = **uncover**, show, reveal, display, exhibit ≠ **hide**; = **make vulnerable**, subject, endanger, leave open, jeopardize

express v = **state**, communicate, convey, articulate, say; = **show**, indicate, exhibit, demonstrate, reveal ▷ adj = **explicit**, clear, plain, distinct, definite; = **specific**, exclusive, particular, sole, special; = **fast**, direct, rapid, priority, prompt

exquisite adj = **beautiful**, elegant, graceful, pleasing, attractive ≠ **unattractive**; = **fine**, beautiful,

lovely, elegant, precious

extend v = **spread out**, reach, stretch; = **stretch**, stretch out, spread out, straighten out; = **last**, continue, go on, stretch, carry on; = **protrude**, project, stand out, bulge, stick out

exterior n = **outside**, face, surface, covering, skin ▷ adj = **outer**, outside, external, surface, outward ≠ **inner**

external adj = **outer**, outside, surface, outward, exterior ≠ **internal**

extinct adj = **dead**, lost, gone, vanished, defunct ≠ **living**

2 wipe out; destroy

extol v **-tolling, -tolled** praise highly

extort v get by force or threats **extortion** n **extortionate** adj excessive

extra ❶ adj **1** additional **2** more than usual ▷ adv **3** additionally **4** more than usually ▷ n **5** extra person or thing **6** something charged as additional

extra- comb. form **1** beyond, as in extramural

extract ❶ v **1** take out, esp. by force **2** get by extortion etc. **3** derive **4** quote ▷ n **5** passage from book, film etc. **6** concentrated solution **extraction** n **1** extracting **2** ancestry

extramural adj outside normal courses etc. of university or college

extraneous adj **1** not essential **2** added from without

extraordinary ❶ adj very unusual **extraordinarily** adv

extrapolate v make inference from known facts

extrasensory adj of perception apparently gained without use of known senses

extravagant ❶ adj **1** wasteful **2** exorbitant **extravagance** n **extravaganza** n elaborate entertainment

extreme ❶ adj **1** of high or highest degree **2** severe **3** going beyond moderation **4** outermost ▷ n **5** utmost degree **6** thing at either end **extremely** adv **extremist** n/adj (one) favouring immoderate methods **extremity** n, pl **-ties 1** end ▷ pl **2** hands and feet

extricate v disentangle

extrovert n lively, outgoing person

extrude v squeeze, force out

exuberant adj high-spirited **exuberance** n

exude v **1** ooze out **2** give off

exult v rejoice, triumph **exultant**

— THESAURUS —

extra adj = **additional**, more, added, further, supplementary ≠ **vital**; = **surplus**, excess, spare, redundant, unused ▷ n = **addition**, bonus, supplement, accessory ≠ **necessity** ▷ adv = **in addition**, additionally, over and above

extract v = **take out**, draw, pull, remove, withdraw; = **pull out**, remove, take out, draw, uproot ▷ n = **passage**, selection, excerpt, cutting, clipping; = **essence**, solution, concentrate, juice,

distillation

extraordinary adj = **remarkable**, outstanding, amazing, fantastic, astonishing ≠ **unremarkable**

extravagant adj = **wasteful**, lavish, prodigal, profligate, spendthrift ≠ **economical**; = **excessive**, outrageous, over the top (Sl), unreasonable, preposterous ≠ **moderate**

extreme adj = **great**, highest, supreme, acute, severe ≠ **mild**; = **severe**, radical, strict, harsh,

adj **exultation** *n*
eye ❶ *n* **1** organ of sight **2** look, glance **3** attention **4** aperture **5** thing resembling eye ▷ *v* **6** look at **7** observe **eyebrow** *n* fringe of hair above eye **eyelash** *n* hair fringing eyelid **eyelet** *n* small hole

eyelid *n* **eye shadow** coloured cosmetic worn on upper eyelids **eyesore** *n* ugly object **eyetooth** *n* canine tooth **eyewitness** *n* one who was present at an event
eyrie *n* nest of bird of prey, esp. eagle

— THESAURUS —

rigid; = **radical**, excessive, fanatical, immoderate ≠ **moderate**; = **farthest**, furthest, far, remotest, far-off ≠ **nearest** ▷ *n* = **limit**, end, edge, opposite, pole

eye *n* = **eyeball**, optic (*Inf*), organ of vision, organ of sight; (*often plural*) = **eyesight**, sight, vision, perception, ability to see ▷ *v* = **look at**, view, study, watch, survey

f

F Fahrenheit

fable n short story with moral **fabulous** adj 1 amazing 2 (Inf) extremely good

fabric ① n 1 cloth 2 structure **fabricate** v 1 construct 2 invent (lie etc.)

face ① n 1 front of head 2 distorted expression 3 outward appearance 4 chief side of anything 5 dignity ▷ v 6 look or front towards 7 meet (boldly) 8 give a covering surface 9 turn **faceless** adj anonymous **face-lift**

n operation to remove wrinkles **face-saving** adj maintaining dignity **facet** n 1 one side of cut gem 2 one aspect **face value** apparent worth **facial** n 1 cosmetic treatment for face ▷ adj 2 of face

facetious adj given to joking

facia pl **-ciae** SEE FASCIA

facile adj 1 easy 2 superficial **facilitate** v make easy **facility** n 1 easiness 2 dexterity ▷ pl 3 opportunities, good conditions 4 means, equipment for doing something

facsimile n exact copy

fact ① n 1 thing known to be true 2 reality **factual** adj

faction ① n 1 (dissenting) minority group 2 dissension

factor ① n 1 something contributing to a result 2 one of numbers which multiplied together give a given number 3 agent

factory ① n, pl **-ries** building where things are manufactured

---

THESAURUS

fabric n = cloth, material, stuff, textile, web; = framework, structure, make-up, organization, frame

face n = countenance, features, profile, mug (Sl), visage; = expression, look, air, appearance, aspect; = side, front, outside, surface, exterior ▷ v = look onto, overlook, be opposite, look out on, front onto; = confront, meet, encounter, deal with, oppose; (often with up to) = accept,

deal with, tackle, acknowledge, cope with

fact n = truth, reality, certainty, verity ≠ fiction; = event, happening, act, performance, incident

faction n = group, set, party, gang, bloc; = dissension, division, conflict, rebellion, disagreement ≠ agreement

factor n = element, part, cause, influence, item

factory n = works, plant, mill,

faculty ❶ n, pl **-ties** 1 inherent power 2 ability 3 aptitude 4 department of university

fad ❶ n short-lived fashion

fade ❶ v 1 lose colour, strength 2 cause to fade

faeces pl n excrement

fag n (Inf) 1 boring task 2 (Sl) cigarette ▷ v (Inf) 3 tire

faggot n 1 ball of chopped liver 2 bundle of sticks

Fahrenheit adj measured by thermometric scale with freezing point of water 32°, boiling point 212°

fail ❶ v 1 be unsuccessful 2 stop working 3 (judge to) be below the required standard 4 disappoint, give no help to 5 be insufficient 6 become bankrupt 7 neglect, forget to do **failing** n 1 deficiency

2 fault ▷ prep 3 in default of **failure** n **without fail** certainly

faint ❶ adj 1 feeble, dim, pale 2 weak 3 dizzy ▷ v 4 lose consciousness temporarily

fair¹ ❶ adj 1 just 2 according to rules 3 blond 4 beautiful 5 of moderate quality or amount 6 favourable ▷ adv 7 honestly **fairly** adv **fairness** n **fairway** n smooth area on golf course between tee and green

fair² ❶ n 1 travelling entertainment with sideshows etc. 2 trade exhibition **fairground** n

fairy ❶ n, pl **fairies** 1 imaginary small creature with powers of magic ▷ adj 2 of fairies 3 delicate, imaginary

workshop, assembly line

faculty n = **ability**, power, skill, facility, capacity ≠ **failing**; = **department**, school, staff, teachers, professors

fad n = **craze**, fashion, trend, rage, vogue

fade v = **become pale**, bleach, wash out, discolour, lose colour; = **make pale**, dim, bleach, wash out, blanch

fail v = **be unsuccessful**, founder, fall, break down, flop (Inf) ≠ **succeed**; = **disappoint**, abandon, desert, neglect, omit; = **stop working**, stop, die, break down, stall; = **wither**, perish, sag, waste away, shrivel up; = **go bankrupt**, collapse, fold (Inf), close down, go under

faint adj = **dim**, low, soft, faded, distant ≠ **clear**; = **slight**, weak, feeble, unenthusiastic, remote; = **dizzy**, giddy, light-headed, weak, exhausted ≠ **energetic** ▷ v = **pass out**, black out, lose consciousness, keel over (Inf), go out

fair¹ adj = **unbiased**, impartial, even-handed, unprejudiced, just ≠ **unfair**; = **respectable**, average, reasonable, decent, acceptable; = **light**, golden, blonde, blond, yellowish; = **fine**, clear, dry, bright, pleasant; = **beautiful**, pretty, attractive, lovely, handsome ≠ **ugly**

fair² n = **carnival**, show, fête, festival, exhibition

fairy n = **sprite**, elf, brownie, pixie, puck

faith ❶ n 1 trust 2 belief (without proof) 3 religion 4 loyalty
faithful adj constant, true
faithfully adv **faithless** adj

fake ❶ v 1 touch up 2 counterfeit ▷ n/adj 3 fraudulent (thing or person)

falcon n small bird of prey

fall ❶ v falling, fell, fallen 1 drop 2 become lower 3 hang down 4 cease to stand 5 perish 6 collapse 7 be captured 8 become 9 happen ▷ n 10 falling 11 amount that falls 12 decrease 13 collapse 14 drop 15 cascade 16 yielding to temptation 17 (US) autumn **fallout** n radioactive particles spread as result of nuclear explosion

fallacy n, pl **-cies** incorrect opinion or argument **fallacious** adj **fallible** adj liable to error

fallow adj ploughed but left without crop

false ❶ adj 1 wrong 2 deceptive 3 faithless 4 artificial **falsely** adv **falsehood** n **falsify** v alter fraudulently

falsetto n, pl **-tos** forced voice above natural range

falter ❶ v 1 hesitate 2 waver 3 stumble

fame ❶ n renown **famed** adj **famous** adj widely known **famously** adv (Inf) excellently

familiar ❶ adj 1 well-known 2 customary 3 intimate 4 acquainted 5 impertinent ▷ n 6 friend 7 demon **familiarity** n **familiarize** v

---

— THESAURUS —

faith n = **confidence**, trust, credit, conviction, assurance ≠ **distrust**; = **religion**, church, belief, persuasion, creed ≠ **agnosticism**

fake adj = **artificial**, false, forged, counterfeit, put-on ≠ **genuine** ▷ n = **forgery**, copy, fraud, reproduction, dummy ▷ v = **forge**, copy, reproduce, fabricate, counterfeit; = **sham**, put on, pretend, simulate, feign

fall v = **drop**, plunge, tumble, plummet, collapse ≠ **rise**; = **decrease**, drop, decline, go down, slump ≠ **increase**; = **be overthrown**, surrender, succumb, submit, capitulate ≠ **triumph**; = **be killed**, die, perish, meet your end ≠ **survive**; = **occur**, happen, come about, chance, take place ▷ n

= **drop**, slip, plunge, dive, tumble; = **decrease**, drop, lowering, decline, reduction; = **collapse**, defeat, downfall, ruin, destruction

false adj = **incorrect**, wrong, mistaken, misleading, faulty ≠ **correct**; = **untrue**, fraudulent, trumped up, fallacious, untruthful ≠ **true**; = **artificial**, forged, fake, reproduction, replica ≠ **real** (Inf)

falter v = **hesitate**, delay, waver, vacillate ≠ **persevere**; = **tumble**, totter; = **stutter**, pause, stumble, hesitate, stammer

fame n = **prominence**, glory, celebrity, stardom, reputation ≠ **obscurity**

familiar adj = **well-known**, recognized, common, ordinary, routine ≠ **unfamiliar**; = **friendly**,

family ❶ *n, pl* **-lies 1** parents and children, relatives **2** group of allied objects

famine ❶ *n* **1** extreme scarcity of food **2** starvation **famished** *adj* very hungry

fan¹ ❶ *n* **1** instrument for producing current of air **2** folding object of paper etc., for cooling the face ▷ *v* **3** blow or cool with fan **4** spread out

fan² ❶ *n* (*Inf*) devoted admirer

fanatic ❶ *adj/n* (person) filled with abnormal enthusiasm **fanatical** *adj* **fanaticism** *n*

fancy ❶ *adj* **-cier, -ciest 1** ornamental ▷ *n* **2** whim **3** liking **4** imagination **5** mental image ▷ *v* **6** imagine **7** be inclined to believe

8 (*Inf*) have a liking for **fancier** *n* one with special interest in something **fanciful** *adj*

fanfare *n* **1** flourish of trumpets **2** ostentatious display

fang *n* **1** snake's tooth, injecting poison **2** long, pointed tooth

fantasy, *Archaic* **phantasy ❶** *n, pl* **-sies 1** power of imagination **2** mental image **3** fanciful invention **fantasize** *v* **fantastic** *adj* **1** quaint, unreal **2** (*Inf*) very good **3** (*Inf*) very large

far ❶ *adv* **farther 1** at or to a great distance or a remote time **2** by very much ▷ *adj* **3** distant **4** more distant **far-fetched** *adj* incredible

farce ❶ *n* **1** comedy of boisterous

——— THESAURUS ———

close, dear, intimate, amicable **≠ formal**; **= relaxed**, easy, friendly, comfortable, intimate; **= disrespectful**, forward, bold, intrusive, presumptuous

family *n* **= relations**, relatives, household, folk (*Inf*), kin; **= children**, kids (*Inf*), offspring, little ones; **= ancestors**, house, race, tribe, clan

famine *n* **= hunger**, want, starvation, deprivation, scarcity

fan¹ *n* **= blower**, ventilator, air conditioner ▷ *v* **= blow**, cool, refresh, air-condition/ventilate

fan² *n* **= supporter**, lover, follower, enthusiast, admirer

fanatic *n* **= extremist**, activist, militant, bigot, zealot

fancy *adj* **= elaborate**, decorative, extravagant, intricate, baroque

≠ plain ▷ *n* **= whim**, thought, idea, desire, urge; **= delusion**, dream, vision, fantasy, daydream ▷ *v* **= wish for**, want, desire, hope for, long for; (*Inf*) **= be attracted to**, find attractive, lust after, like, take to; **= suppose**, think, believe, imagine, reckon

fantasy, *Archaic* **phantasy** *n* **= daydream**, dream, wish, reverie, flight of fancy; **= imagination**, fancy, invention, creativity, originality

far *adv* **= a long way**, miles, deep, a good way, afar; **= much**, greatly, very much, extremely, significantly ▷ *adj* (*often with* **off**) **= remote**, distant, far-flung, faraway, out-of-the-way **≠ near**

farce *n* **= comedy**, satire, slapstick, burlesque, buffoonery; **= mockery**,

humour **2** absurd and futile
proceeding **farcical** adj

fare ❶ n **1** charge for transport
2 passenger **3** food ▷ v **4** get on
5 happen **farewell** interj
1 goodbye ▷ n **2** leave-taking

farm ❶ n **1** tract of land for
cultivation or rearing livestock ▷ v
2 cultivate (land) **3** rear livestock
(on farm) **farmer** n **farmhouse** n
farmyard n

fart (Vulgar) ❶ n **1** (audible)
emission of gas from anus ▷ v
2 break wind

farther, farthest adv/adj
further: comparative of FAR
farthest adv/adj furthest:
superlative of FAR

farthing n formerly, coin worth a
quarter of a penny

fascia n, pl **-ciae, -cias 1** flat
surface above shop window

2 dashboard

fascinate ❶ v attract and delight
fascination n

fascism n authoritarian political
system opposed to democracy and
liberalism **fascist** adj/n

fashion ❶ n **1** (latest) style, esp. of
dress etc. **2** manner **3** type ▷ v
4 shape, make **fashionable** adj

fast¹ ❶ adj **1** (capable of) moving
quickly **2** ahead of true time
3 (Obs) dissipated **4** firm, steady
▷ adv **5** rapidly **6** tightly **fast
food** food, esp. hamburgers etc.,
served very quickly

fast² ❶ v **1** go without food ▷ n
2 fasting n

fasten ❶ v **1** attach, fix, secure
2 become joined **fastener,
fastening** n

fastidious adj hard to please

fat ❶ n **fatter, fattest 1** oily

---

joke, nonsense, parody, shambles

fare n = **charge**, price, ticket price,
ticket money; = **food**, provisions,
board, rations, nourishment ▷ v
= **get on**, do, manage, make out,
prosper

farm n = **smallholding**, ranch
(chiefly US & Canad), farmstead,
vineyard, plantation ▷ v
= **cultivate**, work, plant, grow
crops on, keep animals on

fascinate v = **entrance**, absorb,
intrigue, rivet, captivate ≠ **bore**

fashion n = **style**, look, trend,
rage, custom; = **method**, way,
style, manner, mode ▷ v
= **make**, shape, cast, construct,
form

fast¹ adj = **quick**, flying, rapid, fleet,
swift ≠ **slow**; = **fixed**, firm, sound,
stuck, secure ≠ **unstable**;
= **dissipated**, wild, exciting, loose,
extravagant ▷ adv = **quickly**,
rapidly, swiftly, hastily, hurriedly
≠ **slowly**; = **firmly**, staunchly,
resolutely, steadfastly,
unwaveringly

fast² v = **go hungry**, abstain, go
without food, deny yourself ▷ n
= **fasting**, diet, abstinence

fasten v = **secure**, close, do up

fat adj = **overweight**, large,
heavy, plump, stout ≠ **thin**
= **large**, substantial, profitable
▷ n = **fatness**, flesh, bulk,
obesity, flab

animal substance **2** fat part ▷ *adj*
3 having too much fat **4** greasy
5 profitable **fatten** *v* **fatty** *adj*

fate ❶ *n* **1** power supposed to
predetermine events **2** destiny
3 person's appointed lot **4** death or
destruction **fatal** *adj* ending in
death **fatality** *n* death **fatally**
adv **fated** *adj* destined **fateful** *adj*

father ❶ *n* **1** male parent
2 ancestor **3** (*with cap.*) God
4 originator **5** priest ▷ *v* **6** beget
7 originate **fatherhood** *n*
father-in-law *n, pl* **fathers-in-
law** husband's or wife's father
fatherland *n* native country

fathom ▷ *n* **1** measure of six feet of
water ▷ *v* **2** sound (water)
3 understand

fatigue ▷ *v* **1** tire ▷ *n*
2 weariness **3** toil **4** weakness of
metals etc.

fatuous *adj* very silly, idiotic

faucet (*US & Canad*) *n* valve with
handle, plug etc. to regulate or stop

flow of fluid

fault ❶ *n* **1** defect **2** misdeed
3 blame ▷ *v* **4** find fault in
5 (cause to) commit fault **faultily**
adv **faultless** *adj* **faulty** *adj*

faun *n* mythological woodland
being with tail and horns

fauna *n, pl* **-nas, -nae** animals of
region collectively

faux pas *n, pl* **faux pas** social
blunder or indiscretion

favour ❶ *n* **1** goodwill **2** approval
3 especial kindness **4** partiality ▷ *v*
5 regard or treat with favour
6 oblige **7** treat with partiality
8 support **favourable** *adj*

favourite *n* **1** favoured person or
thing ▷ *adj* **2** chosen, preferred
favouritism *n* practice of showing
undue preference

fawn¹ *n* **1** young deer ▷ *adj* **2** light
yellowish brown

fawn² *v* (*oft. with on*) cringe, court
favour servilely

fax *n* **1** facsimile ▷ *v* **2** send by

THESAURUS

fate *n* = **destiny**, chance, fortune,
luck, the stars; = **fortune**, destiny,
lot, portion, cup

father *n* = **daddy** (*Inf*), dad (*Inf*),
male parent, pop (*US Inf*), old man
(*Brit Inf*); = **founder**, author, maker,
architect, creator; (*usually cap.*)
= **priest**, minister, vicar, parson,
pastor; (*usually plural*) = **forefather**,
predecessor, ancestor, forebear,
progenitor ▷ *v* = **sire**, parent,
conceive, bring to life, beget

fatigue *n* = **tiredness**, lethargy,
weariness, heaviness, languor
≠ **freshness** ▷ *v* = **tire**,

exhaust, weaken, weary, drain
≠ **refresh**

fault *n* = **responsibility**, liability,
guilt, accountability, culpability;
= **mistake**, slip, error, blunder,
lapse; = **failing**, weakness, defect,
deficiency, flaw ≠ **strength** ▷ *v*
= **criticize**, blame, complain,
condemn, moan about

favour *n* = **approval**, goodwill,
commendation, approbation
≠ **disapproval**; = **favouritism**,
preferential treatment ▷ *v*
= **prefer**, opt for, like better, incline
towards, choose ≠ **object to**;

telegraphic facsimile system

FBI (US) Federal Bureau of Investigation

fear ❶ n **1** unpleasant emotion caused by coming danger ▷ v **2** be afraid **3** regard with fear **fearful** adj **fearless** adj **fearsome** adj

feasible ❶ adj able to be done **feasibility** n

feast ❶ n **1** banquet **2** religious anniversary ▷ v **3** eat banquet **4** entertain with feast **5** delight

feat ❶ n notable deed

feather n **1** one of the barbed shafts which form covering of birds **2** anything resembling this ▷ v **3** provide with feathers **4** grow feathers **feathery** adj

feature ❶ n **1** part of face **2** notable part of anything **3** main or special item ▷ v **4** portray **5** be

prominent (in) **featureless** adj without striking features

Feb. February

February n second month

feckless adj ineffectual, irresponsible

federal adj of the government of states which are united but retain internal independence **federalism** n **federalist** n **federate** v form into, become, a federation **federation** n **1** league **2** federal union

fee ❶ n payment for services

feeble ❶ adj **1** weak **2** not effective or convincing

feed ❶ v feeding, fed **1** give food to **2** supply, support **3** take food ▷ n **4** feeding **5** fodder **feedback** n response **fed up** (Inf) bored, dissatisfied

— THESAURUS —

= **indulge**, reward, side with, smile upon

fear n = **dread**, horror, panic, terror, fright ▷ v = **be afraid of**, dread, shudder at, be fearful of, tremble at; = **worry**, expect

feasible adj = **practicable**, possible, reasonable, viable, workable ≠ **impracticable**

feast n = **banquet**, repast, spread (Inf), dinner, treat; = **festival**, holiday, fête, celebration, holy day; = **treat**, delight, pleasure, enjoyment, gratification ▷ v = **eat your fill**, wine and dine, overindulge, consume, indulge

feat n = **accomplishment**, act, performance, achievement, enterprise

feature n = **aspect**, quality, characteristic, property, factor; = **article**, report, story, piece, item; = **highlight**, attraction, speciality, main item ▷ v = **spotlight**, present, emphasize, play up, foreground

fee n = **charge**, price, cost, bill, payment

feeble adj = **weak**, frail, debilitated, sickly, puny ≠ **strong**; = **inadequate**, pathetic, insufficient, lame

feed v = **cater for**, provide for, nourish, provide with food, supply; = **graze**, eat, browse, pasture ▷ n = **food**, fodder, provender, pasturage; (Inf) = **meal**, spread (Inf), dinner, lunch, tea

feel ❶ v **feeling, felt 1** touch **2** experience **3** find (one's way) cautiously **4** be sensitive to **5** show emotion (for) **6** believe, consider ▷ n **7** feeling **8** impression perceived by feeling **9** sense of touch **feeler** n **feeling** n **1** sense of touch **2** sensation **3** emotion **4** sympathy **5** opinion ▷ v **6** susceptibilities **feel like** have an inclination for

feet see FOOT

feign v pretend, sham

feint n **1** sham attack **2** pretence ▷ v **3** make feint

feisty adj **1** (Inf) lively, resilient, and self-reliant **2** (US & Canad) frisky **3** (US & Canad) irritable

felicity n **1** great happiness **2** apt wording **felicitations** pl n congratulations **felicitous** adj

feline adj **1** of cats **2** catlike

fell¹ ❶ v **1** knock down **2** cut down (tree) **feller** n

fell² n mountain, moor

fellow ❶ n (Inf) **1** man, boy **2** associate **3** counterpart **4** member (of society, college etc.) ▷ adj **5** of the same class, associated **fellowship** n

felon n one guilty of felony **felony**

n, pl **-nies** serious crime

felt¹ n **1** soft, matted fabric ▷ v **2** make into, or cover with, felt **3** become matted **felt-tip pen** pen with writing point of pressed fibres

female adj **1** of sex which bears offspring **2** relating to this sex ▷ n **3** one of this sex

feminine ❶ adj **1** of women **2** womanly **feminism** n advocacy of equal rights for women **feminist** n/adj **femininity** n

fen n tract of marshy land

fence ❶ n **1** structure of wire, wood etc. enclosing an area **2** (Sl) dealer in stolen property ▷ v **3** erect fence **4** fight with swords **5** (Sl) deal in stolen property **fencing** n art of swordplay

fend v **1** ward off **2** repel **3** provide (for oneself etc.) **fender** n low metal frame in front of fireplace

fender n (US & Canad) the part of a car body that surrounds the wheels

fennel n fragrant plant

feral adj wild

ferment n **1** substance causing thing to ferment **2** excitement ▷ v **3** (cause to) undergo chemical change with effervescence and

— THESAURUS —

feel v = **experience**, bear; = **touch**, handle, manipulate, finger, stroke, detect, discern, experience, note = **grope**, explore ▷ n = **texture**, finish, touch, surface, surface quality; = **impression**, feeling, air, sense, quality

fell¹ v = **cut down**, cut, level, demolish, knock down

fellow n (Old-fashioned) = **man**, person, individual, character, guy; (Inf) = **associate**, colleague, peer, partner, companion

feminine adj = **womanly**, pretty, soft, gentle, tender ≠ **masculine**

fence n = **barrier**, wall, defence, railings, hedge ▷ v (often with **in** or **off**) = **enclose**, surround, bound,

alteration of properties
fermentation n

fern n plant with feathery fronds

ferocious ❶ adj fierce, savage,
cruel **ferocity** n

ferret n **1** tamed animal like weasel
▷ v **2** drive out with ferrets
3 search about

ferric, ferrous adj pert. to,
containing, iron

ferry ❶ n, pl **-ries 1** boat etc. for
transporting people, vehicles,
across water ▷ v **2** carry, travel, by
ferry

fertile ❶ adj **1** (capable of)
producing offspring, bearing crops
etc. **2** producing abundantly
fertility n **fertilize** v make fertile
fertilization n **fertilizer** n

fervent, fervid adj ardent,
intense **fervour** n

fester v **1** (cause to) form pus
2 rankle **3** become embittered

festival ❶ n **1** day, period of
celebration **2** organized series of
events, performances etc. **festive**
adj joyous, merry **festivity** n, pl
-ties 1 gaiety **2** rejoicing ▷ pl
3 festive proceedings

festoon n **1** loop of flowers,

ribbons etc. ▷ v **2** form, adorn with
festoons

fete n **1** gala, bazaar etc., esp. one
held out of doors ▷ v **2** honour
with festive entertainment

fetid adj stinking

fetish n **1** object believed to have
magical powers **2** object, activity,
to which excessive devotion is paid

fetter n **1** chain for feet **2** check
▷ pl **3** captivity ▷ v **4** chain up
5 restrain

fettle n state of health

fetus, foetus n, pl **-tuses** fully
developed embryo **fetal, foetal**
adj

feud ❶ n **1** long bitter hostility ▷ v
2 carry on feud

fever ❶ n **1** condition of illness
with high body temperature
2 intense nervous excitement
fevered adj **feverish** adj

few ❶ adj **1** not many ▷ pron **2** small
number

fez n, pl **fezzes** red, brimless cap
with tassel

fiancé n person engaged to be
married

fiasco ❶ n, pl **-cos, -coes**
breakdown, total failure

— THESAURUS —

protect, pen

ferocious adj = **fierce**, violent,
savage, ravening, predatory
≠ gentle

ferry n = **ferry boat**, boat, ship,
passenger boat, packet boat ▷ v
= **transport**, bring, carry, ship, take

fertile adj = **productive**, rich, lush,
prolific, abundant **≠ barren**

festival n = **celebration**, fair,

carnival, gala, fête; = **holy day**,
holiday, feast, commemoration,
feast day

feud n = **hostility**, row, conflict,
argument, disagreement ▷ v
= **quarrel**, row, clash, dispute, fall
out

fever n = **excitement**, frenzy,
ferment, agitation, fervour

fiasco n = **flop**, failure, disaster,

fib n/v (tell) trivial lie

fibre ❶ n 1 filament forming part of animal or plant tissue 2 substance that can be spun **fibrous** adj **fibreglass** n material made out of fine glass fibres

fickle adj changeable

fiction ❶ n literary works of the imagination **fictional** adj **fictitious** adj 1 false 2 imaginary

fiddle ❶ n 1 violin 2 (Inf) fraudulent arrangement ▷ v 3 play fiddle 4 fidget 5 (Sl) cheat **fiddling** adj trivial **fiddly** adj small, awkward to handle

fidelity ❶ n faithfulness

fidget v 1 move restlessly ▷ n 2 (oft. pl) restless mood 3 one who fidgets **fidgety** adj

field ❶ n 1 area of (farming) land 2 tract of land rich in specified product 3 players in a game or sport collectively 4 battlefield

5 sphere of knowledge ▷ v 6 (Cricket) stop and return ball 7 send player, team, on to sports field **fielder** n **field day** exciting occasion **fieldwork** n investigation made away from classroom or laboratory

fiend n 1 devil 2 person addicted to something **fiendish** adj

fierce ❶ adj 1 savage, wild, violent 2 intense **fiercely** adv

fiery ❶ adj fierier, fieriest 1 consisting of, or like, fire 2 irritable **fierily** adv

fiesta n carnival

fifteen SEE FIVE

fig n 1 soft, pear-shaped fruit 2 tree bearing this

fight ❶ v fighting, fought 1 struggle against or contend with in battle 2 maintain against opponent 3 settle by combat ▷ n 4 fighting **fighter** n person or

THESAURUS

mess (Inf), catastrophe

fibre n = **thread**, strand, filament, tendril, pile

fiction n = **tale**, story, novel, legend, myth; = **lie**, invention, fabrication, falsehood, untruth

fiddle v (usually with with) = **fidget**, play, finger, tamper, mess about or around; (usually with with) = **tinker**, adjust, interfere, mess about or around ▷ n (Brit Inf) = **fraud**, racket, scam (Sl), fix, swindle

fidelity n = **loyalty**, devotion, allegiance, constancy, faithfulness ≠ **disloyalty**; = **accuracy**, precision, correspondence, closeness, faithfulness

≠ **inaccuracy**

field n = **meadow**, land, green, lea (Poet), pasture; = **speciality**, line, area, department, territory; = **line**, reach, sweep ▷ **retrieve**, return, stop, catch, pick up

fierce adj = **ferocious**, wild, dangerous, cruel, savage ≠ **gentle**; = **intense**, strong, keen, relentless, cut-throat

fiery adj = **burning**, flaming, blazing, on fire, ablaze; = **excitable**, fierce, passionate, irritable, impetuous

fight v = **oppose**, campaign against, dispute, contest, resist; = **battle**, combat, do battle;

aircraft that fights

figment n imaginary thing

figure ❶ n **1** numerical symbol **2** amount, number **3** (bodily) shape **4** (conspicuous) appearance **5** space enclosed by lines **6** diagram, illustration ▷ v **7** calculate **8 figurative** adj (of language) symbolic **figurine** n statuette **figurehead** n nominal leader

filament n **1** fine wire **2** threadlike body

filch v steal, pilfer

file¹ ❶ n **1** (box, folder etc. holding) papers for reference **2** orderly line ▷ v **3** arrange (papers etc.) and put them away for reference **4** march in file **filing** n

file² ❶ n/v (use) roughened tool for smoothing or shaping **filing** n scrap of metal removed

filial adj of, befitting, son or daughter

filibuster v **1** obstruct legislation by making long speeches ▷ n **2** filibustering

filigree n fine tracery or openwork of metal

fill ❶ v **1** make full **2** occupy completely **3** discharge duties of **4** stop up **5** satisfy **6** fulfil **7** become full ▷ n **8** full supply **9** as much as desired **filling** n/adj of metal

fillet n **1** boneless slice of meat, fish **2** narrow strip ▷ v **3** cut into fillets, bone **filleted** adj

fillip n stimulus

filly n, pl **-lies** young female horse

film ❶ n **1** sequence of images projected on screen, creating illusion of movement **2** sensitized celluloid roll used in photography,

— THESAURUS —

= **engage in**, conduct, wage, pursue, carry on ▷ n = **battle**, campaign, movement, struggle; = **conflict**, clash, contest, encounter, confrontation

figure n = **digit**, character, symbol, number, numeral; = **shape**, build, body, frame, proportions; = **personage**, person, individual, character, personality; = **diagram**, drawing, picture, illustration, representation; = **design**, shape, pattern ▷ v (usually with **in**) = **feature**, act, appear, contribute to, play a part; = **calculate**, work out, compute, tot up, total

file¹ n = **folder**, case, portfolio, binder; = **dossier**, record,

information, data, documents ▷ v = **register**, record, enter, log, put on record; = **march**, troop, parade, walk in line, walk behind one another

file² v = **smooth**, shape, polish, rub, scrape

fill v = **swell**, expand, become bloated, extend, balloon; = **pack**, crowd, squeeze, cram, throng; = **stock**, supply, pack, load; = **plug**, close, stop, seal, cork; = **saturate**, charge, pervade, permeate, imbue

film n = **movie**, picture, flick (SI), motion picture; = **cinema**, the movies ▷ v = **photograph**, record, shoot, video, videotape cinematography **3** thin skin or layer ▷ *adj* **4** connected with cinema ▷ *v* **5** photograph with cine camera **6** make cine film of **7** cover, become covered, with film **filmy** *adj* gauzy

filth *n* **1** disgusting dirt **2** obscenity **filthiness** *n* **filthy** *adj*

fin *n* **1** propelling organ of fish **2** anything like this

final ❶ *adj* **1** at the end **2** conclusive ▷ *n* **3** game, heat, examination etc., coming at end of series **finale** *n* closing part of musical composition **finalist** *n* competitor in a final **finalize** *v* **finally** *adv*

finance ❶ *n* **1** management of money **2** money resources ▷ *v* **3** find capital for **financial** *adj* **financier** *n*

finch *n*, *pl* **finches** one of family of small singing birds

find ❶ *v* **finding**, **found 1** come across **2** experience, discover

3 (*Law*) give verdict ▷ *n* **4** (valuable) thing found **finding** *n* conclusion from investigation

fine¹ ❶ *adj* **1** of high quality **2** not rainy **3** delicate **4** subtle **5** pure **6** in small particles **7** (*Inf*) healthy, at ease **8** satisfactory **finery** *n* showy dress **finesse** *n* skilful management **fine art** art produced for its aesthetic value **fine-tune** *v* make small adjustments

fine² ❶ *n* **1** sum fixed as penalty ▷ *v* **2** punish by fine

finger ❶ *n* **1** one of the jointed branches of the hand **2** various things like this ▷ *v* **3** touch with fingers **fingerprint** *n* impression of tip of finger

finicky *adj* fussy

finish ❶ *v* **1** bring, come to an end, conclude **2** complete **3** perfect ▷ *n* **4** end **5** way in which thing is finished **6** final appearance

finite *adj* bounded, limited

fiord see FJORD

——————————— THESAURUS ———————————

final *adj* = **last**, latest, closing, finishing, concluding ≠ **first**; = **irrevocable**, absolute, definitive, decided, settled

finance *v* = **fund**, back, support, pay for, guarantee ▷ *n* = **economics**, business, money, banking, accounts

find *v* = **discover**, uncover, spot, locate, detect ≠ **lose**; = **obtain**, get, come by ▷ *n* = **discovery**, catch, asset, bargain, acquisition

fine¹ *adj* = **excellent**, good, striking, masterly, very good ≠ **poor**;

= **satisfactory**, good, all right, suitable, acceptable; = **thin**, light, narrow, wispy, light; = **stylish**, expensive, elegant, refined, tasteful; = **exquisite**, delicate, fragile, dainty; = **minute**, exact, precise, nice

fine² *n* = **penalty**, damages, punishment, forfeit, financial penalty ▷ *v* = **penalize**, charge, punish

finger *v* = **touch**, feel, handle, play with, manipulate

finish *v* = **stop**, close, complete,

fir n coniferous tree

fire ❶ n 1 state of burning 2 mass of burning fuel 3 destructive burning 4 device for heating a room etc. 5 shooting of guns 6 ardour ▷ v 7 discharge (firearm) 8 (Inf) dismiss from employment 9 bake 10 make burn 11 inspire 12 explode 13 begin to burn 14 become excited **firearm** n gun, rifle, pistol etc. **fire brigade** organized body to put out fires **fire engine** vehicle with apparatus for extinguishing fires **fire escape** means, esp. stairs, for escaping from burning buildings **firefly** n, pl -flies beetle that glows in dark **fireguard** n protective grating in front of fire **fireman** n member of fire brigade **fireplace** n recess in room for fire **fire station** building housing fire-fighting vehicles and equipment **firework** n 1 device to give spectacular effects by explosions and coloured sparks ▷ pl 2 outburst of temper **firing squad** group of soldiers ordered to execute offender

firm ❶ adj 1 solid, fixed, stable ▷ v 2 make, become firm ▷ n 3 commercial enterprise

first adj 1 earlier in time or order 2 foremost in rank or position **First Nations** pl n (Canad) Canadian aboriginal communities **First Peoples** pl n (Canad) a collective term for the Native Canadian peoples, the Inuit, and the Métis

fiscal adj of government finances

fish n, pl fish, fishes 1 vertebrate cold-blooded animal with gills, living in water ▷ v 2 (attempt to) catch fish 3 try to get information indirectly **fishy** adj 1 of, like, or full of fish 2 (Inf) suspicious **fisherman** n **fishmonger** n seller of fish

fissure n cleft, split **fission** n 1 splitting 2 reproduction by division of living cells 3 splitting of atomic nucleus

fist n clenched hand **fisticuffs** pl n fighting

— THESAURUS —

conclude, cease ≠ **start**; = **end**, stop, conclude, wind up, terminate; = **consume**, dispose of, devour, polish off, eat; = **use up**, empty, exhaust; = **coat**, polish, stain, texture, wax ▷ n = **end**, close, conclusion, run-in, completion ≠ **beginning**; = **surface**, polish, shine, texture, glaze

fire n = **flames**, blaze, combustion, inferno, conflagration; = **passion**, energy, spirit, enthusiasm, excitement; = **bombardment**, shooting, firing, shelling, hail ▷ v = **let off**, shoot, shell, set off, discharge; = **shoot**, explode, discharge, detonate, pull the trigger; (Inf) = **dismiss**, sack (Inf), get rid of, discharge, lay off

firm adj = **hard**, solid, dense, set, stiff ≠ **soft**, fixed, rooted, stable, steady ≠ **unstable**; = **secure**, close, tight, steady, unshakeable; = **strong**, close, tight, steady, unshakeable; = **determined**, resolved, definite, set on, adamant ≠ **wavering**

fit¹ ❶ v **fitting, fitted** 1 be suited to 2 be properly adjusted 3 adjust 4 supply ▷ adj 5 well-suited 6 proper 7 in good health ▷ n 8 way anything fits **fitness** n **fitter** n **fitting** adj 1 appropriate ▷ n 2 attachment 3 action of fitting

fit² ❷ n 1 seizure with convulsions 2 passing state, mood **fitful** adj spasmodic

five adj/n cardinal number after four **fifth** adj ordinal number **fifteen** adj/n ten plus five **fifteenth** adj **fiftieth** adj **fifty** adj/n ten tens

fix ❶ v 1 fasten, make firm 2 determine 3 repair 4 (Inf) influence unfairly ▷ n 5 difficult situation 6 position of ship, aircraft ascertained by radar, observation etc. 7 (Sl) dose of narcotic drug **fixation** n obsession **fixed** adj **fixture** n 1 thing fixed in position 2 (date for) sporting event

fizz ❶ v 1 hiss ▷ n 2 hissing noise 3 effervescent liquid **fizzy** adj

fizzle v splutter weakly **fizzle out** (Inf) fail

fjord, fiord n (esp. in Norway) long, narrow inlet of sea

flabby adj **-bier, -biest** 1 limp 2 too fat 3 weak and lacking purpose **flabbiness** n

flag¹ ❶ n 1 banner, piece of bunting as standard or signal ▷ v 2 inform by flag signals **flagpole, flagstaff** n pole for flag **flagship** n 1 admiral's ship 2 most important item

flag² ❷ v lose vigour

flagon n large bottle

flagrant adj blatant

flail n 1 instrument for threshing corn by hand ▷ v 2 beat with, move as, flail

flair ❶ n 1 natural ability 2 elegant style

flak n 1 anti-aircraft fire 2 (Inf) adverse criticism

— THESAURUS —

fit¹ v = **adapt**, shape, arrange, alter, adjust; = **place**, insert, connect; = **suit**, meet, match, belong to, conform to ▷ adj = **appropriate**, suitable, right, becoming, seemly ≠ **inappropriate**; = **healthy**, strong, robust, sturdy, well ≠ **unfit**

fit² n = **seizure**, attack, bout, spasm, convulsion; = **bout**, burst, outbreak, outburst, spell

fix v = **place**, join, stick, attach, set; = **decide**, set, choose, establish, determine; = **arrange**, organize, sort out, see to, fix up; = **repair**,

mend, service, correct, restore; = **focus**, direct at, fasten on; (Inf) = **rig**, set up (Inf), influence, manipulate, fiddle (Inf) ▷ n (Inf) = **mess**, corner, difficulty, dilemma, embarrassment

fizz v = **bubble**, froth, fizzle, effervesce, produce bubbles

flag¹ v = **banner**, standard, colours, pennant, ensign

flag² v = **weaken**, fade, weary, falter, wilt

flair n = **ability**, feel, talent, gift, genius; = **style**, taste, dash, chic,

flake ❶ n 1 small, thin piece
2 piece chipped off ▷ v 3 (cause to)
peel off in flakes **flaky** adj

flambé v flambéing, flambéed
cook in flaming brandy

flamboyant ❶ adj showy
flamboyance n

flame ❶ n 1 burning gas, esp.
above fire ▷ v 2 give out flames

flamenco n, pl -cos rhythmical
Spanish dance

flamingo n, pl -gos, -goes large
pink bird with long neck and legs

flammable adj liable to catch fire

flan n open sweet or savoury tart

flange n projecting rim

flank ❶ n 1 part of side between
hips and ribs 2 side of anything ▷ v
3 be at, move along either side of

flannel n 1 soft woollen fabric
2 small piece of cloth for washing
face

flap ❶ v flapping, flapped
1 move (wings, arms etc.) as bird
flying ▷ n 2 act of flapping
3 broad piece of anything hanging

from one side 4 (Inf) state of panic

flapjack n chewy biscuit

flare ❶ v 1 blaze with unsteady
flame 2 spread outwards
▷ n 3 instance of flaring 4 signal
light

flash ❶ n 1 sudden burst of light or
flame 2 very short time ▷ v
3 break into sudden flame 4 move
very fast 5 (cause to) gleam **flash,
flashy** adj showy, sham
flashback n break in narrative to
introduce what has taken place
previously

flask n type of bottle

flat¹ ❶ adj flatter, flattest 1 level
2 at full length 3 smooth
4 downright 5 dull 6 (Mus) below
true pitch 7 (of tyre) deflated 8 (of
battery) dead ▷ n 9 what is flat
10 (Mus) note half tone below
natural pitch **flatly** adv **flatten** v
flatfish n type of fish with broad,
flat body **flat rate** the same in all
cases **flat out** at, with maximum
speed or effort

---

elegance

flake n = chip, scale, layer, peeling,
shaving ▷ v = chip, peel (off),
blister

flamboyant adj = showy,
elaborate, extravagant, ornate,
ostentatious; = colourful, striking,
brilliant, glamorous, stylish

flame n = fire, light, spark, glow,
blaze ▷ v = burn, flash, shine,
glow, blaze

flank n = side, hip, thigh, loin

flap v = flutter, wave, flail ▷ n
= flutter, beating, waving, shaking,

swinging; (Inf) = panic, state (Inf),
agitation, commotion, sweat (Inf)

flare n = flame, burst, flash, blaze,
glare ▷ v = blaze, flame, glare,
flicker, burn up

flash n = blaze, burst, spark, beam,
streak ▷ v = blaze, shine, beam,
sparkle, flare; = speed, race, shoot,
fly, tear; (Inf) = show quickly,
display, expose, exhibit, flourish
▷ adj (Inf) = ostentatious, smart,
trendy, showy

flat¹ adj = even, level, levelled,
smooth, horizontal ≠ uneven;

flat² ❶ *n* suite of rooms in larger building

flatter ❶ *v* **1** praise insincerely **2** gratify **flatterer** *n* **flattery** *n*

flattie *n* (*NZ & S Afr, Inf*) flat tyre

flatulent *adj* suffering from, generating (excess) gases from intestines **flatulence** *n*

flaunt *v* show off

flavour ❶ *n* **1** distinctive taste, savour ▷ *v* **2** give flavour to **flavouring** *n*

flaw ❶ *n* defect, blemish **flawless** *adj*

flax *n* plant grown for its fibres, spun into linen thread **flaxen** *adj* **1** of flax **2** light yellow

flay *v* **1** strip skin of **2** criticize severely

flea *n* small, wingless, jumping, blood-sucking insect

fleck *n/v* (make) small mark(s)

flee ❶ *v* **fleeing, fled** run away from (a place, danger etc.)

fleece *n* **1** sheep's wool ▷ *v* **2** rob **fleecy** *adj*

fleet¹ ❶ *n* **1** number of warships organized as unit **2** number of ships, cars etc.

fleet² *adj* **1** swift **2** nimble **fleeting** *adj* passing quickly

flesh ❶ *n* **1** soft part, muscular substance, between skin and bone **2** in plants, pulp **3** fat **4** sensual appetites **fleshy** *adj* plump, pulpy **in the flesh** in person, actually present

flex ❶ *n* **1** flexible insulated electric cable ▷ *v* **2** bend, be bent **flexible** *adj* **1** easily bent **2** manageable **3** adaptable **flexibility** *n*

flick ❶ *v* **1** strike lightly, jerk ▷ *n* **2** light blow **3** jerk ▷ *pl* **4** (*Sl*) cinema

flicker ❶ *v* **1** burn, shine, unsteadily ▷ *n* **2** unsteady light or

— THESAURUS —

= **punctured**, collapsed, burst, blown out, deflated; = **used up**, finished, empty, drained, expired; = **absolute**, firm, positive, explicit, definite **flat out** (*Inf*) = **at full speed**, all out, to the full, hell for leather (*Inf*), as hard as possible

flat² *n* = **apartment**, rooms, quarters, digs, suite

flatter *v* = **praise**, compliment, pander to, sweet-talk (*Inf*), wheedle; = **suit**, become, enhance, set off, embellish

flavour *n* = **taste**, seasoning, flavouring, savour, relish ≠ **blandness**; = **quality**, feeling, feel, style, character ▷ *v* = **season**, spice, add flavour to, enrich, infuse

flaw *n* = **weakness**, failing, defect, weak spot, fault

flee *v* = **run away**, escape, bolt, fly, take off (*Inf*)

fleet¹ *n* = **navy**, task force, flotilla, armada

flesh *n* = **fat**, muscle, tissue, brawn; = **fatness**, fat, adipose tissue, corpulence, weight; = **physical nature**, carnality, human nature, flesh and blood, sinful nature

flick *v* = **jerk**, pull, tug, lurch, jolt; = **strike**, tap, remove quickly, hit, touch

flicker *v* = **twinkle**, flash, sparkle, flare, shimmer; = **flutter**, waver, movement **3** slight trace

flight¹ ❶ n **1** act or manner of flying through air **2** group of flying birds or aircraft **3** power of flying **4** stairs between two landings **flighty** adj frivolous **flight recorder** electronic device in aircraft storing information about its flight

flight² ❶ n running away

flimsy adj **-sier, -siest 1** delicate **2** weak, thin

flinch v draw back, wince

fling ❶ v **flinging, flung 1** throw, send, move with force ▷ n **2** throw **3** spell of indulgence **4** vigorous dance

flint n hard steel-grey stone

flip ❶ v **flipping, flipped 1** flick lightly **2** turn over **flippant** adj treating serious things lightly **flipper** n limb, fin for swimming

flirt ❶ v play with another's affections ▷ n **2** person who flirts **flirtation** n **flirtatious** adj

flit v **flitting, flitted** pass lightly and rapidly

float ❶ v **1** rest on surface of liquid **2** be suspended freely **3** in commerce, get (company) started **4** obtain loan ▷ n **5** anything small that floats **6** small delivery vehicle **7** motor vehicle carrying tableau etc. **8** sum of money used to provide change **floating** adj moving about, changing **flotation** n

flock ❶ n **1** number of animals of one kind together **2** religious congregation ▷ v **3** gather in a crowd

floe n floating ice

flog ❶ v **flogging, flogged 1** beat with whip, stick etc. **2** (Sl) sell

flood ❶ n **1** inundation, overflow of water **2** rising of tide

quiver, vibrate ▷ n = **glimmer**, flash, spark, flare, gleam; = **trace**, breath, spark, glimmer, iota

flight¹ n = **journey**, trip, voyage; = **aviation**, flying, aeronautics, ability to fly; = **flock**, group, unit, cloud, formation

flight² n = **escape**, fleeing, departure, retreat, exit

fling v = **throw**, toss, hurl, launch, cast ▷ n = **binge**, good time, bash, party, spree (Inf)

flip v = **flick**, switch, snap, slick ▷ n = **toss**, throw, spin, snap, flick

flirt v = **chat up**, lead on (Inf), make advances at, make eyes at,

philander; (usually with **with**) = **toy with**, consider, entertain, play with, dabble in ▷ n = **tease**, philanderer, coquette, heart-breaker

float v = **glide**, sail, drift, move gently, bob; = **be buoyant**, hang, hover ≠ **sink**; = **launch**, offer, sell, set up, promote ≠ **dissolve**

flock n = **herd**, group, flight, drove, colony; = **crowd**, company, group, host, collection ▷ v = **stream**, crowd, mass, swarm, throng

flog v = **beat**, whip, lash, thrash, whack

flood n = **deluge**, downpour, inundation, tide, overflow;

3 outpouring ▷ *v* **4** inundate **5** cover, fill with water **6** arrive, move etc. in great numbers

floodlight *n* broad, intense beam of artificial light **floodlit** *adj*

floor ❶ *n* **1** lower surface of room **2** set of rooms on one level **3** (right to speak in) legislative hall ▷ *v* **4** supply with floor **5** knock down **6** confound **flooring** *n* material for floors

flop ❶ *v* flopping, flopped **1** bend, fall, collapse loosely **2** fall flat on water etc. **3** (*Inf*) fail ▷ *n* **4** flopping movement or sound **5** (*Inf*) failure **floppy** *adj* **floppy disk** (*Comp*) flexible magnetic disk that stores information

flora *n* plants of a region **floral** *adj* of flowers **florist** *n* dealer in flowers

floret *n* small flower

florid *adj* **1** with red, flushed complexion **2** ornate

floss *n* mass of fine, silky fibres

flotilla *n* **1** fleet of small vessels **2** group of destroyers

flotsam *n* floating wreckage

flounce¹ *v* **1** go, move abruptly and impatiently ▷ *n* **2** fling, jerk of body or limb

flounce² *n* ornamental gathered strip on woman's garment

flounder¹ ❶ *v* plunge and struggle, esp. in water or mud

flounder² *n* flatfish

flour *n* powder prepared by sifting and grinding wheat etc.

flourish ❶ *v* **1** thrive **2** brandish **3** wave about ▷ *n* **4** ornamental curve **5** showy gesture **6** fanfare

flow ❶ *v* **1** glide along as stream **2** circulate, as the blood **3** hang loose **4** be present in abundance ▷ *n* **5** act, instance of flowing **6** quantity that flows **7** rise of tide

flower ❶ *n* **1** brightly coloured part of plant from which fruit is developed **2** bloom, blossom **3** choicest part ▷ *v* **4** produce

— THESAURUS —

= **torrent**, flow, rush, stream, tide; = **series**, stream, avalanche, barrage, spate ▷ *v* = **immerse**, swamp, submerge, inundate, drown; = **pour over**, swamp, run over, overflow, inundate

floor *v* (*Inf*) = **disconcert**, stump, baffle, confound, throw (*Inf*); = **knock down**, fell, knock over, prostrate, deck (*Sl*)

flop *v* = **slump**, fall, drop, collapse, sink; = **hang down**, hang, dangle, sag, droop ▷ *n* (*Inf*) = **failure**, disaster, fiasco, debacle, washout (*Inf*) ≠ **success**

flounder¹ *v* = **falter**, struggle, stall, slow down, run into trouble

flourish *v* = **thrive**, increase, advance, progress, boom ≠ **fail**; = **succeed**, move ahead, go places (*Inf*) ▷ *n* = **wave**, sweep, brandish, swish, swing; = **show**, display, parade, fanfare

flow *v* = **run**, course, rush, sweep, move; = **pour**, move, sweep, flood, stream; = **issue**, follow, result, emerge, spring ▷ *n* = **stream**, current, movement, motion, course

flower *n* = **bloom**, blossom, efflorescence; = **elite**, best, prime, flowers **5** come to prime condition **flowery** adj **flowerbed** n ground for growing flowers

fl. oz. fluid ounce

flu n short for INFLUENZA

fluctuate ❶ v vary, rise and fall, undulate **fluctuation** n

flue n chimney

fluent ❶ adj speaking, writing easily and well **fluency** n

fluff n **1** soft, feathery stuff ▷ v **2** make or become soft, light **3** (Inf) make mistake **fluffy** adj

fluid ❶ adj **1** flowing easily **2** flexible ▷ n **3** gas or liquid **fluid ounce** unit of capacity 1/20 of pint

fluke n stroke of luck

flummox v bewilder, perplex

flunky, flunkey pl **flunkies, flunkeys 1** liveried manservant **2** servile person

fluoride n salt containing fluorine **fluorine** n nonmetallic element, yellowish gas

flurry ❶ n, pl -**ries 1** gust **2** bustle **3** fluttering ▷ v **4** agitate

flush¹ ❶ v **1** blush **2** flow suddenly or violently **3** be excited **4** cleanse (e.g. toilet) by rush of water **5** excite ▷ n **6** blush **7** rush of water **8** excitement **9** freshness

flush² ❶ adj **1** level with surrounding surface **2** overflowing

fluster v **1** make or become nervous, agitated ▷ n **2** agitation

flute n **1** wind instrument with blowhole in side **2** groove ▷ v **3** play on flute **4** make grooves in

flutter ❶ v **1** flap (as wings) rapidly **2** quiver **3** be or make agitated ▷ n **4** flapping movement **5** agitation **6** (Inf) modest wager

flux n **1** discharge **2** constant succession of changes **3** substance mixed with metal in soldering etc.

fly¹ ❶ v flying, flew, flown pl **flies 1** move through air on wings or in aircraft **2** pass quickly **3** float

----- THESAURUS -----

finest, pick ▷ v = **bloom**, open, mature, flourish, unfold; = **blossom**, grow, develop, progress, mature

fluctuate v = **change**, swing, vary, alternate, waver

fluent adj = **effortless**, natural, articulate, well-versed, voluble

fluid n = **liquid**, solution, juice, liquor, sap ▷ adj = **liquid**, flowing, watery, molten, melted ≠ **solid**

flurry n = **commotion**, stir, bustle, flutter, excitement; = **gust**, shower, gale, swirl, squall

flush¹ v = **blush**, colour, glow, redden, turn red; (often with **out**)

= **cleanse**, wash out, rinse out, flood, swill ▷ n = **blush**, colour, glow, reddening, redness

flush² adj = **level**, even, true, flat, square

flutter v = **beat**, flap, tremble, ripple, waver ▷ n = **tremor**, tremble, shiver, shudder, palpitation; = **vibration**, twitching, quiver; = **agitation**, state (Inf), confusion, excitement, flap (Inf)

fly¹ v = **take wing**, soar, glide, wing, sail; = **pilot**, control, operate, steer, manoeuvre; = **airlift**, send by plane, take by plane, take in an aircraft;

loosely **4** run away **5** operate aircraft **6** cause to fly **7** set flying ▷ *n* **8** (zip or buttons fastening) opening in trousers **flyer, flier** *n* **1** small advertising leaflet **2** aviator **flying** *adj* hurried, brief **flying colours** conspicuous success **flying saucer** unidentified disc-shaped flying object **flying squad** special detachment of police, soldiers etc., ready to act quickly **flying start** very good start **flyover** *n* road passing over another by bridge **flywheel** *n* heavy wheel regulating speed of machine

fly² *n, pl* **flies** two-winged insect, esp. common housefly

foal *n* young of horse

foam ❶ *n* **1** collection of small bubbles on liquid **2** light cellular solid ▷ *v* **3** (cause to) produce foam **foamy** *adj*

fob *v* (with *off*) ignore, dismiss in offhand manner

focus ❶ *n, pl* **-cuses, -ci** point at which rays meet **2** state of optical image when it is clearly defined **3** point on which interest, activity is

centred ▷ *v* **4** bring to focus **5** concentrate **focal** *adj*

fodder *n* bulk food for livestock

foe ❶ *n* enemy

fog ❶ *n* **1** thick mist ▷ *v* **2** cover in fog **3** puzzle **foggy** *adj* **foghorn** *n* large horn to warn ships

fogey, fogy *n, pl* **-geys, -gies** old-fashioned person

foible *n* minor weakness, slight peculiarity of character

foil¹ ❶ *v* **1** baffle, frustrate ▷ *n* **2** blunt sword for fencing

foil² ❶ *n* **1** metal in thin sheet **2** anything which sets off another thing to advantage

foist *v* (usu. with *on*) force, impose on

fold¹ ❶ *v* **1** double up, bend part of **2** interlace (arms) **3** clasp (in arms) **4** (*Cookery*) mix gently **5** become folded **6** admit of being folded **7** (*Inf*) fail ▷ *n* **8** folding **9** line made by folding **folder** *n* binder, file for loose papers

fold² *n* enclosure for sheep

foliage *n* leaves collectively

folio *n, pl* **-lios 1** sheet of paper folded in half to make two leaves of

= **flutter**, wave, float, flap; = **display**, show, flourish, brandish; = **rush**, race, shoot, career, speed

foam *n* = **froth**, spray, bubbles, lather, suds ▷ *v* = **bubble**, boil, fizz, froth, lather

focus *v* = **concentrate**, centre, spotlight, direct, aim ▷ *n* = **centre**, focal point, central point, heart, target

foe *n* = **enemy**, rival, opponent,

adversary, antagonist ≠ **friend**

fog *n* = **mist**, gloom, haze, smog, murk

foil¹ *v* = **thwart**, stop, defeat, disappoint, counter

foil² *n* = **complement**, relief, contrast, antithesis

fold¹ *v* = **bend**, crease, double over; (*Inf*) = **go bankrupt**, fail, crash, collapse, founder ▷ *n* = **crease**, gather, bend, overlap, wrinkle book **2** book of largest common size

folk ❶ *n* **1** people in general **2** family, relative **3** race of people **folksy** *adj* simple, unpretentious **folklore** *n* tradition, customs, beliefs popularly held

follicle *n* small sac

follow ❶ *v* **1** go or come after **2** accompany **3** keep to **4** be a consequence of **5** take as guide **6** grasp meaning of **7** have keen interest in **follower** *n* disciple, supporter **following** *adj* **1** about to be mentioned ▷ *n* **2** body of supporters

folly ❶ *n, pl* **-lies** foolishness

foment *v* foster, stir up

fond ❶ *adj* tender, loving **fondness** *n* fond of having liking for

fondant *n* flavoured paste of sugar and water

fondle *v* caress

font *n* bowl for baptismal water

fontanelle *n* soft, membranous gap between bones of baby's skull

food ❶ *n* **1** solid nourishment **2** what one eats

fool¹ ❶ *n* **1** silly, empty-headed person **2** (*Hist*) jester ▷ *v* **3** delude **4** dupe **5** act as fool **foolhardy** *adj* foolishly adventurous **foolish** *adj* **1** silly, stupid **2** unwise **foolishness** *n* **foolproof** *adj* unable to fail **foolscap** *n* size of paper

fool² *n* dessert made from fruit and cream

foot ❶ *n, pl* **feet 1** lowest part of leg, from ankle down **2** lower part of anything, base, stand **3** end of bed etc. **4** measure of twelve inches ▷ *v* **5** pay cost of **footage** *n* amount of film used **footing** *n* basis, foundation **football** *n* **1** game played with large blown-up ball **2** the ball **footballer** *n*

folk *n* = **people**, persons, individuals, men and women, humanity; (*usually plural*) = **family**, parents, relations, relatives, tribe

follow *v* = **accompany**, attend, escort, go behind, tag along behind; = **pursue**, track, dog, hunt, chase ≠ **avoid**; = **come after**, go after, come next ≠ **precede**; = **result**, issue, develop, spring, flow; = **obey**, observe, adhere to, stick to, heed ≠ **ignore**; = **succeed**, replace, come after, take over from, come next; = **understand**, realize, appreciate, take in, grasp

folly *n* = **foolishness**, nonsense,

madness, stupidity, indiscretion ≠ **wisdom**

fond *adj* = **loving**, caring, warm, devoted, tender ≠ **indifferent**; = **unrealistic**, empty, naive, vain, foolish ≠ **sensible**

food *n* = **nourishment**, fare, diet, rations, nutrition

fool¹ *n* = **simpleton**, idiot, mug (*Brit Sl*), dummy (*Sl*), git (*Brit Sl*) ≠ **genius**; = **dupe**, mug (*Brit Sl*), sucker (*Sl*), stooge (*Sl*), laughing stock; = **jester**, clown, harlequin, buffoon, court jester ▷ *v* = **deceive**, mislead, delude, trick, take in

foothills pl n hills at foot of mountain **foothold** n place giving secure grip for the foot **footlights** pl n lights across front of stage

footloose adj free from ties

footman n male servant in livery

footnote n note of reference or explanation printed at foot of page

footprint n mark left by foot

footstep n 1 step in walking 2 sound made by walking

footwear n anything worn to cover feet **footwork** n skilful use of the feet in football etc.

footle v (Inf) loiter aimlessly **footling** adj trivial

for prep 1 directed to 2 because of 3 instead of 4 towards 5 on account of 6 in favour of 7 respecting 8 during 9 in search of 10 in payment of 11 in the character of 12 in spite of ▷ conj 13 because

forage n 1 food for cattle and horses ▷ v 2 collect forage 3 make roving search

foray ❶ n raid, inroad

forbear v 1 cease 2 refrain (from) 3 be patient **forbearance** n

forbid ❶ v 1 prohibit 2 refuse to allow **forbidden** adj **forbidding**

adj uninviting, threatening

force ❶ n 1 strength, power 2 compulsion 3 that which tends to produce a change in a physical system 4 body of troops, police etc. 5 group of people organized for particular task 6 validity 7 vigour ▷ v 8 compel 9 produce by effort, strength 10 break open 11 hasten maturity of **forced** adj 1 compulsory 2 unnatural **forceful** adj powerful, persuasive **forcible** adj done by force

forceps pl n surgical pincers

ford n 1 shallow place where river may be crossed ▷ v 2 cross river

fore adj 1 in front ▷ n 2 front part

forearm n 1 arm between wrist and elbow ▷ v 2 arm beforehand

forebear n ancestor

forecast ❶ v -casting, -cast 1 estimate beforehand (esp. weather) ▷ n 2 prediction

forecastle n forward raised part of ship

foreclose v take away power of redeeming (mortgage)

forecourt n open space in front of building

forefather n ancestor

THESAURUS

foray n = raid, sally, incursion, inroad, attack

forbid v = prohibit, ban, disallow, exclude, rule out ≠ permit

force v = compel, make, drive, press, oblige; = push, thrust, propel; = break open, blast, wrench, prise, wrest ▷ n = compulsion, pressure, violence,

constraint, oppression; = power, might, pressure, energy, strength ≠ weakness; = intensity, vigour, vehemence, fierceness, emphasis; = army, unit, company, host, troop

forecast n = prediction, prognosis, guess, prophecy, conjecture ▷ v = predict, anticipate, foresee, foretell, divine

forefinger *n* finger next to thumb

forefront ❶ *n* most active prominent position

foregoing *adj* going before, preceding **foregone** *adj* determined beforehand

foreground *n* part of view nearest observer

forehand *adj* (of stroke in racket games) made with inner side of wrist leading

forehead *n* part of face above eyebrows and between temples

foreign ❶ *adj* 1 not of, or in, one's own country 2 relating to other countries 3 strange **foreigner** *n*

foreman *n* 1 one in charge of work 2 leader of jury

foremost *adj/adv* first in time, place, importance etc.

forensic *adj* connected with a court of law **forensic medicine** application of medical knowledge in legal matters

forerunner *n* one who goes before, precursor

foresee ❶ *v* see beforehand

foreshadow *v* show, suggest beforehand

foresight *n* 1 foreseeing 2 care for future

foreskin *n* skin that covers the tip of the penis

forest *n* area with heavy growth of trees **forestry** *n*

forestall *v* prevent, guard against in advance

foretaste *n* experience of something to come

foretell *v* prophesy

forethought *n* thoughtful consideration of future events

forever, for ever ❶ *adv* 1 always 2 eternally 3 (*Inf*) for a long time

forewarn *v* warn, caution in advance

foreword *n* preface

forfeit ❶ *n* 1 thing lost by crime or fault 2 penalty, fine ▷ *adj* lost by crime or fault ▷ *v* 4 lose by penalty

forge¹ *v* advance steadily

forge² ❶ *n* 1 place where metal is worked, smithy ▷ *v* 2 shape (metal) by heating and hammering 3 counterfeit **forger** *n* **forgery** *n* 1 counterfeiting 2 counterfeit thing

forefront *n* = **lead**, centre, front, fore, spearhead

foreign *adj* = **alien**, exotic, unknown, strange, imported ≠ **native**; = **uncharacteristic**, inappropriate, inapposite

foremost *adj* = **leading**, best, highest, chief, prime

foresee *v* = **predict**, forecast, anticipate, envisage, prophesy

forever *adv* = **evermore**, always, ever, for good, for keeps; = **constantly**, always, all the time, continually, endlessly

forfeit *v* = **relinquish**, lose, give up, surrender, renounce ▷ *n* = **penalty**, fine, damages, forfeiture, loss

forge² *v* = **form**, build, create, establish, set up; = **fake**, copy, reproduce, imitate, counterfeit; = **create**, make, work, found, form

forget ❶ v -getting, -got, -gotten lose memory of, neglect, overlook **forgetful** adj liable to forget **forget-me-not** n plant with small blue flowers

forgive ❶ v -giving, -gave, -given 1 cease to blame or hold resentment against 2 pardon **forgiveness** n

forgo v 1 go without 2 give up

fork ❶ n 1 pronged instrument for eating food 2 pronged tool for digging or lifting 3 division into branches ▷ v 4 branch 5 dig, lift, throw, with fork 6 make fork-shaped

forlorn adj 1 forsaken 2 desperate

form ❶ n 1 shape, visible appearance 2 structure 3 nature 4 species, kind 5 regularly drawn up document 6 condition 7 class in school 8 customary way of

doing things 9 bench ▷ v 10 shape, organize 11 conceive 12 make part of 13 come into existence or shape **formation** n 1 forming 2 thing formed **formative** adj

formal ❶ adj 1 ceremonial, according to rule 2 of outward form 3 stiff **formality** n, pl -ties 1 observance required by custom 2 condition of being formal **formalize** v make official **formally** adv

format ❶ n size and shape of book etc.

former ❶ adj 1 earlier in time 2 of past times 3 first named ▷ pron 4 first named thing or person or fact **formerly** adv previously

Formica® n material used for heat-resistant surfaces

formidable ❶ adj 1 to be feared

——————————— THESAURUS ———————————

forget v = **neglect**, overlook, omit, not remember, be remiss; = **leave behind**, lose, lose sight of, mislay, ignore

forgive v = **excuse**, pardon, not hold something against, understand, acquit ≠ **blame**

fork v = **branch**, part, separate, split, divide

form n = **type**, sort, kind, variety, class; = **shape**, formation, configuration, structure, pattern; = **condition**, health, shape, nick (Inf), fitness; = **document**, paper, sheet, questionnaire, application; = **procedure**, etiquette, use, custom, convention; = **class**, year, set, rank, grade ▷ v = **arrange**,

combine, line up, organize, assemble; = **make**, produce, fashion, build, create; = **constitute**, make up, compose, comprise, start; = **take shape**, grow, develop, materialize, rise; = **draw up**, devise, formulate, organize

formal adj = **serious**, stiff, detached, official, correct ≠ **informal**; = **official**, authorized, endorsed, certified, solemn; = **ceremonial**, traditional, solemn, ritualistic, dressy

format n = **arrangement**, form, style, make-up, look

former adj = **previous**, one-time, erstwhile, earlier, prior ≠ **current**

formidable adj = **impressive**,

2 overwhelming **3** likely to be
difficult

formula ❶ n, pl **-las, -lae 1** set
form of words, rule **2** (Maths) rule,
fact expressed in symbols and
figures **formulate** v

forsake v **-saking, -sook, -saken**
1 abandon, desert **2** give up

forswear v **-swearing, -swore,**
-sworn 1 renounce, deny
2 perjure

fort ❶ n stronghold

forte¹ ❶ n one's strong point, that
in which one excels

forte² adv (Mus) loudly

forth ❶ adv onwards, into view
forthcoming adj **1** about to come
2 ready when wanted **3** willing to
talk **forthwith** adv at once

forthright adj outspoken

fortify ❶ v **-fying, -fied**
strengthen **fortification** n

fortitude ❶ n endurance

fortnight n two weeks

fortress ❶ n fortified place

fortuitous adj accidental

fortune ❶ n **1** good luck **2** wealth
3 chance **fortunate** adj
fortunately adv

forty pl **-ties** see FOUR

forum n (place or medium for)
meeting, discussion or debate

forward ❶ adj **1** lying in front of
2 onward **3** presumptuous
4 advanced **5** relating to the future
▷ n **6** player in various team games
▷ adv **7** towards the future
8 towards the front, to the front,
into view ▷ v **9** help forward
10 send, dispatch **forwards** adv

fossick v (Aust & NZ) search, esp.
for gold or precious stones

fossil n remnant or impression of
animal or plant, preserved in earth

THESAURUS

great, powerful, tremendous,
mighty; = **intimidating**,
threatening, terrifying, menacing,
dismaying ≠ **encouraging**

formula n = **method**, plan, policy,
rule, principle

fort n = **fortress**, keep, camp,
tower, castle

forte¹ n = **speciality**, strength,
talent, strong point, métier ≠ **weak**
point

forth adv (Formal or Old-fashioned)
= **forward**, out, away, ahead,
onward

fortify v = **protect**, defend,
strengthen, reinforce, support;
= **strengthen**, add alcohol to

fortitude n = **courage**, strength,

resolution, grit, bravery

fortress n = **castle**, fort,
stronghold, citadel, redoubt

fortune n = **wealth**, means,
property, riches, resources
≠ **poverty**; = **luck**, fluke (Inf),
stroke of luck, serendipity, twist of
fate; = **chance**, fate, destiny,
providence, the stars

forward adv = **forth**, on, ahead,
onwards ≠ **backward(s)** ▷ adj
= **leading**, first, head, front,
advance; = **future**, advanced,
premature, prospective;
= **presumptuous**, familiar, bold,
cheeky, brash ≠ **shy** ▷ v = **further**,
advance, promote, assist, hurry;
= **send on**, send, post, pass on,

fossilize v 1 turn into fossil
2 petrify

foster ❶ v 1 promote
development of 2 bring up child,
esp. not one's own

foul ❶ adj 1 loathsome, offensive
2 stinking 3 dirty 4 unfair
5 obscene ▷ n 6 act of unfair play
7 breaking of a rule ▷ v 8 make,
become foul 9 jam 10 collide with

found¹ ❶ v 1 establish 2 lay base
of 3 base **foundation** n 1 basis
2 lowest part of building
3 founding 4 endowed institution
etc. **founder** n

found² v 1 melt and run into
mould 2 cast **foundry** n place for
casting

founder ❶ v 1 collapse 2 sink

foundling n deserted infant

fount n 1 fountain 2 source

fountain ❶ n 1 jet of water, esp.
ornamental one 2 spring
3 source

four n/adj cardinal number next
after three **fourth** adj ordinal
number **fourteen** n/adj four plus
ten **fourteenth** adj **forty** n/adj
four tens **fortieth** adj **foursome**
n group of four people

fowl n 1 domestic cock or hen
2 bird, its flesh

fox n 1 red bushy-tailed animal
2 its fur 3 cunning person ▷ v
4 perplex 5 act craftily **foxy** adj

foxglove n tall flowering plant

foxtrot n (music for) ballroom
dance

foyer ❶ n entrance hall in theatres,
hotels etc.

fracas n, pl **-cas** noisy quarrel

fraction ❶ n 1 numerical quantity
not an integer 2 fragment

fracture ❶ n 1 breakage
2 breaking of bone
▷ v 3 break

fragile ❶ adj 1 breakable
2 delicate **fragility** n

—— THESAURUS ——

dispatch

foster v = **bring up**, mother, raise,
nurse, look after; = **develop**,
support, further, encourage, feed
≠ **suppress**

foul adj = **dirty**, unpleasant,
stinking, filthy, grubby ≠ **clean**;
= **obscene**, crude, indecent, blue,
abusive; = **unfair**, illegal, crooked,
shady (Inf), fraudulent; = **offensive**,
bad, wrong, evil, corrupt
≠ **admirable** ▷ v = **dirty**, stain,
contaminate, pollute, taint ≠ **clean**

found¹ v = **establish**, start, set up,
begin, create

founder v = **fail**, collapse, break

down, fall through, be
unsuccessful; = **sink**, go down, be
lost, submerge, capsize

fountain n = **font**, spring,
reservoir, spout, fount; = **jet**,
stream, spray, gush; = **source**,
fount, wellspring, cause, origin

foyer n = **entrance hall**, lobby,
reception area, vestibule, anteroom

fraction n = **percentage**, share,
section, slice, portion

fracture n = **break**, split, crack ▷ v
= **break**, crack

fragile adj = **unstable**, weak,
vulnerable, delicate, uncertain;
= **fine**, weak, delicate, frail, brittle

DICTIONARY

fragrant ❶ adj sweet-smelling **fragrance** n

frail ❶ adj 1 fragile 2 in weak health **frailty** n, pl **-ties**

frame ❶ n 1 that in which thing is set, as square of wood round picture etc. 2 structure 3 build of body ▷ v 4 make 5 put into words 6 put into frame 7 bring false charge against **framework** n supporting structure

franc n monetary unit in France, Switzerland etc.

franchise n 1 right of voting 2 citizenship 3 privilege or right

frank ❶ adj 1 candid, outspoken 2 sincere ▷ n 3 official mark on letter either cancelling stamp or ensuring delivery without stamp ▷ v 4 mark letter thus

frankfurter n smoked sausage

frankincense n aromatic gum

resin burned as incense

frantic ❶ adj 1 distracted with rage, grief, joy etc. 2 frenzied **frantically** adv

fraternal adj of brother, brotherly **fraternity** n 1 brotherliness 2 brotherhood **fraternize** v 1 associate 2 make friends

fraud ❶ n 1 criminal deception 2 impostor **fraudulent** adj

fraught adj filled (with), involving

fray ❶ v make, become ragged at edge

fray² n 1 fight 2 noisy quarrel

frazzle (Inf) ▷ v 1 make or become exhausted ▷ n 2 exhausted state

freak ❶ n/adj abnormal (person or thing)

freckle n light brown spot on skin, esp. caused by sun

free ❶ adj **freer, freest** 1 able to act at will, not under compulsion or

THESAURUS

≠ **durable**

fragrant adj = **aromatic**, perfumed, balmy, redolent, sweet-smelling ≠ **stinking**

frail adj = **feeble**, weak, puny, infirm ≠ **strong**; = **flimsy**, weak, vulnerable, delicate, fragile

frame n = **casing**, framework, structure, shell, construction; = **physique**, build, form, body, figure ▷ v = **mount**, case, enclose; = **surround**, ring, enclose, encompass, envelop; = **devise**, draft, compose, sketch, put together

frank adj = **candid**, open, direct, straightforward, blunt ≠ **secretive**

frantic adj = **frenzied**, wild, furious, distracted, distraught ≠ **calm**; = **hectic**, desperate, frenzied, fraught (Inf), frenetic

fraud n = **deception**, deceit, treachery, swindling, trickery ≠ **honesty**; = **scam**, deception

fray² v = **wear thin**, wear, rub, wear out, chafe

freak adj = **abnormal**, chance, unusual, exceptional, unparalleled ▷ n (Inf): = **enthusiast**, fan, nut (Sl), addict, buff (Inf); = **aberration**, eccentric, anomaly, oddity, monstrosity

free adj = **complimentary**, for free (Inf), for nothing, unpaid, for love; = **allowed**, permitted, unrestricted, restraint **2** self-ruling **3** not restricted or affected by **4** not subject to cost or tax **5** not in use **6** (of person) not occupied **7** loose, not fixed ▷ v **8** set at liberty **9** remove (obstacles, pain etc.) **10** rid (of) **freedom** n **free-for-all** n brawl **freehold** n tenure of land without obligation of service or rent **freelance** adj/n (of) self-employed person **freeloader** n (Sl) scrounger **free-range** adj kept, produced in natural, nonintensive conditions **free speech** right to express opinions publicly **freewheel** v travel downhill on bicycle without pedalling

freeze ⊕ v freezing, froze, frozen **1** change (by reduction of temperature) from liquid to solid, as water to ice **2** preserve (food etc.) by extreme cold **3** fix (prices etc.) **4** feel very cold **5** become rigid

freezer n insulated cabinet for long-term storage of perishable foodstuffs
freight ⊕ n **1** commercial transport (esp. by railway, ship) **2** cost of this **3** goods so carried ▷ v **4** send as or by freight **freighter** n
frenetic adj frenzied
frenzy ⊕ n, pl -zies **1** violent mental derangement **2** wild excitement **frenzied** adj
frequent ⊕ adj **1** happening often **2** common **3** numerous ▷ v **2** go often to **frequency** n, pl -cies **1** rate of occurrence **2** in radio etc., cycles per second of alternating current
fresco n, pl -coes, -cos (method of) painting on wet plaster
fresh ⊕ adj **1** not stale **2** new **3** additional **4** different **5** recent **6** inexperienced **7** pure **8** not pickled, frozen etc. **9** not faded

THESAURUS

unimpeded, clear; **= at liberty**, loose, liberated, at large, on the loose ≠ **confined**; **= independent**, unfettered, footloose **= non-working**, leisure, unemployed, idle, unoccupied; **= available**, empty, spare, vacant, unused ▷ v **= clear**, disengage, cut loose, release, rescue; **= release**, liberate, let out, set free, deliver ≠ **confine**
freeze v **= ice over** or **up**, harden, stiffen, solidify, become solid; **= fix**, hold, limit, hold up
freight n **= transportation**, traffic, delivery, carriage, shipment;

= cargo, goods, load, delivery, burden
frenzy n **= fury**, passion, rage, seizure, hysteria ≠ **calm**
frequent adj **= common**, repeated, usual, familiar, everyday ≠ **infrequent** ▷ v **= visit**, attend, haunt, be found at, patronize ≠ **keep away**
fresh adj **= additional**, more, new, other, added; **= natural**, unprocessed, unpreserved ≠ **preserved**; **= new**, original, novel, different, recent ≠ **old**; **= invigorating**, clean, pure, crisp, bracing ≠ **stale**; **= cool**, cold,

10 not tired **11** (of wind) strong

freshen v **freshman, fresher** n first-year student

fret[1] ❶ v **fretting, fretted 1** be irritated, worry ▷ n **2** irritation **fretful** adj

fret[2] n **1** repetitive geometrical pattern ▷ v **2** ornament with carved pattern **fretwork** n

friable adj easily crumbled

friar n member of religious order

fricassee n dish of stewed pieces of meat

friction ❶ n **1** rubbing **2** resistance met with by body moving over another **3** clash of wills etc.

Friday n sixth day of the week

fridge n (Inf) refrigerator

friend ❶ n one well known to another and regarded with affection and loyalty **friendly** adj **1** kind **2** favourable **friendship** n

frieze n ornamental band, strip (on wall)

frigate n fast warship

fright ❶ n **1** sudden fear **2** shock **3** alarm **4** grotesque or ludicrous person or thing **frighten** v cause fear, fright in **frightening** adj

frightful adj **1** terrible, calamitous **2** shocking **3** (Inf) very great, very large **frightfully** adv

frigid adj **1** formal **2** (sexually) unfeeling **3** cold

frill n **1** strip of fabric gathered at one edge **2** ruff of hair, feathers around neck of dog, bird etc. **3** unnecessary words **4** superfluous thing **5** adornment **frilly** adj

fringe ❶ n **1** ornamental edge of hanging threads, tassels etc. **2** hair cut in front and falling over brow **3** edge ▷ adj **4** (of theatre etc.) unofficial

frisk v **1** move, leap, playfully **2** (Inf) search (person) **frisky** adj

frisson n shiver of excitement

fritter[1] v waste

fritter[2] n piece of food fried in batter

frivolous adj **1** not serious, unimportant **2** flippant **frivolity** n

frizz v **1** crisp, curl into small curls ▷ n **2** frizzed hair **frizzy** adj

frock n **1** woman's dress **2** various similar garments

frog n tailless amphibious animal

—— THESAURUS ——

refreshing, brisk, chilly; **= lively**, keen, alert, refreshed, vigorous **≠ weary**

fret[1] v **= worry**, brood, agonize, obsess, lose sleep

friction n **= conflict**, hostility, resentment, disagreement, animosity; **= resistance**, rubbing, scraping, grating, rasping

friend n **= companion**, pal, mate

(Inf), buddy (Inf), best friend **≠ foe**; **= supporter**, ally, associate, sponsor, patron

fright n **= fear**, shock, alarm, horror, panic **≠ courage**

fringe n **= border**, edging, edge, trimming, hem; **= edge**, limits, border, margin, outskirts ▷ adj **= unofficial**, alternative, radical, innovative, avant-garde

developed from tadpole **frogman**
n underwater swimmer with
rubber suit

frolic *n* **-icking, -icked**
1 merrymaking ▷ *v* **2** behave
playfully

from *prep* expressing point of
departure, source, distance, cause,
change of state etc.

frond *n* plant organ consisting of
stem and foliage

front ➊ *n* **1** fore part **2** position
directly before or ahead **3** seaside
promenade **4** outward aspect
5 (*Inf*) thing serving as respectable
cover ▷ *v* **6** look, face **7** (*Inf*) be a
cover for ▷ *adj* **8** of, at the front
frontal *adj* **frontage** *n* **1** façade
of building **2** extent of front
frontier *n* part of country which
borders on another **frontispiece** *n*
illustration facing title page of book

frost ➊ *n* **1** frozen dew or mist
2 act or state of freezing ▷ *v*
3 cover, be covered with frost or
something similar in appearance
frosted *adj* (of glass) opaque
frosty *adj* **1** accompanied by frost
2 cold **3** unfriendly **frostbite** *n*
destruction of tissue by cold

froth *n* **1** collection of small

bubbles, foam ▷ *v* **2** (cause to)
foam **frothy** *adj*

frown ➊ *v* **1** wrinkle brows
2 (with *on*) disapprove of ▷ *n*
3 expression of disapproval

frugal *adj* **1** sparing **2** thrifty,
economical **3** meagre

fruit ➊ *n* **1** seed and its envelope,
esp. edible one **2** vegetable
product **3** (*usu. pl*) result, benefit
▷ *v* **4** bear fruit **fruitful** *adj*
fruition *n* **1** enjoyment
2 realization of hopes **fruitless** *adj*
fruity *adj*

frump *n* dowdy woman **frumpy**
adj

frustrate ➊ *v* **1** thwart
2 disappoint **frustration** *n*

fry[1] *v* **frying, fried 1** cook with fat
2 be cooked thus

fry[2] *pl n* young fishes

ft. 1 feet **2** foot

fuchsia *n* shrub with purple-red
flowers

fuddle *v* (cause to) be intoxicated,
confused

fuddy-duddy *n, pl* **-dies** (*Inf*)
(elderly) dull person

fudge[1] *n* soft, variously flavoured
sweet

fudge[2] *v* avoid definite decision

————————— THESAURUS —————————

front *n* = **head**, start, lead,
forefront; = **exterior**, face, façade,
frontage; = **foreground**, fore,
forefront, nearest part; = **front
line**, trenches, vanguard, firing line;
(*Inf*) = **disguise**, cover, blind, mask,
cover-up ▷ *adj* = **foremost**, at the
front ≠ **back** ▷ *v* = **face onto**,
overlook, look out on, have a view

of, look over *or* onto

frost *n* = **hoarfrost**, freeze, rime

frown *v* = **glare**, scowl, glower,
make a face, look daggers

fruit *n* = **produce**, crop, yield,
harvest; (*often plural*) = **result**,
reward, outcome, end result, return

frustrate *v* = **thwart**, stop, check,
block, defeat ≠ **further**

DICTIONARY

fuel ❶ n 1 material for burning as source of heat or power ▷ v 2 provide with fuel

fugitive ❶ n 1 one who flees, esp. from arrest ▷ adj 2 elusive

fugue n musical composition in which themes are repeated in different parts

fulcrum n, pl -crums, -cra point on which a lever is placed for support

fulfil ❶ v -filling, -filled 1 satisfy 2 carry out **fulfilment** n

full ❶ adj 1 containing as much as possible 2 abundant 3 complete 4 ample 5 plump ▷ adv 6 very 7 quite 8 exactly **fully** adv **full-blooded** adj vigorous, enthusiastic **full-blown** adj fully developed **full stop** punctuation

mark (.) at end of sentence

fulminate v (esp. with against) criticize harshly

fulsome adj insincerely excessive

fumble v 1 grope about 2 handle awkwardly ▷ n 3 awkward attempt

fume ❶ v 1 be angry 2 emit smoke or vapour ▷ n 3 smoke 4 vapour **fumigate** v apply fumes or smoke to, esp. for disinfection

fun ❶ n anything enjoyable, amusing etc. **funny** adj 1 comical 2 odd **funnily** adv **funfair** n entertainment with rides and stalls

function ❶ n 1 work a thing is designed to do 2 (large) social event 3 duty 4 profession ▷ v 5 operate, work **functional** adj

fund ❶ n 1 stock or sum of money

THESAURUS

fuel = **incitement**, ammunition, provocation, incentive, power

fugitive n = **runaway**, refugee, deserter, escapee

fulfil v = **carry out**, perform, complete, achieve, accomplish ≠ **neglect**; = **achieve**, realize, satisfy, attain, consummate; = **satisfy**, please, content, cheer, refresh

full adj = **filled**, stocked, brimming, replete, complete; = **satiated**, having had enough, replete; = **extensive**, complete, generous, adequate, ample ≠ **incomplete**; = **comprehensive**, complete, exhaustive, all-embracing; = **rounded**, strong, rich, powerful, intense; = **plump**, rounded, voluptuous, shapely, well-rounded; = **voluminous**, large, loose, baggy,

billowing ≠ **tight**; = **rich**, strong, deep, loud, distinct ≠ **thin**

fumble v = **grope**, flounder, scrabble, feel around

fume v = **rage**, seethe, see red (Inf), storm, rant ▷ pl n = **smoke**, gas, exhaust, pollution/vapour

fun n = **amusement**, sport, pleasure, entertainment, recreation; = **enjoyment**, pleasure, mirth ≠ **gloom**

function n = **purpose**, business, job, use, role; = **reception**, party, affair, gathering, bash (Inf) ▷ v = **work**, run, operate, perform, go; = **act**, operate, perform, behave, do duty

fund n = **reserve**, stock, supply, store, collection ▷ v = **finance**, back, support, pay for, subsidize

2 supply ▷ pl **3** money resources ▷ v **4** provide or obtain funds

fundamental ❶ adj **1** of, affecting, or serving as, the base **2** essential, primary ▷ n **3** basic rule or fact **fundamentalism** n strict interpretation of religion **fundamentalist** n/adj

fundi n (SAfr) expert or boffin

funeral ❶ n (ceremony associated with) burial or cremation of dead **funereal** adj **1** like a funeral **2** dark **3** gloomy

fungus n, pl **-gi, -guses** plant without leaves, flowers, or roots, as mushroom, mould **fungicide** n substance that destroys fungi

funk n style of dance music **funky** adj **funkier, funkiest**

funnel n **1** cone-shaped vessel or tube **2** chimney of locomotive or ship ▷ v **3** (cause to) move as through funnel

fur n **1** soft hair of animal **2** garment of this **furry** adj

furious ❶ adj **1** extremely angry **2** violent

furl v roll up and bind

furlong n eighth of mile

furnace n apparatus for applying great heat to metals

furnish ❶ v **1** fit up house with furniture **2** supply **furnishings** pl n **furniture** n

furore ❶ n very angry or excited reaction to something

furrow n **1** trench **2** groove ▷ v **3** make furrows in

further, farther ❶ adv **1** more **2** in addition **3** at or to a greater distance or extent ▷ adj **4** more distant **5** additional: comparative of FAR ▷ v **6** promote **furthermore** adv besides **furthermost** adj **furthest** adj/ adv superlative of FAR

furtive adj stealthy, sly, secret

fury ❶ n, pl **-ries** wild rage, violence

fuse v **1** blend by melting **2** melt with heat **3** (cause to) fail as a result of blown fuse ▷ n **4** soft wire used as safety device in electrical systems **5** device for igniting bomb etc. **fusion** n

——————————— THESAURUS ———————————

fundamental adj = **central**, key, basic, essential, primary ≠ **incidental**; = **basic**, essential, underlying, profound, elementary

funeral n = **burial**, committal, laying to rest, cremation, interment

furious adj = **angry**, raging, fuming, infuriated, incensed ≠ **pleased**; = **violent**, intense, fierce, savage, turbulent

furnish v = **decorate**, fit out, stock, equip; = **supply**, give, offer, provide, present

furore n = **commotion**, to-do, stir, disturbance, outcry

further, farther adv = **in addition**, moreover, besides, furthermore, also ▷ adj = **additional**, more, new, other, extra ▷ v = **promote**, help, develop, forward, encourage ≠ **hinder**

fury n = **anger**, passion, rage, madness, frenzy ≠ **calmness**; = **violence**, force, intensity, severity, ferocity ≠ **peace**

fuselage *n* body of aircraft

fuss **❶** *n* **1** needless bustle or concern **2** complaint **3** objection ▷ *v* **4** make fuss **fussy** *adj*

fusty *adj* **-tier, -tiest 1** mouldy **2** smelling of damp **3** old-fashioned

futile **❶** *adj* useless, ineffectual, trifling **futility** *n*

futon *n* Japanese padded quilt

future **❶** *n* **1** time to come **2** what will happen ▷ *adj* **3** that will be **4** of, relating to, time to come **futuristic** *adj* appearing to belong to some future time

fuzz *n* **1** fluff **2** frizzed hair **3** blur **4** (*Sl*) police **fuzzy** *adj* **fuzzier, fuzziest**

THESAURUS

fuss *n* = **commotion**, to-do, bother, stir, excitement; = **bother**, trouble, struggle, hassle (*Inf*), nuisance ▷ *v* = **worry**, flap (*Inf*), fret, fidget, take pains

futile *adj* = **useless**, vain, unsuccessful, pointless, worthless

≠ **useful**

future *n* = **time to come**, hereafter, what lies ahead; = **prospect**, expectation, outlook ▷ *adj* = **forthcoming**, coming, later, approaching, to come

≠ **past**

g

g gram

gabardine, gaberdine n fine twill cloth like serge

gabble v talk, utter inarticulately or too fast

gable n triangular upper part of wall at end of ridged roof

gad v **gadding, gadded** (esp. with *about*) go around in search of pleasure

gadget ❶ n small mechanical device

gaffe n tactless remark

gaffer n 1 old man 2 (*Inf*) foreman, boss

gag¹ ❶ v **gagging, gagged** 1 stop up (person's mouth) 2 (*Sl*) retch, choke ▷ n 3 cloth etc. tied across mouth

gag² n joke, funny story

gaggle n flock of geese

gain ❶ v 1 obtain (as profit) 2 earn 3 reach 4 increase, improve 5 get nearer ▷ n 6 profit 7 increase, improvement

gainsay v **-saying, -said** deny, contradict

gait n manner of walking

gala ❶ n 1 festive occasion 2 show 3 sporting event

galaxy n, pl **-axies** system of stars **galactic** adj

gale ❶ n 1 strong wind 2 (*Inf*) outburst, esp. of laughter

gall¹ ❶ v 1 make sore by rubbing 2 irritate

gall² n (*Inf*) 1 impudence 2 bitterness **gall bladder** sac for bile

gallant adj 1 fine, stately, brave 2 chivalrous **gallantry** n

galleon n large sailing ship

gallery n, pl **-ries** 1 projecting upper floor in church, theatre etc. 2 place for showing works of art

galley n 1 one-decked vessel with

THESAURUS

gadget n = **device**, thing, appliance, machine, tool

gag¹ n = **muzzle**, tie, restraint ▷ v = **suppress**, silence, muffle, curb, stifle; = **retch**, heave

gain v = **acquire**, get, receive, pick up, secure; = **profit**, get, land, secure, collect ≠ **lose** = **put on**, increase in, gather, build up ▷ n = **rise**, increase, growth, advance,

improvement; = **profit**, return, benefit, advantage, yield ≠ **loss**

gala n = **festival**, fête, celebration, carnival, festivity

gale n = **storm**, hurricane, tornado, cyclone, blast; (*Inf*) = **outburst**, scream, roar, fit, storm

gall¹ v = **annoy**, provoke, irritate, trouble, disturb sails and oars **2** kitchen of ship or aircraft

gallivant v gad about

gallon n liquid measure of eight pints (4.55 litres)

gallop ❶ n **1** horse's fastest pace **2** ride at this pace ▷ v **3** go, ride at gallop **4** move fast

gallows n structure for hanging criminals

galore adv in plenty

galoshes pl n waterproof overshoes

gambit n opening move, comment etc. intended to secure an advantage

gamble ❶ v **1** play games of chance to win money **2** act on expectation of ▷ n **3** risky undertaking **4** bet **gambler** n **gambling** n

gambol v **-bolling, -bolled** skip, jump playfully

game¹ ❶ n **1** pastime **2** jest **3** contest for amusement **4** scheme **5** animals or birds hunted **6** their flesh ▷ adj **7** brave

8 willing **gaming** n gambling

gamekeeper n man employed to breed game, prevent poaching

game² adj lame

gammon n cured or smoked ham

gamut n whole range or scale

gander n male goose

gang ❶ n **1** (criminal) group **2** organized group of workmen ▷ v **3** (esp. with *up*) form gang

gangling adj lanky

gangplank n portable bridge for boarding or leaving vessel

gangrene n death or decay of body tissue as a result of disease or injury

gangster ❶ n member of criminal gang

gangway n **1** bridge from ship to shore **2** anything similar **3** passage between rows of seats

gannet n predatory sea bird

gantry n, pl **-tries** structure to support crane, railway signals etc.

gaol n see JAIL

gap ❶ n opening, interval

--- THESAURUS ---

gallop v = **run**, race, career, speed, bolt

gamble n = **risk**, chance, venture, lottery, speculation ≠ **certainty**; = **bet**, flutter (Inf), punt (chiefly Brit), wager ▷ v = **take a chance**, speculate, stick your neck out (Inf); = **risk**, chance, hazard, wager

game¹ n = **pastime**, sport, activity, entertainment, recreation ≠ **job**; = **match**, meeting, event, competition, tournament; = **amusement**, joke,

entertainment, diversion; = **wild animals** or **birds**, prey, quarry ▷ adj = **willing**, prepared, ready, keen, eager; = **brave**, courageous, spirited, daring, persistent ≠ **cowardly**

gang n = **group**, crowd, pack, company, band

gangster n = **hoodlum** (chiefly US), crook (Inf), bandit, hood (US SI), robber

gap n = **opening**, space, hole, break, crack; = **interval**, pause,

gape ❶ v 1 stare in wonder 2 open mouth wide 3 be, become wide open

garage n 1 (part of) building to house cars 2 refuelling and repair centre for cars

garb n/v dress

garbage n (US & Canad) rubbish

garden n 1 ground for cultivation ▷ v 2 cultivate garden **gardener** n **gardening** n

gargantuan adj immense

gargle v 1 wash throat with liquid kept moving by the breath ▷ n 2 gargling 3 preparation for this purpose

gargoyle n grotesque carving on church etc.

garish adj 1 showy 2 gaudy

garland ❶ n wreath of flowers as decoration

garlic n (bulb of) plant with strong smell and taste, used in cooking and seasoning

garment n article of clothing

garner v store up, collect

garnet n red semiprecious stone

garnish ❶ v 1 decorate (esp. food) ▷ n 2 material for this

garret n attic

garrison ❶ n 1 troops stationed in town, fort etc. 2 fortified place ▷ v 3 occupy with garrison

garrotte, garotte v execute by strangling

garrulous adj talkative

garter n band worn round leg to hold up sock or stocking

gas n, pl **gases, gasses** 1 airlike substance 2 fossil fuel in form of gas 3 gaseous anaesthetic 4 gaseous poison or irritant 5 (Inf, US & Canad) petrol ▷ v 6 poison with gas 7 talk idly, boastfully **gaseous** adj of, like gas

gash n 1 gaping wound, slash ▷ v 2 cut deeply

gasket n seal between metal faces, esp. in engines

gasp ❶ v 1 catch breath as in exhaustion or surprise ▷ n 2 gasping

gastric adj of stomach

gastroenteritis n inflammation of stomach and intestines

gastronomy n art of good eating

gate ❶ n 1 opening in wall, fence etc. 2 barrier for closing it 3 any entrance or way out **gate-crash** v enter social function etc. uninvited

— THESAURUS —

interruption, respite, lull

gape v = **stare**, wonder, goggle, gawp (Brit sl), gawk; = **open**, split, crack, yawn

garland n = **wreath**, band, bays, crown, honours

garnish n = **decoration**, embellishment, adornment, ornamentation, trimming ▷ v = **decorate**, adorn, ornament,

embellish, trim **≠ strip**

garrison n = **troops**, group, unit, section, command; = **fort**, fortress, camp, base, post ▷ v = **station**, position, post, install, assign

gasp v = **pant**, blow, puff, choke, gulp ▷ n = **pant**, puff, gulp, sharp intake of breath

gate n = **barrier**, opening, door, entrance, exit

gateway n 1 entrance with gate 2 means of access

gâteau n, pl **-teaux** elaborate, rich cake

gather ● v 1 (cause to) assemble 2 increase gradually 3 draw together 4 collect 5 learn, understand **gathering** n assembly

gaudy adj **gaudier, gaudiest** showy in tasteless way

gauge ● n 1 standard measure, as of diameter of wire etc. 2 distance between rails of railway 3 instrument for measuring ▷ v 4 measure 5 estimate

gaunt adj lean, haggard

gauntlet n (armoured) glove covering part of arm

gauze n thin transparent fabric of silk, wire etc.

gavel n auctioneer's mallet

gay ● adj 1 homosexual 2 merry 3 bright **gaiety** n **gaily** adv

gaze ● v 1 look fixedly ▷ n 2 fixed look

gazebo n, pl **-bos, -boes** summerhouse

gazelle n small graceful antelope

gazette ● n official newspaper for announcements **gazetteer** n geographical dictionary

GB Great Britain

GBH grievous bodily harm

GCE General Certificate of Education

GCSE General Certificate of Secondary Education

gear ● n 1 set of wheels working together, esp. by engaging cogs 2 equipment 3 clothing 4 (Sl) drugs ▷ v 5 adapt (one thing) so as to conform with another **gearbox** n case protecting gearing of bicycle, car etc.

geese pl of GOOSE

geezer n (Inf) (old or eccentric) man

geisha n, pl **-sha, -shas** in Japan, professional female companion for men

gel n jelly-like substance

g

---

gather v = **congregate**, assemble, collect, meet, mass ≠ **scatter**; = **assemble**, collect, bring together, muster, call together ≠ **disperse**; = **collect**, assemble, accumulate, mass, muster; = **pick**, harvest, pluck, reap, garner; = **build up**, rise, increase, grow, expand

gauge v = **measure**, calculate, evaluate, value, determine; = **judge**, estimate, guess, assess, evaluate ▷ n = **meter**, dial, measuring instrument

gay adj = **homosexual**, lesbian,

queer (Inf, offens); = **cheerful**, lively, sparkling, merry, upbeat (Inf) ≠ **sad**; = **colourful**, rich, bright, brilliant, vivid ≠ **drab**

gaze v = **stare**, look, view, watch, regard ▷ n = **stare**, look, fixed look

gazette n = **newspaper**, paper, journal, periodical, news-sheet

gear n = **mechanism**, works, machinery, cogs, cogwheels; = **equipment**, supplies, tackle, tools, instruments; = **clothing**, wear, dress, clothes, outfit ▷ v **with to** or **towards** = **equip**, fit, adjust,

gelatine, gelatin n substance prepared from animal bones etc., producing edible jelly

geld v castrate **gelding** n castrated horse

gelignite n powerful explosive consisting of dynamite in gelatine form

gem ❶ n precious stone. esp. when cut and polished

gen n (Inf) information

gender n sex, male or female

gene n biological factor determining inherited characteristics

genealogy n, pl **-gies** study or account of descent from ancestors

general ❶ adj 1 widespread 2 not particular or specific 3 usual 4 miscellaneous ▷ n 5 army officer of rank above colonel **generally** adv **generalize** v draw general conclusions **general practitioner** doctor serving local area

generate ❶ v 1 bring into being 2 produce **generation** n 1 bringing into being 2 all persons born about same time 3 time

between generations (about 30 years) **generator** n apparatus for producing (steam, electricity etc.)

generous ❶ adj 1 free in giving 2 abundant **generosity** n

genesis ❶ n, pl **-eses** 1 origin 2 mode of formation

genial adj 1 cheerful 2 mild

genie n in fairy tales, servant appearing by, and working, magic

genital adj relating to sexual organs or reproduction **genitals** pl n sexual organs

genius ❶ n (person with) exceptional power or ability

genocide n murder of entire race of people

genome n all the genetic material within an organism

genre ❶ n style of literary work

gent n (Inf) gentleman **gents** n men's public lavatory

genteel adj 1 well-bred 2 affectedly proper **gentility** n respectability

gentile adj 1 n 2 (person) of race other than Jewish

gentle ❶ adj 1 mild, not rough or

— THESAURUS —

adapt

gem n = **precious stone**, jewel, stone; = **treasure**, prize, jewel, pearl, masterpiece

general adj = **widespread**, accepted, popular, public, common ≠ **individual**; = **overall**, complete, total, global, comprehensive ≠ **restricted**; = **universal**, overall, widespread, collective, across-the-board ≠ **exceptional**

generate v = **produce**, create, make, cause, give rise to ≠ **end**

generous adj = **liberal**, lavish, charitable, hospitable, bountiful ≠ **mean**; = **magnanimous**, kind, noble, good, high-minded; = **plentiful**, lavish, ample, abundant, full ≠ **meagre**

genesis n = **beginning**, origin, start, birth, creation ≠ **end**

genius n = **brilliance**, ability, talent, capacity, gift

genre n = **type**, group, order, sort, kind

gentle adj = **kind**, kindly, tender,

severe **2** moderate **3** well-born
gently adv **gentleness** n quality
of being gentle **gentleman** n
1 chivalrous well-bred man **2** man
(used as a mark of politeness)
gentry n people just below nobility
in social rank
genuine ❶ adj **1** real **2** sincere
genus n, pl **genera** class, order,
group (esp. of insects, animals etc.)
with common characteristics
geography n science of earth's
form, physical features, climate,
population etc. **geographer** n
geographical adj
geology n science of earth's crust,
rocks, strata etc. **geological** adj
geologist n
geometry n science of properties
and relations of lines, surfaces etc.
geometrical, -metric adj
geranium n plant with red, pink or
white flowers
gerbil n desert rodent of Asia and
Africa
geriatrics n science of old age and
its diseases **geriatric** adj/n old

(person), esp. a patient
germ ❶ n **1** microbe, esp. causing
disease **2** rudiment
germinate v (cause to) sprout or
begin to grow
gestation n carrying of young in
womb
gesticulate v use expressive
movements of hands and arms
when speaking
gesture ❶ n/v (make) movement
to convey meaning
get ❶ v **getting, got 1** obtain
2 catch **3** cause to go or come
4 bring into position or state
5 induce **6** be in possession of,
have (to do) **7** become
geyser n **1** hot spring throwing up
spout of water **2** water heater
ghastly ❶ adj **-lier, -liest**
1 deathlike **2** (Inf) horrible ▷ adv
3 sickly
gherkin n small pickled cucumber
ghetto n, pl **-tos, -toes** densely
populated (esp. by one racial group)
slum area **ghetto blaster** (Inf)
large portable cassette recorder

g

— THESAURUS —

mild, humane **≠** unkind; **= slow,**
easy, slight, moderate, gradual;
= moderate, light, soft, slight, mild
≠ violent
genuine adj **= authentic,** real,
actual, true, valid **≠ counterfeit**;
= heartfelt, sincere, honest,
earnest, real **≠ affected**
germ n **= microbe,** virus, bug (Inf),
bacterium, bacillus; **= beginning,**
root, seed, origin, spark
gesture n **= sign,** action, signal,
motion, indication ▷ v **= signal,**

sign, wave, indicate, motion
get v **= become,** grow, turn, come
to be; **= persuade,** convince,
induce, influence, entice; (Inf)
= annoy, upset, anger, disturb,
trouble; **= obtain,** receive, gain,
acquire, win; **= fetch,** bring, collect;
= understand, follow, catch, see,
realize; **= catch,** develop, contract,
succumb to, fall victim to; **= arrest,**
catch, grab, capture, seize
ghastly adj **= horrible,** shocking,
terrible, awful, dreadful **≠ lovely**

ghost ❶ n 1 dead person appearing again 2 spectre 3 faint trace **ghostly** adj

ghoul n 1 malevolent spirit 2 person with morbid interests **ghoulish** adj

giant ❶ n 1 mythical being of superhuman size 2 very tall person, plant etc. ▷ adj 3 huge **gigantic** adj enormous, huge

gibber v make meaningless sounds with mouth **gibberish** n meaningless speech or words

gibbon n type of ape

gibe, jibe v/n jeer

giblets pl n internal edible parts of fowl

gidday, g'day interj (Aust & NZ) expression of greeting

giddy adj -dier, -diest 1 dizzy 2 liable to cause dizziness 3 flighty

gift ❶ n 1 thing given, present 2 faculty, power **gifted** adj talented

gig n performance by pop or jazz musicians

gigabyte n (Comp) 1024 megabytes

gigantic ❶ see GIANT

giggle ❶ v 1 laugh nervously, foolishly ▷ n 2 such a laugh

gild v gilding, gilded put thin layer of gold on **gilt** n thin layer of gold put on **gilt-edged** adj

gill¹ n (usu. pl) breathing organ in fish

gill² n liquid measure, quarter of pint (0.142 litres)

gimmick n stratagem etc., esp. designed to attract attention or publicity

gin n spirit flavoured with juniper berries

ginger n 1 plant with hot-tasting spicy root 2 the root ▷ v 3 stimulate **gingerbread** n cake flavoured with ginger

gingerly adv cautiously

gingham n cotton cloth, usu. checked

gingivitis n inflammation of gums

ginseng n plant root used as tonic

Gipsy pl -sies see GYPSY

giraffe n Afr. animal with very long neck

gird v girding, girded 1 put belt round 2 prepare (oneself) **girder** n large beam

girdle n 1 corset 2 waistband

girl ❶ n 1 female child 2 young (unmarried) woman **girlfriend** n man's female companion

giro n, pl -ros system operated by banks and post offices for the transfer of money

girth n 1 measurement round thing 2 band put round horse to

— THESAURUS —

ghost n = **spirit**, soul, phantom, spectre, spook (Inf); = **trace**, shadow, suggestion, hint, suspicion

giant adj = **huge**, vast, enormous, tremendous, immense ≠ **tiny** ▷ n = **ogre**, monster, titan, colossus

gift n = **donation**, offering, present,

guaranteed

contribution, grant; = **talent**, ability, capacity, genius, power

gigantic adj = **huge**, large, giant, massive, enormous ≠ **tiny**

giggle n = **laugh**, chuckle, snigger, chortle, titter

girl n = **female child**, lass, lassie

hold saddle etc.

gist n substance, main point (of remarks etc.)

give ⊕ v n giving, gave, given 1 make present of 2 deliver 3 assign 4 utter 5 yield, give way ▷ n 6 yielding, elasticity

glacé adj 1 crystallized 2 iced

glacier n slow-moving river of ice **glacial** adj

glad ⊕ adj gladder, gladdest 1 pleased 2 happy **gladden** v make glad **gladly** adv

glade n grassy space in forest

gladiator n trained fighter in Roman arena

gladiolus n, pl **-lus, -li, -luses** kind of iris, with sword-shaped leaves

glamour ⊕ n alluring charm, fascination **glamorous** adj

glance ⊕ v 1 look rapidly or briefly 2 glide off something struck ▷ n 3 brief look

gland n organ controlling different bodily functions by chemical means **glandular** adj

glare ⊕ v 1 look fiercely 2 shine intensely ▷ n 3 glaring **glaring** adj conspicuous

glass n 1 hard transparent substance 2 things made of it 3 tumbler 4 its contents ▷ pl 5 spectacles **glassy** adj 1 like glass 2 expressionless

glaucoma n eye disease

glaze ⊕ v 1 furnish with glass 2 cover with glassy substance 3 become glassy ▷ n 4 transparent coating 5 substance used for this **glazier** n one who glazes windows

gleam ⊕ n/v (give out) slight or passing beam of light

glean n 1 pick up 2 gather

glee n mirth, merriment **gleeful** adj

glen n narrow valley

glib adj **glibber, glibbest** fluent but insincere or superficial

g

(Inf), miss, maiden (Archaic)

give v = **perform**, do, carry out, execute; = **communicate**, announce, transmit, pronounce, utter; = **produce**, make, cause, occasion, engender; = **present**, contribute, donate, provide, supply ≠ **take**; = **concede**, allow, grant; = **surrender**, yield, devote, hand over, relinquish

glad adj = **happy**, pleased, delighted, contented, gratified ≠ **unhappy**; (Archaic) = **pleasing**, happy, cheering, pleasant, cheerful

glamour n = **charm**, appeal, beauty, attraction, fascination

glance v = **peek**, look, view, glimpse, peep ≠ **scrutinize** ▷ n = **peek**, look, glimpse, peep, dekko (Sl) ≠ **good look**

glare v = **scowl**, frown, glower, look daggers, lour or lower; = **dazzle**, blaze, flare, flame ▷ n = **scowl**, frown, glower, dirty look, black look; = **dazzle**, glow, blaze, flame, brilliance

glaze n = **coat**, finish, polish, shine, gloss ▷ v = **coat**, polish, gloss, varnish, enamel

gleam v = **shine**, flash, glow, sparkle, glitter ▷ n = **glimmer**, flash, beam, glow, sparkle; = **trace**,

glide ❶ v 1 pass smoothly and continuously ▷ n 2 smooth, silent movement **glider** n aircraft without engine

glimmer v 1 shine faintly ▷ n 2 faint light

glimpse ❶ n 1 brief view ▷ v 2 catch glimpse of

glint v/n flash

glisten v gleam by reflecting light

glitter ❶ v 1 shine with bright quivering light, sparkle ▷ n 2 lustre 3 sparkle

gloat v regard with smugness or malicious satisfaction

globe ❶ n 1 sphere with map of earth or stars 2 ball **global** adj 1 relating to whole world 2 total, comprehensive

globule n small round drop

glockenspiel n percussion instrument played with hammers

gloom ❶ n 1 darkness 2 melancholy **gloomy** adj **gloomier, gloomiest**

glory ❶ n, pl **-ries** 1 renown 2 splendour 3 heavenly bliss ▷ v 4 take pride (in) **glorify** v 1 make glorious 2 praise **glorious** adj 1 illustrious 2 splendid 3 (Inf) delightful **gloriously** adv

gloss¹ ❶ n 1 surface shine, lustre ▷ v 2 put gloss on 3 (esp. with over) (try to) cover up, pass over (fault, error) **glossy** adj **-sier, -siest** smooth, shiny

gloss² ❶ n 1 interpretation of word 2 comment ▷ v 3 interpret 4 comment **glossary** n dictionary of special words

glove n 1 covering for the hand ▷ v 2 cover as with glove

glow ❶ v 1 give out light and heat without flames 2 be or look hot ▷ n 3 shining heat **glow-worm** n insect giving out light

glower v/n scowl

glucose n type of sugar found in fruit etc.

———————————— THESAURUS ————————————

≠ **happiness**

glide v = **slip**, sail, slide

glimpse n = **look**, sighting, sight, glance, peep ▷ v = **catch sight of**, spot, sight, view, spy

glitter v = **shine**, flash, sparkle, glare, gleam ▷ n = **glamour**, show, display, splendour, tinsel; = **sparkle**, flash, shine, glare, gleam

globe n = **planet**, world, earth, sphere, orb

gloom n = **darkness**, dark, shadow, shade, twilight ≠ **light**; = **depression**, sorrow, woe, melancholy, unhappiness

glory n = **honour**, praise, fame, distinction, acclaim ≠ **shame**; = **splendour**, majesty, greatness, grandeur, nobility ▷ v = **triumph**, boast, relish, revel, exult

gloss¹ n = **shine**, gleam, sheen, polish, brightness

gloss² n = **interpretation**, comment, note, explanation, commentary ▷ v = **interpret**, explain, comment, translate, annotate

glow n = **light**, gleam, splendour, glimmer, brilliance ≠ **dullness** ▷ v

suggestion, hint, flicker, glimmer

glue ❶ n/v (fasten with) sticky substance **gluey** adj

glum adj **glummer, glummest** sullen, gloomy

glut n 1 surfeit, excessive amount ▷ v 2 feed, gratify to the full or to excess

glutton n 1 greedy person 2 one with great liking or capacity for something **gluttonous** adj **gluttony** n

glycerine, glycerin n colourless sweet liquid

GMT Greenwich Mean Time

gnarled adj knobby, twisted

gnash v grind (teeth) together as in anger or pain

gnat n small, biting fly

gnaw v **gnawing, gnawed** bite or chew steadily

gnome n legendary creature like small old man

gnu n oxlike antelope

go ❶ v **going, went, gone** 1 move along 2 depart 3 function 4 fare 5 fail 6 elapse 7 be able to be put 8 become ▷ n 9 going 10 energy 11 attempt 12 turn **go-between** n intermediary

goad n 1 spiked stick for driving cattle 2 anything that urges to action ▷ v 3 urge on 4 torment

goal ❶ n 1 end of race 2 object of effort 3 posts through which ball is to be driven in football etc. 4 the score so made

goat n animal with long hair, horns and beard **goatee** n small pointed beard

gobble¹ v eat hastily, noisily or greedily

gobble² n/v (make) cry of turkey

gobbledegook, gobbledygook n unintelligible language

goblet n drinking cup

goblin n (Folklore) small, usu. malevolent spirit

god n 1 superhuman being worshipped as having supernatural power 2 object of worship, idol 3 (with cap.) the Supreme Being, creator and ruler of universe **godly** adj devout, pious **godfather** n sponsor at baptism **godforsaken** adj desolate, dismal **godsend** n something unexpected but welcome

gogga n (S Afr, Inf) any small insect

goggle v 1 (of eyes) bulge 2 stare ▷ pl n 3 protective spectacles

---

THESAURUS

= **shine**, burn, gleam, brighten, glimmer

glue n = **adhesive**, cement, gum, paste

go v = **move**, travel, advance, journey, proceed ≠ **stay**; = **leave**, withdraw, depart, move out, slope off; = **elapse**, pass, flow, fly by, expire; = **be given**, be spent, be

awarded, be allotted; = **function**, work, run, move, operate ≠ **fail**; = **match**, blend, correspond, fit, suit ▷ n = **attempt**, try, effort, bid, shot (Inf); = **turn**, shot (Inf), stint, fossick through (Aust & NZ)

goal n = **aim**, end, target, purpose, object

go-kart, go-cart n miniature, low-powered racing car

gold n 1 yellow precious metal 2 coins of this 3 colour of gold ▷ adj 4 of, like gold **golden** adj **golden wedding** fiftieth wedding anniversary **goldfinch** n bird with yellow feathers **goldfish** n any of various ornamental pond or aquarium fish

golf n outdoor game in which small ball is struck into holes **golfer** n

gondola n Venetian canal boat **gondolier** n rower of gondola

gong n metal plate which sounds when struck with soft mallet

good ⓘ adj better, best 1 commendable 2 right 3 beneficial 4 well-behaved 5 virtuous 6 sound 7 valid ▷ n 8 benefit 9 wellbeing 10 profit ▷ pl 11 property 12 wares **goodly**

adj large, considerable **goodness** n **goodwill** n kindly feeling

goodbye ⓘ interj/n form of address on parting

gooey adj **gooier, gooiest** (Inf) sticky, soft

goose n, pl **geese** 1 web-footed bird 2 its flesh 3 simpleton

gooseberry n 1 thorny shrub 2 its hairy fruit

gore¹ ⓘ n (dried) blood from wound **gory** adj

gore² ⓘ v pierce with horns

gorge ⓘ n 1 ravine 2 disgust, resentment ▷ v 3 feed greedily

gorgeous ⓘ adj splendid, showy

gorilla n largest anthropoid ape, found in Africa

gormless adj (Inf) stupid

gorse n prickly shrub

gosling n young goose

gospel ⓘ n 1 unquestionable

— THESAURUS —

good adj = excellent, great, fine, pleasing, acceptable ≠ bad; = proficient, able, skilled, expert, talented ≠ bad; = beneficial, useful, helpful, favourable, wholesome ≠ harmful; = honourable, moral, worthy, ethical, upright ≠ bad; = well-behaved, polite, orderly, obedient, dutiful ≠ naughty; = kind, kindly, friendly, obliging, charitable ≠ unkind; = true, real, genuine, proper; = full, complete, extensive ≠ scant ▷ n = benefit, interest, gain, advantage, use ≠ disadvantage; = virtue, goodness, righteousness, worth, merit ≠ evil

goodbye n = farewell, parting, leave-taking ▷ interj = farewell, see you, see you later, ciao (Italian), cheerio

gore¹ n = blood, slaughter, bloodshed, carnage, butchery

gore² v = pierce, wound, transfix, impale

gorge n = ravine, canyon, pass, chasm, cleft ▷ v = overeat, devour, gobble, wolf, gulp

gorgeous adj = magnificent, beautiful, superb, spectacular, splendid ≠ shabby; = delightful, good, great, wonderful, excellent ≠ awful

gospel n = doctrine, news, teachings, message, revelation;

truth **2** (*with cap.*) any of first four
books of New Testament
gossamer *n* filmy substance like
spider's web
gossip ❶ *n* **1** idle (malicious) talk
about other persons **2** one who
talks thus ▷ *v* **3** engage in gossip
gouge *v* **1** scoop out **2** force out
▷ *n* **3** chisel with curved cutting
edge
goulash *n* stew seasoned with
paprika
gourd *n* **1** large fleshy fruit **2** its
rind as vessel
gourmand *n* glutton
gourmet ❶ *n* **1** connoisseur of
wine, food **2** epicure
gout *n* disease with inflammation,
esp. of joints
govern ❶ *v* **1** rule, control
2 determine **governess** *n* woman
teacher, esp. in private household
government *n* **1** exercise of
political authority in directing a

people, state etc. **2** system by
which community is ruled
3 governing group **4** control
governor ❶ *n* **1** one who governs
2 chief administrator of an
institution **3** member of
committee responsible for an
organization or institution
gown ❶ *n* **1** loose flowing outer
garment **2** woman's (long) dress
3 official robe
GP General Practitioner
grab ❶ *v* grabbing, grabbed
1 grasp suddenly **2** snatch ▷ *n*
3 sudden clutch **4** quick attempt
to seize
grace ❶ *n* **1** charm, elegance
2 goodwill, favour **3** sense of
propriety **4** postponement
granted **5** short thanksgiving for
meal ▷ *v* **6** add grace to, honour
graceful *adj* **gracious** *adj* **1** kind
2 condescending
grade ❶ *n* **1** step, stage **2** class

g

= **truth**, fact, certainty, the last
word
gossip *n* **=** **idle talk**, scandal,
hearsay, tittle-tattle, small talk;
= **busybody**, chatterbox (*Inf*),
chatterer, scandalmonger,
gossipmonger ▷ *v* **=** **chat**, chatter,
jaw (*Sl*), blether
gourmet *n* **=** **connoisseur**, foodie
(*Inf*), bon vivant (*Fr*), epicure,
gastronome
govern *v* **=** **rule**, lead, control,
command, manage; **=** **restrain**,
control, check, master, discipline
gown *n* **=** **dress**, costume,
garment, robe, frock

grab *v* **=** **snatch**, catch, seize,
capture, grip
grace *n* **=** **elegance**, poise, ease,
polish, refinement ≠ **ungainliness**;
= **manners**, decency, etiquette,
consideration, propriety ≠ **bad
manners**; **=** **indulgence**, mercy,
pardon, reprieve; **=** **benevolence**,
favour, goodness, goodwill,
generosity ≠ **ill will**; **=** **prayer**,
thanks, blessing, thanksgiving,
benediction ▷ *v* **=** **adorn**, enhance,
decorate, enrich, set off; **=** **honour**,
favour, dignify ≠ **insult**
grade *v* **=** **classify**, rate, order,
class, group, degree

3 rating **4** slope ▷ v **5** arrange in classes **6** assign grade to
gradation n **1** series of steps **2** each of them
gradient n (degree of) slope
gradual ❶ adj **1** taking place by degrees **2** slow and steady **3** not steep **gradually** adv
graduate ❶ v **1** take university degree **2** divide into degrees ▷ n **3** holder of university degree **graduation** n
graffiti pl n (oft. obscene) writing, drawing on walls
graft¹ ❶ n **1** shoot of plant set in stalk of another **2** the process **3** surgical transplant of skin, tissue ▷ v **4** insert (shoot) in another stalk **5** transplant (living tissue in surgery)
graft² n (Inf) **1** hard work **2** self-advancement, profit by unfair means
grain ❶ n **1** (seed, fruit of) cereal plant **2** small hard particle **3** very small unit of weight **4** arrangement of fibres **5** any very small amount
gram, gramme n one

thousandth of a kilogram
grammar n **1** science of structure and usages of language **2** use of words **grammatical** adj
grammar school state-maintained secondary school providing academic education
gramophone n record player
gran n (Inf) grandmother
granary n, pl **-ries** storehouse for grain
grand ❶ adj **1** magnificent **2** noble **3** splendid **4** eminent **grandeur** n **1** nobility **2** magnificence **3** dignity **grandiose** adj **1** imposing **2** affectedly grand **grandchild** n child of one's child **grandson** n, **granddaughter** n **grandparent** n parent of parent **grandfather** n, **grandmother** n **grandstand** n structure with tiered seats for spectators
granite n hard crystalline rock
grant ❶ v **1** consent to fulfil (request) **2** permit **3** admit ▷ n **4** sum of money provided for specific purpose, esp. education **5** gift **6** allowance, concession

—————— THESAURUS ——————

gradual adj = **steady**, slow, regular, gentle, progressive ≠ **sudden**
graduate v = **mark off**, grade, proportion, regulate, gauge; = **classify**, rank, grade, group, order
graft¹ n = **shoot**, bud, implant, sprout, splice ▷ v = **join**, insert, transplant, implant, splice
grain n = **seed**, kernel, grist; = **cereal**, corn; = **bit**, piece, trace,

scrap, particle; = **texture**, pattern, surface, fibre, weave
grand adj = **impressive**, great, large, magnificent, imposing ≠ **unimposing**; = **ambitious**, great, grandiose
grant n = **award**, allowance, donation, endowment, gift ▷ v = **give**, allow, present, award, permit; = **accept**, allow, admit, acknowledge, concede

granule *n* small grain

grape *n* small fruit, used to make wine **grapevine** *n* **1** grape-bearing plant **2** (*Inf*) unofficial way of spreading news

grapefruit *n* subtropical citrus fruit

graph *n* drawing depicting relation of different numbers, quantities etc.

graphic ❶ *adj* **1** vividly descriptive **2** of writing, drawing, painting etc. ▷ *pl n* **3** diagrams etc. used on television, computer screen etc.

graphite *n* form of carbon (used in pencils)

grapple ❶ *v* **1** wrestle **2** struggle

grasp ❶ *v* **1** (try, struggle to) seize hold **2** understand ▷ *n* **3** grip **4** comprehension **grasping** *adj* greedy, avaricious

grass *n* **1** common type of plant with jointed stems and long narrow leaves **2** such plants grown as lawn **3** pasture **4** (*Sl*) marijuana **5** (*Sl*) informer **grassy** *adj* **-sier, -siest** **grasshopper** *n* jumping, chirping insect **grass roots** ordinary

members of group

grate¹ *n* framework of metal bars for holding fuel in fireplace **grating** *n* framework of bars covering opening

grate² *v* **1** rub into small bits on rough surface **2** rub with harsh noise **3** irritate **grater** *n* utensil with rough surface for reducing substance to small particles **grating** *adj* **1** harsh **2** irritating

grateful ❶ *adj* **1** thankful **2** appreciative **3** pleasing **gratefully** *adv* **gratitude** *n* sense of being thankful

gratify *v* **-fying, -fied 1** satisfy **2** please **gratification** *n*

gratis *adv/adj* free, for nothing

gratuitous *adj* **1** given free **2** uncalled for **gratuity** *n* gift of money for services rendered, tip

grave¹ ❶ *n* hole dug to bury corpse **graveyard** *n*

grave² ❶ *adj* **1** serious **2** solemn

grave³ *n* accent (`) over letter

gravel *n* **1** small stones **2** coarse sand **gravelly** *adj*

graphic *adj* = **vivid**, clear, detailed, striking, explicit ≠ **vague**; = **pictorial**, visual, diagrammatic ≠ **impressionistic**

grapple *v* = **deal**, tackle, struggle, take on, confront; = **struggle**, fight, combat, wrestle, battle

grasp *v* = **grip**, hold, catch, grab, seize; = **understand**, realize, take in, get, see ▷ *n* = **grip**, hold, possession, embrace, clutches; = **understanding**, knowledge,

grip, awareness, mastery

grateful *adj* = **thankful**, obliged, in (someone's) debt, indebted, appreciative

gratitude *n* = **thankfulness**, thanks, recognition, obligation, appreciation ≠ **ingratitude**

grave¹ *n* = **tomb**, vault, crypt, mausoleum, sepulchre

grave² *adj* = **serious**, important, critical, pressing, threatening ≠ **trifling**; = **solemn**, sober,

graven adj carved, engraved

gravitate v 1 move by gravity
2 tend (towards) centre of
attraction 3 sink, settle down

gravity ❶ n, pl **-ties** 1 force of
attraction of one body for another,
esp. of objects to the earth
2 heaviness 3 importance
4 seriousness

gravy n, pl **-vies** 1 juices from
meat in cooking 2 sauce made
from these

graze¹ ❶ v feed on grass, pasture

graze² ❶ v 1 touch lightly in
passing, scratch, scrape ▷ n
2 grazing 3 abrasion

grease n 1 soft melted fat of
animals 2 thick oil as lubricant ▷ v
3 apply grease to **greasy** adj
greasier, greasiest greasepaint
n theatrical make-up

great ❶ adj 1 large 2 important
3 pre-eminent 4 (Inf) excellent
▷ comb. form 5 one degree further
removed in relationship, as in

great-grandfather **greatly** adv

greed, greediness ❶ n
excessive consumption of, desire
for, food, wealth **greedy** adj

green ❶ adj 1 of colour between
blue and yellow 2 grass-coloured
3 unripe 4 inexperienced
5 envious ▷ n 6 colour 7 area of
grass, esp. for playing bowls etc.
▷ pl 8 green vegetables **greenery**
n vegetation **greenfly** n aphid,
small green garden pest
greengrocer n dealer in
vegetables and fruit **greenhouse**
n glass building for rearing plants

greet ❶ v 1 meet with expressions
of welcome 2 salute 3 receive
greeting n

gregarious adj sociable

gremlin n imaginary being blamed
for mechanical malfunctions

grenade n bomb thrown by hand
or shot from rifle **grenadier** n
soldier of Grenadier Guards
grenadine n syrup made from

——— THESAURUS ———

sombre, dour, unsmiling
≠ **carefree**

gravity n = **seriousness**,
importance, significance, urgency,
severity ≠ **triviality**; = **solemnity**,
seriousness, gravitas ≠ **frivolity**

graze¹ v = **feed**, crop, browse,
pasture

graze² v = **scratch**, skin, scrape,
chafe, abrade; = **touch**, brush, rub,
scrape, shave ▷ v = **scratch**,
scrape, abrasion

great adj = **large**, big, huge, vast,
enormous ≠ **small**; = **important**,
serious, significant, critical, crucial

≠ **unimportant**; = **famous**,
outstanding, remarkable,
prominent, renowned; (Inf)
= **excellent**, fine, wonderful,
superb, fantastic (Inf) ≠ **poor**

greed, greediness n
= **gluttony**, voracity

green adj = **verdant**, leafy, grassy;
= **inexperienced**, new, raw,
naive, immature; = **jealous**,
grudging, resentful, envious,
covetous ▷ n = **lawn**, common,
turf, sward

greet v = **salute**, hail, say hello to,
address, accost

pomegranate juice, for sweetening and colouring drinks

grey ❶ adj **1** between black and white **2** clouded **3** turning white **4** aged **5** intermediate, indeterminate ▷ n **6** grey colour

greyhound n swift slender dog

grid n **1** network of horizontal and vertical lines, bars etc. **2** any interconnecting system of links

griddle n flat iron plate for cooking

gridiron n frame of metal bars for grilling

grief ❶ n deep sorrow **grievance** n real or imaginary cause for complaint **grieve** v **1** feel grief **2** cause grief to **grievous** adj **1** painful, oppressive **2** very serious

grill n **1** device on cooker to radiate heat downwards **2** food cooked under grill **3** gridiron ▷ v **4** cook (food) under grill **5** subject to severe questioning

grille, grill n grating

grim ❶ adj **grimmer, grimmest 1** stern **2** relentless **3** joyless

grimace n/v (pull) wry face

grime n ingrained dirt, soot **grimy** n

grin n/v **grinning, grinned** (give) broad smile

grind ❶ v **grinding, ground 1** crush to powder **2** make sharp, smooth **3** grate ▷ n **4** (Inf) hard work **5** action of grinding

grip ❶ n **1** firm hold **2** mastery **3** handle **4** travelling bag ▷ v **5** hold tightly **6** hold attention of

gripe v (Inf) **1** complain (persistently) ▷ n **2** intestinal pain (esp. in infants) **3** (Inf) complaint

grisly adj **-lier, -liest** causing terror

grist n corn to be ground

gristle n cartilage, tough flexible tissue

grit n **1** rough particles of sand **2** courage ▷ v **3** clench (teeth)

grizzle v (Inf) whine

grizzled adj grey (haired)

grizzly n, pl **-zlies** large Amer. bear

groan ❶ v/n (make) low, deep sound of grief or pain

grocer n dealer in foodstuffs **groceries** pl n commodities sold by a grocer **grocery** n, pl **-ceries** trade, premises of grocer

g

— THESAURUS —

grey adj = **dull**, dark, dim, gloomy, drab; = **boring**, dull, anonymous, faceless, colourless

grief n = **sadness**, suffering, regret, distress, misery ≠ **joy**

grim adj = **terrible**, severe, harsh, forbidding, formidable

grind v = **crush**, mill, powder, grate, pulverize; = **press**, push, crush, jam, mash; = **grate**, scrape, gnash ▷ n = **hard work** (Inf),

labour, sweat (Inf), chore, toil

grip v = **grasp**, hold, catch, seize, clutch; = **engross**, fascinate, absorb, entrance, hold ▷ n = **clasp**, hold, grasp; = **control**, rule, influence, command, power

grit n = **gravel**, sand, dust, pebbles; = **courage**, spirit, resolution, determination, guts (Inf) ▷ v = **clench**, grind, grate, gnash

groan v = **moan**, cry, sigh; (Inf)

grog n spirit (esp. rum) and water

groggy adj (Inf) shaky, weak

groin n fold where legs meet abdomen

groom 1 n 1 person caring for horses 2 bridegroom ▷ v 3 tend or look after 4 brush or clean (esp. horse) 5 train

groove 1 n 1 narrow channel 2 routine ▷ v 3 cut groove in

grope 1 v feel about, search blindly

gross 1 adj 1 very fat 2 total, not net 3 coarse 4 flagrant ▷ n 5 twelve dozen

grotesque 1 adj 1 (horribly) distorted 2 ugly or repulsive

grotto n, pl -toes, -tos cave

grotty adj -tier, -tiest (Inf) nasty, in bad condition

grouch (Inf) ▷ n 1 persistent grumbler 2 discontented mood ▷ v 3 grumble

ground 1 n 1 surface of earth 2 soil, earth 3 reason 4 special area ▷ pl 5 dregs 6 enclosed land round house ▷ v 7 establish 8 instruct 9 place on ground 10 run ashore **grounded** adj (of aircraft) unable or not permitted to fly **grounding** n basic knowledge of subject **groundless** adj without reason **groundwork** n preliminary work

group 1 n 1 number of persons or things together 2 small musical band 3 class ▷ v 4 place, fall into group

grouse[1] n 1 game bird 2 its flesh

grouse[2] v 1 grumble, complain ▷ n 2 complaint

grout n 1 thin fluid mortar ▷ v 2 fill up with grout

grove 1 n small group of trees

grovel v -elling, -elled 1 abase oneself 2 lie face down

————————— THESAURUS —————————

= **complain**, object, moan, grumble, gripe (Inf) ▷ n = **moan**, cry, sigh, whine; (Inf) = **complaint**, protest, objection, grumble, grouse

groom n = **stableman**, stableboy, hostler or ostler (Archaic) ▷ v = **brush**, clean, tend, rub down, curry; = **smarten up**, clean, tidy, preen, spruce up; = **train**, prime, prepare, coach, ready

groove n = **indentation**, cut, hollow, channel, trench

grope v = **feel**, search, fumble, flounder, fish

gross adj = **flagrant**, blatant, rank, sheer, utter ≠ **qualified**; = **vulgar**, offensive, crude, obscene, coarse

≠ **decent**; = **fat**, overweight, hulking, corpulent ≠ **slim**; = **total**, whole, entire, aggregate, before tax ≠ **net**

grotesque adj = **unnatural**, bizarre, strange, fantastic, distorted ≠ **natural**; = **absurd**, preposterous ≠ **natural**

ground n = **earth**, land, dry land, terra firma ▷ v = **base**, found, establish, set, settle; = **instruct**, train, teach, initiate, tutor

group n = **crowd**, party, band, pack, gang ▷ v = **arrange**, order, sort, class, classify

grove n = **wood**, plantation, covert, thicket, copse

grow ❶ v *growing, grew, grown*
1 develop naturally 2 increase
3 be produced 4 become by
degrees 5 produce by cultivation

growth n 1 growing 2 increase
3 what has grown or is growing

grown-up adj/n adult

growl v/n (make) low guttural
sound of anger

grub v 1 dig 2 root up 3 rummage
▷ n 4 short, legless larva of certain
insects 5 (Sl) food

grubby adj **-bier, -biest** dirty

grudge ❶ v 1 be unwilling to give,
allow ▷ n 2 ill will

gruel n food of oatmeal etc., boiled
in milk or water

gruelling ❶ adj exhausting

gruesome ❶ adj horrible,
grisly

gruff adj rough-voiced, surly

grumble ❶ v 1 complain
2 rumble ▷ n 3 complaint

grumpy adj **grumpier, grumpiest**
ill-tempered, surly

grunt v/n (make) sound
characteristic of pig

G-string n very small covering for
genitals

guarantee ❶ n 1 formal assurance
(esp. in writing) that product etc.
will meet certain standards ▷ v
2 give guarantee 3 secure (against
risk etc.) **guarantor** n

guard ❶ v 1 protect, defend
2 take precautions (against) ▷ n
3 person, group that protects
4 sentry 5 official in charge of train
6 protection **guarded** adj
cautious, noncommittal **guardian**
n 1 keeper, protector 2 person
having custody of infant etc.

guava n tropical tree with fruit
used to make jelly

guerrilla, guerilla ❶ n member
of irregular armed force

g

——— THESAURUS ———

grow v = **develop**, get bigger
≠ **shrink**; = **get bigger**, spread,
swell, stretch, expand; = **cultivate**,
produce, raise, farm, breed;
= **become**, get, turn, come to be;
= **originate**, spring, arise, stem,
issue

grudge n = **resentment**,
bitterness, grievance, dislike,
animosity ≠ **goodwill** ▷ v
= **resent**, mind, envy, covet,
begrudge ≠ **welcome**

gruelling adj = **exhausting**,
demanding, tiring, taxing, severe
≠ **easy**

gruesome adj = **horrific**,
shocking, terrible, horrible, grim

≠ **pleasant**

grumble v = **complain**, moan,
gripe (Inf), whinge (Inf), carp;
= **rumble**, growl, gurgle ▷ n
= **complaint**, protest, objection,
moan, grievance

guarantee v = **ensure**, secure,
assure, warrant, make certain ▷ n
= **promise**, pledge, assurance,
certainty, word of honour

guard v = **protect**, defend, secure,
mind, preserve ▷ n = **sentry**,
warder, warden, custodian, watch;
= **shield**, security, defence, screen,
protection

guerrilla n = **freedom fighter**,
partisan, underground fighter

guess ❶ v 1 estimate 2 conjecture 3 (US & Canad) think ▷ n 4 conclusion reached by guessing

guest ❶ n 1 one entertained at another's house 2 one living in hotel

guffaw n/v (make) burst of boisterous laughter

guide ❶ n 1 one who shows the way 2 adviser 3 book of instruction or information ▷ v 4 lead, act as guide to **guidance** n **guideline** n set principle

guild ❶ n 1 organization for mutual help, or with common object

guile n cunning, deceit

guillotine n 1 machine for beheading 2 machine for cutting paper ▷ v 3 use guillotine on

guilt ❶ n 1 fact, state of having done wrong 2 responsibility for offence **guiltless** adj innocent **guilty** adj having committed an offence

guinea n formerly, sum of 21

shillings **guinea pig** 1 rodent originating in S Amer 2 (Inf) person or animal used in experiments

guise ❶ n external appearance, esp. one assumed

guitar n stringed instrument played by plucking or strumming **guitarist** n

gulch n (US & Canad) a narrow ravine cut by a fast stream

gulf ❶ n 1 large inlet of the sea 2 chasm 3 large gap

gull n long-winged web-footed sea bird

gullet n food passage from mouth to stomach

gullible adj easily imposed on, credulous

gully n, pl -lies channel or ravine worn by action of water

gulp v/n 1 swallow 2 gasp

gum¹ ❶ n 1 sticky substance issuing from certain trees

— THESAURUS —

guess v = **estimate**, predict, work out, speculate, conjecture ≠ **know**; = **suppose**, think, believe, suspect, judge ▷ n = **estimate**, speculation, judgment, hypothesis, conjecture ≠ **certainty**

guest n = **visitor**, company, caller

guide n = **handbook**, manual, guidebook, instructions, catalogue; = **directory**, street map; = **escort**, leader, usher; = **pointer**, sign, landmark, marker, beacon ▷ v = **lead**, direct, escort, conduct, accompany; = **steer**, control, manage, direct, handle

guild n = **society**, union, league, association, company

guilt n = **shame**, regret, remorse, contrition, guilty conscience ≠ **pride**; = **culpability**, blame, responsibility, misconduct, wickedness ≠ **innocence**

guise n = **form**, appearance, shape, aspect, mode; = **pretence**, disguise, aspect, semblance

gulf n = **bay**, bight, sea inlet; = **chasm**, opening, split, gap, separation

gum¹ n = **glue**, adhesive, resin, cement, paste ▷ v = **stick**, glue, affix, cement, paste

2 adhesive **3** chewing gum ▷ v
4 stick with gum **gumboots** pl n
boots of rubber **gumtree** n any
species of eucalypt
gum² n firm flesh in which teeth
are set
gumption n **1** resourcefulness
2 shrewdness, sense
gun ⊕ n **1** weapon with metal
tube from which missiles are
discharged by explosion
2 cannon, pistol etc. ▷ v **3** shoot
4 pursue vigorously **gunner** n
gunpowder n explosive
mixture of saltpetre, sulphur,
charcoal **gunshot** n **1** shot or
range of gun ▷ adj **2** caused by
missile from gun
gunge n (Inf) any sticky,
unpleasant substance
gunwale, gunnel n upper edge
of ship's side
guppy n, pl **-pies** small colourful
aquarium fish
gurgle n/v (make) bubbling noise
guru ⊕ n **1** spiritual teacher, esp. in
India
gush ⊕ v **1** flow out suddenly and
copiously, spurt ▷ n **2** sudden and
copious flow
gusset n triangle or diamond-
shaped piece of material let into
garment
gust n **1** sudden blast of wind

2 burst of rain, anger, passion etc.
gusto n enjoyment, zest
gut ⊕ n **1** intestines **2** material
made from guts of animals, e.g. for
violin strings etc. ▷ pl **3** (Inf)
courage ▷ v **4** remove guts from
(fish etc.) **5** remove, destroy
contents of (house)
gutter ⊕ n **1** shallow trough for
carrying off water from roof or side
of street
guttural adj harsh-sounding, as if
produced in the throat
guy¹ ⊕ n **1** effigy of Guy Fawkes
burnt on Nov. 5th **2** (Inf) person
(usu. male) ▷ v **3** make fun of
4 ridicule
guy² n rope, chain to steady, secure
something, e.g. tent
guzzle v eat or drink greedily
gym n short for GYMNASIUM or
GYMNASTICS
gymkhana n competition or
display of horse riding
gymnasium n place equipped for
muscular exercises, athletic
training **gymnastics** pl n
muscular exercises **gymnast** n
gynaecology n branch of
medicine dealing with functions
and diseases of women
gynaecologist n
gypsum n chalklike mineral, used
for making plaster

g

--- THESAURUS ---

gun n = **firearm**, shooter (Sl), piece
(Sl), handgun
guru n = **authority**, expert, leader,
master, pundit
gush v = **flow**, run, rush, flood,
pour ▷ n = **stream**, flow, rush,

flood, jet
gut v = **disembowel**, clean;
= **ravage**, empty, clean out, despoil
gutter n = **drain**, channel, ditch,
trench, trough
guy¹ n (Inf) = **man**, person, fellow,

Gypsy, Gipsy ❼ *n, pl* **-sies** one of
wandering race orig. from NW
India

gyrate *v* move in circle, spiral
gyroscope *n* disc rotating on axis
that can turn in any direction

————————— THESAURUS —————————

lad, bloke *(Brit Inf)*
Gypsy, Gipsy *n* = **traveller**,
roamer, wanderer, Bohemian, rover

g

h

haberdasher *n* dealer in articles of dress, ribbons, pins, needles etc. **haberdashery** *n*

habit ❶ *n* **1** settled tendency or practice **2** customary apparel, esp. of nun or monk **habitual** *adj* **1** formed or acquired by habit **2** usual, customary

habitable *adj* fit to live in **habitat** *n* natural home (of animal etc.) **habitation** *n* abode

hack¹ ❶ *v* **1** cut, chop (at) violently **2** (*Inf*) utter harsh, dry cough ▷ *n* **3** violent blow **hacker** *n* (*Sl*) computer enthusiast who breaks into computer system of company or government

hack² ❶ *n* **1** horse for ordinary riding **2** inferior writer

hackles *pl n* hairs on back of neck of dog and other animals which are raised in anger

hackneyed *adj* (of words etc.) stale, trite because of overuse

hacksaw *n* handsaw for cutting metal

haddock *n* large, edible sea fish

haemoglobin *n* colouring and oxygen-bearing matter of red blood corpuscles

haemophilia *n* illness in which blood does not clot **haemophiliac** *n*

haemorrhage *n* profuse bleeding

haemorrhoids *pl n* swollen veins in rectum

hag *n* **1** ugly old woman **2** witch

haggard *adj* anxious, careworn

haggis *n* Scottish dish made from sheep's offal, oatmeal etc.

haggle *v* bargain over price

hail¹ ❶ *v* **1** greet **2** acclaim **3** call **4** come (from)

hail² ❶ *n* **1** (shower of) pellets of ice **2** barrage ▷ *v* **3** pour down as shower of hail **hailstone** *n*

hair ❶ *n* **1** filament growing from skin of animal, as covering of man's head **2** such filaments collectively

THESAURUS

habit *n* = **mannerism**, custom, way, practice, characteristic

hack¹ *v* = **cut**, chop, slash, mutilate, mangle

hack² *n* = **reporter**, writer, correspondent, journalist, scribbler

hail¹ *v* = **acclaim**, honour, acknowledge, cheer, applaud **≠ condemn**; = **salute**, greet,

address, welcome, say hello to **≠ snub**; = **flag down**, summon, signal to, wave down

hail² *n* = **hailstones**, sleet, hailstorm, frozen rain; = **shower**, rain, storm, battery, volley ▷ *v* = **rain**, shower, pelt

hair *n* = **locks**, mane, tresses, shock, mop

hairy adj **hairdo** n way of dressing hair **hairdresser** n one who cuts and styles hair **hairgrip** n small, tightly bent metal hairpin **hairpin** n pin for keeping hair in place **hairpin bend** U-shaped turn of road

hale ❶ adj robust, healthy

half ❶ n, pl **halves** 1 either of two equal parts of thing ▷ adj 2 forming half ▷ adv 3 to the extent of half **half-baked** adj (Inf) poorly planned **half-breed, half-caste** n (Offens) person with parents of different races **half-brother, -sister** n brother, sister by one parent only **half-hearted** adj unenthusiastic **halfwit** n feeble-minded person

halibut n large edible flatfish

halitosis n bad-smelling breath

hall ❶ n 1 (entrance) passage 2 large room or building used for esp. public assembly

hallelujah n/interj exclamation of praise to God

hallmark ❶ n 1 mark used to indicate standard of tested gold and silver 2 mark of excellence

3 distinguishing feature

hallo interj see HELLO

hallowed adj holy

hallucinate v suffer illusions **hallucination** n **hallucinatory** adj

halo n, pl **-loes, -los** circle of light

halt ❶ n 1 interruption or end to progress etc. (esp. as command to stop marching) ▷ v 2 (cause to) stop **halting** adj hesitant, lame

halter n 1 rope with headgear to fasten horse 2 low-cut dress style with strap passing behind neck 3 noose for hanging person

halve ❶ v 1 cut in half 2 reduce to half 3 share

ham n 1 meat (esp. salted or smoked) from thigh of pig 2 actor adopting exaggerated style 3 amateur radio enthusiast **ham-fisted** adj clumsy

hamburger n fried cake of minced beef

hamlet n small village

hammer ❶ n 1 tool usu. with heavy head at end of handle, for beating, driving nails etc. ▷ v 2 strike as with hammer

──────────── THESAURUS ────────────

hale adj = **healthy**, well, strong, sound, fit

half n = **fifty per cent**, equal part ▷ adj = **partial**, limited, moderate, halved ▷ adv = **partially**, partly, in part

hall n = **passage**, lobby, corridor, hallway, foyer; = **meeting place**, chamber, auditorium, concert hall, assembly room

hallmark n = **trademark**, sure

sign, telltale sign; (Brit) = **mark**, sign, device, stamp, seal

halt v = **stop**, break off, stand still, wait, rest ≠ **continue**; = **come to an end**, stop, cease ▷ n = **stop**, end, close, pause, standstill ≠ **continuation**

halve v = **cut in half**, reduce by fifty per cent, decrease by fifty per cent, lessen by fifty per cent

hammer v = **hit**, drive, knock,

hammock n bed of canvas etc., hung on cords

hamper¹ n large covered basket

hamper² ❶ v impede, obstruct

hamster n type of rodent, sometimes kept as pet

hamstring n tendon at back of knee

hand ❶ n 1 extremity of arm beyond wrist 2 side 3 style of writing 4 cards dealt to player 5 manual worker 6 help 7 pointer of dial 8 applause ▷ v 9 pass 10 deliver 11 hold out **handful** n 1 small quantity 2 (Inf) person, thing causing problems **handiness** n 1 dexterity 2 state of being near, available **handy** adj 1 convenient 2 clever with hands **handbag** n woman's bag **handbook** n small instruction book **handcuff** n 1 fetter for wrist, usu. joined in pair ▷ v 2 secure thus **handicraft** n manual occupation or skill **handiwork** n thing done by particular person **handkerchief** n

small square of fabric for wiping nose etc. **hand-out** n 1 thing given free 2 written information given out at talk etc. **handwriting** n way person writes **handyman** n man employed to do various tasks

handicap ❶ n 1 something that hampers or hinders 2 race, contest in which chances are equalized 3 (Offens) any physical disability ▷ v 4 hamper, impose handicaps on

handle ❶ n 1 part of thing to hold it by ▷ v 2 touch, feel with hands 3 manage 4 deal with 5 trade **handler** n person who controls animal **handlebars** pl n curved metal bar to steer cycle

handsome ❶ adj 1 of fine appearance 2 generous 3 ample

hang ❶ v **hanging, hung** 1 suspend 2 attach, set up (wallpaper, doors etc.) 3 be suspended, cling 4 (past **hanged**) kill by suspension by neck **hanger** n frame on which clothes etc. can be hung **hangdog** adj sullen,

h

— THESAURUS —

beat, strike

hamper² v = **hinder**, handicap, prevent, restrict, frustrate ≠ help

hand n = **palm**, fist, paw (Inf), mitt (Sl); = **worker**, employee, labourer, workman, operative; = **round of applause**, clap, ovation, big hand; = **writing**, script, handwriting, calligraphy ▷ v = **give**, pass, hand over, present to, deliver

handicap n = **disadvantage**, barrier, restriction, obstacle, limitation, drawback

≠ **advantage**; = **advantage**, head start ▷ v = **hinder**, limit, restrict, burden, hamstring ≠ help

handle n = **grip**, hilt, haft, stock ▷ v = **manage**, deal with, tackle, cope with; = **deal with**, manage

handsome adj = **good-looking**, attractive, gorgeous, elegant, personable ≠ **ugly**; = **generous**, large, princely, liberal, considerable ≠ mean

hang v = **dangle**, swing, suspend; = **execute**, lynch, string up (Inf) dejected **hang-glider** n glider with light frame from which pilot hangs in harness **hangman** n person who executes people by hanging **hangover** n aftereffects of too much drinking **hang-up** n (*Inf*) emotional or psychological problem

hangar n large shed for aircraft

hanker v crave

hanky, hankie n, pl **hankies** (*Inf*) handkerchief

haphazard adj random, careless

hapless adj unlucky

happen ❶ v 1 come about, occur 2 chance to do **happening** n occurrence, event

happy ❶ adj **-pier, -piest** 1 glad, content 2 lucky **happily** adv **happiness** n

harangue n 1 vehement speech 2 tirade ▷ v 3 address vehemently

harass ❶ v worry, torment **harassment** n

harbour ❶ n 1 shelter for ships ▷ v 2 give shelter 3 maintain

(secretly)

hard ❶ adj 1 firm, resisting pressure 2 solid 3 difficult to do, understand 4 unfeeling 5 heavy ▷ adv 6 vigorously 7 persistently 8 close **harden** v **hardly** adv 1 unkindly, harshly 2 scarcely, not quite 3 only just **hardship** n 1 ill luck 2 severe toil, suffering 3 instance of this **hard-headed** adj shrewd **hard-hearted** adj unfeeling **hard shoulder** n motorway verge for emergency stops **hardware** n 1 tools, implements 2 (*Comp*) mechanical and electronic parts **hardwood** n wood from deciduous trees

hardy ❶ adj **hardier, hardiest** 1 robust, vigorous 2 bold 3 (of plants) able to grow in the open all the year round

hare n animal like large rabbit **harebell** n round-leaved bell-shaped flower **harebrained** adj rash, wild **harelip** n fissure of upper lip

harem n 1 women's part of Muslim

─────── THESAURUS ───────

happen v. = **occur**, take place, come about; = **result**, develop; = **chance**, turn out

happy adj = **pleased**, delighted, content, thrilled, glad; = **fortunate**, lucky, timely, favourable, auspicious ≠ **unfortunate**

harass v = **annoy**, trouble, bother, harry, plague

harbour n = **port**, haven, dock, mooring, marina ▷ v = **hold**, bear, maintain, nurse, retain; = **shelter**, protect, hide, shield, provide

refuge

hard adj = **tough**, strong, firm, solid, stiff ≠ **soft**; = **difficult**, involved, complicated, puzzling, intricate ≠ **easy**; = **exhausting**, tough, exacting, rigorous, gruelling ≠ **easy**; = **harsh**, cold, cruel, stern, callous ≠ **kind**; = **grim**, painful, distressing, harsh, unpleasant ▷ adv = **intently**, closely, carefully, sharply, keenly

hardy adj = **strong**, tough, robust, sound, rugged ≠ **frail**

dwelling **2** one's man's wives

hark v listen

harlequin n masked clown in diamond-patterned costume

harlot n whore, prostitute

harm ❶ n/v damage **harmful** adj **harmless** adj unable or unlikely to hurt

harmony ❶ n, pl **-nies** **1** agreement **2** combination of notes to make chords **3** melodious sound **harmonic** adj of harmony **harmonica** n mouth organ **harmonious** adj **harmonium** n small organ **harmonize** v **1** bring into harmony **2** cause to agree **3** reconcile **4** be in harmony

harness ❶ n **1** equipment for attaching horse to cart, plough etc. ▷ v **2** put on, in harness **3** utilize energy or power of

harp n **1** musical instrument of strings played by hand ▷ v **2** play on harp **3** dwell on continuously **harpsichord** n stringed instrument like piano

harpoon n/v (use) barbed spear for catching whales

harrier n **1** hound used in hunting hares **2** falcon

harrow n **1** implement for smoothing, levelling or stirring up soil ▷ v **2** draw harrow over **3** distress greatly **harrowing** adj distressful

harry ❶ v **-rying, -ried 1** harass **2** ravage

harsh ❶ adj **1** rough, discordant **2** severe **3** unfeeling **harshly** adv

harvest ❶ n **1** (season for) gathering grain **2** gathering **3** crop ▷ v **4** reap and gather in **harvester** n

has third person sing. of HAVE **has-been** (Inf) one who is no longer successful

hash n **1** dish of chopped meat etc. **2** mess ▷ v **3** cut up small, chop **4** mix up

hashish n resinous extract of Indian hemp, esp. used as hallucinogen

hassle ❶ n (Inf) **1** quarrel **2** a lot of bother, trouble ▷ v **3** bother

hassock n kneeling cushion

haste n **1** speed, hurry ▷ v

---

harm v = **injure**, hurt, wound, abuse, ill-treat ≠ **heal** ▷ n = **injury**, suffering, damage, ill, hurt

harmony n = **accord**, peace, agreement, friendship, sympathy ≠ **conflict**; = **tune**, melody, unison, tunefulness, euphony ≠ **discord**

harness v = **exploit**, control, channel, employ, utilize ▷ n = **equipment**, tackle, gear, tack

harry v = **pester**, bother, plague, harass, hassle (Inf)

harsh adj = **severe**, hard, tough, stark, austere; = **bleak**, freezing, severe, icy

harvest n = **harvesting**, picking, gathering, collecting, reaping; = **crop**, yield, year's growth, produce ▷ v = **gather**, pick, collect, bring in, pluck

hassle (Inf) ▷ n = **trouble**, problem, difficulty, bother, grief (Inf) ▷ v = **bother**, bug (Inf), annoy, hound, harass

2 hasten **hasten** v (cause to) hurry **hastily** adv **hasty** adj

hat n head covering usu. with brim **hat trick** set of three achievements

hatch¹ ❶ v **1** (of young birds etc.) (cause to) emerge from egg **2** contrive, devise **hatchery** n

hatch² n **1** hatchway **2** trapdoor over it **3** opening in wall, to facilitate service of meals etc. **hatchback** n car with lifting rear door **hatchway** n opening in deck of ship etc.

hatchet n small axe

hate ❶ v **1** dislike strongly **2** bear malice towards ▷ n **3** this feeling **4** that which is hated **hateful** adj detestable **hatred** n

haughty adj **-tier, -tiest** proud, arrogant **haughtily** adv

haul ❶ v **1** pull, drag with effort ▷ n **2** hauling **3** what is hauled **haulage** n **haulier** n

haunch n human hip or fleshy hindquarter of animal

haunt ❶ v **1** visit regularly **2** visit in form of ghost **3** recur to ▷ n **4** place frequently visited **haunted** adj **1** frequented by ghosts **2** worried **haunting** adj extremely beautiful or sad

have ❶ v **has, having, had 1** hold, possess **2** be affected with **3** be obliged (to do) **4** cheat **5** contain **6** contain **7** allow **8** cause to be done **9** give birth to **10** as auxiliary, forms perfect and other tenses

haven ❶ n place of safety

haversack n canvas bag for provisions etc. carried on back

havoc ❶ n **1** devastation, ruin **2** (Inf) confusion, chaos

hawk¹ n **1** bird of prey smaller than eagle **2** advocate of warlike policies

hawk² v offer (goods) for sale, esp. in street **hawker** n

hawthorn n thorny shrub or tree

— THESAURUS —

hatch¹ v = **incubate**, breed, sit on, brood, bring forth; = **devise**, design, invent, put together, conceive

hate v = **loathe**, despise, dislike, abhor ≠ **love**; = **dislike**, detest, shrink from, recoil from, not be able to bear ≠ **like** ▷ n = **dislike**, hostility, hatred, loathing, animosity ≠ **love**

haul v = **drag**, draw, pull, heave ▷ n = **yield**, gain, spoils, catch, harvest

haunt v = **plague**, trouble, obsess, torment, possess ▷ n = **meeting**

place, hangout (Inf), rendezvous, stamping ground

have v = **own**, keep, possess, hold, retain; = **get**, obtain, take, receive, accept; = **suffer**, experience, undergo, sustain, endure; = **give birth to**, bear, deliver, bring forth, beget; = **experience**, go through, undergo, meet with, come across

haven n = **sanctuary**, shelter, retreat, asylum, refuge

havoc n (Inf) = **disorder**, confusion, chaos, disruption, mayhem

hay n grass mown and dried **hay fever** allergic reaction to pollen, dust etc. **haystack** n large pile of hay **haywire** adj 1 crazy 2 disorganized

hazard ❶ n 1 chance 2 risk, danger ▷ v 3 expose to risk 4 run risk of **hazardous** adj risky

haze ❶ n 1 mist 2 obscurity **hazy** adj 1 misty 2 vague

hazel n 1 bush bearing nuts ▷ adj 2 light brown

he pron 1 person, animal already referred to ▷ comb. form 2 male, as in he-goat

head ❶ n 1 upper part of body, containing mouth, sense organs and brain 2 upper part of anything 3 chief of organization, school etc. 4 chief part 5 aptitude, capacity 6 crisis 7 person, animal considered as unit ▷ adj 8 chief, principal 9 (of wind) contrary ▷ v 10 be at the top 11 lead 12 provide with head 13 hit (ball) with head

14 make for 15 form a head **heading** n title **heady** adj apt to intoxicate or excite **headache** n continuous pain in head **headland** n area of land jutting into sea **headlight** n powerful lamp on front of vehicle etc. **headline** n news summary, in large type in newspaper **headlong** adv in rush **headphones** pl n two small loudspeakers strapped against ears **headquarters** pl n centre of operations **head start** advantage **headstrong** adj self-willed **headway** n progress

heal ❶ v make or become well

health ❶ n 1 soundness of body 2 condition of body 3 toast drunk in person's honour **healthy** adj **healthier, healthiest** **health food** vegetarian food etc., eaten for dietary value

heap ❶ n 1 pile 2 great quantity ▷ v 3 pile, load with

hear ❶ v **hearing, heard**

THESAURUS

hazard n = **danger**, risk, threat, problem, menace ▷ v = **jeopardize**, risk, endanger, threaten, expose

haze n = **mist**, cloud, fog, obscurity, vapour

head n = **skull**, crown, pate, nut (Sl), loaf (Sl); = **mind**, reasoning, understanding, thought, sense; = **top**, crown, summit, peak, crest (Inf); = **leader**, president, director, manager, chief ▷ adj = **chief**, main, leading, first, prime ▷ v = **lead**, precede, be the leader of, be or go first, be or go at the front of; = **top**,

lead, crown, cap; = **be in charge of**, run, manage, lead, control

heal v (sometimes with **up**) = **mend**, get better, get well, cure, regenerate

health n = **condition**, state, shape, constitution, fettle; = **wellbeing**, strength, fitness, vigour, good condition ≠ **illness**

heap n = **pile**, lot, collection, mass, stack; often plural (Inf) = **a lot**, lots (Inf), plenty, masses, load(s) (Inf) ▷ v (sometimes with **up**) = **pile**, collect, gather, stack, accumulate

hear v = **overhear**, catch, detect;

h

1 perceive sound by ear **2** listen to
3 (*Law*) try (case) **4** heed **5** learn
hearing *n* **1** ability to hear
2 earshot **3** judicial examination
hearsay *n* rumour

hearken *v* listen

hearse *n* funeral carriage for coffin

heart ❶ *n* **1** organ which makes
blood circulate **2** seat of emotions
and affections **3** mind, soul,
courage **4** central part **5** suit at
cards **hearten** *v* make, become
cheerful **heartless** *adj* unfeeling
hearty *adj* **1** friendly **2** vigorous
3 in good health **4** satisfying
heart attack sudden severe
malfunction of heart **heartbeat** *n*
single pulsation of heart
heartbreak *n* intense grief
heartfelt *adj* felt sincerely
heart-rending *adj* agonizing **by
heart** by memory

hearth *n* **1** part of room where fire
is made **2** home

heat ❶ *n* **1** hotness **2** sensation of
this **3** hot weather **4** warmth of
feeling, anger etc. **5** sexual
excitement in female animals

6 one of many eliminating races
etc. ▷ *v* **7** make, become hot
heated *adj* angry **heater** *n*

heath *n* tract of waste land

heathen *adj/n* **1** (one) not
adhering to a religious system
2 pagan

heather *n* shrub growing on
heaths and mountains

heave *v* **1** lift (and throw) with
effort **2** utter (sigh) **3** swell, rise
4 feel nausea ▷ *n* **5** act of heaving

heaven ❶ *n* **1** abode of God
2 place of bliss **3** (*also pl*) sky
heavenly *adj*

heavy ❶ *adj* **heavier, heaviest**
1 weighty **2** dense **3** sluggish
4 severe **5** sorrowful **6** serious
7 dull **heavily** *adv*

heckle *v* interrupt (speaker) by
questions, taunts etc.

hectare *n* one hundred ares or
10 000 square metres (2.471
acres)

hectic *adj* **1** rushed, busy

hedge ❶ *n* **1** fence of bushes ▷ *v*
2 surround with hedge **3** be
evasive **4** secure against loss

— THESAURUS —

(*Law*) = **try**, judge, examine,
investigate; = **learn**, discover, find
out, pick up, gather

heart *n* = **nature**, character, soul,
constitution, essence; = **courage**,
will, spirit, purpose, bottle (*Brit Inf*)

heat *v* (*sometimes with* up) = **warm
(up)**, cook, boil, roast, reheat
≠ **chill** ▷ *n* = **warmth**, hotness,
temperature ≠ **cold**; = **hot
weather**, warmth, closeness, high
temperature, heatwave

heaven *n* = **paradise**, next world,
hereafter, nirvana (*Buddhism,
Hinduism*), bliss; (*Inf*) = **happiness**,
paradise, ecstasy, bliss, utopia

heavy *adj* = **weighty**, large,
massive, hefty, bulky ≠ **light**;
= **intensive**, severe, serious,
concentrated, fierce

hectic *adj* = **frantic**, chaotic,
heated, animated, turbulent
≠ **peaceful**

hedge *v* = **prevaricate**, evade,

hedgehog n small animal covered with spines

hedonism n pursuit of pleasure **hedonist** n

heed 🔊 v take notice of **heedless** adj careless

heel¹ 🔊 n **1** hind part of foot **2** part of shoe supporting this **3** (SI) undesirable person ▷ v **4** supply with heel

heel² v lean to one side

hefty 🔊 adj **heftier, heftiest 1** bulky **2** weighty **3** strong

heifer n young cow

height 🔊 n **1** measure from base to top **2** quality of being high **3** elevation **4** highest degree **5** hilltop **heighten** v **1** make higher **2** intensify

heinous adj atrocious, extremely wicked, detestable

heir 🔊 n person entitled to inherit property or rank **heirloom** n thing that has been in family for generations

helicopter n aircraft lifted by rotating blades

helium n very light, nonflammable gaseous element

helix n, pl **helices, helixes** spiral

hell 🔊 n **1** abode of the damned **2** abode of the dead generally **3** place of torture **hellish** adj **hell-bent** adj intent

hello, hallo 🔊 interj expression of greeting

helm 🔊 n tiller, wheel for turning ship's rudder

helmet n defensive or protective covering for head

help 🔊 v/n **1** aid **2** support **3** remedy **helper** n **helpful** adj **helping** n single portion of food **helpless** adj **1** incompetent **2** unaided **3** unable to help

helter-skelter adv/adj/n **1** (in) hurry and confusion ▷ n **2** high spiral slide at fairground

h

THESAURUS

sidestep, duck, dodge

heed v = **pay attention to**, listen to, take notice of, follow, consider ≠ **ignore**

heel¹ n (SI) = **swine**, cad (Brit Inf), bounder (old-fashioned Brit SI), rotter (SI, chiefly Brit)

hefty adj (Inf) = **big**, strong, massive, strapping, robust ≠ **small**

height n = **tallness**, stature, highness, loftiness ≠ **shortness**; = **altitude**, measurement, highness, elevation, tallness ≠ **depth**; = **peak**, top, crown, summit, crest ≠ **valley**

heir n = **successor**, beneficiary, inheritor, heiress (fem.), next in line

hell n = **the underworld**, the abyss, Hades (Greek myth), hellfire, the inferno; (Inf) = **torment**, suffering, agony, nightmare, misery

hello interj = **hi** (Inf), greetings, how do you do?, good morning, good evening

helm n = **tiller**, wheel, rudder

help v (sometimes with out) = **aid**, support, assist, cooperate with, abet ≠ **hinder**; = **improve**, ease, relieve, facilitate, alleviate ≠ **make worse**; = **assist**, aid, support ▷ n = **assistance**, aid, support, advice, guidance ≠ **hindrance**

hem ① n 1 edge of cloth, folded and sewn down ▷ *v* **2** sew thus **3** confine, shut in

hemisphere *n* **1** half sphere **2** half of the earth

hemlock *n* poisonous plant

hemp *n* **1** Indian plant **2** its fibre used for rope etc. **3** any of several narcotic drugs

hen *n* female of domestic fowl and others **henpecked** *adj* (of man) dominated by wife

hence ① adv 1 from this point **2** for this reason **henceforward, henceforth** *adv* from now onwards

henchman *n* trusty follower

henna *n* **1** flowering shrub **2** reddish dye made from it

hepatitis *n* inflammation of the liver

heptagon *n* figure with seven angles

her *pron* object of SHE ▷ *adj* of, belonging to her **hers** *pron* of her **herself** *pron* emphatic or reflexive form of SHE

herald ① n 1 messenger, envoy ▷ *v* **2** announce **heraldic** *adj* **heraldry** *n* study of (right to have) heraldic bearings

herb *n* plant used in cookery or medicine **herbaceous** *adj* **1** of, like herbs **2** perennial flowering

herbal *adj* **herbicide** *n* chemical which destroys plants **herbivore** *n* animal that feeds on plants **herbivorous** *adj*

herd ① n 1 company of animals feeding together ▷ *v* **2** crowd together **3** tend (herd) **herdsman** *n*

here *adv* **1** in this place **2** at or to this point **hereabouts** *adv* near here **hereafter** *adv* **1** in time to come ▷ *n* **2** future existence **hereby** *adv* as a result of this **herein** *adv* in this place **herewith** *adv* with this

heredity *n* tendency of organism to transmit its nature to its descendants **hereditary** *adj* descending by inheritance or heredity

heresy *n, pl* **-sies** unorthodox opinion or belief **heretic** *n* **heretical** *adj*

heritage ① n what may be or is inherited

hermaphrodite *n* person or animal with characteristics, or reproductive organs, of both sexes

hermetic *adj* sealed so as to be airtight **hermetically** *adj*

hermit *n* one living in solitude **hermitage** *n* hermit's dwelling

hernia *n* projection of organ

━━━━━━━━━━ THESAURUS ━━━━━━━━━━

hem *n* = **edge**, border, margin, trimming, fringe

hence *conj* = **therefore**, thus, consequently, for this reason, in consequence

herald *v* = **indicate**, promise, usher in, presage, portend ▷ *n*

= **messenger**, courier, proclaimer, announcer, crier

herd *n* = **flock**, crowd, collection, mass, drove

heritage *n* = **inheritance**, legacy, birthright, tradition, endowment through lining

hero ❶ *n, pl* **heroes 1** one greatly regarded for achievements or qualities **2** principal character in story **heroic** *adj* **heroism** *n*

heroin *n* highly addictive drug

heron *n* long-legged wading bird

herring *n* important food fish

hertz *n, pl* **hertz** SI unit of frequency

hesitate ❶ *v* **1** hold back **2** feel, or show indecision **3** be reluctant **hesitancy, hesitation** *n* **hesitant** *adj*

hessian *n* coarse jute cloth

heterogeneous *adj* composed of diverse elements **heterogeneity** *n*

heterosexual *n/adj* (person) sexually attracted to members of the opposite sex

hew *v* **hewing, hewed 1** chop, cut with axe **2** carve

hexagon *n* figure with six angles **hexagonal** *adj*

hey *interj* expression of surprise or for catching attention

heyday *n* bloom, prime

hiatus *n, pl* **-tuses, -tus** break or gap

hibernate *v* pass the winter, esp. in a torpid state **hibernation** *n*

hiccup, hiccough *n/v* (have) spasm of the breathing organs with an abrupt sound

hickory *n, pl* **-ries 1** N Amer. nut-bearing tree **2** its tough wood

hide ❶ *v* **hiding, hid, hidden 1** put, keep out of sight **2** conceal oneself

hide² ❶ *n* skin of animal **hiding** *n* (Sl) thrashing **hidebound** *adj* **1** restricted **2** narrow-minded

hideous ❶ *adj* repulsive, revolting

hierarchy ❶ *n, pl* **-chies** system of persons or things arranged in graded order **hierarchical** *adj*

hieroglyphic *adj* **1** of picture writing, as used in ancient Egypt ▷ *n* **2** symbol representing object, concept or sound

hi-fi *adj* short for HIGH-FIDELITY *n* high-fidelity equipment

high ❶ *adj* **1** tall, lofty **2** far up **3** (of sound) acute in pitch

h

— THESAURUS —

hero *n* = **protagonist**, leading man; = **star**, champion/victor, superstar, conqueror

hesitate *v* = **waver**, delay, pause, wait, doubt ≠ **be decisive**; = **be reluctant**, be unwilling, shrink from, think twice, scruple ≠ **be determined**

hide¹ *v* = **conceal**, stash (Inf), secrete, put out of sight ≠ **display**; = **go into hiding**, take cover, hole up, lie low; = **keep secret**, suppress, withhold, keep

quiet about, hush up ≠ **disclose**

hide² *n* = **skin**, leather, pelt

hideous *adj* = **ugly**, revolting, ghastly, monstrous, grotesque ≠ **beautiful**

hierarchy *n* = **grading**, ranking, social order, pecking order, class system

high *adj* = **tall**, towering, soaring, steep, elevated ≠ **short**; = **extreme**, great, acute, severe, extraordinary ≠ **low**; = **strong**, violent, extreme, blustery, squally; = **important**,

4 expensive 5 of great importance, quality, or rank 6 (*Inf*) in state of euphoria ▷ *adv* 7 at, to a height **highly** *adv* **highness** *n* 1 quality of being high 2 (*with cap.*) title of royal person **highbrow** *n/adj* intellectual **high-fidelity** *adj* of high-quality sound reproducing equipment **high-handed** *adj* domineering **highlands** *pl n* area of relatively high ground **highlight** *n* 1 outstanding feature ▷ *v* 2 emphasize **highly strung** excitable, nervous **high-rise** *adj* of building that has many storeys **high-tech** *adj* using sophisticated technology **high time** latest possible time **highwayman** *n* formerly, horseman who robbed travellers

highway *n* (*US & Canad*) main road for fast-moving traffic

hijack ❶ *v* divert or wrongfully take command of a vehicle (esp. aircraft) **hijacker** *n*

hike ❶ *v* 1 walk a long way (for pleasure) in country 2 pull (up), hitch **hiker** *n*

hill ❶ *n* 1 natural elevation, small mountain 2 mound **hillock** *n* little hill **hilly** *adj*

hilt *n* handle of sword etc.

him *pron* object of HE **himself** *pron* emphatic form of HE

hind[1] *n* female of deer

hind[2] *adj* **hinder, hindmost** at the back, posterior

hinder ❶ *v* obstruct, impede, delay **hindrance** *n*

hinge *n* 1 movable joint, as that on which door hangs ▷ *v* 2 attach with hinge 3 depend on

hint ❶ *n* 1 slight indication 2 piece of advice 3 small amount ▷ *v* 4 give hint

hinterland *n* district lying behind coast, port etc.

hip *n* **hipper, hippest** 1 either side of body below waist and above thigh 2 fruit of rose

hippie *n* person who rejects conventional dress and lifestyle

hippopotamus *n, pl* **-muses, -mi** large Afr. animal living in rivers

hire ❶ *v* 1 obtain temporary use of by payment 2 engage for wage ▷ *n*

— THESAURUS —

chief, powerful, superior, eminent ≠ **lowly**; = **high-pitched**, piercing, shrill, penetrating, strident ≠ **deep** ▷ *adv* = **way up**, aloft, far up, to a great height

hijack *v* = **seize**, take over, commandeer, expropriate

hike *v* = **walk**, march, trek, ramble, tramp; = **hitch up**, raise, lift, pull up, jack up

hill *n* = **mount**, fell, height, mound, hilltop

hinder *v* = **obstruct**, stop, check, block, delay ≠ **help**

hint *n* = **clue**, suggestion, implication, indication, pointer; *often plural* = **advice**, help, tip(s), suggestion(s), pointer(s); = **trace**, touch, suggestion, dash, suspicion ▷ *v* (*sometimes with at*) = **suggest**, indicate, imply, intimate, insinuate

hire *v* = **employ**, commission, take on, engage, appoint; = **rent**, charter, lease, let, engage ▷ *n*

DICTIONARY

3 hiring or being hired **4** payment for use of thing **hire-purchase** n purchase of goods by instalments

hirsute adj hairy

his pron/adj belonging to him

hiss ⊙ v **1** make sharp sound of letter s **2** express disapproval with ▷ n **3** hissing

history ⊙ n, pl **-ries 1** (record of) past events **2** study of these **historian** n **historic** adj **historical** adj

histrionic adj excessively theatrical, insincere, artificial in manner **histrionics** pl n behaviour like this

hit ⊙ v **hitting, hit 1** strike with blow or missile **2** affect injuriously **3** find **4** light (upon) ▷ n **5** blow **6** success **hit man** hired assassin

hitch ⊙ v **1** fasten with loop etc. **2** raise with jerk **3** be caught or fastened ▷ n **4** difficulty **5** knot **6** jerk **hitchhike** v travel by begging free rides **hitchhiker** n

hither adv to this place **hitherto** adv up to now

HIV human immunodeficiency virus

hive n structure in which bees live

hive off transfer

hives pl n eruptive skin disease

HM His (or Her) Majesty

HMS His (or Her) Majesty's Service or Ship

hoard n **1** store, esp. hidden ▷ v **2** amass and hide

hoarding n large board for displaying advertisements

hoarse adj sounding husky

hoary adj **hoarier, hoariest 1** grey with age **2** greyish-white **3** very old **hoarfrost** n frozen dew

hoax n **1** practical joke ▷ v **2** play trick upon

hob n top area of cooking stove

hobble v **1** walk lamely **2** tie legs together ▷ n **3** limping gait

hobby ⊙ n, pl **-bies** favourite occupation as pastime **hobbyhorse** n **1** favourite topic **2** toy horse

hobgoblin n mischievous fairy

hobnob v **-nobbing, -nobbed 1** drink together **2** be familiar (with)

hobo n, pl **-bos** (US & Canad) shiftless, wandering person

hock¹ n backward-pointing joint on

h

THESAURUS

= **rental**, hiring, rent, lease

hiss v = **whistle**, wheeze, whiz, whirr, sibilate; = **jeer**, mock, deride ▷ n = **fizz**, buzz, hissing, fizzing, sibilation

history n = **the past**, antiquity, yesterday, yesteryear, olden days; = **chronicle**, record, story, account, narrative

hit v = **strike**, beat, knock, bang, slap; = **affect**, damage, harm, ruin,

devastate; = **reach**, gain, achieve, arrive at, accomplish ▷ n = **blow**, knock, stroke, belt (Inf), rap; = **success**, winner, triumph, smash (Inf), sensation

hitch n = **problem**, catch, difficulty, hold-up, obstacle ▷ v (Inf) = **hitchhike**, thumb a lift; = **fasten**, join, attach, couple, tie

hobby n = **pastime**, relaxation, leisure pursuit, diversion, avocation

hock¹ *n* leg of horse etc.

hock² *n* dry white wine

hockey *n* 1 team game played on a field with ball and curved sticks 2 (US & Canad) ice hockey

hod *n* 1 small trough for carrying bricks etc. 2 coal scuttle

hoe *n* 1 tool for weeding, breaking ground etc. ▷ *v* 2 work with hoe

hog *n* 1 pig 2 greedy person ▷ *v* 3 (Inf) eat, use (something) selfishly

hoist ❶ *v* raise aloft, raise with tackle etc.

hold¹ **❶** *v* **holding, held** 1 keep in hands 2 maintain in position 3 contain 4 occupy 5 carry on 6 detain 7 be in force 8 occur ▷ *n* 9 grasp 10 influence **holdall** *n* 1 large travelling bag **holder** *n* **holding** *n* property **hold-up** *n* 1 armed robbery 2 delay

hold² *n* space in ship or aircraft for cargo

hole ❶ *n* 1 hollow place 2 perforation 3 opening 4 (Inf) unattractive place **holey** *adj*

holiday ❶ *n* day(s) of rest from work etc., esp. spent away from home

holistic *adj* considering the complete person, esp. in treatment of disease

hollow ❶ *adj* 1 having a cavity, not solid 2 empty 3 insincere ▷ *n* 4 cavity, hole, valley ▷ *v* 5 make hollow 6 excavate

holly *n* evergreen shrub with prickly leaves and red berries

hollyhock *n* tall plant bearing many large flowers

holocaust ❶ *n* great destruction of life, esp. by fire

hologram *n* three-dimensional photographic image

holster *n* leather case for pistol, hung from belt etc.

─────────── THESAURUS ───────────

hoist *v* = **raise**, lift, erect, elevate, heave

hold¹ keep ▷ *v* = **embrace**, grasp, clutch, hug, squeeze; = **accommodate**, take, contain, seat, have a capacity for; = **occupy**, have, fill, maintain, retain; = **conduct**, convene, call, run, preside over ≠ **cancel** ▷ *n* = **grip**, grasp, clasp; = **foothold**, footing; = **control**, influence, mastery

hole *n* = **cavity**, pit, hollow, chamber, cave; = **opening**, crack, tear, gap, breach; (Inf) = **hovel**, dump (Inf), dive (Sl), slum

holiday *n* = **vacation**, leave, break, time off, recess

hollow *adj* = **empty**, vacant, void, unfilled ≠ **solid**; = **worthless**, useless, vain, meaningless, pointless ≠ **meaningful** ▷ *n* = **cavity**, hole, bowl, depression, pit ≠ **mound**; = **valley**, dale, glen, dell, dingle ≠ **hill** ▷ *v* (often followed by out) = **scoop out**, dig out, excavate, gouge out

holocaust *n* = **devastation**, destruction, genocide, annihilation, conflagration

holy *adj* = **sacred**, blessed, hallowed, venerable, consecrated ≠ **unsanctified**; = **devout**, godly,

holy ❶ adj **-lier, -liest**
1 belonging, devoted to God **2** free
from sin **3** divine **4** consecrated
holily adv **holiness** n

homage ❶ n tribute, respect

home ❶ n **1** dwelling-place
2 residence ▷ adj **3** of home
4 native **5** in home ▷ adv **6** to, at,
one's home **7** to the point ▷ v
8 direct or be directed onto a point
or target **homeless** adj
homelessness n **homely** adv
1 unpretentious **2** domestic
homeward adj/adv **homewards**
adv **home-made** adj **homesick**
adj depressed by absence from
home **homesickness** n
homespun adj **1** domestic
2 simple **homework** n school
work done at home

homeopathy n treatment of
disease by small doses of drug
that produces symptoms of the
disease in healthy people
homeopathic adj

homestead n **1** a house or estate
and the adjoining land and
buildings, esp. on a farm **2** land

assigned to a N American settler

homicide ❶ n **1** killing of human
being **2** killer **homicidal** adj

homily n, pl **-lies** sermon

homogeneous adj **1** formed of
uniform parts **2** similar
homogeneity n **homogenize** v
break up fat globules in milk and
cream to distribute them evenly

homonym n word of same form
as another, but of different sense

homosexual n/adj (person)
sexually attracted to members of
the same sex **homosexuality** n

hone ❶ v sharpen (on whetstone)

honest ❶ adj **1** not cheating,
lying, stealing etc. **2** genuine
honestly adv **honesty** n

honey n sweet fluid made by bees
honeycomb n **1** wax structure in
hexagonal cells ▷ v **2** fill with cells
or perforations **honeymoon** n
holiday taken by newly wedded pair
honeysuckle n climbing plant

honk n **1** call of wild goose **2** sound of
motor-horn ▷ v **3** make this sound

honour ❶ n **1** personal integrity
2 renown **3** reputation ▷ v

─────── THESAURUS ───────

religious, pure, righteous ≠ **sinful**

homage n = **respect**, honour,
worship, devotion, reverence
≠ **contempt**

home n = **dwelling**, house,
residence, abode, habitation;
= **birthplace**, homeland, home
town, native land ▷ adj
= **domestic**, local, internal, native

homicide n = **murder**, killing,
manslaughter, slaying, bloodshed

hone v = **improve**, better, enhance,

upgrade, refine

honest adj = **trustworthy**,
upright, ethical, honourable,
reputable ≠ **dishonest**; = **open**,
direct, frank, plain, sincere
≠ **secretive**

honour n = **integrity**, morality,
honesty, goodness, fairness
≠ **dishonour**; = **prestige**, credit,
reputation, glory, fame ≠ **disgrace**;
= **reputation**, standing, prestige,
image, status; = **acclaim**, praise,

4 respect highly **5** confer honour on **6** accept or pay (bill etc.) when due **honourable** adj **honorary** adj conferred for the sake of honour only

hood n **1** covering for head and neck **2** hoodlike thing **hoodwink** v deceive

hoodlum n gangster

hoof n, pl **hooves, hoofs** horny casing of foot of horse etc.

hook ❶ n **1** bent piece of metal etc., for catching hold, hanging up etc. **2** something resembling hook in shape or function ▷ v **3** grasp, catch, hold, as with hook **hooked** adj **1** shaped like hook **2** caught **3** (Sl) addicted

hooligan ❶ n violent, irresponsible (young) person **hooliganism** n

hoon n (Aust & NZ, Sl) loutish youth who drives irresponsibly

hoop ❶ n rigid circular band of metal, wood etc.

hooray interj see HURRAH

hoot n **1** owl's cry or similar sound **2** cry of derision **3** (Inf) funny person or thing ▷ v **4** utter hoot **hooter** n device (e.g. horn) to emit hooting sound

Hoover® n **1** vacuum cleaner ▷ v **2** (without cap.) vacuum

hop¹ ❶ v hopping, hopped **1** spring on one foot ▷ n **2** leap, skip

hop² n **1** climbing plant with bitter cones used to flavour beer etc. ▷ pl **2** the cones

hope ❶ n **1** expectation of something desired **2** thing that gives, or object of, this feeling ▷ v **3** feel hope (for) **hopeful** adj **hopefully** adv **hopeless** adj

hopper n **1** one who hops **2** device for feeding material into mill

hopscotch n children's game of hopping in pattern drawn on ground

horde ❶ n large crowd

horizon ❶ n line where earth and sky seem to meet **horizontal** adj parallel with horizon, level

THESAURUS

recognition, compliments, homage ≠ contempt ▷ v = acclaim, praise, decorate, commemorate, commend; = respect, value, esteem, prize, appreciate ≠ scorn; = fulfil, keep, carry out, observe, discharge; = pay, take, accept, pass, acknowledge ≠ refuse

hook n = fastener, catch, link, peg, clasp ▷ v = fasten, fix, secure, clasp; = catch, land, trap, entrap

hooligan n = delinquent, vandal, ruffian, lager lout, yob or yobbo (Brit Sl)

hoop n = ring, band, loop, wheel, round

hop¹ v = jump, spring, bound, leap, skip ▷ n = jump, step, spring, bound, leap

hope v = believe, look forward to, cross your fingers ▷ n = belief, confidence, expectation, longing, dream ≠ despair

horde n = crowd, mob, swarm, host, band

horizon n = skyline, view, vista

hormone n substance secreted from gland which stimulates organs of the body

horn n **1** hard projection on heads of certain animals **2** various things made of, or resembling it **3** wind instrument **4** device (esp. in car) emitting sound **horny** adj
hornpipe n sailor's lively dance

hornet n large insect of wasp family

horoscope n telling of person's fortune by studying positions of planets etc. at his or her birth

horrendous adj horrific

horror ❶ n **1** terror **2** loathing, fear **3** its cause **horrible** adj **1** exciting horror, hideous, shocking **2** disagreeable **horribly** adv
horrid adj **1** unpleasant, repulsive **2** (Inf) unkind **horrific** adj particularly horrible **horrify** v **1** cause horror (in) **2** shock

hors d'oeuvre n small dish served before main meal

horse ❶ n **1** four-footed animal used for riding **2** cavalry **3** frame for support etc. **horsy** adj **1** devoted to horses **2** like a horse
horse chestnut tree with white or pink flowers and large nuts
horsefly n large bloodsucking fly

horseman n rider on horse
horsepower n unit of power of engine etc. **horseradish** n plant with pungent root **horseshoe** n protective U-shaped piece of iron nailed to horse's hoof

horticulture n art or science of gardening

hose n **1** flexible tube for conveying liquid or gas **2** stockings ▷ v **3** water with hose **hosiery** n stockings

hoser n **1** (US, Sl) a person who swindles or deceives others **2** (Canad, Sl) an unsophisticated, esp. rural, person

hospice n home for care of the terminally ill

hospital n institution for care of sick **hospitalize** v send or admit to hospital

hospitality ❶ n friendly and liberal reception of strangers or guests **hospitable** adj

host¹, hostess ❶ n **1** one who entertains another **2** innkeeper **3** compere of show ▷ v **4** act as a host

host² ❶ n large number

hostage ❶ n person taken or given as pledge or security

horror n = **terror**, fear, alarm, panic, dread

horse n = **nag**, mount, mare, colt, filly

hospitality n = **welcome**, warmth, kindness, friendliness, sociability

host¹, hostess n = **master of ceremonies**, proprietor, innkeeper, landlord or landlady; = **presenter**, compere (Brit), anchorman or anchorwoman ▷ v = **present**, introduce, compere (Brit), front (Inf)

host² n = **multitude**, lot, load (Inf), wealth, array

hostage n = **captive**, prisoner, pawn

h

hostel n building providing accommodation at low cost for students etc.

hostile ❶ adj 1 antagonistic 2 warlike 3 of an enemy **hostility** n, pl **-ties** 1 enmity ▷ pl 2 acts of warfare

hot ❶ adj **hotter, hottest** 1 of high temperature 2 angry 3 new 4 spicy **hotly** adv **hot air** (Inf) empty talk **hotbed** n 1 bed of heated earth for young plants 2 any place encouraging growth **hot-blooded** adj excitable **hot dog** hot sausage in split bread roll **hotfoot** v/adv (go) quickly **hothead** n intemperate person **hothouse** n heated greenhouse **hotline** n direct telephone link for emergency use **hotplate** n heated plate on electric cooker **hot spot** 1 place where there is a lot of exciting activity 2 area where there is a concentration of violence or political unrest 3 (Comp) place (esp. a public building or commercial premises) offering a Wi-Fi connection

hotchpotch n 1 medley 2 dish of many ingredients

hotel n commercial establishment providing lodging and meals **hotelier** n

hound ❶ n 1 hunting dog ▷ v 2 chase, urge, pursue

hour n 1 twenty-fourth part of day 2 sixty minutes 3 appointed time ▷ pl 4 fixed periods for work etc. **hourly** adv/adj **hourglass** n timing device in which sand trickles between two glass compartments

house ❶ n 1 building for human habitation 2 legislative assembly 3 family 4 business firm ▷ v 5 give or receive shelter, lodging, or storage 6 cover or contain **housing** n 1 (providing of) houses 2 part designed to cover, protect, contain **houseboat** n boat used as home **household** n inmates of house collectively **housekeeper** n person managing affairs of household **housekeeping** n (money for) running household

━━━━━━━━━━━━━━━━ THESAURUS ━━━━━━━━━

hostile adj = antagonistic, opposed, contrary, ill-disposed; = **unfriendly**, belligerent, antagonistic, rancorous, ill-disposed ≠ **friendly**

hot adj = heated, boiling, steaming, roasting, searing; = **warm**, close, stifling, humid, torrid ≠ **cold**; = spicy, pungent, peppery, piquant, biting ≠ **mild**; = intense, passionate, heated, spirited, fierce; = **new**, latest, fresh, recent, up to date ≠ **old**

hound v = harass, harry, bother, provoke, annoy

house n = home, residence, dwelling, pad (Sl), homestead; = **household**, family; = **firm**, company, business, organization, outfit (Inf); = **assembly**, parliament, Commons, legislative body ▷ v = **accommodate**, quarter, take in, put up, lodge; = contain, keep, hold, cover, store; = **take**, accommodate, sleep, provide shelter for, give a bed to

housewife n woman who runs her own household

hovel n lowly dwelling

hover ❶ v 1 hang in the air 2 loiter 3 be in state of indecision **hovercraft** n type of craft which can travel over both land and sea on a cushion of air

how adv 1 in what way 2 by what means 3 in what condition 4 to what degree **however** conj 1 nevertheless ▷ adv 2 in whatever way, degree 3 all the same

howl ❶ v/n (utter) long loud cry **howler** n (Inf) stupid mistake

HP, h.p. hire-purchase

HQ headquarters

HRH His (or Her) Royal Highness

hub ❶ n 1 middle part of wheel 2 central point of activity

hubbub n confused noise

huddle ❶ n 1 crowded mass 2 (Inf) impromptu conference ▷ v 3 heap, crowd together 4 hunch

hue ❶ n colour

huff n 1 passing mood of anger ▷ v 2 make or become angry 3 blow

hug ❶ v hugging, hugged 1 clasp tightly in the arms 2 keep close to ▷ n 3 fond embrace

huge ❶ adj very big **hugely** adv very much

hulk n 1 body of abandoned vessel 2 large, unwieldy person or thing **hulking** adj

hull ❶ n 1 frame, body of ship 2 calyx of strawberry etc. ▷ v 3 remove shell, hull from (fruit, seeds)

hullabaloo n, pl **-loos** 1 uproar 2 clamour

hum ❶ v humming, hummed 1 make low continuous sound 2 sing with closed lips ▷ n 3 humming sound **hummingbird** n very small Amer. bird whose wings make humming noise

human ❶ adj 1 of man 2 relating to, characteristic of, man's nature

h

─────── THESAURUS ───────

hover v = **float**, fly, hang, drift, flutter; = **linger**, loiter, hang about or around (Inf); = **waver**, fluctuate, dither (chiefly Brit), oscillate, vacillate

howl v = **cry**, scream, roar, weep, yell ▷ n = **baying**, cry, bay, bark, barking

hub n = **centre**, heart, focus, core, middle

huddle v = **curl up**, crouch, hunch up; = **crowd**, press, gather, collect, squeeze ▷ n (Inf) = **discussion**, conference, meeting, powwow, confab (Inf)

hue n = **colour**, tone, shade, dye, tint

hug v = **embrace**, cuddle, squeeze, clasp, enfold ▷ n = **embrace**, squeeze, bear hug, clinch (Sl), clasp

huge adj = **enormous**, large, massive, vast, tremendous ≠ **tiny**

hull n = **framework**, casing, body, covering, frame

hum v = **drone**, buzz, murmur, throb, vibrate

human adj = **mortal**, manlike ≠ **nonhuman** ▷ n = **human being**, person, individual, creature, mortal ≠ **nonhuman**

humane adj 1 kind 2 merciful
humanism n belief in human effort rather than religion
humanitarian n 1 philanthropist ▷ adj 2 philanthropic **humanity** n 1 human nature 2 human race 3 kindliness ▷ pl 4 study of literature, philosophy, the arts **humanize** v
humble ● adj 1 lowly, modest ▷ v 2 humiliate **humbly** adv
humbug n 1 imposter 2 sham, nonsense 3 sweet of boiled sugar
humdrum adj commonplace, dull
humid adj moist, damp **humidifier** n device for increasing amount of water vapour in air in room etc. **humidity** n
humiliate ● v lower dignity of, abase, mortify **humiliation** n
humility n 1 state of being humble 2 meekness
hummock n low knoll, hillock
humour ● n 1 faculty of saying or perceiving what excites amusement 2 amusing speech,

writing etc. 3 state of mind, mood ▷ v 4 gratify, indulge **humorist** n person who acts, speaks, writes humorously **humorous** adj
hump n 1 normal or deforming lump, esp. on back ▷ v 2 make hump-shaped 3 (Sl) carry or heave **humpback** n person with hump
humus n decayed vegetable and animal mould
hunch ● n (Inf) 1 intuition 2 hump ▷ v 3 bend into hump **hunchback** n humpback
hundred n/adj cardinal number, ten times ten **hundredth** adj ordinal number **hundredweight** n weight of 112 lbs (50.8 kg), 20th part of ton
hunger ● n/v 1 (have) discomfort from lack of food 2 (have) strong desire **hungrily** adv **hungry** adj having keen appetite
hunk ● n thick piece
hunt ● v 1 seek out to kill or capture for sport or food 2 search (for)

——————— THESAURUS ———————

humble adj = **modest**, meek, unassuming, unpretentious, self-effacing ≠ **proud**; = **lowly**, poor, mean, simple, ordinary ≠ **distinguished**; ▷ v = **humiliate**, disgrace, crush, subdue, chasten ≠ **exalt**
humiliate v = **embarrass**, shame, humble, crush, put down ≠ **honour**
humour n = **comedy**, funniness, fun, amusement, funny side ≠ **seriousness**; = **mood**, spirits, temper, disposition, frame of mind ▷ v = **indulge**, accommodate, go

along with, flatter, gratify ≠ **oppose**
hunch n = **feeling**, idea, impression, suspicion, intuition ▷ v = **crouch**, bend, curve, arch, draw in
hunger n = **appetite**, emptiness, hungriness, ravenousness; = **starvation**, famine, malnutrition, undernourishment; = **desire**, appetite, craving, ache, lust
hunk n = **lump**, piece, chunk, block, mass
hunt v = **stalk**, track, chase,

▷ *n* **3** chase, search **4** (party organized for) hunting
hunter *n*

hurdle ❶ *n* **1** portable frame of bars for temporary fences or for jumping over **2** obstacle ▷ *v* **3** race over hurdles

hurdy-gurdy *n, pl* **-dies** mechanical musical instrument

hurl ❶ *v* throw violently

hurly-burly *n* loud confusion

hurrah, hurray *interj* exclamation of joy or applause

hurricane ❶ *n* very strong, violent wind or storm

hurry ❶ *v* **-rying, -ried 1** (cause to) move or act in great haste ▷ *n* **2** undue haste **3** eagerness
hurriedly *adv*

hurt ❶ *v* **hurting, hurt 1** injure, damage, give pain to **2** feel pain ▷ *n* **3** wound, injury, harm
hurtful *adj*

hurtle ❶ *v* rush violently

husband ❶ *n* **1** married man ▷ *v* **2** economize **3** use to best advantage **husbandry** *n* **1** farming **2** economy

hush ❶ *v* **1** make or be silent ▷ *n* **2** stillness **3** quietness

husk *n* **1** dry covering of certain seeds and fruits ▷ *v* **2** remove husk from **husky** *adj* **1** rough in tone **2** hoarse, throaty

husky *n* **huskier, huskiest** *pl* **huskies** Arctic sledge dog

hussy *n, pl* **-sies** cheeky young woman

hustings *pl n* political campaigning

hustle ❶ *v* **1** push about, jostle, hurry ▷ *n* **2** lively activity

hut ❶ *n* small house or shelter

hutch *n* cage for rabbits etc.

hyacinth *n* bulbous plant with bell-shaped flowers

hybrid ❶ *n* **1** offspring of two plants or animals of different species ▷ *adj* **2** crossbred

— THESAURUS —

pursue, trail ▷ *n* = **search**, hunting, investigation, chase, pursuit

hurdle *n* = **obstacle**, difficulty, barrier, handicap, hazard; = **fence**, barrier, barricade

hurl *v* = **throw**, fling, launch, cast, pitch

hurricane *n* = **storm**, gale, tornado, cyclone, typhoon

hurry *v* = **rush**, fly, dash, scurry, scoot ≠ **dawdle** ▷ *n* = **rush**, haste, speed, urgency, flurry ≠ **slowness**

hurt *v* = **injure**, damage, wound, cut, disable ≠ **heal**; = **ache**, be sore, be painful, burn, smart; = **harm**,

injure, ill-treat, maltreat ▷ *n* = **distress**, suffering, pain, grief, misery ≠ **happiness**

hurtle *v* = **rush**, charge, race, shoot, fly

husband *n* = **partner**, spouse, mate, better half (*humorous*) ▷ *v* = **conserve**, budget, save, store, hoard ≠ **squander**

hush *v* = **quieten**, silence, mute, muzzle, shush ▷ *n* = **quiet**, silence, calm, peace, tranquillity

hut *n* = **cabin**, shack, shanty, hovel

hybrid *n* = **crossbreed**, cross, mixture, compound, composite; = **mixture**, compound, composite,

hydrangea n ornamental shrub

hydrant n water-pipe with nozzle for hose

hydraulic adj concerned with, operated by, pressure transmitted through liquid in pipe

hydro adj (Canad) electricity as supplied to a residence, business, institution, etc.

hydrochloric acid strong colourless acid

hydroelectric adj pert. to generation of electricity by use of water

hydrofoil n fast, light vessel with hull raised out of water at speed

hydrogen n colourless gas which combines with oxygen to form water **hydrogen bomb** atom bomb of enormous power **hydrogen peroxide** colourless liquid used as antiseptic and bleach

hydrophobia n aversion to water, esp. as symptom of rabies

hyena n wild animal related to dog

hygiene ❶ n (study of) principles and practice of health and cleanliness **hygienic** adj

hymen n membrane partly covering vagina of virgin

hymn ❶ n 1 song of praise, esp. to God ▷ v 2 praise in song

hype ❶ n 1 intensive publicity ▷ v 2 publicize

hyperbole n rhetorical exaggeration

hypermarket n huge self-service store

hypertension n abnormally high blood pressure

hyphen n short line (-) indicating that two words or syllables are to be connected **hyphenate** v **hyphenated** adj

hypnosis n induced state like deep sleep in which subject acts on external suggestion **hypnotic** adj **hypnotism** n **hypnotize** v affect with hypnosis

hypochondria n morbid depression without cause, about one's own health **hypochondriac** adj/n

hypocrisy ❶ n, pl -sies 1 assuming of false appearance of virtue 2 insincerity **hypocrite** n **hypocritical** adj

hypodermic adj 1 introduced, injected beneath the skin ▷ n 2 hypodermic syringe or needle

hypotenuse n side of right-angled triangle opposite the right angle

hypothermia n condition of having body temperature reduced to dangerously low level

---
THESAURUS
---

amalgam

hygiene n = **cleanliness**, sanitation, disinfection, sterility

hymn n = **religious song**, song of praise, carol, chant, anthem

hype n (Sl) = **publicity**, promotion, plugging (Inf), razzmatazz (Sl), brouhaha

hypocrisy n = **insincerity**, pretence, deception, cant, duplicity ≠ **sincerity**

hypothesis ❶ *n, pl* **-ses**
1 suggested explanation of
something 2 assumption as
basis of reasoning
hypothetical *adj*
hysterectomy *n, pl* **-mies**

surgical operation for removing
uterus
hysteria ❶ *n* 1 mental disorder
with emotional outbursts 2 fit of
crying or laughing **hysterical** *adj*
hysterics *pl n* fits of hysteria

THESAURUS
---

hypothesis *n* = **theory**, premise,
proposition, assumption, thesis

hysteria *n* = **frenzy**, panic,
madness, agitation, delirium

I pron the pronoun of the first person singular

ibis n storklike bird

ice n 1 frozen water 2 ice cream ▷ v 3 cover, become covered with ice 4 cool with ice 5 cover with icing **icicle** n hanging spike of ice **icing** n mixture of sugar and water etc. used to decorate cakes **icy** adj **icier, iciest** 1 covered with ice 2 cold 3 unfriendly **iceberg** n large floating mass of ice **ice cream** sweet creamy frozen dessert **ice hockey** team game played on ice with puck **ice skate** boot with steel blade for gliding over ice **ice-skate** v

icon n religious image **iconoclast** n one who attacks established ideas

idea ❶ n 1 notion 2 conception 3 plan, aim **ideal** n 1 idea of perfection 2 perfect person or thing ▷ adj 3 perfect **idealism** n tendency to seek perfection in everything **idealist** n 1 one who strives after the ideal 2 impractical person **idealistic** adj **idealization** n **idealize** v portray as ideal **ideally** adv

identity ❶ n, pl **-ties** 1 individuality 2 state of being exactly alike **identical** adj very same **identifiable** adj **identification** n 1 recognition 2 identifying document **identify** v 1 establish identity of 2 associate (oneself) with 3 treat as identical

ideology n, pl **-gies** body of ideas, beliefs of group, nation etc. **ideological** adj

idiom n expression peculiar to a language or group **idiomatic** adj

idiosyncrasy n, pl **-sies** peculiarity of mind

idiot ❶ n 1 mentally deficient person 2 stupid person **idiocy** n **idiotic** adj utterly stupid

idle ❶ adj 1 unemployed 2 lazy 3 useless 4 groundless ▷ v 5 be idle 6 run slowly in neutral gear **idleness** n **idler** n **idly** adv

——————————————— **THESAURUS** ———————————————

idea n = **notion**, thought, view, teaching, opinion; = **intention**, aim, purpose, object, plan

identity n = **individuality**, self, character, personality, existence

idiot n = **fool**, moron, twit (Inf, chiefly Brit), chump, imbecile

idle adj = **unoccupied**, unemployed, redundant, inactive ≠ occupied; = **unused**, inactive, out of order, out of service; = **lazy**, slow, slack, sluggish, lax ≠ busy; = **useless**, vain, pointless, unsuccessful, ineffective ≠ useful

idol ❶ n 1 image worshipped as deity 2 object of excessive devotion **idolatry** n **idolize** v love or admire to excess

idyll n (poem describing) picturesque or charming scene or episode **idyllic** adj delightful

i.e. that is

if ❶ conj 1 on condition or supposition that 2 whether 3 although

igloo n, pl **-loos** domed house made of snow

ignite ❶ v (cause to) burn **ignition** n 1 act of kindling or setting on fire 2 car's electrical firing system

ignoble adj 1 mean, base 2 of low birth

ignominy n 1 public disgrace 2 shameful act **ignominious** adj

ignore ❶ v disregard, leave out of account **ignoramus** n ignorant person **ignorance** n lack of knowledge **ignorant** adj

1 lacking knowledge 2 uneducated

iguana n large tropical American lizard

ill ❶ adj 1 not in good health 2 bad, evil 3 harmful ▷ n 4 evil, harm ▷ adv 5 badly 6 hardly **illness** n

ill-advised adj imprudent

ill-disposed adj unsympathetic

ill-fated adj unfortunate

ill-gotten adj obtained dishonestly **ill-treat** v treat cruelly **ill will** hostility

illegal ❶ adj against the law

illegible adj unable to be read

illegitimate adj 1 born to unmarried parents 2 irregular **illegitimacy** n

illicit ❶ adj 1 illegal 2 prohibited, forbidden

illiterate adj 1 unable to read or write ▷ n 2 illiterate person **illiteracy** n

illogical adj not logical

illuminate ❶ v 1 light up 2 clarify 3 decorate with lights or

—————— THESAURUS ——————

idol n = **hero**, pin-up, favourite, pet, darling; = **graven image**, god, deity

if conj = **provided**, assuming, given that, providing, supposing

ignite v = **catch fire**, burn, burst into flames, inflame, flare up; = **set fire to**, light, set alight, torch, kindle

ignore v = **pay no attention to**, neglect, disregard, slight, overlook ≠ **pay attention to**

ill adj = **unwell**, sick, poorly (Inf), diseased, weak ≠ **healthy**; = **harmful**, bad, damaging, evil,

foul ≠ **favourable** ▷ n = **problem**, trouble, suffering, worry, injury ▷ adv = **badly**, unfortunately, unfavourably, inauspiciously; = **hardly**, barely, scarcely, just, only just ≠ **well**

illegal adj = **unlawful**, banned, forbidden, prohibited, criminal ≠ **legal**

illicit adj = **illegal**, criminal, prohibited, unlawful, illegitimate ≠ **legal**; = **forbidden**, improper, immoral, guilty, clandestine

illuminate v = **light up**, brighten ≠ **darken**; = **explain**, interpret, colours **illumination** n

illusion n deceptive appearance or belief **illusionist** n conjuror **illusory** adj

illustrate v 1 provide with pictures or examples 2 explain by examples **illustration** n 1 picture, diagram 2 example

illustrious adj 1 famous 2 glorious

image n 1 likeness 2 optical counterpart 3 double, copy 4 general impression 5 word picture **imagery** n images collectively

imagine v 1 picture to oneself 2 think 3 conjecture **imaginable** adj **imaginary** adj existing only in fantasy **imagination** n 1 faculty of making mental images of things not present 2 fancy **imaginative** adj

imbalance n lack of balance in emphasis or proportion

imbecile n 1 idiot ▷ adj 2 idiotic

imbibe v drink (in)

imbue v -buing, -bued instil, fill

imitate v 1 take as model 2 copy **imitation** n 1 act of imitating 2 copy 3 counterfeit ▷ adj 4 synthetic **imitative** adj

immaculate adj 1 spotless 2 pure

immaterial adj 1 unimportant 2 not consisting of matter

immature adj 1 not fully developed 2 lacking wisdom because of youth

immediate adj 1 occurring at once 2 closest **immediately** adv

immense adj huge, vast **immensely** adv **immensity** n

immerse v 1 submerge in liquid 2 involve 3 engross **immersion** n

immigrant n settler in foreign country

imminent adj liable to happen soon **imminence** n

_____ THESAURUS _____

make clear, clarify, clear up ≠ obscure

illusion n = **delusion**, misconception, misapprehension, fancy, fallacy; = **fantasy**, vision, hallucination, trick, spectre

illustrate v = **demonstrate**, emphasize

image n = **thought**, idea, vision, concept, impression, likeness, mirror image; = **figure**, idol, icon, fetish, talisman

imagine v = **envisage**, see, picture, plan, think of; = **believe**, think, suppose, assume, suspect

imitate v = **copy**, follow, repeat,

echo, emulate

immaculate adj = **clean**, spotless, neat, spruce, squeaky-clean ≠ **dirty**; = **pure**, perfect, impeccable, flawless, faultless ≠ **corrupt**

immediate adj = **instant**, prompt, instantaneous, quick, on-the-spot ≠ **later**; = **nearest**, next, direct, close, near ≠ **far**

immense adj = **huge**, great, massive, vast, enormous ≠ **tiny**

immerse v = **engross**, involve, absorb, busy, occupy; = **plunge**, dip, submerge, sink, duck

imminent adj = **near**, coming,

immobile *adj* unable to move
immobility *n* **immobilize** *v*
immolate *v* kill, sacrifice
immoral ❶ *adj* **1** corrupt
2 promiscuous **immorality** *n*
immortal ❶ *adj* **1** deathless
2 famed for all time ▷ *n* **3** person
living forever **immortality** *n*
immortalize *v*
immune *adj* **1** protected (against a
disease etc.) **2** exempt **immunity**
n, pl **-ties** **immunization** *n*
process of making immune to
disease **immunize** *v*
imp *n* **1** little devil **2** mischievous
child
impact ❶ *n* **1** collision **2** profound
effect **impacted** *adj* wedged
impair ❶ *v* weaken, damage
impairment *n*
impala *n* S Afr. antelope
impale *v* pierce with sharp
instrument
impart *v* **1** communicate **2** give
impartial *adj* **1** unbiased **2** fair
impartiality *n*

impassable *adj* blocked
impasse ❶ *n* deadlock
impassioned *adj* full of feeling,
ardent
impassive *adj* **1** showing no
emotion **2** calm
impatient *adj* **1** irritable
2 restless **impatience** *n*
impeach *v* **1** charge, esp. with
treason or crime in office
2 denounce **impeachable** *adj*
impeachment *n*
impeccable ❶ *adj* faultless
impede *v* hinder **impediment** *n*
1 obstruction **2** defect
impel *v* **-pelling, -pelled 1** induce
2 drive
impending ❶ *adj* imminent
imperative ❶ *adj* **1** necessary
2 peremptory **3** (*Grammar*)
expressing command ▷ *n*
4 (*Grammar*) imperative mood
imperfect *adj* **1** having faults
2 not complete **imperfection** *n*
imperial ❶ *adj* **1** of empire, or
emperor **2** majestic **3** denoting

—— THESAURUS ——

close, approaching, gathering
≠ remote
immoral *adj* = **wicked**, bad,
wrong, corrupt, indecent **≠** moral
immortal *adj* = **timeless**, eternal,
everlasting, lasting, traditional
≠ ephemeral ▷ *n* = **hero**, genius,
great; = **god**, goddess, deity, divine
being, immortal being
impact *n* = **effect**, influence,
consequences, impression,
repercussions; = **collision**, contact,
crash, knock, stroke
impair *v* = **worsen**, reduce,

damage, injure, harm **≠** improve
impasse *n* = **deadlock**, stalemate,
standstill, dead end, standoff
impeccable *adj* = **faultless**,
perfect, immaculate, flawless,
squeaky-clean **≠** flawed
impending *adj* = **looming**,
coming, approaching, near,
forthcoming
imperative *adj* = **urgent**,
essential, pressing, vital, crucial
≠ unnecessary
imperial *adj* = **royal**, regal, kingly,
queenly, princely

weights and measures formerly official in Brit. **imperialism** n policy of acquiring empire

imperil v **-illing, -illed** endanger

imperious adj domineering

impersonal adj objective

impersonate v pretend to be **impersonation** n **impersonator** n

impertinent adj insolent, rude **impertinence** n

imperturbable adj calm, not excitable

impervious adj **1** impossible to penetrate **2** unaffected by

impetigo n contagious skin disease

impetuous adj rash **impetuosity** n

impetus ① n, pl **-tuses 1** incentive **2** momentum

impinge v encroach (upon)

impious adj irreverent

implacable adj not to be placated

implant ① v insert firmly

implement ① n 1 tool, instrument ▷ **v 2** carry out

implore v entreat earnestly

imply ① v -plying, -plied 1 hint **2** mean **implicate** v involve **implication** n something implied **implicit** adj **1** implied **2** absolute

import ① v 1 bring in ▷ **n 2** thing imported **3** meaning **importation** n **importer** n

important ① adj 1 of great consequence **2** eminent, powerful **importance** n

impose v **1** place (upon) **2** take advantage (of) **imposing** adj impressive **imposition** n

impossible ① adj 1 not possible **2** unreasonable **impossibility** n, pl **-ties impossibly** adv

impotent adj **1** powerless **2** (of males) incapable of sexual intercourse **impotence** n

impound v seize legally

impoverish ① v make poor or weak

---

impetus n = **incentive**, push, spur, motivation, impulse; = **force**, power, energy, momentum

implant v = **insert**, fix, graft; = **instil**, infuse, inculcate

implement v = **carry out**, effect, carry through, complete, apply ≠ **hinder** ▷ n = **tool**, machine, device, instrument, appliance

imply v = **suggest**, hint, insinuate, indicate, intimate; = **involve**, mean, entail, require, indicate

import v = **bring in**, buy in, ship in, introduce ▷ n (Formal) = **significance**, concern/value,

weight, consequence; = **meaning**, implication, significance, sense, intention

important adj = **significant**, critical, substantial, urgent, serious ≠ **unimportant**; = **powerful**, prominent, commanding, dominant, influential

impossible adj = **not possible**, out of the question, impracticable, unfeasible; = **unachievable**, out of the question/vain, unthinkable, inconceivable ≠ **possible**

impoverish v = **bankrupt**, ruin, beggar, break

impractical adj not sensible

impregnable adj proof against attack

impregnate v 1 saturate 2 make pregnant

impresario n, pl **-ios** 1 organizer of public entertainment 2 manager of opera, ballet etc.

impress ❶ v 1 affect deeply, usu. favourably 2 imprint, stamp **impression** n 1 effect 2 notion, belief 3 imprint 4 comic impersonation **impressionable** adj susceptible **impressive** adj making deep impression

imprint ❶ n 1 mark made by pressure ▷ v 2 stamp 3 fix in mind

imprison ❶ v put in prison **imprisonment** n

improbable ❶ adj unlikely

impromptu adv/adj 1 without preparation ▷ n 2 improvisation

improper ❶ adj 1 indecent 2 incorrect **impropriety** n

improve ❶ v make or become better **improvement** n

improvident adj thriftless

improvise ❶ v 1 make use of materials at hand 2 perform, speak without preparation **improvisation** n

impudent adj impertinent **impudence** n

impugn v call in question, challenge

impulse ❶ n 1 sudden inclination to act 2 impetus **impulsive** adj rash

impunity n **with impunity** without punishment

impure adj 1 having unwanted substances mixed in 2 immoral, obscene **impurity** n

impute v attribute to **imputation** n reproach

in prep 1 expresses inclusion within limits of space, time, circumstance, sphere etc. ▷ adv 2 in or into state, place etc. 3 (Inf) in vogue etc. ▷ adj 4 (Inf) fashionable

inability n lack of means or skill to do something

inaccurate ❶ adj not correct

impress v = **excite**, move, strike, touch, affect

imprint n = **mark**, impression, stamp, indentation ▷ v = **engrave**, print, stamp, impress, etch

imprison v = **jail**, confine, detain, lock up, put away ≠ **free**

improbable adj = **doubtful**, unlikely, dubious, questionable, fanciful ≠ **probable**

improper adj = **inappropriate**, unfit, unsuitable, out of place, unwarranted ≠ **appropriate**; = **indecent**, vulgar, suggestive,

unseemly, untoward ≠ **decent**

improve v = **enhance**, better, add to, upgrade, touch up ≠ **worsen**; = **get better**, pick up, develop, advance, rally

improvise v = **devise**, contrive, concoct, throw together; = **ad-lib**, invent, busk, wing it (Inf), play it by ear (Inf)

impulse n = **urge**, longing, wish, notion, yearning

inaccurate adj = **incorrect**, wrong, mistaken, faulty, unreliable ≠ **accurate**

inaccuracy n, pl -cies
inadequate **❶** adj 1 not enough
2 incapable inadequacy n
inane adj foolish
inanimate adj lifeless
inappropriate adj not suitable
inarticulate adj unable to express
oneself clearly
inaugurate v 1 initiate 2 admit
to office inaugural adj
inauguration n formal initiation
(to office etc.)
inauspicious adj unlucky
inborn adj existing from birth
incalculable adj 1 beyond
calculation 2 very great
incandescent adj 1 glowing
2 produced by glowing filament
incantation n magic spell
incapable adj helpless
incapacitate v 1 disable
2 disqualify
incarcerate v imprison
incarnate adj 1 in human form
2 typified incarnation n
incendiary adj 1 designed to
cause fires 2 inflammatory ▷ n
3 fire-bomb
incense¹ **❶** v enrage
incense² **❶** n 1 gum, spice giving
perfume when burned 2 its smoke

incentive **❶** n something that
stimulates effort
inception n beginning
incessant adj unceasing
incest n sexual intercourse
between close relatives
incestuous adj
inch n 1 one twelfth of a foot, or
0.0254 metre ▷ v 2 move very
slowly
incident **❶** n 1 event, occurrence
2 public disturbance incidence n
extent or frequency of occurrence
incidental adj occurring as a
minor, inevitable, or chance
accompaniment incidentally adv
1 by chance 2 by the way
incidentals pl n accompanying
items
incinerate v burn up completely
incinerator n
incipient adj beginning
incise v cut into incision n
incisive adj sharp incisor n
cutting tooth
incite v urge, stir up
inclement adj severe
incline **❶** v 1 lean, slope 2 (cause
to) be disposed ▷ n 3 slope
inclination n 1 liking, tendency
2 degree of deviation

——————— THESAURUS ———————

inadequate adj = insufficient,
meagre, poor, lacking, scant
≠ adequate; = incapable,
incompetent, faulty, deficient,
unqualified ≠ capable
incense v = anger, infuriate,
enrage, irritate, madden
incentive n = inducement,
encouragement, spur, lure, bait

≠ disincentive
incident n = disturbance, scene,
clash, disorder, confrontation;
= adventure, drama, excitement,
crisis, spectacle
incline v = predispose, influence,
persuade, prejudice, sway ▷ n
= slope, rise, dip, grade,
descent

DICTIONARY

include ● v 1 have as (part of) contents 2 add in **inclusion** n **inclusive** adj including (everything)

incognito adv/adj 1 under an assumed identity ▷ n 2 assumed identity

incoherent adj 1 lacking clarity 2 inarticulate **incoherence** n

income ● n money received from salary, investments etc.

incoming ● adj 1 coming in 2 about to come into office 3 next

incomparable adj beyond comparison

incompatible ● adj inconsistent, conflicting

incompetent ● adj lacking necessary ability **incompetence** n

inconceivable adj impossible to imagine

inconclusive adj not giving a final decision

incongruous adj not appropriate **incongruity** n, pl **-ties**

inconsequential adj 1 trivial

2 haphazard

incontinent adj not able to control bladder or bowels

incontrovertible adj undeniable

inconvenience ● n trouble, difficulty **inconvenient** adj

incorporate ● v 1 include 2 form into corporation

incorrigible adj beyond correction or reform

increase ● v 1 make or become greater in size, number etc. ▷ n 2 growth, enlargement **increasingly** adv more and more

incredible ● adj 1 unbelievable 2 (Inf) amazing **incredibly** adv

incredulous adj unbelieving **incredulity** n

increment n increase

incriminate v imply guilt of

incubate v 1 provide eggs, bacteria etc. with heat for development 2 develop in this way **incubation** n **incubator** n apparatus for hatching eggs or rearing premature babies

THESAURUS

include v = **contain**, involve, incorporate, cover, consist of ≠ **exclude**; = **add**, enter, put in, insert

income n = **revenue**, earnings, pay, returns, profits

incoming adj = **arriving**, landing, approaching, entering, returning ≠ **departing**

incompatible adj = **inconsistent**, conflicting, contradictory, incongruous, unsuited ≠ **compatible**

incompetent adj = **inept**,

useless, incapable, floundering, bungling ≠ **competent**

inconvenience n = **trouble**, difficulty, bother, fuss, disadvantage ▷ v = **trouble**, bother, disturb, upset, disrupt

incorporate v = **include**, contain, take in, embrace, integrate

increase v = **raise**, extend, boost, expand, develop ≠ **decrease** ▷ n = **growth**, rise, development, gain, expansion

incredible adj (Inf) = **amazing**, wonderful, stunning, extraordinary,

inculcate v fix in the mind

incumbent n holder of office

incur ① v **-curring, -curred** bring upon oneself **incursion** n invasion

indebted adj owing gratitude or money

indecent ① adj 1 offensive 2 unseemly

indeed ① adv 1 really 2 in fact ▷ interj 3 denoting surprise, doubt etc.

indefatigable adj untiring

indefensible adj not justifiable

indefinite adj without exact limits

indelible adj that cannot be blotted out **indelibly** adv

indelicate adj coarse, embarrassing

indemnity n, pl **-ties** 1 compensation 2 security against loss **indemnify** v give indemnity to

indent v 1 set in (from margin etc.) 2 notch 3 order by indent ▷ n 4 notch 5 requisition **indentation** n

independent ① adj 1 not subject to others 2 self-reliant 3 free 4 valid in itself **independence** n 1 being independent 2 self-reliance 3 self-support

indescribable adj beyond description

indeterminate adj uncertain

index n, pl **indices** 1 alphabetical list of references 2 indicator 3 (Maths) exponent 4 forefinger ▷ v 5 provide with, insert in index

indicate ① v 1 point out 2 state briefly 3 signify **indication** n **indicative** adj 1 pointing to 2 (Grammar) stating fact **indicator** n

indict ① v accuse, esp. by legal process **indictment** n

indifferent ① adj 1 uninterested 2 mediocre **indifference** n

indigenous adj native

indigent adj poor, needy

indigestion n (discomfort caused by) poor digestion

indigo n 1 blue dye obtained from plant 2 the plant ▷ adj 3 deep blue

overwhelming; = **unbelievable**, unthinkable, improbable, inconceivable, preposterous

incur v = **sustain**, experience, suffer, gain, earn

indecent adj = **obscene**, lewd, dirty, inappropriate, rude ≠ **decent**; = **unbecoming**, unsuitable, vulgar, unseemly, undignified ≠ **proper**

indeed adv = **certainly**, yes, definitely, surely, truly

independent adj = **separate**,

unattached, uncontrolled, unconstrained ≠ **controlled**; = **self-sufficient**, free, liberated, self-contained, self-reliant

indicate v = **imply**, suggest, hint, intimate, signify; = **register**, show, record, read, express

indict v = **charge**, accuse, prosecute, summon, impeach

indifferent adj = **unconcerned**, detached, cold, cool, callous ≠ **concerned**; = **mediocre**, ordinary, moderate, so-so (Inf),

indirect ❶ adj 1 done, caused by someone or something else 2 not by straight route

indiscreet adj tactless in revealing secrets **indiscretion** n

indiscriminate adj 1 lacking discrimination 2 jumbled

indispensable ❶ adj essential

indisposed adj 1 unwell 2 disinclined

indisputable adj without doubt

indissoluble adj permanent

individual ❶ adj 1 single 2 distinctive ▷ n 3 single person or thing **individuality** n distinctive personality **individually** adv singly

indoctrinate v implant beliefs in the mind of

indolent adj lazy **indolence** n

indoor adj 1 within doors 2 under cover **indoors** adv

indubitable adj beyond doubt

induce ❶ v 1 persuade 2 bring on **inducement** n incentive

induct v install in office **induction** n 1 inducting 2 general inference

from particular inferences 3 production of electric or magnetic state by proximity

indulge ❶ v 1 gratify 2 pamper **indulgence** n 1 indulging 2 extravagance 3 favour, privilege **indulgent** adj

industry ❶ n, pl **-tries** 1 manufacture, processing etc. of goods 2 branch of this 3 diligence **industrial** adj of industries, trades **industrialize** v **industrious** adj diligent

inedible adj not eatable

ineffable adj unutterable

ineligible adj not fit or qualified (for something)

inept adj 1 absurd 2 out of place 3 clumsy **ineptitude** n

inert adj 1 without power of motion 2 sluggish 3 unreactive **inertia** n 1 inactivity 2 tendency to continue at rest or in uniform motion

inescapable adj unavoidable

inestimable adj immeasurable

inevitable ❶ adj 1 unavoidable

passable ≠ **excellent**

indirect adj = **related**, secondary, subsidiary, incidental, unintended; = **circuitous**, roundabout, curving, wandering, rambling ≠ **direct**

indispensable adj = **essential**, necessary, needed, key, vital ≠ **dispensable**

individual adj = **separate**, independent, isolated, lone, solitary ≠ **collective**; = **unique**, special, fresh, novel, exclusive ≠ **conventional** ▷ n = **person**, being, human, unit, character

induce v = **cause**, produce, create, effect, lead to ≠ **prevent**; = **persuade**, encourage, influence, convince, urge ≠ **dissuade**

indulge v = **gratify**, satisfy, feed, give way to, yield to; = **spoil**, pamper, cosset, humour, give in to

industry n = **business**, production, manufacturing, trade, commerce; = **trade**, world, business, service, line

inevitable adj = **unavoidable**, inescapable, inexorable, sure, certain ≠ **avoidable**

2 sure to happen **inevitability** n
inexorable adj relentless
inexplicable adj impossible to explain
infallible adj not liable to fail or err
infamous ❶ adj **1** notorious
2 shocking **infamy** n
infant ❶ n very young child
infancy n **1** babyhood **2** early stage of development **infantile** adj childish
infantry n foot soldiers
infect ❶ v **1** affect (with disease)
2 contaminate **infection** n
infectious adj catching
infer v -**ferring**, -**ferred** deduce, conclude **inference** n
inferior ❶ adj **1** of poor quality
2 lower ▷ n **3** one lower (in rank etc.) **inferiority** n
infernal adj **1** devilish **2** hellish
3 (Inf) irritating, confounded
inferno n, pl -**nos** **1** intense, raging fire **2** hell
infertile adj barren, not productive
infest v inhabit or overrun in dangerously or unpleasantly large numbers
infidelity n, pl -**ties**

1 unfaithfulness **2** religious disbelief **infidel** n unbeliever
infiltrate ❶ v **1** trickle through
2 gain access surreptitiously
infinite ❶ adj boundless
infinitely adv exceedingly
infinitesimal adj extremely small **infinity** n unlimited extent
infinitive n form of verb without tense, person, or number
infirm adj physically or mentally weak **infirmary** n hospital, sick quarters **infirmity** n, pl -**ties**
inflame ❶ v **1** rouse to anger, excitement **2** cause inflammation in **inflammable** adj **1** easily set on fire **2** excitable **inflammation** n painful infected swelling **inflammatory** adj
inflate ❶ v **1** blow up with air, gas
2 swell **3** raise prices, esp. artificially **inflatable** adj **inflation** n increase in prices and fall in value of money
inflection, inflexion n
1 modification of word
2 modulation of voice
inflexible adj **1** incapable of being bent **2** stubborn

— THESAURUS —

infamous adj = **notorious**, ignominious, disreputable, ill-famed ≠ **esteemed**
infant n = **baby**, child, babe, toddler, tot
infect v = **pollute**, poison, corrupt, contaminate, taint
inferior adj = **lower**, minor, secondary, subsidiary, lesser ≠ **superior** (Aust Sl) ▷ n = **underling**, junior, subordinate,

lesser, menial
infiltrate v = **penetrate**, pervade, permeate, percolate, filter through to
infinite adj = **limitless**, endless, unlimited, eternal, never-ending ≠ **finite**
inflame v = **enrage**, stimulate, provoke, excite, anger ≠ **calm**
inflate v = **blow up**, pump up, swell, dilate, distend ≠ **deflate**

inflict ① v impose, deliver forcibly **infliction** n

influence ① n 1 power to affect other people, events etc. 2 person, thing possessing such power ▷ v 3 sway 4 induce 5 affect **influential** adj

influenza n contagious viral disease

influx ① n 1 flowing in 2 inflow

inform ① v give information (about) **informant** n one who tells **information** n what is told, knowledge **informative** adj **informer** n.

informal ① adj 1 relaxed and friendly 2 appropriate for everyday use **informally** adv **informality** n

infrared adj below visible spectrum

infrastructure n basic structure or fixed capital items of an organization or economic system

infringe v transgress, break

infuriate ① v enrage

infuse v 1 soak to extract flavour etc. 2 instil **infusion** n 1 infusing 2 extract obtained

ingenious ① adj 1 clever at contriving 2 cleverly contrived **ingenuity** n

ingenuous adj 1 frank 2 innocent

ingot n block of cast metal, esp. gold

ingrained adj 1 deep-rooted 2 inveterate

ingratiate v get (oneself) into favour

ingredient ① n component part of a mixture

inhabit ① v -habiting, -habited dwell in **inhabitant** n

inhale ① v breathe in (air etc.) **inhalation** n **inhaler** n container with medical preparation inhaled to help breathing

inherent ① adj existing as an inseparable part

————— THESAURUS —————

embroider, embellish

inflict v = **impose**, administer, visit, apply, deliver

influence n = **control**, power, authority, direction, command; = **power**, authority, pull (Inf), importance, prestige ▷ v = **affect**, have an effect on, have an impact on, control, concern

influx n = **arrival**, rush, invasion, incursion, inundation

inform v = **tell**, advise, notify, instruct, enlighten

informal adj = **natural**, relaxed, casual, familiar, unofficial

infuriate v = **enrage**, anger, provoke, irritate, incense **≠ soothe**

ingenious adj = **creative**, original, brilliant, clever, bright **≠ unimaginative**

ingredient n = **component**, part, element, feature, piece

inhabit v = **live in**, occupy, populate, reside in, dwell in

inhale v = **breathe in**, gasp, draw in, suck in, respire **≠ exhale**

inherent adj = **intrinsic**, natural, essential, native, fundamental **≠ extraneous**

inherit ➊ v **-heriting, -herited**
1 receive, succeed as heir **2** derive
from parents **inheritance** n

inhibit ➊ v **-hibiting, -hibited**
1 restrain **2** hinder **inhibition** n
repression of emotion, instinct

inhospitable adj **1** unfriendly
2 harsh

inhuman adj **1** cruel, brutal **2** not
human

inhumane adj cruel, brutal
inhumanity n

inimical adj unfavourable, hostile

inimitable adj defying imitation

iniquity n, pl **-ties 1** gross
injustice **2** sin **iniquitous** adj

initial ➊ adj **1** of, occurring at
the beginning ▷ n **2** initial letter,
esp. of person's name ▷ v **3** mark,
sign with one's initials **initially**
adv

initiate ➊ v **1** originate **2** admit
into closed society **3** instruct
initiation n **initiative** n **1** lead
2 ability to act independently

inject ➊ v **1** put (fluid, medicine
etc.) into body with syringe

2 introduce (new element)
injection n

injunction ➊ n (judicial) order

injustice ➊ n **1** want of justice
2 wrong **3** unjust act

ink n **1** fluid used for writing or
printing ▷ v **2** mark, cover with ink
inky adj

inkling n hint, vague idea

inland ➊ adj/adv **1** in, towards the
interior **2** away from the sea

inlay v **1** embed **2** decorate with
inset pattern ▷ n **3** inlaid piece or
pattern

inlet n **1** entrance **2** mouth of
creek **3** piece inserted

inmate n occupant, esp. of prison,
hospital, etc.

inmost adj most inward, deepest

inn n **1** public house providing food
and accommodation **2** hotel
innkeeper n

innards pl n (Inf) internal parts,
esp. of body

innate adj **1** inborn **2** inherent

inner ➊ adj lying within
innermost adj

————— **THESAURUS** —————

inherit v = **be left**, come
into, be willed, succeed to, fall heir
to

inhibit v = **hinder**, check, frustrate,
curb, restrain ≠ **further**

initial adj = **opening**, first, earliest,
beginning, primary ≠ **final**

initiate v = **begin**, start, open,
launch, kick off (Inf); = **introduce**,
admit, enlist, enrol, launch ▷ n
= **novice**, member, pupil, convert,
amateur

inject v = **vaccinate**, administer,

inoculate; = **introduce**, bring in,
insert, instil, infuse

injunction n = **order**, ruling,
command, instruction,
mandate

injustice n = **unfairness**,
discrimination, prejudice, bias,
inequality ≠ **justice**

inland adj = **interior**, internal,
upcountry

inner adj = **inside**, internal, interior,
inward ≠ **outer**; = **central**, middle,
internal, interior, personal

innings n (Sport) **1** player's or side's turn of batting **2** turn

innocent ❶ adj **1** guiltless **2** without experience of evil ▷ n **3** innocent person **innocence** n

innocuous adj harmless

innuendo n, pl **-does** indirect accusation

innumerable adj countless

inoculate v immunize by injecting vaccine **inoculation** n

inoperable adj (Med) not able to be operated on **inoperative** adj not operative

inordinate adj excessive

inorganic adj **1** not organic **2** not containing carbon

input n material, data, current etc. fed into a system

inquest ❶ n **1** coroner's inquiry into cause of death **2** detailed inquiry

inquire, enquire ❶ v seek information **inquirer, enquirer** n **inquiry, enquiry** n **1** question **2** investigation

inquisition n **1** searching investigation (Hist) **2** (with cap.) tribunal for suppression of heresy

inquisitor n

inquisitive adj **1** curious **2** prying

insane ❶ adj **1** mentally deranged **2** crazy **insanely** adv **1** madly **2** excessively **insanity** n

insatiable adj incapable of being satisfied

inscribe v write, engrave (in or on something) **inscription** n words inscribed

inscrutable adj **1** enigmatic **2** incomprehensible

insect n small, usu. winged animal with six legs **insecticide** n preparation for killing insects

insecure ❶ adj **1** not safe or firm **2** anxious

insensible adj **1** unconscious **2** without feeling **3** not aware **insensibly** adv imperceptibly

insensitive adj unaware of other people's feelings

insert ❶ v **1** put into or between ▷ n **2** something inserted **insertion** n

inset n something extra inserted **inset** v

inshore adv/adj near shore

THESAURUS

innocent adj = **not guilty**, in the clear, blameless, clean, honest **≠ guilty**; = **naive**, open, trusting, simple, childlike **≠ worldly**; = **harmless**, innocuous, inoffensive, well-meant, unobjectionable

inquest n = **inquiry**, investigation, probe, inquisition

inquire, enquire v = **ask**, question, query, quiz

insane adj = **mad**, crazy, mentally ill, crazed, demented **≠ sane**; = **stupid**, foolish, daft (Inf), irresponsible, irrational **≠ reasonable**

insecure worried, anxious, afraid ▷ adj = **unsafe**, exposed, vulnerable, wide-open, unprotected **≠ safe**

insert v = **put**, place, position, slip, slide

inside ❶ n **1** inner part ▷ pl **2** (Inf) stomach, entrails ▷ adj/adv/prep **3** in, on, into the inside

insidious adj unseen but deadly

insight ❶ n discernment

insignia pl n, pl **-nias, -nia** badges, emblems

insignificant ❶ adj not important **insignificance** n

insincere adj pretending what one does not feel **insincerity** n, pl **-ties**

insinuate v **1** hint **2** introduce subtly **insinuation** n

insipid adj dull, tasteless

insist ❶ v **1** demand persistently **2** maintain **3** emphasize **insistence** n **insistent** adj

insole n inner sole of shoe or boot

insolent adj impudent **insolence** n

insoluble adj **1** incapable of being solved **2** incapable of being dissolved

insolvent adj unable to pay one's debts **insolvency** n

insomnia n inability to sleep **insomniac** adj/n

inspect ❶ v examine (closely or officially) **inspection** n **inspector** n

inspire ❶ v **1** arouse creatively **2** give rise to **inspiration** n **1** good idea **2** creative influence

install ❶ v **1** place in position **2** formally place (person) in position or rank **installation** n **1** act of installing **2** equipment installed

instalment ❶ n **1** part payment **2** one of a series of parts

instance ❶ n **1** example ▷ v **2** cite

instant ❶ n **1** moment ▷ adj **2** immediate **3** (of foods) requiring little preparation **instantaneous** adj happening in an instant **instantly** adv at once

——————— THESAURUS ———————

inside n = **interior**, contents, core, nucleus ▷ adj = **inner**, internal, interior, inward ≠ **outside**; = **confidential**, private, secret, internal, exclusive ▷ adv = **indoors**, in, within, under cover

insight n = **understanding**, perception, sense, knowledge, vision

insignificant adj = **unimportant**, minor, irrelevant, petty, trivial ≠ **important**

insist v = **demand**, order, require, command, dictate; = **assert**, state, maintain, claim, declare

inspect v = **examine**, check, look at, view, survey

inspire stimulate ▷ v = **give rise to**, produce, result in, engender

install v = **set up**, put in place, position, station; = **institute**, establish, introduce, invest, ordain

instalment n = **payment**, repayment, part payment

instance n = **example**, case, occurrence, occasion, sample ▷ v = **name**, mention, identify, point out, advance

instant n = **moment**, second, flash, split second, jiffy (Inf); = **time**, point, hour, moment, stage ▷ adj = **immediate**, prompt,

instead ❶ *adv* in place (of)

instep *n* top of foot between toes and ankle

instigate *v* incite, urge **instigation** *n* **instigator** *n*

instil *v* **-stilling, -stilled** implant

instinct ❶ *n* 1 inborn impulse 2 unconscious skill **instinctive**

institute ❶ *v* 1 establish 2 set *adj* going ▷ *n* 3 society for promoting science etc. **institution** *n* 1 setting up 2 establishment for care or education 3 established custom, law etc. **institutional** *adj* 1 of institutions 2 routine

instruct ❶ *v* 1 teach 2 inform 3 order **instruction** *n* 1 teaching, order ▷ *pl* 2 directions **instructive** *adj* informative **instructor** *n*

instrument ❶ *n* 1 thing used to make, do, measure etc. 2 mechanism for producing musical sound **instrumental** *adj* 1 acting as instrument or means 2 produced by musical instruments

insubordinate *adj* mutinous, rebellious **insubordination** *n*

insufferable *adj* unbearable

insular *adj* 1 of an island 2 narrow-minded

insulate ❶ *v* 1 prevent or reduce transfer of electricity, heat, sound etc. 2 isolate, detach **insulation** *n* **insulator** *n*

insulin *n* hormone used in treatment of diabetes

insult ❶ *v* 1 behave rudely to 2 offend ▷ *n* 3 affront **insulting** *adj*

insuperable *adj* not able to be overcome

insurance *n* agreement to pay compensation if damage, loss or death occurs

intact ❶ *adj* 1 untouched 2 uninjured

intake *n* 1 thing, amount taken in 2 opening

integer *n* whole number

integral ❶ *adj* essential **integrate** *v* combine into one whole **integration** *n*

instantaneous, direct, quick; = **ready-made**, fast, convenience, ready-mixed, ready-cooked

instead *adv* = **rather**, alternatively, preferably, in preference, in lieu

instinct *n* = **talent**, skill, gift, capacity, bent

institute *v* = **establish**, start, found, launch, set up ≠ **end**

instruct *v* = **order**, tell, direct, charge, bid; = **teach**, school, train, coach, educate

instrument *n* = **tool**, device, implement, mechanism, appliance;

= **agent**, means, medium, agency, vehicle (*SI*)

insulate *v* = **isolate**, protect, screen, defend, shelter

insult *v* = **offend**, abuse, wound, slight, put down ≠ **praise** ▷ *n* = **jibe**, slight, put-down, abuse, snub

intact *adj* = **undamaged**, whole, complete, sound, perfect ≠ **damaged**

integral *adj* = **essential**, basic, fundamental, necessary, component ≠ **inessential**

integrity ❶ n honesty

intellect ❶ n power of thinking and reasoning **intellectual** adj **1** of, appealing to intellect **2** having good intellect ▷ n **3** intellectual person

intelligent ❶ adj clever **intelligence** n **1** intellect **2** information, esp. military **intelligent design** theory that a sentient being designed and created the universe and all life **intelligible** adj understandable

intemperate adj **1** drinking alcohol to excess **2** immoderate

intend ❶ v propose, mean

intense ❶ adj **1** very strong or acute **2** emotional **intensify** v **-fying, -fied** increase **intensity** n **intensive** adj

intent ❶ n **1** purpose ▷ adj **2** concentrating (on) **3** resolved **intention** n purpose, aim **intentional** adj

inter ❶ v **-terring, -terred** bury **interment** n

inter- comb. form between, among, mutually, as in interglacial, interrelation

interact v act on each other **interaction** n **interactive** adj

intercede v plead in favour of, mediate **intercession** n

intercept ❶ v **1** cut off **2** seize, stop in transit **interception** n

interchange v **1** (cause to) exchange places ▷ n **2** motorway junction **interchangeable** adj able to be exchanged in position or use

intercom n internal communication system

intercontinental adj **1** connecting continents **2** (of missile) able to reach one continent from another

intercourse ❶ n **1** act of having sex **2** communications or dealings between individuals or groups

interest ❶ n **1** concern, curiosity **2** thing exciting this **3** sum paid for borrowed money **4** advantage

— THESAURUS —

integrity n = **honesty**, principle, honour, virtue, goodness ≠ **dishonesty**; = **unity**, unification, cohesion, coherence, wholeness

intellect n = **intelligence**, mind, reason, understanding, sense

intelligent adj = **clever**, bright, smart, sharp, enlightened ≠ **stupid**

intend v = **plan**, mean, aim, propose, purpose

intense adj = **extreme**, great, severe, fierce, deep ≠ **mild**; = **fierce**, tough

intent adj = **absorbed**, intense,

fascinated, preoccupied, enthralled ≠ **indifferent** ▷ n = **intention**, aim, purpose, meaning, end ≠ **chance**

inter v = **bury**, lay to rest, entomb, consign to the grave

intercept v = **catch**, stop, block, seize, cut off

intercourse n = **sexual intercourse**, sex (Inf), copulation, coitus, carnal knowledge; = **contact**, communication, commerce, dealings

interest n often plural = **hobby**,

5 right, share ▷ *v* **6** excite, cause to feel interest **interested** *adj*
interesting *adj*
interface ❶ *adj* area, surface, boundary linking two systems
interfere ❶ *v* **1** meddle, intervene **2** clash **interference** *n* **1** act of interfering **2** (*Radio*) atmospherics
interim ❶ *n* **1** meantime ▷ *adj* **2** temporary
interior ❶ *adj* **1** inner **2** inland **3** indoors ▷ *n* **4** inside **5** inland region
interject *v* interpose (remark etc.) **interjection** *n* **1** exclamation **2** interjected remark
interlock *v* lock together firmly
interloper *n* intruder
interlude *n* **1** interval **2** something filling an interval
intermarry *v* **1** (of families, races, religions) become linked by marriage **2** marry within one's family **intermarriage** *n*
intermediate ❶ *adj* **1** coming between **2** interposed

intermediary *n*
interminable *adj* endless
intermission *n* interval
intermittent *adj* occurring at intervals
intern *v* confine to special area or camp **internment** *n*
internal ❶ *adj* **1** inward **2** interior **3** within (a country, organization)
international ❶ *adj* **1** of relations between nations ▷ *n* **2** game or match between teams of different countries
internecine *adj* **1** mutually destructive **2** deadly
interplanetary *adj* of, linking planets
interplay *n* action and reaction of things upon each other
interpolate *v* **1** insert new matter **2** interject
interpose *v* **1** insert **2** say as interruption
interpret ❶ *v* **1** explain **2** translate, esp. orally **3** represent **interpretation** *n* **interpreter** *n*

i

— THESAURUS —

activity, pursuit, entertainment, recreation; *often plural*
= advantage, good, benefit, profit; **= stake**, investment ▷ *v* **= arouse your curiosity**, fascinate, attract, grip, entertain ≠ **bore**
interface *n* **= connection**, link, boundary, border, frontier
interfere *v* **= meddle**, intervene, intrude, butt in, tamper
interim *adj* **= temporary**, provisional, makeshift, acting, caretaker
interior *n* **= inside**, centre, heart,

middle, depths ▷ *adj* **= inside**, internal, inner ≠ **exterior**;
= mental, emotional, psychological, private, personal
intermediate *adj* **= middle**, mid, halfway, in-between (*Inf*), midway
internal *adj* **= domestic**, home, national, local, civic; **= inner**, inside, interior ≠ **external**
international *adj* **= global**, world, worldwide, universal, cosmopolitan
interpret *v* **= take**, understand, explain, construe; **= translate**,

interrogate v question, esp. closely or officially **interrogation** n **interrogative** n word used in asking question **interrogator** n

interrupt ❶ v 1 break in (upon) 2 stop 3 block **interruption** n

intersect v 1 divide by passing across or through 2 meet and cross **intersection** n

interstellar adj between stars

interstice n slit, crevice

intertwine v twist together

interval ❶ n 1 intervening time or space 2 pause, break 3 difference (of pitch)

intervene ❶ v 1 come into a situation in order to change it 2 be, come between or among 3 occur in the meantime 4 interpose **intervention** n

interview ❶ n 1 meeting, esp. one involving questioning ▷ v 2 have interview with **interviewee** n **interviewer** n

intestate adj not having made a will

intestine n (usu. pl) lower part of alimentary canal between stomach and anus **intestinal** adj

intimate¹ ❶ adj 1 closely acquainted, familiar 2 private 3 having cosy atmosphere ▷ n 4 intimate friend **intimacy** n

intimate² ❶ v 1 announce 2 imply in indirect way **intimation** n

intimidate ❶ v frighten into submission **intimidation** n

into prep 1 expresses motion to a point within 2 indicates change of state 3 indicates coming up against, encountering 4 indicates arithmetical division

intolerable adj more than can be endured

intolerant adj narrow-minded

intone v chant **intonation** n accent

intoxicate v make drunk

intractable adj difficult

intransigent adj uncompromising

— THESAURUS —

transliterate; = **explain**, make sense of, decode, decipher, elucidate

interrupt v = **intrude**, disturb, intervene, interfere (with), break in; = **suspend**, stop, end, delay, cease

interval n = **break**, spell, space ▷ n = **break**, interlude, intermission, rest, gap; = **delay**, gap, hold-up, stoppage

intervene v = **step in** (Inf), interfere, mediate, intrude, intercede; = **interrupt**, involve yourself

interview v = **examine**, talk to

intimate¹ adj = **close**, dear, loving, near, familiar ≠ **distant**; = **private**,

personal, confidential, special, individual ≠ **public**; = **detailed**, minute, full, deep, particular; = **cosy**, relaxed, friendly, informal, harmonious ▷ n = **friend**, close friend, crony, confidant or confidante, (constant) companion ≠ **stranger**

intimate² v = **suggest**, indicate, hint, imply, insinuate; = **announce**, state, declare, communicate, make known

intimidate v = **frighten**, pressure, threaten, scare, bully

intravenous adj into a vein
intrepid adj fearless, undaunted
intricate ❶ adj complex
 intricacy n, pl **-cies**
intrigue ❶ n 1 underhand plot
 2 secret love affair ▷ v 3 carry on
 intrigue 4 interest, puzzle
intrinsic adj inherent, essential
introduce ❶ v 1 make
 acquainted 2 present 3 bring in
 4 insert **introduction** n
 1 introducing 2 preliminary part of
 book etc. **introductory** adj
 preliminary
introvert n (Psychiatry) one who
 looks inward **introverted** adj
intrude v thrust (oneself) in
 intruder n **intrusion** n
 intrusive adj
intuition ❶ n spontaneous
 insight **intuitive** adj

Inuit n indigenous inhabitant of North
 America or Greenland
Inuk n a member of any Inuit people
Inuktitut n (Canad) the language
 of the Inuit
inundate v 1 flood 2 overwhelm
 inundation n
inured adj hardened
invade ❶ v 1 enter by force
 2 overrun **invader** n **invasion** n
invalid¹ n 1 one suffering from
 ill health ▷ v 2 retire because of
 illness etc.
invalid² ❶ adj having no legal force
 invalidate v
invaluable ❶ adj priceless
invasion ❶ SEE INVADE
invective n bitter verbal attack
inveigle v entice
invent ❶ v 1 devise, originate
 2 fabricate **invention** n 1 that

—————— THESAURUS ——————

intricate adj = **complicated**,
 involved, complex, fancy, elaborate
 ≠ **simple**
intrigue n = **plot**, scheme,
 conspiracy, manoeuvre, collusion;
 = **affair**, romance, intimacy, liaison,
 amour ▷ v = **interest**, fascinate,
 attract, rivet, titillate; = **plot**,
 scheme, manoeuvre, connive
introduce v = **bring in**, establish,
 set up, start, found; = **present**,
 acquaint, make known, familiarize,
 air; = **add**, insert, inject, throw in
 (Inf) infuse
intuition n = **instinct**, perception,
 insight, sixth sense
invade v = **attack**, storm, assault,
 capture, occupy; = **infest**, swarm,

overrun, ravage, beset
invalid¹ n = **patient**, sufferer,
 convalescent, valetudinarian ▷ adj
 = **disabled**, ill, sick, ailing, frail
invalid² adj = **null and void**, void,
 worthless, inoperative ≠ **valid**;
 = **unfounded**, false, illogical,
 irrational, unsound ≠ **sound**
invaluable adj = **precious**,
 valuable, priceless, inestimable,
 worth your or its weight in gold
 ≠ **worthless**
invasion n = **attack**, assault,
 capture, takeover, raid;
 = **intrusion**, breach, violation,
 disturbance, disruption
invent v = **create**, make, produce,
 design, discover; = **make up**,
 devise, concoct, forge, fake

which is invented **2** ability to invent
inventive adj **1** resourceful
2 creative **inventor** n
inventory ❶ n, pl **-tories**
detailed list
invert v **1** turn upside down
2 reverse **inverse** adj **1** inverted
2 opposite **inversion** n
invertebrate n/adj (animal)
without backbone
invest ❶ v **1** lay out (money, time,
effort etc.) for profit or advantage
2 install **3** endow **investiture** n
formal installation in office or rank
investment n **1** investing
2 money invested **3** stocks and
shares bought **investor** n
investigate ❶ v **1** inquire into
2 examine **investigation** n
investigative adj **investigator** n
inveterate adj **1** deep-rooted
2 confirmed
invidious adj likely to cause ill will
invigilate v supervise
examination candidates
invigilator n
invigorate v give vigour to
invincible adj unconquerable
inviolable adj not to be violated
inviolate adj not violated
invisible ❶ adj not able to be seen

invite ❶ v **1** request the company
of **2** ask courteously **3** ask for
4 attract, call forth **invitation** n
invoice n **1** list of goods or services
sold, with prices ▷ v **2** make,
present an invoice
invoke ❶ v **1** call on **2** appeal to
3 ask earnestly for **4** summon
invocation n
involuntary adj **1** unintentional
2 instinctive
involve ❶ v **1** include **2** entail
3 implicate (person) **4** concern
5 entangle **involved** adj
1 complicated **2** concerned (in)
inward adj **1** internal **2** situated
within **3** mental ▷ adv **4** (also
inwards) towards the inside **5** into
the mind **inwardly** adv **1** in the
mind **2** internally
iodine n nonmetallic element
found in seaweed
ion n electrically charged atom
IOU n signed paper acknowledging
debt
IP address (Comp) internet
protocol address: unique code that
identifies each computer connected
to the internet
IQ intelligence quotient
ire n anger **irascible** adj hot-tempered

─────────────────── THESAURUS ───────────────────

inventory n = **list**, record,
catalogue, listing, account
invest v = **spend**, expend, advance,
venture, put in; = **empower**,
provide, charge, sanction, license
investigate v = **examine**, study,
research, go into, explore
invisible adj = **unseen**,
imperceptible, indiscernible,

unseeable ≠ **visible**
invite v = **request**, look for, bid for,
appeal for; = **encourage**, attract,
cause, court, ask for (Inf)
invoke v = **apply**, use, implement,
initiate, resort to; = **call upon**,
appeal to, pray to, petition, beseech
involve v = **entail**, mean, require,
occasion, imply

DICTIONARY

irate *adj* angry

iridescent *adj* exhibiting changing colours

iris *n* **1** circular membrane of eye containing pupil **2** plant with sword-shaped leaves and showy flowers

irk *v* irritate, vex **irksome** *adj* tiresome

iron ❶ *n* **1** common metallic element **2** tool etc. of this metal **3** appliance used to smooth cloth **4** metal-headed golf club ▷ *pl* **5** fetters ▷ *adj* **6** of, like, iron **7** unyielding **8** robust ▷ *v* **9** press **ironmonger** *n* dealer in hardware

irony ❶ *n, pl* **-nies 1** use of words to mean the opposite of what is said **2** event, situation opposite of that expected **ironic, ironical** *adj* of, using, irony

irradiate *v* **1** treat with light or beams of particles **2** shine upon **irradiation** *n*

irrational ❶ *adj* not based on logic

irregular ❶ *adj* **1** not regular or even **2** unconventional **irregularity** *n, pl* **-ties**

irrelevant ❶ *adj* not connected with the matter in hand **irrelevance** *n*

irreparable *adj* not able to be repaired or remedied

irresistible ❶ *adj* **1** too strong to resist **2** enchanting, seductive

irrevocable *adj* not able to be changed

irrigate *v* water by artificial channels, pipes etc. **irrigation** *n*

irritate ❶ *v* **1** annoy **2** inflame **irritable** *adj* easily annoyed **irritant** *adj/n* (person or thing) causing irritation **irritation** *n*

is third person sing. of BE

Islam *n* Muslim faith or world **Islamic** *adj*

island ❶ *n* **1** piece of land surrounded by water **2** anything like this **islander** *n* inhabitant of island

isle *n* island **islet** *n* little island

THESAURUS

iron *adj* = **ferrous**, ferric;
= **inflexible**, hard, strong, tough, rigid ≠ **weak**

irony *n* = **sarcasm**, mockery, ridicule, satire, cynicism;
= **paradox**, incongruity

irrational *adj* = **illogical**, crazy, absurd, unreasonable, preposterous ≠ **rational**

irregular *adj* = **variable**, erratic, occasional, random, casual ≠ **steady**; = **uneven**, rough, ragged, crooked, jagged ≠ **even**; = **inappropriate**, unconventional,

unethical, unusual, extraordinary

irrelevant *adj* = **unconnected**, unrelated, unimportant, inappropriate, peripheral ≠ **relevant**

irresistible *adj* = **overwhelming**, compelling, overpowering, urgent, compulsive

irritate *v* = **annoy**, anger, bother, needle (*Inf*), infuriate ≠ **placate**; = **inflame**, pain, rub, scratch, scrape

island *n* = **isle**, atoll, islet, ait or eyot (*dialect*), cay or key

isobar *n* line on map connecting places of equal mean barometric pressure

isolate ❶ *v* place apart or alone **isolation** *n*

isomer *n* substance with same molecules as another but different atomic arrangement

isometric *adj* **1** having equal dimensions **2** relating to muscular contraction without movement **isometrics** *pl n* system of isometric exercises

isotope *n* atom having different atomic weight from other atoms of same element

issue ❶ *n* **1** topic of discussion or dispute **2** edition of newspaper etc. **3** offspring **4** outcome ▷ *v* **5** go out **6** result in **7** arise (from)

8 give, send out **9** publish

isthmus *n, pl* **-muses** neck of land between two seas

it *pron* neuter pronoun of the third person **its** *adj* belonging to it **it's** it is **itself** *pron* emphatic form of IT

italic *adj* (of type) sloping **italics** *pl n* this type, used for emphasis etc. **italicize** *v* put in italics

itch ❶ *v/n* (feel) irritation in the skin **itchy** *adj*

item ❶ *n* **1** single thing **2** piece of information **3** entry **itemize** *v*

itinerant *adj* travelling from place to place **itinerary** *n* **1** plan of journey **2** route

ivory *n* hard white substance of the tusks of elephants etc.

ivy *n, pl* **ivies** climbing evergreen plant

THESAURUS

---

isolate *v* = **separate**, break up, cut off, detach, split up

issue *n* = **topic**, point, matter, problem, question; = **point**, question, bone of contention; = **edition**, printing, copy, publication, number; = **children**, offspring, babies, kids (*Inf*), heirs ≠ **parent** ▷ *v* = **give out**, release,

publish, announce, deliver

itch *v* = **prickle**, tickle, tingle; = **long**, ache, crave, pine, hunger ▷ *n* = **irritation**, tingling, prickling, itchiness; = **desire**, longing, craving, passion, yen (*Inf*)

item *n* = **article**, thing, object, piece, unit; = **matter**, point, issue, case, question

J

jab ❶ *v* **jabbing, jabbed 1** poke roughly **2** thrust, stab ▷ *n* **3** poke **4** (*Inf*) injection

jabber *v* **1** chatter **2** talk incoherently

jack *n* **1** device for lifting heavy weight, esp. motorcar **2** lowest court card **3** (*Bowls*) ball aimed at **4** socket and plug connection in electronic equipment **5** small flag, esp. national, at sea ▷ *v* **6** (usu. with *up*) lift with a jack

jackal *n* doglike scavenging animal of Asia and Africa

jackass *n* **1** male ass **2** blockhead

jackboot *n* large military boot

jackdaw *n* small kind of crow

jacket ❶ *n* **1** outer garment, short coat **2** outer casing, cover

jackknife *n* **1** clasp knife ▷ *v* **2** angle sharply, esp. the parts of an articulated lorry

jackpot ❶ *n* large prize, accumulated stake, as pool in poker

Jacuzzi® *n* bath with device that swirls water

jade *n* **1** ornamental semiprecious stone, usu. dark green **2** this colour ▷ *adj* **3** of this colour

jaded *adj* **1** tired **2** off colour

jaguar *n* large S Amer. cat

jail ❶ *n* **1** building for confinement of criminals or suspects ▷ *v* **2** send to, confine in prison **jailer** *n*

jam ❶ *v* **jamming, jammed 1** pack together **2** (cause to) stick and become unworkable **3** (*Radio*) block (another station) ▷ *n* **4** fruit preserved by boiling with sugar **5** crush **6** hold-up of traffic **7** awkward situation

jamb *n* side post of door, fireplace etc.

jamboree *n* large gathering or rally of Scouts

Jan. January

jangle *v* **1** (cause to) sound harshly, as bell **2** (of nerves) be irritated

janitor *n* caretaker

January *n* first month

THESAURUS

jab *v* = **poke**, dig, punch, thrust, tap ▷ *n* = **poke**, dig, punch, thrust, tap

jacket *n* = **covering**, casing, case, cover, skin

jackpot *n* = **prize**, winnings, award, reward, bonanza

jail *n* = **prison**, penitentiary (*US*), confinement, dungeon, nick (*Brit Sl*)

▷ *v* = **imprison**, confine, detain, lock up, put away

jam *n* = **predicament**, tight spot, situation, trouble, hole (*Sl*) ▷ *v* = **pack**, force, press, stuff, squeeze; = **crowd**, throng, crush, mass, surge; = **congest**, block, clog, stick, stall

DICTIONARY

jar¹ ❶ *n* **1** round vessel of glass, earthenware etc. **2** (*Inf*) glass of esp. beer

jar² ❷ *v* **jarring, jarred 1** grate, jolt **2** have distressing effect on ▷ *n* **3** jarring sound **4** shock etc.

jargon ❸ *n* **1** special vocabulary for particular subject **2** pretentious language

jasmine *n* shrub with sweet-smelling flowers

jaundice *n* disease marked by yellowness of skin **jaundiced** *adj* prejudiced, bitter etc.

jaunt *n/v* (make) short pleasure excursion

jaunty *adj* **-tier, -tiest 1** sprightly **2** brisk

javelin *n* spear, esp. for throwing in sporting events

jaw ❹ *n* **1** one of bones in which teeth are set ▷ *pl* **2** mouth **3** gripping part of vice etc.

jay *n* noisy bird of brilliant plumage

jazz *n* **1** syncopated music and dance ▷ *v* **2** (with *up*) make more lively **jazzy** *adj* flashy, showy

jealous ❺ *adj* **1** envious

2 suspiciously watchful **jealousy** *n, pl* **-sies**

jeans *pl n* casual trousers, esp. of denim

Jeep® *n* light four-wheel-drive motor vehicle

jeer ❻ *v/n* scoff, taunt

jell *v* **1** congeal **2** (*Inf*) assume definite form

jelly *n, pl* **-lies 1** sweet, preserve etc. becoming softly stiff as it cools **2** anything of similar consistency **jellyfish** *n* small jelly-like sea animal

jemmy *n, pl* **-mies** short steel crowbar

jeopardy ❼ *n* danger **jeopardize** *v* endanger

jerk ❽ *n* **1** sharp push or pull **2** (*Sl*) stupid person ▷ *v* **3** move or throw with a jerk **jerky** *adj* **1** uneven **2** spasmodic

jerkin *n* sleeveless jacket

jersey *n* **1** knitted jumper **2** machine-knitted fabric

jest *n/v* joke **jester** *n* **1** joker **2** (*Hist*) professional fool at court

jet¹ ❾ *n* **1** aircraft driven by jet

THESAURUS

jar¹ *n* = **pot**, container, drum, vase, jug

jar² *v usually with* **on** = **irritate**, annoy, offend, nettle, irk; = **jolt**, rock, shake, bump, rattle

jargon *n* = **parlance**, idiom, usage, argot

jaw *v* (*Inf*) = **talk**, chat, gossip, chatter, spout

jealous *adj* = **suspicious**, protective, wary, doubtful, sceptical ≠ **trusting**; = **envious**,

grudging, resentful, green, green with envy ≠ **satisfied**

jeer *v* = **mock**, deride, heckle, barrack, ridicule ≠ **cheer** ▷ *n* = **mockery**, abuse, ridicule, taunt, boo ≠ **applause**

jeopardy *n* = **danger**, risk, peril, vulnerability, insecurity

jerk *v* = **jolt**, bang, bump, lurch ▷ *n* = **lurch**, movement, thrust, twitch, jolt

jet¹ *n* = **stream**, current, spring,

propulsion **2** stream of liquid, gas etc. **3** spout, nozzle ▷ v **4** shoot out **5** shoot forth **jet lag** fatigue caused by crossing time zones in aircraft **jet propulsion** propulsion by jet of gas or liquid **jet-propelled** *adj*

jet² *n* hard black mineral **jet-black** *adj* glossy black

jetsam *n* goods thrown overboard **jettison** v **1** abandon **2** throw overboard

jetty *n, pl* **-ties** small pier, wharf

Jew *n* one of Hebrew religion or ancestry **Jewish** *adj*

jewel ❶ *n* **1** precious stone **2** ornament containing one **3** precious thing **jeweller** *n* dealer in jewels **jewellery** *n*

jib *n* **1** jibbing, jibbed **1** triangular sail set forward of mast **2** arm of crane ▷ v **3** (of horse, person) stop and refuse to go on

jibe see GIBE

jig *n* **1** lively dance **2** music for it **3** guide for cutting etc. ▷ v **4** dance jig **5** make jerky up-and-down movements **jigsaw** *n* machine fret saw **jigsaw puzzle** picture cut into pieces, which the user tries to fit together again

jilt v reject (lover)

jingle *n* **1** light metallic noise **2** catchy rhythmic verse, song etc.

▷ v **3** (cause to) making jingling sound

jingoism *n* aggressive nationalism

jinks *pl n* **high jinks** boisterous merrymaking

jinx *n* **1** force, person, thing bringing bad luck ▷ v **2** cause bad luck

jitters *pl n* worried nervousness, anxiety **jittery** *adj* nervous

jive *n* **1** (dance performed to) popular music, esp. of 1950s ▷ v **2** do this dance

job ❶ *n* **1** piece of work, task **2** post **3** (*Inf*) difficult task **jobbing** *adj* doing single, particular jobs for payment **jobless** *adj/pl n* unemployed (people)

jockey *n* **1** rider in horse races ▷ v **2** manoeuvre

jockstrap *n* belt with pouch to support genitals

jocular *adj* **1** joking **2** given to joking **jocularity** *n*

jodhpurs *pl n* tight-legged riding breeches

jog ❶ v **1** jogging, jogged **1** run slowly, trot, esp. for exercise **2** nudge **3** stimulate ▷ n **4** jogging **jogger** *n* **jogging** *n*

Johnny Canuck *n* (*Canad*) **1** an informal name for a Canadian **2** a personification of Canada

join ❶ v **1** fasten, unite **2** become

flow, rush ▷ v = **fly**, wing, cruise, soar, zoom

jewel *n* = **gemstone**, gem, ornament, sparkler (*Inf*), rock (*Sl*); = **treasure**, wonder, darling, pearl, gem

job *n* = **task**, duty, work, venture, enterprise

jog v = **run**, trot, canter, lope; = **nudge**, push, shake, prod, stir

join v = **enrol in**, enter, sign up for, enlist in; = **connect**, unite, couple, a member (of) **3** become connected **4** (with *up*) enlist **5** take part (in) ▷ *n* **6** (place of) joining **joiner** *n* maker of finished woodwork **joinery** *n* joiner's work

joint ❶ *n* **1** arrangement by which two things fit together **2** place of this **3** meat for roasting, oft. with bone **4** (*Sl*) disreputable bar or nightclub **5** (*Sl*) marijuana cigarette ▷ *adj* **6** shared ▷ *v* **7** connect by joints **8** divide at the joints **jointly** *adv* **out of joint** **1** dislocated **2** disorganized

joist *n* beam supporting floor or ceiling

joke ❶ *n* **1** thing said or done to cause laughter **2** ridiculous thing ▷ *v* **3** make jokes **joker** *n* **1** one who jokes **2** (*Sl*) fellow **3** extra card in pack **jokey** *adj*

jolly ❶ *adj* **-lier, -liest 1** jovial **2** merry ▷ *v* **3** make person, occasion happier **jollification** *n* **jollity** *n*

jolt ❶ *n/v* **1** jerk **2** jar **3** shock **joss stick** incense stick

jostle *v* knock or push

jot *n* **1** jotting, jotted **1** small amount ▷ *v* **2** note **jotter** *n* notebook

joual *n* nonstandard Canadian French dialect, esp. as associated with ill-educated speakers

joule *n* (*Electricity*) unit of work or energy

journal ❶ *n* **1** newspaper or other periodical **2** daily record **journalism** *n* editing, writing in periodicals **journalist** *n*

journey ❶ *n* **1** going to a place, excursion **2** distance travelled ▷ *v* **3** travel

journeyman *n* qualified craftsman

jovial *adj* convivial, merry **joviality** *n*

joy ❶ *n* **1** gladness, pleasure, delight **2** cause of this **joyful** *adj* **joyous** *adj* extremely happy **joy ride** trip, esp. in stolen car **joystick** *n* **1** control column of aircraft **2** control device for video game

link, combine ≠ **detach**
joint *adj* = **shared**, mutual, collective, communal, united ▷ *n* = **junction**, connection, brace, bracket, hinge
joke *n* = **jest**, gag (*Inf*), wisecrack (*Inf*), witticism, crack (*Inf*); = **laugh**, jest, jape, trick, practical joke ▷ *v* = **jest**, kid (*Inf*), mock, tease, taunt
jolly *adj* = **happy**, cheerful, merry, upbeat (*Inf*), playful ≠ **miserable**
jolt *v* = **jerk**, push, shake, knock, jar; = **surprise**, stun, disturb, stagger,

startle ▷ *n* = **jerk**, start, jump, shake, bump; = **surprise**, blow, shock, setback, bombshell
journal *n* = **magazine**, publication, gazette, periodical; = **newspaper**, paper, daily, weekly, monthly
journey *n* = **trip**, drive, tour, flight, excursion ▷ *v* = **travel**, go, move, tour, progress
joy *n* = **delight**, pleasure, satisfaction, ecstasy, enjoyment ≠ **sorrow**

JP Justice of the Peace

jubilant adj exultant **jubilation** n

jubilee ❶ n time of rejoicing, esp. 25th or 50th anniversary

judder v 1 shake, vibrate ▷ n 2 vibration

judge ❶ n 1 officer appointed to try cases in law courts 2 one who decides in a dispute, contest etc. 3 one able to form a reliable opinion ▷ v 4 act as judge (of, for) **judgment, judgement** n 1 faculty of judging 2 sentence of court 3 opinion **judgmental, judgemental** adj

judicial ❶ adj of, by a court or judge **judiciary** n judges collectively **judicious** adj well-judged, sensible

judo n modern sport derived from jujitsu

jug ❶ n 1 vessel for liquids, with handle and small spout 2 its contents

juggernaut n 1 large heavy lorry 2 irresistible, destructive force

juggle ❶ v 1 keep several objects in the air simultaneously 2 manipulate to deceive **juggler** n

juice ❶ n 1 liquid part of vegetable, fruit or meat 2 (Inf) electric current 3 (Inf) petrol **juicy** adj 1 succulent 2 interesting

jujitsu n Japanese art of wrestling and self-defence

jukebox n automatic, coin-operated record player

July n seventh month

jumble ❶ v 1 mix in confused heap ▷ n 2 confused heap or state **jumble sale** sale of miscellaneous, usu. second-hand, items

jumbo ❶ n (Inf) 1 elephant 2 anything very large

jump ❶ v 1 (cause to) spring, leap (over) 2 move hastily 3 pass or skip (over) 4 rise steeply 5 start (with astonishment etc.) ▷ n 6 act of jumping 7 obstacle to be jumped 8 distance, height jumped 9 sudden rise **jumper** n sweater, pullover **jumpy** adj nervous

---------- THESAURUS ----------

jubilee n = **celebration**, holiday, festival, festivity

judge n = **magistrate**, justice, beak (Brit Sl), His, Her or Your Honour's; = **referee**, expert, specialist, umpire, mediator; = **critic**, assessor, arbiter ▷ v = **adjudicate**, referee, umpire, mediate, officiate; = **evaluate**, rate, consider, view, value

judicial adj = **legal**, official

jug n = **container**, pitcher, urn, carafe, creamer (US & Canad)

juggle v = **manipulate**, change,

alter, modify, manoeuvre

juice n = **liquid**, extract, fluid, liquor, sap

jumble n = **muddle**, mixture, mess, disorder, confusion ▷ v = **mix**, mistake, confuse, disorder, shuffle

jumbo adj = **giant**, large, huge, immense, gigantic ≠ **tiny**

jump v = **leap**, spring, bound, bounce, hop; = **recoil**, start, jolt, flinch, shake; = **increase**, rise, climb, escalate, advance; = **miss**, avoid, skip, omit, evade ▷ n = **leap**,

junction n 1 place where routes meet 2 point of connection

juncture n state of affairs

June n sixth month

jungle n 1 equatorial forest 2 tangled mass 3 condition of intense competition

junior ⊕ n 1 younger 2 of lower standing ▷ n 3 junior person

juniper n evergreen shrub

junk n 1 useless objects **junkie** n (Sl) drug addict **junk food** food of low nutritional value **junk mail** unsolicited mail

junket n 1 flavoured curdled milk 2 excursion

junta n group holding power in country

jurisdiction ⊕ n 1 authority 2 territory covered by it

jury n, pl **-ries** 1 body of persons

sworn to render verdict in court of law 2 judges of competition **juror** n

just ⊕ adj 1 fair 2 upright, honest 3 right, equitable ▷ adv 4 exactly 5 barely 6 at this instant 7 merely 8 really **justice** n 1 moral or legal fairness 2 judge, magistrate

justice of the peace person who can act as judge in local court

justify v 1 prove right 2 vindicate **justifiable** adj **justification** n

jut v jutting, jutted project, stick out, protrude

jute n plant fibre used for rope, canvas etc.

juvenile ⊕ adj 1 of, for young children 2 immature ▷ n 3 young person, child

juxtapose v put side by side **juxtaposition** n

— THESAURUS —

spring, skip, bound, hop; **= rise**, increase, upswing, advance, upsurge

junior adj = **minor**, lower, secondary, lesser, subordinate

junk n = **rubbish**, refuse, waste, scrap, litter

jurisdiction n = **authority**, power, control, rule, influence; **= range**, area, field, bounds, province

just adv = **recently**, lately, only now; **= merely**, only, simply, solely; **= barely**, hardly, by a whisker, by the skin of your teeth ▷ adj = **fair**, good, legitimate, upright, honest ≠ **unfair**; **= fitting**, due, correct, deserved, appropriate ≠ **inappropriate**

juvenile n = **child**, youth, minor, girl, boy ≠ **adult** ▷ adj = **immature**, childish, infantile, puerile, young

k

Kabloona n a person who is not of Inuit ancestry, esp. a White person

kaftan n woman's long, loose dress with sleeves

kak n (S Afr, Sl) 1 faeces 2 rubbish

kaleidoscope n 1 optical toy producing changing patterns 2 any complex pattern **kaleidoscopic** adj

kamik n (Canad) a traditional Inuit boot made of caribou hide or sealskin

kamikaze n 1 Japanese suicide pilot ▷ adj 2 (of action) certain to kill or injure the doer

kangaroo n/pl -roos Aust. marsupial with strong hind legs for jumping

karate n Japanese system of unarmed combat

karma n person's actions affecting fate for next incarnation

kayak n 1 Inuit canoe 2 any similar canoe

kebab n 1 dish of small pieces of meat, tomatoes etc. grilled on skewers 2 grilled minced lamb served in split slice of unleavened bread

kedgeree n dish of fish cooked with rice, eggs etc.

keel n lowest longitudinal support on which ship is built **keel over** 1 turn upside down 2 (Inf) collapse suddenly

keen ❶ adj 1 sharp 2 acute 3 eager 4 shrewd 5 (of price) competitive

keep ❶ v keeping, kept 1 retain possession of, not lose 2 hold 3 (cause to) remain 4 maintain 5 remain good 6 continue ▷ n 7 maintenance 8 central tower of castle **keeper** n **keeping** n 1 harmony 2 care, charge **keepsake** n gift treasured for sake of the giver

keg n 1 small barrel 2 container for beer

kelp n large seaweed

THESAURUS

keen adj = **eager**, intense, enthusiastic, passionate, ardent ≠ **unenthusiastic**; = **sharp**, incisive, cutting, edged, razor-like ≠ **dull**; = **perceptive**, quick, sharp, acute, smart ≠ **obtuse**; = **intense**, strong, fierce, relentless, cut-throat

keep v usually with from = **prevent**, restrain, hinder, keep back; = **hold on to**, maintain, retain, save, preserve ≠ **lose**; = **store**, put, place, house, hold; = **carry**, stock, sell, supply, handle; = **support**, maintain, sustain, provide for, mind ▷ n = **board**, food, maintenance, living, hold

ken n **kenning, kenned** range of knowledge

kennel n shelter for dog

kerb n stone edging to footpath

kernel n 1 inner seed of nut or fruit stone 2 central, essential part

kerosene n (US & Canad) another name for PARAFFIN

kestrel n small falcon

ketchup n sauce of vinegar, tomatoes etc.

kettle n metal vessel with spout and handle, esp. for boiling water

kettledrum n musical instrument made of membrane stretched over copper hemisphere

key ● n 1 instrument for operating lock, winding clock etc. 2 explanation, means of achieving an end etc. 3 (Mus) set of related notes 4 operating lever of typewriter, piano, organ etc. ▷ adj 5 most important **keyboard** n set of keys on piano, computer etc.

keyhole n opening for key

keynote n dominant idea

kg kilogram

khaki adj 1 dull, yellowish-brown ▷ n 2 khaki cloth 3 military uniform

kibbutz n/pl **kibbutzim** communal agricultural settlement in Israel

kick ● v 1 strike (out) with foot 2 recoil 3 resist 4 (Inf) free oneself of (habit etc.) ▷ n 5 blow with foot 6 thrill 7 strength (of flavour, alcoholic drink etc.) 8 recoil **kick off** start (a game of football) **kick out** dismiss or expel forcibly

kid ● n 1 young goat 2 leather of its skin 3 (Inf) child ▷ v 4 (Inf) tease, deceive 5 behave, speak in fun

kidnap ● v -napping, -napped seize and hold to ransom **kidnapper** n

kidney n 1 either of the pair of organs which secrete urine 2 animal kidney used as food

kill ● v 1 deprive of life 2 put an end to 3 pass (time) ▷ n 4 act of killing 5 animals etc. killed **killer** n **killing** adj 1 (Inf) very tiring 2 very funny

kiln furnace, oven

kilo n short for KILOGRAM

kilo- comb. form one thousand, as in kilometre, kilowatt

kilogram, kilogramme n 1000 grams

kilohertz n 1000 cycles per second

kilt n pleated tartan skirt worn orig. by Scottish Highlanders

key n = **opener**, door key, latchkey ▷ adj = **essential**, leading, major, main, important ≠ minor

kick v = **boot**, knock, punt; (Inf) = **give up**, break, stop, abandon, quit ▷ n (Inf) = **thrill**, buzz (Sl), tingle, high (Sl)

kid (Inf) n = **child**, baby, teenager, youngster, infant, ankle-biter (Aust Sl) ▷ v (Inf) = **tease**, joke, trick, fool, pretend

kidnap v = **abduct**, capture, seize, snatch (Sl), hijack

kill v = **slay**, murder, execute, slaughter, destroy; (Inf) = **destroy**, crush, scotch, stop, halt

kimono n, pl -nos loose Japanese robe

kin, kinsfolk n relatives **kindred** n 1 relatives ▷ adj 2 similar 3 related **kinsman** n

kind ❶ n 1 sort, type, class ▷ adj 2 considerate 3 gentle **kindly** adj -lier, -liest 1 kind, genial ▷ adv 2 gently **kindness** n **kind-hearted** adj

kindergarten n class, school for children of about four to six years old

kindle v 1 set alight 2 arouse 3 catch fire **kindling** n small wood to kindle fires

kindy, kindie n/pl -dies (Aust & NZ, Inf) kindergarten

kinetic adj relating to motion

king ❶ n 1 male ruler 2 chess piece 3 highest court card 4 (Draughts) crowned piece **kingdom** n 1 state ruled by king 2 realm 3 sphere **kingpin** n (Inf) chief thing or person **king-size** (Inf) very large

kingfisher n small brightly-coloured bird

kink n 1 tight twist in rope, wire, hair etc. ▷ v 2 make, become kinked **kinky** adj 1 full of kinks 2 (Inf) deviant

kiosk n 1 small, sometimes movable booth 2 public telephone box

kip n/v kipping, kipped (Inf) sleep

kipper n smoked herring

kirk n in Scotland, church

kismet n fate, destiny

kiss ❶ n 1 touch or caress with lips 2 light touch ▷ v 3 touch with lips **kiss of life** mouth-to-mouth resuscitation

kist n (SAfr) large wooden chest

kit ❶ n 1 outfit, equipment 2 personal effects, esp. of traveller 3 set of pieces of equipment sold ready to be assembled ▷ v 4 (with out) provide with kit **kitbag** n bag for soldier's or traveller's kit

kitchen n room used for cooking

kite n 1 light papered frame flown in wind 2 large hawk

kitsch n vulgarized, pretentious art

kitten n young cat **kittenish** adj playful

kitty n/pl -ties 1 in some card games, pool 2 communal fund

kiwi n 1 NZ flightless bird 2 (Inf) New Zealander **kiwi fruit** edible fruit with green flesh

klaxon n loud horn

kleptomania n compulsion to steal **kleptomaniac** n

kloof n (SAfr) mountain pass or gorge

km kilometre

knack ❶ n 1 acquired facility or dexterity 2 trick 3 habit

k

─────── THESAURUS ───────

kind n = **class**, sort, type, variety, brand

king n = **ruler**, monarch, sovereign, leader, lord

kiss v = **peck** (Inf), osculate, neck

(Inf) ▷ n = **peck** (Inf), snog, smacker (Sl), French kiss, osculation

kit n = **equipment**, materials, tackle, tools, apparatus

knack n = **skill**, art, ability, facility,

knacker n buyer of worn-out horses etc. for killing **knackered** adj (Sl) exhausted

knapsack n haversack

knave n 1 jack at cards 2 (Obs) rogue **knavish** adj

knead v 1 work into dough 2 massage

knee n joint between thigh and lower leg **kneecap** n bone in front of knee **kneejerk** adj (of reaction) automatic and predictable **knees-up** n (Inf) party

kneel ⊕ v **kneeling, kneeled** fall, rest on knees

knell n/v (ring) death bell

knickers ⊕ pl n woman's undergarment for lower half of body

knick-knack n trinket

knife ⊕ n, pl **knives** 1 cutting blade, esp. one in handle, used as implement or weapon ▷ v 2 cut or stab with knife

knight n 1 man of rank below baronet 2 member of medieval order of chivalry 3 piece in chess ▷ v 4 confer knighthood on **knighthood** n

knit ⊕ v **knitting, knitted** 1 form (garment etc.) by linking loops of yarn 2 draw together 3 unite **knitter** n **knitting** n 1 knitted work 2 act of knitting

knob n rounded lump **knobbly** adj

knock ⊕ v 1 strike, hit 2 (Inf) disparage 3 rap audibly 4 (of engine) make metallic noise ▷ n 5 blow, rap **knocker** n appliance for knocking on door **knock back** 1 (Inf) drink quickly 2 reject **knock-kneed** adj having incurved legs **knock out** 1 render unconscious 2 (Inf) overwhelm, amaze **knockout** n

knoll n small hill

knot ⊕ n 1 fastening of strands by looping and pulling tight 2 cluster 3 hard lump, esp. in timber 4 nautical miles per hour ▷ v 5 tie with knot, in knots **knotty** adj 1 full of knots 2 puzzling, difficult

know ⊕ v **knowing, knew, known** 1 be aware (of), have information (about) 2 be acquainted with 3 understand 4 feel certain **knowing** adj

—————————— THESAURUS ——————————

talent ≠ **ineptitude**

kneel v = **genuflect**, stoop

knickers pl n = **underwear**, smalls, briefs, drawers, panties

knife n = **blade**, carver, cutter ▷ v = **cut**, wound, stab, slash, thrust

knit v = **join**, unite, link, tie, bond; = **furrow**, tighten, knot, wrinkle, crease

knock v = **bang**, strike, tap, rap, thump; = **hit**, strike, punch, belt (Inf), smack; (Inf) = **criticize**,

condemn, put down, run down, abuse ▷ n = **knocking**, pounding, beating, tap, bang; = **bang**, blow, impact, jar, collision

knot n = **connection**, tie, bond, joint, loop ▷ v = **tie**, secure, bind, loop, tether

know v = **have knowledge of**, see, understand, recognize, perceive; = **be acquainted with**, recognize, be familiar with, be friends with, be friendly with ≠ **be unfamiliar with**

shrewd **knowingly** *adv*
1 shrewdly **2** deliberately
knowledge *n* **1** knowing **2** what
one knows **3** learning
knowledgable, knowledgeable
adj well-informed
knuckle *n* bone at finger joint
knuckle down get down (to work)
knuckle-duster *n* metal appliance
on knuckles to add force to blow
knuckle under submit
KO knockout
koala *n* marsupial Aust. animal,
native bear

kohl *n* cosmetic powder
Koran *n* sacred book of Muslims
kosher *adj* **1** conforming to Jewish
dietary law **2** (*Inf*) legitimate,
authentic
kowtow *v* **1** prostrate oneself
2 be obsequious
krypton *n* rare atmospheric gas
kudos *n* **1** fame **2** credit
kugel [koog]-el *n* (*S Afr*) rich,
fashion-conscious, materialistic
young woman
kung fu *n* Chinese martial art

k

fabric **2** cord, usu. one of pair, to draw edges together ▷ v **3** fasten with laces **4** flavour with spirit
lacy adj fine, like lace
lacerate v tear, mangle
lachrymose adj tearful
lack ❶ n **1** deficiency ▷ v **2** need, be short of
lackadaisical adj languid
lackey n **1** servile follower **2** footman
lacklustre adj lacking brilliance or vitality
laconic adj terse
lacquer n **1** hard varnish ▷ v **2** coat with this
lacrosse n ball game played with long-handled racket
lad ❶ n boy, young fellow
ladder n **1** frame with rungs, for climbing **2** line of torn stitches, esp. in stockings
laden ❶ adj heavily loaded
ladle n **1** spoon with long handle and large bowl ▷ v **2** serve out liquid with a ladle
lady ❶ n, pl **-dies 1** female counterpart of gentleman **2** polite term for a woman **3** title of some women of rank **ladybird** n small

l litre
lab n (Inf) short for LABORATORY
label ❶ n **1** slip of paper, metal etc., giving information **2** descriptive phrase ▷ v **3** give label
laboratory n, pl **-ries** place for scientific investigations or for manufacture of chemicals
labour n **1** exertion of body or mind **2** workers collectively
labrador n breed of large, smooth-coated retriever dog
laburnum n tree with yellow hanging flowers
labyrinth n **1** maze **2** perplexity
lace ❶ n **1** patterned openwork

━━━━━━━━━━━━━━━━━━━━━ THESAURUS ━━━━━━━━━

label n = **tag**, ticket, tab, marker, sticker ▷ v = **tag**, mark, stamp, ticket, tab
lace n = **netting**, net, filigree, meshwork, openwork; = **cord**, tie, string, lacing, shoelace ▷ v = **fasten**, tie, tie up, do up, secure; = **mix**, drug, doctor, add to, spike; = **intertwine**, interweave, entwine, twine, interlink

lack n = **shortage**, want, absence, deficiency, need ≠ **abundance** ▷ v = **miss**, want, need, require, not have ≠ **have**
lad n = **boy**, kid (Inf), guy (Inf), youth, fellow
laden adj = **loaded**, burdened, full, charged, weighed down
lady n = **gentlewoman**, duchess, noble, dame, baroness; = **woman**,

beetle, usu. red with black spots
ladylike adj gracious

lag¹ ❶ v go too slowly, fall behind
laggard n one who lags

lag² ❶ v wrap boiler, pipes etc. with insulating material **lagging** n this material

lag³ ❶ n (Sl) convict

lager n light-bodied beer

lagoon n saltwater lake, enclosed by atoll or sandbank

laid see LAY¹ **laid-back** adj (Inf) relaxed

lair n den of animal

laird n Scottish landowner

laissez-faire n principle of nonintervention

laity n people not belonging to clergy

lake ❶ n expanse of inland water

lama n Buddhist priest in Tibet or Mongolia

lamb n **1** young of the sheep **2** its meat **3** innocent or helpless creature ▷ v **4** give birth to lamb

lambast, lambaste v **1** beat, thrash **2** reprimand severely

lame ❶ adj **1** crippled in leg **2** limping **3** unconvincing ▷ v **4** cripple

lamé n/adj (fabric) interwoven with gold or silver thread

lament ❶ v **1** express sorrow (for) ▷ n **2** expression of grief **3** song of grief **lamentable** adj deplorable, disappointing **lamentation** n

laminate v **1** make (sheet of material) by bonding together two or more thin sheets **2** cover with thin sheet ▷ n **3** laminated sheet **lamination** n

lamington n (Aust & NZ) sponge cake coated with a sweet frosting

lamp n appliance (esp. electrical) that produces, light, heat etc. **lamppost** n post supporting lamp in street

lampoon n/v (make subject of) a satire

lamprey n fish like an eel

lance n **1** horseman's spear ▷ v **2** pierce with lance or lancet **lancet** n pointed two-edged surgical knife **lance corporal** lowest noncommissioned army rank

land ❶ n **1** solid part of earth's surface **2** ground **3** country **4** estate ▷ v **5** come to land **6** disembark **7** arrive on ground **8** bring to land **9** (Inf) obtain **10** catch **11** (Inf) strike **landed** adj

female, girl, damsel

lag¹ v = **hang back**, delay, trail, linger, loiter

lake n = **pond**, pool, reservoir, loch (Scot), lagoon

lame adj = **disabled**, handicapped, crippled, limping, hobbling; = **unconvincing**, poor, pathetic, inadequate, thin

lament v = **bemoan**, grieve, mourn, weep over, complain about ▷ n = **complaint**, moan, wailing, lamentation; = **dirge**, requiem, elegy, threnody

land n = **ground**, earth, dry land, terra firma; = **soil**, ground, earth, clay, dirt; = **countryside**, farmland; (Law) = **property**, grounds, estate,

possessing, consisting of lands
landing n **1** act of landing
2 platform between flights of stairs
landlocked adj completely
surrounded by land **landlord** n
1 person who lets land or houses
etc. **2** master or mistress of inn,
boarding house etc. **landlubber** n
person ignorant of the sea and
ships **landmark** n **1** conspicuous
object **2** event, decision etc.
considered as important stage in
development of something
landscape n **1** piece of inland
scenery **2** picture of this ▷ v
3 create, arrange garden, park etc.
landslide n **1** falling of soil, rock
etc. down mountainside
2 overwhelming election victory
lane ❶ n **1** narrow road or street
2 specified air, sea route **3** area of
road for one stream of traffic
language ❶ n **1** system of
sounds, symbols etc. for
communicating thought **2** style of
speech or expression
languish ❶ v **1** be or become
weak or faint **2** droop, pine

languid adj lacking energy,
spiritless **languor** n **1** lack of
energy **2** tender mood
languorous adj
lank adj **1** lean **2** limp **lanky** adj
lantern n transparent case for
lamp or candle
lap¹ ❶ n **1** the part between waist
and knees of a person when sitting
2 single circuit of track **3** stage or
part of journey ▷ v **4** enfold, wrap
round **5** overtake opponent to be
one or more circuits ahead
lap² ❶ v **1** drink by scooping up
with tongue **2** (of waves etc.) beat
softly
lapel n part of front of coat folded
back towards shoulders
lapwing n type of plover
larceny n, pl **-nies** theft
larch n deciduous conifer tree
lard n **1** prepared pig's fat ▷ v
2 insert strips of bacon in (meat)
3 intersperse
larder n storeroom for food
large ❶ adj **1** great in size, number
etc. ▷ adv **2** in a big way **largely**
adv **largesse** n **1** generosity

THESAURUS

real estate, realty; **= country**,
nation, region, state, district ▷ v
= arrive, dock, put down, moor,
alight; (Inf) **= gain**, get, win, secure,
acquire
lane n **= road**, street, track, path,
way
language n **= tongue**, dialect,
vernacular, patois; **= speech**,
communication, expression,
speaking, talk
languish v **= decline**, fade away,

wither away, flag, weaken
≠ flourish; (Lit) **= waste away**,
suffer, rot, be abandoned, be
neglected **≠ thrive**; often with **for**
= pine, long, desire, hunger, yearn
lap¹ n **= circuit**, tour, leg, stretch,
circle
lap² v **= ripple**, wash, splash, swish,
gurgle; **= drink**, sip, lick, swallow,
gulp
large adj **= big**, great, huge, heavy,
massive **≠ small**; **= massive**, great,

2 gift at large 1 free **2** in general

large-scale adj wide-ranging, extensive

largo adv/n, pl **-gos** (Mus) (passage played) in slow and dignified manner

lariat n (US & Canad) another word for LASSO

lark¹ n **1** small, brown singing bird **2** skylark

lark² n **1** frolic, spree ▷ v **2** indulge in lark

larrikin n (Aust or NZ, Old-fashioned Sl) mischievous or unruly person

larva n, pl **-vae** immature insect **larval** adj

larynx n, pl **larynges** part of throat containing vocal cords **laryngitis** n inflammation of this

lasagne, lasagna n pasta formed in wide, flat sheets

lascivious adj lustful

laser n device for concentrating electromagnetic radiation in an intense, narrow beam

lash¹ ❶ n **1** stroke with whip **2** flexible part of whip **3** eyelash

▷ v **4** strike with whip etc. **5** dash against **6** attack verbally, ridicule **7** flick, wave sharply to and fro **8** (with **out**) hit, kick

lash² ❶ v fasten or bind tightly

lashings pl n (Inf) abundance

lass, lassie n girl

lassitude n weariness

lasso n, pl **-sos, -soes 1** rope with noose for catching cattle etc. ▷ v **2** catch with this

last¹ ❶ adj/adv **1** after all others **2** most recent(ly) ▷ adj **3** only remaining ▷ n **4** last person or thing **lastly** adv finally **last-ditch** adj done as final resort **last straw** small irritation that, coming after others, is too much to bear **last word 1** final comment in argument **2** most recent or best example

last² ❶ v continue, hold out

latch ❶ n **1** fastening for door ▷ v **2** fasten with latch **3** (with **onto**) become attached to

late ❶ adj **1** coming after the appointed time **2** recent **3** recently dead ▷ adv **4** after

— THESAURUS —

big, huge, vast ≠ **small** = **plentiful**, comprehensive, lavish, bountiful, profuse

lash¹ v = **pound**, beat, strike, hammer, drum; = **censure**, attack, blast, put down, criticize; = **whip**, beat, thrash, birch, flog ▷ n = **blow**, hit, strike, stroke, stripe

lash² v = **fasten**, tie, secure, bind, strap

last¹ adj = **most recent**, latest, previous; = **hindmost**, final, at the end, remotest, furthest behind

≠ **foremost**

last² v = **continue**, remain, survive, carry on, endure ≠ **end**

latch n = **fastening**, catch, bar, lock, hook ▷ v = **fasten**, bar, secure, bolt, make fast

late adj = **overdue**, delayed, last-minute, belated, tardy ≠ **early**; = **dead**, deceased, departed, passed on, former ≠ **alive**; = **recent**, new, advanced, fresh ≠ **old** ▷ adv = **behind time**, belatedly, tardily, behindhand, dilatorily ≠ **early**

proper time **5** recently **6** at, till late hour **lately** adv not long since

latent adj **1** existing but not developed **2** hidden

lateral adj of, at, from the side

latex n sap or fluid of plants, esp. of rubber tree

lath n thin strip of wood

lathe n machine for turning and shaping

lather n **1** soapy froth **2** frothy sweat ▷ v **3** make frothy

Latin n **1** language of ancient Romans ▷ adj **2** of ancient Romans or their language

latitude ❶ n **1** angular distance in degrees N or S of equator **2** scope ▷ pl **3** regions

latrine n in army etc., lavatory

latter ❶ adj **1** second of two **2** later **3** more recent **latterly** adv **latter-day** adj modern

lattice n **1** network of strips of wood, metal etc. **2** window so made

laud v praise **laudable** adj praiseworthy

laudanum n sedative from opium

laugh ❶ v/n (make) sound of amusement, merriment or scorn **laughable** adj ludicrous **laughter** n **laughing stock** object of general derision

launch[1] ❶ v **1** set afloat **2** set in motion **3** begin **4** propel (missile, spacecraft) into space

launch[2] n large power-driven boat

laureate adj crowned with laurels **poet laureate** poet with appointment to Royal Household

laurel n **1** glossy-leaved shrub, bay tree ▷ pl **2** its leaves, emblem of victory or merit

lava n molten matter thrown out by volcano

lavatory ❶ n, pl **-ries** toilet, water closet

lavender n **1** shrub with fragrant, pale-lilac flowers **2** this colour

lavish ❶ adj **1** plentiful, rich **2** very generous ▷ v **3** spend, bestow, profusely

law ❶ n **1** rule binding on community **2** system of such rules

latitude n = **scope**, liberty, freedom, play, space

latter adj = **last**, ending, closing, final, concluding ≠ earlier

laugh v = **chuckle**, giggle, snigger, cackle, chortle ▷ n = **chortle**, giggle, chuckle, snigger, guffaw, (Inf) = **joke**, scream (Inf), hoot (Inf), lark, prank; (Inf) = **clown**, character (Inf), scream (Inf), entertainer, card (Inf)

launch[1] v = **propel**, fire, dispatch, discharge, project; = **begin**, start,

open, initiate, introduce

lavatory n = **toilet**, bathroom, loo (Brit Inf), privy, cloakroom (Brit)

lavish adj = **grand**, magnificent, splendid, abundant, copious ≠ stingy; = **extravagant**, wild, excessive, exaggerated, wasteful ≠ thrifty; = **generous**, free, liberal, bountiful, open-handed ≠ stingy ▷ v = **shower**, pour, heap, deluge, dissipate ≠ stint

law n = **constitution**, code, legislation, charter; = **statute**, act,

3 legal science **4** general principle deduced from facts **lawful** *adj* allowed by law **lawless** *adj* **1** ignoring laws **2** violent **lawyer** *n* professional expert in law **lawsuit** *n* prosecution of claim in court

lawn *n* tended turf in garden etc.

lawyer ❶ see LAW

lax *adj* **1** not strict **2** slack

laxative *adj/n* (substance) having loosening effect on bowels **laxity, laxness** *n*

lay¹ *v* **laying, laid 1** deposit, set, cause to lie **2** devise (plan) **3** attribute (blame) **4** place (bet) **5** (of animal) produce eggs **layer** *n* **1** single thickness as stratum or coating ▷ *v* **2** form layer **lay-by** *n* stopping place for traffic beside road **lay off** *v* dismiss staff during slack period **lay-off** *n* the act of suspending employees **layout** *n* arrangement

lay² ❶ *adj* not clerical or professional **layman** *n* ordinary person

lay ❶³ past tense of LIE **layabout** *n* lazy person, loafer

layette *n* clothes for newborn child

lazy ❶ *adj* **lazier, laziest** averse to work **laze** *v* be lazy **lazily** *adv*

lbw (Cricket) leg before wicket

lead¹ ❶ *v* **leading, led 1** guide, conduct **2** persuade **3** direct **4** be, go, play first **5** spend (one's life) **6** result **7** give access to ▷ *n* **8** that which leads or is used to lead **9** example **10** front or principal place, role etc. **11** cable bringing current to electrical instrument **leader** *n* **1** one who leads **2** editorial article in newspaper **leadership** *n*

lead² ❶ *n* **1** soft, heavy grey metal **2** graphite in pencil **3** plummet **leaded** *adj* (of windows) made from small panes held together by lead strips **leaden** *adj* **1** sluggish **2** dull grey **3** made from lead

— THESAURUS —

bill, rule, order; **= principle**, code, canon, precept, axiom

lawyer *n* **= legal adviser**, attorney, solicitor, counsel, advocate

lay¹ *v* **= place**, put, set, spread, plant; **= devise**, plan, design, prepare, work out; **= produce**, bear, deposit; **= arrange**, prepare, make, organize, position; **= attribute**, assign, allocate, allot, ascribe; **= put forward**, offer, present, advance, lodge; **= bet**, stake, venture, gamble, chance

lay² *adj* **= nonclerical**, secular, non-ordained; **= nonspecialist**,

amateur, unqualified, untrained, inexpert

lazy *adj* **= idle**, inactive, indolent, slack, negligent **≠ industrious**; **= lethargic**, languorous, slow-moving, languid, sleepy **≠ quick**

lead *v* **= go in front (of)**, head, be in front, be at the head (of), walk in front (of); **= guide**, conduct, steer, escort, precede; **= connect to**, link, open onto; **= be ahead (of)**, be first, exceed, be winning, excel; **= command**, rule, govern, preside over, head; **= live**, have, spend,

leaf ❶ *n, pl* **leaves 1** organ of photosynthesis in plants, consisting of a flat, usu. green blade on stem **2** two pages of book etc. **3** thin sheet ▷ *v* **4** turn through (pages etc.) cursorily **leaflet** *n* **1** small leaf **2** single printed and folded sheet, handbill **leafy** *adj*

league¹ ❶ *n* **1** agreement for mutual help **2** parties to it **3** federation of clubs etc. **4** (*Inf*) class, level

league² ❷ *n* former measure of distance, about 3 miles

leak ❶ *n* **1** defect that allows escape or entrance of liquid, gas, radiation etc. **2** disclosure ▷ *v* **3** let fluid etc. in or out **4** (of fluid etc.) find its way through leak

5 (allow to) become known little by little **leakage** *n* **1** leaking **2** gradual escape or loss **leaky** *adj*

lean¹ ❶ *v* **leaning, leaned 1** rest against **2** incline **3** tend (towards) **4** rely (on) **leaning** *n* tendency

lean-to *n* room, shed built against existing wall

lean² ❶ *adj* **1** lacking fat **2** thin **3** meagre ▷ *n* **4** lean part of meat

leap ❶ *v* **leaping, leapt 1** spring, jump **2** spring over ▷ *n* **3** jump **leapfrog** *n/v* vault over person bending down **leap year** year with extra day

learn ❶ *v* **learning, learned 1** gain skill, knowledge **2** memorize **3** find out **learned** *adj* showing much learning **learner** *n* **learning**

THESAURUS

experience, pass ▷ *n* = **first place**, winning position, primary position/ vanguard; = **advantage**, start, edge, margin, winning margin; = **example**, direction, leadership, guidance, model; = **clue**, suggestion, hint, indication, pointer; = **leading role**, principal, protagonist, title role, principal part ▷ *adj* = **main**, prime, top, leading, first

leaf *n* = **frond**, blade, cotyledon; = **page**, sheet, folio

league *n* = **association**, union, alliance, coalition, group; (*Inf*) = **class**, group, level, category, conspiring with

leak *v* = **escape**, pass, spill, release, drip; = **disclose**, tell, reveal, pass on, give away ▷ *n* = **leakage**, discharge, drip, seepage,

percolation; = **hole**, opening, crack, puncture, aperture; = **disclosure**, exposé, exposure, admission, revelation

lean¹ *v* = **bend**, tip, slope, incline, tilt; = **rest**, prop, be supported, recline, repose; = **tend**, prefer, favour, incline, be prone to

lean² *adj* = **thin**, slim, slender, skinny, angular ≠ **fat**

leap *v* = **jump**, spring, bound, bounce, hop ▷ *n* = **jump**, spring, bound, vault; = **rise**, change, increase, soaring, surge

learn *v* = **master**, grasp, pick up, take in, familiarize yourself with; = **discover**, hear, understand, find out about, become aware; = **memorize**, commit to memory, learn by heart, learn by rote, learn parrot-fashion *n* knowledge got by study

lease ① *n* 1 contract by which land or property is rented ▷ *v* 2 let, rent by lease **leasehold** *adj* held on lease

leash *n* lead for dog

least *adj* 1 smallest: superlative of LITTLE *n* 2 smallest one ▷ *adv* 3 in smallest degree

leather *n* prepared skin of animal **leathery** *adj* like leather, tough

leave¹ ① *v* **leaving, left** 1 go away 2 allow to remain 3 entrust 4 bequeath

leave² ① *n* 1 permission, esp. to be absent from duty 2 period of such absence 3 formal parting

leaven *n* 1 yeast ▷ *v* 2 raise with leaven

lecherous *adj* 1 full of lust 2 lascivious **lecher** *n* lecherous man **lechery** *n*

lectern *n* reading desk

lecture ① *n* 1 instructive discourse 2 speech of reproof ▷ *v* 3 deliver discourse 4 reprove

lecturer *n*

ledge *n* 1 narrow shelf sticking out from wall, cliff etc. 2 ridge below surface of sea

ledger *n* book of debit and credit accounts

lee ① *n* 1 shelter 2 side, esp. of ship, away from wind **leeward** *adj/adv/n* (on, towards) lee side **leeway** *n* 1 leeward drift of ship 2 room for movement within limits

leech *n* species of bloodsucking worm

leek *n* plant like onion with long bulb and thick stem

leer *v/n* glance with malign or lascivious expression

lees ① *pl n* 1 sediment 2 dregs

left¹ ① *adj* 1 on or to the west 2 opposite to the right 3 radical, socialist ▷ *adv* 4 on or towards the left ▷ *n* 5 the left hand or part 6 *(Politics)* reforming or radical party **leftist** *n/adj* (person) of the political left

left¹ ① *n* ² past tense past participle of

— THESAURUS —

lease *v* = **hire**, rent, let, loan, charter

leave *v* = **depart from**, withdraw from, go from, escape from, quit **≠ arrive**; = **quit**, give up, get out of, resign from, drop out of; = **give up**, abandon, dump (*Inf*), drop, surrender **≠ stay with**; = **entrust**, commit, delegate, refer, hand over; = **bequeath**, will, transfer, endow, confer; = **forget**, leave behind, mislay ▷ *n* = **holiday**, break, vacation, time off, sabbatical; = **permission**, freedom, sanction,

liberty, concession **≠ refusal**; = **departure**, parting, withdrawal, goodbye, farewell **≠ arrival**

lecture *n* = **talk**, address, speech, lesson, instruction; = **telling-off** (*Inf*), rebuke, reprimand, talking-to (*Inf*), scolding ▷ *v* = **talk**, speak, teach, address, discourse; = **tell off** (*Inf*), berate, scold, reprimand, censure

lees *pl n* = **sediment**, grounds, deposit, dregs

left¹ *adj* = **left-hand**, port, larboard (*Naut*)

LEAVE¹ **leftover** n unused portion

leg ❶ n 1 one of limbs on which person or animal walks, runs, stands 2 part of garment covering leg 3 support, as leg of table 4 stage **leggings** pl n covering of leather or other material (for legs) **leggy** adj long-legged **legless** adj 1 without legs 2 (Sl) very drunk

legacy ❶ n, pl **-cies** 1 bequest 2 thing handed down to successor

legal ❶ adj in accordance with law **legality** n **legalize** v make legal **legally** adv

legate n messenger, representative

legatee n recipient of legacy

legato adv, pl **-tos** (Mus) smoothly

legend ❶ n 1 traditional story 2 notable person or event 3 inscription **legendary** adj

legible adj readable **legibility** n

legion ❶ n 1 various military bodies 2 association of veterans 3 notable number ▷ adj 4 countless **legionary** adj/n **legionnaire** n

member of legion **legionnaire's disease** serious bacterial disease similar to pneumonia

legislate v make laws **legislation** n 1 act of legislating 2 laws which are made **legislative** adj

legitimate ❶ adj 1 born in wedlock 2 lawful, regular ▷ v 3 make lawful **legitimacy** n **legitimize** v

legume n pod

leisure ❶ n spare time **leisurely** adj 1 unhurried ▷ adv 2 slowly

lekker adj (S Afr, Sl) 1 attractive or nice 2 tasty

lemming n rodent of arctic regions

lemon n 1 pale yellow fruit 2 its colour 3 (Sl) useless person or thing **lemonade** n drink made from lemon juice **lemon curd** creamy spread made of lemons, butter etc.

lemur n nocturnal animal like monkey

lend v 1 give temporary use of 2 let out at interest 3 bestow

leg n = **limb**, member, shank, lower limb, pin (Inf); = **support**, prop, brace, upright; = **stage**, part, section, stretch, lap

legacy n = **bequest**, inheritance, gift, estate, heirloom

legal adj = **judicial**, judiciary, forensic, juridical, jurisdictive; = **lawful**, allowed, sanctioned, constitutional, valid

legend n = **myth**, story, tale, fiction, saga; = **celebrity**, star, phenomenon, genius, prodigy;

= **inscription**, title, caption, device, motto

legion n = **army**, company, force, division, troop; = **multitude**, host, mass, drove, number

legitimate adj = **lawful**, legal, genuine, authentic, authorized ≠ **unlawful**; = **reasonable**, correct, sensible, valid, warranted ≠ **unreasonable** ▷ v = **legitimize**, allow, permit, sanction, authorize

leisure n = **spare**, free, rest, ease, relaxation ≠ **work**

DICTIONARY

length ❶ n 1 measurement from end to end 2 duration 3 extent 4 piece of a certain length
lengthen v make, become, longer
lengthy adj very long
lenient adj not strict **leniency** n
lens n, pl **lenses** glass etc. shaped to converge or diverge light rays
lent SEE LEND
Lent n period of fasting from Ash Wednesday to Easter Eve
lentil n edible seed of leguminous plant
leopard n large, spotted, carnivorous cat
leotard n tight-fitting garment covering most of body
leper n 1 (Offens) one ill with leprosy 2 person shunned **leprosy** n ulcerous skin disease
leprechaun n mischievous Irish elf
lesbian ❶ n 1 homosexual woman ▷ adj 2 (of woman) homosexual
lesion n harmful sore on bodily organ
less ❶ adj comparative of LITTLE 1 not so much ▷ n 2 smaller part,

quantity 3 a lesser amount ▷ adv 4 to a smaller extent ▷ prep 5 minus **lessen** v 1 diminish 2 reduce **lesser** adj 1 smaller 2 minor
lesson ❶ n 1 instalment of course of instruction 2 content of this 3 experience that teaches 4 portion of Scripture read in church
lest conj for fear that
let¹ ❶ v letting, let 1 allow, enable, cause 2 rent 3 be leased **let down** 1 disappoint 2 lower 3 deflate **let off** 1 excuse 2 fire, explode 3 emit **let up** v diminish, stop
let² n 1 hindrance 2 in some games, minor infringement or obstruction
lethal ❶ adj deadly
lethargy n apathy, lack of energy **lethargic** adj
letter ❶ n 1 alphabetical symbol 2 written message 3 strict meaning, interpretation ▷ pl 4 literature ▷ v 5 mark with, in, letters

THESAURUS

length n = distance, reach, measure, extent, span; = duration, term, period, space, stretch; = piece, measure, section, segment, portion
lesbian adj = homosexual, gay, sapphic
less prep = minus, without, lacking, excepting, subtracting
lesson n = class, schooling, period, teaching, coaching; = example, warning, message, moral,

deterrent
let¹ v = allow, permit, authorize, give the go-ahead, give permission; = lease, hire, rent, rent out, hire out
lethal adj = deadly, terminal, fatal, dangerous, devastating ≠ harmless
letter n = message, line, note, communication, dispatch; = character, mark, sign, symbol, education

lettuce n salad plant
leukaemia n progressive blood disease
level ❶ adj 1 horizontal 2 even, flat ▷ n 3 horizontal line or surface 4 instrument for establishing horizontal plane 5 position on scale 6 grade ▷ v 7 make, become level 8 knock down 9 aim (gun, accusation etc.) **level crossing** point where railway and road cross **level-headed** adj not apt to be carried away by emotion
lever ❶ n 1 rigid bar pivoted about a fulcrum to transfer a force with mechanical advantage 2 operating handle ▷ v 3 prise, move, with lever **leverage** n 1 action, power of lever 2 influence
leveret n young hare
leviathan n 1 sea monster 2 anything huge or formidable
levitation n raising of solid body into the air supernaturally **levitate**

v (cause to) do this
levity n, pl **-ties** (undue) frivolity
levy ❶ v **levying, levied** 1 impose (tax) 2 raise (troops) ▷ n 3 imposition or collection of taxes
lewd adj 1 lustful 2 indecent
lexicon n dictionary
liable ❶ adj 1 answerable 2 exposed (to) 3 subject (to) 4 likely (to) **liability** n 1 state of being liable 2 debt 3 hindrance, disadvantage ▷ pl 4 debts
liar ❶ n see LIE²
lib n (Inf) short for LIBERATION
libel ❶ n 1 published statement falsely damaging person's reputation ▷ v 2 defame falsely **libellous** adj defamatory
liberal ❶ adj 1 (also with cap.) of political party favouring democratic reforms and individual freedom 2 generous 3 tolerant 4 abundant ▷ n 5 one who has liberal ideas or opinions **liberality** n generosity

——————— THESAURUS ———————

level n = **position**, standard, degree, grade, standing ▷ adj = **equal**, balanced, at the same height; = **horizontal**, even, flat, smooth, uniform ≠ slanted; = **even**, tied, equal, drawn, neck and neck ▷ v = **equalize**, balance, even up; = **destroy**, devastate, demolish, flatten, knock down ≠ build; = **direct**, point, turn, train, aim; = **flatten**, plane, smooth, even off or out
lever n = **handle**, bar ▷ v = **prise**, force
levy n = **tax**, fee, toll, tariff, duty

▷ v = **impose**, charge, collect, demand, exact
liable adj = **likely**, tending, inclined, disposed, prone; = **vulnerable**, subject, exposed, prone, susceptible
liar n = **falsifier**, perjurer, fibber, fabricator
libel n = **defamation**, misrepresentation, denigration, smear, calumny ▷ v = **defame**, smear, slur, blacken, malign
liberal adj = **tolerant**, open-minded, permissive, indulgent, easy-going

DICTIONARY

liberalize v make (laws etc.) less restrictive **liberally** adv

liberate ❶ v set free **liberation** n **liberator** n

libertine n 1 morally dissolute person ▷ adj 2 dissolute

liberty ❶ n, pl **-ties** freedom **libertarian** n/adj (person) believing in freedom of thought and action **at liberty** 1 free 2 having the right **take liberties** be presumptuous

libido n, pl **-dos** 1 psychic energy 2 sexual drive **libidinous** adj lustful

library n, pl **-braries** 1 room, building where books are kept 2 collection of books, records etc. **librarian** n keeper of library

libretto n, pl **-tos, -ti** words of opera **librettist** n

lice n pl of LOUSE

licence ❶ n 1 permit

2 permission 3 excessive liberty 4 dissoluteness **license** v grant licence to **licensee** n holder of licence

license plate n the US and Canadian term for NUMBERPLATE

licentious adj dissolute

lichen n small flowerless plants on rocks, trees etc.

licit adj lawful

lick ❶ v 1 pass tongue over 2 touch slightly 3 (SI) defeat ▷ n 4 act of licking 5 small amount (esp. of paint etc.) 6 (SI) speed **licking** n (SI) beating

licorice n see LIQUORICE

lid n 1 movable cover 2 eyelid

lido n, pl **-dos** pleasure centre with swimming and boating

lie¹ ❶ v **lying, lied, 1** make false statement ▷ n 2 deliberate falsehood **liar** n person who tells lies

THESAURUS

≠ **intolerant**; = **progressive**, radical, reformist, libertarian, forward-looking ≠ **conservative**; = **abundant**, generous, handsome, lavish, ample ≠ **limited**; = **generous**, kind, charitable, extravagant, open-hearted ≠ **stingy**

liberate v = **free**, release, rescue, save, deliver ≠ **imprison**

liberty n = **independence**, sovereignty, liberation, autonomy, immunity = **freedom**, liberation, emancipation, deliverance ≠ **restraint**

licence n = **certificate**, document, permit, charter, warrant;

= **permission**, the right, authority, leave, sanction ≠ **denial**; = **freedom**, creativity, latitude, independence, liberty ≠ **restraint**; = **laxity**, excess, indulgence, irresponsibility, licentiousness ≠ **moderation**

lick v = **taste**, lap, tongue; (Inf) = **beat**, defeat, overcome, rout, outstrip; (of flames) = **flicker**, touch, flick, dart, ripple ▷ n = **dab**, bit, touch, stroke; (Inf) = **pace**, rate, speed, clip (Inf)

lie¹ n = **falsehood**, deceit, fabrication, fib, fiction ▷ v = **fib**, fabricate, falsify, prevaricate, not tell the truth

lie² ❷ v lying, lay, lain 1 be
horizontal, at rest 2 be situated
3 be in certain state 4 exist ▷ n
5 state (of affairs etc.) **lie in**
remain in bed late **lie-in** n
remain in bed late **lie-in** n

lieu n in lieu of in place of

lieutenant n 1 deputy 2 junior
army or navy officer

life ❶ n, pl lives 1 active principle
of existence 2 time that it lasts
3 story of a person's life 4 way of
living 5 vigour, vivacity **lifeless**
adj 1 dead 2 insensible 3 dull
lifelike adj **lifelong** adj lasting a
lifetime **life belt, jacket** n
device to keep person afloat
lifeline n 1 means of help 2 rope
thrown to person in danger **life
preserver** n buoyant device to
keep afloat a person in danger of
drowning **lifestyle** n particular
habits, attitudes etc. of person or
group **lifetime** n time person,
animal or object lives or functions

lift ❷ v 1 move upwards in
position, status, mood, volume etc.

2 take up and remove 3 (Inf) steal
4 disappear ▷ n 5 cage in vertical
shaft for raising and lowering
people or goods 6 act of lifting
7 ride in car etc., as passenger
8 boost **liftoff** n moment rocket
leaves the ground

ligament n band of tissue joining
bones **ligature** n 1 anything
which binds 2 thread for tying up
artery

light¹ ❶ n 1 electromagnetic
radiation by which things are
visible 2 source of this, lamp
3 window 4 means or act of
setting fire to 5 understanding
▷ pl 6 traffic lights ▷ adj 7 bright
8 pale, not dark ▷ v 9 set on fire
10 give light to 11 brighten
lighten v give light to **lighting**
n apparatus for supplying artificial
light **lightning** n visible discharge
of electricity in atmosphere
lighthouse n tower with a light to
guide ships **light year** distance
light travels in one year

THESAURUS

lie² v = recline, rest, lounge, sprawl,
stretch out; = be placed, be, rest,
exist, be situated; = be situated,
sit, be located, be positioned, reside

life n = being, existence, vitality,
sentience; = existence, being,
lifetime, time, days; = way of life,
situation, conduct, behaviour, life
style; = liveliness, energy, spirit,
vitality, animation; = biography,
story, history, profile, confessions

lift v = raise, pick up, hoist, draw
up, elevate ≠ lower; = revoke, end,
remove, withdraw, stop ≠ impose;

= disappear, clear, vanish,
disperse, dissipate ▷ n = boost,
encouragement, stimulus,
pick-me-up, fillip ≠ blow;
= elevator (chiefly US), hoist,
paternoster; = ride, run, drive, hitch
(Inf)

light¹ n = brightness, illumination,
luminosity, brightness, glow ≠ dark;
= lamp, torch, candle, flare,
beacon; = match, spark, flame,
lighter; = aspect, context, angle,
point of view, interpretation ▷ adj
= bright, brilliant, shining,

light² ❶ *adj* of, or bearing, little weight **2** not severe **3** easy **4** trivial **5** not clumsy **6** not serious or profound **7** (industry) producing small, usu. consumer goods, using light machinery ▷ *adv* **8** in light manner ▷ *v* **9** come by chance (upon) **lighten** *v* reduce, remove (load etc.) **lightly** *adv* **lights** *pl n* lungs of animal **light-fingered** *adj* likely to steal **light-headed** *adj* dizzy, delirious **light-hearted** *adj* carefree **lightweight** *n/adj* (person) of little weight or importance

lighter *n* **1** device for lighting cigarettes etc. **2** flat-bottomed boat for unloading ships

like¹ ❶ *adj* **1** resembling **2** similar **3** characteristic of ▷ *adv* **4** in the manner of ▷ *pron* **5** similar thing **likelihood** *n* probability **likely** *adj* **1** probable **2** promising ▷ *adv* **3** probably **liken** *v* compare **likeness** *n* resemblance

2 portrait **likewise** *adv* in like manner

like² *v* find agreeable, enjoy, love **likeable** *adj* **liking** *n* **1** fondness **2** inclination, taste

lilac *n* shrub bearing pale mauve or white flowers

lilt *n* rhythmical swing **lilting** *adj*

lily *n, pl* **lilies** bulbous flowering plant **lily of the valley** small garden plant with fragrant white flowers

limb ❶ *n* **1** arm or leg **2** wing **3** branch of tree

limber *adj* pliant, lithe **limber up** loosen stiff muscles by exercise

limbo¹ *n* **1** region between Heaven and Hell for the unbaptized **2** indeterminate place or state

limbo² *n* West Indian dance in which dancers lean backwards to pass under a bar

lime¹ *n* **1** calcium compound used in fertilizer, cement ▷ *v* **2** treat (land) with lime **limelight** *n* glare of publicity **limestone** *n*

illuminated, luminous ≠ **dark**; = **pale**, fair, faded, blonde, blond ≠ **dark** ▷ *v* = **illuminate**, light up, brighten ≠ **darken**; = **ignite**, inflame, kindle, touch off, set alight ≠ **put out**

light² *adj* = **insubstantial**, thin, slight, portable, buoyant ≠ **heavy**; = **weak**, soft, gentle, moderate, slight ≠ **strong**; = **digestible**, modest, frugal ≠ **substantial**; = **insignificant**, small, slight, petty, trivial ≠ **serious**; = **light-hearted**, funny,

entertaining, amusing, witty ≠ **serious**; = **nimble**, graceful, deft, agile, sprightly ≠ **clumsy**

like¹ *adj* = **similar to**, same as, equivalent to, parallel to, identical to ≠ **different**

like² *v* = **enjoy**, love, delight in, go for, relish ≠ **dislike**; = **admire**, approve of, appreciate, prize, take to ≠ **dislike**; = **wish**, want, choose, prefer, desire

limb *n* = **part**, member, arm, leg, wing; = **branch**, spur, projection, offshoot, bough sedimentary rock used in building

lime² n small acid fruit like lemon
lime-green adj greenish-yellow

lime³ n tree

limerick n humorous verse of five lines

limit ❶ n 1 utmost extent or duration 2 boundary ▷ v 3 restrict, restrain, bound **limitation** n **limited company** one whose shareholders' liability is restricted

limousine n large, luxurious car

limp¹ ❶ v 1 walk lamely ▷ n 2 limping walk

limp² ❶ adj without firmness or stiffness

limpet n shellfish that sticks tightly to rocks

limpid adj 1 clear 2 translucent

linchpin, lynchpin n 1 pin to hold wheel on its axle 2 essential person or thing

linctus n, pl **-tuses** syrupy cough medicine

line ❶ n 1 long narrow mark 2 row 3 series, course 4 telephone

connection 5 progeny 6 province of activity 7 shipping company 8 railway track 9 any class of goods 10 cord 11 approach, policy ▷ v 12 cover inside 13 mark with lines 14 bring into line **lineage** n descent from, descendants of an ancestor **lineament** n feature **linear** adj of, in lines **liner** n large ship or aircraft of passenger line **linesman** n sporting official who helps referee **line-up** n people or things assembled for particular purpose

linen adj 1 made of flax ▷ n 2 linen cloth 3 linen articles collectively

linger ❶ v 1 delay, loiter 2 remain long

lingerie n women's underwear or nightwear

linguist n one skilled in languages or language study **linguistic** adj of languages or their study **linguistics** pl n study, science of language

liniment n embrocation

lining n covering for inside of garment etc.

———————————————— THESAURUS ————————————————

limit n = **end**, ultimate, deadline, breaking point, extremity; = **boundary**, edge, border, frontier, perimeter ▷ v = **restrict**, control, check, bound, confine

limp¹ v = **hobble**, stagger, stumble, shuffle, hop ▷ n = **lameness**, hobble

limp² adj = **floppy**, soft, slack, drooping, flabby ≠ **stiff**

line n = **stroke**, mark, score, band, scratch; = **wrinkle**, mark, crease,

furrow, crow's foot; = **row**, queue, rank, file, column; = **string**, cable, wire, rope, thread; = **trajectory**, way, course, track, channel; = **boundary**, limit, edge, border, frontier; = **occupation**, work, calling, business, job ▷ v = **border**, edge, bound, fringe; = **mark**, crease, furrow, rule, score; = **under control**, in order, in check

linger v = **stay**, remain, stop, wait, delay

link ❶ *n* **1** ring of chain
2 connection ▷ *v* **3** join with, as
with, link **4** intertwine **linkage** *n*
links *pl n* golf course
linnet *n* songbird of finch family
lino *n* short for LINOLEUM
linoleum *n* floor covering of
powdered cork, linseed oil etc.
backed with hessian
linseed *n* seed of flax plant
lint *n* soft material for dressing
wounds
lintel *n* top piece of door or window
lion *n* large animal of cat family
lip ❶ *n* **1** either edge of the mouth
2 edge or margin **3** (*Sl*) impudence
lip-reading *n* method of
understanding speech by
interpreting lip movements **lip
service** insincere tribute or respect
lipstick *n* cosmetic for colouring lips
liqueur *n* alcoholic liquor flavoured
and sweetened
liquid ❶ *adj* **1** fluid, not solid or
gaseous **2** flowing smoothly **3** (of
assets) easily converted into money
▷ *n* **4** substance in liquid form

liquefy *v* make or become liquid
liquidity *n* state of being able to
meet debts **liquidize** *v* **liquidizer**
n
liquidate *v* **1** pay (debt) **2** arrange
affairs of, and dissolve (company)
3 wipe out, kill **liquidation** *n*
1 clearing up of financial affairs
2 bankruptcy **liquidator** *n* official
appointed to liquidate business
liquor ❶ *n* alcoholic liquid
liquorice *n* black substance used
in medicine and as a sweet
lira *n*, *pl* **-re**, **-ras** monetary unit of
Italy (former) and Turkey
lisp *v/n* (speak with) faulty
pronunciation of *s* and *z*
lissom, lissome *adj* supple, agile
list¹ ❶ *n* **1** inventory, register
2 catalogue ▷ *v* **3** place on list
list² ❶ *v* **1** (of ship) lean to one side
▷ *n* **2** inclination of ship
listen ❶ *v* try to hear, attend to
listener *n*
listless *adj* indifferent, languid
litany *n*, *pl* **-nies** prayer with
responses

— THESAURUS —

link *n* = **connection**, relationship,
association, tie-up, affinity ▷ *v*
= **associate**, relate, identify,
connect, bracket; = **connect**, join,
unite, couple, tie ≠ **separate**
lip *n* = **edge**, rim, brim, margin,
brink; (*Sl*) = **impudence**, insolence,
impertinence, cheek (*Inf*),
effrontery
liquid *n* = **fluid**, solution, juice, sap
▷ *adj* = **fluid**, running, flowing,
melted, watery; (of assets)
= **convertible**, disposable,

negotiable, realizable
liquor *n* = **alcohol**, drink, spirits,
booze (*Inf*), hard stuff (*Inf*); = **juice**,
stock, liquid, extract, broth
list¹ *n* = **inventory**, record, series,
roll, index ▷ *v* = **itemize**, record,
enter, register, catalogue
list² *v* = **lean**, tip, incline, tilt, heel
over ▷ *n* = **tilt**, leaning, slant, cant
listen *n* = **hear**, attend, pay
attention, lend an ear, prick up your
ears; = **pay attention**, observe,
obey, mind, heed

literal ❶ adj 1 according to the strict meaning of the words, not figurative 2 actual, true **literally** adv

literate ❶ adj 1 able to read and write 2 educated **literacy** n

literature ❶ n books and writings of a country, period or subject **literary** adj

lithe adj supple, pliant

lithium n metallic chemical element

lithography n method of printing using the antipathy of grease and water **lithograph** n 1 print so produced ▷ v 2 print thus

litmus n blue dye turned red by acids and restored to blue by alkali

litre n measure of volume of fluid, one cubic decimetre, about 1.75 pints

litter ❶ n 1 untidy refuse 2 young of animal produced at one birth 3 kind of stretcher for wounded ▷ v 4 strew with litter 5 give birth to young

little ❶ adj 1 small, not much 2 young ▷ n 3 small quantity ▷ adv 4 slightly

liturgy n, pl -gies prescribed form of public worship **liturgical** adj

live¹ ❶ v 1 have life 2 pass one's life 3 continue in life 4 continue, last 5 dwell **living** n 1 action of being in life 2 people now alive 3 means of living 4 church benefice ▷ adj 5 alive **living room** room in house for relaxation and entertainment

live² ❷ adj 1 living, alive, active, vital 2 flaming 3 (of electrical conductor) carrying current 4 (of broadcast) transmitted during the actual performance **liveliness** n **lively** adj brisk, active, vivid **liven** v (esp. with up) make (more) lively

livelihood ❶ n means of living

— THESAURUS —

literal adj = **exact**, close, strict, accurate, faithful; = **actual**, real, true, simple, plain

literate adj = **educated**, informed, knowledgeable

literature n = **writings**, letters, compositions, lore, creative writing

litter n = **rubbish**, refuse, waste, junk, debris; = **brood**, young, offspring, progeny ▷ v = **clutter**, mess up, clutter up, be scattered about, disorder; = **scatter**, spread, shower, strew

little adj = **small**, minute, short, tiny, wee ≠ **big**; = **young**, small, junior, infant, immature ▷ adv

= **hardly**, barely, scarcely ≠ **much**; = **rarely**, seldom, scarcely, not often, infrequently ≠ **always** ▷ n = **bit**, touch, spot, trace, hint ≠ **lot**

live¹ v = **dwell**, board, settle, lodge, occupy; = **exist**, last, prevail, be, have being; = **survive**, get along, make a living, make ends meet, subsist; = **thrive**, flourish, prosper, have fun, enjoy yourself

live² adj = **living**, alive, breathing, animate; = **active**, unexploded; = **topical**, important, pressing, current, hot

livelihood n = **occupation**, work, employment, living, job

liver n **1** organ secreting bile
2 animal liver as food **liverish** adj
1 unwell, as from liver upset
2 touchy, irritable

livery n, pl **-eries** distinctive dress,
esp. servant's

livestock n farm animals

livid adj (Inf) **1** angry, furious
2 discoloured, as by bruising

lizard n four-footed reptile

llama n woolly animal of S America

load ❶ n **1** something carried
2 quantity carried **3** burden
4 amount of power used ▷ v **5** put
load on or into **6** charge (gun)
7 weigh down **loaded** adj
1 carrying a load **2** (of dice)
dishonestly weighted **3** (of
question) containing hidden trap or
implication **4** (of weapon) charged
with ammunition **5** (Sl) wealthy
6 (Sl) drunk

loaf¹ ❶ n, pl **loaves 1** mass of
baked bread **2** shaped mass of food

loaf² ❶ v idle, loiter **loafer** n idler

loam n fertile soil

loan ❶ n **1** act of lending **2** thing
lent **3** money borrowed at interest
▷ v **4** lend

loath, loth adj unwilling **loathe**
v feel strong disgust for **loathing**
n disgust **loathsome** adj

lob n **1** in tennis etc., shot pitched
high in air ▷ v **2** throw, pitch shots
thus

lobby ❶ n, pl **-bies 1** corridor into
which rooms open **2** group which
tries to influence legislature ▷ v
3 try to enlist support (of)

lobe n **1** soft, hanging part of ear
2 rounded segment **lobotomy** n
surgical incision into lobe of brain

lobelia n garden plant with lobed
flowers

lobster n shellfish with long tail
and claws, turning red when boiled

local ❶ adj **1** of, existing in
particular place **2** confined to
particular place ▷ n **3** person from
district **4** (Inf) (nearby) pub **locale**
n scene of event **locality** n
neighbourhood **localize** v assign,
restrict to definite place **locally**
adv

locate ❶ v **1** find **2** situate
location n **1** placing **2** situation
3 site of film production away from
studio

--- THESAURUS ---

load v = **fill**, stuff, pack, pile, stack;
= **make ready**, charge, prime ▷ n
= **cargo**, delivery, haul, shipment,
batch

loaf¹ n = **lump**, block, cake, cube,
slab; (Sl) = **head**, mind, sense,
common sense, nous (Brit Sl)

loaf² v = **idle**, hang around, take it
easy, lie around, loiter

loan n = **advance**, credit, overdraft
▷ v = **lend**, advance, let out

lobby v = **campaign**, press,
pressure, push, influence ▷ n
= **pressure group**, group, camp,
faction, lobbyists; = **corridor**,
passage, entrance, porch, hallway

local adj = **community**, regional;
= **confined**, limited, restricted ▷ n
= **resident**, native, inhabitant

locate v = **find**, discover, detect,
come across, track down; = **place**,
put, set, position, seat

loch n Scottish lake or long narrow bay

lock¹ ❶ n 1 appliance for fastening door, lid etc. 2 arrangement for moving boats from one level of canal to another 3 extent to which vehicle's front wheels will turn 4 block, jam ▷ v 5 fasten, make secure with lock 6 place in locked container 7 join firmly 8 jam 9 embrace closely **locker** n small cupboard with lock **lockjaw** n tetanus **lockout** n exclusion of workers by employers as means of coercion **locksmith** n one who makes and mends locks **lockup** n garage, storage area away from main premises

lock² n tress of hair

locket n small hinged pendant for portrait etc.

locomotive n engine for pulling carriages on railway tracks **locomotion** n action, power of moving

locum (Lat) substitute, esp. for doctor or clergyman

locus n, pl **loci** curve traced by all points satisfying specified mathematical condition

locust n destructive winged insect

lodge ❶ n 1 house, cabin used seasonally or occasionally, e.g. for hunting, skiing 2 gatekeeper's house 3 branch of Freemasons etc. ▷ v 4 house 5 deposit 6 bring (a charge etc.) 7 live in another's house at fixed charge 8 come to rest (in, on) **lodger** n **lodgings** pl n rented accommodation in another person's house

loft n space under roof **loftily** adv haughtily **lofty** adj 1 of great height 2 elevated 3 haughty

log¹ ❶ n 1 trimmed portion of felled tree 2 record of voyages of ship, aircraft etc. ▷ v 3 enter in a log 4 record 5 cut logs **logbook** n

log² n logarithm

loganberry n purplish-red fruit

logarithm n one of series of arithmetical functions tabulated for use in calculation

loggerheads pl n **at loggerheads** quarrelling, disputing

logic ❶ n 1 science of reasoning 2 reasoned thought or argument 3 coherence of various facts, events etc. **logical** adj 1 of logic 2 according to reason 3 reasonable 4 apt to reason correctly

lock¹ v = **fasten**, close, secure, shut, bar; = **unite**, join, link, engage, clench; = **embrace**, press, grasp, clutch, hug ▷ n = **fastening**, catch, bolt, clasp, padlock

lodge n = **cabin**, shelter, cottage, hut, chalet; = **society**, group, club, section, wing ▷ v = **register**, enter, file, submit, put on record; = **stay**,

room, board, reside, house; = **stick**, remain, implant, come to rest, imbed

log¹ n = **stump**, block, branch, chunk, trunk; = **record**, account, register, journal, diary ▷ v = **record**, enter, note, register, chart

logic n = **reason**, reasoning, sense, good sense

logistics pl n (with sing or pl v) the handling of supplies and personnel **logistical** adj

logo n, pl **-os** company emblem or similar device

loin n **1** part of body between ribs and hip **2** cut of meat from this ▷ pl **3** hips and lower abdomen **loincloth** n garment covering loins only

loiter v **1** dawdle, hang about **2** idle **loiterer** n

loll v **1** sit, lie lazily **2** (esp. of the tongue) hang out

lollipop n sweet on small wooden stick

lolly n, pl **-ies** (Inf) **1** lollipop or ice lolly **2** (Sl) money

lone ❶ adj solitary **loneliness** n **lonely** adj **1** sad because alone **2** unfrequented **3** solitary **loner** n one who prefers to be alone

lonesome adj (chiefly US and Canad) another word for LONELY

long¹ ❶ adj **1** having length, esp. great length, in space or time **2** extensive **3** protracted ▷ adv **4** for a long time **long-distance** adj going between places far apart **longhand** n words written in full **long-range** adj **1** into the

future **2** able to travel long distances without refuelling **3** (of weapons) designed to hit distant target **long shot** competitor, undertaking, bet etc. with small chance of success **long-sighted** adj able to see distant objects in focus but not nearby ones **long-standing** adj existing for a long time **long-suffering** adj enduring trouble or unhappiness without complaint **long-winded** adj tediously loquacious

long² ❷ v have keen desire, yearn (for) **longing** n yearning

longevity n long life

longitude n distance east or west from standard meridian

longshoreman n a man employed in the loading or unloading of ships

loo n (Inf) lavatory

look ❶ v **1** direct eyes (at) **2** face **3** seem **4** search (for) **5** hope (for) **6** (with after) take care of ▷ n **7** looking **8** view **9** search **10** (oft. pl) appearance **lookalike** n person who is double of another **lookout** n **1** watchman **2** place for watching **3** prospect

— THESAURUS —

lone adj = **solitary**, single, one, only, sole

long¹ adj = **elongated**, extended, stretched, expanded, extensive ≠ **short**; = **prolonged**, sustained, lengthy, lingering, protracted ≠ **brief**

long² v = **desire**, want, wish, burn, pine

look v = **see**, view, consider, watch, eye; = **search**, seek, hunt, forage; = **consider**, contemplate; = **face**, overlook; = **hope**, expect, await, anticipate, reckon on ▷ n = **glimpse**, view, glance, observation, sight; = **appearance**, bearing, air, style, aspect

loom ❶ v 1 appear dimly 2 seem ominously close

loonie n (Canad, Sl) 1 a Canadian dollar coin with a loon bird on one of its faces 2 the Canadian currency

loony n/adj (Sl) foolish or insane (person)

loop n 1 figure made by curved line crossing itself ▷ v 2 form loop **loophole** n means of evading rule without infringing it

loose ❶ adj 1 slack 2 not fixed or restrained 3 vague 4 dissolute ▷ v 5 free 6 unfasten 7 slacken 8 shoot, let fly **loosen** v make loose **loose-leaf** adj allowing addition or removal of pages

loot ❶ n/v plunder

lop v lopping, lopped 1 cut away twigs and branches 2 chop off

lope v run with long, easy strides

lopsided adj with one side lower

than the other

loquacious adj talkative

lord ❶ n 1 British nobleman 2 ruler 3 (with cap.) God ▷ v 4 domineer **lordly** adj 5 imperious 6 fit for a lord **lordship** n

lore n 1 learning 2 body of facts and traditions

lorry n, pl **-ries** motor vehicle for heavy loads, truck

lose ❶ v losing, lost 1 be deprived of, fail to retain or use 2 fail to get 3 (of clock etc.) run slow 4 be defeated in **loser** n **loss** n 1 act of losing 2 what is lost **lost** adj 1 unable to be found 2 unable to find one's way 3 bewildered 4 not won 5 not utilized

lot ❶ pron 1 great number ▷ n 2 collection 3 large quantity 4 share 5 fate 6 item at auction 7 object used to make decision by chance 8 area of land ▷ pl 9 (Inf)

— THESAURUS —

loom v = **appear**, emerge, hover, take shape, threaten

loop n = **curve**, ring, circle, twist, curl ▷ v = **twist**, turn, roll, knot, curl

loose adj = **free**, detached, insecure, unfettered, unrestricted; = **slack**, easy, relaxed, sloppy, loose-fitting ≠ **tight**; (Old-fashioned) = **promiscuous**, fast, abandoned, immoral, dissipated ≠ **chaste**; = **vague**, random, inaccurate, rambling, imprecise ≠ **precise** ▷ v = **free**, release, liberate, detach, unleash ≠ **fasten**

loot v = **plunder**, rob, raid, sack, rifle ▷ n = **plunder**, goods, prize, haul, spoils

lord n = **peer**, nobleman, count, duke, gentleman; = **ruler**, leader, chief, master, governor

lose v = **be defeated**, be beaten, lose out, come to grief; = **mislay**, drop, forget, be deprived of, lose track of; = **forfeit**, miss, yield, be deprived of, pass up (Inf)

lot n = **bunch** (Inf), group, crowd, crew, set; = **destiny**, situation, circumstances, fortune, chance

great numbers or quantity **a lot**
(Inf) a great deal

lotion ❶ n liquid for washing
wounds, improving skin etc.

lottery ❶ n, pl **-teries 1** method
of raising funds by selling tickets
that win prizes by chance
2 gamble

lotus n legendary plant whose
fruits induce forgetfulness

loud ❶ adj **1** strongly audible
2 noisy **3** (Fig) garish **loudly** adv
loudspeaker n instrument for
converting electrical signals into
sound audible at a distance

lounge ❶ v **1** recline, move at ease
▷ n **2** living room of house **3** public
room, area for sitting **lounge suit**
man's suit for daytime wear

lour see LOWER

louse n parasitic insect **lousy** adj
(Sl) **1** bad **2** (Sl) nasty **3** having lice

lout n crude, oafish person

louvre n one of set of slats slanted

to admit air but not rain

love ❶ n **1** warm affection
2 benevolence **3** sexual passion
4 sweetheart. **5** (Tennis) score of
nothing ▷ v **6** admire passionately
7 delight in **lovable** adj **lovelorn**
adj pining for a lover **lovely** adj
beautiful, delightful **lover** n
loving adj **1** affectionate **2** tender
make love (to) have sexual
intercourse (with)

low ❶ adj **1** not tall, high or
elevated **2** humble **3** vulgar
4 unwell **5** below what is usual
6 not loud **lower** v **1** cause, allow
to move down **2** diminish, degrade
▷ adj **3** below **4** at an early stage,
period **lowly** adj modest, humble
lowbrow n/adj nonintellectual
(person) **lowdown** n (Inf) inside
information **low-down** adj (Inf)
mean, shabby **lower case** (Inf)
letters **low-key** adj not intense
lowland n low-lying country

lotion n = **cream**, solution, balm,
salve, liniment

lottery n = **raffle**, draw, lotto
(Brit, NZ, & S Afr), sweepstake;
= **gamble**, chance, risk, hazard,
toss-up (Inf)

loud adj = **noisy**, booming, roaring,
thundering, forte (Mus) ≠ **quiet**;
= **garish**, bold, glaring, flamboyant,
brash ≠ **sombre**

lounge v = **relax**, loaf, sprawl, lie
about, take it easy

love v = **adore**, care for, treasure,
cherish, prize ≠ **hate**; = **enjoy**, like,
appreciate, relish, delight in
≠ **dislike** ▷ n = **passion**, affection,

warmth, attachment, intimacy
≠ **hatred**; = **liking**, taste, bent for,
weakness for, relish for; = **beloved**,
dear, dearest, lover, darling
≠ **enemy**; = **sympathy**,
understanding, pity, humanity,
warmth

low adj = **small**, little, short, stunted,
squat ≠ **tall**; = **inferior**, bad, poor,
inadequate, unsatisfactory; = **quiet**,
soft, gentle, whispered, muted
≠ **loud**; = **dejected**, depressed,
miserable, fed up, moody ≠ **happy**;
= **coarse**, common, rough, crude,
rude; = **ill**, weak, frail, stricken,
debilitated ≠ **strong**

lower, lour *v* **1** (of sky) look threatening **2** scowl

loyal ❶ *adj* faithful, true to allegiance **loyalist** *n* **loyalty** *n*

lozenge *n* **1** small sweet or tablet of medicine **2** diamond shape

LP long-playing record

L-plate *n* sign on car driven by learner driver

LSD **1** lysergic acid diethylamide (hallucinogenic drug) **2** pounds, shillings, and pence

lubricate *v* oil, grease **2** make slippery **lubricant** *n* substance used for this **lubrication** *n*

lucerne *n* fodder plant

lucid *adj* **1** clear **2** easily understood **3** sane **lucidity** *n*

luck ❶ *n* **1** chance, whether good or bad **2** good fortune **luckily** *adv* fortunately **luckless** *adj* having bad luck **lucky** *adj* having good luck

lucrative ❶ *adj* very profitable

ludicrous ❶ *adj* ridiculous

lug¹ *v* drag with effort

lug² *n* **1** projection, serving as handle or support **2** (*Inf*) ear

luggage ❶ *n* traveller's baggage

lugubrious *adj* doleful

lukewarm *adj* **1** tepid **2** indifferent

lull ❶ *v* **1** soothe, sing to sleep **2** calm **3** subside ▷ *n* **4** quiet spell **lullaby** *n* lulling song, esp. for children

lumbago *n* rheumatism of the lower part of the back

lumber¹ ❶ *n* **1** disused articles, useless rubbish **2** sawn timber ▷ *v* **3** (*Inf*) burden with something unpleasant **lumberjack** *n* (*US & Canad*) man who fells trees and prepares logs

lumber² ❶ *v* move heavily

luminous *adj* **1** shedding light **2** glowing **luminary** *n* famous person **luminescence** *n* emission of light without heat

lump¹ ❶ *n* **1** shapeless piece or mass **2** swelling **3** large sum ▷ *v* **4** throw together **lumpy** *adj* **1** full

— THESAURUS —

loyal *adj* = **faithful**, true, devoted, dependable, constant ≠ **disloyal**

luck *n* **1** = **good fortune**, success, advantage, prosperity, blessing; = **fortune**, lot, stars, chance, accident

lucrative *adj* = **profitable**, rewarding, productive, fruitful, well-paid

ludicrous *adj* = **ridiculous**, crazy, absurd, preposterous, silly ≠ **sensible**

luggage *n* = **baggage**, things,

cases, bags, gear

lull *n* = **respite**, pause, quiet, silence, calm ▷ *v* = **calm**, soothe, subdue, quell, allay

lumber¹ *v* (*Brit Inf*) = **burden**, land, load, saddle, encumber ▷ *n* (*Brit*) = **junk**, refuse, rubbish, trash, clutter

lumber² *v* = **plod**, shuffle, shamble trudge, stump

lump¹ *n* = **piece**, ball, block, mass, chunk; = **swelling**, growth, bump, tumour, bulge ▷ *v* = **group**, throw, mass, combine, collect of lumps **2** uneven

lump² v (Inf) tolerate

lunar adj relating to the moon

lunatic ❶ adj/n **1** foolish or irresponsible (person) **2** insane (person) **lunacy** n

lunch n **1** meal taken in middle of day ▷ v **2** eat, entertain to lunch **luncheon** n lunch **luncheon meat** tinned ground mixture of meat and cereal

lung n one of the two organs of respiration in vertebrates

lunge ❶ v **1** thrust with sword etc. ▷ n **2** thrust **3** sudden movement of body, plunge

lupin n leguminous plant with spikes of flowers

lurch ❶ n **1** sudden roll to one side ▷ v **2** stagger **leave in the lurch** leave in difficulties

lure ❶ n **1** bait **2** power to attract ▷ v **3** entice **4** attract

lurid adj **1** sensational **2** garish

lurk ❶ v lie hidden **lurking** adj (of suspicion) not definite

luscious adj **1** sweet, juicy **2** extremely attractive

lush ❶ adj **1** (of plant growth) luxuriant **2** luxurious

lust ❶ n **1** strong desire for sexual gratification **2** any strong desire ▷ v **3** have passionate desire **lustful** adj **lusty** adj vigorous, healthy

lustre n **1** gloss, sheen **2** renown **3** metallic pottery glaze **lustrous** adj shining

lute n old stringed musical instrument played like a guitar

luxury ❶ n, pl **-ries 1** possession and use of costly, choice things for enjoyment **2** enjoyable, comfortable surroundings **3** enjoyable but not essential thing **luxuriance** n abundance **luxuriant** adj **1** growing thickly **2** abundant **luxuriate** v **1** indulge in luxury **2** flourish profusely **3** take delight (in) **luxurious** adj **1** fond of luxury **2** self-indulgent **3** sumptuous

lunatic n = **madman**, maniac, psychopath, nutcase (Sl) ▷ adj = **mad**, crazy, insane, irrational, daft

lunge v = **pounce**, charge, dive, leap, plunge ▷ n = **thrust**, charge, pounce, spring, swing

lurch v = **tilt**, roll, pitch, list, rock; = **stagger**, reel, stumble, weave, sway

lure v = **tempt**, draw, attract, invite, trick ▷ n = **temptation**, attraction, incentive, bait, carrot (Inf)

lurk v = **hide**, sneak, prowl, lie in wait, slink

lush adj = **abundant**, green, flourishing, dense, rank; = **luxurious**, grand, elaborate, lavish, extravagant

lust n = **lechery**, sensuality, lewdness, lasciviousness; = **desire**, longing, passion, appetite, craving

luxury n = **opulence**, splendour, richness, extravagance, affluence ≠ **poverty**; = **extravagance**, treat, extra, indulgence, frill ≠ **necessity**

lychee *n* Chinese fruit

Lycra® *n* fabric used for tight-fitting garments

lymph *n* colourless body fluid, mainly white blood cells **lymphatic** *adj*

lynch *v* put to death without trial

lynx *n* animal of cat family

lyre *n* instrument like harp

lyric *n* **1** songlike poem expressing personal feelings ▷ *pl* **2** words of popular song **lyrical** *adj* **1** expressed in this style **2** enthusiastic **lyricist** *n*

Supplement:
Punctuation
and Spelling

The apostrophe (')

Misusing or omitting the apostrophe is one of the commonest punctuation errors.

Showing possession

The apostrophe (') is used to show that something belongs to someone. It is usually added to the end of a word and followed by an -s.

- -'s is added to the end of singular words.

    a baby's pushchair
    Hannah's book

- -'s is added to the end of plural words not ending in -s.

    children's games
    women's clothes

- An apostrophe alone (') is added to plural words ending in -s.

    Your grandparents are your parents' parents.
    We're campaigning for workers' rights.

- **-'s** is added to the end of names and singular words ending in -s.

  > James**'s** car
  > the octopus**'s** tentacles

- **-'s** is added to the end of certain professions or occupations to indicate workplaces.

  > She's on her way to the doctor**'s**.
  > James is at the hairdresser**'s**.

- **-'s** is added to the end of people or their names to indicate that you are talking about their home.

  > I'm going over to Harry**'s** for tea tonight.
  > I popped round to Mum**'s** this afternoon,
  >   but she wasn't in.

* Note that if the word is a classical Greek name, or a historical building, an apostrophe only is sometimes preferred.

  > Dickens**'** novels
  > St Giles**'** Cathedral

-'s can also be added to:

- whole phrases

  > My next-door neighbour**'s** dog was barking away
  >   like mad.
  > John and Cath**'s** house was on TV last night.

- indefinite pronouns such as somebody or anywhere

  > Is this anybody**'s** pencil case?
  > It's nobody**'s** fault but mine.

- each other

  > We're getting used to each other**'s** habits.
  > We kept forgetting each other**'s** names

When the possessor is an inanimate object (rather than a living thing), the apostrophe is not used and the word order is changed.

> the middle of the street (not the street's middle)
> the front of the house (not the house's front)

To test whether an apostrophe is in the right place, think about who the owner is.

> the boy**'s** books [= the books belonging to the boy]
> the boys**'** books [= the books belonging to the boys]

Note that:

- An apostrophe is not used to form possessive pronouns such as its, yours, or theirs.

- An apostrophe is not used to form the plurals of words such as potatoes or tomatoes.

With letters and numbers

An apostrophe is used in front of two figures referring to a year or decade.

> French students rioted in **'68** [short for '1968'].

> He worked as a schoolteacher during the **'60s** and early **'90s**.

An apostrophe can be used in plurals of letters and numbers to make them more readable.

> Mind your p**'s** and q**'s**.
> His 2**'s** look a bit like 7**'s**.
> She got straight A**'s** in her exams.

Contracted forms

An apostrophe is used in shortened forms of words to show that one or more letters have been missed out. Contractions are usually shortened forms of auxiliary verbs

be	**have**
I'**m**	I/we/they'**ve** (have)
We/you/they'**re** (are)	He/she/it/one'**s** (has)
He/she/it/one'**s** (is)	I/we/you/he/she/it/one/they'**d** (had)

would
I/we/you/he/she/it/one/they'**d** (would)

or the negative *not*.

not
We/you/they aren'**t**
He/she/it/one isn'**t**
I/we/they haven'**t**
He/she/it/one hasn'**t**

7

In order to work out what the contracted forms **'s** and **'d** represent, you need to look at what follows it:

- If **'s** is followed by an *-ing* form, it represents the auxiliary *is*.

    > She**'s reading** a book about the ancient Egyptians.
    > He**'s going** to Ibiza for his holidays.

- If 's is followed by an adjective or a noun phrase, it represents the main verb is.

    > She**'s nervous** about meeting my parents.
    > That**'s brilliant** news!

- If **'s** is followed by a past participle, it can represent *is* as it is used in the passive,

    > He**'s portrayed** by the media as a kindly old
    >   grandfather.
    > It**'s** often **said** that rock stars are frustrated actors.

- or *has* as it is used in the present perfect.

    > She**'s broken** her wrist.
    > It**'s been** ages since we last saw you.

- If **'s** is followed by *got*, it represents the auxiliary *has*.

  > She**'s got** two brothers and one sister.
  > It**'s got** everything you could want.

- If **'d** is followed by a past participle, it represents the auxiliary *had*.

  > I**'d raced** against him before, but never in a marathon.
  > She couldn't believe what she**'d done**.

- If **'d** is followed by a base form, it represents the modal auxiliary *would*.

  > I**'d give up** now, if I were you.
  > When we were kids we**'d spend** hours out on our bikes.

- If **'d** is followed by *rather* or *better*, it represents the modal auxiliary *would*.

  > We**'d better** go home soon.
  > I**'d rather** not talk about that.

The comma (,)

The comma marks a short pause between elements in a sentence.

Separating main clauses

Main clauses that are joined together with *and* or *but* do not normally have a comma before the conjunction unless the two clauses have different subjects.

> *You go out of the door and turn immediately left.*
> *It was cold outside, but we decided to go out for a walk anyway.*

Separating subordinate clauses from main clauses

Commas are normally used if the subordinate clause comes before the main clause.

> *If you have any problems, just call me.*
> *Just call me if you have any problems.*

Sometimes a comma is used even when the main clause comes first, if the clauses are particularly long.

> *We should be able to finish the work by the end*
> *of the week, if nothing unexpected turns up*
> *between now and then.*

Separating relative clauses from main clauses

Commas are used to mark off non-defining relative clauses. This is the type of clause that adds to information about a noun or noun phrase.

> *My next-door neighbour, who works from home,*
> *is keeping an eye on the house while we're away.*
> *She moved to Los Angeles, where she was*
> *immediately signed as a singer songwriter.*

Commas are not required in defining relative clauses, since these simply postmodify the noun.

> *Let's make sure the money goes to the people*
> *who need it most.*
> *The computer **(that) I borrowed** kept on crashing.*

Separating items in a list

Commas are used to separate three or more items in a list or series.

> *She got out bread, butter, and jam (but bread and butter).*

Note that the comma is often not given before the final *and* or *or*.

> *They breed dogs, cats, rabbits and hamsters.*
> *We did canoeing, climbing and archery.*

Separating adjectives

Commas are used between adjectives, whether they come before the noun (i.e. used attributively) or after a linking verb (i.e. used predicatively).

> *It was a hot, dry and dusty road.*
> *It's wet, cold and windy outside.*

A comma is not usually used before an adjective that is followed by *and*.

With adverbials

When an adverbial such as *however, therefore* or *unfortunately* modifies a whole sentence, it is separated from the rest of the sentence by a comma.

> *However, police would not confirm this rumour.*
> *Therefore, I try to avoid using the car as much as possible.*

With question tags and short responses

Commas are used before question tags and after *yes* or *no* in short responses.

> *It's quite cold today, isn't it?*
> *He's up to date with all his injections, isn't he?*
> *Are you the mother of these children? – Yes, I am.*
> *You're Amy Osborne, aren't you? – No, I'm not.*

With vocatives

Commas are used to separate the name of a person or group being addressed from the rest of the sentence.

> *And now, ladies and gentlemen, please raise your glasses in a toast to the happy couple.*
> *Dad, can you come and help me, please?*

With discourse markers

Commas are used to separate discourse markers like *Well* and *Now then* from the rest of the sentence.

13

Well, believe it or not, I actually passed!
Now then, let's see what's on TV tonight.

In reported speech

Commas are used to follow direct speech
(if there is no question or exclamation mark after
the quotation), or to show that it comes next.

'I don't understand this question,' said Peter.
Peter said, 'I don't understand this question.'

It is also possible to punctuate reported speech of
the type *Peter said, '...'* using a colon instead of a comma.
This is a particularly common practice in American
English.

Peter said: 'Dream on.'

In dates

A comma must be used between the day of the
month and the year, when the two numbers are next
to each other.

March 31, 2011

Quotation marks (' ') or (" ")

Direct speech

Direct speech gives the actual words that a speaker used. It is common in novels and other writing where the actual words of a speaker are quoted.

The words spoken are enclosed in single or double quotation marks.

> *'Have you been to the new shopping precinct yet?' enquired Shona.*
> *"I've already seen it," John replied.*

* The comma comes inside the quotation marks, unless the reporting verb is positioned inside a reported sentence that itself does not require a comma.

> *'There is', Monica said, 'nothing we can do about it.'*

Other uses

Single quotation marks are sometimes used:

- to draw attention to a word

    *The word **'book'** can be used as a noun or a verb.*

- to indicate an unusual use of a word

    *She pointed out that websites used for internet voting could be **'spoofed'**.*

- to suggest that the writer wants to be distanced from a word.

    *I don't agree with this **'mercy killing'** business.*

* Note that the full stop comes after the quotation marks in such cases.

Capital letters

A capital (or 'upper case') letter is used to mark the beginning of a sentence.

When I was 20, I dropped out of university and became a model.

Capital letters are also used for the first letter in proper nouns. These include:

- people's names

    Jenny Forbes   *William Davidson*

- days of the week

    Wednesday   *Saturday*

- months of the year

    August   *January*

- public holidays

    Christmas   *Yom Kippur*

- nationalities

    Spanish   *Iraqi*

- languages

    Swahili   *Flemish*

- geographical locations

    Australia   *Loch Ness*

    Mount Everest   *The Mediterranean Sea*

- company names

    Dyson   *Harper Collins*

- religions

    Islam   *Buddhism*

Capital letters are also used for the first letter in titles of books, magazines, newspapers, TV shows, films, etc. Where there are several words, a capital letter is usually used for all the main content words in the title (i.e. not the prepositions or the determiners – unless they are the first word in the title).

> *The Times*   *Hello!*
> *Twelfth Night*   *The Secret Garden*
> *Newsnight*   *Mamma Mia!*

The full stop (.)

Full stops are used:

- to mark the end of a sentence

    Let's have some lunch.
    I have to catch a bus in ten minutes.

- to mark the end of a sentence fragment

    Are you cold? – Yes, a bit.
    Do you like this sort of music? Not really.

- in initials for people's names, although this practice is becoming less frequent

    J.K. Rowling   *Iain M. Banks*
    M.C. Hammer   *Ronald G. Hardie*

- after abbreviations, although this practice is becoming less frequent.

    P.S. Do pop in next time you're passing.
    She's moved to the I.T. department
    R.S.V.P. to Helen Douglas on 01234 676240.
    The U.S. government reacted strongly to the accusation.

19

When an abbreviation consists of a shortened word such as *Re.* or *Prof.*, a full stop is needed.

> *Re. your suggestion that we shorten the lunch hour, could we arrange a quick meeting to discuss the various options?*
> *Prof. John Johansson will be speaking on the subject of 'Discourse in the Electronic Age'.*
> *Flight BA 345: dep. 09.44 arr. 11.10.*

When an abbreviation contains the last letter of the shortened word, a full stop is not needed.

> **Dr** *McDonald*
> **St** *Mary's School*
> *41, Douglas* **Rd**
> *Universal Pictures (UK)* **Ltd**

* Note that full stops are not used in many common sets of initials,

> *Did you see that programme on* **BBC** *4 last night?*
> *Millions of people now call the* **NHS** *Direct helpline each year.*

or at the end of headlines, headings and titles.

Fear grips global stock markets
Teaching grammar as a liberating force
Wuthering Heights

Remember that a full stop, and not a question mark, is used after an indirect question or a polite request.

He asked if the bus had left.
Will you open your books on page 14.
I wonder what's happened.
She asked him where he was going.

In American English, the full stop is called a period.

The question mark (?)

The question mark marks the end of a question.

> *When will we be arriving?*
> *Why did you do that?*
> *Does any of this matter?*
> *He's certain to be elected, isn't he?*

Question marks are used in direct questions, i.e. when the actual words of a speaker are used. A reported question should end with a full stop.

> *The lady said, 'Where are you going?'*
> *The lady asked where she was going.*

Note that you put a question mark at the end of a question, even if the words in the sentence are not in the normal question order, or some words are omitted. Care is needed here as such a sentence can look, at first sight, like a statement rather than a question.

> *You know he doesn't live here any longer?*

A full stop, rather than a question mark, is used after an indirect question.

> *I'd like to know what you've been doing all this time.*
> *I wonder what's happened.*

A full stop also replaces a question mark at the end of a sentence which looks like a question if, in fact, it is really a polite request.

> *Will you please return the completed forms to me.*
> *Would you please call my brother and ask him to collect my car.*

The exclamation mark (!)

The exclamation mark is used after exclamations and emphatic expressions.

> *I can't believe it!*
> *Oh, no! Look at this mess!*

The exclamation mark loses its effect if it is overused. It is better to use a full stop after a sentence expressing mild excitement or humour.

> *It was such a beautiful day.*
> *I felt like a perfect banana.*

The colon (:)

The colon indicates a break between two main clauses which is stronger than a comma but weaker than a full stop. A colon is used:

- in front of a list

    I used three colours: green, blue and pink.
    Make sure you wear clothes made from natural fibres: cotton, silk and wool.

- in front of an explanation or a reason

    Nevertheless, the main problem remained:
        what should be done with the two men?
    I decided against going away this weekend:
        the weather forecast was dreadful.

- after introductory headings

    Cooking time: about five minutes.
    Start time: 10 o'clock.

- in more formal writing, between two main clauses that are connected

> It made me feel claustrophobic: what, I wonder,
> would happen to someone who was really
> unable to tolerate being locked into such
> a tiny space?
>
> Be patient: the next book in the series has not yet
> been published.

- in front of the second part of a book title

  > Farming and wildlife: a study in compromise
  > Beyond single words: the most frequent
  > collocations in spoken English.

- to introduce direct speech, especially in
  American English, or when the quotation is
  particularly long.

  > He said: 'You owe me three dollars'
  > The Health Minister said: 'The NHS I.T.
  > programme will mean that patients will get
  > access to more comprehensive information to
  > help them make choices.'

The semicolon (;)

The semicolon is used to mark a break between two main clauses when there is a balance or a contrast between the clauses.

> Compare:
>
> *The engine roared into life. The propellers began to turn. The plane taxied down the runway ready for takeoff.*
>
> with:
>
> *The engine roared into life; the propellers began to turn; the plane taxied down the runway ready for takeoff.*

A useful test to work out when to use a semicolon is to ask yourself whether the two clauses could be written instead as separate sentences. If the answer is 'yes', then you can use a semicolon.

Note that it is quite acceptable to use a full stop in these cases, but a semicolon is preferable if you wish to convey the sense of a link or continuity between the clauses in your narrative.

> I'm not that interested in jazz; I prefer classical
> music.
> He knew everything about me; I had never even
> heard of him.

A semicolon is also used to separate items in a list, especially if the listed items are phrases or clauses, which may already contain commas.

> The holiday was a disaster: the flight was four
> hours late; the hotel, which was described as
> 'luxury', was dirty; and it rained for the whole
> fortnight.

Brackets ( )

Brackets (also called **parentheses**) are used to enclose a word or words which can be left out and still leave a meaningful sentence.

> *The wooded area (see map below) is approximately 4,000 hectares.*
> *This is a process which Hayek (a writer who came to rather different conclusions) also observed.*

Brackets are also used to show alternatives or options.

> *Any student(s) interested in taking part should e-mail me.*
> *A goat should give from three to six pints (1.7 to 3.4 litres) of milk a day.*

Note that when the structure of the sentence as a whole demands punctuation after a bracketed section, the punctuation is given *outside* the brackets.

> *I haven't yet spoken to John (I mean John Maple, my boss), but I have a meeting with him on Friday.*

> For lunch we had sandwiches (*pastrami on rye and so on*), *salami, coleslaw, fried chicken, and potato salad.*

Punctuation is given before the closing brackets only when it applies to the bracketed section rather than to the sentence as a whole.

> He's very handsome (*positively gorgeous in fact!*) and still single.

Square brackets [ ]

Square brackets are used, usually in books and articles, when supplying words that make a quotation clearer or that comment on it, although they were not originally said or written.

> Mr Runcie concluded: 'The novel is at its strongest when describing the dignity of Cambridge [a slave] and the education of Emily [the daughter of an absentee landlord].'

The hyphen (-)

The hyphen joins words or parts of words.

Hyphens are used at the ends of lines where a word has been split, to warn the reader that the word continues on the next line. If the word you need to split is clearly made up of two or more smaller words or elements, you should put the hyphen after the first of these parts. Otherwise, you put the hyphen at the end of a syllable.

> *wheel-barrow*   *inter-national*
> *listen-ing*   *compli-mentary*
> *infor-mation*

It is best not to add a hyphen if the word is a short one, or if it would mean writing just one or two letters at the end or beginning of a line. For example, it would be better to write 'unnatural' on the line below, rather than writing 'un-' on one line and 'natural' on the next.

Prefixes that are used in front of a word beginning with a capital letter always have a hyphen after them.

> *a wave of anti-British feeling*
> *a neo-Byzantine cathedral*

A hyphen is used to join two or more words that together form an adjective, where this adjective is used *before* the noun it describes.

> *an up-to-date account*
> *a last-minute rush*
> *a six-year-old boy*

The hyphen is omitted when the adjective so formed comes after the noun or pronoun it describes.

> *The accounts are up to date.*
> *It was all rather last minute.*
> *He's six years old.*

Some common compound nouns are usually written with hyphens.

> *mother-in-law*   *great-grandmother*

Hyphens can be used to split words that have been formed by adding a prefix to another word, especially to avoid an awkward combination of letters or confusion with another word.

> *re-elect*
> *re-covering furniture*
> *re-creation*

The dash (–)

A spaced dash (i.e. with a single space before and after it) is used:

- at the beginning and end of a comment that interrupts the flow of a sentence.

    Now children – Kenneth, stop that immediately! – open your books on page 20.

- to separate off extra information.

    Boots and shoes – all shapes, sizes and colours – tumbled out.

An unspaced dash (i.e. with no space before or after it) is used:

- to indicate a range.

    pages 26–42

- between two adjectives or noun modifiers that indicate that two countries or groups are involved in something or that an individual has two roles or aspects.

> *Swedish–Norwegian relations improved*
> *the United States–Canada free trade pact*
> *a mathematician–philosopher*

- to indicate that something such as a plane or a train goes between two places.

> *the Anguilla–St Kitts flight*
> *the New York–Montreal train*

The slash (/)

The slash separates letters, words or numbers.
It is used to indicate alternatives, ratios and ranges,
and in website addresses.

>*he/she/it*
>*200 km/hr*
>*the 2001/02 accounting year*
>*http://www.abcdefg.com*

Punctuation in numbers

Dates

Full stops or slashes are often used in dates.

	American usage
12.3.09	3/12/09
2.28.11	2/28/11

Scientific usage

Full stops are not used in scientific abbreviations.

12 kg	50 cm

Times

Full stops and occasionally colons are used in times.

| 4.15 p.m | 21.15 |
| 3:30 a.m | 20:30 |

Long numbers

Commas are used in numbers to mark off units of thousands and millions.

1,359   2,543,678

Decimals

Full stops indicate decimal points.

1.5   25.08

Spelling

The spelling rules you really need to know

English has a small number of rules that underpin how certain words and types of words ought to be spelled. If you can learn these rules, you will be on your way to becoming a better and more confident speller. Don't be put off if the rule sounds complicated – look at the examples and you will begin to see spelling patterns emerging. Once you are familiar with these patterns, you can make a good attempt at guessing how a word ought to be spelled. Then check it in your dictionary.

Rule 1

- *i* before *e* except after *c*

When the letters **i** and **e** are combined to make the 'ee' sound, the **i** comes before the **e**.

Examples

achieve	field	relief
brief	hygiene	siege
chief	niece	thief

protein	seize

When they follow the letter **c** in a word, the **e** comes before the **i**.

Examples

ceiling	deceit	receipt
conceive	deceive	receive

Rule 2

• *-ize* or *-ise?*

The question of whether a verb should end in **-ize** or **-ise** is one that raises temperatures. Historically, both endings have always been used in English. The **-ize** spelling has been preferred in American English for over a century, and this had led some people to think that **-ize** is an Americanism, and object to its use in British English. Collins Dictionaries (and all other leading British dictionary publishers) show **-ize** as the main spelling form for these verbs, and **-ization** and **-izer** as the preferred forms of their derivatives. It is perfectly correct to use **-ise**, **-isation**

41

and **-iser**. The most important thing is to be consistent and stick to one style.

(!) *The exceptions*

Some words are always spelled with **-ise**

advertise	disguise	'to force
advise	excise	open')
chastise	exercise	revise
comprise	franchise	supervise
compromise	improvise	surprise
despise	prise	televise
devise	(meaning	

Some words are always spelled with **-ize**

capsize
prize (meaning 'to value highly')

Rule 3 – Suffixes

• Adding a suffix to words that end with a silent *e*

Many English words end with a silent *e* – that means the *e* is not pronounced. When you add a suffix that begins with a vowel onto these words, you drop the *e*.

Examples

abbreviate + -ion = abbreviation
appreciate + -ive = appreciative
desire + -able = desirable
guide + -ance = guidance
hope + -ing = hoping
response + -ible = responsible
ventilate + -ed = ventilated

! The exceptions

When the word ends in **ce** and sounds like **s** or the word ends in **ge** and sounds like **j**, you do not drop the final **e**.

notice + -able = noticeable
change + -able = changeable
outrage + -ous = outrageous

Rule 4 – Suffixes

• Adding a suffix to words that end with a consonant

In words of one syllable ending in a short vowel plus a consonant, you double the final consonant when you add a suffix that begins with a vowel.

Examples

run + ing = running
pot + ed = potted
thin + est = thinnest
swim + er = swimmer

In words of more than one syllable ending in a single vowel plus a consonant, if the stress is on the end of the word when it is pronounced, you double the final consonant when you add a suffix that begins with a vowel.

Examples

admit + -ance = admittance
begin + -ing = beginning
commit + -ed = committed
occur + -ence = occurrence

When you add a suffix that begins with a vowel to a word that ends in a single vowel plus **l** or **p**, you double the **l** or **p**.

Examples

appal + -ing = appalling
cancel + -ation = cancellation
dial + -er = dialler
fulfil + -ed = fulfilled
handicap + -ed = handicapped
kidnap + -er = kidnapper
slip + -age = slippage
wrap + -ing = wrapping

When you add a suffix that begins with **e**, **i** or **y** to a word that ends in **c**, you add a **k** after the **c**. This is to keep the hard **k** sound when it is pronounced.

Examples

mimic + -ed = mimicked
picnic + -ing = picnicking
panic + -y = panicky

The exceptions

arc + -ed = arced
arc + -ing = arcing

Rule 5 – Suffixes

• Adding a suffix to words that end with *our*

When you add the suffixes **-ous** or **-ary** to a word that ends with **our**, you drop the **u** from **our**.

Examples

glamour + -ous = glamorous
humour + -ous = humorous
honour + -ary = honorary

Rule 6 – Suffixes

• Adding the **-ly** suffix to words that end with *le*

When you make an adverb by adding the suffix **-ly** to an adjective that ends with **le**, you drop the **le** from the adjective.

Examples

gentle + -ly = gently
idle + -ly = idly
subtle + -ly = subtle

Rule 7 – Suffixes

• Adding a suffix to words that end with **y**

When you add a suffix to a word that ends with a consonant plus **y**, you change the **y** to **i**.

Examples

apply + -ance = appliance
beauty + -ful = beautiful
crazy + -ly = crazily
happy + -ness = happiness
smelly + -er = smellier
woolly + -est = woolliest

(!) *The exceptions*

In certain short adjectives that end with a consonant followed by **y**, you keep the **y** when you add the ending **-ly** to make an adverb.

shy + -ly = shyly
spry + -ly = spryly
wry + -ly = wryly

Rule 8 – Suffixes

• Words ending in *ful*

You always spell the suffix **-ful** with just one **l**.

Examples

beautiful	faithful	hopeful
cupful	grateful	painful

Rule 9 – Prefixes

• Words beginning with *al-*

When **all** and another word are joined to make an unhyphenated word, you drop the second l.

Examples

| all + mighty = almighty |
| all + ready = already |
| all + though = although |
| all + together = altogether |

If you are making a hyphenated form, you keep both ls.

Examples

| all + important = all-important |
| all + inclusive = all-inclusive |
| all + powerful = all-powerful |

Rule 10 – Plurals

• Making plurals of words that end with a consonant followed by **y**

When you make a plural of a word that ends with a consonant plus **y**, you change the **y** to **i** and add **-es**.

Examples

fairy + -es = fairies
pantry + -es = pantries
quality + -es = qualities
spy + -es = spies
story + -es = stories

Rule 11 – Plurals

• Making plurals of words that end with a vowel followed by **y**

When you make a plural of a word that ends with a vowel plus **y**, you add **-s**.

Examples

boy + -s = boys
day + -s = days
donkey + -s = donkeys
guy + -s = guys

Rule 12 – Plurals

• Making plurals of words that end with **s**, **x**, **z**, **sh** or **ch**

When you make a plural of a word that ends with **s**, **x**, **z**, **sh** or **ch**, you add **-es**.

Examples

bus + -es = buses
kiss + -es = kisses
jinx + -es = jinxes
buzz + es = buzzes
rash + -es = rashes
match + -es = matches

Rule 13 – Plurals

• Making plurals of words that end with *eau*

When you make a plural of a word that ends with **eau**, you add **-x** or **-s**. Words that end with **eau** are French words that have come into English. The **-x** ending is the French plural, and the **-s** ending is the English one. Both forms are acceptable for these words.

Examples

bureau + -x = bureaux
bureaus + -s = bureaus
chateau + -x = chateaux
chateau + -s = chateaus
gateau + -x = gateaux
gateau + -s = gateaus

Rule 14 – Plurals

• Making plurals of words that end with a single *o*

When you make a plural of a word that ends with a single **o**, you add **-s**.

Examples

memo + -s = memos
solo + -s = solos
taco + -s = tacos
zero + -s = zeros

! The exceptions

There are a number of words that end with a single **o** that add -**es** when they are plural.

echo + -es = echoes
hero + -es = heroes
potato + -es = potatoes
tomato + -es = tomatoes
veto + -es = vetoes

Tips for looking up words

Sometimes words are not spelled the way they are pronounced. This can make finding them in the dictionary very difficult. Here are some tips that should help.

If the word sounds like it should begin with C...
Some words which sound as if they might begin with *ch* are spelled with *c* alone, for example *cello*.

If the word sounds like it should begin with D...
Words that sound as if they should start with *di* are often spelled with *de* instead, for example *determination* and *dessert*.

If the word sounds like it should begin with E...
The words *aesthetic*, *oesophagus* and *oestrogen* sound as if they should start with letter *e*, but in British English they are spelled with *ae* and *oe*. These two combinations of letters, which both sound like *ee*, can come in the middle of words too, for example in *anaesthetic* and *amoeba*.

If the word sounds like it should begin with F...
Some words which sound as if they should begin
with the letter f actually begin with the letters ph,
for example *pharmacy*, *pharaoh* and *phrase*. The *ph*
combination, pronounced like f, comes in the middle
of some words too. for example *amphetamine* and
emphasis.

If the word sounds like it should begin with G...
Some words which sound as if they might begin
with g alone, are actually spelled with the letters *gh*,
for example *ghastly* and *ghost*. Some words which
sound as if they might begin with the letter n, are
spelled with *gn*, for example *gnaw*, *gnome* and *gnu*.
Also take care with the spelling of words that start
with *gu*- followed by the vowels a, e or i, because the
u is not pronounced, for example *guarantee*, *guard*,
guerrilla and *guile*.

If the word sounds like it should begin with H...
Some words which sound as if they might begin
with letter h, instead begin with the letters *wh*, for
example *who*, *whole*, *wholly*, *whom*, *whore* and *whose*.

If the word sounds like it should begin with J...
Many words which sound as if they ought to begin with letter *j* are spelled instead with letter *g*, for example *gender*, *geranium*, *giraffe* and *gym*.

If the word sounds like it should begin with K...
Some words that begin with a *k-* sound are spelled with the letters *ch-*, for example *chlorophyll*, *chlorine*, and *choir*. Some words that begin with a *k-* sound are spelled with letter *q*, for example *quite* and *quiet*.

If the word sounds like it should begin with N...
Some words which sound as if they should begin with letter *n*, are spelled with *gn*, for example *gnaw*, *gnome* and *gnu*. Other words that sound as if they ought to begin with letter *n* are actually spelled with *kn*, for example *knee*, *knight*, *knock* and *knot*. Other words that sound as if they ought to begin with letter *n* are actually spelled with *pn*, for example *pneumatic* and *pneumonia*.

If the word sounds like it should begin with R...
Some words which sound as if they should begin with letter *r* are spelled with *wr*, for example *wrangle*, *wretch*, *write* and *wrong*. Other words which sound as

if they ought to begin with letter r alone are actually spelled with rh, for example *rhapsody*, *rheumatism*, *rhino* and *rhododendron*.

If the word sounds like it should begin with S…

Some words which sound as if they begin with *s* actually begin with *c*, for example *city* and *centre*. Some words which sound as if they begin with *sh* actually begin with *ch*, for example *chute*. Other words which sound as if they begin with *s* actually begin with the letters *ps*, for example *psychiatry* and *psychology*.

If the word sounds like it should begin with Z…

Many words which sound as if they begin with letter *z* actually begin with letter *x*, for example *Xerox*, *xylem* and *xylophone*.

Hints and tips on how to improve your spelling

- Learn spellings that are personal to you, your studies and your needs. At the back of each subject file or exercise book for school, stick a sheet of paper with a list of words you find difficult to spell.

- Key words you find difficult to spell into a Word document on your computer, save them on your mobile, or buy an address book with alphabet tabs and make your own personalized spelling help book.

- Different people learn spelling in different ways. Find out how you learn best.

- Feeling the patterning of word through writing or tracing the letters many times can help with spelling.

- Break words down into small chunks to copy or spell. Start by taking 3-letter strings at a time and then build up your ability to remember more letters.

- Writing a spelling down to see if it 'looks right' can help people with a strong visual memory.

- Make a habit of highlighting difficult vowel sounds.

- With a particular word that is difficult – picture it in your head, make the font really big, colour the difficult part of the word, look at it forwards and backwards.

- There are only 3 verbs in English that end in -ceed: succeed, proceed, and exceed. All the other verbs with that sound end in -cede. There's only one English verb that ends in -sede: supersede

- The sound "full" at the end of a word is spelled with only one l.
  For example:

  careful   graceful   healthful   hopeful

  The word "Full" itself is the only exception.

- Break up words and exaggerate their pronunciation in your head, for example, **bus-i-ness** or **Wed-nes-day**

- Make a habit of looking up any words you are doubtful about in a reliable dictionary, such as *Collins School Dictionary*

List of commonly misspelled words

accommodation
achieve
actually
address
advertise
alcohol
although
amateur
anaesthetic
analyse/
 analysis
anoint
apartment
appal
appalling
aqueduct
archaeology
argument
artefact
assessment
atmosphere

audible
audience
autumn
beautiful
beginning
beige
believe
beneath
besiege
biased
blatant
broccoli
budget
buried
business
camouflage
cappuccino
Caribbean
caught
cemetery
chocolate

climb
cinnamon
column
commemorate
commitment
committee
comparative
compatible
concentration
conclusion
connoisseur
conscience
conscious
consensus
consequence
contemporary
continuous
creation
curriculum
daughter
deceive

decide/decision	exaggerate	hamster
definite	excellent	handkerchief
design	excerpt	happened
despair	exist	harass
desperate	explanation	health
detach	extraordinary	height
development	extrovert	nonorary
diamond	facetious	humorous
diary	fascinate	hygiene
disappear	February	hypocrisy
disappoint	fierce	idiosyncrasy
disastrous	fluorescent	imaginary
dissatisfied	foreign	improvise
ecstasy	forty	independent
eighth	freight	indict
embarrass	fulfil	industrial
energy	furthermore	innocuous
engagement	gauge	inoculate
enquire	glamorous	instalment
enthral	gorgeous	integrate
evaluation	government	intelligent
environment	guarantee	interesting
espresso	guard	interrupt
euthanasia	guardian	introvert
evidence	haemorrhage	irritable

issue	memento	performance
itinerary	millennium	permanent
jealous/	millionaire	persuade/
jealousy	miniature	persuasion
jeopardy	minuscule	pharaoh
jewellery	miscellaneous	phlegm
knight	mischievous	physical
knowledge	moreover	piece
label	mortgage	pigeon
laboratory	murmur	playwright
liaison	necessary	possession
lieutenant	nervous	potential
listening	niece	prejudice
lonely	occasion	preparation
lovely	occurrence	prioritize
maintenance	omit	privilege
manoeuvre	original	process
margarine	outrageous	professor
marriage	parallel	pronunciation
material	participation	proportion
mathematician	pattern	proposition
mayonnaise	peaceful	psychology
meanwhile	people	query
medieval	peculiar	questionnaire
Mediterranean	perceive	queue

reaction
receipt
receive
recommend
reconnaissance
reference
refrigerator
relief
remember
research
resources
rhinoceros
rhythm
sacrilege
safety
satellite
Saturday
sausage
schedule
secondary
seize
separate
sequence
sergeant
shoulder

siege
sieve
silhouette
sincerely
skilful
soldier
sovereign
stomach
straight
strategy
strength
successful
supersede
suppress
surely
surprise
survey
technique
technology
temperature
texture
threshold
tomorrow
truly
unconscious

unfortunately
usual
until
unwieldy
vacuum
vague
vegetable
vehicle
veil
veterinary
Wednesday
weight
weird
whinge
wilful
withhold
xylophone
yield

m metre
MA Master of Arts
mac n (Inf) mackintosh
macabre adj gruesome, ghastly
macaroni n pasta in thin tubes
macaroon n biscuit containing almonds
macaw n kind of parrot
mace¹ n staff of office
mace² n spice made of nutmeg shell
machete n broad, heavy knife
Machiavellian adj (politically) unprincipled, crafty
machine ❶ n 1 apparatus with several parts to apply mechanical force 2 controlling organization 3 mechanical appliance ▷ v 4 shape etc. with machine
machinery n 1 machines or

machine parts 2 procedures by which system functions **machinist** n **machine gun** automatic gun firing repeatedly
macho ❶ adj exhibiting exaggerated pride in masculinity **machismo** n strong, exaggerated masculinity
mackerel n edible sea fish
mackintosh n waterproof raincoat
macramé n ornamental work of knotted cord
macrocosm n 1 the universe 2 any large system
mad ❶ adj madder, maddest 1 suffering from mental disease, foolish 2 enthusiastic (about) 3 excited 4 (Inf) furious **madden** v make mad **madness** n
madam n polite title for a woman
madcap adj/n reckless (person)
made past tense and past participle of MAKE
Madonna n Virgin Mary
madrigal n unaccompanied part song
maelstrom n great whirlpool
maestro n, pl **-tri, -tros** 1 outstanding musician, conductor 2 master of any art
magazine ❶ n 1 periodical

——— THESAURUS ———

machine n = **appliance**, device, apparatus, engine, tool; = **system**, structure, organization, machinery, setup (Inf)
macho adj = **manly**, masculine, chauvinist, virile
mad adj = **insane**, crazy (Inf), nuts (Sl), raving, unstable ≠ **sane**;

= **foolish**, absurd, wild, stupid, daft (Inf) ≠ **sensible**; (Inf) = **angry**, furious, incensed, enraged, livid (Inf) ≠ **calm**; = **enthusiastic**, wild, crazy (Inf), ardent, fanatical ≠ **nonchalant**; = **frenzied**, wild, excited, frenetic, uncontrolled
magazine n = **journal**,

publication **2** appliance for supplying cartridges to gun **3** storehouse for arms etc.

magenta adj/n (of) deep purplish-red

maggot n grub, larva **maggoty** adj

magic ❶ n **1** art of supposedly invoking supernatural powers to influence events etc. **2** witchcraft, conjuring **3** fascinating quality or power ▷ adj **4** of, using magic **magical** adj **magician** n wizard, conjuror

magistrate ❶ n civil officer administering law **magisterial** adj **1** of magistrate **2** authoritative

magnanimous adj generous, not petty **magnanimity** n

magnate n influential person

magnesium n metallic element **magnesia** n white powder used in medicine

magnet n piece of iron, steel having properties of attracting iron, steel **magnetic** adj of magnet

2 exerting powerful attraction **magnetism** n **magnetize** v

magneto n apparatus for ignition in internal-combustion engine

magnetic tape coated plastic strip for recording sound or video signals

magnificent ❶ adj **1** splendid **2** imposing **3** excellent **magnificence** n

magnify ❶ v -fying, -fied **1** increase apparent size of, as with lens **2** exaggerate **magnification** n

magnitude ❶ n **1** importance **2** size

magnolia n tree with white, sweet-scented flowers

magnum n large wine bottle

magpie n black-and-white bird

maharajah n former title of some Indian princes

mahogany n tree yielding reddish-brown wood

maiden ❶ n (Lit) **1** young unmarried woman ▷ adj

— THESAURUS —

publication, supplement, rag (Inf), issue

magic n = **sorcery**, wizardry, witchcraft, enchantment, black art; = **conjuring**, illusion, trickery, sleight of hand, legerdemain; = **charm**, power, glamour, fascination, magnetism ▷ adj = **miraculous**, entrancing, charming, fascinating, marvellous

magistrate n = **judge**, justice, justice of the peace, J.P.

magnificent adj = **splendid**, impressive, imposing, glorious,

gorgeous ≠ **ordinary**; = **brilliant**, fine, excellent, outstanding, superb

magnify v = **enlarge**, increase, boost, expand, intensify ≠ **reduce**; = **make worse**, exaggerate, intensify, worsen, exacerbate

magnitude n = **importance**, consequence, significance, moment, note ≠ **unimportance**; = **immensity**, size, extent, enormity, volume ≠ **smallness**

maiden n (Lit) = **girl**, maid, lass, damsel, virgin ▷ adj = **first**, initial, inaugural, introductory;

2 unmarried **3** first **maid** n
1 woman servant **2** (Lit) maiden
maiden name woman's surname
before marriage

mail¹ ⓝ n **1** letters etc. transported
and delivered by the post office
2 postal system **3** train etc.
carrying mail ▷ v **4** send by mail

mail² n armour of interlaced rings

mailbox n (US & Canada) **1** public
box into which letters are put for
collection and delivery **2** private
box outside house where
occupant's mail is delivered

mailman n person who collects or
delivers mail

maim v cripple, mutilate

main ⓝ adj **1** chief, principal ▷ n
2 principal pipe, line carrying water
etc. **3** (Obs) sea **mainframe** n
1 high-speed general-purpose
computer **2** central processing
unit of computer **mainland** n
stretch of land which forms main
part of a country **mainstay** n
chief support **mainstream** n

prevailing cultural trend

maintain ⓥ v **1** carry on
2 support **3** assert **4** support by
argument **maintenance** n
1 maintaining **2** means of support
3 upkeep of buildings etc.

maisonette n part of house fitted
as self-contained dwelling

maize n type of corn

majesty ⓤ n, pl **-ties**
1 stateliness **2** sovereignty
majestic adj

major ⓝ n **1** army officer above
captain **2** scale in music **3** (US &
Canad) an academic subject chosen
as a field of specialization ▷ adj
4 greater in number, extent etc.
majority n **1** greater number
2 coming of age

make ⓥ v making, made
1 construct **2** produce **3** create
4 establish **5** appoint **6** amount
to **7** cause to do **8** reach **9** earn
10 tend **11** contribute ▷ n
12 brand, type **maker** n **making**
n **make-believe** n fantasy,

m

= **unmarried**, unwed

mail¹ n = **letters**, post,
correspondence ▷ v = **post**, send,
forward, e-mail, dispatch

main adj = **chief**, leading, head,
central, essential ≠ minor

maintain v = **continue**, retain,
preserve, sustain, carry on ≠ end;
= **assert**, state, claim, insist,
declare ≠ disavow; = **look after**,
care for, take care of, conserve, keep
in good condition

majesty n = **grandeur**, glory,
splendour, magnificence, nobility

≠ triviality

major adj = **important**, critical,
significant, great, serious; = **main**,
higher, greater, bigger, leading
≠ minor

make v = **produce**, cause, create,
effect, lead to; = **perform**, do,
effect, carry out, execute; = **force**,
cause, compel, drive, require;
= **create**, build, produce,
manufacture, form; = **earn**, get,
gain, net, win; = **amount to**, total,
constitute, add up to, count as ▷ n
= **brand**, sort, style, model, kind

pretence **make do** manage with inferior alternative **make it** (Inf) be successful **makeshift** adj serving as temporary substitute **make-up** n **1** cosmetics **2** characteristics **3** layout

mal- comb. form ill, badly, as in malformation, malfunction

maladjusted adj badly adjusted, as to society

malady n, pl **-dies** disease

malaise n vague feeling of discomfort

malapropism n ludicrous misuse of word

malaria n infectious disease transmitted by mosquitoes

malcontent adj/n discontented (person)

male ❶ adj **1** of sex that fertilizes female **2** of men or male animals ▷ n **3** male person or animal

malevolent adj full of ill will **malevolence** n

malice n **1** ill will **2** spite **malicious** adj spiteful

malign adj **1** causing evil ▷ v **2** slander **malignancy** n **malignant** adj **1** feeling ill will **2** (of disease) resistant to therapy

malinger v feign illness to escape duty

mall n shopping centre

mallard n wild duck

malleable adj **1** capable of being hammered into shape **2** adaptable

mallet n (wooden) hammer

malnutrition n inadequate nutrition

malodorous adj evil-smelling

malpractice n immoral, illegal or unethical conduct

malt n grain used for brewing

maltreat v treat badly

mammal n animal of type that suckles its young **mammalian** adj

mammary adj of, relating to breast

mammon n wealth regarded as source of evil

mammoth ❶ n **1** extinct animal like an elephant ▷ adj **2** colossal

man ❶ n, pl **men 1** human being **2** human race **3** adult male **4** piece used in chess etc. ▷ v **5** supply with men **manful** adj brave **manly** adj **manhandle** v treat roughly **manhole** n opening through which person may pass to a sewer etc. **mankind** n human beings **manslaughter** n unintentional homicide

mana n (NZ) authority, influence

manacle n/v fetter

manage ❶ v **1** be in charge of **2** succeed in doing **3** control **4** handle **manageable** adj **management** n **1** those who

male adj = masculine, manly, macho, virile ≠ female

mammoth adj = colossal, huge, giant, massive, enormous ≠ tiny

man n = male, guy (Inf), fellow (Inf), gentleman, bloke (Brit Inf);

= human, human being, person, individual, soul; = mankind, humanity, people, human race, humankind ▷ v = staff, people, crew, occupy, garrison

manage v = be in charge of, run,

manage **2** administration

manager n **managerial** adj

mandarin n **1** small orange **2** high-ranking bureaucrat

mandate ❶ n **1** command of, or commission to act for, another **2** instruction from electorate to representative or government

mandatory adj compulsory

mandible n lower jawbone

mandolin n stringed musical instrument

mane n long hair on neck of horse, lion etc.

manganese n metallic element

mange n skin disease of dogs etc. **mangy** adj

manger n eating trough in stable

mangle¹ n **1** machine for rolling clothes etc. to remove water ▷ v **2** press in mangle

mangle² v mutilate

mango n, pl **-goes, -gos** tropical fruit

mangrove n tropical tree which grows on muddy river banks

mania n **1** madness **2** prevailing craze **maniac** adj/n mad (person)

maniacal, manic adj affected by mania

manicure n **1** treatment and care of fingernails and hands ▷ v **2** treat, care for hands

manifest ❶ adj **1** clear, undoubted ▷ v **2** make manifest **manifestation** n **manifesto** n declaration of policy by political party etc.

manifold adj **1** numerous and varied ▷ n **2** in engine, pipe with several outlets

manila, manilla n **1** fibre used for ropes **2** tough paper

manipulate ❶ v **1** handle skilfully **2** manage **3** falsify **manipulation** n

manna n **1** nourishment **2** unexpected gift

mannequin n woman who models clothes

manner ❶ n **1** way, style **2** bearing **3** sort, kind ▷ pl **4** social behaviour **mannered** adj affected **mannerism** n person's distinctive habit

manoeuvre ❶ n **1** complicated, perhaps deceptive plan or action

handle, direct, conduct;
= organize, use, handle, regulate;
= cope, survive, succeed, carry on, make do; **= perform**, do, achieve, carry out, undertake, operate

mandate n **= command**, order, commission, instruction, decree

manifest adj **= obvious**, apparent, patent, evident, clear ≠ **concealed** ▷ v **= display**, show, reveal, express, demonstrate ≠ **conceal**

manipulate v **= influence**, control, direct, negotiate, exploit; **= work**, use, operate, handle

manner n **= style**, way, fashion, method, custom; **= behaviour**, air, bearing, conduct, aspect; **= type**, form, sort, kind, variety

manoeuvre v **= scheme**, wangle (Inf), machinate ▷ n **= stratagem**, scheme, trick, tactic, intrigue; often plural **= movement**, operation,

▷ v 2 employ stratagems 3 (cause to) perform manoeuvres

manor n large country house with land

manse n house of minister in some religious denominations

mansion ❶ n large house

mantle ❶ n 1 loose cloak 2 covering ▷ v 3 cover

mantra n sacred word or syllable in Hinduism and Buddhism

manual ❶ adj 1 done with the hands 2 by human labour, not automatic ▷ n 3 handbook

manufacture ❶ v 1 make (materials) into finished articles 2 concoct 3 making of articles, esp. in large quantities

manufacturer n

manure n 1 dung or chemical fertilizer used to enrich land

manuscript n 1 book etc. written by hand 2 copy for printing

many adj **more, most** 1 numerous ▷ n 2 large number

map n 1 flat representation of the earth ▷ v 2 make map of 3 (with

out) plan

maple n tree of sycamore family

maple sugar n (US & Canad) sugar made from the sap of the sugar maple

mar ❶ v **marring, marred** spoil

Mar. March

maraca n shaken percussion instrument

marathon n 1 long-distance race 2 endurance contest

marble n 1 kind of limestone 2 small ball used in children's game

march ❶ v 1 walk with military step 2 go, progress ▷ n 3 action of marching 4 distance marched 5 marching tune

March n third month

marchioness n wife, widow of marquis

mare n female horse

margarine n butter substitute made from vegetable fats

margin ❶ n 1 border, edge 2 space round printed page 3 amount allowed beyond what is necessary **marginal** adj

—————————— THESAURUS ——————————

exercise, war game

mansion n = **residence**, manor, hall, villa, seat

mantle n = **covering**, screen, curtain, blanket, veil; = **cloak**, wrap, cape, hood, shawl

manual adj = **physical**, human; = **hand-operated**, hand, non-automatic ▷ n = **handbook**, guide, instructions, bible

manufacture v = **make**, build, produce, construct, create; = **concoct**, make up, invent, devise,

fabricate ▷ n = **making**, production, construction, assembly, creation

mar v = **ruin**, spoil, scar, flaw, impair ≠ **improve**

march v = **parade**, walk, file, pace, stride; = **walk**, strut, storm, sweep, stride ▷ n = **walk**, trek, slog, yomp (Brit Inf), routemarch; = **progress**, development, advance, evolution, progression

margin n = **edge**, side, border, boundary, verge

marigold n plant with yellow flowers

marijuana ❶ n dried flowers and leaves of hemp plant, used as narcotic

marina n mooring facility for pleasure boats

marinade n liquid in which food is soaked before cooking **marinate** v soak in marinade

marine ❶ adj 1 of the sea or shipping ▷ n 2 soldier trained for land or sea combat 3 fleet **mariner** n sailor

marionette n puppet

marital ❶ adj of marriage

maritime ❶ adj 1 of seafaring 2 near the sea

mark ❶ n 1 dot, scar etc. 2 sign, token 3 letter, number showing evaluation of schoolwork etc. 4 indication 5 target ▷ v 6 make mark on 7 distinguish 8 notice 9 assess 10 stay close to sporting opponent **marked** adj noticeable **marker** n **marksman** n person skilled in shooting

market ❶ n 1 place for buying and selling 2 demand for goods ▷ v 3 offer for sale **marketable** adj **market garden** place where fruit and vegetables are grown for sale

marmalade n preserve made of oranges, lemons etc.

marmoset n small bushy-tailed monkey

maroon¹ ❶ v 1 leave on deserted island etc. 2 isolate

maroon² adj/n (of) brownish-crimson colour

marquee n large tent

marquetry n inlaid work, wood mosaic

marquis n nobleman of rank below duke

marrow n 1 fatty substance inside bones 2 vital part 3 plant with long, green-striped fruit, eaten as vegetable

marry ❶ v -rying, -ried 1 join as husband and wife 2 unite closely **marriage** n 1 being married

marijuana n = **cannabis**, pot (Sl), dope (Sl), grass (Sl), hemp

marine adj = **nautical**, maritime, naval, seafaring, seagoing

marital adj = **matrimonial**, nuptial, conjugal, connubial

maritime adj = **nautical**, marine, naval, oceanic, seafaring; = **coastal**, seaside, littoral

mark n = **spot**, stain, streak, smudge, line; = **characteristic**, feature, standard, quality, measure; = **brand**, impression, label, device, flag; = **target**, goal, aim, purpose,

object ▷ v = **scar**, scratch, stain, streak, blot; = **label**, identify, brand, flag, stamp; = **grade**, correct, assess, evaluate, appraise; = **distinguish**, show, illustrate, exemplify, denote; = **observe**, mind, note, notice, attend to

market n = **fair**, mart, bazaar, souk (Arabic) ▷ v = **sell**, promote, retail, peddle, vend

maroon¹ v = **abandon**, leave, desert, strand, leave high and dry (Inf)

marry v = **tie the knot** (Inf), wed,

2 wedding ceremony

marsh ❶ n low-lying wet land **marshy** adj

marshal ❶ n 1 high officer of state **2** (US) law enforcement officer **3** high-ranking officer in the army, air force ▷ v **4** arrange **5** conduct with ceremony

marshmallow n spongy pink or white sweet

marsupial n animal that carries its young in pouch

marten n weasel-like animal

martial ❶ adj 1 of war **2** warlike

martin n species of swallow

martinet n strict disciplinarian

martyr ❶ n 1 one who suffers or dies for his beliefs ▷ v **2** make martyr of

marvel ❶ v -velling, -velled 1 wonder ▷ n **2** wonderful thing **marvellous** adj

marzipan n paste of almonds, sugar etc.

mascara n cosmetic for darkening eyelashes

mascot n person, animal or thing

supposed to bring luck

masculine ❶ adj 1 relating to males **2** manly

mash n/v (crush into) soft mass or pulp

mask ❶ n 1 covering for face **2** disguise, pretence ▷ v **3** disguise

masochism n abnormal condition where pleasure (esp. sexual) is derived from pain **masochist** n

mason n worker in stone **masonry** n stonework

masquerade n **1** masked ball ▷ v **2** appear in disguise

mass ❶ n 1 quantity of matter **2** (Physics) amount of matter in body **3** large quantity ▷ v **4** form into mass **massive** adj large and heavy **mass-market** adj appealing to many people **mass-produce** v produce standardized articles in large quantities

Mass n service in R.C. Church

massacre ❶ n 1 indiscriminate, large-scale killing ▷ v **2** kill indiscriminately

m

——————————————— THESAURUS ———————————————

get hitched (SI); = **unite**, join, link, bond, ally

marsh n = **swamp**, bog, slough, fen, quagmire

marshal v = **conduct**, take, lead, guide, steer; = **arrange**, group, order, line up, organize

martial adj = **military**, belligerent, warlike, bellicose

marvel v = **be amazed**, wonder, gape, be awed ▷ n = **wonder**, phenomenon, miracle, portent

masculine adj = **male**, manly, mannish, manlike, virile

mask n = **façade**, disguise, front, cover, screen ▷ v = **disguise**, hide, conceal, obscure, cover (up)

mass n = **lot**, collection, load, pile, quantity; = **piece**, block, lump, chunk, hunk; = **size**, matter, weight, extent, bulk ▷ adj = **large-scale**, general, widespread, extensive, universal ▷ v = **gather**, assemble, accumulate, collect, rally

massacre n = **slaughter**, murder, holocaust, carnage, extermination ▷ v = **slaughter**, kill, murder, butcher, wipe out

massage ❶ n 1 rubbing and kneading of muscles etc. as curative treatment ▷ v 2 perform massage
masseur n one who practises massage

mast n 1 pole for supporting ship's sails 2 tall support for aerial etc.

mastectomy n/pl **-mies** surgical removal of breast

master ❶ n 1 one in control 2 employer 3 owner 4 document etc. from which copies are made 5 expert 6 teacher ▷ adj 7 expert, skilled ▷ v 8 overcome 9 acquire skill in **masterful** adj 1 expert, skilled 2 domineering **masterly** adj showing great skill **mastery** n 1 understanding (of) 2 expertise 3 victory **mastermind** v 1 plan, direct ▷ n 2 one who directs complex operation **masterpiece** n outstanding work

masticate v chew

mastiff n large dog

masturbate v fondle genital organs **masturbation** n

mat¹ n 1 small rug 2 piece of fabric to protect another surface 3 thick tangled mass ▷ v 4 form into such mass

mat² adj dull, lustreless

matador n man who kills bull in bullfights

match¹ ❶ n 1 contest, game 2 equal 3 person, thing corresponding to another 4 marriage ▷ v 5 get something corresponding to 6 oppose, put in competition (with) 7 correspond **matchmaker** n person who schemes to bring about marriage

match² n small stick with head which ignites when rubbed **matchbox** n **matchstick** n

mate ❶ n 1 comrade 2 husband, wife 3 one of pair 4 officer in merchant ship ▷ v 5 marry 6 pair **matey** adj (Inf) friendly

material ❶ n 1 substance from which thing is made 2 cloth

---------- THESAURUS ----------

massage n = **rub-down**, manipulation ▷ v = **rub down**, manipulate, knead

master n = **lord**, ruler, commander, chief, director ≠ **servant**; = **expert**, maestro, ace (Inf), genius, wizard ≠ **amateur**; = **teacher**, tutor, instructor ≠ **student** ▷ adj = **main**, principal, chief, prime, foremost ≠ **lesser** ▷ v = **learn**, understand, pick up, grasp, get the hang of (Inf); = **overcome**, defeat, conquer, tame, triumph over ≠ **give in to**

match² n = **game**, test,

competition, trial, tie; = **marriage**, pairing, alliance, partnership; = **equal**, rival, peer, counterpart ▷ v = **correspond with**, go with, fit with, harmonize with; = **correspond**, agree, accord, square, coincide

mate n (Inf) = **friend**, pal (Inf), companion, buddy (Inf), comrade; = **partner**, lover, companion, spouse, consort; = **assistant**, subordinate, apprentice, helper, accomplice ▷ v = **pair**, couple, breed

material n = **substance**, matter,

3 information on which piece of
work is based ▷ adj 4 of body
5 affecting physical wellbeing
6 important **materialism** n
1 excessive interest in money and
possessions 2 doctrine that
nothing but matter exists
materialistic adj **materialize** v
come into existence or view
materially adv appreciably
maternal ❶ adj of mother
maternity n motherhood
math n (US & Canad) mathematics
mathematics pl n science of
number, quantity, shape and space
mathematical adj
mathematician n
maths n (Inf) mathematics
matinée n afternoon performance
in theatre
matins pl n morning service
matriarch n mother as head of
family **matriarchal** adj
matriculate v enrol, be enrolled
in college or university
matrimony n marriage

matrimonial adj
matrix n/pl **matrices**
1 substance, situation in which
something originates, is enclosed
2 mould
matron ❶ n 1 married woman
2 woman who superintends
domestic arrangements of public
institution: former name for
NURSING OFFICER
matter ❶ n 1 substance of which
thing is made 2 affair 3 business
4 trouble 5 pus ▷ v 6 be of
importance
mattress n stuffed flat (sprung)
case used as part of bed
mature ❶ adj 1 ripe, completely
developed 2 grown-up ▷ v
3 bring, come to maturity
maturity n
maudlin adj weakly sentimental
maul ❶ v handle roughly
mausoleum n stately building as
a tomb
mauve adj/n pale purple
maverick ❶ n independent,

─────── THESAURUS ───────

stuff; = **cloth**, fabric, textile;
= **information**, details, facts,
notes, evidence ▷ adj = **physical**,
solid, substantial, concrete, bodily;
= **relevant**, important, significant,
essential, vital
maternal adj = **motherly**,
protective, nurturing, maternalistic
matter n = **situation**, concern,
business, question, event;
= **substance**, material, body, stuff
▷ v = **be important**, make a
difference, count, be relevant, make
any difference

mature v = **develop**, grow up,
bloom, blossom, come of age ▷ adj
= **matured**, seasoned, ripe,
mellow; = **grown-up**, adult, of age,
fully fledged, full-grown
≠ **immature**
maul v = **mangle**, claw, lacerate,
tear; = **ill-treat**, abuse, batter,
molest, manhandle
maverick n = **rebel**, radical,
dissenter, individualist, protester
≠ **traditionalist** ▷ adj = **rebel**,
radical, dissenting, individualistic,
eccentric

unorthodox person

maw n stomach

mawkish adj 1 maudlin 2 sickly

maxim n 1 general truth 2 rule of conduct

maximum ❶ adj/n, pl **-mums, -ma** greatest (size or number)

maximize v increase to maximum

may v, past tense **might** expresses possibility, permission, opportunity etc. **maybe** adv 1 perhaps 2 possibly

May n 1 fifth month 2 (without cap.) hawthorn or its flowers

mayfly n short-lived aquatic insect

Mayday n international distress signal

mayhem ❶ n violent destruction

mayonnaise n creamy sauce, esp. for salads

mayor n head of municipality

mayoress n 1 mayor's wife 2 lady mayor

maze ❶ n 1 labyrinth 2 network of paths, lines 3 state of confusion

MBE Member of the Order of the British Empire

MD Doctor of Medicine

me pron object of ı

mead n alcoholic drink made from honey

meadow ❶ n piece of grassland

meagre adj lean, scanty

meal¹ n 1 occasion when food is served and eaten 2 the food

meal² n grain ground to powder

mealy-mouthed adj not outspoken enough

mean¹ ❶ v meaning, meant 1 intend 2 signify 3 have a meaning 4 have the intention of behaving **meaning** n

meaningful adj of great significance

mean² ❶ adj 1 ungenerous, petty 2 miserly 3 callous 4 shabby

mean³ ❶ n 1 middle point ▷ pl 2 that by which thing is done 3 money 4 resources ▷ adj 5 intermediate 6 average

meantime, meanwhile adv/n (during) time between one happening and another

meander v 1 flow windingly 2 wander aimlessly ▷ n

m

maximum adj = **greatest**, highest, supreme, paramount, utmost ≠ **minimal** ▷ n = **top**, peak, ceiling, utmost, upper limit ≠ **minimum**

mayhem n = **chaos**, trouble, violence, disorder, destruction

maze n = **web**, confusion, tangle, labyrinth, imbroglio

meadow n = **field**, pasture, grassland, lea (Poet)

mean¹ v = **signify**, indicate, represent, express, stand for; = **intend**, want, plan, expect, design

mean² adj = **miserly**, stingy, parsimonious, niggardly, mercenary ≠ **generous**; = **dishonourable**, petty, shameful, shabby, vile ≠ **honourable**

mean³ n = **average**, middle, balance, norm, midpoint ▷ adj = **average**, middle, standard

3 wandering course

measles *n* infectious disease producing rash of red spots
measly *adj* (Inf) meagre
measure ❶ *n* **1** size, quantity **2** unit, system of measuring **3** course of action **4** law ▷ *v* **5** ascertain size, quantity of **6** be (so much) in size or quantity **7** indicate measurement of
measurable *adj* **measured** *adj* **1** slow and steady **2** carefully considered **measurement** *n* **1** measuring **2** size
meat ❶ *n* **1** animal flesh as food **2** food **meaty** *adj*
mechanic *n* **1** one who works with machinery ▷ *pl* **2** scientific theory of motion **mechanical** *adj* **1** of, by machine **2** acting without thought
mechanism ❶ *n* **1** structure of machine **2** piece of machinery **3** process, technique
mechanization *n* **mechanize** *v* **1** equip with machinery **2** make automatic
medal *n* piece of metal with inscription etc. used as reward or

memento **medallion** (design like) large medal
meddle *v* interfere
media *n* pl of MEDIUM used esp. of the mass media, radio, television etc.
median *adj/n* middle (point or line)
mediate ❶ *v* intervene to reconcile
mediation *n* **mediator** *n*
medic *n* (Inf) doctor or medical student
medicine ❶ *n* **1** drug or remedy for treating disease **2** science of preventing, curing disease
medical *adj* **medicate** *v* impregnate with medicinal substances **medication** *n* (treatment with) medicinal substance **medicinal** *adj* curative
medieval *adj* of Middle Ages
mediocre ❶ *adj* **1** ordinary, middling **2** second-rate
mediocrity *n* **1** state of being mediocre **2** mediocre person
meditate *v* **1** reflect deeply, esp. on spiritual matters **2** think about, plan **meditation** *n*
medium ❶ *adj* **1** between two qualities, degrees etc. ▷ *n* **2** middle

——————————— THESAURUS ———————————

measure *v* = **quantify**, determine, assess, weigh, calculate ▷ *n* = **quantity**, share, amount, allowance, portion; = **action**, act, step, procedure, means; = **gauge**, rule, scale, metre, ruler; = **law**, act, bill, legislation, resolution
meat *n* = **food**, flesh
mechanism *n* = **process**, way, means, system, operation; = **machine**, device, tool,

instrument, appliance
mediate *v* = **intervene**, step in (Inf), intercede, referee, umpire
medicine *n* = **remedy**, drug, cure, prescription, medication
mediocre *adj* = **second-rate**, average, ordinary, indifferent, middling ≠ **excellent**
medium *adj* = **average**, mean, middle, middling, fair
≠ **extraordinary** ▷ *n*

quality **3** means **4** agency of communicating news etc. to public **5** surroundings

medley n mixture

meek adj submissive, humble

meet ❶ v **meeting, met 1** come face to face (with) **2** satisfy **3** pay **4** converge **5** assemble **6** come into contact **meeting** n

megabyte n (Comp) 1 048 576 bytes

megalith n great stone

megalomania n desire for, delusions of grandeur, power etc. **megalomaniac** adj/n

megaphone n cone-shaped instrument to amplify voice

megaton n explosive power of 1 000 000 tons of TNT

melancholy ❶ n **1** sadness, dejection ▷ adj **2** gloomy, dejected

melanin n dark pigment found in hair, skin etc.

mêlée n confused fight

mellifluous adj (of sound)

smooth, sweet

mellow ❶ adj **1** ripe **2** softened by age, experience **3** not harsh **4** genial ▷ v **5** make, become mellow

melodrama n play full of sensational situations **melodramatic** adj

melody ❶ n, pl **-dies 1** series of musical notes which make tune **2** sweet sound **melodic** adj **melodious** adj

melon n large, fleshy, juicy fruit

melt ❶ v **1** (cause to) become liquid by heat **2** dissolve **3** soften **4** disappear

member ❶ n **1** individual making up body or society **2** limb **3** any part of complex whole **membership** n

membrane n thin flexible tissue in plant or animal body

memento n, pl **-tos, -toes** reminder, souvenir

memo n, pl **memos** short for MEMORANDUM

m

THESAURUS

= **spiritualist**, seer, clairvoyant, fortune teller, channeller; = **middle**, mean, centre, average, compromise

meet v = **encounter**, come across, run into, happen on, find ≠ **avoid**; = **gather**, collect, assemble, get together, come together ≠ **disperse**; = **fulfil**, match (up to), answer, satisfy, discharge ≠ **fall short of**; = **experience**, face, suffer, bear, go through

melancholy adj = **sad**, depressed, miserable, gloomy, glum ≠ **happy** ▷ n = **sadness**, depression, misery,

gloom, sorrow ≠ **happiness**

mellow adj = **full-flavoured**, rich, sweet, delicate; = **ripe**, mature, ripened ≠ **unripe** ▷ v = **relax**, improve, settle, calm, mature

melody n = **tune**, song, theme, air, music; = **tunefulness**, harmony, musicality, euphony, melodiousness

melt v = **dissolve**, run, soften, fuse, thaw; often with away = **disappear**, fade, vanish, dissolve, disperse; = **soften**, relax, disarm, mollify

member n = **representative**,

memoir ❶ n autobiography, personal history

memory ❶ n, pl **-ries 1** faculty of recalling to mind **2** recollection **3** thing remembered **4** commemoration **memorable** adj worthy of remembrance **memorandum** n **1** note to help the memory etc. **2** informal letter **memorial** n **1** thing which serves to keep in memory ▷ adj **2** serving as a memorial **memorize** v commit to memory **memory card** small removable data storage device, used in mobile phones, digital cameras, etc. **memory stick, USB memory stick** (Comp) same as USB DRIVE

men n pl of MAN

menace ❶ n **1** threat ▷ v **2** threaten

menagerie n collection of wild animals

mend ❶ v **1** repair **2** correct, put right **3** improve ▷ n **4** repaired breakage

menial adj **1** requiring little skill **2** servile ▷ n **3** servant

meningitis n inflammation of the membranes of the brain

menopause n final cessation of menstruation

menstruation n monthly discharge of blood from womb **menstrual** adj **menstruate** v

mensuration n measuring

mental ❶ adj **1** of, by the mind **2** (Inf) mad **mentality** n way of thinking

menthol n substance found in peppermint

mention ❶ v **1** refer to briefly ▷ n **2** acknowledgment **3** reference to

mentor ❶ n wise adviser

menu ❶ n list of dishes served

———————————— THESAURUS ————————————

associate, supporter, fellow, subscriber

memoir n = **account**, life, record, journal, essay

memory n = **recall**, mind, retention, ability to remember, powers of recall; = **recollection**, reminder, reminiscence, impression, echo; = **commemoration**, respect, honour, recognition, tribute

menace n (Inf) = **nuisance**, plague, pest, annoyance, troublemaker; = **threat**, warning, intimidation, ill-omen, ominousness ▷ v = **bully**, threaten, intimidate, terrorize, frighten

mend v = **repair**, fix, restore,

renew, patch up; = **darn**, repair, patch, stitch, sew; = **heal**, improve, recover, get better, be all right

mental adj = **intellectual**, rational, theoretical, cognitive, brain; (Inf) = **insane**, mad, disturbed, unstable, mentally ill

mention v = **refer to**, point out, bring up, state, reveal ▷ n often with of = **reference to**, observation, indication, remark on, allusion to; = **acknowledgment**, recognition, tribute, citation, honourable mention

mentor n = **guide**, teacher, coach, adviser, tutor

menu n = **bill of fare**, tariff (chiefly Brit), set menu, table d'hôte, carte

mercantile adj of trade

mercenary adj 1 influenced by greed 2 working merely for reward ▷ n 3 hired soldier

merchant ❶ n 1 one engaged in trade 2 wholesale trader **merchandise** n trader's wares **merchant navy** ships engaged in a nation's commerce

mercury n silvery metal, liquid at ordinary temperature **mercurial** adj lively, changeable

mercy ❶ n, pl -cies 1 refraining from infliction of suffering by one who has right, power to inflict it 2 fortunate occurrence **merciful** adj

mere ❶ adj 1 only 2 nothing but **merely** adv

merge ❶ v (cause to) lose identity or be absorbed **merger** n combination esp. of business firms

meridian n 1 circle of the earth passing through poles 2 highest point

meringue n baked mixture of white of eggs and sugar

merit ❶ n 1 excellence, worth 2 quality of deserving reward ▷ v 3 deserve

mermaid n imaginary sea creature half woman, half fish

merry ❶ adj -rier, -riest joyous, cheerful **merriment** n **merry-go-round** n roundabout

mesh ❶ n 1 (one of the open spaces of, or wires etc. forming) network, net ▷ v 2 (cause to) entangle, engage

mesmerize ❶ v hypnotize

mess ❶ n 1 untidy confusion 2 trouble 3 (place where) group regularly eat together ▷ v 4 potter (about) 5 muddle **messy** adj

message ❶ n 1 communication sent 2 meaning, moral **messenger** n

Messiah n 1 promised saviour 2 Christ

met past tense past participle of MEET

metabolism n chemical process

du jour (Fr)

merchant n = **tradesman**, dealer, trader, broker, retailer

mercy n = **compassion**, pity, forgiveness, grace, kindness ≠ **cruelty**; = **blessing**, boon, godsend

mere adj = **simple**, nothing more than, common, plain, pure

merge v = **combine**, blend, fuse, amalgamate, unite ≠ **separate**

merit n = **advantage**, value, quality, worth, strength ▷ v = **deserve**, warrant, be entitled to, earn, have a right to

merry adj = **cheerful**, happy, carefree, jolly, festive ≠ **gloomy**; (Brit Inf) = **tipsy**, happy, mellow, tiddly (Sl, chiefly Brit), squiffy (Brit Inf)

mesh n = **net**, netting, network, web, tracery ▷ v = **engage**, combine, connect, knit, coordinate

mess n = **untidiness**, disorder, confusion, chaos, litter

message n = **communication**, note, bulletin, word, letter; = **point**, meaning, idea, moral, theme of living body **metabolic** adj

metal n mineral substance, malleable and capable of conducting heat and electricity **metallic** adj **metallurgist** n **metallurgy** n scientific study of metals

metamorphosis n, pl **-phoses** change of shape, character etc.

metaphor ❶ n figure of speech in which term is transferred to something it does not literally apply to **metaphorical** adj

mete v **mete out 1** distribute **2** allot

meteor n small, fast-moving celestial body, visible as streak of incandescence if it enters earth's atmosphere **meteoric** adj **1** of meteor **2** brilliant but short-lived **meteorite** n fallen meteor

meteorology n study of climate, weather **meteorological** adj **meteorologist** n

meter n instrument for recording, measuring

methane n flammable gas, compound of carbon and hydrogen

method ❶ n **1** way, manner **2** technique **3** orderliness **methodical** adj orderly

meths n (Inf) methylated spirits

methylated spirits alcoholic mixture used as fuel etc.

meticulous adj particular about details

metre n **1** unit of length in decimal system **2** SI unit of length **3** rhythm of poem **metric** adj of system of weights and measures in which metre is a unit **metrical** adj **1** of measurement **2** of poetic metre

metronome n instrument which marks musical time by means of ticking pendulum

metropolis n chief city of a region **metropolitan** adj

mettle n courage, spirit

mew n/v (utter) cry of cat

mews pl n (with sing or pl v) yard, street orig. of stables, now oft. converted to houses

mezzanine n intermediate storey, balcony between two main storeys

mezzo-soprano n voice, singer between soprano and contralto

mg milligram

miasma n unwholesome atmosphere

mica n mineral found as glittering scales, plates

microbe n **1** minute organism **2** disease germ

microchip n small wafer of silicon containing electronic circuits

microcosm n miniature representation of larger system

microfiche n microfilm in sheet form

microfilm n miniaturized recording of manuscript, book on roll of film

microphone n instrument for

───────── THESAURUS ─────────

metaphor n = figure of speech, image, symbol, analogy, conceit (Lit)

method n = manner, process, approach, technique, way; = orderliness, planning, order, amplifying, transmitting sounds

microprocessor n integrated circuit acting as central processing unit in small computer

microscope n instrument by which very small body is magnified **microscopic** adj very small

microwave n 1 electromagnetic wave with wavelength of a few centimetres, used in cooking etc. 2 oven using microwaves

mid adj intermediate **midday** n noon **midnight** n twelve o'clock at night **midway** adj/adv halfway

middle ⊙ adj 1 equidistant from two extremes ▷ n 2 middle point or part **middling** adj mediocre 2 moderate **middle age** period of life between youth and old age **middle class** social class of businessmen, professional people etc. **middleman** n trader between producer and consumer **middle-of-the-road** adj moderate

midge n gnat or similar insect

midget n 1 (Offens) very small person 2 very small thing

midriff n middle part of body

midst ⊙ n **in the midst of** 1 surrounded by 2 at a point during

midtown n (US & Canad) the centre of a town

midwife n trained person who assists at childbirth **midwifery** n

mien n person's manner or appearance

might¹ ⊙ n power, strength **mightily** adv **mighty** adj

might² past tense of MAY

migraine n severe headache

migrate ⊙ v move from one place to another **migrant** n/adj **migration** n

mike n (Inf) microphone

mild ⊙ adj 1 not strongly flavoured 2 gentle 3 temperate **mildly** adv

mildew n destructive fungus on plants or things exposed to damp

mile n measure of length, 1760 yards, 1.609 km **mileage** n 1 travelling expenses per mile 2 miles travelled (per gallon of petrol) **mileometer** n device that records miles travelled by vehicle **milestone** n significant event

milieu n, pl **milieux, milieus** environment

militant ⊙ adj 1 aggressive, vigorous in support of cause 2 prepared to fight **militancy** n

m

system, purpose

middle n = **centre**, heart, midst, halfway point, midpoint ▷ adj = **central**, medium, mid, intervening, halfway; = **intermediate**, intervening

might¹ n = **power**, force, energy, strength, vigour

migrate v = **move**, travel, journey, wander, trek

mild adj = **gentle**, calm, easy-going, meek, placid ≠ **harsh**; = **temperate**, warm, calm, moderate, tranquil ≠ **cold**; = **bland**, thin, smooth, tasteless, insipid

militant adj = **aggressive**, active, vigorous, assertive, combative ≠ **peaceful**

military ❶ *adj* **1** of, for, soldiers, armies or war ▷ *n* **2** armed forces **militarism** *n* enthusiasm for military force and methods **militia** *n* military force of citizens for home service

militate *v* (esp. with *against* or *for*) have strong influence, effect on

milk ❶ *n* **1** white fluid with which mammals feed their young **2** fluid in some plants ▷ *v* **3** draw milk from **milky** *adj*

mill ❶ *n* **1** factory **2** machine for grinding, pulverizing corn, paper etc. ▷ *v* **3** put through mill **4** cut fine grooves across edges of (e.g. coins) **5** move in confused manner **miller** *n* **millstone** *n* flat circular stone for grinding

millennium *n/pl* **-nia, -niums** **1** period of a thousand years **2** period of peace, happiness

millet *n* cereal grass

milli- *comb. form* thousandth part of, as in **milligram, millilitre; millimetre**

milliner *n* maker of women's hats

million *n* 1000 thousands **millionaire** *n* owner of a million pounds, dollars etc. **millionth** *adj/n*

millipede *n* small animal with many pairs of legs

mime ❶ *n* acting without words ▷ *v* **2** perform mime

mimic ❶ *v* **-icking, -icked 1** imitate, esp. for satirical effect ▷ *n* **2** one who does this **mimicry** *n*

mimosa *n* plant with fluffy, yellow flowers

minaret *n* tall slender tower of mosque

mince ❶ *v* **1** cut, chop small **2** soften (words etc.) ▷ *n* **3** minced meat **mincer** *n* **mincing** *adj* affected in manner **mincemeat** *n* mixture of currants, spices, suet etc. **mince pie** pie containing mincemeat

mind ❶ *n* **1** intellectual faculties **2** memory **3** intention **4** taste

——————————— THESAURUS ———————————

military *adj* = **warlike**, armed, soldierly, martial ▷ *n* = **armed forces**, forces, services, army

milk *v* = **exploit**, pump, take advantage of

mill *n* = **grinder**, crusher, quern; = **factory**, works, plant, workshop, foundry ▷ *v* = **grind**, pound, crush, powder, grate

mimic *v* = **imitate**, do (*Inf*), take off (*Inf*), ape, parody ▷ *n* = **imitator**, impressionist, copycat (*Inf*), impersonator, caricaturist

mince *v* = **cut**, grind, crumble, dice,

hash; = **tone down**, spare, moderate, weaken, soften

mind *n* = **memory**, recollection, remembrance; = **intelligence**, reason, reasoning, understanding, sense; = **intention**, wish, desire, urge, fancy; = **sanity**, reason, senses, judgment, wits ▷ *v* = **take offence at**, dislike, care about, object to, resent; = **be careful**, watch, take care, be wary, be cautious; = **look after**, watch, protect, tend, guard; = **pay**

5 sanity ▷ v **6** take offence at **7** care for **8** attend to **9** heed

minder n (Sl) bodyguard

mindful adj heedful **mindless** adj **1** stupid **2** requiring no thought **3** careless

mine¹ ❶ n **1** deep hole for digging out coal, metals etc. **2** hidden deposit of explosive to blow up ship etc. **3** profitable source ▷ v **4** dig from mine **5** place explosive mines in, on **miner** n **minefield** n area of land or sea containing mines **minesweeper** n ship for clearing mines

mine² pron belonging to me

mineral n/adj (of) naturally occurring inorganic substance **mineralogy** n science of minerals **mineral water** water containing dissolved mineral salts

minestrone n soup containing vegetables and pasta

mingle ❶ v **1** mix, blend **2** mix socially

mini n **1** something small or miniature **2** short skirt ▷ adj **3** small

miniature ❶ n **1** small painted

portrait **2** anything on small scale ▷ adj **3** on small scale **miniaturize** v make to very small scale

minim n (Mus) note half the length of semibreve

minimum ❶ n/pl -mums, -ma **1** lowest size or quantity ▷ adj **2** least possible **minimal** adj **minimize** v reduce to minimum

minion n servile dependant

minister ❶ n **1** person in charge of department of State **2** diplomatic representative **3** clergyman ▷ v **4** take care of **ministerial** adj **ministration** n rendering help **ministry** n/pl -tries **1** office of clergyman **2** government department

mink n **1** variety of weasel **2** its fur

minnow n small freshwater fish

minor ❶ adj **1** lesser **2** under age ▷ n **3** person below age of legal majority **4** scale in music **minority** n **1** lesser number, group **2** state of being a minor

minster n cathedral, large church

minstrel n medieval singer,

attention to, mark, note, listen to, observe

mine¹ n = **pit**, deposit, shaft, colliery, excavation; = **source**, store, fund, stock, supply ▷ v = **dig up**, extract, quarry, unearth, excavate

mingle v = **mix**, combine, blend, merge, unite ≠ **separate**; = **associate**, consort, socialize, rub shoulders (Inf), hobnob ≠ **dissociate**

miniature adj = **small**, little, minute, tiny, toy ≠ **giant**

minimum ❶ n = **lowest**, smallest, least, slightest, minimal ≠ **maximum** ▷ n = **lowest**, least, lowest level, nadir

minister n = **clergyman**, priest, vicar, parson, preacher ▷ v often with **to** = **attend**, serve, tend, take care of, cater to

minor adj = **small**, lesser, slight, petty, trivial ≠ **major**

musician, poet

mint¹ ❶ n 1 place where money is coined ▷ adj 2 brand-new ▷ v 3 coin, invent

mint² n aromatic plant

minuet n stately dance

minus prep/adj 1 less 2 lacking 3 negative ▷ n 4 the sign of subtraction (-)

minuscule adj very small

minute¹ ❶ n 1 60th part of hour or degree ▷ pl 2 record of proceedings of meeting etc.

minute² ❶ adj 1 very small 2 precise

minx n bold, flirtatious woman

miracle ❶ n 1 supernatural event 2 marvel **miraculous** adj

mirage n deceptive image in atmosphere

mire n swampy ground, mud

mirror ❶ n 1 glass or polished surface reflecting images ▷ v 2 reflect in or as if in mirror

mirth n merriment, gaiety

mis- comb. form wrong, bad

misadventure n unlucky chance

misanthrope n hater of mankind

misapprehension n misunderstanding

misappropriate v 1 put to dishonest use 2 embezzle

miscellaneous adj mixed **miscellany** n medley

mischief n 1 annoying behaviour 2 inclination to tease 3 harm, annoyance **mischievous** adj

misconception n wrong idea

misconduct ❶ n unethical behaviour

miscreant n evildoer

misdemeanour n minor offence

miser n hoarder of money

miserable ❶ adj 1 very unhappy 2 causing misery 3 worthless 4 squalid **misery** n, pl **-eries**

misfire v fail to fire, start etc.

misfit n person not suited to environment

misfortune ❶ n (piece of) bad luck

misgiving n (oft. pl) feeling of fear, doubt etc.

— THESAURUS —

mint¹ v = **make**, produce, strike, cast, stamp

minute¹ n = **moment**, second, bit, flash, instant

minute² adj = **small**, little, tiny, miniature, microscopic ≠ **huge**; = **precise**, close, detailed, critical, exact ≠ **imprecise**

miracle n = **wonder**, phenomenon, sensation, marvel, amazing achievement

mirror n = **looking-glass**, glass

(Brit), reflector ▷ v = **reflect**, follow, copy, echo, emulate

misconduct n = **immorality**, wrongdoing, mismanagement, malpractice, impropriety

miserable adj ≠ **happy**; = **pathetic**, sorry, shameful, despicable, deplorable ≠ **respectable**

misfortune n often plural = **bad luck**, adversity, hard luck, ill luck, infelicity

misguided ❶ adj foolish

mishap n minor accident

misjudge v judge wrongly

mislay v put in place which cannot later be remembered

mislead ❶ v give false information to

mismanage v organize badly

misnomer n wrong name or term

misogyny n hatred of women **misogynist** n

misprint n printing error

miss v 1 fail to hit, reach, catch etc. 2 not be in time for 3 notice or regret absence of 4 avoid 5 omit ▷ n 6 fact, instance of missing **missing** adj lost, absent

Miss n 1 title of unmarried woman 2 (without cap.) girl

missal n book containing prayers, rites etc.

missile ❶ n that which may be thrown, shot etc. to damage or destroy

mission ❶ n 1 specific duty 2 delegation 3 those sent **missionary** n/pl **-aries** one sent to a place, society to spread religion

missive n letter

mist ❶ n water vapour in fine drops **misty** adj

mistake ❶ n 1 error ▷ v 2 fail to understand 3 take (person or thing) for another **mistaken** adj

mistletoe n evergreen parasitic plant

mistress ❶ n 1 illicit lover of married man 2 woman with mastery or control 3 title formerly given to married woman

mistrust v 1 not trust ▷ n 2 lack of trust

misunderstand ❶ v fail to understand properly **misunderstanding** n

misuse ❶ n 1 incorrect use ▷ v 2 use wrongly 3 treat badly

mite n 1 very small insect 2 anything very small

mitigate v make less severe **mitigation** n

mitre n 1 bishop's headdress 2 right-angled joint

mitt n covering for hand

mitten n glove with one compartment for thumb and

m

— THESAURUS —

misguided adj = **unwise**, mistaken, misplaced, deluded, ill-advised

mislead v = **deceive**, fool, delude, take someone in (Inf), misdirect

missile n = **projectile**, weapon, shell, rocket

mission n = **task**, job, commission, duty, undertaking

mist n = **fog**, cloud, steam, spray, film

mistake n = **error**, blunder, oversight, slip, gaffe ▷ v = **confuse with**, take for, mix up with; = **misunderstand**, misinterpret, misjudge, misread, misconstrue

mistress n = **lover**, girlfriend, concubine, kept woman, paramour

misunderstand v = **misinterpret**, misread, mistake, misjudge, misconstrue

misuse n = **waste**, squandering, desecration ▷ v = **abuse**, misapply, prostitute another for fingers

mix ❶ v **1** put together, combine, blend **2** be mixed **3** associate **mixed** adj of different elements, races etc. **mixer** n **mixture** n **mix-up** n confused situation

mm millimetre

mnemonic n something to help the memory

moan ❶ v/n (utter) low murmur, usually of pain

moat n deep wide ditch, esp. round castle

mob ❶ n **1** disorderly crowd ▷ v **2** attack in mob, hustle

mobile ❶ adj **1** capable of movement **2** easily changed ▷ n **3** hanging structure designed to move in air currents **mobility** n

mobilize ❶ v prepare, esp. for military service **mobilization** n

moccasin n Amer. Indian soft shoe, usu. of deerskin

mocha n **1** strong dark coffee **2** flavouring of coffee and chocolate

mock ❶ v **1** ridicule **2** mimic ▷ adj **3** sham **mockery** n **1** derision **2** travesty

mode ❶ n **1** manner **2** prevailing fashion **modish** adj fashionable

model ❶ n **1** miniature representation **2** pattern **3** one worthy of imitation **4** person employed to pose, or display clothing ▷ adj **5** made as (miniature) copy **6** exemplary ▷ v **7** make model of **8** mould **9** display (clothing)

modem n device for connecting two computers by telephone line

moderate ❶ adj **1** not going to extremes ▷ n **2** person of

mix v = **combine**, blend, merge, join, cross; = **socialize**, associate, hang out (Inf), mingle, circulate ▷ n = **mixture**, combination, blend, fusion, compound

moan v = **groan**, sigh, sob, whine, lament; (Inf) = **grumble**, complain, groan, whine, carp ▷ n = **groan**, sigh, sob, lament, wail; (Inf) = **complaint**, protest, grumble, whine, grouse

mob n = **crowd**, pack, mass, host, drove; (Sl) = **gang**, group, set, lot, crew (Inf) ▷ v = **surround**, besiege, jostle, fall on, set upon

mobile adj = **movable**, moving, travelling, wandering, portable

mobilize v = **rally**, organize, stimulate, excite, prompt;

= **deploy**, prepare, ready, rally, assemble

mock v = **laugh at**, tease, ridicule, taunt, scorn ≠ **respect** ▷ adj = **imitation**, false, artificial, fake, false ≠ **genuine**

mode n = **method**, way, system, form, process; = **fashion**, style, trend, rage, vogue

model n = **representation**, image, copy, miniature, dummy; = **pattern**, example, standard, original, ideal; = **sitter**, subject, poser, wear, display, sport ▷ v = **shape**, form, design, fashion, carve

moderate adj = **mild**, reasonable, controlled, limited, steady ≠ **extreme**; = **average**, middling, fair, ordinary, indifferent ▷ v moderate views ▷ v **3** make, become less excessive **4** preside over **moderation** n **moderator** n arbitrator

modern ❶ adj **1** of present or recent times **2** in, of current fashion **modernity** n **modernize** v bring up to date

modest ❶ adj **1** not overrating one's qualities or achievements **2** moderate, decent **modesty** n

modicum n small quantity

modify ❶ v **-fying, -fied** change slightly **modification** n

modulate v **1** regulate **2** vary in tone **modulation** n

module n (detachable) component with specific function

mogul ❶ n powerful person

mohair n cloth of goat's hair

moist ❶ adj slightly wet **moisten** v **moisture** n liquid, esp. diffused or in drops

molar n/adj (tooth) for grinding

molasses n syrup, by-product of sugar refining

mole¹ n small dark spot on skin

mole² n small burrowing animal

molecule n simplest freely existing chemical unit **molecular** adj

molest v pester, interfere with so as to annoy or injure

moll n (Sl) gangster's female accomplice

mollify v **-fying, -fied** calm down, placate **mollification** n

mollusc n soft-bodied, usu. hard-shelled animal, e.g. snail

mollycoddle v pamper

molten SEE MELT

mom n (chiefly US and Canad) an informal word for MOTHER

moment ❶ n short space of, (present) point in, time **momentarily** adv **momentary** adj lasting only a moment

momentous ❶ adj of great importance

momentum ❶ n **1** force of a moving body **2** impetus gained from motion

—— THESAURUS ——

= **soften**, control, temper, regulate, curb

modern adj = **current**, contemporary, recent, present-day, latter-day; = **up-to-date**, fresh, new, novel, newfangled ≠ **old-fashioned**

modest adj = **moderate**, small, limited, fair, ordinary; = **unpretentious**, reserved, retiring, shy, coy

modify v = **change**, reform, convert, alter, adjust; = **tone down**, lower, qualify, ease, moderate

mogul n = **tycoon**, baron, magnate, big shot (Inf), big noise (Inf)

moist adj = **damp**, wet, soggy, humid, clammy

molecule n = **particle**, jot, speck

moment n = **instant**, second, flash, twinkling, split second; = **time**, point, stage, juncture

momentous adj = **significant**, important, vital, critical, crucial ≠ **unimportant**

momentum n = **impetus**, force, power, drive, push

m

monarch ❶ n sovereign ruler
monarchist n supporter of
monarchy **monarchy** n 1 state
ruled by sovereign 2 government
by sovereign

monastery ❶ n, pl **-teries** house
occupied by religious order
monastic adj

Monday n second day of the
week

money ❶ n banknotes, coins etc.,
used as medium of exchange
monetary adj **moneyed, monied**
adj rich

mongoose n, pl **-gooses** small
animal of Asia and Africa

mongrel n/adj 1 (animal) of mixed
breed 2 hybrid

monitor ❶ n 1 person or device
which checks, controls, warns,
records 2 pupil assisting teacher
with odd jobs 3 type of large lizard
▷ v 4 watch, check on

monk ❶ n one of a religious
community of men living apart
under vows

monkey ❶ n 1 long-tailed
primate 2 mischievous child ▷ v
3 meddle with

mono- comb. form single, as in
monosyllabic

monochrome adj of one colour

monocle n single eyeglass

monogamy n custom of being
married to one person at a time

monogram n design of letters
interwVn

monograph n short book on
single subject

monolith n large upright block of
stone **monolithic** adj

monologue n long speech by one
person

monopoly n exclusive possession
of trade, privilege etc. **monopolize**
v claim, take exclusive possession
of

monotone n speech on one note
monotonous adj lacking variety,
dull **monotony** n

monsoon n 1 seasonal wind of SE
Asia 2 very heavy rainfall season

monster ❶ n 1 fantastic
imaginary beast 2 huge or
misshapen person, animal or thing
▷ adj 3 huge **monstrosity** n
1 monstrous being 2 deformity
monstrous adj 1 horrible
2 shocking 3 enormous

month n one of twelve periods into
which the year is divided **monthly**
adj/adv once a month

THESAURUS

monarch n = **ruler**, king or queen,
sovereign, tsar, potentate

monastery n = **abbey**, convent,
priory, cloister, nunnery

money n = **cash**, capital, currency,
hard cash, readies (Inf)

monitor v = **check**, follow, watch,
survey, observe ▷ n = **guide**,
observer, supervisor, invigilator;

= **prefect** (Brit), head girl, head boy,
senior boy, senior girl

monk n = **friar**, brother

monkey n = **simian**, ape, primate;
= **rascal**, horror, devil, rogue, imp

monster n = **giant**, mammoth,
titan, colossus, monstrosity;
= **brute**, devil, beast, demon/villain
▷ adj = **huge**, massive, enormous,

monument ❶ n anything that commemorates, esp. a building or statue **monumental** adj

mooch v (Sl) loaf, slouch

mood¹ ❶ n 1 state of mind and feelings 2 sulk **moody** adj 1 gloomy 2 changeable in mood

mood² n (Grammar) form indicating function of verb

moon ❶ n 1 satellite which revolves round earth 2 any secondary planet ▷ v 3 go about dreamily **moonlight** n

moor¹ ❶ n tract of open uncultivated land **moorhen** n small black water bird

moor² ❶ v secure (ship) with chains or ropes **moorings** pl n ropes etc. for mooring

moose n N Amer. deer

moot adj debatable

mop ❶ n 1 yarn, cloth etc. on end of stick, used for cleaning 2 tangle (of hair etc.) ▷ v 3 clean, wipe as with mop

mope v be gloomy, apathetic

moped n light motorized bicycle

moral ❶ adj 1 pert. to right and wrong conduct 2 of good conduct ▷ n 3 practical lesson, e.g. of fable ▷ pl 4 habits with respect to right and wrong **morality** n 1 good moral conduct 2 moral goodness or badness **moralize** v write, think about moral aspect of things

morale ❶ n degree of confidence, hope

morass n 1 marsh 2 mess

moratorium ❶ n, pl **-ria, -riums** authorized postponement of payments etc.

morbid adj 1 unduly interested in death 2 gruesome 3 diseased

mordant adj 1 biting 2 corrosive

more ❶ adj, pron 1 greater or additional (amount or number): comparative of MANY and MUCH adv 2 to a greater extent 3 in addition **moreover** adv besides

mores pl n customs and conventions of society

morgue n mortuary

moribund adj 1 dying 2 without force or vitality

tremendous, immense

monument n = **memorial**, cairn, marker, shrine, tombstone

mood¹ n = **state of mind**, spirit, humour, temper, disposition

moon v = **idle**, drift, loaf, languish, waste time

moor¹ n = **moorland**, fell (Brit), heath

moor² v = **tie up**, secure, anchor, dock, lash

mop n = **squeegee**, sponge, swab; = **mane**, shock, mass, tangle, mat

moral adj = **good**, just, right, principled, decent ≠ **immoral** ▷ n = **lesson**, meaning, point, message, teaching

morale n = **confidence**, heart, spirit, self-esteem, team spirit

moratorium n = **postponement**, freeze, halt, suspension, standstill

more adj = **extra**, additional, new, other, added ▷ adv = **to a greater extent**, longer, better, further, some more

morning ❶ n early part of day until noon **morn** n (Poet) morning

moron n (Offens) mentally deficient person

morose adj sullen, moody

morphine, morphia n extract of opium used to relieve pain

morrow n (Poet) next day

Morse n telegraphic signalling in which letters are represented by dots and dashes

morsel n small piece

mortal ❶ adj 1 subject to death 2 causing death ▷ n 3 mortal creature **mortality** n 1 state of being mortal 2 death rate 3 great loss of life

mortar n 1 mixture of lime, sand and water for holding bricks together 2 small cannon 3 vessel in which substances are pounded **mortarboard** n square academic cap

mortgage n 1 conveyance of property as security for debt ▷ v 2 pledge as security

mortify v **-fying, -fied** 1 humiliate 2 subdue by self-denial 3 (of flesh) be affected with gangrene **mortification** n

mortuary n/pl **-aries** building where corpses are kept before

burial or cremation

mosaic n picture or pattern of small bits of coloured stone, glass etc.

mosque n Muslim temple

mosquito n/pl **-toes, -tos** flying, biting insect

moss n small plant growing in masses on moist surfaces **mossy** adj

most adj/n 1 (of) greatest number, amount or degree: superlative of MUCH and MANY adv 2 in the greatest degree **mostly** adv generally

motel n roadside hotel for motorists

moth n usu. nocturnal insect like butterfly **mothball** n 1 small ball of chemical to repel moths from stored clothing etc. ▷ v 2 store, postpone **moth-eaten** adj 1 damaged by grub of moth 2 scruffy

mother ❶ n 1 female parent 2 head of religious community of women ▷ adj 3 inborn ▷ v 4 act as mother to **motherhood** n **motherly** adj **mother-in-law** n mother of one's wife or husband **mother of pearl** iridescent lining of certain shells

motif ❶ n dominating theme

morning n = before noon, forenoon, morn (Poet), a.m.

mortal adj = human, worldly, passing, fleshly, temporal; = fatal, killing, terminal, deadly, destructive ▷ n = human being, being, man, woman, person

mother n = female parent, mum (Brit Inf), ma (Inf), mater, dam ▷ v = nurture, raise, protect, tend, nurse ▷ adj = native, natural, innate, inborn

motif n = design, shape, decoration, ornament; = theme,

motion ❶ n 1 process or action or way of moving 2 proposal in meeting ▷ v 3 direct by sign

motive ❶ n that which makes person act in particular way **motivate** v incite **motivation** n

motley adj 1 varied 2 multicoloured

motocross n motorcycle race over rough course

motor n 1 that which imparts movement 2 machine to supply power to move ▷ v 3 travel by car **motorist n motorhome** n large motor vehicle designed for living in while travelling **motorize** v equip with a motor or motor transport **motorbike, motorcycle** n **motorcar** n **motorway** n main road for fast-moving traffic

mottled adj marked with blotches

motto ❶ n, pl **-toes, -tos** saying adopted as rule of conduct

mould¹ ❶ n 1 hollow object in which metal etc. is cast 2 character 3 shape ▷ v 4 shape

moulding n ornamental edging

mould² ❶ n fungoid growth caused by dampness **mouldy** adj

mould³ n loose or surface earth **moulder** v decay

moult v 1 cast or shed fur, feathers etc. ▷ n 2 moulting

mound ❶ n 1 heap 2 small hill

mount ❶ v 1 rise 2 increase 3 get on (horse) 4 frame (picture) 5 set up ▷ n 6 support 7 horse 8 hill

mountain ❶ n hill of great size **mountaineer** n one who lives among or climbs mountains **mountainous** adj **mountain bike** bicycle with straight handlebars and heavy-duty tyres

mountebank n charlatan, fake

Mountie n (Inf) a member of the Royal Canadian Mounted Police

mourn ❶ v feel, show sorrow (for)

m

———— THESAURUS ————

idea, subject, concept, leitmotif

motion n = **movement**, mobility, travel, progress, flow; = **proposal**, suggestion, recommendation, proposition, submission ▷ v = **gesture**, direct, wave, signal, nod

motive n = **reason**, ground(s), purpose, object, incentive

motto n = **saying**, slogan, maxim, rule, adage

mould¹ n = **cast**, shape, pattern; = **design**, style, fashion, build, form; = **nature**, character, sort, kind, quality ▷ v = **shape**, make, work, form, create; = **influence**, make, form, control, direct

mould² n = **fungus**, blight, mildew

mound n = **heap**, pile, drift, stack, rick; = **hill**, bank, rise, dune, embankment

mount v = **increase**, build, grow, swell, intensify ≠ **decrease**; = **accumulate**, increase, collect, gather, build up; = **ascend**, scale, climb (up), go up, clamber up ≠ **descend** ▷ n = **horse**, steed (Lit); = **backing**, setting, support, stand, base

mountain n = **peak**, mount, horn, ridge, fell (Brit); = **heap**, mass, masses, pile, a great deal

mourn v often with **for** = **grieve for**,

mourner n **mournful** adj **1** sad
2 dismal **mourning** n **1** grieving
2 clothes of mourner

mouse n, pl **mice** small rodent
mousy adj like mouse, esp. in
colour

mousse n dish of flavoured cream

moustache n hair on upper lip

mouth ❶ n **1** opening in head for
eating, speaking etc. **2** opening,
entrance ▷ v **3** form (words) with
lips without speaking **mouth
organ** small musical instrument
mouthpiece n end of anything
placed between lips

move ❶ v **1** change position, place
2 (cause to) be in motion **3** stir
emotions of **4** incite **5** propose
6 change one's dwelling etc. ▷ n
7 a moving **8** motion **movement**
n **1** moving **2** moving parts
3 group with common aim
4 division of piece of music **movie**
n (Inf) film

mow ❶ v **mowing, mowed** cut
(grass etc.) **mower** n

MP 1 Member of Parliament
2 Military Police

mph miles per hour

much ❶ adj **more, most**
1 existing in quantity ▷ n **2** large
amount **3** important matter ▷ adv
4 in a great degree **5** nearly

muck ❶ n **1** dung **2** dirt **mucky**
adj

mucus n fluid secreted by mucous
membranes

mud ❶ n wet and soft earth
muddy adj **mudguard** n cover
over wheel **mudpack** n cosmetic
paste to improve complexion

muddle ❶ v **1** (esp. with up)
confuse **2** bewilder **3** mismanage
▷ n **4** confusion

muesli n mixture of grain, nuts,
dried fruit etc.

muff¹ n tube-shaped covering to
keep hands warm

muff² v bungle, fail in

muffin n light round yeast cake

muffle v wrap up, esp. to deaden
sound **muffler** n scarf

lament, weep for, wail for

mouth n = **lips**, jaws, gob (Sl, esp.
Brit), maw, cakehole (Brit Sl);
= **entrance**, opening, gateway,
door, aperture; = **inlet**, outlet,
estuary, firth, outfall

move v = **transfer**, change, switch,
shift, transpose; = **go**, advance,
progress, shift, proceed; = **relocate**,
leave, remove, quit, migrate;
= **drive**, cause, influence, persuade,
shift ≠ **discourage**; = **touch**, affect,
excite, impress, stir; = **propose**,
suggest, urge, recommend, request

▷ n = **action**, step, manoeuvre;
= **ploy**, action, measure, step,
initiative

mow v = **cut**, crop, trim, shear,
scythe

much adv = **greatly**, a lot,
considerably, decidedly, exceedingly
≠ **hardly**

muck n = **dirt**, mud, filth, ooze,
sludge; = **manure**, dung, ordure

mud n = **dirt**, clay, ooze, silt,
sludge

muddle n = **confusion**, mess,
disorder, chaos, tangle ▷ v

mug¹ ❶ n drinking cup

mug² ❶ n (Sl) 1 face 2 (Sl) fool, simpleton ▷ v 3 rob violently **mugger** n

mug³ v **mugging, mugged** (Inf) (esp. with up) study hard

muggy adj **-gier, -giest** damp and stifling

mulberry n tree whose leaves are used to feed silkworms

mulch n 1 straw, leaves etc. spread as protection for roots of plants ▷ v 2 protect thus

mule n 1 cross between horse and ass 2 hybrid **mulish** adj obstinate

mull v 1 heat (wine) with sugar and spices 2 think (over)

multi- comb. form many, as in multistorey

multifarious adj of various kinds or parts

multiple ❶ adj 1 having many parts ▷ n 2 quantity which contains another an exact number of times **multiplication** n **multiplicity** n variety, greatness in number **multiply** v 1 (cause to)

increase 2 combine (two numbers) by multiplication 3 increase by reproduction

multitude ❶ n great number

mum n (Inf) mother

mumble v speak indistinctly

mummy¹ n, pl **-mies** embalmed body **mummify** v

mummy² n (Inf) mother

mumps pl n infectious disease marked by swelling in neck

munch v chew vigorously

mundane ❶ adj 1 ordinary, everyday 2 earthly

municipal ❶ adj belonging to affairs of city or town **municipality** n city or town with self-government

munificent adj very generous **munificence** n

munted adj (NZ Sl) 1 destroyed or ruined 2 abnormal or peculiar

mural n painting on wall

murder ❶ n 1 unlawful premeditated killing of human being ▷ v 2 kill thus **murderer** n **murderous** adj

murk n darkness **murky** adj

m

= **jumble**, disorder, scramble, tangle, mix up; = **confuse**, bewilder, daze, confound, perplex

mug¹ n = **cup**, pot, beaker, tankard

mug² n = **face**, features, countenance, visage; = **fool**, sucker (Sl), chump (Inf), simpleton, easy or soft touch (Sl)

multiple adj = **many**, several, various, numerous, sundry

multitude n = **great number**,

host, army, mass, horde

mundane adj = **ordinary**, routine, commonplace, banal, everyday ≠ **extraordinary**; = **earthly**, worldly, secular, mortal, terrestrial ≠ **spiritual**

municipal adj = **civic**, public, local, council, district

murder n = **killing**, homicide, massacre, assassination, slaying ▷ v = **kill**, massacre, slaughter, assassinate, eliminate (Sl)

murmur ⊕ *n* -muring, -mured
1 low, indistinct sound ▷ *v* 2 make,
utter such a sound 3 complain

muscle ⊕ *n* 1 part of body which
produces movement by contracting
2 system of muscles **muscular** *adj*
1 strong 2 of muscle

muse ⊕ *v* 1 ponder 2 be lost in
thought ▷ *n* 3 musing 4 reverie
5 goddess inspiring creative artist

museum *n* (place housing)
collection of historical etc. objects

mush¹ *n* soft pulpy mass **mushy**
adj

mush² *interj* order to dogs in sled
team to advance

mushroom *n* 1 fungoid growth,
typically with stem and cap ▷ *v*
2 shoot up rapidly

music *n* 1 art form using
harmonious combination of notes
2 composition in this art **musical**
adj 1 of, like, interested in music
▷ *n* 2 show, film in which music
plays essential part **musician** *n*

musk *n* scent obtained from gland
of deer **musky** *adj* **muskrat** *n*
1 N Amer. rodent found near water
2 its fur

muskeg *n* (Canad) bog or swamp

musket *n* (Hist) infantryman's gun

Muslim, Moslem *n* 1 follower of

religion of Islam ▷ *adj* 2 of Islam

muslin *n* fine cotton fabric

muss *v* (US & Canad, Inf) to make
untidy

mussel *n* bivalve shellfish

must ⊕ *v* 1 be obliged to, or
certain to ▷ *n* 2 necessity

mustang *n* wild horse

mustard *n* powder made from the
seeds of a plant, used in paste as a
condiment

muster ⊕ *v* 1 assemble ▷ *n*
2 assembly, esp. for exercise,
inspection

musty *adj* **mustier, mustiest**
mouldy, stale

mute ⊕ *adj* 1 (Offens) unable to
speak 2 silent ▷ *n* 3 (Mus)
contrivance to soften tone of
instruments **muted** *adj* 1 muffled
2 subdued

mutilate *v* 1 deprive of a limb etc.
2 damage

mutiny *n, pl* -nies 1 rebellion
against authority, esp. against
officers of disciplined body ▷ *v*
2 commit mutiny **mutineer** *n*
mutinous *adj*

mutter ⊕ *v* 1 speak, utter
indistinctly 2 grumble ▷ *n*
3 muttered sound

mutton *n* flesh of sheep used as food

———————— THESAURUS ————————

murmur *v* = **mumble**, whisper,
mutter ▷ *n* = **whisper**, drone, purr

muscle *n* = **tendon**, sinew;
= **strength**, might, power, weight,
stamina

muse *v* = **ponder**, consider, reflect,
contemplate, deliberate

must *n* = **necessity**, essential,

requirement, fundamental,
imperative

muster *v* = **summon up**, marshal
▷ *n* = **assembly**, meeting,
collection, gathering, rally

mute *v* = **silent**, dumb,
unspoken, tacit, wordless

mutter *v* = **grumble**, complain,

mutual ❶ adj 1 done, possessed etc. by each of two with respect to the other 2 (Inf) common

muzzle n 1 mouth and nose of animal 2 cover for these to prevent biting 3 open end of gun ▷ v 4 put muzzle on

muzzy adj -zier, -ziest indistinct, confused

my adj belonging to me **myself** pron emphatic or reflexive form of I

mynah n Indian bird related to starling

myopia n short-sightedness **myopic** adj

myriad ❶ adj 1 innumerable ▷ n 2 large number

myrrh n aromatic gum, formerly used as incense

myrtle n flowering evergreen shrub

myself see MY

mystery ❶ n, pl -teries 1 obscure or secret thing 2 anything strange or inexplicable **mysterious** adj

mystic ❶ n one who seeks divine, spiritual knowledge, esp. by prayer, contemplation etc. **mystical** adj

mystify v -fying, -fied bewilder, puzzle

mystique n aura of mystery, power etc.

myth ❶ n 1 tale with supernatural characters or events 2 imaginary person or object **mythical** adj **mythology** n myths collectively

myxomatosis n contagious, fatal disease of rabbits

—— THESAURUS ——

murmur, rumble, whine

mutual adj = **shared**, common, joint, returned, reciprocal

myriad n = **multitude**, host, army, swarm, horde ▷ adj = **innumerable**, countless, untold, incalculable, immeasurable

mystery n = **puzzle**, problem, question, secret, riddle

mystical adj = **supernatural**, mysterious, transcendental, occult, metaphysical

myth n = **legend**, story, fiction, saga, fable; = **illusion**, story, fancy, fantasy, imagination

m

n

nadir n lowest point

naff adj (Sl) inferior or useless

nag¹ ❶ v **nagging, nagged**
1 scold or trouble constantly ▷ n
2 nagging 3 one who nags

nag² ❷ n (Inf) horse

nail ❶ n 1 horny shield at ends of
fingers, toes 2 small metal spike for
fixing wood etc. ▷ v 3 fix with nails

naive, naïve ❶ adj simple,
unaffected, ingenuous **naiveté,
naivety** n

naked ❶ adj 1 without clothes
2 exposed, bare 3 undisguised

name ❶ n 1 word by which
person, thing etc. is denoted
2 reputation ▷ v 3 give name to
4 call by name 5 appoint
6 mention **nameless** adj
1 without a name 2 unknown
3 indescribable **namely** adv that
is to say **namesake** n person with
same name as another

nanny n, pl **-nies** child's nurse
nanny goat she-goat

nap¹ ❶ v 1 take short sleep ▷ n
2 short sleep

nap² ❷ n downy surface on cloth
made by projecting fibres

nape n back of neck

napkin ❶ n 1 cloth, paper for
wiping fingers or lips at table
2 nappy

nappy n, pl **-pies** towelling cloth
to absorb baby's excrement

narcissism n abnormal
admiration for oneself

narcissus n, pl **-cissi** genus
of bulbous plants including
daffodil, esp. one with white
flowers

────────── THESAURUS ──────────

nab v = **catch**, arrest, apprehend,
seize, grab

nag¹ v = **scold**, harass, badger,
pester, worry ▷ n = **scold**,
complainer, grumbler, virago,
shrew

nag² n = **horse** (US), hack

nail v = **fasten**, fix, secure, attach,
pin

naive, naïve adj = **gullible**,
trusting, credulous, unsuspicious,
green ≠ **worldly**

naked adj = **nude**, stripped,
exposed, bare, undressed
≠ **dressed**

name n = **title**, nickname,
designation, term, handle (Sl) ▷ v
= **call**, christen, baptize, dub, term;
= **nominate**, choose, select,
appoint, specify

nap¹ v = **sleep**, rest, kip (Brit Sl),
siesta, catnap ▷ v = **sleep**, rest,
drop off (Inf), doze, kip (Brit Sl)

nap² n = **pile**, down, fibre, weave,
grain

napkin n = **serviette**, cloth

DICTIONARY

narcotic ❶ n/adj (drug) producing numbness and stupor

nark v (Sl) annoy, irritate

narrate v tell (story) **narration** n **narrative** n account, story **narrator** n

narrow ❶ adj 1 of little breadth 2 limited ▷ v 3 make, become narrow **narrow-minded** adj 1 illiberal 2 bigoted

nasal adj 1 of nose ▷ n 2 sound partly produced in nose

nasturtium n garden plant with red or orange flowers

nasty ❶ adj -tier, -tiest 1 foul, unpleasant 2 spiteful

nation ❶ n people or race organized as a state **national** adj 1 of, characteristic of, a nation ▷ n 2 citizen **nationalism** n 1 devotion to one's country 2 movement for independence **nationalist** n/adj **nationality** n fact of belonging to a particular nation **nationalization** n acquisition and management of

industries by the state **nationalize** v **National Health Service** system of medical services financed mainly by taxation **national service** compulsory military service

native ❶ adj 1 inborn 2 born in particular place ▷ n 3 native person, animal or plant

NATO North Atlantic Treaty Organization

natter (Inf) ▷ v 1 talk idly ▷ n 2 idle talk

natty adj -tier, -tiest neat and smart

nature ❶ n 1 innate qualities of person or thing 2 class, sort 3 (oft. with cap.) power underlying all phenomena 4 natural unspoilt scenery **natural** adj 1 of nature 2 inborn 3 normal 4 unaffected ▷ v 5 something, somebody well suited for something 6 (Mus) character used to remove effect of sharp or flat preceding it **naturalist** n one who studies

THESAURUS

narcotic adj = **sedative**, calming, hypnotic, analgesic, soporific

narrow adj = **thin**, fine, slim, slender, tapering ≠ **broad**; = **limited**, restricted, confined, tight, close ≠ **wide**; = **insular**, prejudiced, partial, dogmatic, intolerant ≠ **broad-minded** ▷ v = **restrict**, limit, reduce, constrict

nasty adj = **unpleasant**, ugly, disagreeable ≠ **pleasant**; = **spiteful**, mean, offensive, vicious, unpleasant ≠ **pleasant**;

= **disgusting**, unpleasant, offensive, vile, distasteful

nation n = **country**, state, realm

native adj = **mother**, indigenous, vernacular, local, indigenous, home ▷ n = **inhabitant**, national, resident, citizen, countryman

nature n = **creation**, world, earth, environment, universe; = **quality**, character, make-up, constitution, essence; = **temperament**, character, personality, disposition, outlook

n

animals and plants **naturalize** v
admit to citizenship **naturally** adv

naturism ① n nudism

naughty ① adj **-tier, -tiest**
1 disobedient 2 (Inf) mildly indecent

nausea ① n feeling that precedes
vomiting **nauseate** v sicken
nauseous adj

nautical adj of seamen or ships
nautical mile 1852 metres

nave n main part of church

navel n small depression in
abdomen where umbilical cord was
attached

navigate v 1 direct, plot path of
ship etc. 2 travel **navigable** adj
navigation n **navigator** n

navvy n, pl **-vies** labourer
employed on roads, railways etc.

navy ① n, pl **-vies** 1 fleet
2 warships of country with their
crews ▷ adj 3 navy-blue **naval** adj
of the navy **navy-blue** adj very
dark blue

nay adv (Obs) no

NB note well

near ① prep 1 close to ▷ adv 2 at

or to a short distance ▷ adj 3 close
at hand 4 closely related 5 stingy
▷ v 6 approach **nearby** adj
adjacent **nearly** adv 1 closely
2 almost **nearside** n side of
vehicle nearer kerb

neat ① adj 1 tidy, orderly 2 deft
3 undiluted 4 (US & Canad) good or
pleasing

nebulous adj vague

necessary ① adj 1 that must be
done 2 inevitable ▷ n 3 what is
needed **necessarily** adv
necessitate v make necessary
necessity n 1 something needed
2 constraining power
3 compulsion 4 poverty

neck n 1 part of body joining head
to shoulders 2 narrow part of
anything **neckerchief** n cloth tied
round the neck **necklace** n
ornament round the neck

nectar n honey of flowers

nectarine n variety of peach

née adj indicating maiden name of
married woman

need ① v 1 want, require ▷ n

naughty adj = disobedient, bad,
mischievous, badly behaved,
wayward ≠ **good**; = obscene,
vulgar, improper, lewd, risqué
≠ **clean**

nausea n = sickness, vomiting,
retching, squeamishness,
queasiness

navy n = fleet, flotilla, armada

near adj = close, neighbouring,
nearby, adjacent, adjoining ≠ far;
= imminent, forthcoming,
approaching, looming, impending

≠ **far-off**

neat adj = tidy, trim, orderly,
spruce, shipshape ≠ **untidy**;
= methodical, tidy, systematic,
fastidious ≠ **disorganized**;
= smart, trim, tidy, spruce, dapper

necessary adj = needed, required,
essential, vital, compulsory
≠ **unnecessary**; = inevitable,
certain, unavoidable, inescapable
≠ **avoidable**

need v = want, miss, require, lack,
have to have ▷ n = requirement,

2 (state, instance of) want **3** requirement **4** necessity **5** poverty **needful** adj necessary **needless** adj unnecessary **needy** adj poor, in want

needle ❶ n 1 thin pointed piece of metal for sewing, knitting **2** stylus for record player **3** leaf of fir tree ▷ v **4** (Inf) goad, provoke **needlework** n sewing, embroidery

nefarious adj wicked

negate v deny, nullify **negation** n

negative ❶ adj 1 expressing denial or refusal **2** lacking enthusiasm **3** not positive **4** (of electrical charge) having the same polarity as the charge of an electron ▷ n **5** negative word or statement **6** (Photog) picture in which lights and shades are reversed

neglect ❶ v 1 take no care of **2** fail to do **3** fact of neglecting or being neglected

negligee v woman's light dressing gown

negligence ❶ n carelessness **negligent** adj **negligible** adj very small or unimportant

negotiate ❶ v 1 discuss with view to mutual settlement **2** arrange by conference **3** transfer (bill, cheque etc.) **4** get over (obstacle) **negotiable** adj **negotiation** n **negotiator** n

neigh n/v (utter) cry of horse

neighbour n one who lives near another **neighbourhood** n **1** district **2** people of district **neighbouring** adj nearby **neighbourly** adj 1 friendly **2** helpful

neither adj, pron 1 not the one or the other ▷ adv **2** not on the one hand **3** not either ▷ conj **4** nor yet

nemesis n, pl -ses retribution/vengeance

neologism n newly-coined word or phrase

neon n inert gas in the atmosphere, used to illuminate signs and lights

nephew n brother's or sister's son

nepotism n undue favouritism towards one's relations

nerve ❶ n 1 bundle of fibres

THESAURUS

demand, essential, necessity, requisite; = **necessity**, call, demand, obligation; = **emergency**, want, necessity, urgency, exigency

needle v = **irritate**, provoke, annoy, harass, taunt

negative adj = **pessimistic**, cynical, unwilling, gloomy, jaundiced ≠ **optimistic**; = **dissenting**, contradictory, refusing, denying, rejecting ≠ **assenting** ▷ n = **denial**, no, refusal, rejection, contradiction

neglect v = **disregard**, ignore, fail to look after ≠ **look after**; = **shirk**, forget, overlook, omit, evade ▷ n = **negligence**, inattention ≠ **care**

negligence n = **carelessness**, neglect, disregard, dereliction, slackness

negotiate v = **bargain**, deal, discuss, debate, mediate; = **arrange**, work out, bring about, transact

nerve n = **bravery**, courage, bottle (Brit Sl), resolution, daring; (Inf) carrying feeling, impulses to motion etc. to and from brain **2** assurance **3** coolness in danger **4** audacity ▷ pl **5** sensitiveness to fear, annoyance etc. ▷ v **6** give courage to **nervous** adj **1** excitable **2** apprehensive **nervy** adj nervous, jumpy **nerve-racking** adj very distressing

nestle ❶ v settle comfortably close to something

net¹ ❶ n **1** openwork fabric of meshes of cord etc. ▷ v **2** cover with, or catch in, net **netting** n string or wire net **netball** n game in which ball has to be thrown through high net

net², nett ❶ adj **1** left after all deductions ▷ v **2** gain, yield as clear profit

nether adj lower

nettle n **1** plant with stinging hairs ▷ v **2** irritate

network ❶ n **1** system of intersecting lines, roads etc. **2** interconnecting group **3** linked broadcasting stations

neural adj of the nerves

neuralgia n pain in, along nerves

neurosis n, pl **-ses** relatively mild mental disorder **neurotic** adj/n

neuter adj **1** neither masculine nor feminine ▷ v **2** castrate (animals)

neutral ❶ adj **1** taking neither side in war, dispute etc. **2** without marked qualities ▷ n **3** neutral nation or subject of one **4** position of disengaged gears **neutrality** n **neutralize** v make ineffective

neutron n electrically neutral particle of nucleus of an atom

never ❶ adv at no time **nevertheless** adv for all that

new ❶ adj **1** not existing before, fresh **2** unfamiliar ▷ adv **3** newly **newly** adv recently, freshly **newcomer** n recent arrival **newfangled** adj objectionably or unnecessarily modern

news ❶ n **1** report of recent happenings **2** interesting fact not previously known **newsagent** n shopkeeper selling newspapers, magazines etc. **newsflash** n brief

---

THESAURUS

= **impudence**, cheek (Inf), audacity, boldness, temerity

nestle v = **snuggle**, cuddle, huddle, curl up, nuzzle

net¹ n = **mesh**, netting, network, web, lattice ▷ v = **catch**, bag, capture, trap, entangle

net², nett adj = **after taxes**, final, clear, take-home, ultimate ▷ v = **earn**, make, clear, gain, realize

network n = **web**, system, arrangement, grid, lattice; = **maze**, warren, labyrinth

neutral adj = **unbiased**, impartial, disinterested, even-handed, uninvolved ≠ biased; = **expressionless**, dull

never adv = **at no time**, not once, not ever ≠ always

new adj = **modern**, recent, contemporary, up-to-date, latest ≠ old-fashioned; = **extra**, more, added, new-found, supplementary

news n = **information**, latest (Inf), report, story, exposé news item, oft. interrupting programme **newspaper** n periodical publication containing news **newsprint** n inexpensive paper **newsreel** n film giving news

newt n small, tailed amphibian

newton n unit of force

next ❶ adj/adv 1 nearest 2 immediately following **next-of-kin** n closest relative

NF Newfoundland

NHS National Health Service

nib n (split) pen point

nibble v 1 take little bits of ▷ n 2 little bite

nice ❶ adj 1 pleasant 2 friendly 3 kind 4 subtle, fine 5 careful, exact **nicely** adv **nicety** n minute distinction or detail

niche ❶ n recess in wall

nick ❶ v 1 make notch in, indent 2 (Sl) steal ▷ n 3 notch 4 (Inf) condition 5 (Sl) prison

nickel n 1 silver-white metal much used in alloys and plating 2 (US & Canad) five cent piece

nickname ❶ n familiar name

nicotine n poisonous oily liquid in tobacco

niece n brother's or sister's daughter

nifty adj **-tier, -tiest** (Inf) 1 smart 2 quick

niggard n mean, stingy person **niggardly** adj/adv

niggle v 1 find fault continually 2 annoy

nigh adj/adv/prep (Obs) near

night ❶ n time of darkness between sunset and sunrise **nightie, nighty** n nightdress **nightly** adj/adv (happening, done) every night **nightcap** n drink taken before bedtime **nightclub** n place for dancing, music etc., open late at night **nightdress** n woman's loose robe worn in bed **nightingale** n small bird which sings at night **nightmare** n 1 very bad dream 2 terrifying experience **nightshade** n various plants of potato family, some with very poisonous berries **night-time** n

n

next adj = **following**, later, succeeding, subsequent; = **adjacent**, closest, nearest, neighbouring, adjoining ▷ adv = **afterwards**, then, later, following, subsequently

nice adj = **pleasant**, delightful, agreeable, good, attractive ≠ **unpleasant**; = **kind**, helpful, obliging, considerate ≠ **unkind**; = **likable** or **likeable**, friendly, engaging, charming, pleasant;

= **polite**, courteous, well-mannered ≠ **vulgar**

niche n = **recess**, opening, corner, hollow, nook; = **position**, calling, place, slot (Inf), vocation

nick v (Sl) = **steal**, pinch (Inf), swipe (Sl), pilfer; = **cut**, mark, score, chip, scratch ▷ n = **cut**, mark, scratch, chip, scar

nickname n = **pet name**, label, diminutive, epithet, sobriquet

night n = **darkness**, dark,

nil ❶ n nothing, zero
nimble adj agile, quick, dexterous
nimbus n, pl **-bi, -buses** 1 rain or
storm cloud 2 halo
nincompoop n (Inf) stupid person
nine adj/n cardinal number next
above eight **ninth** adj ordinal
number **nineteen** adj/n nine
more than ten **nineteenth** adj
ninetieth adj **ninety** adj/n nine
tens
nip ❶ v **nipping, nipped** 1 pinch
sharply 2 detach by pinching, bite
3 check growth (of plants) thus
4 (Inf) hurry ▷ n 5 pinch 6 sharp
coldness of weather 7 short drink
nipper n 1 thing that nips 2 (Inf)
small child **nippy** adj **-pier, -piest**
1 (Inf) cold 2 quick
nipple n 1 point of breast, teat
2 anything like this
nit n 1 egg of louse or other parasite
2 (Inf) nitwit **nit-picking** adj (Inf)
overconcerned with insignificant
detail **nitwit** n (Inf) fool
nitrogen n one of the gases
making up air **nitrate** n
compound of nitric acid and an

alkali **nitric** adj **nitroglycerine** n
explosive liquid
no ❶ adj 1 not any, not a 2 not at
all ▷ adv 3 expresses negative reply
▷ n 4 refusal 5 denial 6 negative
vote or voter **no-one, no one**
nobody
no. number
noble ❶ adj 1 of the nobility
2 having high moral qualities
3 impressive ▷ n 4 member of the
nobility **nobility** n 1 class holding
special rank 2 being noble
nobleman n **nobly** adv
nobody ❶ n 1 no person 2 person
of no importance
no-brainer n (Sl) something that
requires little or no mental effort
nocturnal adj of, in, by, night
nod ❶ v **nodding, nodded** 1 bow
head slightly and quickly in assent,
command etc. 2 let head droop
with sleep ▷ n 3 act of nodding
node n knot or knob
nodule n 1 little knot 2 rounded
irregular mineral mass
noise ❶ n 1 any sound, esp.
disturbing one ▷ v 2 rumour

nil n = **nothing**, love, zero
nip v = **pop**, go, run, rush, dash
no interj = **not at all**, certainly not,
of course not, absolutely not, never
≠ **yes** ▷ n = **refusal**, rejection,
denial, negation ≠ **consent**
noble adj = **worthy**, generous,
upright, honourable, virtuous
≠ **despicable**; = **dignified**, great,
imposing, impressive, distinguished
≠ **lowly**; = **aristocratic**, lordly,

titled, patrician, blue-blooded
≠ **humble** ▷ n = **lord**, peer,
aristocrat, nobleman ≠ **commoner**
nobody n = **nonentity**,
lightweight (Inf), zero, cipher
≠ **celebrity**
nod v = **signal**, indicate, motion,
gesture; = **salute**, acknowledge
▷ n = **signal**, sign, motion, gesture,
indication
noise n = **sound**, row, racket,
clamour, din ≠ **silence**

night-time

DICTIONARY

noisy *adj*

nomad *n* **1** member of wandering tribe **2** wanderer **nomadic** *adj*

nomenclature *n* system of names

nominal ① ** *adj* **1 in name only **2** (of fee etc.) small

nominate ① ** *v* **1 propose as candidate **2** appoint to office **nomination** *n* **nominee** *n* candidate

non- *comb. form* indicates the negative of a word

nonchalant *adj* casually unconcerned, indifferent

noncommissioned officer (Mil) subordinate officer, risen from the ranks

noncommittal *adj* avoiding definite preference or pledge

nonconformist *n* dissenter, esp. from Established Church

nondescript *adj* lacking distinctive characteristics

none ① ** *pron* **1 no-one, not any ▷ *adv* **2** in no way **nonetheless** *adv* despite that, however

nonentity *n/pl* **-ties** insignificant person, thing

nonevent *n* disappointing or insignificant occurrence

nonflammable *adj* not easily set on fire

nonpareil *n/adj* (person or thing) unequalled or unrivalled

nonplussed *adj* disconcerted

nonsense ① ** *n* **1 absurd language **2** absurdity **3** silly conduct

non sequitur statement with little relation to what preceded it

nook *n* sheltered corner

**noon ① ** *n* midday, twelve o'clock

noose *n* **1** loop on end of rope **2** snare

nor *conj* and not

norm ① ** *n* **1 average level **2** standard **normal** *adj* **1** ordinary **2** usual **3** conforming to type **normality** *n* **normally** *adv*

north ① ** *n* **1 direction to the right of person facing the sunset ▷ *adv/ adj* **2** from, towards or in the north **northerly** *adj/n* wind from the north **northern** *adj* **northwards** *adv*

nose ① ** *n* **1 organ of smell, used also in breathing **2** any projection resembling a nose ▷ *v* **3** (cause to)

THESAURUS

nominal *adj* = **titular**, formal, purported, in name only, supposed; = **token**, small, symbolic, minimal, trivial

nominate *v* = **propose**, suggest, recommend, put forward; = **appoint**, name, choose, select, elect

none *pron* = **not any**, nothing, zero, not one, nil

nonsense *n* = **rubbish**, hot air

(Inf), twaddle, drivel, tripe (Inf) ≠ **sense**

noon *n* = **midday**, high noon, noonday, twelve noon, noontide

norm *n* = **standard**, rule, pattern, average, par

north *adj* = **northern**, polar, arctic, boreal, northerly ▷ *adv* = **northward(s)**, in a northerly direction

nose *n* = **snout**, bill, beak, hooter (Sl),

move forward slowly and carefully **4** touch with nose **5** smell, sniff **6** pry **nosy** *adj* (*Inf*) inquisitive **nose dive** sudden drop

nosh (*Sl*) ▷ *n* **1** food ▷ *v* **2** eat

nostalgia ❶ *n* longing for past events **nostalgic** *adj*

nostril *n* one of the two external openings of the nose

not *adv* expressing negation, refusal, denial

notable ❶ *adj/n* remarkable (person) **notably** *adv*

notary *n, pl* **-ries** person authorized to draw up deeds, contracts

notation *n* representation of numbers, quantities by symbols

notch ❶ *n/v* (make) V-shaped cut

note ❶ *n* **1** brief comment or record **2** short letter **3** banknote **4** symbol for musical sound

5 single tone **6** fame **7** notice ▷ *v* **8** observe, record **9** heed **noted** *adj* well-known **notebook** *n* small book with blank pages for writing

nothing *n* **1** no thing **2** not anything, nought ▷ *adv* **3** not at all, in no way

notice ❶ *n* **1** observation **2** attention **3** warning, announcement ▷ *v* **4** observe, mention **5** give attention to

notify ❶ *v* **-fying, -fied** give notice of or to

notion ❶ *n* **1** concept **2** opinion **3** whim

notorious ❶ *adj* known for something bad **notoriety** *n*

notwithstanding ❶ *prep* **1** in spite of ▷ *adv* **2** all the same ▷ *conj* **3** although

nougat *n* chewy sweet containing nuts, fruit etc.

proboscis ▷ *v* = **ease forward**, push, edge, shove, nudge

nostalgia *n* = **reminiscence**, longing, pining, yearning, remembrance

notable *adj* = **remarkable**, striking, unusual, extraordinary, outstanding ≠ **imperceptible** ▷ *n* = **celebrity**, big name, dignitary, luminary, personage

notch *n* = **level** (*Inf*), step, degree, grade; = **cut**, nick, incision, indentation, mark ▷ *v* = **cut**, mark, score, nick, scratch

note *n* = **message**, letter, communication, memo, memorandum ▷ *v* = **notice**, see, observe, perceive; = **bear in mind**,

be aware, take into account; = **mention**, record, mark, indicate, register

notice *v* = **observe**, see, note, spot, distinguish ≠ **overlook** ▷ *n* = **notification**, warning, advice, intimation, news; = **attention**, interest, note, regard, consideration ≠ **oversight**

notify *v* = **inform**, tell, advise, alert to, announce

notion *n* = **idea**, view, opinion, belief, concept; = **whim**, wish, desire, fancy, impulse

notorious *adj* = **infamous**, disreputable, opprobrious

notwithstanding *prep* = **despite**, in spite of, regardless of

nought n 1 nothing 2 figure o

noun n word used as name of person, idea or thing

nourish ① v 1 feed 2 nurture **nourishment** n

Nov. November

novel¹ ① n fictitious tale in book form **novelist** n

novel² ① adj 1 new, recent 2 strange **novelty** n 1 newness 2 something new 3 small trinket

November n eleventh month

novice ① n beginner

now ① adv 1 at the present time 2 immediately 3 recently ▷ *conj* 4 seeing that, since **nowadays** *adv* in these times

nowhere *adv* not in any place or state

noxious *adj* poisonous, harmful

nozzle n pointed spout, esp. at end of hose

NS Nova Scotia

nuance n delicate shade of difference

NSW New South Wales

nub n 1 small lump 2 main point

nubile *adj* 1 sexually attractive 2 marriageable

nucleus ① n, pl **-clei** 1 centre, kernel 2 core of atom **nuclear** *adj* of, pert. to atomic nucleus **nuclear energy** energy released by nuclear fission **nuclear fission** disintegration of atom

nude ① n/adj naked (person) **nudism** n practice of nudity **nudist** n **nudity** n

nudge ① v 1 touch slightly with elbow ▷ n 2 such touch

nugget n lump of gold

nuisance ① n something or someone annoying

nuke v (Sl) attack or destroy with nuclear weapons

null *adj* of no effect, void **nullify** v 1 cancel 2 make useless

numb ① adj 1 deprived of feeling ▷ v 2 make numb

number ① n 1 sum or aggregate 2 word or symbol saying how many 3 single issue of a paper etc.

n

------- THESAURUS -------

nourish v = **feed**, supply, sustain, nurture; = **encourage**, support, maintain, promote, sustain

novel¹ n = **story**, tale, fiction, romance, narrative

novel² *adj* = **new**, different, original, fresh, unusual ≠ **ordinary**

novice n = **beginner**, pupil, amateur, newcomer, trainee ≠ **expert**

now *adv* = **nowadays**, at the moment; = **immediately**, promptly, instantly, at once, straightaway

nucleus n = **centre**, heart, focus, basis, core

nude *adj* = **naked**, stripped, bare, undressed, stark-naked ≠ **dressed**

nudge v = **push**, touch, dig, elbow, bump

nuisance n = **trouble**, problem, trial, drag (*Inf*), bother (*Inf*) ≠ **benefit**

numb *adj* = **unfeeling**, dead, frozen, paralysed, insensitive ≠ **sensitive** knock out, deaden ▷ v = **deaden**, freeze, dull, paralyse, immobilize

number n = **numeral**, figure,

4 company, collection
5 identifying number ▷ v 6 count
7 class, reckon 8 give a number to
numberless adj countless
numeral n sign or word denoting a
number **numeracy** n ability to
use numbers in calculations
numerate adj **numerator** n top
part of fraction **numerical** adj of
numbers **numerous** adj many
numskull n dolt, dunce
nun n woman living (in convent)
under religious vows **nunnery** n
convent of nuns
nuptial adj of marriage **nuptials**
pl n wedding
nurse ❶ n 1 person trained for
care of sick or injured ▷ v 2 act as
nurse to 3 suckle **nursery** n
1 room for children 2 rearing place
for plants **nursing home** private
hospital or home for old people
nursing officer administrative
head of nursing staff of hospital

nurture ❶ n 1 bringing up
2 rearing ▷ v 3 bring up 4 educate
5 nourish
nut ❶ n 1 fruit consisting of hard
shell and kernel 2 hollow metal
collar into which a screw fits 3 (Inf)
head 4 (Sl) crank, maniac **nutty**
adj **nutmeg** n aromatic seed of
Indian tree
nutrient adj 1 nourishing ▷ n
2 something nutritious
nutrition ❶ n 1 receiving foods
2 act of nourishing **nutritional,
nutritious, nutritive** adj
nuzzle v 1 burrow, press with nose
2 nestle
NWT Northwest Territories
nylon n 1 synthetic material used
for fabrics etc. ▷ pl 2 stockings of
this
nymph n legendary spirit of sea,
woods etc.
nymphomaniac n woman with
abnormally intense sexual desire

———— THESAURUS ————

character, digit, integer; = **amount**,
quantity, collection, aggregate
≠ **shortage**; = **crowd**, horde,
multitude, throng; = **group**, set,
band, crowd, gang ▷ v = **amount
to**, come to, total, add up to
nurse v = **look after**, treat, tend,
care for, take care of; = **harbour**,
have, maintain, preserve, entertain;
= **breast-feed**, feed, nurture,

nourish, suckle
nurture v = **bring up**, raise, look
after, rear, care for ≠ **neglect** ▷ n
= **upbringing**, training, education,
instruction, rearing
nut n (Sl) = **madman**, psycho (Sl),
crank (Inf), lunatic, maniac; (Sl)
= **head**, skull
nutrition n = **food**, nourishment,
sustenance, nutriment

O

oaf n 1 lout 2 dolt

oak n common deciduous tree

OAP old age pensioner

oar n wooden lever with broad blade worked by the hands to propel boat

oasis n, pl **-ses** fertile spot in desert

oat n 1 (usu. pl) grain of cereal plant 2 the plant **oatmeal** n

oath ❶ n 1 confirmation of truth of statement by naming something sacred 2 curse

obdurate adj stubborn, unyielding

OBE Officer of the Order of the British Empire

obelisk n tapering rectangular stone column

obese adj very fat **obesity** n

obey ❶ v 1 do the bidding of 2 do as ordered

obituary n, pl **-aries** 1 notice, record of death 2 biographical sketch of deceased person

object¹ ❶ n 1 material thing 2 that to which feeling or action is directed 3 end or aim 4 (Grammar) word dependent on verb or preposition

object² ❶ v express or feel dislike or reluctance to something **objection** n **objectionable** adj

objective ❶ adj 1 external to the mind 2 impartial ▷ n 3 thing or place aimed at

oblige ❶ v 1 compel 2 do favour for (someone) **obligate** v bind, esp. by legal contract **obligation** n 1 binding duty, promise 2 debt of gratitude **obligatory** adj 1 required 2 binding **obliging** adj ready to serve others, helpful

oblique adj 1 slanting 2 indirect

obliterate ❶ v 1 blot out, efface 2 destroy completely

oblong adj 1 rectangular, with adjacent sides unequal ▷ n

o

THESAURUS

oath n = **promise**, bond, pledge, vow, word; = **swear word**, curse, obscenity, blasphemy, expletive

obey v = **carry out**, follow, implement, act upon, carry through ≠ **disregard**

object¹ n = **thing**, article, body, item, entity; = **purpose**, aim, end, point, plan; = **target**, victim, focus, recipient

object² v with **to** = **protest against**, oppose, argue against, draw the line at, take exception to ≠ **accept**

objective n = **purpose**, aim, goal, end, plan ▷ adj = **factual**, real

oblige v = **compel**, make, force, require, bind; = **help**, assist, benefit, please, humour ≠ **bother**

2 oblong figure

obnoxious adj offensive, odious

oboe n woodwind instrument

obscene ⊕ adj indecent, repulsive **obscenity** n

obscure ⊕ adj 1 unclear, indistinct ▷ v 2 make unintelligible 3 dim 4 conceal **obscurity** n 1 indistinctness 3 lack of intelligibility 3 obscure place or position

obsequious adj servile, fawning

observe ⊕ v 1 notice, remark 2 watch 3 note systematically 4 keep, follow **observance** n 1 keeping of custom 2 ritual, ceremony **observant** adj quick to notice **observation** n **observatory** n place for watching stars etc. **observer** n

obsess v haunt, fill the mind **obsession** n

obsolete ⊕ adj not current; disused, out of date **obsolescent** adj going out of use

obstacle ⊕ n obstruction

obstetrics pl n branch of medicine concerned with childbirth **obstetrician** n

obstinate adj 1 stubborn 2 hard to overcome or cure **obstinacy** n

obstreperous adj unruly, noisy

obstruct ⊕ v 1 block up 2 hinder 3 impede **obstruction** n **obstructive** adj

obtain ⊕ v 1 get 2 acquire 3 be customary **obtainable** adj

obtrude v thrust forward unduly **obtrusive** adj

obtuse adj 1 dull of perception 2 stupid 3 greater than right angle 4 not pointed

obverse n 1 complement 2 principal side of coin, medal etc.

obviate v remove, make unnecessary

obvious ⊕ adj clear, evident **obviously** adv

—————— THESAURUS ——————

obscene adj = **indecent**, dirty, offensive, filthy, improper ≠ **decent**; = **offensive**, shocking, evil, disgusting, outrageous

obscure adj = **unknown**, little-known, humble, unfamiliar, out-of-the-way ≠ **famous**; = **abstruse**, complex, confusing, mysterious, vague ≠ **straightforward**; = **unclear**, uncertain, confused, mysterious, doubtful ≠ **well-known** ▷ v = **obstruct**, hinder

observe v = **watch**, study, view, look at, check; = **notice**, see, note, discover, spot; = **remark**, say,

comment, state, note; = **comply with**, keep, follow, respect, carry out ≠ **disregard**

obsolete adj = **outdated**, old, passé, old-fashioned, discarded ≠ **up-to-date**

obstacle n = **obstruction**, block, barrier, hurdle, snag

obstruct v = **block**, close, bar, plug, barricade; = **hold up**, stop, check, block, restrict

obtain v = **get**, gain, acquire, land, net ≠ **lose**; = **achieve**, get, gain, accomplish, attain

obvious adj = **clear**, plain, apparent, evident, distinct

occasion ❶ n 1 time when thing happens 2 reason, need 3 opportunity 4 special event ▷ v 5 cause **occasional** adj happening, found now and then **occasionally** adv

Occident n the West **Occidental** adj

occult adj 1 secret, mysterious 2 supernatural

occupy ❶ v -pying, -pied 1 inhabit, fill 2 employ 3 take possession of **occupancy** n fact of occupying **occupant** n **occupation** n employment, pursuit 2 tenancy 3 military control of country by foreign power **occupational** adj **occupier** n

occur ❶ v -curring, -curred 1 happen 2 come to mind **occurrence** n happening

ocean n 1 great body of water 2 large division of this 3 the sea

ochre n earth used as yellow or

brown pigment

o'clock adv by the clock

Oct. October

octagon n figure with eight angles **octagonal** adj

octane n chemical found in petrol

octave n (Mus) 1 eighth note above or below given note 2 this space

octet n (music for) group of eight

October n tenth month

octopus n, pl -puses mollusc with eight arms covered with suckers

odd ❶ adj 1 strange, queer 2 incidental, random 3 left over or additional 4 not even 5 not part of a set **oddity** n 1 odd person or thing 2 quality of being odd **oddments** pl n things left over **odds** pl n 1 advantage conceded in betting 2 likelihood **odds and ends** odd fragments or scraps

ode n lyric poem

≠ **unclear**

occasion n = **time**, moment, point, stage, instance; = **function**, event, affair, do (Inf), happening; = **opportunity**, chance, time, opening, window; = **reason**, cause, call, ground(s), excuse ▷ v (Formal) = **cause**, produce, lead to, inspire, result in

occupy v = **inhabit**, own, live in, dwell in, reside in ≠ **vacate**; = **invade**, take over, capture, seize, conquer ≠ **withdraw**; = **hold**, control, dominate, possess; = **take**

up, consume, tie up, monopolize

occur v = **happen**, take place, come about, turn up (Inf), crop up (Inf); = **exist**, appear, be found, develop, turn up

odd adj = **peculiar**, strange, unusual, extraordinary, bizarre; = **unusual**, strange, rare, extraordinary, remarkable ≠ **normal**; = **occasional**, various, random, casual, irregular ≠ **regular**; = **spare**, remaining, extra, surplus, solitary ≠ **matched**

odium n hatred, widespread dislike **odious** adj

odour ❶ n smell **odorous** adj 1 fragrant 2 scented

odyssey ❶ n long eventful journey

oesophagus n, pl **-gi** passage between mouth and stomach

of prep denotes removal, separation, ownership, attribute, material, quality

off ❶ adv 1 away ▷ prep 2 away from ▷ adj 3 not operative 4 cancelled or postponed 5 bad, sour etc. **offhand** adj/adv 1 without previous thought 2 curt **off-licence** n place where alcoholic drinks are sold for consumption elsewhere **offline** adj/adv not connected to the internet **offset** v counterbalance, compensate **offspring** n children, issue

offal n 1 edible entrails of animal 2 refuse

offend ❶ v 1 hurt feelings of, displease 2 do wrong 3 disgust

offence n 1 wrong 2 crime 3 insult **offender** n **offensive** adj 1 causing displeasure 2 aggressive ▷ n 3 position or movement of attack

offer ❶ v 1 present for acceptance or refusal 2 tender 3 propose 4 attempt ▷ n 5 offering, bid

office ❶ n 1 room(s), building, in which business, clerical work etc. is done 2 commercial or professional organization 3 official position 4 service 5 duty 6 form of worship ▷ pl 7 task 8 service **officer** n 1 one in command in army, navy, ship etc. 2 official

official ❶ adj 1 with, by, authority ▷ n 2 one holding office

officiate v perform duties of office, ceremony

officious adj 1 importunate in offering service 2 interfering

offside adj/adv (Sport) illegally forward

often ❶ adv many times

ogle v stare, look (at) amorously

— THESAURUS —

odour n = **smell**, scent, perfume, fragrance, stink

odyssey n = **journey**, tour, trip, quest, trek

off adv = **away**, out, apart, elsewhere, aside ▷ adj = **absent**, gone, unavailable; = **cancelled**, abandoned, postponed, shelved

offend v = **distress**, upset, outrage, wound, slight ≠ **please**

offer v = **provide**, present, furnish, afford ≠ **withhold**; = **volunteer**, come forward, offer your services; = **propose**, suggest, advance, submit; = **give**, show, bring,

provide, render ▷ n = **proposal**, suggestion, proposition, submission; = **bid**, tender, bidding price

office n = **place of work**, workplace, base, workroom, place of business

official adj = **authorized**, formal, sanctioned, licensed, proper ≠ **unofficial**; = **formal**, bureaucratic, ceremonial, solemn, ritualistic ▷ n = **officer**, executive, agent, representative, bureaucrat

often adv = **frequently**, generally, commonly, repeatedly, time and

o

▷ *n* **2** this look

ogre *n* **1** man-eating giant **2** monster

oh *interj* exclamation of surprise, pain etc.

ohm *n* unit of electrical resistance

oil ❶ *n* **1** any viscous liquid with smooth, sticky feel **2** petroleum ▷ *v* **3** lubricate with oil **oily** *adj* **oilskin** *n* cloth treated with oil to make it waterproof

ointment *n* greasy preparation for healing or beautifying the skin

O.K., okay (*Inf*) ▷ *adj/adv, interj* **1** all right ▷ *v* **2** agree to, endorse

old ❶ *adj* **1** aged, having lived or existed long **2** belonging to earlier period **olden** *adj* old **old-fashioned** *adj* **1** in style of earlier period, out of date **2** fond of old ways

olfactory *adj* of smelling

oligarchy *n, pl* **-chies** government by small group

olive *n* **1** evergreen tree **2** its oil-yielding fruit **3** its wood ▷ *adj* **4** greyish-green

ombudsman *n* official who investigates complaints against government organizations

omelette *n* dish of eggs beaten and fried

omen *n* prophetic happening **ominous** *adj* boding evil, threatening

omit ❶ *v* omitting, omitted leave out, leave undone **omission** *n*

omnibus *n* **1** book etc. containing several works **2** bus ▷ *adj* **3** serving, containing several objects

omnipotent *adj* all-powerful

omniscient *adj* knowing everything

omnivorous *adj* eating both animals and plants **omnivore** *n*

on ❶ *prep* **1** above and touching, at, near, towards etc. **2** attached to **3** concerning **4** performed upon **5** during **6** taking regularly ▷ *adj* **7** operating **8** taking place ▷ *adv* **9** so as to be on **10** forwards **11** continuously etc. **12** in progress **oncoming** *adj* approaching from the front **ongoing** *adj* in progress, continuing **online** *adj/adv* connected to the internet

once ❶ *adv* **1** one time **2** formerly **3** ever **at once 1** immediately **2** simultaneously **once-over** *n* (*Inf*) quick examination

one *adj* **1** lowest cardinal number **2** single **3** united **4** only, without others **5** identical ▷ *n* **6** number or figure 1 **7** unity **8** single specimen ▷ *pron* **9** particular but not stated person **10** any person **oneself** *pron* **one-sided** *adj*

again ≠ never

oil *v* = **lubricate**, grease

old *adj* = **aged**, elderly, ancient, mature, venerable ≠ **young**; = **out of date**, dated, antique, obsolete, archaic ≠ **up-to-date**

omit *v* = **leave out**, drop, exclude, eliminate, skip ≠ **include**; = **forget**, overlook, neglect, pass over, lose sight of

once *adv* = **on one occasion**, one time, one single time; = **at one**

DICTIONARY

1 partial **2** uneven

onerous *adj* burdensome

onion *n* edible bulb of pungent flavour

onlooker ❶ *n* person who watches without taking part

only ❶ *adj* **1** being the one specimen ▷ *adv* **2** solely, merely, exclusively ▷ *conj* **3** but then **4** excepting that

onset ❶ *n* beginning

onslaught ❶ *n* attack

onto *prep* on top of

onus *n, pl* **onuses** responsibility, burden

onward *adj* **1** advanced or advancing ▷ *adv* **2** in advance, ahead, forward **onwards** *adv*

onyx *n* variety of quartz

ooze ❶ *v* **1** pass slowly out, exude ▷ *n* **2** sluggish flow **3** wet mud

opal ❶ *n* glassy gemstone displaying variegated colours

opaque *adj* not transparent

open ❶ *adj* **1** not shut or blocked up **2** without lid or door **3** bare **4** undisguised **5** not enclosed, covered or exclusive **6** spread out, accessible **7** frank ▷ *v* **8** make or become open ▷ *n* **9** begin ▷ *n* **10** clear space, unenclosed country

opening *n* **1** hole, gap **2** beginning **3** opportunity ▷ *adj* **4** first **5** initial **openly** *adv* without concealment

open-minded *adj* unprejudiced

opera *n* musical drama **operatic** *adj* **operetta** *n* light opera

operation *n* **1** the act or method of operating **2** the condition of being in action **3** a surgical procedure carried out to remove, replace or repair a diseased or damaged part of the body

ophthalmic *adj* of eyes

opinion ❶ *n* **1** what one thinks about something **2** belief, judgment **opinionated** *adj*

THESAURUS

time, previously, formerly, long ago, once upon a time

onlooker *n* = **spectator**, witness, observer, viewer, looker-on

only *adj* = **sole**, one, single, individual, exclusive ▷ *adv* = **just**, simply, purely, merely

onset *n* = **beginning**, start, birth, outbreak, inception ≠ **end**

onslaught *n* = **attack**, charge, campaign, strike, assault ≠ **retreat**

onward, onwards *adv* = **forward**, on, forwards, ahead, beyond

ooze *v* = **seep**, well, escape, leak, drain

open *v* = **unfasten**, unlock ≠ **close**; = **unwrap**, uncover, undo, unravel, untie ≠ **wrap** ▷ *adj* = **unclosed**, unlocked, ajar, unfastened, yawning ≠ **closed**; = **unsealed**, unstoppered ≠ **unopened**; = **extended**, unfolded, stretched out, unfurled, straightened out ≠ **shut**; = **frank**, direct, straightforward, sincere, transparent ≠ **sly**; = **receptive**, sympathetic, responsive, amenable, subject; = **unresolved**, unsettled, undecided, debatable, moot

opinion ❶ *n* = **belief**, feeling, view,

stubborn in one's opinions

opium *n* narcotic drug made from poppy **opiate** *n* drug containing opium

opossum *n* small Amer. and Aust. marsupial

opponent ❶ *n* adversary, antagonist

opportunity ❶ *n* **1** favourable time or condition **2** good chance **opportunity shop** (Aust & NZ) shop selling second-hand clothes, sometimes for charity

oppose ❶ *v* resist, set against **opposite** *adj* **1** contrary **2** facing ▷ *n* **3** the contrary ▷ *prep, adv* **4** facing **5** on the other side **opposition** *n* **1** resistance **2** hostility **3** group opposing another

oppress ❶ *v* **1** govern by tyranny **2** weigh down **oppression** *n* **oppressive** *adj* **1** tyrannical **2** hard to bear **3** (of weather) hot and tiring

opt ❶ *v* make a choice

optic *adj* of eye or sight **optical** *adj* **optician** *n* maker of, dealer in spectacles, optical instruments

optimism *n* disposition to look on the bright side **optimist** *n* **optimistic** *adj*

optimum ❶ *adj/n, pl* **-ma, -mums** the best, the most favourable

option ❶ *n* **1** choice **2** thing chosen **optional** *adj* leaving to choice

optometrist *n* person testing eyesight, prescribing corrective lenses

opulent *adj* **1** rich **2** copious **opulence** *n*

opus ❶ *n, pl* **opuses, opera 1** work **2** musical composition

or *conj* **1** introducing alternatives **2** if not

oracle *n* **1** divine utterance, prophecy given at shrine of god **2** the shrine **3** wise adviser

oral ❶ *adj* **1** spoken **2** by mouth ▷ *n* **3** spoken examination

orange *adj* **1** reddish-yellow ▷ *n* **2** reddish-yellow citrus fruit

orang-utan, orang-utang *n* large reddish-brown ape

O

idea, theory

opponent *n* = **adversary**, rival, enemy, competitor, challenger ≠ **ally**

opportunity *n* = **chance**, opening, time, turn, moment

oppose *v* = **be against**, fight (against), block, take on, counter ≠ **support**

oppress *v* = **subjugate**, abuse, suppress, wrong, master ≠ **liberate**; = **depress**, burden,

discourage, torment, harass

opt *v* = **choose**, decide, prefer, select, elect ≠ **reject**

optimum *adj* = **ideal**, best, highest, finest, optimal, perfect ≠ **worst**

option *n* = **choice**, alternative, selection, preference, freedom of choice

opus *n* = **work**, piece, production, creation, composition

oral *adj* = **spoken/vocal**, verbal,

orator n 1 maker of speech 2 skilful speaker **oration** n formal speech **oratory** n 1 speeches 2 eloquence

orb n globe

orbit ❶ n 1 track of planet, satellite, comet etc. around another heavenly body 2 field of influence ▷ v 3 move in, or put into, an orbit

orchard n (area for) fruit trees

orchestra n 1 band of musicians 2 place for such band in theatre etc. **orchestral** adj **orchestrate** v 1 arrange (music) for orchestra 2 organize (something) to particular effect

orchid n genus of various flowering plants

ordain ❶ v 1 confer holy orders upon 2 decree, enact

ordeal ❶ n severe, trying experience

order n 1 regular, proper or peaceful arrangement or condition 2 command

ordinal number number

showing position in series

ordinance n decree, rule

ordinary ❶ adj 1 usual, normal 2 commonplace **ordinarily** adv

ordnance n 1 artillery 2 military stores **ordnance survey** official geographical survey of Britain

ore n mineral which yields metal

oregano n aromatic herb

organ ❶ n 1 musical wind instrument of pipes and stops, played with keys 2 member of animal or plant with particular function 3 medium of information **organist** n organ player

organism ❶ n plant, animal **organic** adj 1 of, derived from, living organisms 2 of bodily organs 3 (Chem) of compounds formed from carbon 4 organized, systematic

organize ❶ v 1 give definite structure 2 arrange 3 unite in a society **organization** n 1 act of organizing 2 structure 3 association, group **organizer** n

orgasm n sexual climax

— THESAURUS —

unwritten

orbit n = **path**, course, cycle, circle, revolution; = **sphere of influence**, reach, range, influence, province ▷ v = **circle**, ring, go round, revolve around, encircle

ordain v = **appoint**, name, commission, select, invest; (Formal) = **order**, will, rule, demand, require

ordeal n = **hardship**, trial, difficulty, test, suffering ≠ **pleasure**

ordinary adj = **usual**, standard,

normal, common, regular; = **commonplace**, plain, modest, humble, mundane

organ n = **body part**, part of the body, element, biological structure; = **newspaper**, medium, voice, vehicle, gazette

organism n = **creature**, being, thing, body, animal

organize v = **arrange**, run, plan, prepare, set up ≠ **disrupt**; = **put in order**, arrange, group, list, file ≠ **muddle**

DICTIONARY

orgy n/pl **-gies 1** drunken or licentious revel **2** unrestrained bout

orient, orientate ❶ n (with cap.) East ▷ v **2** determine (one's) position (also) **oriental** adj/n **orientation** n

orifice n opening, mouth

origami n art of paper folding

origin ❶ n **1** beginning **2** source **3** parentage **original** adj **1** earliest **2** new, not copied **3** thinking or acting for oneself ▷ n **4** thing from which another is copied **originality** n **originally** adv **originate** v **1** come or bring into existence, begin **2** create, pioneer

ornament ❶ n **1** any object used to adorn or decorate ▷ v **2** adorn **ornamental** adj

ornate adj highly decorated or elaborate

ornithology n science of birds

orphan n child whose parents are dead **orphanage** n institution for care of orphans

orthodox ❶ adj **1** holding accepted views **2** conventional

orthodoxy n

oscillate v **1** swing to and fro **2** waver

osmosis n movement of liquid through membrane from higher to lower concentration

osprey n fishing hawk

ossify v **-fying, -fied 1** turn into bone **2** grow rigid

ostensible adj **1** apparent **2** professed

ostentation n show, pretentious display **ostentatious** adj

osteopathy n art of treating disease by manipulation of bones **osteopath** n

ostracize n exclude, banish from society **ostracism** n

ostrich n large flightless bird

other ❶ adj **1** not this **2** not the same **3** alternative ▷ pron **4** other person or thing **otherwise** adv **1** differently ▷ conj **2** or else, if not

otter n furry aquatic fish-eating mammal

ouch interj exclamation of sudden pain

ought v expressing obligation or advisability or probability

THESAURUS

orient, orientate v = **adjust**, adapt, alter, accustom, align; = **get your bearings**, establish your location

origin n = **beginning**, start, birth, launch, foundation ≠ **end**; = **root**, source, basis, base, seed

ornament n = **decoration**, trimming, accessory, festoon, trinket; = **embellishment**,

decoration, embroidery, elaboration, adornment ▷ v = **decorate**, adorn, array, do up (Inf), embellish

orthodox adj = **established**, official, accepted, received, common ≠ **unorthodox**

other adj = **additional**, more, further, new, added; = **different**, alternative, contrasting, distinct, diverse

DICTIONARY

ounce ❶ n unit of weight, sixteenth of pound (28.4 grams)

our adj belonging to us **ours** pron **ourselves** pron emphatic or reflexive form of WE

oust ❶ v put out, expel

out ❶ adv/adj **1** from within, away **2** wrong **3** not burning **4** not allowed **5** (Sport) dismissed **outer** adj away from the inside **outermost, outmost** adj on extreme outside **outing** n pleasure excursion **outward** adj/adv

outbreak ❶ n sudden occurrence

outburst ❶ n sudden expression of emotion

outcast n rejected person

outcome ❶ n result

outcry ❶ n, pl **-cries** expression of widespread protest

outdoors adv in the open air **outdoor** adj

outfit ❶ n **1** equipment **2** clothes and accessories **3** (Inf) group or association regarded as a unit

outgoing ❶ adj **1** leaving **2** sociable **outgoings** pl n expenses

outlandish adj queer, extravagantly strange

outlaw ❶ n **1** one beyond protection of the law ▷ v **2** make (someone) an outlaw **3** ban

outlay n expenditure

outline ❶ n **1** rough sketch **2** general plan **3** lines enclosing visible figure ▷ v **4** sketch **5** summarize

outlook ❶ n **1** point of view **2** probable outcome

outlying adj remote

outmoded adj no longer fashionable or accepted

outpatient n patient who does

THESAURUS

ounce n = **shred**, bit, drop, trace, scrap

oust v = **expel**, turn out, dismiss, exclude, exile

out adj = **not in**, away, elsewhere, outside, gone; = **extinguished**, ended, finished, dead, exhausted

outbreak n = **eruption**, burst, explosion, epidemic, rash

outburst n = **explosion**, fit, surge, outbreak, flare-up

outcome n = **result**, end, consequence, conclusion, payoff (Inf)

outcry n = **protest**, complaint, objection, dissent, outburst

outfit n = **costume**, dress, clothes, clothing, kit; (Inf) = **group**, company, team, party, unit

outgoing adj = **leaving**, former, previous, retiring, withdrawing ≠ **incoming**; = **sociable**, open, social, warm, friendly ≠ **reserved**

outlaw v = **ban**, bar, veto, forbid, exclude ≠ **legalise**; = **banish**, put a price on (someone's) head ▷ n (Hist) = **bandit**, criminal, thief, robber, fugitive

outline v = **summarize**, draft, plan, trace, sketch (in); = **silhouette**, etch ▷ n = **summary**, review, résumé, rundown, synopsis; = **shape**, lines, form, figure, profile

outlook n = **attitude**, opinion, position, approach, mood;

not stay in hospital overnight
outport n (Canad) isolated fishing village, esp. in Newfoundland
outpost n outlying settlement
output ❶ n 1 quantity produced 2 (Comp) information produced
outrage ❶ n 1 violation of others' rights 2 shocking act 3 anger arising from this ▷ v 4 commit outrage **outrageous** adj 1 shocking 2 offensive
outright ❶ adj 1 complete 2 definite ▷ adv 3 completely
outset ❶ n beginning
outside ❶ n 1 exterior ▷ adv 2 not inside ▷ adj 3 on exterior 4 unlikely 5 greatest possible **outsider** n 1 person outside specific group 2 contestant thought unlikely to win

outsize, outsized adj larger than normal
outskirts ❶ pl n outer areas, districts, esp. of city
outspan v (S Afr) relax
outspoken ❶ adj frank, candid
outstanding ❶ adj 1 excellent 2 remarkable 3 unsettled, unpaid
outweigh ❶ v be more important than
outwit v -witting, -witted get the better of by cunning
oval ❶ adj/n egg-shaped, elliptical (thing)
ovary n, pl -ries female egg-producing organ **ovarian** adj
ovation ❶ n enthusiastic burst of applause
oven n heated chamber for baking
over ❶ adv 1 above 2 beyond 3 in

THESAURUS

= prospect(s), future, expectations, forecast, prediction
output n = production, manufacture, manufacturing, yield, productivity
outrage v = offend, shock, upset, wound, insult ▷ n = indignation, shock, anger, rage, fury
outright adj = absolute, complete, total, perfect, sheer; = definite, clear, certain, flat, absolute ▷ adv = openly, frankly, plainly, overtly, candidly; = absolutely, completely, totally, fully, entirely
outset n = beginning, start, opening, onset, inauguration ≠ finish
outside n = exterior, face, front, covering, skin ▷ adj = external,

outer, exterior, outward, extraneous ≠ inner; = remote, small, unlikely, slight, slim
outskirts pl n = edge, boundary, suburbs, fringe, perimeter
outspoken adj = forthright, open, frank, straightforward, blunt ≠ reserved
outstanding adj = excellent, good, great, important, special ≠ mediocre; = unpaid, remaining, due, pending, payable
outweigh v = override, cancel (out), eclipse, offset, compensate for
oval adj = elliptical, egg-shaped, ovoid
ovation n = applause, hand, cheers, praise, tribute ≠ derision
over prep = above, on top of; = on

O

— DICTIONARY —

excess **4** finished **5** in repetition **6** across **7** downwards ▷ *prep* **8** above **9** upon **10** more than **11** along ▷ *n* **12** (Cricket) delivery of six balls from one end

over- *comb. form* too, too much, in excess, above

overall ❶ *n* **1** (*also pl*) loose garment worn as protection against dirt etc. ▷ *adj* **2** total

overbearing *adj* domineering

overboard *adv* from a boat into water **go overboard** go to extremes

overcast *adj* cloudy

overcome ❶ *v* **1** conquer **2** surmount **3** make incapable or powerless

overdose *n/v* (take) excessive dose of drug

overdraft *n* withdrawal of more money than is in bank account

overdrive *n* very high gear in motor vehicle

overgrown *adj* thickly covered with plants

overhaul ❶ *v* **1** examine and set in order ▷ *n* **2** examination and repair

overhead ❶ *adj/adv* over one's head, above

overland *adj/adv* by land

overlap *v* **1** share part of same space or period of time ▷ *n* **2** area overlapping

overlook ❶ *v* **1** fail to notice **2** disregard

overseas *adj/adv* **1** foreign **2** from or to a place over the sea

overshadow ❶ *v* reduce significance of

oversight *n* **1** failure to notice **2** mistake

overt ❶ *adj* open, unconcealed

— THESAURUS —

o

top of, on, across, upon ▷ *adv*
= **above**, overhead, in the sky, on high, aloft; = **extra**, more, further, beyond, additional ▷ *adj*
= **finished**, done (with), through, ended, closed

overall *adj* = **total**, full, whole, general, complete ▷ *adv* = **in general**, generally, mostly, all things considered, on average

overcome *v* = **defeat**, beat, conquer, master, overwhelm; = **conquer**, beat, master, subdue, triumph over ▷ *adj*
= **overwhelmed**, moved, affected, emotional, choked

overhaul *v* = **check**, service, maintain, examine, restore;

= **overtake**, pass, leave behind, catch up with, get past ▷ *n*
= **check**, service, examination, going-over (*Inf*), inspection

overhead *adj* = **raised**, suspended, elevated, aerial, overhanging ▷ *adv* = **above**, in the sky, on high, aloft, up above ≠ **underneath**

overlook *v* = **look over** or **out on**, have a view of; = **miss**, forget, neglect, omit, disregard ≠ **notice**; = **ignore**, excuse, forgive, pardon, disregard

overshadow *v* = **spoil**, ruin, mar, wreck, blight; = **outshine**, eclipse, surpass, dwarf, tower above

overt *adj* = **open**, obvious, plain,

overtake ❶ v **1** move past
2 catch up

overthrow ❶ v **1** overturn
2 defeat ▷ n **3** ruin **4** fall

overtime n **1** time at work,
outside normal working hours
2 payment for this time **3** (US &
Canad) period of extra time in a
contest or game

overtone n additional meaning

overture n (Mus) **1** orchestral
introduction **2** opening of
negotiations

overwhelm ❶ v **1** crush
2 submerge **overwhelming** adj
irresistible

overwrought adj overexcited

owe ❶ v be bound to repay, be

indebted for **owing** adj owed,
due **owing to** caused by, as
result of

owl n night bird of prey

own ❶ adj **1** emphasizes
possession ▷ v **2** possess
3 acknowledge **4** confess **owner**
n **ownership** n possession

ox n, pl **oxen** castrated bull

oxide n compound of oxygen and
one other element

oxygen n gas in atmosphere
essential to life

oyster n edible mollusc

Oz n (Sl) Australia

oz. ounce

ozone n form of oxygen with
pungent odour

public, manifest ≠ hidden

overtake v = **pass**, leave behind,
overhaul, catch up with, get past;
= **outdo**, top, exceed, eclipse,
surpass

overthrow v = **defeat**, overcome,
conquer, bring down, oust
≠ **uphold** ▷ n = **downfall**, fall,
defeat, collapse, destruction
≠ **preservation**

overwhelm v = **overcome**,

devastate, stagger, bowl over (Inf),
knock (someone) for six (Inf);
= **destroy**, defeat, overcome,
crush, massacre

owe v = **be in debt (to)**, be in
arrears (to), be overdrawn (by), be
obligated or indebted (to)

own adj = **personal**, special,
private, individual, particular
▷ v = **possess**, have, keep, hold,
enjoy

O

p

p 1 page 2 pence 3 penny 4 (Mus) piano (softly)

pace ❶ n 1 step 2 rate of movement ▷ v 3 step 4 set speed for 5 measure **pacemaker** n 1 electronic device to regulate heartbeat 2 person who sets speed for race

pacifier n (US & Canad) a baby's dummy or teething ring

pacify v **-fying, -fied** calm **pacifism** n **pacifist** n 1 advocate of abolition of war 2 one who refuses to help in war

pack ❶ n 1 bundle 2 band of animals 3 large set of people or things ▷ v 4 put together in suitcase etc. 5 make into a bundle 6 cram 7 fill **package** n 1 parcel 2 set of items offered together ▷ v 3 put into packages **packet** n 1 small parcel 2 small container (and contents)

packsack n a US and Canadian word for HAVERSACK

pact ❶ n covenant, agreement

pad ❶ n 1 soft stuff used as a cushion, protection etc. 2 block of sheets of paper 3 foot or sole of various animals ▷ v 4 make soft, fill in, protect etc., with pad 5 walk with soft step

paddle¹ ❶ n 1 short oar with broad blade ▷ v 2 move by, as with, paddles

paddle² ❶ v walk with bare feet in shallow water

paddock n small grass enclosure

paddy field field where rice is grown

pademelon, paddymelon [pad]-ee-mel-an n small Australian wallaby

padlock n/v (fasten with) detachable lock with hinged hoop

THESAURUS

pace n = **speed**, rate, tempo, velocity; = **step**, walk, stride, tread, gait ▷ v = **stride**, walk, pound, patrol, march up and down

pack v = **package**, load, store, bundle, stow; = **cram**, crowd, press, fill, stuff ▷ v = **packet**, box, package, carton; = **bundle**, parcel, load, burden, rucksack

pact n = **agreement**, alliance, treaty, deal, understanding

pad n = **wad**, dressing, pack, padding, compress; = **cushion**, filling, stuffing, pillow, bolster; = **notepad**, block, notebook, jotter, writing pad; (Sl) = **home**, flat, apartment, place ▷ v = **pack**, fill, protect, stuff, cushion = **lengthen**, stretch, elaborate, fill out, spin out

paddle¹ n = **oar**, scull ▷ v = **row**, pull, scull

paddle² v = **wade**, splash (about),

paediatrics pl n branch of medicine dealing with diseases of children **paediatrician** n

paella n Spanish dish of rice, chicken, shellfish etc.

pagan ① adj/n heathen

page¹ ① n one side of leaf of book etc.

page² ① n **1** boy attendant ▷ v **2** summon by loudspeaker announcement or electronic device **pager** n small portable electronic signalling device

pageant n show of persons in costume in procession, dramatic scenes etc.

pagoda n pyramidal temple of Chinese or Indian type

pail n bucket

pain ① n **1** bodily or mental suffering ▷ pl **2** trouble ▷ v **3** inflict pain upon **painful** adj **painkiller** n drug that reduces pain **painstaking** adj careful

paint ① n **1** colouring matter spread on a surface ▷ v **2** colour,

coat, or make picture of, with paint **painter** n **painting** n

pair ① n **1** set of two ▷ v **2** arrange in twos

pal ① n (Inf) friend

palace n **1** residence of king, bishop etc. **2** stately mansion **palatial** adj

palate n **1** roof of mouth **2** sense of taste **palatable** adj agreeable to eat

palaver n fuss

pale ① adj **1** wan, whitish ▷ v **2** whiten **3** lose superiority

palette n artist's flat board for mixing colours on

palindrome n word etc., that is the same when read backwards or forwards

paling n upright plank in fence

pall¹ n cloth spread over a coffin **pallbearer** n one carrying coffin at funeral

pall² v **1** become tiresome **2** cloy

pallet n portable platform for storing and moving goods

THESAURUS

slop

pagan adj = **heathen**, infidel, polytheistic, idolatrous ▷ n = **heathen**, infidel, polytheist, idolater

page¹ n = **folio**, side, leaf, sheet

page² v = **call**, summon, send for ▷ n = **attendant**, pageboy; = **servant**, attendant, squire, pageboy

pain n = **suffering**, discomfort, hurt, irritation, tenderness; = **ache**, stinging, aching, cramp, throb ▷ v = **distress**, hurt, torture, grieve,

torment

paint n = **colouring**, colour, stain, dye, tint ▷ v = **colour**, cover, coat, stain, whitewash; = **depict**, draw, portray, picture, represent

pair v = **team**, match (up), join, couple, twin

pal n (Inf) = **friend**, companion, mate (Inf), buddy (Inf), comrade

pale adj = **light**, soft, faded, subtle, muted; = **dim**, weak, faint, feeble, thin ▷ v = **become pale**, blanch, whiten, go white, lose colour

palliate v **1** relieve without curing **2** excuse **palliative** adj/n

pallid adj pale **pallor** n

palm n **1** inner surface of hand **2** tropical tree **3** its leaf as symbol of victory **palmistry** n fortune-telling from lines on palm of hand

palomino n, pl **-nos** golden horse with white mane and tail

palpable adj obvious

palpitate v throb

palsy n paralysis

paltry adj **-trier, -triest** worthless

pamper ❶ v overindulge, spoil

pamphlet ❶ n thin unbound book

pan¹ ❶ n **1** broad, shallow vessel **2** bowl of lavatory **3** depression in ground ▷ v **4** (Inf) criticize harshly

pan² ❶ v **panning, panned** move film camera slowly while filming

pan- comb. form all, as in pan-American

panacea n universal remedy

panache n dashing style

pancake n thin cake of batter fried in pan

pancreas n digestive gland behind stomach

panda n large black and white bearlike mammal of China

pandemonium n din and uproar

pander v **1** (esp. with to) give gratification to ▷ n **2** pimp

pane n sheet of glass

panegyric n speech of praise

panel n **1** compartment of surface, usu. raised or sunk, e.g. in door **2** team in quiz game etc. **3** list of jurors, doctors etc. ▷ v **4** adorn with panels

pang n sudden pain

panic ❶ n **1** sudden and infectious fear ▷ v **2** (cause to) feel panic **panicky** adj

pannier n basket carried by beast of burden, bicycle etc.

panoply n magnificent array

panorama ❶ n wide view

pansy n, pl **-sies 1** flower, species of violet **2** (Offens) effeminate man

pant ❶ v/n gasp

pantechnicon n large van, esp. for carrying furniture

panther n variety of leopard

pantomime n theatrical show, usu. at Christmas time, often founded on a fairy tale

pantry n, pl **-tries** room for storing food or utensils

pants ❶ pl n **1** undergarment for

pamper v = **spoil**, indulge, pet, cosset, coddle

pamphlet n = **booklet**, leaflet, brochure, circular, tract

pan¹ n = **pot**, container, saucepan ▷ v (Inf) = **criticize**, knock, slam (Sl), censure, tear into (Inf); = **sift out**, look for, search for

pan² v = **move along** or **across**, follow, track, sweep

panic n = **fear**, alarm, terror, anxiety, hysteria ▷ v = **go to pieces**, become hysterical, lose your nerve

panorama n = **view**, prospect, vista

pant v = **puff**, blow, breathe, gasp, wheeze

pants pl n (Brit) = **underpants**, briefs, drawers, knickers, panties;

lower trunk **2** (US & Canad) trousers

pap n soft food

papacy n, pl **-cies** office of Pope **papal** adj of the Pope

paper ❶ n **1** material made by pressing pulp of rags, wood etc., into thin sheets **2** sheet of paper **3** newspaper **4** essay ▷ pl **5** documents etc. ▷ v **6** cover with paper **paperback** n book with flexible covers

papier-mâché n paper pulp mixed with paste, shaped and dried hard

paprika n red pepper

papyrus n, pl **-ri, -ruses 1** species of reed **2** paper made from this

par n **1** equality of value or standing **2** face value **3** (Golf) estimated standard score **parity** n **1** equality **2** analogy

parable n allegory, story with moral lesson

parachute n **1** apparatus extending like umbrella used to slow the descent of falling body ▷ v **2** drop by parachute

parade ❶ n **1** display **2** muster of troops ▷ v **3** march **4** display

paradise ❶ n **1** Heaven **2** state of bliss **3** Garden of Eden

paradox ❶ n statement that seems self-contradictory **paradoxical** adj

paraffin n waxlike or liquid hydrocarbon mixture used as fuel, solvent, etc.

paragon n pattern or model of excellence

paragraph ❶ n **1** section of chapter or book ▷ v **2** arrange in paragraphs

parakeet n small parrot

parallel ❶ adj/n **1** (line or lines) continuously at equal distances **2** (thing) precisely corresponding ▷ v **3** represent as similar **parallelogram** n four-sided figure with opposite sides parallel

paralysis ❶ n incapacity to move or feel **paralyse** v **1** affect with paralysis **2** make immobile **paralytic** adj/n

paramedic n person working in

P

(US) = **trousers**, slacks

paper n = **newspaper**, daily, journal, gazette; = **essay**, article, treatise, dissertation ▷ v = **wallpaper**, hang

parade n = **procession**, march, pageant, cavalcade ▷ v = **march**, process, promenade; = **flaunt**, display, exhibit, show off (Inf)

paradise n = **heaven**, Promised Land, Happy Valley (Islam), Elysian fields; = **bliss**, delight, heaven, felicity, utopia

paradox n = **contradiction**, puzzle, anomaly, enigma, oddity

paragraph n = **section**, part, item, passage, clause

parallel n = **equivalent**, counterpart, match, equal, twin ≠ **opposite** ▷ adj = **matching**, corresponding, like, similar, resembling ≠ **different**; = **equidistant**, alongside, side by side ≠ **divergent**

paralysis n = **immobility**, palsy

support of medical profession
parameter ❶ n limiting factor
paramilitary adj organized on military lines
paramount ❶ adj supreme
paranoia n mental disease with delusions of persecution etc. **paranoid** adj/n
parapet n low wall along edge of bridge etc.
paraphernalia pl n 1 (used as sing) belongings 2 equipment
paraphrase v express in other words
paraplegia n paralysis of lower body **paraplegic** n/adj
parasite ❶ n animal or plant living in or on another **parasitic** adj
parasol n sunshade
paratroops pl n troops trained to descend by parachute
parboil v boil until partly cooked
parcel ❶ n 1 packet ▷ v 2 wrap up 3 divide into parts
parch v make, become hot and dry
parchment n sheep, goat, calf skin prepared for writing
pardon ❶ v 1 forgive, excuse ▷ n

2 forgiveness 3 release from punishment
pare v 1 peel, trim 2 decrease
parent ❶ n father or mother **parentage** n descent, extraction **parental** adj **parenthood** n
parenthesis n, pl **-ses** word(s) inserted in passage **parentheses** pl n round brackets, (), used to mark this
pariah n social outcast
parish ❶ n district under one clergyman **parishioner** n inhabitant of parish
parity see PAR
park ❶ n 1 large area of land in natural state for recreational use ▷ v 2 leave for short time 3 manoeuvre (car) into suitable space
parka n warm waterproof coat
parkade n (Canad) a building used as a car park
parkette n (Canad) a small public park
parking lot n (US & Canad) area or building where vehicles may be left for a time

up
parameter n (Inf) usually plural = **limit**, restriction, framework, limitation, specification
paramount adj = **principal**, prime, first, chief, main ≠ secondary
parasite n = **sponger** (Inf), leech, hanger-on, scrounger (Inf), bloodsucker (Inf)
parcel n = **package**, case, box, pack, bundle ▷ v often with **up** = **wrap**, pack, package, tie up, do

pardon v = **forgive**, excuse ≠ condemn ▷ n = **forgiveness**, absolution ≠ condemnation; = **acquittal**, amnesty, exoneration ≠ punishment
parent n = **father** or **mother**, sire, progenitor, procreator, old (Aust & NZ Inf)
parish n = **district**, community
park n = **recreation ground**, garden, playground, pleasure

parlance n particular way of speaking

parley v/n (hold) discussion about terms

parliament ❶ n law-making assembly of country
parliamentary adj

parlor, US **parlour** ❶ n sitting room

parochial adj 1 narrow, provincial 2 of a parish

parody ❶ n/v, pl **-dies** (write) satirical, amusing imitation of a work

parole n 1 release of prisoner on condition of good behaviour ▷ v 2 release on parole

paroxysm n sudden attack of pain, rage, laughter

parquet n flooring of wooden blocks

parrot ❶ n 1 brightly coloured bird

which can imitate speaking ▷ v 2 repeat words without thinking

parry ❶ v **-rying, -ried** ward off, turn aside

parsimony n stinginess
parsimonious adj

parsley n herb used for seasoning, garnish etc.

parsnip n root vegetable

parson ❶ n clergyman

part ❶ n 1 portion 2 role 3 duty 4 region 5 component ▷ v 6 divide 7 separate **parting** n 1 division of hair on head 2 separation 3 leave-taking **partly** adv in part

partake v **-taking, -took, -taken** 1 take or have share in 2 take food or drink

partial ❶ adj 1 not complete 2 prejudiced 3 fond of **partially** adv partly

---

THESAURUS

garden, playpark

parliament n = **assembly**, council, congress, senate, convention

parlour, US **parlor** n (Old-fashioned) = **sitting room**, lounge, living room, drawing room, front room

parody n = **takeoff** (Inf), satire, caricature, send-up (Brit Inf), spoof (Inf) ▷ v = **take off** (Inf), caricature, send up (Brit Inf), burlesque, satirize

parrot v = **repeat**, echo, imitate, copy, mimic

parry v = **evade**, avoid, dodge, sidestep; = **ward off**, block, deflect, repel, rebuff

parson n = **clergyman**, minister, priest, vicar, preacher

part n = **piece**, share, proportion, percentage, bit ≠ **entirety**; often plural = **region**, area, district, neighbourhood, quarter; = **component**, bit, unit, constituent; = **branch**, division, office, section, wing ▷ v = **divide**, separate, break, tear, split ≠ **join**; = **part company**, separate, split up ≠ **meet**

partial adj = **incomplete**, unfinished, imperfect, uncompleted ≠ **complete**; = **biased**, prejudiced, discriminatory, partisan, unfair ≠ **unbiased**

p

DICTIONARY

participate ❶ v 1 share in 2 take part **participant** n **participation** n

participle n (Grammar) verbal adjective

particle ❶ n minute portion

particular ❶ adj 1 relating to one 2 distinct 3 fussy ▷ n 4 detail, item ▷ pl 5 items of information **particularly** adv

partisan ❶ n 1 adherent of a party 2 guerilla ▷ adj 3 adhering to faction 4 prejudiced

partition ❶ n 1 division 2 interior dividing wall ▷ v 3 divide into sections

partner ❶ n 1 ally or companion 2 spouse **partnership** n

partridge n game bird

party ❶ n, pl **-ties** 1 social assembly 2 group of persons organized together, esp. with common political aim 3 person

pashmina pash-[mee]-na n shawl or scarf made from fine soft goat's wool

pass ❶ v 1 go by, beyond, through etc. 2 exceed 3 transfer 4 spend 5 elapse 6 undergo examination successfully 7 bring a law into force ▷ n 8 way, esp. through mountains 9 permit 10 successful result **passable** adj (just) acceptable **passing** adj 1 transitory 2 casual **pass away** die **pass out** faint

THESAURUS

participate v = **take part**, be involved, perform, join, partake ≠ **refrain from**

particle n = **bit**, piece, scrap, grain, shred

particular adj = **specific**, special, exact, precise, distinct ≠ **general**; = **special**, exceptional, notable, uncommon, marked; = **fussy**, demanding, fastidious, choosy (Inf), picky (Inf) ≠ **indiscriminate** ▷ n usually plural = **detail**, fact, feature, item, circumstance

partisan adj = **prejudiced**, one-sided, biased, partial, sectarian ≠ **unbiased** ▷ n = **supporter**, devotee, adherent, upholder ≠ **opponent**; = **underground fighter**, guerrilla, freedom fighter, resistance fighter

partition n = **screen**, wall, barrier; = **division**, separation, segregation

▷ v = **separate**, screen, divide

partner n = **spouse**, consort, significant other (US Inf), mate, husband or wife; = **companion**, ally, colleague, associate, mate

party n = **faction**, set, side, league, camp; = **get-together** (Inf), celebration, do (Inf), gathering, function; = **group**, team, band, company, unit

pass v = **go by** or **past**, overtake, drive past, lap, leave behind ≠ **stop**; = **go**, move, travel, progress, flow; = **run**, move, stroke; = **give**, hand, send, transfer, deliver; = **be left**, come, be bequeathed, be inherited by; = **kick**, hit, loft, head, lob; = **elapse**, progress, go by, lapse, wear on ▷ n = **licence**, ticket, permit, passport, warrant; = **gap**, route, canyon, gorge, ravine

passage ❶ n 1 opening
2 corridor 3 part of book etc.
4 voyage, fare
passé adj out-of-date
passenger ❶ n traveller, esp. by
public conveyance
passion ❶ n 1 ardent desire 2 any
strong emotion 3 great
enthusiasm **passionate** adj
passive ❶ adj 1 submissive
2 inactive
passport n official document
granting permission to travel
abroad etc.
password n secret word to ensure
admission etc.
past ❶ adj 1 ended 2 gone by
3 elapsed ▷ n 4 bygone times
▷ adv 5 by 6 along ▷ prep
7 beyond 8 after
pasta n any of several preparations

of dough, e.g. spaghetti
paste ❶ n 1 soft mixture
2 adhesive ▷ v 3 fasten with paste
pasting n 1 (Sl) defeat 2 strong
criticism **pasty** adj 1 like paste
2 white 3 sickly
pastel ❶ n 1 coloured crayon
2 drawing with crayons 3 pale,
delicate colour ▷ adj 4 (of colour)
pale
pasteurize v sterilize by heat
pastiche n work of art that mixes
or copies styles
pastille n lozenge
pastime ❶ n recreation
pastor ❶ n clergyman **pastoral**
adj 1 of rural life 2 of pastor
pastry n, pl -ries article of food
made chiefly of flour, fat and water
pasture ❶ n 1 ground on which
cattle graze ▷ v 2 (cause to) graze

_____ THESAURUS _____

passage n = **corridor**, hall, lobby,
vestibule; = **alley**, way, close (Brit);
course; road; = **extract**, reading,
piece, section, text; = **journey**,
crossing, trip, trek, voyage;
= **safe-conduct**, right to travel,
freedom to travel, permission to
travel
passenger n = **traveller**, rider,
fare, commuter, fare payer
passion n = **love**, desire, lust,
infatuation, ardour; = **emotion**,
feeling, fire, heat, excitement
≠ **indifference**; = **mania**,
enthusiasm, obsession, bug (Inf),
craving
passive adj = **submissive**,
compliant, receptive, docile,
quiescent ≠ **spirited**

past n = **former times**, long ago,
days gone by, the olden days
≠ **future**; = **background**, life,
history, past life, life story ▷ adj
= **former**, early, previous, ancient,
bygone ≠ **future**; = **previous**,
former, one-time, ex- ▷ prep
= **after**, beyond, later than
paste ▷ n = **adhesive**, glue, cement,
gum ▷ v = **stick**, glue, cement,
gum
pastel adj = **pale**, light, soft,
delicate, muted ≠ **bright**
pastime n = **activity**, game,
entertainment, hobby, recreation
pastor n = **clergyman**, minister,
priest, vicar, parson
pasture n = **grassland**, grass,
meadow, grazing

DICTIONARY

pasty n, pl **pasties** small pie of meat and crust, baked without a dish

pat¹ **❶** v **patting, patted** 1 tap ▷ n 2 tap 3 small mass, as of butter

pat² adv 1 exactly 2 fluently

patch ❶ n 1 piece of cloth sewed on garment 2 spot 3 plot of ground ▷ v 4 mend 5 repair clumsily **patchy** adj of uneven quality **patchwork** n needlework of different pieces sewn together

pate n 1 head 2 top of head

pâté n spread of finely minced liver etc.

patent ❶ n 1 exclusive right to invention ▷ adj 2 open 3 evident ▷ v 4 secure a patent **patently** adv obviously

paternal adj 1 fatherly 2 of a father **paternity** n fatherhood

path ❶ n 1 way, track 2 course of action

pathetic ❶ adj moving to pity

pathology n science of diseases **pathological** adj **pathologist** n

pathos n power of exciting tender emotions

patient ❶ adj 1 bearing troubles calmly ▷ n 2 person under medical treatment **patience** n

patio n, pl **-tios** paved area adjoining house

patriarch n father and ruler of family

patrician n/adj (one) of noble birth

patriot ❶ n person that loves his or her country **patriotic** adj **patriotism** n

patrol ❶ n 1 regular circuit by guard 2 person, small group patrolling ▷ v 3 go round on guard

patron ❶ n 1 one who aids artists, charities etc. 2 regular customer 3 guardian saint **patronage** n support given by patron **patronize** v 1 assume air of superiority towards 2 be regular customer

THESAURUS

pat¹ v = **stroke**, touch, tap, pet, caress ▷ n = **tap**, stroke, clap

patch n = **spot**, bit, scrap, shred, small piece; = **plot**, area, ground, land, tract; = **reinforcement**, piece of fabric, piece of cloth, piece of material, piece sewn on ▷ v often with **up** = **mend**, cover, repair, reinforce, stitch (up)

patent n = **copyright**, licence, franchise, registered trademark ▷ adj = **obvious**, apparent, evident, clear, glaring

path n = **way**, road, walk, track, trail; = **route**, way, course, direction

pathetic adj = **sad**, moving, touching, affecting, distressing ≠ **funny**

patient adj = **sick person**, case, sufferer, invalid ▷ adj = **forbearing**, understanding, forgiving, mild, tolerant ≠ **impatient**

patriot n = **nationalist**, loyalist, chauvinist

patrol v = **police**, guard, keep watch (on), inspect, safeguard ▷ n = **guard**, watch, watchman, sentinel, patrolman

patron n = **supporter**, friend,

DICTIONARY

patter n **1** quick succession of taps **2** (Inf) glib, rapid speech ▷ v **3** make quick tapping noise

pattern ❶ n **1** arrangement of repeated parts **2** design **3** plan for cutting cloth etc. **4** model ▷ v **5** model

paunch n belly

pauper n very poor person

pause ❶ v/n stop, rest

pave ❶ v form surface with stone **pavement** n paved footpath

pavilion n **1** clubhouse on playing field etc. **2** building for exhibition etc. **3** large tent

paw ❶ n **1** foot of animal ▷ v **2** scrape with forefoot **3** maul

pawn¹ v deposit (article) as security for money borrowed **pawnbroker** n lender of money on goods deposited

pawn² n **1** piece in chess **2** person used as mere tool

pay ❶ v **paying, paid 1** give money etc., for goods or services

2 give **3** be profitable to **4** spend ▷ n **5** wages **payable** adj justly due **payee** n person to whom money is paid or due **payment** n **payday** n day when wages are paid

PC 1 personal computer **2** Police Constable **3** Privy Councillor

PE physical education

pea n **1** edible seed, growing in pods, of climbing plant **2** the plant

peace ❶ n **1** freedom from war **2** harmony **3** calm **peaceable** adj disposed to peace **peaceful** adj

peach n fruit of delicate flavour

peacock n male bird with fanlike tail

peak ❶ n **1** pointed end of anything, esp. hilltop **2** highest point

peal n **1** (succession of) loud sound(s) ▷ v **2** sound loudly

peanut n **1** pea-shaped nut ▷ pl **2** (Inf) trifling amount of money

THESAURUS

champion, sponsor, backer; **= customer**, client, buyer, frequenter, shopper

pattern n **= order**, plan, system, method, sequence; **= design**, arrangement, motif, figure, device; **= plan**, design, original, guide, diagram

pause v **= stop briefly**, delay, break, wait, rest ≠ **continue** ▷ n **= stop**, break, interval, rest, gap ≠ **continuance**

pave v **= cover**, floor, surface, concrete, tile

paw v (Inf) **= manhandle**, grab, maul, molest, handle roughly

pay v **= reward**, compensate, reimburse, recompense, requite; **= spend**, give, fork out (Inf), remit, shell out (Inf); **= bring in**, earn, return, net, yield ▷ n **= wages**, income, payment, earnings, fee

peace n **= truce**, ceasefire, treaty, armistice ≠ **war**; **= stillness**, rest, quiet, silence, calm; **= serenity**, calm, composure, contentment, repose; **= harmony**, accord, agreement, concord

peak n **= high point**, crown, climax, culmination, zenith; **= point**, top, tip, summit, brow ▷ v **= culminate**, climax, come to a

pear n 1 tree yielding sweet, juicy fruit 2 the fruit **pear-shaped** adj shaped like a pear, heavier at the bottom than the top

pearl n hard, lustrous structure found esp. in oyster and used as jewel

peasant ❶ n member of low social class, esp. in rural district

peat n decomposed vegetable substance

pebble n small roundish stone

peccadillo n, pl **-loes, -los** 1 slight offence 2 petty crime

peck ❶ v 1 strike with or as with beak 2 nibble at 3 (Inf) kiss quickly ▷ n 4 pecking movement **peckish** adj (Inf) hungry

pectoral n of the breast

peculiar ❶ adj 1 strange 2 particular 3 belonging to **peculiarity** n, pl **-ties** 1 oddity 2 characteristic 3 distinguishing feature

pedal n 1 foot lever ▷ v 2 propel bicycle by using its pedals 3 use pedal

pedant n one who insists on petty details of book-learning,

grammatical rules etc. **pedantic** adj

peddle v go round selling goods

pedestal n base of column

pedestrian ❶ n 1 one who walks on foot ▷ adj 2 going on foot 3 commonplace 4 dull

pedestrian crossing place marked where pedestrians may cross road

pedigree ❶ n 1 register of ancestors 2 genealogy

pedlar n 1 one who sells 2 hawker

peek v/n peep, glance

peel ❶ v 1 strip off skin, rind or covering 2 flake off, as skin, rind ▷ n 3 rind, skin

peep ❶ v 1 look slyly or quickly ▷ n 2 such a look

peer¹ ❶ v look closely

peer² ❶ n 1 nobleman 2 one of the same rank **peerage** n **peerless** adj without match or equal **peer group** group of people of similar age, status etc. **peer pressure** influence from one's peer group

peeved adj (Inf) sulky, irritated

peevish adj 1 fretful 2 irritable

——————— THESAURUS

head

peasant n = **rustic**, countryman

peck v = **pick**, hit, strike, tap, poke

peculiar adj = **odd**, strange, unusual, bizarre, funny ≠ **ordinary**; = **special**, particular, unique, characteristic ≠ **common**

pedestrian n = **walker**, foot-traveller ≠ **driver** ▷ adj = **dull**, ordinary, boring, commonplace, mundane ≠ **exciting**

pedigree n = **lineage**, family, line, race, stock

peel n = **rind**, skin, peeling ▷ v = **skin**, scale, strip, pare, shuck

peep v = **peek**, look, eyeball (Sl), sneak a look, steal a look ▷ n = **look**, glimpse, peek, look-see (Sl)

peer¹ v = **squint**, look, spy, gaze, scan

peer² n = **noble**, lord, aristocrat, nobleman; = **equal**, like, fellow,

peewit n lapwing

peg ❶ n **1** pin for joining, fastening, marking etc. **2** (mark of) level, standard etc. ▷ v **3** fasten with pegs **4** stabilize (prices) **5** (with *away*) persevere

pejorative adj (of words etc.) with disparaging connotation

pelican n waterfowl with large pouch beneath its bill **pelican crossing** road crossing with pedestrian-operated traffic lights

pellet n little ball

pelmet n ornamental drapery or board, concealing curtain rail

pelt¹ v **1** throw missiles **2** rain persistently **3** rush

pelt² n raw hide or skin

pelvis n bony cavity at base of human trunk **pelvic** adj

pen¹ ❶ n **1** instrument for writing ▷ v **2** compose **3** write **pen friend** friend with whom one corresponds without meeting **penknife** n small knife with folding blade

pen² ❶ n/v (put in) enclosure

penal adj of punishment **penalize** v impose penalty on **penalty** n, pl **-ties 1** punishment **2** forfeit **3** (Sport) handicap

penance n suffering submitted to as expression of penitence

pence n pl of PENNY

penchant n inclination, decided taste

pencil n **1** instrument, esp. of graphite, for writing etc. ▷ v **2** draw **3** mark with pencil

pendant n hanging ornament

pendent adj hanging

pending ❶ prep **1** during, until ▷ adj **2** awaiting settlement **3** imminent

pendulous adj hanging, swinging **pendulum** n suspended weight swinging to and fro

penetrate ❶ v **1** enter into **2** pierce **3** arrive at meaning of **penetrating** adj **1** sharp **2** easily heard **3** quick to understand **penetration** n

penguin n flightless bird

penicillin n antibiotic drug

peninsula n portion of land nearly surrounded by water **peninsular** adj

penis n male organ of copulation and urination

penitent adj **1** affected by sense of guilt ▷ n **2** one that repents **penitence** n sorrow for sin **penitentiary** adj, pl **-ries** ▷ n (US) prison

pennant n long narrow flag

penny n, pl **pence**, **pennies** Brit.

contemporary, compeer

peg v = **fasten**, join, fix, secure, attach

pen¹ v = **write (down)**, draft, compose, pencil, draw up

pen² n = **enclosure**, pound, fold, cage, coop ▷ v = **enclose**, confine,

cage, fence in, coop up

pending adj = **undecided**, unsettled, in the balance, undetermined

penetrate v = **pierce**, enter, go through, bore, stab (Inf); = **grasp**, work out, figure out (Inf),

bronze coin, 100th part of pound
penniless adj having no money
pension ❶ n 1 regular payment to
old people, soldiers etc. ▷ v 2 grant
pension to **pensioner** n
pensive adj thoughtful
pentagon n figure with five angles
penthouse n apartment, flat on
top of building
penultimate adj next before the
last
penury n extreme poverty
peony n, pl **-nies** plant with
showy red, pink, or white flowers
people ❶ pl n 1 persons generally,
nation 2 race 3 family ▷ v
4 populate
pep n (Inf) 1 vigour 2 energy ▷ v
3 give energy, enthusiasm **pep
talk** (Inf) talk designed to increase
confidence, enthusiasm etc.
pepper ❶ n 1 pungent aromatic
spice 2 slightly pungent vegetable
▷ v 3 season with pepper
4 sprinkle 5 pelt with missiles
peppermint n 1 plant noted for
aromatic pungent liquor distilled
from it 2 sweet flavoured with this
pepper spray aerosol spray
causing temporary blindness and

breathing difficulty, used esp. for
self-defence
per prep 1 for each 2 by 3 in
manner of
perambulate v 1 walk through
or over 2 walk about
perambulator n pram
per annum (Lat) by the year
per capita (Lat) for each person
perceive ❶ v 1 obtain knowledge
of through senses 2 understand
perceptible adj **perception** n
perceptive adj
percentage n proportion or rate
per hundred **per cent** in each
hundred
perch¹ ❶ n 1 resting place, as for
bird ▷ v 2 place, as on perch
3 alight on branch etc. 4 balance
on
perch² n freshwater fish
perchance adv (Obs) perhaps
percolate v 1 pass through fine
mesh as liquor 2 filter **percolator**
n coffeepot with filter
percussion n striking of one thing
against another
peremptory adj imperious
perennial ❶ adj 1 lasting through
the years 2 perpetual ▷ n 3 plant

——— THESAURUS ———

pension n = **allowance**, benefit,
welfare, annuity, superannuation
people pl n = **persons**, individuals,
folk (Inf), men and women,
humanity; = **nation**, public,
community, subjects, population;
= **race**, tribe ▷ v = **inhabit**, occupy,
settle, populate, colonize
pepper n = **seasoning**, flavour,

spice ▷ v = **pelt**, hit, shower, blitz,
rake; = **sprinkle**, spot, scatter, dot,
fleck
perceive v = **see**, notice, note,
identify, discover; = **understand**,
gather, see, learn, realize
perch¹ v = **sit**, rest, balance, settle
▷ n = **resting place**, post, branch,
pole
perennial adj = **continual**,

lasting more than two years
perfect ⊕ *adj* **1** complete
2 unspoilt **3** correct, precise
4 excellent ▷ *v* **5** improve **6** make
skilful **perfection** *n*
perfectionist *n* one who demands
highest standards **perfectly** *adv*
perforate *v* make holes in,
penetrate **perforation** *n*
perform ⊕ *v* **1** fulfil **2** function
3 act part **4** play, as on musical
instrument **performance** *n*
perfume ⊕ *n* **1** agreeable scent
▷ *v* **2** imbue with an agreeable
odour
perfunctory *adj* done
indifferently
perhaps ⊕ *adv* possibly
peril ⊕ *n* **1** danger **2** exposure to
injury **perilous** *adj*
perimeter ⊕ *n* **1** outer boundary
of area **2** length of this
period ⊕ *n* **1** particular portion of

time **2** series of years **3** single
occurrence of menstruation **4** full
stop ▷ *adj* **5** (of furniture, dress
etc.) belonging to a particular time
in history **periodic** *adj* recurring
at regular intervals **periodical** *adj*
1 periodic ▷ *n* **2** publication issued
at regular intervals **periodic table**
(*Chem*) chart showing relationship
of elements to each other
peripatetic *adj* travelling about
periphery *n, pl* **-eries**
1 circumference **2** outside
peripheral *adj* unimportant
periscope *n* instrument used for
giving view of objects on different
level
perish ⊕ *v* **1** die **2** rot **perishable**
adj that will not last long
perishing *adj* (*Inf*) very cold
perk ⊕ *n* incidental benefit from
employment
perm *n* **1** long-lasting curly

lasting, constant, enduring,
persistent
perfect *adj* = **faultless**, correct,
pure, impeccable, exemplary
≠ **deficient**; = **excellent**, ideal,
supreme, superb, splendid;
= **immaculate**, impeccable,
flawless, spotless, unblemished
≠ **flawed**; = **complete**, absolute,
sheer, utter, consummate ≠ **partial**
▷ *v* = **improve**, develop, polish,
refine ≠ **mar**
perform *v* = **do**, achieve, carry out,
complete, fulfil; = **fulfil**, carry out,
execute, discharge
perfume *n* = **fragrance**, scent
perhaps *adv* = **maybe**, possibly, it

may be, it is possible (that),
conceivably
peril *n* = **danger**, risk, threat,
hazard, menace
perimeter *n* = **boundary**,
edge, border, bounds, limit
≠ **centre**
period *n* = **time**, term, season,
space, run
perish *v* = **die**, be killed, expire,
pass away, lose your life; = **be
destroyed**, fall, decline,
collapse, disappear; = **rot**,
waste away, decay, disintegrate,
decompose
perk *n* (*Brit Inf*) = **bonus**, benefit,
extra, plus, fringe benefit

hairstyle ▷ v **2** give a perm
permanent ❶ adj **1** continuing in
same state **2** lasting **permanence**
n
permeate v **1** pervade **2** pass
through pores of **permeable** adj
permit ❶ v -mitting, -mitted
1 allow **2** give leave to ▷ n
3 warrant or licence to do
something **permissible** adj
permission n **permissive** adj
(too) tolerant, esp. sexually
permutation n (Maths)
arrangement of a number of
quantities in every possible order
pernicious adj **1** wicked
2 harmful
pernickety adj (Inf) fussy
peroxide n short for HYDROGEN
PEROXIDE
perpendicular adj/n **1** (line) at
right angles to another
2 (something) exactly upright
perpetrate v perform or be
responsible for (something bad)
perpetual ❶ adj **1** continuous
2 lasting forever **perpetuate** v
1 make perpetual **2** not to allow to
be forgotten **perpetuity** n

perplex v **1** puzzle **2** bewilder
perplexity n/pl -ties
persecute ❶ v oppress because of
race, religion etc. **persecution** n
persevere v persist, maintain
effort **perseverance** n
persist ❶ v continue in spite of
obstacles or objections
persistence n **persistent** adj
person ❶ n **1** individual (human)
being **2** body of human being
3 (Grammar) classification of
pronouns and verb forms according
to the person speaking, spoken to,
or of **personable** adj pleasant in
looks and personality **personal**
adj **1** individual, private **2** of
grammatical person **personality**
n **1** distinctive character
2 celebrity **personally** adv
1 independently **2** in one's own
opinion **personal computer**
small computer for word processing
or computer games **personal
stereo** portable cassette player
with headphones
persona n, pl -nae someone's
personality as presented to
others

——— THESAURUS ———

permanent adj = **lasting**,
constant, enduring, persistent,
eternal ≠ **temporary**
permit v = **allow**, grant, sanction,
let, entitle ≠ **forbid** ▷ n = **licence**,
pass, document, certificate,
passport ≠ **prohibition**
perpetual adj = **everlasting**,
permanent, endless, eternal,
lasting ≠ **temporary**; = **continual**,
repeated, constant, endless,

continuous ≠ **brief**
persecute v = **victimize**, torture,
torment, oppress, pick on
≠ **mollycoddle**; = **harass**, bother,
annoy, tease, hassle (Inf) ≠ **leave
alone**
persist v = **continue**, last, remain,
carry on, keep up; = **persevere**,
continue, go on, carry on, keep on
person n = **individual**, being,
body, human, soul

personify v -fying, -fied
1 represent as person 2 typify
personification n
personnel ❶ n staff employed in organization
perspective ❶ n 1 mental view
2 method of drawing on flat surface to give effect of relative distances and sizes
Perspex® n transparent acrylic substitute for glass
perspicacious adj having quick mental insight
perspire v sweat **perspiration** n
persuade ❶ v 1 make (one) do something by argument, charm etc. 2 convince **persuasion** n
1 art, act of persuading 2 belief **persuasive** adj
pert adj forward, saucy
pertain v belong, relate, have reference (to)
pertinacious adj persistent
pertinent adj to the point **pertinence** n relevance
perturb v 1 disturb 2 alarm
peruse v read in careful or leisurely

manner **perusal** n
pervade v spread through
pervasive adj
pervert ❶ v 1 turn to wrong use
2 lead astray ▷ n 3 one who practises sexual perversion
perverse adj 1 obstinately or unreasonably wrong 2 wayward
perversion n 1 sexual act considered abnormal 2 corruption
perversity n
peseta n Spanish monetary unit
pessimism n tendency to see worst side of things **pessimist** n
pessimistic adj
pest ❶ n 1 troublesome or harmful thing, person or insect **pesticide** n chemical for killing pests, esp. insects
pester v 1 vex 2 harass
pestilence n epidemic disease
pestle n instrument with which things are pounded
pet ❶ n 1 animal or person kept or regarded with affection ▷ adj
2 favourite ▷ v 3 make pet of
4 (Inf) fondle
petal n white or coloured leaflike

personnel n = **employees**, people, staff, workers, workforce
perspective n = **outlook**, attitude, context, angle, frame of reference
persuade v = **talk (someone) into**, urge, influence, win (someone) over, induce
≠ **dissuade**; = **cause**, lead, move, influence, motivate
pervert v = **distort**, abuse, twist, misuse, warp; = **corrupt**, degrade, deprave, debase, debauch ▷ n

= **deviant**, degenerate, sicko (Inf), weirdo or weirdie (Inf)
pest n = **infection**, bug, insect, plague, epidemic; = **nuisance**, trial, pain (Inf), drag (Inf), bother
pet adj = **favourite**, favoured, dearest, cherished, fave (Inf) ▷ n
= **favourite**, treasure, darling, jewel, idol ▷ v = **fondle**, pat, stroke, caress; = **pamper**, spoil, indulge, cosset, baby; (Inf)
= **cuddle**, kiss, snog (Brit Sl), smooch (Inf), neck (Inf)

part of flower

petite adj small, dainty

petition ❶ n 1 request, esp. to sovereign or parliament ▷ v 2 present petition to

petrel n sea bird

petrify v -fying, -fied 1 turn to stone 2 make motionless with fear

petroleum n mineral oil **petrol** n refined petroleum as used in motorcars etc.

petticoat n woman's underskirt

pettifogging adj overconcerned with unimportant detail

petty ❶ adj -tier, -tiest 1 unimportant 2 small-minded **petty cash** cash kept to pay minor expenses **petty officer** noncommissioned officer in navy

petulant adj 1 irritable 2 peevish

petunia n garden plant

pew n fixed seat in church

pewter n greyish alloy of tin and lead

phallus n, pl -luses, -li 1 penis 2 symbol of it used in primitive rites **phallic** adj

phantom ❶ n 1 apparition 2 ghost

Pharaoh n title of ancient Egyptian kings

pharmaceutical adj of drugs or pharmacy **pharmacist** n person qualified to dispense drugs **pharmacology** n study of drugs **pharmacy** n 1 preparation and dispensing of drugs 2 dispensary

phase ❶ n distinct stage in development **phase in, out** introduce or discontinue gradually

PhD Doctor of Philosophy

pheasant n game bird

phenomenon ❶ n, pl -ena 1 anything observed 2 remarkable person or thing **phenomenal** adj

phial n small bottle

philanthropy n practice of doing good to one's fellow men **philanthropic** adj **philanthropist** n

philately n stamp collecting **philatelist** n

philistine n/adj ignorant (person)

philosophy ❶ n, pl -phies 1 study of realities and general principles 2 system of theories on nature of things or on conduct **philosopher** n **philosophical** adj 1 of, like philosophy 2 wise, learned 3 calm, stoical

petition n = **appeal**, round robin, list of signatures ▷ v = **appeal**, plead, ask, pray, beg

petty adj = **trivial**, insignificant, little, small, slight ≠ **important**; = **small-minded**, mean, shabby, spiteful, ungenerous ≠ **broad-minded**

phantom n = **spectre**, ghost, spirit, shade (Lit), spook (Inf)

phase n = **stage**, time, point, position, step

phenomenon n = **occurrence**, happening, fact, event, incident; = **wonder**, sensation, exception, miracle, marvel

philosophy n = **thought**, knowledge, thinking, reasoning, wisdom; = **outlook**, values, principles, convictions, thinking

phlegm n thick yellowish substance formed in throat **phlegmatic** adj not easily agitated

phobia n fear or aversion

phoenix n legendary bird

phone ❶ n 1 telephone 2 telephone call ▷ v 3 telephone **phonecard** n card used to operate some public telephones

phonetic adj of vocal sounds **phonetics** pl n science of vocal sounds

phoney, phony (Inf) ▷ adj 1 sham 2 suspect ▷ n 3 phoney person or thing

phosphorus n nonmetallic element which appears luminous in the dark **phosphate** n compound of phosphorus **phosphorescence** n faint glow in the dark

photo n, pl **photos** (Inf) photograph **photo finish** finish of a race in which the contestants are so close that a photograph is needed to decide the result **Photoshop®** n 1 software application for managing and editing digital images ▷ v 2 (Inf) alter (a digital image) using Photoshop or a similar application

photocopy n, pl **-copies**

1 photographic reproduction ▷ v 2 make photocopy of

photogenic adj tending to look attractive when photographed

photograph ❶ n 1 picture made by chemical action of light on sensitive film ▷ v 2 take photograph of **photographer** n **photographic** adj **photography** n

photosynthesis n process by which green plant uses sun's energy to make carbohydrates

phrase ❶ n 1 group of words 2 expression ▷ v 3 express in words **phraseology** n choice of words

physical ❶ adj 1 of the body, as contrasted with the mind or spirit 2 of material things or nature

physics pl n science of properties of matter and energy **physical** adj 1 bodily, as opposed to mental 2 material **physician** n qualified medical practitioner **physicist** n one skilled in, or student of, physics

physiognomy n face

physiology n science of living things

physiotherapy n therapeutic use of physical means, as massage etc. **physiotherapist** n

physique n bodily structure, constitution

phone n = **telephone**, blower (Inf), mobile, landline ▷ v = **call**, telephone, ring (up) (Inf, chiefly Brit), give someone a call, give someone a ring (Inf, chiefly Brit), give someone a buzz (Inf)

photograph n = **picture**, photo (Inf), shot, print, snap (Inf), selfie (Inf) ▷ v = **take a picture of**, record,

film, shoot, snap (Inf)

phrase n = **expression**, saying, remark, construction, quotation ▷ v = **express**, say, word, put, voice

physical adj = **corporal**, fleshly, bodily, corporeal; = **earthly**, fleshly, mortal, incarnate

physician n = **doctor**, doc (Inf), medic (Inf), general practitioner,

pi n (Maths) ratio of circumference of circle to its diameter

piano n, pl **pianos** 1 musical instrument with keyboard ▷ adj/adv 2 (Mus) softly **pianist** n performer on piano

picador n mounted bullfighter with lance

piccalilli n pickle of vegetables in mustard sauce

piccolo n, pl **-los** small flute

pick¹ ▷ v 1 choose, select carefully 2 pluck, gather 3 find occasion for ▷ v 4 act of picking 5 choicest part **pick on** find fault with **pickpocket** n thief who steals from someone's pocket **pick up** 1 lift 2 obtain 3 collect 4 get better 5 accelerate **pick-up** n 1 small truck 2 device for conversion of mechanical energy into electric signals

pick² tool with curved iron crossbar **pickaxe** n pick

picket ❶ n 1 pointed stake

2 party of trade unionists posted to deter would-be workers during strike ▷ v 3 post as picket

pickle ❶ n 1 food preserved in brine, vinegar etc. 2 awkward situation ▷ v 3 preserve in pickle

picnic ❶ n 1 pleasure excursion including meal out of doors ▷ v 2 take part in picnic

picture ❶ n 1 drawing or painting 2 mental image 3 film, movie ▷ pl 4 cinema ▷ v 5 represent in, or as in, a picture **pictorial** adj 1 of, in, with pictures ▷ v 2 newspaper with pictures **picturesque** adj visually striking

pidgin n language made up of two or more other languages

pie n baked dish of meat, fruit etc. usu. with pastry crust

piebald adj irregularly marked with black and white **pied** adj 1 piebald 2 variegated

piece ❶ n 1 bit, part, fragment 2 single object 3 literary or musical

——————— THESAURUS —————

medical practitioner

pick¹ v = **select**, choose, identify, elect, nominate **≠ reject**; = **gather**, pull, collect, take in, harvest; = **provoke**, start, cause, stir up, incite; = **open**, force, crack (Inf), break into, break open ▷ n = **choice**, decision, option, selection, preference; = **best**, prime, finest, elect, elite

picket v = **blockade**, boycott, demonstrate outside ▷ n = **demonstration**, strike, blockade; = **protester**, demonstrator, picketer; = **lookout**, watch, guard,

patrol, sentry

pickle v = **preserve**, marinade, steep ▷ n = **chutney**, relish, piccalilli

picnic n = **excursion**, barbecue, barbie (Inf), cookout (US & Canad), alfresco meal

picture n = **representation**, drawing, painting, portrait, image; = **photograph**, photo, still, shot, selfie (Inf), image ▷ v = **imagine**, see, envision, visualize, conceive of; = **represent**, show, draw, paint, illustrate

piece n = **bit**, slice, part, block,

DICTIONARY

composition etc. ▷ v **4** mend, put together **piecemeal** adv by, in, or into pieces, a bit at a time

pier ❶ n **1** structure running into sea **2** piece of solid upright masonry

pierce ❶ v **1** make hole in **2** make a way through **piercing** adj **1** shrill **2** alert, probing

piety n, pl **-ties 1** godliness **2** devoutness

pig ❶ n **1** wild or domesticated mammal killed for pork, ham, bacon **2** (Inf) greedy, dirty person **piggish, piggy** adj **pig-headed** adj obstinate

pigeon n bird of wild and domesticated varieties **pigeonhole** n **1** compartment for papers in desk etc. ▷ v **2** defer **3** classify

piggyback n ride on the back

pigment ❶ n colouring matter, paint or dye

pigtail n plait of hair on either side of head

pike¹ n predatory freshwater fish

pike² n long-handled spear

pikelet n (Aust & NZ) small thick pancake

pilau, pilaf, pilaff n Oriental dish of meat or fowl boiled with rice, spices etc.

piker n (Aust & NZ, Sl) shirker

pilchard n small sea fish like herring

pile¹ ❶ n **1** heap ▷ v **2** heap (up) **3** (with in or out) crowd ▷ n **4** heap **pile-up** n (Inf) traffic accident with several vehicles

pile² ❶ n beam driven into the ground, esp. as foundation

pile³ ❶ n nap of cloth

piles pl n haemorrhoids

pilfer v steal small items

pilgrim ❶ n one who journeys to sacred place **pilgrimage** n

pill ❶ n small ball of medicine swallowed whole **the pill** oral contraceptive

pillage v/n plunder

pillar ❶ n **1** upright support

p

THESAURUS

quantity; = **component**, part, section, bit, unit

pier n = **jetty**, wharf, quay, promenade, landing place; = **pillar**, support, post, column, pile

pierce v = **penetrate**, stab, spike, enter, bore

pig n = **hog**, sow, boar, swine, porker; (Inf) = **slob** (Sl), glutton

pigment n = **colour**, colouring, paint, stain, dye

pile¹ n = **heap**, collection, mountain, mass, stack; (Inf) often plural = **lot(s)**, mountain(s), load(s)

(Inf), oceans, wealth; = **mansion**, building, residence, manor, country house ▷ v = **load**, stuff, pack, stack, charge; = **crowd**, pack, rush, climb, flood

pile² n = **foundation**, support, post, column, beam

pile³ n = **nap**, fibre, down, hair, fur

pilgrim n = **traveller**, wanderer, devotee, wayfarer

pill n = **tablet**, capsule, pellet

pillar n = **support**, post, column, prop, shaft; = **supporter**, leader, mainstay, leading light (Inf),

2 strong supporter **pillar box** red pillar-shaped letter box

pillion |- n seat behind rider of motorcycle or horse

pillory n, pl **-ries** 1 frame with holes for head and hands in which offender was confined ▷ v

2 expose to ridicule and abuse

pillow n cushion for the head, esp. in bed **pillowcase** n removable cover for pillow

pilot ❶ v 1 person qualified to fly an aircraft or spacecraft 2 one qualified to take charge of ship entering or leaving harbour etc.

3 guide ▷ adj **4** experimental and preliminary ▷ v **5** act as pilot to **6** steer **pilot light** small flame lighting main one in gas appliance

pimento, pimiento n, pl **-tos** **1** allspice **2** sweet red pepper

pimp n 1 one who solicits for prostitute ▷ v 2 act as pimp

pimpernel n plant with small scarlet, blue, or white flowers

pimple n small pus-filled spot on skin **pimply** adj

pin ❶ n 1 piece of stiff wire with point and head, for fastening

2 wooden or metal peg or rivet ▷ v **3** fasten with pin **4** seize and hold fast **pinpoint** v identify exactly **pinstripe** n very narrow stripe in fabric **pin-up** n picture of sexually attractive person

pinafore n 1 apron 2 dress with bib top

pincers pl n 1 tool for gripping **2** claws of lobster etc.

pinch ❶ v 1 nip, squeeze 2 stint **3** (Inf) steal **4** (Inf) arrest ▷ n **5** nip **6** small amount **7** emergency

pine¹ ❶ v 1 yearn 2 waste away with grief etc.

pine² ❶ n 1 evergreen coniferous tree 2 its wood

pineapple n tropical plant bearing large edible fruit

pinion n 1 bird's wing ▷ v

2 confine by binding wings, arms etc.

pink ❶ n 1 pale red colour **2** garden plant **3** best condition ▷ adj **4** of the colour pink ▷ v **5** pierce **6** cut indented edge **7** (of engine) knock

pinnacle ❶ n 1 highest point **2** mountain peak **3** pointed turret

— THESAURUS —

upholder

pilot n = **airman**, flyer, aviator, aeronaut; = **helmsman**, navigator, steersman ▷ v = **fly**, operate, be at the controls of ▷ adj = **trial**, test, model, sample, experimental

pin v = **fasten**, stick, attach, join, fix; = **hold fast**, hold down, constrain, immobilize, pinion

pinch v = **nip**, press, squeeze,

grasp, compress; = **hurt**, crush, squeeze, pain, cramp; (Brit Inf) = **steal**, lift (Inf), nick (Sl, chiefly Brit), swipe (Sl), knock off (Sl) ▷ n = **nip**, squeeze

pine¹ v = **waste**, decline, sicken, fade, languish

pink adj = **rosy**, rose, salmon, flushed, reddish

pinnacle n = **summit**, top, height, peak

pint n 1 liquid measure 2 1/8 gallon (.568 litre)

pioneer ❶ n 1 explorer 2 early settler 3 originator ▷ v 4 act as pioneer

pious adj 1 devout 2 self-righteous

pip¹ n seed in fruit

pip² n 1 high-pitched sound as time signal on radio 2 spot on cards, dice etc. 3 (Inf) star on junior officer's shoulder showing rank

pipe ❶ n 1 tube of metal or other material 2 tube with small bowl at end for smoking tobacco 3 musical instrument ▷ pl 4 bagpipes ▷ v 5 play on pipe 6 utter in shrill tone 7 convey by pipe 8 ornament with piping **piper** n **piping** n 1 system of pipes 2 decoration of icing on cake 3 fancy edging on clothes **pipeline** n long pipe for transporting oil, water etc.

piquant adj pungent

pique n 1 feeling of injury ▷ v 2 hurt pride of 3 irritate

piranha n fierce tropical Amer. fish

pirate ❶ n 1 sea robber

2 publisher etc. who infringes copyright 3 person broadcasting illegally ▷ v 4 use or reproduce (artistic work etc.) illicitly **piracy** n

pirouette n/v (perform) act of spinning round on toe

pistachio n, pl **-chios** small hard-shelled, sweet-tasting nut

piste n ski slope

pistol n small firearm for one hand

piston n in engine, cylindrical part propelled to and fro in hollow cylinder

pit ❶ n 1 deep hole in ground 2 mine or its shaft 3 depression 4 part of theatre occupied by orchestra 5 servicing area on motor-racing track ▷ v 6 set to fight, match 7 mark with small dents **pitfall** n hidden danger

pitch¹ ❶ v 1 throw 2 set 3 set the key of (a tune) 4 fall headlong ▷ n 5 act of pitching 6 degree, height, intensity 7 slope 8 degree of highness or lowness of sound 9 (Sport) field of play **pitchfork** 1 fork for lifting hay etc. ▷ v 2 throw with, as with, pitchfork

pioneer n = **founder**, leader, developer, innovator, trailblazer; = **settler**, explorer, colonist ▷ v = **develop**, create, establish, start, discover

pipe n = **tube**, drain, canal, pipeline, line ▷ v = **convey**, channel, conduct

pirate n = **buccaneer**, raider, marauder, corsair, freebooter ▷ v = **copy**, steal, reproduce, bootleg, appropriate

pit n = **coal mine**, mine, shaft, colliery, mine shaft ▷ v = **scar**, mark, dent, indent, pockmark

pitch¹ n = **sports field**, ground, stadium, arena, park; = **tone**, sound, key, frequency, timbre; = **level**, point, degree, summit, extent; = **talk**, patter, spiel (Inf) ▷ v = **throw**, cast, toss, hurl, fling; = **fall**, drop, plunge, dive, tumble; = **set up**, raise, settle, put up, erect; = **toss (about)**, roll, plunge, lurch

p

pitch² n dark sticky substance obtained from tar or turpentine

pitcher n large jug

pith n 1 tissue in stems and branches of certain plants 2 essential part **pithy** adj 1 terse, concise 2 consisting of pith

pittance n small amount of money

pituitary adj, pl **-taries** of, pert. to, endocrine gland at base of brain

pity ⊕ n, pl **pities** 1 sympathy for others' suffering 2 regrettable fact ▷ v 3 feel pity for **piteous** adj **pitiful** adj 1 woeful 2 contemptible **pitiless** adj 1 feeling no pity 2 hard, merciless

pivot n 1 shaft or pin on which thing turns ▷ v 2 furnish with pivot 3 hinge on one

pixel n smallest constituent unit of an image, as on a computer screen

pixie n fairy

pizza n baked disc of dough covered with savoury toppings

pizzicato adv/adj (Mus) played by plucking strings with finger

placard n notice for posting up or carrying poster

placate v pacify, appease

place ⊕ n 1 locality, spot 2 position 3 duty 4 town, village, residence, buildings 5 employment 6 seat, space ▷ v 7 put in particular place 8 identify 9 make (order, bet etc.)

placebo n, pl **-bos, -boes** inactive substance given to patient in place of active drug

placenta n, pl **-tas, -tae** 1 organ formed in uterus during pregnancy, providing nutrients for fetus 2 afterbirth

placid adj calm

plague ⊕ n 1 highly contagious disease 2 (Inf) nuisance ▷ v 3 trouble, annoy

plaice n flat fish

plaid n 1 long Highland cloak or shawl 2 tartan pattern

plain ⊕ adj 1 flat, level 2 not intricate 3 clear, simple 4 candid, forthright 5 ordinary 6 without

pity n = **compassion**, charity, sympathy, kindness, fellow feeling ≠ **mercilessness**; = **shame**, sin (Inf) misfortune, bummer (Sl), crying shame ▷ v = **feel sorry for**, feel for, sympathize with, grieve for, weep for

place n = **spot**, point, position, site, area; = **region**, quarter, district, neighbourhood, vicinity; = **position**, point, spot, location; = **space**, position, seat, chair ▷ v = **lay (down)**, put (down), set (down), stand, position; = **put**, lay,

set, invest, pin; = **classify**, class, group, put, order, go down (US & Canad)

plague n = **disease**, infection, epidemic, pestilence; = **infestation**, invasion, epidemic, influx, host ▷ v = **torment**, trouble, torture (Inf)

plain adj = **unadorned**, simple, basic, severe, bare ≠ **ornate**; = **clear**, obvious, patent, evident, visible ≠ **hidden**; = **straightforward**, open, direct, frank, blunt ≠ **roundabout**; = **ugly**,

decoration **7** not beautiful ▷ *n*
8 tract of level country ▷ *adv*
9 clearly

plaintiff *n* (*Law*) one who sues in court

plaintive *adj* sad, mournful

plait *n* **1** braid of hair, straw etc. ▷ *v*
2 weave into plaits

plan ❶ *n* **1** scheme **2** way of proceeding **3** project **4** drawing
5 map ▷ *v* **6** make plan of
7 arrange beforehand

plane¹ ❶ *n* aeroplane

plane² ❶ *n* **1** smooth surface
2 level **3** tool for smoothing wood
▷ *v* **4** make smooth with plane
▷ *adj* **5** perfectly flat or level

plane³ *n* tree with broad leaves

planet *n* heavenly body revolving round sun **planetary** *adj*

planetarium *n/pl* **-iums, -ia**
apparatus that shows movement of sun, moon, stars and planets by projecting lights on inside of dome

plank *n* long flat piece of timber

plankton *n* minute animal and vegetable organisms floating in ocean

plant ❶ *n* **1** living organism without power of locomotion
2 building and equipment for manufacturing purposes ▷ *v* **3** set in ground to grow **4** establish
5 (*SI*) hide

plantation *n* **1** estate for cultivation of tea, tobacco etc.
2 wood of planted trees

plaque *n* **1** ornamental tablet
2 plate of brooch **3** deposit on teeth

plasma *n* clear, fluid portion of blood

plaster ❶ *n* **1** mixture of lime, sand etc. for coating walls etc.
2 adhesive dressing for cut, wound etc. ▷ *v* **3** apply plaster to **4** apply like plaster **plastered** *adj* (*SI*) drunk

plastic ❶ *n* **1** synthetic substance,

p

unattractive, homely (*US & Canad*), unlovely, unprepossessing
≠ attractive; **= simple**, common, simple, everyday, commonplace
≠ sophisticated ▷ *n* **= flatland**, plateau, prairie, grassland, steppe

plan *n* **= scheme**, system, design, programme, proposal; **= diagram**, map, drawing, chart, representation ▷ *v* **= devise**, arrange, scheme, plot, draft

plane¹ *n* **= aeroplane**, aircraft, jet, airliner, jumbo jet

plane² *n* **= flat surface**, the flat, horizontal, level surface; **= level**,

position, stage, condition, standard
▷ *adj* **= level**, even, flat, regular, smooth

plant *n* **= flower**, bush, vegetable, herb, weed ▷ *v* **= sow**, scatter, transplant, implant, put in the ground; **= seed**, sow, implant

plaster *n* **= mortar**, stucco, gypsum, plaster of Paris;
= bandage, dressing, sticking plaster, Elastoplast (*Trademark*), adhesive plaster ▷ *v* **= cover**, spread, coat, smear, overlay

plastic *adj* **= pliant**, soft, flexible, supple, pliable **≠ rigid**

easily moulded and extremely durable ▷ *adj* **2** made of plastic **3** easily moulded **plastic surgery** repair, reconstruction of part of body for medical or cosmetic reasons

Plasticine® *n* modelling material like clay

plate ❶ *n* **1** shallow round dish **2** flat thin sheet of metal, glass etc. **3** utensils of gold or silver **4** device for printing illustration in book **5** device to straighten children's teeth **6** (*Inf*) denture ▷ *v* **7** cover with thin coating of metal

plateau ❶ *n, pl* **-teaus; -teaux 1** tract of level high land **2** period of stability

platform ❶ *n* **1** raised level surface, stage **2** raised area in station from which passengers board trains

platinum *n* white heavy malleable metal

platitude *n* commonplace remark

platonic *adj* (of love) purely spiritual, friendly

platoon *n* body of soldiers employed as unit

platter *n* flat dish

platypus, duck-billed platypus *n* Aust. egg-laying amphibious mammal

plausible ❶ *adj* **1** apparently reasonable **2** persuasive

play ❶ *v* **1** amuse oneself **2** contend with in game **3** take part in (game) **4** trifle **5** act the part of **6** perform (music) **7** perform on (instrument) ▷ *n* **8** dramatic piece or performance **9** sport **10** amusement **11** activity **12** free movement **13** gambling **player** *n* **playful** *adj* lively **playboy** *n* rich man who lives for pleasure **playing card** one of set of 52 cards **playing fields** extensive piece of ground for open-air games **playwright** *n* author of plays

plaza *n* open space or square

———— THESAURUS ————

plate *n* = **platter**, dish, dinner plate, salver, trencher (*Archaic*); = **helping**, course, serving, dish, portion; = **layer**, panel, sheet, slab ▷ *v* = **coat**, gild, laminate, cover, overlay

plateau *n* = **upland**, table, highland, tableland; = **levelling off**, level, stage, stability

platform *n* = **stage**, stand, podium, rostrum, dais; = **policy**, programme, principle, objective(s), manifesto

plausible *adj* = **believable**, possible, likely, reasonable, credible ≠ **unbelievable**; = **glib**, smooth, specious, smooth-talking, smooth-tongued

play *v* = **amuse yourself**, have fun, sport, fool, romp; = **take part in**, be involved in, engage in, participate in, compete in; = **compete against**, challenge, take on, oppose, contend against ▷ *n* = **amusement**, pleasure, leisure, games, sport; = **drama**, show, piece, comedy, tragedy

plea ❶ n 1 entreaty 2 statement of prisoner or defendant 3 excuse
plead v 1 make earnest appeal 2 address court of law 3 bring forward as excuse or plea
please ❶ v 1 be agreeable to 2 gratify 3 delight 4 be willing ▷ adv 5 word of request **pleasant** adj pleasing, agreeable
pleasantry n joke, humour
pleased adj **pleasing** adj
pleasurable adj giving pleasure
pleasure n 1 enjoyment 2 satisfaction
pleat n 1 fold made by doubling material ▷ v 2 make into pleats
plebeian adj/n (one) of the common people
plectrum n, pl **-trums, -tra** small implement for plucking strings of guitar etc.
pledge ❶ n 1 solemn promise 2 thing given as security ▷ v 3 promise, swear
plenary adj complete
plenipotentiary adj/n (envoy) having full powers
plenitude n abundance

plenty ❶ n 1 abundance 2 quite enough **plenteous** adj ample
plentiful adj
plethora n oversupply
pleurisy n inflammation of membrane lining chest and covering lungs
pliable adj easily bent or influenced **pliant** adj pliable
pliers pl n tool with hinged arms and jaws for gripping
plight ❶ n distressing state
plight² v promise
plimsolls pl n rubber-soled canvas shoes
plinth n slab as base of column etc.
plod v **plodding, plodded** walk or work doggedly
plonk¹ v put down heavily and carelessly
plonk² n (Inf) cheap inferior wine
plop n 1 sound of object falling into water without splash ▷ v 2 fall with this sound
plot¹ ❶ n 1 secret plan, conspiracy 2 essence of story, play etc. ▷ v 3 plan secretly 4 mark position of 5 make map of
plot² n small piece of land

P

— THESAURUS —

plea n = **appeal**, request, suit, prayer, petition; = **excuse**, defence, explanation, justification
please v = **delight**, entertain, humour, amuse, suit ≠ **annoy**
pledge n = **promise**, vow, assurance, word, undertaking; = **guarantee**, security, deposit, bail, collateral ▷ v = **promise**, vow, swear, contract, engage
plenty n = **abundance**, wealth,

prosperity, fertility, profusion
plight¹ n = **difficulty**, condition, state, situation, trouble
plot¹ n = **plan**, scheme, intrigue, conspiracy, cabal; = **story**, action, subject, theme, outline ▷ v = **plan**, scheme, conspire, intrigue, manoeuvre; = **devise**, design, lay, conceive, hatch
plot² n = **patch**, lot, area, ground, parcel

plough ❶ n 1 implement for turning up soil ▷ v 2 turn up with plough, furrow 3 work at slowly **ploughman** n

plover n shore bird with straight bill and long pointed wings

ploy ❶ n manoeuvre designed to gain advantage

pluck ❶ v 1 pull, pick off 2 strip from 3 sound strings of (guitar etc.) with fingers, plectrum ▷ n 4 courage 5 sudden pull or tug **plucky** adj brave

plug ❶ n 1 thing fitting into and filling hole 2 (Electricity) device connecting appliance to electricity supply 3 (Inf) favourable mention of product etc. intended to promote it ▷ v 4 stop with plug 5 (Inf) advertise product etc. by frequently mentioning it

plum ❶ n 1 fruit with stone 2 tree bearing it 3 choicest part, piece, position etc. ▷ adj 4 choice

plumb ❶ n 1 ball of lead attached to string used for sounding, finding the perpendicular etc. ▷ adj 2 perpendicular ▷ adv 3 exactly 4 perpendicularly ▷ v 5 find depth of 6 equip with, connect to plumbing system **plumber** n worker who attends to water and sewage systems **plumbing** n 1 trade of plumber 2 system of water and sewage pipes **plumb line** cord with plumb attached

plume n 1 feather 2 ornament of feathers etc. ▷ v 3 furnish with plumes 4 pride oneself **plumage** n bird's feathers

plummet ❶ v -meting, -meted 1 plunge headlong ▷ n 2 plumb line

plump¹ ❶ adj 1 fat, rounded ▷ v 2 make, become plump

plump² v 1 drop, fall abruptly 2 choose

plunder ❶ v 1 take by force 2 rob ▷ n 3 booty, spoils

plunge ❶ v 1 put forcibly, throw (into) 2 descend suddenly ▷ n 3 dive **plunger** n suction cap to

plough v = **turn over**, dig, till, cultivate

ploy n = **tactic**, move, trick, device, scheme

pluck v = **pull out** or **off**, pick, draw, collect, gather; = **tug**, catch, snatch, clutch, jerk ▷ n = **courage**, nerve, bottle (Brit Sl), guts (Inf), grit

plug n = **stopper**, cork, bung, spigot; (Inf) = **mention**, advertisement, advert (Brit Inf), push, publicity ▷ v = **seal**, close, stop, fill, block; (Inf) = **mention**, push, promote, publicize, advertise

plum adj = **choice**, prize, first-class

plumb v = **delve into**, explore, probe, go into, penetrate ▷ adv = **exactly**, precisely, bang, slap, spot-on (Brit Inf)

plummet v = **drop**, fall, crash, nose-dive, descend rapidly

plump¹ adj = **chubby**, fat, stout, round, tubby ≠ **scrawny**

plunder v = **loot**, strip, sack, rob, raid

plunge v = **descend**, fall, drop, crash, pitch; = **hurtle**, charge, career, jump, tear ▷ n = **dive**, unblock drains **plunging** *adj* (of neckline) cut low

plural *adj* **1** of, denoting more than one ▷ *n* **2** word in its plural form **plurality** *n* majority

plus ❶ *prep* **1** with addition of (usu. indicated by the sign +) ▷ *adj* **2** positive

plush ❶ *n* **1** fabric with long nap ▷ *adj* **2** luxurious

ply¹ ❷ *v* **plying, plied 1** wield **2** work at **3** supply insistently **4** go to and fro regularly

ply² *n* **1** fold or thickness **2** strand of yarn **plywood** *n* board of thin layers of wood glued together

PM prime minister

p.m. after noon

pneumatic *adj* of, worked by, inflated with wind or air

pneumonia *n* inflammation of the lungs

PO Post Office

poach¹ *v* **1** take (game) illegally **2** encroach **poacher** *n*

poach² *v* simmer (eggs, fish etc.) gently in water etc.

pocket ❶ *n* **1** small bag inserted in garment **2** cavity, pouch or hollow **3** isolated group or area ▷ *v* **4** put into one's pocket **5** appropriate ▷ *adj* **6** small **pocket money** small allowance, esp. for children

pod ❶ *n* long seed vessel, as of peas, beans etc.

podgy *adj* **podgier, podgiest** short and fat

podium ❶ *n, pl* **-diums, -dia** small raised platform

poem ❶ *n* imaginative composition in rhythmic lines **poet** *n* writer of poems **poetic** *adj* **poetry** *n* art or work of poet, verse

poep *n* (Aust & NZ, Sl) emission of gas from the anus

poet ❶ *n* writer of poems

pogey *n* (Canad, Sl) money received from the state while out of work

poignant ❶ *adj* **1** moving **2** keen **poignancy** *n*

point ❶ *n* **1** dot **2** punctuation mark **3** detail **4** unit of value, scoring **5** degree, stage

p

— THESAURUS —

jump, duck, descent

plus *prep* = **and**, with, added to, coupled with ▷ *n* (Inf) = **advantage**, benefit, asset, gain, extra

plush *adj* = **luxurious**, luxury, lavish, rich, sumptuous ≠ **cheap**

ply¹ *v* = **work at**, follow, exercise, pursue, carry on

pocket *n* = **pouch**, bag, sack, compartment, receptacle ▷ *adj* = **small**, compact, miniature,

portable, little ▷ *v* = **steal**, take, lift (Inf), appropriate, pilfer

pod *n* = **shell**, case, hull, husk, shuck

podium *n* = **platform**, stand, stage, rostrum, dais

poem *n* = **verse**, song, lyric, rhyme, sonnet

poet *n* = **bard**, rhymer, lyricist, lyric poet, versifier

poignant *adj* = **moving**, touching, sad, bitter, intense

point *n* = **essence**, meaning,

DICTIONARY

6 moment **7** gist **8** purpose
9 special quality **10** sharp end
11 headland **12** direction mark on
compass **13** movable rail changing
train to other rails **14** power point
▷ v **15** show direction or position
by extending finger **16** direct
17 sharpen **18** fill up joints with
mortar **pointed** adj **1** sharp
2 direct **pointer** n **1** indicating
rod etc. used for pointing
2 indication **3** breed of gun dog
pointless adj futile **point-blank**
adj **1** at short range **2** blunt, direct
▷ adv **3** bluntly

poise n **1** composure
2 self-possession **3** balance
poised adj **1** ready **2** showing
poise

poison ❶ n **1** substance harmful
or fatal to living organism ▷ v
2 give poison to **3** infect
poisonous adj

poke ❶ v **1** push, thrust with
finger, stick etc. **2** thrust forward
3 pry ▷ n **4** act of poking **poker** n

metal rod for poking fire **poky** adj
small, confined, cramped
poker n card game
pole¹ ❶ n long, rounded piece of
wood etc.
pole² ❶ n **1** each of the ends of axis of
earth or celestial sphere **2** each of
opposite poles of magnet, electric
cell etc. **polar** adj **polarize**
v (cause to) form into groups
with opposite views **polar bear**
white bear that lives around
North Pole
poleaxe v stun with heavy blow
polecat n small animal of weasel
family
police ❶ n **1** civil force which
maintains public order ▷ v **2** keep
in order **policeman** n member of
police force
policy¹ ❷ n course of action
adopted, esp. in state affairs
policy² n insurance contract
polio, poliomyelitis n disease
affecting spinal cord, often causing
paralysis

THESAURUS

subject, question, heart;
= **purpose**, aim, object, end,
reason; = **aspect**, detail, feature,
quality, particular; = **place**, area,
position, site, spot; = **moment**,
time, stage, period, phase; = **stage**,
level, position, condition, degree;
= **end**, tip, sharp end, top, spur;
= **score**, tally, mark = **headland**,
head, cape, promontory ▷ v = **aim**,
level, train, direct; = **indicate**,
show, signal, point to, gesture
towards

poison n = **toxin**, venom, bane

(*Archaic*) ▷ v = **murder**, kill, give
someone poison, administer poison
to; = **contaminate**, foul, infect,
spoil, pollute

poke v = **jab**, push, stick, dig, stab
▷ n = **jab**, dig, thrust, nudge, prod

pole¹ n = **rod**, post, support, staff,
bar

police n = **the law** (*Inf*), police
force, constabulary, fuzz (*Sl*), boys in
blue (*Inf*) ▷ v = **control**, patrol,
guard, watch, protect

policy¹ n = **procedure**, plan,
action, practice, scheme

polish ❶ v 1 make smooth and glossy 2 refine ▷ n 3 shine 4 polishing 5 substance for polishing 6 refinement

polite ❶ adj 1 showing regard for others in manners, speech etc. 2 refined, cultured

politics ❶ pl n 1 art of government 2 political affairs **politic** adj wise, shrewd **political** adj of the state or its affairs **politician** n one engaged in politics

polka n 1 lively dance 2 music for it **polka dot** one of pattern of bold spots on fabric etc.

poll ❶ n 1 voting 2 counting of votes 3 number of votes recorded 4 survey of opinion ▷ v 5 receive (votes) 6 take votes of 7 vote **polling booth** voting place

pollen n fertilizing dust of flower **pollinate** v

pollute v 1 make foul 2 corrupt **pollution** n

polo n game like hockey played on horseback **polo neck** (sweater with) tight turned-over collar

poltergeist n spirit believed to move furniture, throw objects around etc.

polyester n synthetic material

polygamy n custom of being married to several persons at a time **polygamist** n

polygon n figure with many angles or sides

polystyrene n synthetic material used esp. as rigid foam for packing etc.

polythene n tough light plastic material

polyunsaturated adj pert. to fats that do not form cholesterol in blood

polyurethane n synthetic material used esp. in paints

pom n (Aust & NZ, Sl) person from England (also **pommy**)

pomegranate n 1 tree 2 its fruit with thick rind containing many seeds in red pulp

pommel n 1 front of saddle 2 knob of sword hilt

pomp n splendid display or ceremony

pompom n decorative tuft of ribbon, wool, feathers etc.

pompous adj 1 self-important 2 ostentatious 3 (of language)

P

─────── THESAURUS ───────

polish n = **varnish**, wax, glaze, lacquer, japan; = **sheen**, finish, glaze, gloss, brightness; = **style**, class (Inf), finish, breeding, grace ▷ v = **shine**, wax, smooth, rub, buff; often with **up** = **perfect**, improve, enhance, refine, finish

polite adj = **mannerly**, civil, courteous, gracious, respectful ≠ **rude**; = **refined**, cultured,

civilized, polished, sophisticated ≠ **uncultured**

politics n = **affairs of state**, government, public affairs, civics

poll n = **survey**, figures, count, sampling, returns; = **election**, vote, voting, referendum, ballot ▷ v = **question**, interview, survey, sample, ballot; = **gain**, return, record, register, tally inflated, stilted, lofty

pond ❶ n small body of still water

ponder v muse, think over

ponderous adj 1 heavy, unwieldy 2 boring

pong n/v (Inf) (give off) strong unpleasant smell

pontiff n 1 Pope 2 bishop **pontificate** v speak dogmatically

pontoon¹ n flat-bottomed boat or metal drum for use in supporting temporary bridge

pontoon² n gambling card game

pony n, pl **ponies** horse of small breed **ponytail** n long hair tied at back of head

poodle n pet dog with long curly hair

pool¹ ❶ n 1 small body of still water 2 deep place in river or stream 3 puddle 4 swimming pool

pool² ❶ n 1 common fund or resources 2 group of people, e.g. typists, shared by several employers 3 collective stakes in various games

▷ v 4 put in common fund

poop n ship's stern

poor ❶ adj 1 having little money 2 unproductive 3 inadequate 4 inferior 5 miserable, wretched **poorly** adj 1 not in good health ▷ adv 2 in poor manner

pop ❶ v popping, popped 1 (cause to) make small explosive sound 2 put or place suddenly ▷ n 3 small explosive sound **popcorn** n maize that puffs up when roasted

Pope n bishop of Rome and head of R.C. Church

poplar n tall slender tree

poplin n corded fabric, usu. of cotton

poppadom n thin round crisp Indian bread

poppy n, pl **-pies** bright-flowered plant yielding opium

Popsicle n (US & Canad) an ice lolly

populace n the common people

popular ❶ adj 1 finding general favour 2 of, by the people **popularity** n **popularize** v

THESAURUS

pond n = **pool**, tarn, small lake, fish pond, duck pond

ponder v = **think about**, consider, reflect on, contemplate, deliberate about

pool¹ n = **swimming pool**, lido, swimming bath(s) (Brit), bathing pool (Archaic); = **pond**, lake, mere, tarn; = **puddle**, drop, patch

pool² n = **supply**, reserve, fall-back ▷ v = **combine**, share, merge, put together, amalgamate

poor adj = **impoverished**, broke (Inf), hard up (Inf), short, needy

≠ **rich**; = **unfortunate**, unlucky, hapless, pitiful, luckless

≠ **fortunate**; = **inferior**, unsatisfactory, mediocre, second-rate, rotten (Inf)

≠ **excellent**; = **meagre**, inadequate, insufficient, lacking, incomplete ≠ **ample**

pop (US & Canad) ▷ n = **bang**, report, crack, noise, burst ▷ v = **burst**, crack, snap, bang, explode

popular adj = **well-liked**, liked, in, accepted, favourite ≠ **unpopular**; = **common**, general, prevailing,

P

DICTIONARY

populate ❶ v fill with inhabitants **population** n (number of) inhabitants **populous** adj thickly populated

porcelain n fine earthenware, china

porch n covered approach to entrance of building

porcupine n rodent covered with long, pointed quills

pore¹ ❶ n minute opening, esp. in skin **porous** adj 1 allowing liquid to soak through 2 full of pores

pore² v study closely

pork n pig's flesh as food

pornography ❶ n indecent literature, films etc. **pornographic** adj

porpoise n blunt-nosed sea mammal like dolphin

porridge n soft food of oatmeal etc. boiled in water

port¹ ❶ n (town with) harbour

port² n left side of ship

port³ n strong red wine

port⁴ n opening in side of ship

porthole n small opening or

window in side of ship

portable ❶ adj easily carried

portcullis n grating above gateway that can be lowered to block entrance

portend v 1 foretell 2 be an omen of **portent** n omen

porter ❶ n 1 person employed to carry luggage etc. 2 doorkeeper

portfolio n, pl **-os** 1 flat portable case for loose papers 2 collection of work, shares etc.

portico n, pl **-coes, -cos** porch, covered walkway

portion ❶ n 1 part, share, helping 2 destiny, lot ▷ v 3 divide into shares

portly adj **-lier, -liest** bulky, stout

portmanteau n, pl **-teaus, -teaux** leather suitcase, esp. one opening into two compartments

portray ❶ v make pictures of, describe **portrait** n likeness of (face of) individual **portraiture** n **portrayal** n act of portraying

pose ❶ v 1 place in attitude 2 put forward 3 assume attitude

P

THESAURUS

current, conventional ≠ rare

populate v = **inhabit**, people, live in, occupy, reside in

pore¹ n = **opening**, hole, outlet, orifice

pornography n = **obscenity**, porn (Inf), dirt, filth, indecency

port¹ n = **harbour**, haven, anchorage, seaport

portable adj = **light**, compact, convenient, handy, manageable

porter n (chiefly Brit) = **doorman**, caretaker, janitor, concierge,

gatekeeper

portion n = **part**, bit, piece, section, scrap; = **helping**, serving, piece, plateful; = **share**, allowance, lot, measure, quantity

portray v = **play**, take the role of, act the part of, represent, personate (rare); = **describe**, present, depict, evoke, delineate; = **represent**, draw, paint, illustrate, sketch

pose v = **position yourself**, sit, model, arrange yourself; = **put on**

4 affect or pretend to be a certain character ▷ n **5** attitude, esp. one assumed for effect

posh ❶ adj **1** luxurious **2** upper-class

position ❶ n **1** place **2** situation **3** attitude **4** status **5** employment ▷ v **6** place in position

positive ❶ adj **1** sure **2** definite **3** assertive **4** constructive **5** not negative ▷ n **6** something positive

possess ❶ v **1** own **2** have mastery of **possession** n **1** act of possessing **2** ownership ▷ pl **3** things a person possesses

possessive adj **1** of, indicating possession **2** with excessive desire to possess, control

possible ❶ adj **1** that can, or may, be, exist, happen or be done **2** worthy of consideration

possibility n, pl **-ties 1** feasibility **2** chance **possibly** adv perhaps

possum see OPOSSUM

post¹ ❶ n **1** upright pole to support or mark something ▷ v **2** display **3** stick up (on notice board etc.)

poster n large advertisement

post² ❶ n **1** official carrying of letters or parcels **2** collection or delivery of these **3** office **4** situation **5** place of duty **6** fort ▷ v **7** put into official box for carriage by post **8** station (soldiers etc.) in particular spot **postage** n charge for carrying letter **postal** adj **postal order** written order for payment of sum of money

postcard n stamped card sent by post **postman** n person who collects and delivers post

postmark n official mark stamped

---

airs, posture, show off (Inf) ▷ n = **posture**, position, bearing, attitude, stance; = **act**, façade, air, front, posturing

posh adj (Inf, chiefly Brit) = **smart**, grand, stylish, luxurious, classy (Sl); = **upper-class**, high-class

position n = **location**, place, point, area, post; = **posture**, attitude, arrangement, pose, stance; = **status**, place, standing, footing, station; = **job**, place, post, opening, office; = **place**, standing, rank, status ▷ v = **place**, put, set, stand, arrange

positive adj = **beneficial**, useful, practical, helpful, progressive ≠ **harmful**; = **certain**, sure, convinced, confident, satisfied

≠ **uncertain**; = **definite**, real, clear, firm, certain ≠ **inconclusive**; (Inf) = **absolute**, complete, perfect, right (Brit Inf), real

possess v = **own**, have, hold, be in possession of, be the owner of; = **be endowed with**, have, enjoy, benefit from, be possessed of

possible adj = **feasible**, viable, workable, achievable, practicable ≠ **unfeasible**; = **likely**, potential, anticipated, probable, odds-on ≠ **improbable**; = **conceivable**, likely, credible, plausible, hypothetical ≠ **inconceivable**

post¹ v = **put something up**, display, affix, pin something up

post² n = **mail**, collection, delivery, postal service, snail mail (Inf);

on letters **post office** place where postal business is conducted

post- *comb. form* after, later than, as in *postwar*

posterior *adj* 1 later, hind ▷ *n* 2 buttocks

posterity *n* 1 later generations 2 descendants

posthaste *adv* with great speed

posthumous *adj* occurring after death

postmortem *n* medical examination of dead body

postpone ❶ *v* put off to later time, defer

postscript *n* addition to letter, book

postulate *v* 1 take for granted ▷ *n* 2 something postulated

posture ❶ *n* 1 attitude, position of body ▷ *v* 2 pose

posy *n, pl* **-sies** bunch of flowers

pot ❶ *n* 1 round vessel 2 cooking vessel ▷ *v* 3 put into, preserve in pot **potluck** *n* whatever is available

potassium *n* white metallic element

potato *n/pl* **-toes** 1 plant with

tubers grown for food 2 one of these tubers

potato chip *n* the US and Canadian term for CRISP

potent ❶ *adj* powerful, influential **potency** *n*

potentate *n* ruler

potential ❶ *adj* 1 that might exist or act but does not now ▷ *n* 2 possibility

pothole *n* 1 hole in surface of road 2 underground cave

potion *n* dose of medicine or poison

potpourri *n* 1 fragrant mixture of dried flower petals 2 medley

potter¹ ❶ *v* work, act in unsystematic way

potter² *n* maker of earthenware vessel **pottery** *n* 1 earthenware 2 where it is made 3 art of making it

potty¹ *adj* (Inf) crazy, silly

potty² *n* bowl used by small child as toilet

pouch *n* 1 small bag 2 pocket ▷ *v* 3 put into pouch

poultice *n* soft composition of mustard, kaolin etc., applied hot to

THESAURUS

= **correspondence**, letters, cards, mail ▷ *v* = **send (off)**, forward, mail, get off, transmit

postpone *v* = **put off**, delay, suspend, adjourn, shelve ≠ **go ahead** *with*

posture *n* = **bearing**, set, attitude, stance, carriage ▷ *v* = **show off** (Inf), pose, affect, put on airs

pot *n* = **container**, bowl, pan,

vessel, basin

potent *adj* = **powerful**, commanding, dynamic, dominant, influential

potential *adj* = **possible**, future, likely, promising, probable ▷ *n* = **ability**, possibilities, capacity, capability, aptitude

potter¹ *v usually with* **around** *or* **about** = **mess about**, tinker, dabble, footle (Inf)

poultry n domestic fowls
pounce ❶ v 1 spring (upon) suddenly, swoop (upon) ▷ n 2 swoop, sudden descent
pound¹ ❶ n enclosure for stray animals or officially removed vehicles
pound² ❶ v 1 beat, thump 2 crush to pieces or powder 3 walk, run heavily
pound³ n 1 British monetary unit 2 unit of weight equal to 0.454 kg
pour ❶ v 1 come out in a stream, crowd etc. 2 flow freely 3 rain heavily ▷ v 4 give out thus
pout ❶ v 1 thrust out lips to look sulky ▷ n 2 act of pouting
poverty ❶ n 1 state of being poor 2 lack of, scarcity
powder ❶ n 1 solid matter in fine dry particles 2 medicine in this

form 3 gunpowder 4 face powder etc. ▷ v 5 apply powder to 6 reduce to powder
powdery adj
power ❶ n 1 ability to do or act 2 strength 3 authority 4 control 5 person or thing having authority 6 mechanical energy 7 electricity supply **powerful** adj **powerless** adj
pp pages
PQ Quebec
PR 1 proportional representation 2 public relations
practical ❶ adj 1 given to action rather than theory 2 sensible, realistic 3 skilled **practicable** adj that can be done, used etc. **practically** adv 1 all but 2 sensibly **practical joke** trick intended to make someone look foolish

pounce v = **attack**, strike, jump, leap, swoop
pound¹ n = **enclosure**, yard, pen, compound, kennels
pound² v sometimes with **on** = **beat**, strike, hammer, batter, thrash; = **crush**, powder, pulverize; = **pulsate**, beat, pulse, throb, palpitate; = **stomp**, tramp, march, thunder (Inf)
pour v = **let flow**, spill, splash, dribble, drizzle; = **flow**, stream, run, course, rush; = **rain**, right (down), teem, bucket down (Inf)
pout v = **sulk**, glower, look petulant, pull a long face ▷ n = **sullen look**, glower, long face

poverty n = **pennilessness**, want, need, hardship, insolvency ≠ **wealth**; = **scarcity**, lack, absence, want, deficit ≠ **abundance**
powder n = **dust**, talc, fine grains, loose particles ▷ v = **dust**, cover, scatter, sprinkle, strew
power n = **control**, authority, influence, command, dominance; = **ability**, capacity, faculty, property, potential ≠ **inability**; = **authority**, right, licence, privilege, warrant
practical adj = **functional**, realistic, pragmatic ≠ **impractical**; = **empirical**, real, applied, actual, hands-on ≠ **theoretical**;

practise ❶ v 1 do repeatedly, work at to gain skill 2 do habitually 3 put into action 4 exercise profession **practice** n 1 habit 2 exercise of art or profession 3 action, not theory

pragmatic ❶ adj concerned with practical consequences

prairie n a treeless grassy plain of the central US and S Canada

praise ❶ n 1 commendation 2 fact of praising 3 expression of thanks to God ▷ v 4 express approval, admiration of 5 express thanks to God **praiseworthy** adj

pram n carriage for baby

prance v/n 1 swagger 2 caper

prank n mischievous trick

prattle v talk like child

prawn n edible sea shellfish like shrimp

pray ❶ v 1 ask earnestly 2 entreat

3 offer prayers, esp. to God **prayer** n 1 action, practice of praying to God 2 earnest entreaty

pre- comb. form before, as in prerecord, preshrunk

preach ❶ v 1 deliver sermon 2 give moral, religious advice 3 advocate **preacher** n

preamble n introductory part of story etc.

precarious ❶ adj insecure, unstable, perilous

precaution ❶ n previous care to prevent evil or secure good

precede ❶ v go, come before in rank, order, time etc. **precedence** n priority in position, rank, time etc. **precedent** n previous case or occurrence taken as rule

precept n rule for conduct

precinct ❶ n 1 enclosed, limited area ▷ pl 2 environs

THESAURUS

= **sensible**, ordinary, realistic, down-to-earth, matter-of-fact ≠ **impractical**; = **feasible**, possible, viable, workable, practicable ≠ **impractical**

practise v = **rehearse**, study, prepare, perfect, repeat; = **do**, train, exercise, drill; = **carry out**, follow, apply, perform, observe

pragmatic adj = **practical**, sensible, realistic, down-to-earth, utilitarian ≠ **idealistic**

praise v = **acclaim**, approve of, honour, cheer, admire ≠ **criticize**; = **give thanks to**, bless, worship, adore, glorify ▷ n = **approval**, acclaim, tribute, compliment, congratulations ≠ **criticism**;

= **thanks**, glory, worship, homage, adoration

pray v = **say your prayers**, offer a prayer, recite the rosary; = **beg**, ask, plead, petition, request

preach v often with **to** = **deliver a sermon**, address, evangelize, preach a sermon; = **urge**, teach, champion, recommend, advise

precarious adj = **insecure**, dangerous, risky, risky, dodgy (Brit, Aust, & NZ Inf) ≠ **secure**

precaution n = **safeguard**, insurance, protection, provision, safety measure

precede v = **go before**, antedate

precinct n = **area**, quarter, section, sector, district

P

precious ➊ adj 1 beloved, cherished 2 of great value

precipice n very steep cliff or rock face

precipitate ➊ v 1 hasten happening of 2 throw headlong 3 (Chem) cause to be deposited in solid form from solution ▷ adj 4 too sudden 5 rash ▷ n 6 substance chemically precipitated **precipitation** n rain, snow etc.

précis n/pl **précis** 1 summary ▷ v 2 summarize

precise ➊ adj 1 definite 2 exact 3 careful in observance **precisely** adv **precision** n

preclude v prevent

precocious adj developed, matured early or too soon

precursor n forerunner

predatory adj preying on other animals **predator** n

predecessor ➊ n one who precedes another in office or position

predicament ➊ n difficult or

perplexing situation

predict ➊ v foretell, prophesy

predictable adj **prediction** n

predispose v 1 incline, influence 2 make susceptible

predominate v be main or controlling element **predominance** n **predominant** adj

pre-eminent adj excelling all others **pre-eminence** n

pre-empt v do in advance of or to exclusion of others

preen v 1 trim (feather) with beak 2 smarten oneself

prefabricated adj (of building) manufactured in shaped sections for rapid assembly

preface n 1 introduction to book etc. ▷ v 2 introduce

prefect n 1 person put in authority 2 schoolchild in position of limited authority over others

prefer ➊ v -ferring, -ferred 1 like better 2 promote **preferable** adj more desirable **preference** n **preferential** adj special, privileged

precious adj = **valuable**, expensive, fine, prized, dear ≠ **worthless**; = **loved**, prized, dear, treasured, darling; = **affected**, artificial, twee (Brit Inf), overrefined, overnice

precipitate v = **quicken**, trigger, accelerate, advance, hurry; = **throw**, launch, cast, hurl, fling ▷ adj = **hasty**, rash, reckless, impulsive, precipitous

precise adj = **exact**, specific,

particular, express, correct ≠ **vague**; = **strict**, particular, exact, formal, careful ≠ **inexact**

predecessor n = **previous job holder**, precursor, forerunner, antecedent; = **ancestor**, forebear, antecedent, forefather

predicament n = **fix** (Inf), situation, spot (Inf), hole (Sl), mess

predict v = **foretell**, forecast, divine, prophesy, augur

prefer v = **like better**, favour, go for, pick, fancy

preferment n promotion
prefix ❶ n 1 group of letters put at beginning of word ▷ v 2 put as introduction 3 put as prefix
pregnant ❶ adj 1 carrying fetus in womb 2 full of meaning, significant **pregnancy** n, pl **-cies**
prehistoric adj before period in which written history begins
prejudice ❶ n 1 preconceived opinion 2 unreasonable or unfair dislike ▷ v 3 influence 4 bias 5 injure **prejudicial** adj
preliminary ❶ adj/n preparatory, introductory (action, statement)
prelude ❶ n (Mus) 1 introductory movement 2 performance, event etc. serving as introduction
premature ❶ adj happening, done before proper time
premeditated adj planned

beforehand
premier ❶ n 1 prime minister ▷ adj 2 chief, foremost 3 first
première n first performance of play etc.
premise, premiss ❶ n (Logic) proposition from which inference is drawn
premises ❶ pl n house, building with its belongings
premium ❶ n 1 bonus 2 sum paid for insurance 3 excess over nominal value 4 great value or regard
premonition n presentiment
preoccupy v **-pying, -pied** occupy to exclusion of other things **preoccupation** n
preordained adj determined in advance

THESAURUS

pregnant adj = expectant, expecting (Inf), with child, in the club (Brit Sl), big or heavy with child; = meaningful, pointed, charged, significant, telling
prejudice n = discrimination, injustice, intolerance, bigotry, unfairness; = bias, preconception, partiality, preconceived notion, prejudgment ▷ v = bias, influence, colour, poison, distort; = harm, damage, hurt, injure, mar
preliminary adj = first, opening, trial, initial, test ▷ n = introduction, opening, beginning, start, prelude
prelude n = introduction, beginning, start; = overture, opening, introduction, introductory

movement
premature adj = early, untimely, before time, unseasonable; = hasty, rash, too soon, untimely, ill-timed
premier n = head of government, prime minister, chancellor, chief minister, P.M. ▷ adj = chief, leading, first, highest, head
premise n = assumption, proposition, argument, hypothesis, assertion
premises pl n = building(s), place, office, property, site
premium n = fee, charge, payment, instalment; = surcharge, extra charge, additional fee or charge

P

prepare ❶ v 1 make, get ready
2 concoct, make **preparation** n
1 making ready beforehand
2 something prepared, as a
medicine **preparatory** adj
1 serving to prepare 2 introductory
prepared adj 1 ready 2 willing
preposition n word marking
relation between noun or pronoun
and other words
prepossessing v impressive
preposterous adj utterly absurd,
foolish
prerequisite n/adj (something)
required as prior condition
prerogative n peculiar power or
right, esp. as vested in sovereign
prescribe ❶ v 1 set out rules for
2 order use of (medicine)
prescription n 1 prescribing
2 thing prescribed 3 written
statement of it
present[1] ❶ adj 1 that is here
2 now existing or happening ▷ n
3 present time or tense **presence**
n 1 being present 2 appearance,

bearing **presently** adv 1 soon
2 (US) at present
present[2] ❶ v 1 introduce formally
2 show 3 give ▷ n 4 gift
presentable adj fit to be seen
presentation n **presenter** n
presentiment n sense of
something about to happen
preserve ❶ v 1 keep from harm,
injury or decay ▷ n 2 special area
3 fruit preserved by cooking in
sugar 4 place where game is kept
for private fishing, shooting
preservation n **preservative** n
1 preserving agent ▷ adj
2 preserving
preside ❶ v be in charge
presidency n **president** n head
of society, company, republic etc.
presidential adj
press ❶ v 1 subject to push or
squeeze 2 smooth 3 urge
4 throng 5 hasten ▷ n 6 machine
for pressing, esp. printing machine
7 printing house 8 newspapers
and journalists collectively

———————————— THESAURUS ————————————

prepare v = **make** or **get ready**,
arrange, adapt, adjust
prescribe v = **specify**, order,
direct, stipulate, write a
prescription for
present[1] adj = **current**, existing,
immediate, contemporary,
present-day; = **here**, there, near,
ready, nearby ≠ **absent**
present[2] n = **gift**, offering, grant,
donation, hand-out ▷ v = **give**,
award, hand over, grant, hand out;
= **put on**, stage, perform, give,
show; = **launch**, display, parade,

exhibit, unveil
preserve v = **maintain**, keep,
continue, sustain, keep up ≠ **end**;
= **protect**, keep, save, maintain,
defend ≠ **attack** ▷ n = **area**,
department, field, territory,
province
preside v = **officiate**, chair,
moderate, be chairperson
press v = **push (down)**, depress,
lean on, press down, force down;
= **push**, squeeze, jam, thrust, ram;
= **hug**, squeeze, embrace, clasp,
crush; = **urge**, beg, petition, exhort,

9 crowd **pressing** adj 1 urgent
2 persistent
pressure ❶ n 1 act of pressing
2 compelling force 3 (Physics)
thrust per unit area
prestige ❶ n 1 reputation
2 influence depending on it
prestigious adj
presto adv (Mus) very quickly
presume ❶ v 1 take for granted
2 take liberties **presumably** adv
presumption n 1 forward,
arrogant opinion or conduct
2 strong probability **presumptive**
adj that may be assumed as true or
valid until contrary is proved
presumptuous adj forward,
impudent
presuppose v assume or take for
granted beforehand
presupposition n
pretend ❶ v 1 claim or allege
(something untrue) 2 make believe

3 lay claim (to) **pretence** n
simulation **pretender** n claimant
(to throne) **pretension** n
pretentious adj 1 making claim to
special merit or importance
2 given to outward show
pretext n 1 excuse
2 pretence
pretty ❶ adj -tier, -tiest
1 appealing in a delicate way ▷ adv
2 moderately
prevail ❶ v 1 gain mastery
2 be generally established
prevalent adj 1 widespread
2 predominant
prevaricate v tell lies or speak
evasively **prevaricator** n
prevent ❶ v stop, hinder
prevention n **preventive** adj/n
preview ❶ n advance showing
previous ❶ adj 1 preceding
2 happening before **previously**
adv

—— THESAURUS ——

implore; = **plead**, present, lodge,
submit, tender; = **compress**, grind,
reduce, mill, crush; = **crowd**, push,
gather, surge, flock
pressure n = force, crushing,
squeezing, compressing, weight;
= **power**, influence, force,
constraint, sway; = **stress**,
demands, strain, heat, load
prestige n = **status**, standing,
credit, reputation, honour
presume v = **believe**, think,
suppose, assume, guess (Inf, chiefly
US & Canad); = **dare**, venture, go so
far as, take the liberty, make so bold
as
pretend v = **feign**, affect, assume,

allege, fake; = **make believe**,
suppose, imagine, act, make up
pretty adj = **attractive**, beautiful,
lovely, charming, fair ≠ **plain** ▷ adv
(Inf) = **fairly**, rather, quite, kind of
(Inf), somewhat
prevail v = **win**, succeed, triumph,
overcome, overrule; = **be
widespread**, abound,
predominate, be current, be
prevalent
prevent v = **stop**, avoid, frustrate,
hamper, foil ≠ **help**
preview n = **sample**, sneak
preview, trailer, taster, foretaste
previous adj = **earlier**, former,
past, prior, preceding ≠ **later**

P

prey ❶ n 1 animal hunted by another for food 2 victim ▷ v 3 (with on) treat as prey 4 worry, obsess

price ❶ n 1 that for which thing is bought or sold 2 cost ▷ v 3 fix, ask price for **priceless** adj invaluable **pricey** adj **pricier**, **priciest** (Inf) expensive

prick ❶ v 1 pierce slightly 2 cause to feel sharp pain ▷ n 3 slight hole made by pricking 4 sting **prickle** n 1 thorn, spike ▷ v 2 feel pricking sensation **prickly** adj 1 thorny 2 stinging 3 touchy

pride ❶ n 1 too high an opinion of oneself 2 worthy self-esteem 3 great satisfaction 4 something causing this 5 best part of something **pride oneself** take pride

priest ❶ n official minister of religion **priesthood** n

prig n smug self-righteous person **priggish** adj

prim adj **primmer**, **primmest** formal and prudish

primacy n, pl **-cies** supremacy

prima donna female opera singer

primary ❶ adj 1 chief 2 earliest 3 elementary

primate¹ n one of order of mammals including monkeys and man

primate² n archbishop

prime ❶ adj 1 fundamental 2 original 3 chief 4 best ▷ n 5 first, best part of anything ▷ v 6 prepare for use **primer** n paint for preliminary coating **Prime Minister** leader of government

primeval adj of earliest age of the world

primitive ❶ adj 1 of an early undeveloped kind 2 crude

primrose n 1 pale yellow spring flower 2 this colour ▷ adj 3 of this colour

prince ❶ n 1 male member of royal family 2 ruler, chief **princely**

THESAURUS

prey n = **quarry**, game, kill; = **victim**, target, mug (Brit Sl), dupe, fall guy (Inf)

price n = **cost**, value, rate, charge, figure; = **consequences**, penalty, cost, result, toll ▷ v = **evaluate**, value, estimate, rate, cost

prick v = **pierce**, stab, puncture, punch, lance ▷ n = **puncture**, hole, wound, perforation, pinhole

pride n = **satisfaction**, achievement, fulfilment, delight, content; = **self-respect**, honour, ego, dignity, self-esteem; = **conceit**, vanity, arrogance,

pretension, hubris ≠ **humility**

priest n = **clergyman**, minister, father, divine, vicar

primary adj = **chief**, main, first, highest, greatest ≠ **subordinate**

prime adj = **main**, leading, chief, central, major; = **best**, top, select, highest, quality ▷ n = **peak**, flower, bloom, height, heyday ▷ v = **inform**, tell, train, coach, brief

primitive adj = **early**, first, earliest, original, primary ≠ **modern**; = **crude**, simple, rough, rudimentary, unrefined ≠ **elaborate**

prince n = **ruler**, lord, monarch,

adj 1 generous 2 magnificent
princess n female member of royal family

principal ❶ adj 1 chief in importance ▷ n 2 person for whom another is agent 3 head of institution, esp. school or college 4 sum of money lent and yielding interest **principality** n territory of prince

principle ❶ n 1 moral rule 2 settled reason of action 3 uprightness 4 fundamental truth

print ❶ v 1 reproduce (words, pictures etc.) by pressing inked types on blocks of paper etc. 2 write in imitation of this 3 (Photog) produce pictures from negatives 4 stamp (fabric) with design ▷ n 5 printed matter 6 photograph 7 impression left by something pressing 8 printed cotton fabric **printer** n

prior ❶ adj 1 earlier ▷ n 2 leader of religious house or order **priority**

n precedence, something given special attention **priory** n, pl **-ries** monastery, nunnery under prior, prioress **prior to** before

prise v force open by levering

prism n transparent solid, usu. with triangular ends and rectangular sides, used to disperse light into spectrum

prison ❶ n jail **prisoner** n 1 one kept in prison 2 captive

pristine adj completely new and pure

private ❶ adj 1 secret, not public 2 not general, individual 3 personal 4 secluded 5 denoting soldier of lowest rank ▷ n 6 private soldier **privacy** n **privatize** v transfer (service etc.) from public to private ownership

privation n lack of comforts or necessities

privet n bushy evergreen shrub used for hedges

privilege n right, advantage granted or belonging only to few

p

sovereign, crown prince
principal adj = **main**, leading, chief, prime, first ≠ **minor** ▷ n = **headmaster** or **headmistress**, head (Inf), dean, head teacher, rector; = **star**, lead, leader, prima ballerina, leading man or lady; = **capital**, money, assets, working capital

principle n = **morals**, standards, ideals, honour, virtue; = **rule**, law, truth, precept

print v = **run off**, publish, copy, reproduce, issue; = **publish**,

release, circulate, issue, disseminate ▷ n = **photograph**, photo, snap; = **picture**, plate, etching, engraving, lithograph; = **copy**, photo (Inf), picture, reproduction, replica

prior adj = **earlier**, previous, former, preceding, foregoing

prison n = **jail**, confinement, nick (Brit Sl), cooler (Sl), jug (Sl)

private adj = **exclusive**, individual, privately owned, own, special ≠ **public**; = **secret**, confidential, covert, unofficial, clandestine

privileged adj enjoying privilege

privy adj **1** admitted to knowledge of secret ▷ n **2** lavatory

prize ❶ n **1** reward given for success in competition **2** thing striven for **3** thing won, e.g. in lottery etc. ▷ adj **4** winning or likely to win prize ▷ v **5** value highly

pro¹ adj/adv in favour of **pros and cons** arguments for and against

pro² n professional

pro- comb. form **1** in favour of **2** instead of

probable ❶ adj likely **probability** n, pl **-ties 1** likelihood **2** anything probable **probably** adv

probate n **1** proving of authenticity of will **2** certificate of this

probation ❶ n **1** system of dealing with lawbreakers by placing them under supervision **2** trial period **probationer** n person on probation

probe ❶ v **1** search into, examine, question closely ▷ n **2** that which probes, or is used to probe **3** thorough inquiry

probity n honesty, integrity

problem ❶ n **1** matter etc. difficult to deal with or solve **2** question set for solution **problematical** adj

proceed ❶ v **1** go forward, continue **2** be carried on **3** arise from **4** go to law **procedure** n act, manner of proceeding **proceeding** n **1** act or course of action ▷ pl **2** minutes of meeting **3** legal action **proceeds** pl n profit

process ❶ n **1** series of actions or changes **2** method of operation **3** state of going on **4** action of law ▷ v **5** handle, treat, prepare by special method of manufacture etc. **procession** n train of persons in formal order

proclaim ❶ v announce publicly, declare **proclamation** n

THESAURUS

≠ **public**; = **personal**, individual, secret, intimate, undisclosed

prize n = **reward**, cup, award, honour, medal ▷ adj = **champion**, best, winning, top, outstanding

probable adj = **likely**, possible, apparent, reasonable to think, credible ≠ **unlikely**

probation n = **trial period**, trial, apprenticeship

probe v often with **into** = **examine**, go into, investigate, explore, search; = **explore**, examine, poke, prod, feel around ▷ n = **investigation**, study, inquiry,

analysis, examination

problem n = **difficulty**, trouble, dispute, plight, obstacle; = **puzzle**, question, riddle, enigma, conundrum

proceed v = **begin**, go ahead; = **continue**, go on, progress, carry on, go ahead ≠ **discontinue**

process n = **procedure**, means, course, system, action; = **development**, growth, progress, movement, advance ▷ v = **handle**, manage, action, deal with, fulfil

proclaim v = **announce**, declare, advertise, publish, indicate ≠ **keep**

P

procrastinate v put off, delay
  procrastination n

procreate v produce offspring
  procreation n

procure v 1 obtain, acquire
  2 bring about 3 act as pimp
  procurement n **procurer** n
  1 one who procures 2 pimp

prod ❶ v prodding, prodded
  1 poke ▷ n 2 prodding 3 pointed
  instrument

prodigal adj 1 wasteful ▷ n
  2 spendthrift

prodigy ❶ n, pl -gies 1 person
  with some marvellous gift 2 thing
  causing wonder **prodigious** adj
  1 very great 2 extraordinary

produce ❶ v 1 bring into
  existence 2 yield 3 bring forward
  4 manufacture 5 present on stage,
  film, television ▷ n 6 that which is
  yielded or made **producer** n
  product n 1 thing produced
  2 consequence **production** n
  1 producing 2 staging of play etc.
  productive adj 1 fertile 2 creative

productivity n

profane adj 1 irreverent,
  blasphemous 2 not sacred ▷ v
  3 treat irreverently **profanity** n/pl
  -ties profane talk

profess ❶ v 1 affirm belief in
  2 claim, pretend **profession** n
  1 calling or occupation, esp.
  learned, scientific or artistic
  2 professing **professional** adj
  1 engaged in a profession 2 taking
  part in sport, music etc. for money
  3 skilled ▷ n 4 paid player
  professor n teacher of highest
  rank in university

proffer v offer

proficient adj 1 skilled 2 expert
  proficiency n

profile ❶ n 1 outline, esp. of face,
  as seen from side 2 brief
  biographical sketch **profiling** n
  practice of categorizing and
  predicting the behaviour of people
  according to certain characteristics
  racial profiling

profit ❶ n 1 money gained

—————— THESAURUS ——————

secret
prod v = **poke**, push, dig, shove,
  nudge; = **prompt**, move, urge,
  motivate, spur ▷ n = **poke**, push,
  dig, shove, nudge; = **prompt**,
  signal, cue, reminder, stimulus

prodigy n = **genius**, talent, wizard,
  mastermind, whizz (Inf)

produce v = **cause**, effect,
  generate, bring about, give rise to;
  = **make**, create, develop,
  manufacture, construct; = **create**,
  develop, write, turn out, compose;
  = **yield**, provide, grow, bear, give

▷ n = **fruit and vegetables**, goods,
  food, products, crops

profess v = **claim**, allege, pretend,
  fake, make out; = **state**, admit,
  announce, declare, confess

profile n = **outline**, lines, form,
  figure, silhouette; = **biography**,
  sketch, vignette, characterization,
  thumbnail sketch

profit n often plural = **earnings**,
  return, revenue, gain, yield ≠ **loss**;
  = **benefit**, good, use, value, gain
  ≠ **disadvantage** ▷ v = **make
  money**, gain, earn; = **benefit**, help,

— DICTIONARY —

2 benefit obtained ▷ v 3 benefit
4 earn **profitable** adj **profiteer** n
1 one who makes excessive profits
at public's expense ▷ v 2 profit
thus

profligate adj 1 recklessly
extravagant 2 depraved, immoral

profound ❶ adj 1 very learned
2 deep 3 heartfelt **profundity** n,
pl **-ties**

profuse adj abundant **profusion**
n

progeny n, pl **-nies** children
progenitor n ancestor

prognosis n, pl **-noses** forecast

programme ❶ n 1 plan of
intended proceedings 2 broadcast
on radio or television **program** n
1 instructions for computer ▷ v
2 feed program into (computer)
3 arrange program

progress ❶ n 1 onward
movement 2 sequence ▷ v 3 go
forward 4 improve **progression**
n 1 moving forward

2 improvement **progressive** adj
1 progressing by degrees
2 favouring political or social
reform

prohibit ❶ v forbid **prohibition**
n 1 act of forbidding 2 ban on sale
or drinking of alcohol **prohibitive**
adj 1 tending to forbid or exclude
2 (of cost) too high to be afforded

project ❶ n 1 plan, scheme ▷ v
2 plan 3 throw 4 cause to appear
on distant background 5 stick out
projectile n heavy missile
projection n 1 bulge 2 forecast
projector n apparatus for
projecting photographic images

proletariat n working class
proletarian adj/n

proliferate v grow or reproduce
rapidly **proliferation** n

prolific ❶ adj 1 fruitful
2 producing much

prologue n preface

prolong ❶ v lengthen

promenade ❶ n 1 leisurely walk

— THESAURUS —

serve, gain, promote

profound adj = **sincere**, acute,
intense, great, keen ≠ **insincere**;
= **wise**, learned, deep, penetrating,
philosophical ≠ **uninformed**

programme n = **schedule**, plan,
agenda, timetable, listing;
= **course**, curriculum, syllabus

progress n = **development**,
growth, advance, gain,
improvement ≠ **regression**;
= **movement forward**, passage,
advancement, course, advance
≠ **movement backward** ▷ v
= **move on**, continue, travel,

advance, proceed ≠ **move back**;
= **develop**, improve, advance,
grow, gain ≠ **get behind**

prohibit v = **forbid**, ban, veto,
outlaw, disallow ≠ **permit**;
= **prevent**, restrict, stop, hamper,
hinder ≠ **allow**

project n = **scheme**, plan, job,
idea, campaign ▷ v = **forecast**,
expect, estimate, predict, reckon;
= **stick out**, extend, stand out,
bulge, protrude

prolific adj = **productive**, creative,
fertile, inventive, copious

prolong v = **lengthen**, continue,

2 place made or used for this ▷ v
3 take leisurely walk

prominent ① adj **1** sticking out
2 conspicuous **3** distinguished
prominence n

promiscuous adj indiscriminate,
esp. in sexual relations
promiscuity n

promise ① v **1** give undertaking
or assurance **2** be likely to ▷ n
3 undertaking to do or not to do
something **4** potential **promising**
adj **1** showing good signs, hopeful
2 likely to succeed

promontory n, pl **-ries** high land
jutting out into sea

promote ① v **1** help forward
2 move up to higher rank or
position **3** encourage sale of
promoter n **promotion** n

prompt ① adj **1** done at once
2 punctual ▷ adv **3** punctually ▷ v

4 urge, suggest **5** help (actor or
speaker) by suggesting next words
▷ n **6** cue, reminder

promulgate v proclaim, publish

prone ① adj **1** lying face
downwards **2** inclined (to)

prong n one spike of fork or similar
instrument

pronoun n word used to replace
noun

pronounce ① v **1** utter (formally)
2 give opinion **pronounced** adj
strongly marked **pronouncement**
n declaration **pronunciation** n
way word etc. is pronounced

proof ① n **1** evidence **2** thing
which proves **3** test,
demonstration **4** trial impression
from type or engraved plate
5 standard of strength of alcoholic
drink ▷ adj **6** giving impenetrable
defence against

THESAURUS

---

perpetuate, draw out, extend
≠ shorten

prominent adj = **famous**, leading,
top, important, main **≠ unknown**;
= **noticeable**, obvious,
outstanding, pronounced,
conspicuous **≠ inconspicuous**

promise v = **guarantee**, pledge,
vow, swear, contract; = **seem
likely**, look like, show signs of,
augur, betoken ▷ n = **guarantee**,
word, bond, vow, commitment;
= **potential**, ability, talent,
capacity, capability

promote v = **help**, back, support,
aid, forward **≠ impede**;
= **advertise**, sell, hype, publicize,
push; = **raise**, upgrade, elevate,

exalt **≠ demote**

prompt v = **cause**, occasion,
provoke, give rise to, elicit;
= **remind**, assist, cue, help out
▷ adj = **immediate**, quick, rapid,
instant, timely **≠ slow** ▷ adv (Inf)
= **exactly**, sharp, promptly, on the
dot, punctually

prone adj = **liable**, given, subject,
inclined, tending **≠ disinclined**;
= **face down**, flat, horizontal,
prostrate, recumbent **≠ face up**

pronounce v = **say**, speak, sound,
articulate, enunciate; = **declare**,
announce, deliver, proclaim, decree

proof n = **evidence**,
demonstration, testimony,
confirmation, verification ▷ adj

P

prop¹ ❶ n/v support

prop² n object used on set of film, play etc.

propaganda ❶ n organized dissemination of information to assist or damage political cause etc.

propagate v **1** reproduce, breed **2** spread **propagation** n

propel v **-pelling, -pelled** cause to move forward **propeller** n revolving shaft with blades for driving ship or aircraft **propulsion** n act of driving forward

propensity n, pl **-ties 1** inclination **2** tendency

proper ❶ adj **1** appropriate **2** correct **3** conforming to etiquette **4** strict **5** (of noun) denoting individual person or place **properly** adv

property ❶ n, pl **-ties 1** that which is owned **2** land, real estate **3** quality, attribute

prophet, prophetess ❶ n **1** inspired teacher or revealer of God's word **2** foreteller of future **prophecy** n, pl **-cies** prediction, prophetic utterance **prophesy** v **-sying, -sied** foretell **prophetic** adj

proponent n one who argues in favour of something

proportion ❶ n **1** relative size or number **2** due relation between connected things or parts **3** share ▷ pl **4** dimensions ▷ v **5** arrange proportions of **proportional, proportionate** adj in due proportion

propose ❶ v **1** put forward for consideration **2** intend **3** offer marriage **proposal** n **proposition** n **1** offer **2** statement

propound v put forward for consideration

proprietor n owner

= **impervious**, strong, resistant, impenetrable, repellent

prop¹ v = **lean**, place, set, stand, position ▷ n = **support**, stay, brace, mainstay, buttress

propaganda n = **information**, advertising, promotion, publicity, hype

proper adj = **real**, actual, genuine, true, bona fide; = **correct**, accepted, established, appropriate, right ≠ **improper**; = **polite**, right, becoming, seemly, fitting ≠ **unseemly**

property n = **possessions**, goods, effects, holdings, capital; = **land**, holding, estate, real estate, freehold; = **quality**, feature, characteristic, attribute, trait

prophet, prophetess n = **soothsayer**, forecaster, diviner, oracle, seer

proportion n = **part**, share, amount, division, percentage; = **relative amount**, relationship, ratio; = **balance**, harmony, correspondence, symmetry, concord ▷ pl n = **dimensions**, size, volume, capacity, extent

propose v = **put forward**, present, suggest, advance, submit; = **intend**, mean, plan, aim, design; = **nominate**, name, present,

propriety n, pl **-ties** properness, correct conduct

propulsion see PROPEL

prosaic adj commonplace, unromantic

proscribe v outlaw, condemn

prose n speech or writing not in verse

prosecute ❶ v carry on, bring legal proceedings against **prosecution** n **prosecutor** n

prospect ❶ n **1** expectation, chance for success **2** view **prospective** adj **1** anticipated **2** future **prospector** n **prospectus** n booklet giving details of university, company etc.

prosper ❶ v be successful **prosperity** n **prosperous** adj **1** successful **2** well-off

prostate n gland around neck of male bladder

prostitute ❶ n **1** one who offers sexual intercourse in return for payment ▷ v **2** make a prostitute

of **3** put to unworthy use **prostitution** n

prostrate adj **1** lying flat **2** overcome ▷ v **3** throw flat on ground **4** reduce to exhaustion

protagonist ❶ n **1** leading character in story **2** proponent

protect ❶ v keep from harm **protection** n **protective** adj **protector** n

protégé n one under another's patronage

protein n any of group of organic compounds which form essential part of food of living creatures

protest ❶ n **1** declaration or demonstration of objection ▷ v **2** object **3** make declaration against **4** assert formally **protestation** n strong declaration

Protestant adj **1** relating to Christian church split from R.C. church ▷ n **2** member of Protestant church

protocol ❶ n **1** diplomatic

--- THESAURUS ---

recommend; **= offer marriage**, pop the question (Inf), ask for someone's hand (in marriage)

prosecute v (Law) **= take someone to court**, try, sue, indict, arraign

prospect n **= likelihood**, chance, possibility, hope, promise; **= idea**, outlook ▷ pl n **= possibilities**, chances, future, potential, expectations ▷ v **= look**, search, seek, dowse

prosper v **= succeed**, advance, progress, thrive, get on

prostitute n **= whore**, hooker (US

SI), pro (SI), tart (Inf), call girl ▷ v **= cheapen**, sell out, pervert, degrade, devalue

protagonist n **= supporter**, champion, advocate, exponent; **= leading character**, principal, central character, hero or heroine

protect v **= keep someone safe**, defend, support, save, guard ≠ **endanger**

protest v **= object**, demonstrate, oppose, complain, disagree; **= assert**, insist, maintain, declare, affirm ▷ n **= demonstration**, march, rally, sit-in, demo (Inf) etiquette **2** (*Comp*) set of rules for transfer of data, esp. between different systems

proton *n* positively charged particle in nucleus of atom

prototype ❶ *n* original, model, after which thing is copied

protract *v* **1** lengthen **2** prolong **protractor** *n* instrument for measuring angles

protrude *v* stick out, project **protrusion** *n*

protuberant *adj* bulging out

proud ❶ *adj* **1** pleased, satisfied **2** arrogant, haughty

prove ❶ *v* **proving, proved 1** establish validity of **2** demonstrate, test **3** turn out to be **proven** *adj* proved

proverb *n* short, pithy saying in common use **proverbial** *adj*

provide ❶ *v* **1** make preparation **2** supply, equip **provided that** on condition that

province ❶ *n* **1** division of country **2** sphere of action ▷ *pl* **3** any part of country outside capital **provincial** *adj* **1** of a province **2** narrow in outlook ▷ *n* **3** unsophisticated person **4** inhabitant of province

provision ❶ *n* **1** providing, esp. for the future **2** thing provided ▷ *pl* **3** food ▷ *v* **4** supply with food **provisional** *adj* temporary

proviso *n, pl* **-sos, -soes** condition

provoke ❶ *v* **1** anger **2** arouse **3** cause **provocation** *n* **provocative** *adj*

prow *n* bow of vessel

prowess ❶ *n* **1** bravery **2** skill

prowl *v* **1** roam stealthily, esp. in search of prey or booty ▷ *n* **2** prowling **prowler** *n*

proximity ❶ *n* nearness

---

protocol *n* = **code of behaviour**, manners, conventions, customs, etiquette

prototype *n* = **original**, model, first, example, standard

proud *adj* = **satisfied**, pleased, content, thrilled, glad ≠ **dissatisfied**; = **conceited**, arrogant, lordly, imperious, overbearing ≠ **humble**

prove *v* = **turn out**, come out, end up; = **verify**, establish, determine, show, confirm ≠ **disprove**

provide *v* = **supply**, give, distribute, outfit, equip ≠ **withhold**; = **give**, bring, add, produce, present

province *n* = **region**, section, district, zone, patch; = **area**, business, concern, responsibility, line

provision *n* = **supplying**, giving, providing, supply, delivery; = **condition**, term, requirement, demand, rider

provoke *v* = **anger**, annoy, irritate, infuriate, hassle (*Inf*) ≠ **pacify**; = **rouse**, cause, produce, promote, occasion ≠ **curb**

prowess *n* = **skill**, ability, talent, expertise, genius ≠ **inability**; = **bravery**, daring, courage, heroism, mettle ≠ **cowardice**

proximity *n* = **nearness**,

DICTIONARY

proxy ⊕ n, pl **proxies**
  1 authorized agent or substitute
  2 writing authorizing one to act as
  this

prude n one who is excessively
  modest or proper **prudish** adj

prudent ⊕ adj 1 careful, discreet
  2 sensible 3 thrifty **prudence** n

prune¹ n dried plum

prune² ⊕ v 1 cut out dead parts,
  excessive branches etc. 2 shorten,
  reduce

pry v **prying, pried** make furtive
  or impertinent inquiries

PS postscript

psalm n sacred song

pseudo- comb. form false

pseudonym n 1 false, fictitious
  name 2 pen name

psychic ⊕ adj 1 of soul or mind
  2 sensitive to phenomena lying
  outside range of normal experience
  psychiatric adj of psychiatry
  psychiatrist n **psychiatry** n
  medical treatment of mental
  diseases **psychoanalysis** n
  method of studying and treating
  mental disorders **psychoanalyse**

v **psychoanalyst** n

psychological adj 1 of psychology
  2 of the mind **psychologist** n

psychology n 1 study of mind
  2 (Inf) person's mental make-up

psychopath n person afflicted
  with severe mental disorder
  psychopathic adj **psychosis** n
  severe mental disorder

psychosomatic adj (of a physical
  disorder) thought to have
  psychological causes

psychotherapy n treatment of
  disease by psychological, not
  physical, means

PTO please turn over

pub ⊕ n public house, building with
  bar and licence to sell alcoholic
  drinks

puberty n sexual maturity

pubic adj of the lower abdomen

public ⊕ adj 1 of or concerning the
  community as a whole 2 not
  private ▷ n 3 the community or its
  members **publican** n keeper of
  public house **public house** see
  PUB **public school** (Brit) private
  fee-paying school

THESAURUS

closeness

proxy n = **representative**, agent,
  deputy, substitute, factor

prudent adj = **cautious**, careful,
  wary, discreet, vigilant ≠ **careless**;
  = **wise**, politic, sensible, shrewd,
  discerning ≠ **unwise**; = **thrifty**,
  economical, sparing, careful, canny
  ≠ **extravagant**

prune² v = **cut**, trim, clip, dock,
  shape; = **reduce**, cut, cut back,
  trim, cut down

psychic adj = **supernatural**,
  mystic, occult; = **mystical**,
  spiritual, magical, other-worldly,
  paranormal

pub, public house n = **tavern**,
  bar, inn, saloon

public n = **people**, society,
  community, nation, everyone ▷ adj
  = **civic**, government, state,
  national, local; = **general**, popular,
  national, shared, common; = **open**,
  accessible, communal, unrestricted

publicity ❶ n **1** process of attracting public attention **2** attention thus gained **publicize** v advertise

publish ❶ v **1** prepare and issue for sale (books, music etc.) **2** make generally known **3** proclaim **publication** n **publisher** n

puck n rubber disc used instead of ball in ice hockey

pucker v **1** gather into wrinkles ▷ n **2** crease, fold

pudding ❶ n **1** sweet, cooked dessert, often made from suet, flour etc. **2** sweet course of meal **3** soft savoury dish with pastry or batter **4** kind of sausage

puddle n small muddy pool

puerile adj childish

puff ❶ n **1** short blast of breath, wind etc. **2** type of pastry **3** laudatory notice or advertisement ▷ v **4** blow abruptly **5** breathe hard **6** send out in a puff **7** inflate **8** advertise **9** smoke hard **puffy** adj swollen

puffin n sea bird with large brightly-coloured beak

pug n small snub-nosed dog

pugnacious adj given to fighting **pugnacity** n

pull ❶ v **1** exert force on object to move it towards source of force **2** remove **3** strain or stretch **4** attract ▷ n **5** act of pulling **6** force exerted by this **7** (Inf) influence

pulley n wheel with groove in rim for cord, used to raise weights

pullover n jersey, sweater without fastening, to be pulled over head

pulmonary adj of lungs

pulp ❶ n **1** soft, moist, vegetable or animal matter **2** flesh of fruit **3** any soft soggy mass ▷ v **4** reduce to pulp

pulpit n (enclosed) platform for preacher

pulse¹ ❶ n **1** movement of blood in arteries corresponding to heartbeat, discernible to touch, e.g. in wrist **2** any regular beat or vibration **pulsate** v throb, quiver,

p

≠ **private**; = **well-known**, leading, important, respected, famous

publicity n = **advertising**, press, promotion, hype, boost

publish v = **put out**, issue, produce, print; = **announce**, reveal, spread, advertise, broadcast

pudding n = **dessert**, afters (Brit Inf), sweet, pud (Inf)

puff v = **smoke**, draw, drag (Sl), suck, inhale; = **breathe heavily**, pant, exhale, blow, gasp ▷ n = **drag**, pull (Sl), smoke; = **blast**, breath, whiff, draught, gust

pull v = **draw**, haul, drag, trail, tow ≠ **push**; = **extract**, pick, remove, gather, take out ≠ **insert**; (Inf) = **attract**, draw, bring in, tempt, lure ≠ **repel**; = **strain**, tear, stretch, rip, wrench ▷ n = **tug**, jerk, yank, twitch, heave ≠ **shove**; = **puff**, drag (Sl), inhalation; (Inf) = **influence**, power, weight, muscle, clout (Inf)

pulp n = **paste**, mash, mush; = **flesh**, meat, soft part ▷ v = **crush**, squash, mash, pulverize

pulse¹ n = **beat**, rhythm, vibration, beating, throb

vibrate **pulsation** n

pulse² n edible seed of pod-bearing plant

pulverize v reduce to powder

puma n large Amer. feline carnivore, cougar

pumice n light porous variety of lava

pummel v -melling, -melled strike repeatedly

pump¹ ❶ n 1 appliance for raising water, or putting in or taking out air or liquid etc. ▷ v 2 raise, put in, take out etc. with pump 3 work like pump

pump² n light shoe

pumpkin n edible gourd

pun n 1 play on words ▷ v 2 make pun

punch¹ ❶ n 1 tool for perforating or stamping 2 blow with fists 3 (Inf) vigour ▷ v 4 stamp, perforate with punch 5 strike with fist

punch² n drink of spirits or wine with fruit juice etc.

punctilious adj 1 making much of details of etiquette 2 very exact, particular

punctual adj in good time, not late **punctuality** n

punctuate ❶ v 1 put in punctuation marks 2 interrupt at intervals **punctuation** n marks put in writing to assist in making sense clear

puncture ❶ n 1 small hole made by sharp object, esp. in tyre ▷ v 2 prick hole in, perforate

pundit n expert who speaks publicly on subject

pungent adj acrid, bitter

punish ❶ v 1 cause to suffer for offence 2 inflict penalty on 3 use or treat roughly **punishable** adj **punishing** adj harsh, difficult **punishment** n **punitive** adj inflicting or intending to inflict punishment

punnet n small basket for fruit

punter ❶ n 1 person who bets 2 member of public

puny adj -nier, -niest small and feeble

pup n young of certain animals, e.g. dog, seal

pupa n, pl -pae -pas stage

THESAURUS

---

pump¹ v = **supply**, send, pour, inject; = **interrogate**, probe, quiz, cross-examine; = **fire**, shoot, discharge, let off

punch¹ v = **hit**, strike, box, smash, belt (Inf) ▷ n = **blow**, hit, sock (Sl), jab, swipe (Inf); (Inf);
= **effectiveness**, bite, impact, drive, vigour

punctuate v = **interrupt**, break, pepper, sprinkle, intersperse

puncture n = **flat tyre**, flat;
= **hole**, opening, break, cut, nick
▷ v = **pierce**, cut, nick, penetrate, prick

punish v = **discipline**, correct, castigate, chastise, sentence

punitive adj = **retaliatory**, in reprisal, retaliative

punter n = **gambler**, better, backer; (Inf) = **person**, man in the street

between larva and adult in
metamorphosis of insect

pupil ❶ n 1 person being taught
2 opening in iris of eye

puppet ❶ n 1 small doll controlled
by operator's hand 2 (*Fig*) stooge,
pawn

puppy n, pl **-pies** young dog

purchase ❶ v 1 buy ▷ n 2 buying
3 what is bought 4 leverage, grip

pure ❶ adj 1 unmixed, untainted
2 simple 3 faultless 4 innocent
5 concerned with theory only
purely adv **purification** v **purify**
v **-fying, -fied** make, become
pure, clear or clean **purist** n
person obsessed with strict
obedience to tradition **purity** n
state of being pure

purée n 1 pulp of cooked fruit or
vegetables ▷ v 2 reduce to pulp

purgatory n place or state of
torment, pain or distress, esp. one

that is temporary

purge ❶ v 1 make clean, purify
2 remove, get rid of 3 clear out ▷ n
4 act, process of purging
purgative adj/n

purl n 1 stitch that forms ridge in
knitting ▷ v 2 knit in purl

purloin v 1 steal 2 pilfer

purple n/adj (of) colour between
crimson and violet

purport ❶ v 1 claim to be (true
etc.) 2 signify, imply ▷ n
3 meaning 4 apparent meaning

purpose ❶ n 1 reason, object
2 design 3 aim, intention
4 determination ▷ v 5 intend **on
purpose** intentionally **purposely**
adv

purr n 1 pleased noise which cat
makes ▷ v 2 utter this

purse ❶ n 1 small bag for money
2 resources 3 money as prize
4 (*US & Canad*) handbag ▷ v

P

pupil n = **student**, schoolboy *or*
schoolgirl, schoolchild ≠ **teacher**

puppet n = **marionette**, doll,
glove puppet, finger puppet;
= **pawn**, tool, instrument,
mouthpiece, stooge

purchase v = **buy**, pay for, obtain,
get, score (*Sl*) ≠ **sell** ▷ n
= **acquisition**, buy, investment,
property, gain; = **grip**, hold,
support, leverage, foothold

pure adj = **unmixed**, real, simple,
natural, straight ≠ **adulterated**;
= **clean**, wholesome, sanitary,
spotless, sterilized
≠ **contaminated**; = **complete**,
total, perfect, absolute, sheer

≠ **qualified**; = **innocent**, modest,
good, moral, impeccable
≠ **corrupt**

purge v = **rid**, clear, cleanse, strip,
empty ▷ n = **removal**, elimination,
expulsion, eradication, ejection

purport v = **claim**, allege, assert,
profess

purpose n = **reason**, point, idea,
aim, object; = **aim**, end, plan, hope,
goal; = **determination**, resolve,
will, resolution, ambition

purse n = **pouch**, wallet,
money-bag; (*US*) = **handbag**, bag,
shoulder bag, pocket book, clutch
bag ▷ v = **pucker**, contract,
tighten, pout, press together

5 pucker **purser** n ship's officer who keeps accounts

pursue ❶ v **1** chase **2** engage in **3** continue **pursuer** n **pursuit** n **1** pursuing **2** occupation

purvey v supply (provisions)

pus n yellowish matter produced by suppuration

push ❶ v **1** move, try to move away by pressure **2** drive or impel **3** make thrust **4** advance with steady effort ▷ n **5** thrust **6** persevering self-assertion **7** big military advance **pusher** n seller of illegal drugs **pushy** adj assertive, ambitious **pushchair** n collapsible chair-shaped carriage for baby

puss, pussy n, pl **pusses, pussies pussy** cat

pustule n pimple containing pus

put ❶ v putting, put **1** place **2** set **3** express **4** throw (esp. shot) ▷ n **5** throw **put off** **1** postpone **2** disconcert **3** repel **put up** **1** erect **2** accommodate

putrid adj **1** decomposed **2** rotten **putrefy** v **-fying, -fied** make or

become rotten

putt v strike (golf ball) along ground **putter** n golf club for putting

putty n paste used by glaziers

puzzle ❶ v **1** perplex or be perplexed ▷ n **2** bewildering, perplexing question, problem or toy

PVC polyvinyl chloride

pygmy n **1** abnormally undersized person **2** (with cap.) member of one of dwarf peoples of Equatorial Africa ▷ adj **3** very small

pyjamas pl n sleeping suit of trousers and jacket

pylon n tower-like erection, esp. to carry electric cables

pyramid n solid figure or structure with sloping sides meeting at apex, esp. in ancient Egypt

pyre n pile of wood for burning dead body

pyromania n urge to set things on fire **pyromaniac** n

pyrotechnics n manufacture, display of fireworks

python n large nonpoisonous snake that crushes its prey

p

— THESAURUS —

pursue v = **engage in**, perform, conduct, carry on, practise; = **try for**, seek, desire, search for, aim for; = **continue**, maintain, carry on, keep on, persist in; = **follow**, track, hunt, chase, dog ≠ **flee**

push v = **shove**, force, press, thrust, drive ≠ **pull**; = **press**, operate, depress, squeeze, activate

▷ n = **shove**, thrust, butt, elbow, nudge ≠ **pull**; (Inf) = **drive**, go (Inf), energy, initiative, enterprise

put v = **place**, leave, set, position, rest; = **express**, state, word, phrase, utter

puzzle v = **perplex**, confuse, baffle, stump, bewilder ▷ n = **problem**, riddle, question, conundrum, poser

q

QC (Brit) Queen's Counsel
QLD Queensland
quack n 1 harsh cry of duck
2 pretender to medical or other skill
▷ v 3 (of duck) utter cry
quadrangle n 1 four-sided figure
2 four-sided courtyard in a building
quadrant n quarter of circle
quadrilateral adj/n four-sided
(figure)
quadruped n four-footed animal
quadruple adj 1 fourfold ▷ v
2 make, become four times as
much
quadruplet n one of four
offspring born at one birth
quaff v drink heartily or in one
draught
quagmire n bog, swamp
quail¹ n small bird belonging to

partridge family
quail² v 1 flinch 2 cower
quaint adj 1 interestingly
old-fashioned or odd
2 curious
quake ❶ v shake, tremble
qualify ❶ v -fying, -fied 1 make
(oneself) competent 2 moderate
3 ascribe quality to **qualification**
n 1 skill needed for activity
2 modifying or limiting condition
qualified adj 1 fully trained
2 conditional, restricted
quality ❶ n, pl -ties 1 attribute
2 (degree of) excellence
qualm n 1 misgiving 2 sudden
feeling of sickness
quandary n, pl -ries state of
perplexity, dilemma
quango n, pl -gos partly
independent official body, set up by
government
quantify v -fying, -fied discover
or express the quantity of
quantity ❶ n, pl -ties (specified
or considerable) amount
quantitative easing n practice
of increasing the supply of money in
order to stimulate economic
activity
quarantine n/v (place in)
isolation to prevent spreading of
infection

THESAURUS

quake v = **shake**, tremble, quiver,
move, rock
qualify v = **certify**, equip,
empower, train, prepare
≠ **disqualify**; = **restrict**, limit,
reduce, ease, moderate
quality n = **standard**, standing,

class, condition, rank;
= **excellence**, status, merit,
position, value; = **characteristic**,
feature, attribute, point, side
quantity n = **amount**, lot, total,
sum, part; = **size**, measure, mass,
volume, length

quarrel ❶ n 1 angry dispute 2 argument ▷ v 3 argue 4 find fault with **quarrelsome** adj

quarry¹ n 1 object of hunt or pursuit 2 prey

quarry² n 1 excavation where stone etc. is dug for building etc. ▷ v 2 get from quarry

quart n liquid measure, quarter of gallon

quarter ❶ n 1 fourth part 2 region, district 3 mercy ▷ pl 4 lodgings ▷ v 5 divide into quarters 6 lodge **quarterly** adj happening, due etc. each quarter of year **quartermaster** n officer responsible for stores

quartet n (music for) group of four musicians

quartz n hard glossy mineral

quash ❶ v 1 annul 2 reject

quasi- comb. form not really, as in quasi-religious

quaver v 1 say or sing in quavering tones 2 tremble, shake, vibrate

▷ n 3 musical note half length of crotchet

quay n 1 solid, fixed landing stage 2 wharf

queasy adj **-sier, -siest** inclined to, or causing, sickness

queen ❶ n 1 female sovereign 2 king's wife 3 piece in chess 4 fertile female bee, wasp etc. 5 court card

queer ❶ adj odd, strange

quell v 1 crush, put down 2 allay

quench v 1 slake 2 extinguish

querulous adj peevish, whining

query ❶ n/v, pl **-ries** question

quest ❶ n/v search

question ❶ n 1 sentence seeking for answer 2 problem 3 point at issue 4 doubt ▷ v 5 ask questions of 6 dispute 7 doubt

questionable adj doubtful

questionnaire n formal list of questions **question mark** punctuation mark (?) written at end of questions

quarrel n = **disagreement**, fight, row, argument, dispute ≠ **accord** ▷ v = **disagree**, fight, argue, row, clash ≠ **get on** or **along (with)**

quarry¹ n = **prey**, victim, game, goal, aim

quarter n = **district**, region, neighbourhood, place, part; = **mercy**, pity, compassion, charity, sympathy ▷ v = **accommodate**, house, lodge, place, board

quash v = **annul**, overturn, reverse, cancel, overthrow; = **suppress**, crush, put down, beat, overthrow

queen n = **sovereign**, ruler,

monarch, leader, Crown; = **leading light**, star, favourite, celebrity, darling

queer adj = **strange**, odd, funny, unusual, extraordinary ≠ **normal**; = **faint**, dizzy, giddy, queasy, light-headed

query n = **question**, inquiry, problem ▷ v = **question**, challenge, doubt, suspect, dispute

quest n = **search**, hunt, mission, enterprise, crusade

question n = **inquiry**, enquiry, query, investigation, examination ≠ **answer**; = **difficulty**, problem,

queue ➊ n 1 line of waiting persons, vehicles ▷ v 2 wait in queue

quibble n/v (make) trivial objection

quiche n savoury flan

quick ➊ adj 1 fast 2 lively 3 hasty ▷ n 4 sensitive flesh ▷ adv 5 rapidly **quicken** v make, become faster or more lively **quickly** adj **quicksand** n loose wet sand that engulfs heavy objects **quicksilver** n mercury **quickstep** n fast ballroom dance

quiet ➊ adj 1 with little noise 2 undisturbed 3 not showy or obtrusive ▷ n 4 quietness ▷ v 5 make, become quiet **quieten** v

quiff n tuft of brushed-up hair

quill n 1 large feather 2 pen made from feather 3 spine of porcupine

quilt ➊ n 1 padded coverlet ▷ v

2 stitch (two pieces of cloth) with pad between

quinine n drug used to treat fever and as tonic

quintessence n most perfect representation of a quality **quintessential** adj

quintet n (music for) group of five musicians

quintuplet n one of five offspring born at one birth

quip ➊ n/v (utter) witty saying

quirk n 1 individual peculiarity of character 2 unexpected twist

quit ➊ v **quitting, quit** 1 stop doing (something) 2 leave 3 give up

quite ➊ adv 1 completely 2 somewhat ▷ interj 3 expression of agreement

quiver¹ v/n shake, tremble

quiver² n case for arrows

doubt, argument, dispute ▷ v = **interrogate**, cross-examine, interview, examine, probe; = **dispute**, challenge, doubt, suspect, oppose ≠ **accept**

queue n = **line**, row, file, train, series

quick adj = **fast**, swift, speedy, express, cracking (Brit Inf) ≠ **slow**; = **brief**, passing, hurried, flying, fleeting ≠ **long**; = **immediate**, instant, prompt, sudden, abrupt; = **excitable**, passionate, irritable, touchy, irascible ≠ **calm**

quiet adj = **soft**, low, muted, lowered, whispered ≠ **loud**; = **peaceful**, silent, hushed, soundless, noiseless ≠ **noisy**;

= **calm**, peaceful, tranquil, mild, serene ≠ **exciting** ▷ n = **peace**, rest, tranquillity, ease, silence ≠ **noise**

quilt n = **bedspread**, duvet, coverlet, eiderdown, counterpane

quip n = **joke**, sally, jest, riposte, wisecrack (Inf)

quit v = **resign (from)**, leave, retire (from), pull out (of), step down (from) (Inf); = **stop**, give up, cease, end, drop ≠ **continue**; = **leave**, depart from, go out of, go away from, pull out from

quite adv = **somewhat**, rather, fairly, reasonably, relatively; = **absolutely**, perfectly, completely, totally, fully

quiz ❶ n, pl **quizzes**
1 entertainment in which knowledge of players is tested by questions **2** examination, interrogation ▷ v **3** question, interrogate **quizzical** adj **1** questioning **2** mocking
quoit n **1** ring for throwing at peg as a game ▷ pl **2** this game

quorum n least number that must be present to make meeting valid **quorate** adj
quota ❶ n share to be contributed or received
quote ❶ v **1** repeat passages from **2** state price for **quotation** n
quotient n number resulting from dividing one number by another

— THESAURUS —

quiz n = **examination**, questioning, interrogation, interview, investigation ▷ v = **question**, ask, interrogate,

examine, investigate
quota n = **share**, allowance, ration, part, limit
quote v = **repeat**, recite, recall

q

r

R 1 King 2 Queen 3 river

rabbi n, pl **-bis** Jewish learned man, spiritual leader

rabbit n small burrowing mammal

rabble n crowd of vulgar, noisy people

rabid adj 1 of, having rabies 2 fanatical

rabies n infectious disease transmitted by dogs etc.

raccoon n small N Amer. mammal

race¹ ❶ n 1 contest of speed 2 rivalry 3 strong current ▷ pl 4 meeting for horse racing ▷ v 5 (cause to) run, move swiftly **racer** n

race² n 1 group of people of common ancestry with distinguishing physical features 2 species **racial** adj **racism, racialism** n 1 belief in superiority of particular race 2 antagonism towards members of different race based on this **racist, racialist** adj/n

rack ❶ n 1 framework for displaying or holding things 2 instrument of torture ▷ v 3 torture

racket¹ ❶ n 1 uproar 2 occupation by which money is made illegally **racketeer** n

racket², racquet n 1 bat used in tennis etc. ▷ pl 2 ball game

raconteur n skilled storyteller

racy adj **racier, raciest** 1 lively 2 piquant

radar n device for locating objects by radio waves, which reflect back to their source

radial see RADIUS

radiate ❶ v 1 emit, be emitted in rays 2 spread out from centre **radiance** n 1 brightness 2 splendour **radiation** n 1 transmission of heat, light etc. from one body to another 2 particles, rays emitted in nuclear decay **radiator** n 1 heating apparatus for rooms 2 cooling

— THESAURUS —

race¹ n = **competition**, contest, chase, dash, pursuit; = **contest**, competition, rivalry ▷ v = **compete against**, run against; = **compete**, run, contend, take part in a race

rack n = **frame**, stand, structure, framework ▷ v = **torture**, torment, afflict, oppress, harrow

racket¹ n = **noise**, row, fuss, disturbance, outcry; = **fraud**, scheme

radiate v = **emit**, spread, send out, pour, shed; = **show**, display, demonstrate, exhibit, emanate apparatus of car engine

radical ❶ *adj* **1** fundamental **2** extreme **3** of root ▷ *n* **4** person of extreme (political) views

radio *n, pl* **-dios 1** use of electromagnetic waves for broadcasting, communication etc. **2** device for receiving, amplifying radio signals **3** broadcasting of radio programmes ▷ *v* **4** transmit message etc. by radio

radioactive *adj* emitting invisible rays that penetrate matter **radioactivity** *n*

radiography *n* production of image on film by radiation

radiology *n* science of use of rays in medicine

radiotherapy *n* diagnosis and treatment of disease by X-rays

radish *n* pungent root vegetable

radium *n* radioactive metallic element

radius *n, pl* **radii, radiuses** straight line from centre to circumference of circle **radial** *adj*

RAF Royal Air Force

raffia *n* prepared palm fibre for making mats etc.

raffle *n* **1** lottery in which article is won by one of those buying tickets ▷ *v* **2** dispose of by raffle

raft *n* floating structure of logs, planks etc.

rafter *n* main beam of roof

rag *n* **1** fragment of cloth **2** torn piece ▷ *pl* **3** tattered clothing **ragged** *adj* **ragtime** *n* style of jazz piano music

ragamuffin *n* ragged, dirty person, esp. child

rage ❶ *n* **1** violent anger **2** fury ▷ *v* **3** speak, act with fury **4** proceed violently, as storm

raglan *adj* (of sleeve) continuing in one piece to the neck

raid ❶ *n* **1** attack **2** foray ▷ *v* **3** make raid on

rail¹ *n* horizontal bar **railing** *n* fence, barrier made of rails supported by posts **railway** *n* track of iron rails on which trains run

rail² *v* **1** utter abuse **2** scold

rain ❶ *n* **1** moisture falling in drops from clouds ▷ *v* **2** pour down as, like rain **rainy** *adj*

rainbow *n* arch of colours in sky

rainforest *n* dense forest in tropics

— THESAURUS —

radical *adj* = **extreme**, complete, entire, sweeping, severe; = **revolutionary**, extremist, fanatical; = **fundamental**, natural, basic, profound, innate ≠ **superficial** ▷ *n* = **extremist**, revolutionary, militant, fanatic ≠ **conservative**

rage *n* = **fury**, temper, frenzy, rampage, tantrum ≠ **calmness** ▷ *v* = **be furious**, blow up (*Inf*), fume, lose it (*Inf*), seethe ≠ **stay calm**

raid *v* = **steal from**, plunder, pillage, sack ▷ *n* = **attack**, invasion, foray, sortie, incursion

rain *n* = **rainfall**, fall, showers, deluge, drizzle ▷ *v* = **pour**, pelt (down), teem, bucket down (*Inf*), drizzle; = **fall**, shower, be dropped, sprinkle, be deposited

raise ❶ v 1 lift up 2 set up 3 build 4 increase 5 heighten, as voice 6 breed 7 collect 8 propose, suggest ▷ n (US & Canad) pay rise

raisin n dried grape

rake¹ ❶ n 1 tool with long handle and teeth for gathering leaves etc. ▷ v 2 gather, smooth with rake 3 search over 4 sweep with shot

rake² n dissolute man

rakish adj 1 dashing 2 speedy

rally ❶ v, pl **-lies** 1 bring together, esp. what has been scattered 2 come together 3 regain health or strength ▷ n 4 assembly, esp. outdoor 5 (Tennis) lively exchange of strokes

ram ❶ n 1 male sheep 2 hydraulic machine 3 battering engine ▷ v

4 force, drive 5 strike against with force 6 stuff

ramble ❶ v 1 walk without definite route 2 talk incoherently ▷ n 3 rambling walk

ramp ❶ n gradual slope joining two level surfaces

rampage ❶ v 1 dash about violently ▷ n 2 angry or destructive behaviour

rampant ❶ adj 1 violent 2 rife 3 rearing

rampart n wall for defence

ramshackle adj rickety

ran past tense of RUN

ranch n Amer. cattle farm

rancid adj smelling or tasting offensively, like stale fat

rancour n bitter hate

random ❶ adj by chance, without plan

raise v = **lift**, elevate, uplift, heave; = **set upright**, lift, elevate; = **increase**, intensify, heighten, advance, boost ≠ **reduce**; = **make louder**, heighten, amplify, louden; = **collect**, gather, obtain, form, mass; = **cause**, start, produce, create, occasion; = **put forward**, suggest, introduce, advance, broach

rake¹ v = **gather**, collect, remove; = **search**, comb, scour, scrutinize

rake² n = **libertine**, playboy, swinger (Sl), lecher, roué ≠ **puritan**

rally n = **gathering**, convention, meeting, congress, assembly; = **recovery**, improvement, revival, recuperation ≠ **relapse** unite ▷ v = **recover**, improve, revive, get

better, recuperate ≠ **get worse**

ram v = **hit**, force, drive into, crash, impact; = **cram**, force, stuff, jam, thrust

ramble n = **walk**, tour, stroll, hike, roaming ▷ v = **walk**, range, wander, stroll, stray; often with on = **babble**, rabbit (on) (Brit Inf), waffle (Inf, chiefly Brit), witter on (Inf)

ramp n = **slope**, incline, gradient, rise

rampage v = **go berserk**, storm, rage, run riot, run amok

rampant adj = **widespread**, prevalent, rife, uncontrolled, unchecked; (Heraldry) = **upright**, standing, rearing, erect

random adj = **chance**, casual,

randy ❶ adj **randier, randiest**
(Sl) sexually aroused

rang past tense of RING²

range ❶ n **1** limits **2** row **3** scope,
distance missile can travel **4** place
for shooting practice **5** kitchen
stove ▷ v **6** set in row **7** extend
8 roam **9** fluctuate **ranger** n
official patrolling park etc. **rangy**
adj with long, slender limbs

rank¹ ❶ n **1** row, line **2** place
where taxis wait **3** order **4** status
5 relative position ▷ pl **6** (also pl)
common soldiers **7** great mass of
people ▷ v **8** draw up in rank
9 have rank, place

rank² ❶ adj **1** growing too thickly
2 rancid **3** flagrant

rankle v continue to cause anger or
bitterness

ransack v **1** search thoroughly
2 pillage

ransom ❶ n **1** release from
captivity by payment **2** amount
paid ▷ v **3** pay ransom for

rant ❶ v rave in violent language

rap ❶ v **rapping, rapped 1** give
smart slight blow to **2** utter
abruptly **3** perform monologue to
music ▷ n **4** smart slight blow
5 punishment **6** monologue set to
music

rapacious adj **1** greedy **2** grasping

rape¹ ❶ v **1** force (woman) to
submit to sexual intercourse ▷ n
2 act of raping **rapist** n

rape² n plant with oil-yielding
seeds

rapid ❶ adj **1** quick, swift ▷ n
2 (esp. pl) part of river with fast,
turbulent current

rapier n fine-bladed sword

rapport n harmony, agreement

rapt adj engrossed **rapture** n
ecstasy

rare¹ ❶ adj **1** uncommon **2** of

accidental, incidental, haphazard
≠ planned

randy adj (Inf) = **lustful**, hot,
turned-on (Sl), aroused, horny (Sl)

range n = **series**, variety, selection,
assortment, lot; = **limits**, reach ▷ v
= **vary**, run, reach, extend, stretch;
= **roam**, wander, rove, ramble,
traverse

rank¹ n = **status**, level, position,
grade, order; = **class**, caste; = **row**,
line, file, column, group ▷ v
= **order**, dispose; = **arrange**, sort,
line up, array, align

rank² adj = **absolute**, complete,
total, gross, sheer; = **foul**, bad,
offensive, disgusting, revolting;

= **abundant**, lush, luxuriant, dense,
profuse

ransom n = **payment**, money,
price, payoff

rant v = **shout**, roar, yell, rave, cry

rap v = **hit**, strike, knock, crack, tap
▷ n = **blow**, knock, crack, tap, clout
(Inf); (Sl) = **rebuke**, blame,
responsibility, punishment

rape¹ v = **sexually assault**, violate,
abuse, ravish, force ▷ n = **sexual
assault**, violation, ravishment,
outrage

rapid adj = **sudden**, prompt,
speedy, express, swift **≠ gradual**

rare¹ adj = **uncommon**, unusual,
few, strange, scarce **≠ common**;

exceptionally high quality **rarely** adv seldom **rarity** n

rare² adj (of meat) lightly cooked

raring ❶ adj **raring to** enthusiastically willing, ready

rascal n 1 rogue 2 naughty (young) person

rash¹ adj hasty, reckless

rash² ❶ n 1 skin eruption 2 outbreak

rasher n slice of bacon

rasp n 1 harsh, grating noise 2 coarse file ▷ v 3 scrape with rasp 4 make scraping noise 5 irritate

raspberry n 1 red, edible berry 2 plant which bears it

Rastafarian n 1 (oft. shortened to **Rasta**) member of Jamaican cult ▷ adj 2 of this cult

rat n 1 small rodent ▷ v 2 inform (on) 3 betray 4 desert **ratty** adj (Inf) irritable **rat race** continual hectic competitive activity

ratchet n set of teeth on bar or wheel allowing motion in one direction only

rate ❶ n 1 proportion between two things 2 charge 3 degree of speed etc. 4 local tax on business property ▷ v 5 value

rather ❶ adv 1 to some extent 2 preferably 3 more willingly

ratify ❶ v **-fying, -fied** confirm **ratification** n

rating ❶ n 1 valuing 2 classification 3 sailor

ratio ❶ n, pl **-tios** 1 proportion 2 relation

ration ❶ n 1 fixed allowance of food etc. ▷ v 2 supply with, limit to certain amount

rational ❶ adj reasonable, capable of reasoning **rationale** n reason for decision **rationalize** v 1 justify by plausible reasoning 2 reorganize to improve efficiency etc.

THESAURUS

= **superb**, great, fine, excellent, superlative

raring adj (in construction raring to do something) = **eager**, impatient, longing, ready, keen

rash¹ adj = **reckless**, hasty, impulsive, imprudent, careless ≠ **cautious**

rash² n = **outbreak of spots**, (skin) eruption; = **spate**, series, wave, flood, plague

rate n = **speed**, pace, tempo, velocity, frequency; = **degree**, standard, scale, proportion, ratio; = **charge**, price, cost, fee, figure ▷ v = **evaluate**, consider, rank, reckon, value; = **deserve**, merit, be entitled

to, be worthy of

rather adv = **preferably**, sooner, more readily, more willingly; = **to some extent**, quite, a little, fairly, relatively

ratify v = **approve**, establish, confirm, sanction, endorse ≠ **annul**

rating n = **position**, placing, rate, order, class

ratio n = **proportion**, rate, relation, percentage, fraction

ration n = **allowance**, quota, allotment, helping, part ▷ v = **limit**, control, restrict, budget

rational adj = **sensible**, sound, wise, reasonable, intelligent

rattle ❶ v 1 (cause to) give out succession of short sharp sounds ▷ n 2 such sound 3 instrument for making it 4 set of horny rings in rattlesnake's tail **rattlesnake** n poisonous snake

raucous adj hoarse

raunchy adj **-chier, -chiest** (Sl) earthy, sexy

ravage ❶ v 1 plunder ▷ n 2 destruction

rave ❶ v 1 talk wildly in delirium or enthusiasm ▷ n 2 wild talk 3 large-scale party with electronic music **raving** adj 1 delirious 2 (Inf) exceptional

raven n 1 black bird ▷ adj 2 jet-black

ravenous adj very hungry

ravine n narrow steep-sided valley

ravioli pl n small squares of pasta with filling

ravish v 1 enrapture 2 rape **ravishing** adj lovely

raw ❶ adj 1 uncooked 2 not

manufactured or refined 3 skinned 4 inexperienced 5 chilly

ray¹ ❶ n 1 narrow beam of light, heat etc. 2 any of set of radiating lines

ray² n marine flatfish

rayon n synthetic fibre

raze v destroy completely

razor n sharp instrument for shaving

razzle-dazzle, razzmatazz n showy activity

RC Roman Catholic

re ❶ prep concerning

RE religious education

re- comb. form again

reach ❶ v 1 arrive at 2 extend 3 touch ▷ n 4 act of reaching 5 grasp 6 range

react ❶ v act in return, opposition or towards former state **reaction** n 1 counter or backward tendency 2 response 3 chemical or nuclear change **reactionary** n/adj (person) opposed to change, esp. in

— THESAURUS —

rattle v = **clatter**, bang, jangle; = **shake**, jolt, vibrate, bounce, jar; (Inf) = **fluster**, shake, upset, disturb, disconcert

ravage v = **destroy**, ruin, devastate, spoil, demolish

rave v = **rant**, rage, roar, go mad (Inf), babble; (Inf) = **enthuse**, praise, gush, be mad about (Inf), be wild about (Inf)

raw adj = **unrefined**, natural, crude, unprocessed, basic ≠ **refined**; = **uncooked**, natural, fresh ≠ **cooked**; = **inexperienced**, new, green, immature, callow

≠ **experienced**; = **chilly**, biting, cold, freezing, bitter

ray¹ n = **beam**, bar, flash, shaft, gleam

re prep = **concerning**, about, regarding, with regard to, with reference to

reach v = **arrive at**, get to, make, attain; = **attain**, get to; = **touch**, grasp, extend to, stretch to, contact ▷ n = **grasp**, range, distance, stretch, capacity; = **jurisdiction**, power, influence

react v = **respond**, act, proceed, behave

r

politics etc. **reactive** adj chemically active **reactor** n apparatus to produce nuclear energy

read ❶ v **reading, read**
1 understand written matter
2 learn by reading **3** read and utter
4 study **5** understand any indicating instrument **reader** n
1 one who reads **2** university lecturer **3** school textbook
reading n

ready ❶ adj **readier, readiest**
1 prepared for action **2** willing
readiness n

real ❶ adj **1** happening **2** actual
3 genuine **realism** n regarding things as they are **realist** n
realistic adj **reality** n real existence **really** adv **real estate** landed property

realize ❶ v **1** grasp significance of

2 make real **3** convert into money

realm ❶ n kingdom

realtor n (US & Canad) agent, esp. accredited one who sells houses, etc. for others

ream n **1** twenty quires of paper
▷ pl **2** (Inf) large quantity of written matter

reap ❶ v cut and gather harvest

rear¹ ❶ n back part **rear admiral** high-ranking naval officer

rear² ❶ v **1** care for and educate (children) **2** breed **3** rise on hind feet

reason ❶ n **1** motive **2** ability to think **3** sanity **4** sensible thought
▷ v **5** think logically **6** persuade by logical argument **reasonable** adj
1 sensible **2** suitable **3** logical

reassure ❶ v restore confidence to

rebate n discount, refund

rebel ❶ v **-belling, -belled 1** resist

— THESAURUS —

read v = **scan**, study, look at, pore over, peruse; = **understand**, interpret, comprehend, construe, decipher; = **register**, show, record, display, indicate

ready adj = **prepared**, set, primed, organized ≠ **unprepared**;
= **completed**, arranged

real adj = **true**, genuine, sincere, factual, unfeigned

realize v = **become aware of**, understand, take in, grasp, comprehend; = **fulfil**, achieve, accomplish, make real

realm n = **field**, world, area, province, sphere; = **kingdom**, country, empire, land, domain

reap v = **get**, gain, obtain, acquire,

derive; = **collect**, gather, bring in, harvest, garner

rear¹ n = **back part**, back ≠ **front**

rear² v = **bring up**, raise, educate; train, foster; = **breed**, keep; = **rise**, tower, soar, loom

reason n = **cause**, grounds, purpose, motive, goal; = **sense**, mind, understanding, judgment, logic ≠ **emotion** ▷ v = **deduce**, conclude, work out, make out, infer

reassure v = **encourage**, comfort, hearten, gee up, restore confidence to

rebate n = **refund**, discount, reduction, bonus, allowance

rebel n = **revolutionary**, insurgent, secessionist, revolutionist ▷ v

DICTIONARY

lawful authority ▷ n 2 one who rebels ▷ adj 3 rebelling **rebellion** n organized open resistance to authority **rebellious** adj

rebound ① v 1 spring back 2 misfire, esp. so as to hurt perpetrator ▷ n 3 recoiling

rebuff ① n/v repulse, snub

rebuke ① n/v reprimand

rebut v **-butting, -butted** refute, disprove **rebuttal** n

recalcitrant adj wilfully disobedient

recall ① v 1 remember 2 call back 3 restore ▷ n 4 summons 5 ability to remember

recant v withdraw statement, opinion etc.

recap v 1 recapitulate ▷ n 2 recapitulation

recapitulate v state again briefly

recapitulation n

recede ① v 1 go back 2 slope backward

receipt ① n 1 written acknowledgment of money received 2 receiving

receive ① v 1 accept, experience 2 greet (guests) **receiver** n 1 officer appointed to take public money 2 one who knowingly takes stolen goods 3 equipment in telephone etc. to convert electrical signals into sound etc.

recent ① adj 1 lately happened 2 new **recently** adv

receptacle n n 1 vessel to contain anything

reception n n 1 receiving 2 formal party 3 area for receiving guests etc. 4 in broadcasting, quality of signals received

THESAURUS

= **revolt**, resist, rise up, mutiny; = **defy**, dissent, disobey

rebound v = **bounce**, ricochet, recoil; = **misfire**, backfire, recoil, boomerang

rebuff v = **reject**, refuse, turn down, cut, slight ≠ **encourage** ▷ n = **rejection**, snub, knock-back, slight, refusal (Sl) ≠ **encouragement**

rebuke v = **scold**, censure, reprimand, castigate, chide ≠ **praise** ▷ n = **scolding**, censure, reprimand, row, dressing down (Inf) ≠ **praise**

recall v = **recollect**, remember, evoke, call to mind ▷ n = **recollection**, memory, remembrance; = **annulment**,

withdrawal, repeal, cancellation, retraction

recede v = **fall back**, withdraw, retreat, return, retire

receipt n = **sales slip**, proof of purchase, counterfoil; = **receiving**, delivery, reception, acceptance

receive v = **get**, accept, be given, pick up, collect; = **experience**, suffer, bear, encounter, sustain; = **greet**, meet, admit, welcome, entertain

recent adj = **new**, modern, up-to-date, late, current ≠ **old**

reception n = **party**, gathering, get-together, social gathering, function (Inf); = **response**, reaction, acknowledgment, treatment, welcome

r

receptionist n person who receives clients etc.

receptive adj quick, willing to receive new ideas

recess ⦿ n 1 alcove 2 hollow 3 suspension of business

recession ⦿ n 1 period of reduction in trade 2 act of receding **recessive** adj receding

recipe ⦿ n directions for cooking food

recipient n one that receives

reciprocal adj 1 complementary 2 mutual 3 moving backwards and forwards **reciprocate** v give and receive mutually

recite ⦿ v repeat aloud, esp. to audience **recital** n 1 musical performance, usu. by one person 2 narration **recitation** n

reckless ⦿ adj incautious

reckon ⦿ v 1 count 2 include 3 think

reclaim ⦿ v 1 make fit for

cultivation 2 bring back 3 reform 4 demand the return of

recline v sit, lie back

recluse n hermit

recognize ⦿ v 1 identify again 2 treat as valid 3 notice **recognition** n

recoil v 1 draw back in horror 2 rebound ▷ n 3 recoiling

recollect v remember **recollection** n

recommend ⦿ v 1 advise 2 praise 3 make acceptable **recommendation** n

recompense v 1 reward 2 compensate ▷ n 3 reward 4 compensation

reconcile ⦿ v 1 bring back into friendship 2 adjust, harmonize **reconciliation** n

reconnoitre v make survey of **reconnaissance** n survey, esp. for military purposes

reconstitute v restore (food) to

recess n = **break**, rest, holiday, interval, vacation; = **alcove**, corner, bay, hollow, niche

recession n = **depression**, drop, decline, slump ≠ **boom**

recipe n = **directions**, instructions, ingredients

recite v = **perform**, deliver, repeat, declaim

reckless adj = **careless**, wild, rash, precipitate, hasty ≠ **cautious**

reckon v (Inf) = **think**, believe, suppose, imagine, assume; = **consider**, rate, account, judge, regard

reclaim v = **retrieve**, regain;

= **regain**, salvage, recapture, reform, redeem

recognize v = **identify**, know, place, remember, spot; = **acknowledge**, allow, accept, admit, grant ≠ **ignore**; = **appreciate**, respect, notice

recommend v = **advocate**, suggest, propose, approve, endorse ≠ **disapprove of**; = **put forward**, approve, endorse, commend, praise

reconcile v = **resolve**, settle, square, adjust, compose; = **reunite**, bring back together, conciliate; = **make peace between**, reunite, propitiate former state, esp. by addition of water

record ❶ n **1** document that records **2** disc with indentations which can be transformed into sound **3** best achievement **4** known facts ▷ v **5** put in writing **6** preserve (sound etc.) for reproduction on playback device **recorder** n **1** one that records **2** type of flute **3** judge in certain courts **record player** instrument for reproducing sound on records

recount ❶ v tell in detail

recoup v recover what has been expended or lost

recourse n (resorting to) source of help

recover ❶ v **1** get back **2** become healthy again **recovery** n

recreation ❶ n agreeable relaxation, amusement

recrimination n mutual abuse and blame

recruit ❶ n **1** newly-enlisted soldier **2** one newly joining ▷ v **3** enlist **recruitment** n

rectangle n oblong four-sided figure with four right angles **rectangular** adj

rectify v -fying, -fied correct

rectitude n honesty

rector n **1** clergyman with care of parish **2** head of academic institution **rectory** n rector's house

rectum n, pl -tums, -ta final section of large intestine

recumbent adj lying down

recuperate v restore, be restored from illness etc.

recur ❶ v -curring, -curred **1** happen again **2** go or come back in mind **recurrence** n **recurrent** adj

recycle ❶ v reprocess substance for use again

red ❶ adj/n redder, reddest **1** (of) colour of blood **2** (Inf) communist **redden** v **reddish** adj

record n = **document**, file, register, log, report; = **evidence**, trace, documentation, testimony, witness; = **disc**, single, album, LP, vinyl ▷ v = **set down**, minute, note, enter, document; = **make a recording of**, video, tape, video-tape, tape-record; = **register**, show, indicate, give evidence of; = **confidential**, private, unofficial, not for publication

recount v = **tell**, report, describe, relate, repeat

recover v = **get better**, improve, get well, recuperate, heal ≠ **relapse**

recreation n = **leisure**, play, sport, fun, entertainment

recruit v = **assemble**, raise, levy, muster, mobilize ▷ n = **beginner**, trainee, apprentice, novice, convert

recur v = **happen again**, return, repeat, persist, revert

recycle v = **reprocess**, reuse, salvage, reclaim, save

red adj = **crimson**, scarlet, ruby, vermilion, cherry; = **flushed**, embarrassed, blushing, florid, shamefaced; (of hair) = **chestnut**, reddish, flame-coloured, sandy, Titian

r

red-blooded adj 1 (Inf) vigorous 2 virile **red carpet** special welcome for important guest **red-handed** adj (Inf) (caught) in the act **red herring** topic introduced to divert attention **red-hot** adj 1 extremely hot 2 very keen **red tape** excessive adherence to rules **redwood** n giant coniferous tree of California

redeem ❶ v 1 buy back 2 set free 3 free from sin 4 make up for **redemption** n

redolent adj 1 smelling strongly 2 reminiscent (of)

redouble v increase, intensify

redoubtable adj dreaded, formidable

redress ❶ v 1 make amends for ▷ n 2 compensation

reduce ❶ v 1 lower 2 lessen 3 bring by necessity to some state 4 slim 5 simplify **reduction** n

redundant ❶ adj 1 superfluous 2 (of worker) deprived of job because no longer needed

redundancy n

reed n 1 various water plants 2 tall straight stem of one 3 (Mus) vibrating strip of certain wind instruments

reef n 1 ridge of rock or coral near surface of sea 2 part of sail which can be rolled up to reduce area

reek v/n (emit) strong unpleasant smell

reel ❶ n 1 spool on which film, thread etc. is wound 2 (Cinema) portion of film 3 lively dance ▷ v 4 wind on reel 5 draw (in) by means of reel 6 stagger

refectory n, pl **-tories** room for meals in college etc.

refer ❶ v **-ferring, -ferred** 1 relate (to) 2 send to for information 3 ascribe to 4 submit for decision **reference** n 1 act of referring 2 citation 3 appeal to judgment of another 4 testimonial 5 one to whom inquiries as to character etc. may be made

referee ❶ n 1 arbitrator 2 umpire ▷ v 3 act as referee

redeem v = reinstate, absolve, restore to favour; = make up for, compensate for, atone for, make amends for; = buy back, recover, regain, retrieve, reclaim; = save, free, deliver, liberate, ransom

redress v = make amends for, make up for, compensate for ▷ n = amends, payment, compensation, reparation, atonement

reduce v = lessen, cut, lower, moderate, weaken ≠ increase; = degrade, downgrade, break,

humble, bring low ≠ promote (Inf, Brit Sl)

redundant adj = superfluous, extra, surplus, unnecessary, unwanted ≠ essential

reel v = stagger, rock, roll, pitch, sway

refer v = direct, point, send, guide

referee n = umpire, judge, ref (Inf), arbiter, arbitrator ▷ v = umpire, judge, mediate, adjudicate, arbitrate

referendum n = public vote, popular vote, plebiscite

r

referendum ❶ n, pl -dums, -da
submitting of question to
electorate

refill v 1 fill again ▷ n
2 subsequent filling 3 replacement
supply

refine ❶ v purify **refined** adj
1 cultured, polite 2 purified
refinement n 1 subtlety
2 elaboration 3 fineness of taste or
manners **refinery** n place where
sugar, oil etc. is refined

reflect ❶ v 1 throw back, esp. light
2 cast (discredit etc.) upon
3 meditate **reflection** n
1 reflecting 2 image of object given
back by mirror etc. 3 thought
4 expression of thought **reflective**
adj **reflector** n

reflex n 1 involuntary action ▷ adj
2 (of muscular action) involuntary
3 bent back **reflexive** adj
(Grammar) describes verb denoting
agent's action on himself

reform ❶ v 1 improve 2 abandon

evil practices ▷ n 3 improvement
reformation n

refract v change course of light
etc. passing from one medium to
another **refraction** n

refractory adj unmanageable

refrain[1] ❶ v **refrain from** abstain
(from)

refrain[2] ❶ n chorus

refresh ❶ v 1 revive 2 renew
3 brighten **refreshment** n that
which refreshes, esp. food, drink

refrigerate ❶ v 1 freeze 2 cool
refrigerant n/adj **refrigeration**
n **refrigerator** n apparatus in
which foods, drinks are kept cool

refuge ❶ n shelter, sanctuary
refugee n one who seeks refuge,
esp. in foreign country

refund ❶ v 1 pay back ▷ n
2 repayment

refurbish ❶ v renovate and
brighten up

refuse[1] ❶ v decline, deny, reject
refusal n

— THESAURUS —

refine v = **purify**, process, filter,
cleanse, clarify; = **improve**, perfect,
polish, hone

reflect v = **show**, reveal, display,
indicate, demonstrate; = **throw
back**, return, mirror, echo,
reproduce; = **consider**, think,
muse, ponder, meditate

reform n = **improvement**,
amendment, rehabilitation,
betterment ▷ v = **improve**,
correct, restore, amend, mend;
= **mend your ways**, go straight
(Inf), shape up (Inf), turn over a new
leaf, clean up your act (Inf)

refrain[1] v = **stop**, avoid, cease,
renounce, abstain

refrain[2] n = **chorus**, tune, melody

refresh v = **revive**, freshen,
revitalize, stimulate, brace;
= **stimulate**, prompt, renew, jog

refuge n = **protection**, shelter,
asylum

refund n = **repayment**,
reimbursement, return ▷ v
= **repay**, return, restore, pay back,
reimburse

refurbish v = **renovate**, restore,
repair, clean up, overhaul

refuse[1] v = **decline**, reject, turn

refuse² ❶ n rubbish
refute v disprove **refutation** n
regain ❶ v 1 get back, recover
2 reach again
regal ❶ adj of, like a king **regalia**
pl n 1 insignia of royalty
2 emblems of high office
regale v 1 give pleasure to 2 feast
regard ❶ v 1 look at 2 consider
3 relate to ▷ n 4 look 5 attention
6 particular respect 7 esteem ▷ pl
8 expression of good will
regardless adj 1 heedless ▷ adv
2 in spite of everything
regatta n meeting for boat races
regenerate v 1 reform 2 re-create
3 reorganize **regeneration** n
regent ❶ n ruler of kingdom during
absence, minority etc. of its
monarch **regency** n
reggae ❶ n popular music with
strong beat
regime ❶ n system of government
regiment n 1 organized body of

troops ▷ v 2 discipline (too)
strictly
regimental adj
region ❶ n 1 area, district 2 part
3 sphere **regional** adj
register ❶ n 1 list 2 catalogue
3 device for registering 4 range of
voice or instrument ▷ v 5 show, be
shown on meter, face etc. 6 enter
in register 7 record **registrar** n
1 keeper of a register 2 senior
hospital doctor **registration** n
registry n 1 registering 2 place
where registers are kept
regress v revert to former place,
condition etc. **regression** n
regret ❶ v -gretting, -gretted
1 feel sorry, distressed for loss of or
on account of ▷ n 2 feeling of
sorrow **regretful** adj **regrettable**
adj
regular ❶ adj 1 normal 2 habitual
3 according to rule 4 periodical
5 straight ▷ n 6 soldier in standing
army **regularity** n

━━━━━━━━━ THESAURUS ━━━━━━━━━

down, say no to
refuse² n = **rubbish**, waste, junk
(Inf), litter, garbage
regain v = **recover**, get back,
retrieve, recapture, win back; = **get
back to**, return to, reach again
regal adj = **royal**, majestic, kingly or
queenly, noble, princely
regard v = **consider**, see, rate,
view, judge; = **look at**, view, eye,
watch, observe ▷ n = **respect**,
esteem, thought, concern, care;
= **look**, gaze, scrutiny, stare,
glance
regime n = **government**, rule,
management, leadership, reign

region n = **area**, place, part,
quarter, section
register n = **list**, record, roll, file,
diary ▷ v = **enrol**, enlist, list, note,
enter; = **record**, catalogue,
chronicle, mark, indicate,
manifest
regret v = **be** or **feel sorry about**,
rue, deplore, bemoan, repent (of)
≠ **be satisfied with**; = **mourn**,
miss, grieve for or over ▷ n
= **remorse**, compunction,
bitterness, repentance, contrition
regular adj = **normal**, common,
usual, ordinary, typical
≠ **infrequent**; = **steady**, consistent

regulate ➊ v 1 adjust 2 arrange 3 govern **regulation** n

regurgitate v 1 vomit 2 bring back (swallowed food) into mouth

rehabilitate v 1 help (person) to readjust to society after illness, imprisonment etc. 2 restore to former position **rehabilitation** n

rehash n 1 old materials presented in new form ▷ v 2 treat thus

rehearse ➊ v 1 practise (play etc.) 2 repeat 3 train **rehearsal** n

reign ➊ n 1 period of sovereign's rule ▷ v 2 rule

reimburse v pay back

rein n 1 strap attached to bit to guide horse 2 instrument for governing

reincarnation n rebirth of soul in successive bodies

reindeer n, pl **-deer, -deers** deer of cold regions

reinforce ➊ v strengthen with

new support, material, force **reinforcement** n

reinstate ➊ v replace, restore

reiterate ➊ v repeat again

reject ➊ v 1 refuse to accept 2 put aside 3 discard 4 renounce ▷ n 5 person or thing rejected **rejection** n

rejig v **-jigging, -jigged** 1 re-equip 2 rearrange

rejoice ➊ v make or be joyful

rejoin ➊ v reply **rejoinder** n

rejuvenate v restore to youth

relapse v 1 fall back into evil, illness etc. ▷ n 2 relapsing

relate ➊ v 1 narrate 2 establish relation between 3 have reference to 4 form sympathetic relationship

relation ➊ n 1 relative condition 2 connection by blood or marriage 3 connection between things 4 narrative **relationship** n

relative adj 1 dependent on

regulate v = **control**, run, rule, manage, direct; = **moderate**, control, modulate, fit, balance

rehearse v = **practise**, prepare, run through, go over, train

reign v = **be supreme**, prevail, predominate, hold sway; = **rule**, govern, be in power, influence, command ▷ n = **rule**, power, control, command, monarchy

reinforce v = **support**, strengthen, fortify, toughen, stress

reinstate v = **restore**, recall, re-establish, return

reiterate v (Formal) = **repeat**, restate, say again, do again

reject v = **rebuff**, jilt, turn down,

spurn, refuse ≠ **accept**; = **deny**, exclude, veto, relinquish, renounce ≠ **approve**; = **discard**, decline, eliminate, scrap, jettison ≠ **accept** ▷ n = **castoff**, second, discard ≠ **treasure**

rejoice v = **be glad**, celebrate, be happy, glory, be overjoyed ≠ **lament**

rejoin v = **reply**, answer, respond, retort, riposte

relate v = **tell**, recount, report, detail, describe

relation n = **similarity**, link, bearing, bond, comparison; = **relative**, kin, kinsman or kinswoman relation to something else **2** having reference (to) ▷ *n* **3** one connected by blood or marriage

relax ❶ *v* **1** make, become loose or slack **2** ease up **3** make, become less strict **relaxation** *n* **1** recreation **2** abatement

relay ❶ *n* **1** fresh set of people or animals relieving others **2** (*Radio, TV*) broadcasting station receiving programmes from another station ▷ *v* **3** pass on, as message **relay race** race between teams of which each runner races part of distance

release ❶ *v* **1** set free **2** permit showing of (film etc.) ▷ *n* **3** releasing **4** permission to show publicly **5** film, record etc. newly issued

relegate ❶ *v* **1** put in less important position **2** demote **relegation** *n*

relent *v* become less severe **relentless** *adj*

relevant ❶ *adj* having to do with the matter in hand **relevance** *n*

reliable ❶ *see* RELY

relic ❶ *n* thing remaining

relief ❶ *n* **1** alleviation of pain etc. **2** money, food given to victims of disaster **3** release from duty **4** one who relieves another **5** bus, plane etc. operating when a scheduled service is full **6** freeing of besieged city **7** projection of carved design from surface **8** prominence **relieve** *v*

religion *n* system of belief in, worship of a supernatural power or god **religious** *adj* **1** of religion **2** pious **3** scrupulous

relinquish ❶ *v* give up

relish ❶ *v* **1** enjoy ▷ *n* **2** liking **3** savoury taste **4** sauce **5** pickle

---

relax *v* = **be** *or* **feel at ease**, chill out (*Sl, chiefly US*), take it easy, lighten up (*Sl*) ≠ **be alarmed**; = **calm down**, calm, unwind; = **make less tense**, rest

relay *v* = **broadcast**, carry, spread, communicate, transmit

release *v* = **set free**, free, discharge, liberate, drop ≠ **imprison**; = **acquit**, let go, let off, exonerate, absolve ▷ *n* = **liberation**, freedom, liberty, discharge, emancipation ≠ **imprisonment**; = **acquittal**, exemption, absolution, exoneration; = **issue**, publication, proclamation

relegate *v* = **demote**, degrade,

downgrade

relevant *adj* = **significant**, appropriate, related, fitting, to the point ≠ **irrelevant**

reliable *adj* = **dependable**, trustworthy, sure, sound, true ≠ **unreliable**

relic *n* = **remnant**, vestige, memento, trace, fragment

relief *n* = **ease**, release, comfort, cure, remedy; = **rest**, respite, relaxation, break, breather (*Inf*); = **aid**, help, support, assistance, succour

relinquish *v* (*Formal*) = **give up**, leave, drop, abandon, surrender

relish *v* = **enjoy**, like, savour, revel in ≠ **dislike** fancy ▷ *n*

DICTIONARY

relocate v move to new place, esp. to work

reluctant ❶ adj unwilling **reluctance** n

rely v **-lying, -lied 1** depend (on) **2** trust **reliability** n **reliable** adj **reliance** n **1** trust **2** confidence

remain ❶ v **1** be left behind **2** continue **3** last **remainder** n **remains** pl n **1** relics **2** dead body

remand v send back, esp. into custody **on remand** in custody

remark ❶ v/n (make) casual comment (on) **remarkable** adj unusual

remedy n, pl **-edies 1** means of curing ▷ v **2** put right **remedial** adj

remember ❶ v retain in, recall to memory **remembrance** n

remind ❶ v cause to remember **reminder** n

reminisce v talk, write of past times, experiences etc. **reminiscence** n **reminiscent** adj

remiss adj careless

remit v **-mitting, -mitted 1** send money for goods etc. **2** refrain from exacting **3** give up **4** return **5** slacken ▷ n **6** area of authority **remission** n **1** abatement **2** reduction of prison term **3** pardon **remittance** n **1** sending of money **2** money sent

remnant ❶ n fragment

remonstrate v protest

remorse ❶ n regret and repentance **remorseful** adj **remorseless** adj pitiless

remote ❶ adj **1** distant **2** aloof **3** slight **remote control** control of apparatus from distance by electrical device

remove ❶ v **1** take, go away **2** transfer **3** withdraw **removal** n

remunerate v reward, pay

THESAURUS

= **enjoyment**, liking, love, taste, fancy ≠ **distaste**; = **condiment**, seasoning, sauce

reluctant adj = **unwilling**, hesitant, loath, disinclined, unenthusiastic ≠ **willing**

remain v = **stay**, continue, go on, stand, dwell; = **stay behind**, wait, delay ≠ **go** be left, linger

remark v = **comment**, say, state, reflect, mention; = **notice**, note, observe, perceive, see ▷ n = **comment**, observation, reflection, statement, utterance

remedy n = **cure**, treatment, medicine, nostrum ▷ v = **put right**, rectify, fix, correct, set to

rights

remember v = **recall**, think back to, recollect, reminisce about, call to mind ≠ **forget**; = **bear in mind**, keep in mind

remind v = **jog your memory**, prompt, make you remember

remnant n = **remainder**, remains, trace, fragment, end

remorse n = **regret**, shame, guilt, grief, sorrow

remote adj = **distant**, far, isolated, out-of-the-way, secluded ≠ **nearby**; = **far**, distant; = **slight**, small, outside, unlikely, slim ≠ **strong**

remove v = **take out**, withdraw,

r

remuneration n **remunerative** adj

renaissance, renascence ❶ n revival, rebirth

renal adj of the kidneys

rend ❶ v **rending, rent 1** tear apart **2** burst

render ❶ v **1** submit **2** give in return **3** cause to become **4** represent **5** melt down **6** plaster

rendezvous n, pl **-vous 1** meeting place **2** appointment

rendition n **1** performance **2** translation

renegade n deserter

renege v go back on (promise etc.)

renew ❶ v **1** begin again **2** make valid again **3** make new **4** restore **5** replenish **renewable** adj **1** able to be renewed **2** (of energy or an energy source) inexhaustible or capable of being perpetually replenished **renewables** pl n

renewable energy sources **renewal** n

renounce ❶ v **1** give up, disown **2** resign, as claim **renunciation** n

renovate ❶ v restore, repair **renovation** n

renown n fame

rent¹ ❶ n **1** payment for use of land, buildings etc. ▷ v **2** hire

rent² ❶ n tear

reorganize v organize in new, more efficient way

repair¹ ❶ v **1** make whole again **2** mend ▷ n **3** repaired part **reparation** n compensation

repair² v go (to)

repartee n **1** witty retort **2** interchange of them

repatriate v send (someone) back to his or her own country **repatriation** n

repay ❶ v **repaying, repaid 1** pay back **2** make return for **repayment** n

THESAURUS

extract ≠ insert

renaissance, renascence n = **rebirth**, revival, restoration, renewal, resurgence

rend v (Lit) = **tear**, rip, separate, wrench, rupture

render v = **make**, cause to become, leave; = **provide**, give, pay, present, supply; = **represent**, portray, depict, do, give

renew v = **recommence**, continue, extend, repeat, resume; = **reaffirm**, resume, recommence; = **replace**, refresh, replenish, restock; = **restore**, repair, overhaul, mend, refurbish

renounce v = **disown**, quit, forsake, recant, forswear

renovate v = **restore**, repair, refurbish, do up (Inf), renew

rent¹ v = **hire**, lease ▷ n = **hire**, rental, lease, fee, payment

rent² n = **tear**, split, rip, slash, slit

repair¹ v = **mend**, fix, restore, heal, patch ≠ **damage**; = **put right**, make up for, compensate for, rectify, redress ▷ n = **mend**, restoration, overhaul; = **darn**, mend, patch

repay v = **pay back**, refund, settle up, return, square

DICTIONARY

repeal ❶ v 1 revoke, cancel ▷ n 2 cancellation

repeat ❶ v 1 say, do again 2 recur ▷ n 3 act, instance of repeating **repetition** n 1 act of repeating 2 thing repeated **repetitive** adj

repel ❶ v -pelling, -pelled 1 drive back 2 be repulsive to **repellent** adj/n

repent v feel regret for deed or omission **repentance** n **repentant** adj

repertoire ❶ n stock of plays, songs etc. that player or company can give **repertory** n repertoire **repetition** ❶ see REPEAT

replace ❶ v 1 substitute for 2 put back **replacement** n

replay n 1 reshowing on TV of sporting incident, esp. in slow motion 2 second sports match, esp. following earlier draw ▷ v 3 play (match, recording etc.) again

replenish v fill up again

replete adj filled, gorged

replica ❶ n exact copy **replicate** v make or be copy of

reply ❶ n/v -plying, -plied answer

report ❶ n 1 account 2 written statement of child's progress at school 3 rumour 4 repute 5 bang ▷ v 6 announce 7 give account of 8 complain about 9 make report 10 present oneself (to) **reporter** n

repose 1 n 2 peace 3 composure 4 sleep ▷ v 5 rest **repository** n place where valuables are deposited for safekeeping

repossess v take back property from one who is behind with payments

reprehensible adj 1 deserving censure 2 unworthy

represent ❶ v 1 stand for 2 deputize for 3 act 4 symbolize

THESAURUS

repeal v = abolish, reverse, revoke, annul, recall ≠ pass ▷ n = abolition, cancellation, annulment, invalidation, rescindment ≠ passing

repeat v = reiterate, restate ▷ n = repetition, echo, reiteration

repel v = drive off, fight, resist, parry, hold off ≠ submit to; = disgust, offend, revolt, sicken, nauseate ≠ delight

repertoire n = range, list, stock, supply, store

repetition n = recurrence, repeating, echo

replace v = take the place of, follow, succeed, oust, take over

from; = substitute, change, exchange, switch, swap

replica n = reproduction, model, copy, imitation, facsimile ≠ original

reply v = answer, respond, retort, counter, rejoin ▷ n = answer, response, reaction, counter, retort

report v = inform of, communicate, recount; often with on = communicate, tell, state, detail, describe, post, tweet ▷ n = article, story, piece, write-up; = account, record, statement, communication, description; often plural = news, word

represent v = act for, speak for;

DICTIONARY

5 make out to be **6** describe

representation n

representative n **1** one chosen to stand for group **2** salesman ▷ adj **3** typical

repress ❶ v keep down or under

repression ❶ n **repressive** adj

reprieve ❶ v **1** suspend execution of (condemned person) ▷ n **2** postponement or cancellation of punishment **3** respite

reprimand n/v rebuke

reprisal n retaliation

reproach v **1** blame, rebuke ▷ n **2** scolding **3** thing bringing discredit **reproachful** adj

reprobate adj/n depraved (person)

reproduce ❶ v **1** produce copy of **2** bring new individuals into existence **reproduction** n **reproductive** adj

reprove v censure, rebuke **reproof** n

reptile n cold-blooded, air breathing vertebrate with scales or plates, as snake

republic n state without monarch governed by elected representatives **republican** adj/n

repudiate v reject authority or validity of

repugnant adj **1** offensive **2** distasteful **3** contrary

repulse v **1** drive back **2** rebuff **3** repel **repulsion** n **repulsive** adj disgusting

reputation ❶ n estimation in which a person is held

request ❶ n **1** asking **2** thing asked for ▷ v **3** ask

Requiem n Mass for the dead

require ❶ v **1** need **2** demand **requirement** n

requisite adj/n essential

requisition n **1** formal demand, e.g. for materials ▷ v **2** demand (supplies) **3** press into service

rescind v cancel

rescue ❶ v **-cuing, -cued 1** save, extricate ▷ n **2** rescuing

THESAURUS

= **stand for**, serve as, symbolize, mean, betoken; = **exemplify**, embody, symbolize, typify, personify

repress v = **control**, suppress, hold back, bottle up, check ≠ **release**; = **hold back**, suppress, stifle

reprieve v = **grant a stay of execution to**, pardon, let off the hook (SI) ▷ n = **stay of execution**, amnesty, pardon, remission, deferment

reproduce v = **copy**, recreate, replicate, duplicate, match; = **print**, copy

reputation n = **name**, standing, character, esteem, stature

request v = **ask for**, appeal for, put in for, demand, desire ▷ n = **appeal**, call, demand, plea, desire

require v = **need**, crave, want, miss, lack; = **order**, demand, command, compel, exact

rescue v = **save**, get out, release, deliver, recover ≠ **desert** ▷ n = **saving**, salvage, deliverance, release, recovery

DICTIONARY

research ❶ n 1 investigation to gather or discover facts ▷ v 2 investigate

resemble ❶ v 1 be like 2 look like **resemblance** n

resent ❶ v show, feel indignation at **resentful** adj **resentment** n

reserve ❶ v 1 hold back, set aside ▷ n 2 (also pl) something, esp. troops, kept for emergencies 3 area of land reserved for particular purpose or group 4 reticence ▷ adj 5 auxiliary, substitute **reservation** n 1 reserving 2 thing reserved 3 doubt 4 limitation **reserved** adj 1 booked 2 not showing one's feelings

reservoir ❶ n 1 enclosed area for storage of water 2 receptacle for liquid, gas etc.

reshuffle n 1 reorganization ▷ v 2 reorganize

reside ❶ v dwell permanently **residence** n home **resident** adj/n **residential** adj

residue ❶ n remainder **residual** adj

resign ❶ v 1 give up (esp. office, job) 2 reconcile (oneself) to **resignation** n

resilient adj 1 elastic 2 (of person) recovering quickly from shock etc. **resilience** n

resin n sticky substance from plants, esp. firs and pines

resist ❶ v withstand, oppose **resistance** n 1 resisting 2 opposition **resistant** adj **resistor** n component of electrical circuit producing resistance to current

resit v 1 retake (exam) ▷ n 2 exam to be retaken

resolute adj determined **resolution** n 1 resolving

THESAURUS

research n = **investigation**, study, analysis, examination, probe ▷ v = **investigate**, study, examine, explore, probe

resemble v = **be like**, look like, mirror, parallel, be similar to

resent v = **be bitter about**, object to, grudge, begrudge, take exception to ≠ **be content with**

reserve v = **book**, prearrange, engage; = **put by**, secure ▷ n = **store**, fund, savings, stock, supply; = **park**, reservation, preserve, sanctuary, tract; = **shyness**, silence, restraint, constraint, reticence; = **reservation**, doubt, delay,

uncertainty, indecision

reservoir n = **lake**, pond, basin; = **store**, stock, source, supply, reserves

reside v (Formal) = **live**, lodge, dwell, stay, abide ≠ **visit**

residue n = **remainder**, remains, remnant, leftovers, rest

resign v = **quit**, leave, step down (Inf), vacate, abdicate; = **give up**, abandon, yield, surrender, relinquish

resist v = **oppose**, battle against, combat, defy, stand up to ≠ **accept**; = **refrain from**, avoid, keep from, forgo, abstain from ≠ **indulge in**; = **withstand**, be

2 firmness 3 thing resolved
4 decision 5 vote
resolve ❶ v 1 decide 2 vote
3 separate component parts of
4 make clear ▷ n 5 absolute
determination
resonance n echoing, esp. in deep
tone **resonant** adj **resonate** v
resort ❶ v 1 have recourse ▷ n
2 place of recreation, e.g. beach
3 recourse
resound ❶ v echo, go on sounding
resource ❶ n 1 ingenuity 2 that
to which one resorts for support
3 expedient ▷ pl 4 stock that can
be drawn on 5 funds **resourceful**
adj
respect ❶ n 1 esteem 2 aspect
3 reference ▷ v 4 treat with
esteem 5 show consideration for
respectability n **respectable** adj

1 worthy of respect 2 fairly good
respectful adj **respecting** prep
concerning **respective** adj
1 relating separately to each
2 separate **respectively** adv
respiration n breathing
respirator n apparatus worn over
mouth and breathed through
respiratory adj
respite ❶ n 1 pause, interval
2 reprieve
resplendent adj brilliant, shining
respond ❶ v 1 answer 2 react
respondent n 1 replying ▷ n
2 one who answers 3 defendant
response n **responsive** adj
readily reacting
responsible ❶ adj 1 in charge
2 liable to answer for 3 dependable
4 involving responsibility
responsibility n, pl **-ties**

proof against
resolve v = **work out**, answer,
clear up, crack, fathom; = **decide**,
determine, agree, purpose, intend
▷ n = **determination**, resolution,
willpower, firmness, steadfastness
≠ **indecision**
resort n = **holiday centre**, spot,
retreat, haunt, tourist centre;
= **recourse to**, reference to
resound v = **echo**, resonate,
reverberate, re-echo
resource n = **means**, course,
resort, device, expedient
respect v = **think highly of**, value,
honour, admire, esteem; = **show
consideration for**, honour,
observe, heed ▷ n = **regard**,
honour, recognition, esteem,

admiration ≠ **contempt**;
= **consideration**, kindness,
deference, tact, thoughtfulness;
= **particular**, way, point, matter,
sense
respite n = **pause**, break, rest,
relief, halt
respond v = **answer**, return,
reply, counter, retort ≠ **remain
silent**; often with **to** = **reply to**,
answer
responsible adj = **to blame**,
guilty, at fault, culpable; = **in
charge**, in control, in authority;
= **accountable**, liable,
answerable ≠ **unaccountable**;
= **sensible**, reliable, rational,
dependable, trustworthy
≠ **unreliable**

DICTIONARY

rest¹ ❶ n 1 repose 2 freedom from exertion etc. 3 pause 4 support ▷ v 5 take, give rest 6 support, be supported **restful** adj **restless** adj unable to rest or be still

rest² n 1 remainder ▷ v 2 remain

restaurant ❶ n commercial establishment serving food

restitution n 1 giving back 2 compensation

restive adj restless

restore ❶ v 1 repair, renew 2 give back **restoration** n **restorative** adj/n

restrain ❶ v 1 hold back 2 prevent **restraint** n 1 self-control 2 anything that restrains

restrict ❶ v limit **restriction** n **restrictive** adj

result ❶ v 1 follow as consequence 2 happen 3 end ▷ n 4 outcome **resultant** adj

resume ❶ v begin again **résumé** n summary **resumption** n

resurgence ❶ n rising again **resurgent** adj

resurrect ❶ v restore to life, use **resurrection** n

resuscitate v restore to consciousness **resuscitation** n

retail n 1 sale in small quantities ▷ adv 2 by retail ▷ v 3 sell, be sold, retail 4 recount **retailer** n

retain ❶ v 1 keep 2 engage services of **retainer** n 1 fee to

THESAURUS

rest¹ v = **relax**, take it easy, sit down, be at ease, put your feet up ≠ **work**; = **stop**, have a break, break off, take a breather (Inf) ≠ **keep going**; = **place**, repose, sit, lean, prop; = **be placed**, sit, lie, be supported, recline ▷ n = **relaxation**, repose, leisure ≠ **work**; = **pause**, break, stop, halt, interval; = **refreshment**, release, relief, ease, comfort; = **support**, stand, base, holder, prop; = **calm**, tranquillity, stillness, still, quiet

restaurant n = **café**, diner (chiefly US & Canad), bistro, cafeteria, tearoom

restore v = **reinstate**, re-establish, reintroduce ≠ **abolish**; = **revive**, build up, strengthen, refresh, revitalize ≠ **make worse**; = **re-establish**, replace, reinstate, give back; = **repair**, refurbish,

renovate, reconstruct, fix (up) ≠ **demolish**

restrain v = **hold back**, control, check, contain, restrict ≠ **encourage**

restrict v = **limit**, regulate, curb, ration ≠ **widen**

result n = **consequence**, effect, outcome, end result, product ≠ **cause** ▷ v = **arise**, follow, issue, happen, appear; = **end in**, bring about, cause, lead to, finish with

resume v = **begin again**, continue, go on with, proceed with, carry on ≠ **discontinue**

resurgence n = **revival**, return, renaissance, resurrection, resumption

resurrect v = **revive**, renew, bring back, reintroduce; = **restore to life**, raise from the dead

retain v = **maintain**, reserve, preserve, keep up, continue to

retain esp. barrister **2** *(Hist)* follower of nobleman etc.
retention n **retentive** adj
retaliate ❶ v repay in kind **retaliation** n
retard ❶ v **1** make slow **2** impede development of **retarded** adj
retch v try to vomit
reticent adj **1** reserved **2** uncommunicative **reticence** n
retina n, pl **-nas, -nae** light-sensitive membrane at back of eye
retinue n band of followers
retire ❶ v **1** give up office or work **2** go away **3** go to bed **retirement** n **retiring** adj unobtrusive, shy
retort ❶ v **1** reply **2** retaliate ▷ n **3** vigorous reply **4** vessel with bent neck used for distilling
retrace v go back over
retract ❶ v **1** draw in or back **2** withdraw statement **retraction** n

retreat ❶ v **1** move back ▷ n **2** withdrawal **3** place to which anyone retires **4** refuge
retrench v reduce expenditure
retribution n recompense, esp. for evil
retrieve ❶ v **1** fetch back again **2** regain **retrieval** n **retriever** n dog trained to retrieve game
retroactive adj applying to the past
retrograde adj going backwards, reverting
retrospect n survey of past **retrospective** adj
return ❶ v **1** go, come back **2** give, send back **3** report officially **4** elect ▷ n **5** returning **6** profit **7** report **returning officer** one conducting election
reunion n gathering of people who have been apart **reunite** v bring, come together again

have; = **keep**, save ≠ **let go**
retaliate v = **pay someone back**, hit back, strike back, reciprocate, take revenge = **turn the other cheek**
retard v = **slow down**, check, arrest, delay, handicap ≠ **speed up**
retire v = **stop working**, give up work; = **withdraw**, leave, exit, go away, depart; = **go to bed**, turn in (*Inf*), hit the sack (*Sl*), hit the hay (*Sl*)
retort v = **reply**, return, answer, respond, counter ▷ n = **reply**, answer, response (*Inf*), comeback, riposte
retreat v = **withdraw**, back off, draw back, leave, go back

≠ **advance** ▷ n = **flight**, retirement, departure, withdrawal, evacuation ≠ **advance**; = **refuge**, haven, shelter, sanctuary, hideaway
retrieve v = **get back**, regain, recover, restore, recapture
return v = **come back**, go back, retreat, turn back, revert ≠ **depart**; = **put back**, replace, restore, reinstate ≠ **keep**; = **give back**, repay, refund, pay back, reimburse ≠ **keep**; = **recur**, repeat, persist, revert, happen again; = **elect**, choose, vote in ▷ n = **restoration**, reinstatement, re-establishment ≠ **removal**

r

Rev., Revd. Reverend

rev *n* (*Inf*) revolution (of engine)

revalue *v* adjust exchange value of currency upwards

revamp ⊕ *v* renovate, restore

reveal ⊕ *v* 1 make known 2 show **revelation** *n*

reveille *n* morning bugle call etc. to waken soldiers

revel ⊕ *v* **-elling, -elled** 1 take pleasure (in) 2 make merry ▷ *n* 3 (*usu. pl*) merrymaking **revelry** *n*

revenge ⊕ *n* 1 retaliation for wrong done ▷ *v* 2 avenge 3 make retaliation for

revenue ⊕ *n* income, esp. of state

reverberate *v* echo, resound **reverberation** *n*

revere ⊕ *v* hold in great regard or religious respect **reverence** *n*

reverend *adj* (esp. as prefix to clergyman's name) worthy of reverence **reverent** *adj*

reverie *n* daydream

reverse ⊕ *v* 1 move (vehicle) backwards 2 turn other way round 3 change completely ▷ *n* 4 opposite 5 side opposite 6 defeat ▷ *adj* 7 opposite **reversal** *n*

revert ⊕ *v* return to former state, subject **reversion** *n*

review ⊕ *v* 1 examine 2 reconsider 3 hold, make, write review of ▷ *n* 4 survey 5 critical notice of book etc. 6 periodical with critical articles 7 (*Mil*) inspection of troops

revile *v* abuse viciously

revamp *v* = **renovate**, restore, overhaul, refurbish, do up (*Inf*)

reveal *v* = **make known**, disclose, give away, make public, tell ≠ **keep secret**; = **show**, display, exhibit, unveil, uncover ≠ **hide**

revel *v* = **celebrate**, carouse, live it up (*Inf*), make merry

revenge *n* = **retaliation**, vengeance, reprisal, retribution, an eye for an eye ▷ *v* = **avenge**, repay, take revenge for, get your own back for (*Inf*)

revenue *n* = **income**, returns, profits, gain, yield ≠ **expenditure**

revere *v* = **be in awe of**, respect, honour, worship, reverence ≠ **despise**

reverse *v* (*Law*) = **change**, cancel, overturn, overthrow, undo ≠ **implement**; = **turn round**, turn over, turn upside down, upend; = **transpose**, change, move, exchange, transfer ▷ *n* = **opposite**, contrary, converse, inverse; = **misfortune**, blow, failure, disappointment, setback; = **back**, rear, other side, wrong side, underside ≠ **front** ▷ *adj* = **opposite**, contrary, converse

revert *v* = **go back**, return, come back, resume

review *n* = **survey**, study, analysis, examination, scrutiny; = **critique**, commentary, evaluation, notice, criticism; = **inspection**, parade, march past; = **magazine**, journal, periodical, zine (*Inf*) ▷ *v* = **reconsider**, revise, rethink, reassess, re-examine; = **assess**, study, judge, evaluate, criticize

r

revise ❶ v 1 look over and correct 2 study again (work done previously) 3 change **revision** n

revive ❶ v bring, come back to life, vigour, use etc. **revival** n

revoke v 1 withdraw 2 cancel **revocation** n

revolt ❶ n 1 rebellion ▷ v 2 rise in rebellion 3 feel disgust 4 affect with disgust **revolting** adj disgusting

revolve ❶ v 1 turn round 2 be centred on 3 rotate **revolution** n 1 violent overthrow of government 2 great change 3 complete rotation **revolutionary** adj/n **revolutionize** v

revue n entertainment with sketches and songs

revulsion n repugnance or abhorrence

reward ❶ n 1 thing given in return for service, conduct etc. ▷ v 2 give reward **rewarding** adj

rewind v run (tape, film etc.) back to earlier point

rewire v provide (house, engine etc.) with new wiring

rhapsody n, pl **-dies** 1 freely

structured, emotional musical piece 2 expression of enthusiasm **rhapsodic** adj **rhapsodize** v

rhesus n small, long-tailed monkey **rhesus factor** feature distinguishing different types of human blood

rhetoric ❶ n 1 art of effective speaking or writing 2 exaggerated language **rhetorical** adj (of question) not requiring an answer

rheumatism n painful inflammation of joints or muscles **rheumatic** adj/n

rhinoceros n, pl **-oses**, **-os** large animal with one or two horns on nose

rhododendron n evergreen flowering shrub

rhombus n, pl **-buses**, **-bi** diamond-shaped figure

rhubarb n garden plant with edible fleshy stalks

rhyme ❶ n 1 identity of final sounds in words 2 word or syllable identical in final sound to another 3 verse marked by rhyme ▷ v 4 (of words) have identical final sounds

revise v = **change**, review; = **edit**, correct, alter, update, amend

revive v = **revitalize**, restore, renew, rekindle, invigorate

revolt n = **uprising**, rising, revolution, rebellion, mutiny ▷ v = **rebel**, rise up, resist, mutiny; = **disgust**, sicken, repel, repulse, nauseate

revolve v = **go round**, circle, orbit

reward n = **punishment**,

retribution, comeuppance (Sl), just deserts ▷ v = **compensate**, pay, repay, recompense, remunerate ≠ **penalize**

rhetoric n = **hyperbole**, bombast, wordiness, verbosity, grandiloquence; = **oratory**, eloquence, public speaking, speech-making, elocution

rhyme n = **poem**, song, verse, ode, planning

DICTIONARY

rhythm ❶ n measured beat of words, music etc. **rhythmic, -ical** adj

rib n 1 one of curved bones springing from spine and forming framework of upper part of body 2 raised series of rows in knitting etc. ▷ v 3 mark with ribs 4 knit to form a rib pattern

ribald adj irreverent, scurrilous

ribbon n 1 narrow band of fabric 2 long strip of anything

rice n 1 Eastern cereal plant 2 its seeds as food

rich ❶ adj 1 wealthy 2 fertile 3 abounding 4 valuable 5 containing much fat or sugar 6 mellow 7 amusing **riches** pl n wealth **richly** adv 1 elaborately 2 fully

rick[1] n stack of hay etc.

rick[2] v/n sprain, wrench

rickets n disease of children marked by softening of bones **rickety** adj shaky, unstable

rickshaw n two-wheeled man-drawn Asian vehicle

ricochet v 1 (of bullet) rebound or be deflected ▷ n 2 rebound

rid ❶ v ridding, rid 1 relieve of 2 free **riddance** n

ridden past participle of RIDE adj afflicted, as in disease-ridden

riddle[1] ❶ n 1 question made puzzling to test one's ingenuity 2 puzzling thing, person

riddle[2] ❶ v 1 pierce with many holes ▷ n 2 coarse sieve

ride ❶ v riding, rode, ridden 1 sit on and control or propel 2 be carried on or across 3 go on horseback or in vehicle 4 lie at anchor ▷ n 5 journey on horse, in vehicle **rider** n 1 one who rides 2 supplementary clause 3 addition to document

ridge n 1 long narrow hill 2 line of meeting of two sloping surfaces ▷ v 3 form into ridges

ridiculous ❶ adj deserving to be laughed at, absurd **ridicule** v 1 laugh at, deride ▷ n 2 derision

rife ❶ adj prevalent, common

riff n short repeated musical phrase

THESAURUS

rhythm n = **beat**, swing, accent, pulse, tempo

rich adj = **wealthy**, affluent, well-off, loaded (Sl), prosperous ≠ **poor**; = **well-stocked**, full, productive, ample, abundant ≠ **scarce**; = **full-bodied**, sweet, fatty, tasty, creamy ≠ **bland**; = **fruitful**, productive, fertile, prolific ≠ **barren**

rid v = **free**, clear, deliver, relieve, purge

riddle[1] n = **puzzle**, problem, conundrum, poser; = **enigma**, question, secret, mystery, puzzle

riddle[2] v = **pierce**, pepper, puncture, perforate, honeycomb

ride v = **control**, handle, manage; = **travel**, be carried, go, move ▷ n = **journey**, drive, trip, lift, outing

ridiculous adj = **laughable**, stupid, silly, absurd, ludicrous ≠ **sensible**

rife adj = **widespread**, rampant, general, common, universal

riffraff n rabble

rifle ❶ v **1** search and rob ▷ n
2 firearm with long barrel

rift ❶ n crack, split

rig ❶ v **rigging, rigged 1** provide
(ship) with ropes etc. **2** equip
3 arrange in dishonest way ▷ n
4 apparatus for drilling for oil
rigging n ship's spars and ropes

right ❶ adj **1** just **2** in accordance
with truth and duty **3** true
4 correct **5** proper **6** of side that
faces east when front is turned to
north **7** (Politics) conservative
8 straight ▷ v **9** make, become
right ▷ n **10** claim, title etc.
allowed or due **11** what is right
12 conservative political party
▷ adv **13** straight **14** properly
15 very **16** on or to right side
rightful adj **right angle** angle of

90 degrees **right-hand man** most
valuable assistant

righteous ❶ adj **1** virtuous
2 good **righteousness** n

rigid ❶ adj **1** inflexible **2** stiff
rigidity n

rigmarole n **1** long, complicated
procedure **2** nonsense

rigor mortis stiffening of body
after death

rigour n **1** severity **2** hardship
rigorous adj

rile v anger

rim ❶ n edge

rind n outer coating of fruits etc.

ring¹ ❶ v **ringing, rang, rung
1** (cause to) give out resonant
sound like bell **2** telephone ▷ n
3 resonant sound

ring² ❶ n **1** circular band, esp. for
finger **2** circle of persons

THESAURUS

rifle v = **ransack**, rob, burgle, loot,
strip

rift n = **breach**, division, split,
separation, falling out (Inf); = **split**,
opening, crack, gap, break

rig v = **fix**, engineer (Inf), arrange,
manipulate, tamper with; (Naut)
= **equip**, fit out, kit out, outfit,
supply

right adj = **correct**, true, genuine,
accurate, exact ≠ **wrong**; = **proper**,
done, becoming, seemly, fitting
≠ **inappropriate**; = **just**, good, fair,
moral, proper ≠ **unfair** ▷ adv
= **correctly**, truly, precisely, exactly,
genuinely ≠ **wrongly**; = **suitably**,
fittingly, appropriately, properly,
aptly ≠ **improperly**; = **exactly**,
squarely, precisely; = **directly**,

straight, precisely, exactly,
unswervingly ▷ n = **prerogative**,
business, power, claim, authority;
= **justice**, truth, fairness, legality,
righteousness ≠ **injustice** ▷ v
= **rectify**, settle, fix, correct, sort
out

righteous adj = **virtuous**, good,
just, fair, moral ≠ **wicked**

rigid adj = **strict**, set, fixed, exact,
rigorous ≠ **flexible**; = **inflexible**,
uncompromising, unbending

rim n = **edge**, lip, brim

ring¹ v = **phone**, call, telephone,
buzz (Inf, chiefly Brit); = **chime**,
sound, toll, reverberate, clang ▷ n
= **call**, phone call, buzz (Inf, chiefly
Brit); = **chime**, knell, peal

ring² n = **circle**, round, band,

3 enclosed area ▷ v **4** put ring round **ringer** n (Inf) identical thing or person **ringleader** n instigator of mutiny, riot etc.
ringlet n curly lock of hair **ring road** main road that bypasses a town (centre) **ringworm** n skin disease
rink n sheet of ice for skating
rinse ❶ v **1** remove soap from by applying water **2** wash lightly ▷ n **3** rinsing **4** liquid to tint hair
riot ❶ n/v (engage in) tumult, disorder **riotous** adj
RIP rest in peace
rip ❶ v/n **ripping, ripped** cut, slash **ripcord** n cord pulled to open parachute **rip off** (Sl) cheat by overcharging
ripe ❶ adj ready to be harvested, eaten etc. **ripen** v
riposte n **1** verbal retort **2** counterattack ▷ v **3** make

riposte
ripple n **1** slight wave **2** soft sound ▷ v **3** form into little waves **4** (of sounds) rise and fall gently
rise ❶ v **rising, rose, risen 1** get up **2** move upwards **3** reach higher level **4** increase **5** rebel **6** have its source ▷ n **7** rising **8** upslope **9** increase **rising** n revolt
risk ❶ n **1** chance of disaster or loss ▷ v **2** put in jeopardy **3** take chance of **risky** adj
risotto n, pl **-tos** dish of rice with vegetables, meat etc.
risqué adj suggestive of indecency
rissole n cake of minced meat coated with breadcrumbs
rite ❶ n **1** formal practice or custom, esp. religious **ritual** n
1 prescribed order of rites
2 stereotyped behaviour ▷ adj
3 concerning rites

— THESAURUS —

circuit, loop; **= arena**, enclosure, circus, rink; **= gang**, group, association, band, circle
rinse v **= wash**, clean, dip, splash, cleanse ▷ n **= wash**, dip, splash, bath
riot n **= disturbance**, disorder, confusion, turmoil, upheaval; **= display**, show, splash, extravaganza, profusion; **= laugh**, joke, scream (Inf), hoot (Inf), lark ▷ v **= rampage**, run riot, go on the rampage
rip v **= tear**, cut, split, burst, rend ▷ n **= tear**, cut, hole, split, rent
ripe adj **= ripened**, seasoned, ready, mature, mellow ≠ **unripe**; **= right**,

suitable
rise v **= get up**, stand up, get to your feet; **= go up**, climb, ascend ≠ **descend**; **= loom**, tower; **= get steeper**, ascend, go uphill, slope upwards ≠ **drop**; **= increase**, mount ≠ **decrease** ▷ n **= upward slope**, incline, elevation, ascent, kopje or koppie (S Afr); **= increase**, upturn, upswing, upsurge ≠ **decrease**; **= pay increase**, raise (US), increment; **= advancement**, progress, climb, promotion
risk n **= danger**, chance, possibility, hazard
rite n **= ceremony**, custom, ritual, practice, procedure

rival ❶ *n* **1** one that competes with another ▷ *adj* **2** in position of rival ▷ *v* **3** vie with **rivalry** *n*

river *n* large natural stream of water

rivet *n* **1** bolt for fastening metal plates, the end being put through holes and then beaten flat ▷ *v* **2** fasten firmly **riveting** *adj* very interesting

rivulet *n* small stream

RN Royal Navy

road ❶ *n* **1** track, way prepared for passengers, vehicles etc. **2** direction, way **3** street **roadblock** *n* barricade across road to stop traffic for inspection **roadworks** *pl n* repairs to road

roam ❶ *v* wander about, rove

roar ❶ *v/n* (utter) loud deep hoarse sound

roast *v* **1** cook in oven or over open fire **2** make, be very hot ▷ *n* **3** roasted joint ▷ *adj* **4** roasted

rob ❶ *v* **robbing, robbed** steal

from **robber** *n* **robbery** *n*

robe ❶ *n* **1** long outer garment ▷ *v* **2** dress **3** put on robes

robin *n* small brown bird with red breast

robot ❶ *n* automated machine, esp. performing functions in human manner

robust ❶ *adj* **1** sturdy **2** strong

rock¹ ❶ *n* **1** stone **2** mass of stone **3** hard sweet in sticks **rockery** *n* mound of stones in garden **rocky** *adj*

rock² ❶ *v* **1** (cause to) sway to and fro ▷ *n* **2** popular music with heavy beat **rocker** *n* **1** curved piece of wood etc. on which thing may rock **2** rocking chair **rock and roll** style of popular music

rock melon *n* (*Aust, NZ & US*) type of melon with sweet orange flesh

rocket *n* **1** self-propelling device powered by burning of explosive contents ▷ *v* **2** move fast, esp. upwards, as rocket

THESAURUS

rival *n* = **opponent**, competitor, contender, contestant, adversary ≠ **supporter** ▷ *v* = **compete with**, match, equal, compare with, come up to ▷ *adj* = **competing**, conflicting, opposing

river *n* = **stream**, brook, creek, waterway, tributary; = **flow**, rush, flood, spate, torrent

road *n* = **roadway**, highway, motorway, track, route

roam *v* = **wander**, walk, range, travel, stray

roar *v* = **guffaw**, laugh heartily, hoot, split your sides (*Inf*); = **cry**,

shout, yell, howl, bellow ▷ *n* = **guffaw**, hoot

rob *v* = **steal from**, hold up, mug (*Inf*); = **raid**, hold up, loot, plunder, burgle

robe *n* = **gown**, costume, habit

robot *n* = **machine**, automaton, android, mechanical man

robust *adj* = **strong**, tough, powerful, fit, healthy ≠ **weak**

rock¹ *n* = **stone**, boulder

rock² *v* = **sway**, pitch, swing, reel, toss; = **shock**, surprise, shake, stun, astonish

rod ❶ n 1 slender straight bar, stick 2 cane

rodent n gnawing animal

rodeo n, pl **-deos** (US & Canad) display of bareback riding, cattle handling etc.

roe¹ n small species of deer

roe² n mass of eggs in fish

rogue ❶ n 1 scoundrel 2 mischief-loving person or child

role, rôle ❶ n 1 actor's part 2 specific task or function

roll ❶ v 1 move by turning over and over 2 wind round 3 smooth out with roller 4 move, sweep along 5 undulate ▷ n 6 act of rolling 7 anything rolled up 8 list 9 small round piece of baked bread 10 continuous sound, as of drums, thunder etc. **roller** n 1 cylinder of wood, stone, metal etc. 2 long wave of sea **roller coaster** narrow undulating railway at funfair **roller skate** skate with wheels instead of runner **rolling pin** cylindrical roller for pastry **rolling stock**

locomotives, carriages etc. of railway

rollicking adj boisterously jovial and merry

roly-poly n 1 pudding of suet pastry ▷ adj 2 round, plump

ROM (Comp) read only memory

Roman adj of Rome or Church of Rome **Roman Catholic** member of that section of Christian Church which acknowledges supremacy of the Pope **Roman numerals** letters used to represent numbers

romance ❶ n 1 love affair 2 mysterious or exciting quality 3 tale of chivalry 4 tale remote from ordinary life ▷ v 5 exaggerate, fantasize **romantic** adj 1 characterized by romance 2 of love 3 (of literature etc.) displaying passion and imagination ▷ n 4 romantic person

Romany adj/n, pl **-nies** Gypsy

romp ❶ v 1 run, play wildly ▷ n 2 spell of romping **rompers** pl n child's overalls

rod n = **stick**, bar, pole, shaft, cane

rogue n = **scoundrel**, crook (Inf), villain, fraud, blackguard; = **scamp**, rascal, scally (Northwest English dialect)

role n = **job**, part, position, post, task; = **part**, character, representation, portrayal

roll v = **turn**, wheel, spin, go round, revolve; = **trundle**, go, move; = **flow**, run, course; often with **up** = **wind**, bind, wrap, swathe, envelop; = **level**, even, press, smooth, flatten ▷ n = **rumble**,

boom, roar, thunder, reverberation; = **register**, record, list, index, census; = **turn**, spin, rotation, cycle, wheel

romance n = **love affair**, relationship, affair, attachment, liaison; = **excitement**, colour, charm, mystery, glamour; = **story**, tale, fantasy, legend, fairy tale

romp v = **frolic**, sport, have fun, caper, cavort ▷ n = **frolic**, lark (Inf), caper = **win easily**, walk it (Inf), win hands down, win by a mile (Inf)

r

roof n, pl **roofs** 1 outside upper covering of building ▷ v 2 put roof on, over

rooibos n (S Afr) tea prepared from the dried leaves of an African plant

rook n bird of crow family

rookie n (Inf) new recruit

room ❶ n 1 space 2 division of house 3 scope ▷ pl 4 lodgings
  roomy adj spacious

roost n/v perch

rooster n (US & Canad) domestic cock

root, rootle ❶ n 1 underground part of plant 2 source, origin 3 (Anat) embedded portion of tooth, hair etc. ▷ pl 4 person's sense of belonging ▷ v 5 (cause to) take root 6 pull by roots 7 dig, burrow

rope ❶ n 1 thick cord ▷ v 2 secure, mark off with rope

rort n (Aust, Inf) dishonest scheme

rosary n, pl **-saries** 1 series of prayers 2 string of beads for counting these prayers

rose n 1 shrub usu. with prickly stems and fragrant flowers 2 the flower 3 pink colour **rosette** n rose-shaped bunch of ribbon **rosy** adj 1 flushed 2 promising **rose-coloured** adj 1 having colour of rose 2 unjustifiably optimistic **rosehip** n

berry-like fruit of rose plant

rosé n pink wine

rosemary n evergreen fragrant flowering shrub

roster n list of turns of duty

rostrum n/pl **-trums, -tra** platform, stage

rot ❶ v **rotting, rotted** 1 decompose, decay 2 deteriorate physically or mentally ▷ n 3 decay 4 any disease producing decomposition of tissue 5 (Inf) nonsense **rotten** adj 1 decomposed 2 very bad 3 corrupt **rotter** n (Inf) despicable person

rota n roster, list

rotary adj (of movement) circular **rotate** v 1 (cause to) move round centre 2 (cause to) follow set sequence **rotation** n

rote n mechanical repetition

rotor n revolving portion of dynamo motor or turbine

rotund adj 1 round 2 plump

rouge n red powder, cream used to colour cheeks

rough ❶ adj 1 not smooth 2 violent, stormy 3 rude 4 approximate 5 in preliminary form ▷ v 6 make rough 7 plan ▷ n 8 rough state or area 9 sketch

---

                THESAURUS

room n = **chamber**, office, apartment; = **space**, area, capacity, extent, expanse; = **opportunity**, scope, leeway, chance, range

root n = **stem**, tuber, rhizome; = **source**, cause, heart, bottom, base

rope n = **cord**, line, cable, strand, hawser

rot v = **decay**, spoil, deteriorate,

perish, decompose ▷ n = **decay**, decomposition, corruption, mould, blight; (Inf) = **nonsense**, rubbish, drivel, twaddle, garbage (chiefly US)

rough adj = **uneven**, broken, rocky, irregular, jagged ≠ **even**; = **boisterous**, hard, tough, arduous; = **ungracious**, blunt, rude,

roughen v **roughage** n unassimilated portion of food **rough it** live without usual comforts etc.

roulette n gambling game played with revolving wheel

round ❶ adj **1** spherical, circular, curved **2** plump **3** complete **4** roughly correct **5** considerable ▷ adv **6** with circular course ▷ n **7** thing round in shape **8** recurrent duties **9** stage in competition **10** customary course **11** game (of golf) **12** period in boxing match etc. **13** cartridge for firearm ▷ prep **14** about **15** on all sides of ▷ v **16** make, become round **17** move round **rounders** pl n ball game **roundly** adv thoroughly **roundabout** n **1** revolving circular platform on which people ride for amusement **2** road junction at which traffic passes round central

island ▷ adj **3** not straightforward **round trip** journey out and back again **round up** drive (cattle) together

rouse ❶ v **1** wake up, stir up, excite **2** waken

rout ❶ n **1** overwhelming defeat, disorderly retreat ▷ v **2** put to flight

route ❶ n road, chosen way

routine ❶ n **1** regularity of procedure ▷ adj **2** ordinary, regular

rove v wander, roam

row¹ ❶ n number of things in a straight line

row² ❶ (Inf) ▷ n **1** dispute **2** disturbance ▷ v **3** quarrel noisily

rowan n tree producing bright red berries, mountain ash

rowdy adj/n **-dier, -diest** disorderly, noisy (person)

rowlock n device to hold oar on gunwale of boat

— THESAURUS —

coarse, brusque ≠ **refined**; = **unpleasant**, hard, difficult, tough, uncomfortable ≠ **easy**; ≈ **approximate**, estimated ≠ **exact**; = **vague**, general, sketchy, imprecise, inexact; = **basic**, crude, unfinished, incomplete, imperfect ≠ **complete** ▷ n = **outline**, draft, mock-up, preliminary sketch

round n = **series**, session, cycle, sequence, succession; = **stage**, turn, level, period, division; = **sphere**, ball, band, ring, circle ▷ adj = **spherical**, rounded, curved, circular, cylindrical ▷ v = **go round**, circle, skirt, flank, bypass

rouse v = **wake up**, call, wake, awaken; = **excite**, move, stir,

provoke, anger

rout v = **defeat**, beat, overthrow, thrash, destroy ▷ n = **defeat**, beating, overthrow, thrashing, pasting (Sl)

route n = **way**, course, road, direction, path

routine n = **procedure**, programme, order, practice, method ▷ adj = **usual**, standard, normal, customary, ordinary ≠ **unusual**

row¹ n = **line**, bank, range, series, file

row² n (Inf) = **quarrel**, dispute, argument, squabble, tiff; = **disturbance**, noise, racket, uproar, commotion ▷ v = **quarrel**, fight, argue, dispute, squabble

royal ❶ adj of king or queen

royalist n supporter of monarchy

royalty n 1 royal power 2 royal persons 3 payment for right, use of invention or copyright

rpm revolutions per minute

RSVP please reply

rub ❶ v rubbing, rubbed 1 apply pressure to with circular or backwards-and-forwards movement 2 clean, polish, dry thus 3 abrade, chafe 4 remove by friction 5 become frayed or worn by friction ▷ n 6 rubbing

rubber n 1 elastic dried sap of certain tropical trees 2 synthetic material resembling this 3 piece of rubber etc. used for · erasing ▷ adj 4 made of rubber **rubbery** adj

rubbish ❶ n 1 refuse 2 anything worthless 3 nonsense ▷ v 4 (Inf) criticize

rubble n fragments of stone

rubella n mild contagious viral disease, German measles

ruby n, pl -bies 1 precious red gem

2 its colour ▷ adj 3 of this colour

ruck¹ n 1 crowd 2 common herd

ruck² n/v crease

rucksack n pack carried on back, knapsack

rudder n steering device for boat, aircraft

ruddy adj -dier, -diest of healthy red colour

rude ❶ adj 1 impolite 2 coarse 3 vulgar 4 roughly made

rudiments pl n elements, first principles **rudimentary** adj

rue ❶ v ruing, rued 1 grieve for 2 regret **rueful** adj

ruff n 1 frilled collar 2 natural collar of feathers, fur etc. on some birds and animals **ruffle** v 1 rumple, annoy, frill ▷ n 2 frilled trimming

ruffian n violent, lawless person

rug n 1 small floor mat 2 woollen coverlet

rugby n form of football in which the ball may be carried

rugged ❶ adj 1 rough 2 strong-featured

royal adj = **regal**, kingly, queenly, princely, imperial; = **splendid**, grand, impressive, magnificent, majestic

rub v = **stroke**, massage, caress; = **polish**, clean, shine, wipe, scour; = **chafe**, scrape, grate, abrade ▷ n = **massage**, caress, kneading

rubbish n = **waste**, refuse, scrap, junk (Inf), litter; = **nonsense**, garbage (chiefly US), twaddle, rot, trash

rude adj = **impolite**, insulting,

cheeky, abusive, disrespectful ≠ **polite**; = **uncivilized**, rough, coarse, brutish, boorish; = **unpleasant**, sharp, sudden, harsh, startling

rue v (Lit) = **regret**, mourn, lament, repent, be sorry for

rugged adj = **rocky**, broken, rough, craggy, difficult ≠ **even**; = **strong-featured**, rough-hewn, weather-beaten ≠ **delicate**; = **well-built**, strong, tough, robust, sturdy; = **tough**, strong, robust,

ruin ❶ *n* 1 destruction 2 downfall
3 fallen or broken state 4 loss of
wealth etc. ▷ *pl* 5 ruined buildings
etc. ▷ *v* 6 bring or come to ruin
ruinous *adj*
rule ❶ *n* 1 principle 2 government
3 what is usual 4 measuring stick
▷ *v* 5 govern 6 decide 7 mark with
straight lines **ruler** *n* 1 one who
governs 2 stick for measuring or
ruling lines **ruling** *n* formal decision
rum *n* spirit distilled from sugar
cane
rumba *n* lively ballroom dance
rumble *v/n* (make) noise as of
distant thunder
ruminate *v* 1 chew cud 2 ponder
over **ruminant** *adj/n*
cud-chewing (animal)
rummage *v* search thoroughly
rummy *n* card game
rumour ❶ *n* 1 hearsay, unproved
statement ▷ *v* 2 put around as
rumour
rump *n* 1 tail end 2 buttocks

rumple *v* make untidy, dishevelled
rumpus *n, pl* **-puses** disturbance
run ❶ *v* **running, ran, run** 1 move
with more rapid gait than walking
2 go quickly 3 flow 4 flee
5 compete in race, contest, election
6 cross by running 7 expose
oneself (to risk etc.) 8 cause to run
9 manage 10 operate ▷ *n* 11 act,
spell of running 12 rush
13 tendency, course 14 enclosure
for domestic fowls 15 ride in car
16 unravelled stitches 17 score of
one at cricket **runner** *n* 1 racer
2 messenger 3 curved piece of
wood on which sleigh slides
4 stem of plant forming new roots
5 strip of cloth, carpet **running**
adj 1 continuous 2 consecutive
3 flowing ▷ *n* 4 act of moving or
flowing quickly 5 ride in car
6 continuous period or sequence
runny *adj* **rundown** *n* summary
run-down *adj* 1 exhausted
2 decrepit, broken-down **run**

muscular, sturdy ≠ **delicate**
ruin *v* = **destroy**, devastate, wreck,
defeat, smash ≠ **create**;
= **bankrupt**, break, impoverish,
beggar, pauperize ▷ *n*
= **bankruptcy**, insolvency,
destitution; = **disrepair**, decay,
disintegration, ruination,
wreckage; = **destruction**, fall,
breakdown, defeat, collapse
≠ **preservation**
rule *n* = **regulation**, law, direction,
guideline, decree; = **precept**,
principle, canon, maxim, tenet;
= **custom**, procedure, practice,

routine, tradition ▷ *v* = **govern**,
control, direct, have power over,
command over; = **reign**, govern, be
in power, be in authority = **control**,
monopolize, tyrannize
rumour *n* = **story**, news, report,
talk, word
run *v* = **race**, rush, dash, hurry,
sprint ≠ **dawdle**; = **flee**, escape,
take off (*Inf*), bolt, beat it (*Sl*)
≠ **stay**; = **take part**, compete;
= **continue**, go, stretch, reach,
extend ≠ **stop**; (*chiefly US & Canad*)
= **compete**, stand, contend, be a
candidate, put yourself up for;

r

down 1 stop working **2** reduce **3** exhaust **4** denigrate

run-of-the-mill adj ordinary **run out** be completely used up

runway n level stretch where aircraft take off and land

rune n character of old Germanic alphabet

rung n crossbar in ladder

runt n unusually small animal

rupture ❶ n **1** breaking, breach **2** hernia ▷ v **3** break **4** burst, sever

rural ❶ adj **1** of the country **2** rustic

ruse n stratagem, trick

rush¹ ❶ v **1** hurry or cause to hurry **2** move violently or rapidly ▷ n **3** rushing ▷ adj **4** done with speed

rush hour period when many people travel to or from work

rush² n marsh plant with slender pithy stem

rusk n kind of biscuit

russet n/adj reddish-brown (colour)

rust ❶ n **1** reddish-brown coating formed on iron **2** disease of plants ▷ v **3** affect with rust **rusty** adj **1** corroded **2** reddish-brown **3** out of practice

rustic adj **1** simple, homespun **2** rural **3** uncouth. boorish ▷ n **4** countryman

rustle¹ v/n (make) sound as of blown dead leaves etc.

rustle² v (US) steal (cattle) **rustler** n

rut n **1** furrow made by wheel **2** settled habit

rutabaga n the US and Canadian name for SWEDE

ruthless ❶ adj merciless

rye n grain plant bearing it

——————————— THESAURUS ———————————

= **manage**, lead, direct, be in charge of, head; = **go**, work, operate, perform, function; = **perform**, carry out; = **work**, go, operate, function; = **pass**, go, move, roll, glide ▷ n = **race**, rush, dash, sprint, gallop; = **ride**, drive, trip, spin (Inf), outing; = **sequence**, period, stretch, spell, course; = **enclosure**, pen, coop

rupture n = **break**, tear, split, crack, rent ▷ v = **break**, separate, tear, split, crack

rural adj = **agricultural**, country

rush¹ v = **hurry**, run, race, shoot, fly ≠ **dawdle**; = **push**, hurry, press, hustle; = **attack**, storm, charge at ▷ n = **dash**, charge, race, scramble, stampede; = **hurry**, haste, hustle ▷ adj = **hasty**, fast, quick, hurried, rapid ≠ **leisurely**

rust n = **corrosion**, oxidation; = **mildew**, must, mould, rot, blight ▷ v = **corrode**, oxidize

ruthless adj = **merciless**, harsh, cruel, brutal, relentless ≠ **merciful**

DICTIONARY

Sabbath n day of worship and rest, observed on Saturday in Judaism, on Sunday by Christians **sabbatical** adj/n (pert. to) leave for study

sabotage ❶ n 1 intentional damage done to roads, machines etc., esp. secretly in war ▷ v 2 damage intentionally **saboteur** n

sabre n curved cavalry sword

sac n pouchlike structure in animal or plant

saccharin n artificial sweetener

sachet n small envelope or bag, esp. one holding liquid

sack ❶ n 1 large bag, esp. of coarse material 2 pillaging 3 (Inf) dismissal ▷ v 4 pillage (captured town) 5 (Inf) dismiss **sackcloth** n coarse fabric used for sacks

sacrament n one of certain ceremonies of Christian Church

sacred ❶ adj 1 dedicated, regarded as holy 2 revered 3 inviolable

sacrifice ❶ n 1 giving something up for sake of something else 2 thing so given up 3 making of offering to a god 4 thing offered ▷ v 5 offer as sacrifice 6 give up **sacrificial** adj

sacrilege n misuse, desecration of something sacred **sacrilegious** adj

sacrosanct adj preserved by religious fear against desecration or violence

sad ❶ adj sadder, saddest 1 sorrowful 2 unsatisfactory, deplorable **sadden** v make sad **sadness** n

saddle ❶ n 1 rider's seat on horse,

THESAURUS

sabotage v = **damage**, destroy, wreck, disable, disrupt ▷ n = **damage**, destruction, wrecking

sack n = **bag**, pocket, sac, pouch, receptacle; = **dismissal**, discharge, the boot (Sl), the axe (Inf), the push (Sl) ▷ v (Inf) = **dismiss**, fire (Inf), axe (Inf), discharge, give (someone) the push (Inf)

sacred adj = **holy**, hallowed, blessed, divine, revered ≠ **secular**; = **religious**, holy, ecclesiastical, hallowed ≠ **unconsecrated**;

= **inviolable**, protected, sacrosanct, hallowed, inalienable

sacrifice v = **offer**, offer up, immolate; = **give up**, abandon, relinquish, lose, surrender ▷ n = **offering**, oblation; = **surrender**, loss, giving up, rejection, abdication

sad adj = **unhappy**, down, low, blue, depressed ≠ **happy**; = **tragic**, moving, upsetting, depressing, dismal; = **deplorable**, bad, sorry, terrible, unfortunate ≠ **good**

saddle v = **burden**, load,

S

DICTIONARY

bicycle etc. **2** joint of meat
▷ *v* **3** put saddle on **4** lay burden on
sadism *n* love of inflicting pain
sadist *n* **sadistic** *adj*
safari *n, pl* **-ris** expedition to hunt
or observe wild animals, esp. in
Africa
safe ❶ *adj* **1** secure, protected
2 uninjured, out of danger **3** not
involving risk **4** trustworthy
5 sure ▷ *n* **6** strong lockable
container **safely** *adv* **safety** *n*
safeguard *n* **1** protection ▷ *v*
2 protect **safety pin** pin with
guard over the point when closed
saffron *n* **1** crocus **2** orange-
coloured flavouring obtained from
it **3** orange colour ▷ *adj* **4** orange
sag ❶ *v* **sagging, sagged 1** sink in
middle **2** curve downwards under
pressure **3** hang loosely ▷ *n*
4 droop
saga ❶ *n* **1** legend of Norse heroes
2 any long (heroic) story
sage ❶ *n* **1** very wise man ▷ *adj*
2 wise

sago *n* starchy cereal from
powdered pith of palm tree
said past tense and past participle
of SAY
sail ❶ *n* **1** piece of fabric stretched
to catch wind for propelling ship
etc. **2** act of sailing **3** arm of
windmill ▷ *v* **4** travel by water
5 move smoothly **6** begin voyage
sailor *n* **1** seaman **2** one who sails
saint *n* **1** person recognized as
having gained a special place in
heaven **2** exceptionally good
person
sake ❶ *n* **1** cause, account **2** end,
purpose **for the sake of 1** on
behalf of **2** to please or benefit
salad *n* mixed raw vegetables or
fruit used as food
salami *n* variety of highly-spiced
sausage
salary ❶ *n, pl* **-ries** fixed regular
payment to persons employed usu.
in nonmanual work
sale ❶ *n* **1** selling **2** selling of
goods at unusually low prices

THESAURUS

lumber (*Brit Inf*), encumber
safe *adj* = **protected**, secure,
impregnable, out of danger, safe
and sound ≠ **endangered**; = **all
right**, intact, unscathed, unhurt,
unharmed; = **risk-free**, sound,
secure, certain, impregnable ▷ *n*
= **strongbox**, vault, coffer,
repository, deposit box
sag *v* = **sink**, bag, droop, fall, slump;
= **drop**, sink, slump, flop, droop
saga *n* = **carry-on** (*Inf*, chiefly *Brit*),
performance (*Inf*), pantomime
(*Inf*)

sage *n* = **wise man**, philosopher,
guru, master, elder ▷ *adj* = **wise**,
sensible, judicious, sagacious,
sapient
sail *v* = **go by water**, cruise,
voyage, ride the waves, go by sea;
= **set sail**, embark, get under way,
put to sea, put off; = **pilot**, steer
sake *n* = **purpose**, interest, reason,
end, aim
salary *n* = **pay**, income, wage, fee,
payment
sale *n* = **selling**, marketing,
dealing, transaction, disposal

3 auction **salesman** n **1** shop assistant **2** one travelling to sell goods

salient adj **1** prominent, noticeable **2** jutting out

saline adj **1** containing, consisting of a chemical salt, esp. common salt **2** salty

saliva n liquid which forms in mouth, spittle

sallow adj of unhealthy pale or yellowish colour

sally n, pl **-lies 1** rushing out, esp. by troops **2** witty remark ▷ v **3** rush **4** set out

salmon n **1** large silvery fish with orange-pink flesh valued as food **2** colour of its flesh ▷ adj **3** of this colour

salmonella n, pl **-lae** bacterium causing food poisoning

salon n **1** (reception room for) guests in fashionable household **2** commercial premises of hairdressers, beauticians etc.

saloon n **1** public room, esp. on passenger ship **2** car with fixed roof **saloon bar** first-class bar in hotel etc.

salt ❶ n **1** white powdery or crystalline substance consisting mainly of sodium chloride, used to season or preserve food **2** chemical compound of acid and metal ▷ v **3** season, sprinkle with, preserve with salt ▷ adj **4** preserved in salt

salty adj of, like salt **saltcellar** n small vessel for salt at table

salubrious adj favourable to health, beneficial

salutary adj producing beneficial result

salute ❶ v **1** greet with words or sign **2** acknowledge with praise **3** perform military salute ▷ n **4** word, sign by which one greets another **5** motion of arm as mark of respect to military superior **6** firing of guns as military greeting of honour

salvation ❶ n fact or state of being saved, esp. of soul

salve n **1** healing ointment ▷ v **2** anoint with such, soothe

salver n (silver) tray for presentation of food, letters etc.

salvo n, pl **-vos, -voes** simultaneous discharge of guns etc.

same ❶ adj **1** identical, not different, unchanged **2** uniform **3** just mentioned previously

sample ❶ n **1** specimen ▷ v **2** take, give sample of **3** try

sampler n beginner's exercise in

S

salt marine, seafarer

salute v = **greet**, welcome, acknowledge, address, hail; = **honour**, acknowledge, recognize, pay tribute or homage to ▷ n = **greeting**, recognition, salutation, address

salvation n = **saving**, rescue, recovery, salvage, redemption ≠ **ruin**

same adj = **identical**, similar, alike, equal, twin ≠ **different**; = **the very same**, one and the same, selfsame; = **aforementioned**, aforesaid

sample n = **specimen**, example, model, pattern, instance ▷ v embroidery

sanatorium n/pl **-riums, -ria**
1 hospital, esp. for chronically ill
2 health resort

sanctify v **-fying, -fied 1** set
apart as holy **2** free from sin
sanctity n sacredness **sanctuary**
n **1** holy place **2** place of refuge
3 nature reserve

sanctimonious adj making
affected show of piety

sanction ❶ n **1** permission,
authorization **2** penalty for
breaking law ▷ pl **3** boycott or
other coercive measure, esp. by one
state against another ▷ v **4** allow,
authorize

sand n **1** substance consisting of
small grains of rock or mineral, esp.
on beach or in desert ▷ pl
2 stretches or banks of this ▷ v
3 polish, smooth with sandpaper
4 cover, mix with sand **sandy** adj
1 like sand **2** sand-coloured
3 consisting of, covered with sand
sandbag n **1** bag filled with sand
or earth as protection against
gunfire, floodwater etc. and as
weapon ▷ v **2** beat, hit with
sandbag **sandpaper** n paper with
sand stuck on it for scraping or

polishing **sandpiper** n shore bird
with long bill **sandstone** n rock
composed of sand

sandal n shoe consisting of sole
attached by straps

sandwich n **1** two slices of bread
with meat or other substance
between ▷ v **2** insert between two
other things

sane ❶ adj **1** of sound mind
2 sensible, rational **sanity** n

sang past tense of SING

sanguine adj **1** cheerful, confident
2 ruddy in complexion

sanitary adj helping protection of
health against dirt etc. **sanitation**
n measures, apparatus for
preservation of public health

sap¹ ❶ n **1** moisture which
circulates in plants **2** (Inf) foolish
person **sapling** n young tree

sap² ❶ v **sapping, sapped**
1 undermine **2** weaken

sapphire n **1** (usu. blue) precious
stone **2** deep blue ▷ adj **3** of deep
blue colour

sarcasm n **1** bitter or wounding
ironic remark **2** (use of) such
remarks **sarcastic** adj

sarcophagus n, pl **-gi, -guses**
stone coffin

THESAURUS

= **test**, try, experience, taste,
inspect

sanction v = **permit**, allow,
approve, endorse, authorize
≠ **forbid** ▷ n often plural = **ban**,
boycott, embargo, exclusion,
penalty ≠ **permission**;
= **permission**, backing, authority,
approval, authorization ≠ **ban**

sane adj = **rational**, all there (Inf),
of sound mind, compos mentis
(Lat), in your right mind ≠ **insane**;
= **sensible**, sound, reasonable,
balanced, judicious ≠ **foolish**

sap¹ n = **juice**, essence, vital fluid,
lifeblood; (Sl) = **fool**, jerk (Sl, chiefly
US & Canad), idiot, wally (Sl), twit (Inf)

sap² v = **weaken**, drain, undermine,

sardine n small fish of herring family

sardonic adj characterized by irony, mockery or derision

sari, saree n long garment worn by Hindu women

sarmie n (S Afr, Sl) sandwich

sartorial adj of tailor, tailoring, or men's clothes

sash n decorative belt, ribbon, wound around the body

Satan n the devil **satanic** adj devilish

satchel n small bag, esp. for school books

satellite n 1 celestial body or man-made projectile orbiting planet 2 person, country etc. dependent on another

satin n fabric (of silk, rayon etc.) with glossy surface on one side

satire ❶ n use of ridicule or sarcasm to expose vice and folly **satirical** adj **satirize** v make object of satire

satisfy ❶ v **-fying, -fied 1** please, meet wishes of **2** fulfil, supply adequately **3** convince **satisfaction** n **satisfactory** adj

satsuma n kind of small orange

saturate ❶ v soak thoroughly **saturation** n act, result of saturating

Saturday n seventh day of the week

satyr n **1** woodland deity, part man, part goat **2** lustful man

sauce n **1** liquid added to food to enhance flavour ▷ v **2** add sauce to **saucy** adj impudent **saucepan** n cooking pot with long handle

saucer n **1** curved plate put under cup **2** shallow depression

sauerkraut n dish of shredded cabbage fermented in brine

sauna n steam bath

saunter v **1** walk in leisurely manner, stroll ▷ n **2** leisurely walk or stroll

sausage n minced meat enclosed in thin tube of animal intestine or synthetic material **sausage roll** pastry cylinder filled with sausage

sauté v **-téing** fry quickly

savage ❶ adj **1** wild **2** ferocious **3** brutal **4** uncivilized, primitive ▷ n **5** member of savage tribe, barbarian ▷ v **6** attack ferociously

S

exhaust, deplete

satire n = **mockery**, irony, ridicule; = **parody**, mockery, caricature, lampoon, burlesque

satisfy v = **content**, please, indulge, gratify, pander to ≠ **dissatisfy**; = **convince**, persuade, assure, reassure ≠ **dissuade**; = **comply with**, meet, fulfil, answer, serve ≠ **fail to meet**

saturate v = **flood**, overwhelm, swamp, overrun

savage adj = **cruel**, brutal, vicious, fierce, harsh ≠ **gentle**; = **wild**, fierce, ferocious, unbroken, feral ≠ **tame**; = **primitive**, undeveloped, uncultivated, uncivilized ▷ n = **lout**, yob (Brit Sl), barbarian, yahoo, boor ▷ v = **maul**, tear, claw, attack, mangle (Inf)

save ❶ v 1 rescue, preserve 2 keep for future 3 prevent need of 4 lay by money ▷ n 5 (Sport) act of preventing goal etc. ▷ prep 6 except **saving** adj 1 redeeming ▷ prep 2 excepting ▷ n 3 economy ▷ pl 4 money put by for future use

saviour ❶ n 1 person who rescues another 2 (with cap.) Christ

savour ❶ n 1 characteristic taste or smell ▷ v 2 have particular taste or smell 3 give flavour to 4 have flavour of 5 enjoy **savoury** adj 1 attractive to taste or smell 2 not sweet

saw¹ n 1 tool with toothed edge for cutting wood etc. ▷ v 2 cut with saw 3 make movements of sawing **sawdust** n fine wood fragments made in sawing

saw² past tense of SEE

saxophone n keyed wind instrument

say ❶ v saying, said 1 speak 2 pronounce 3 state 4 express 5 take as example or near

enough 6 form and deliver opinion ▷ n 7 what one has to say 8 chance of saying it 9 share in decision **saying** n maxim, proverb

scab n 1 crust formed over wound 2 skin disease 3 disease of plants

scabbard n sheath for sword or dagger

scaffold n 1 temporary platform for workmen 2 gallows **scaffolding** n (material for building) scaffold

scald v 1 burn with hot liquid or steam 2 heat (liquid) almost to boiling point ▷ n 3 injury by scalding

scale¹ ❶ n 1 one of the thin, overlapping plates covering fishes and reptiles 2 thin flake 3 crust which forms in kettles etc. ▷ v 4 remove scales from 5 come off in scales

scale² ❶ n 1 graduated table or sequence of marks at regular intervals used as reference in making measurements 2 series of

— THESAURUS —

save v = **rescue**, free, release, deliver, recover ≠ **endanger**; = **keep**, reserve, set aside, store, collect ≠ **spend**; = **protect**, keep, guard, preserve, look after

saviour n = **rescuer**, deliverer, defender, protector, liberator

savour v = **relish**, delight in, revel in, luxuriate in; = **enjoy**, appreciate, relish, delight in, revel in ▷ n = **flavour**, taste, smell, relish, smack

say v = **state**, declare, remark, announce, maintain; = **speak**,

utter, voice, express, pronounce; = **suggest**, express, imply, communicate, disclose; = **suppose**, supposing, imagine, assume, presume ▷ v = **influence**, power, control, authority, weight; = **chance to speak**, vote, voice

scale¹ n = **flake**, plate, layer, lamina

scale² n = **degree**, size, range, extent, dimensions, measuring system; = **ranking**, ladder, hierarchy, series, sequence ▷ v = **climb up**, mount, ascend, surmount, clamber up

S

musical notes **3** ratio of size
between a thing and a model or
map of it **4** (relative) degree,
extent ▷ v **5** climb ▷ adj
6 proportionate

scale³ n (usu. pl) weighing
instrument

scallop n **1** edible shellfish
2 edging in small curves like scallop
shell ▷ v **3** shape like scallop shell

scalp n **1** skin and hair of top of
head ▷ v **2** cut off scalp of

scalpel n small surgical knife

scamp n mischievous person

scamper v **1** run about **2** run
hastily ▷ n **3** scampering

scampi pl n large prawns

scan ❶ v scanning, scanned
1 look at carefully **2** examine,
search using radar or sonar beam
3 glance over quickly **4** (of verse)
conform to metrical rules ▷ n
5 scanning **scanner** n device, esp.
electronic, which scans

scandal ❶ n **1** something
disgraceful **2** malicious gossip
scandalize v shock **scandalous**
adj

scant ❶ adj barely sufficient or not
sufficient **scanty** adj

scapegoat ❶ n person bearing
blame due to others

scar ❶ n **1** mark left by healed
wound, burn or sore **2** change
resulting from emotional distress
▷ v **3** mark, heal with scar

scarce ❶ adj **1** hard to find
2 existing or available in insufficient
quantity **3** uncommon **scarcely**
adv **1** only just **2** not quite
3 definitely or probably not
scarcity, scarceness n

scare ❶ v **1** frighten ▷ n **2** fright,
sudden panic **scary** adj

scarecrow n **1** thing set up to
frighten birds from crops **2** badly
dressed person

scarf n, pl **scarves, scarfs** long
narrow strip of material to put
round neck, head etc.

scarlet n **1** brilliant red colour
▷ adj **2** of this colour **3** immoral,
esp. unchaste **scarlet fever**
infectious fever with scarlet rash

scathing adj harshly critical

scatter ❶ v **1** throw in various

scan v = **glance over**, skim, look
over, eye, check; = **survey**, search,
investigate, sweep, scour

scandal n = **disgrace**, crime,
offence, sin, embarrassment;
= **gossip**, talk, rumours, dirt,
slander; = **shame**, disgrace, stigma,
infamy, opprobrium

scant adj = **inadequate**, meagre,
sparse, little, minimal ≠ **adequate**

scapegoat n = **fall guy** (Inf),
whipping boy

scar n = **mark**, injury, wound,
blemish ▷ v = **mark**, disfigure,
damage, mar, mutilate

scarce adj = **in short supply**,
insufficient ≠ **plentiful**; = **rare**, few,
uncommon, few and far between,
infrequent ≠ **common**

scare v = **frighten**, alarm, terrify,
panic, shock ▷ n = **fright**, shock,
start

scatter v = **throw about**, spread,
sprinkle, strew, shower ≠ **gather**;

S

directions **2** put here and there **3** sprinkle **4** disperse

scatterbrain n empty-headed person

scavenge v search for (anything usable), esp. among discarded material **scavenger** n **1** person who scavenges **2** animal, bird which feeds on refuse

scenario n, pl **-rios 1** summary of plot of play or film **2** imagined sequence of future events

scene ❶ n **1** place of action of novel, play etc. **2** place of any action **3** subdivision of play **4** view **5** episode **6** display of strong emotion **scenery** n **1** natural features of district **2** constructions used on stage to represent scene of action **scenic** adj picturesque

scent ❶ n **1** distinctive smell, esp. pleasant one **2** perfume ▷ v **4** detect or track (by smell) **5** sense **6** fill with fragrance

sceptic ❶ n one who maintains doubt or disbelief **sceptical** adj

scepticism n

sceptre n ornamental staff as symbol of royal power

schedule ❶ n **1** plan of procedure for project **2** list **3** timetable ▷ v **4** enter into schedule **5** plan to occur at certain time

scheme ❶ n **1** plan, design **2** project **3** outline ▷ v **4** devise, plan, esp. in underhand manner **scheming** adj

schism n (group resulting from) division in political party, church etc.

schizophrenia n mental disorder involving deterioration of, confusion about personality **schizophrenic** adj/n

school ❶ n **1** institution for teaching children or for giving instruction in any subject **2** buildings of such institution **3** group of thinkers, writers, artists etc. with principles or methods in common ▷ v **4** educate **5** bring under control, train **scholar** n **1** learned person **2** one taught in

——————— THESAURUS ———————

= **disperse**, dispel, disband, dissipate ≠ **assemble**

scene n = **act**, part, division, episode; = **setting**, set, background, location, backdrop; = **site**, place, setting, area, position; (Inf) = **world**, business, environment, arena; = **view**, prospect, panorama, vista, landscape; = **fuss**, to-do, row, performance, exhibition

scent n = **fragrance**, smell, perfume, bouquet, aroma; = **trail**, track, spoor ▷ v = **smell**, sense,

detect, sniff, discern

sceptic n = **doubter**, cynic, disbeliever

schedule n = **plan**, programme, agenda, calendar, timetable ▷ v = **plan**, set up, book, programme, arrange

scheme n = **plan**, programme, strategy, system, project; = **plot**, ploy, ruse, intrigue, conspiracy ▷ v = **plot**, plan, intrigue, manoeuvre, conspire

school n = **academy**, college, institution, institute, seminary;

S

school **scholarly** adj learned
scholarship n 1 learning 2 prize, grant to student for payment of school or college fees **scholastic** adj of schools or scholars
school² n shoal (of fish, whales etc.)
schooner n 1 fore-and-aft rigged vessel with two or more masts 2 tall glass
science ❶ n 1 systematic study and knowledge of natural or physical phenomena 2 any branch of study concerned with observed material facts 3 skill, technique **scientific** adj 1 of the principles of science 2 systematic **scientist** n **science fiction** stories making imaginative use of scientific knowledge
scimitar n curved oriental sword
scintillating adj 1 sparkling 2 animated, witty, clever
scissors pl n cutting instrument of two blades pivoted together
scoff¹ ❶ v express derision for

scoff² ❶ v (Sl) eat rapidly
scold v 1 find fault 2 reprimand
scone n small plain cake baked on griddle or in oven
scope ❶ n 1 range of activity or application 2 room, opportunity
scorch ❶ v 1 burn, be burnt, on surface ▷ n 2 slight burn
score ❶ n 1 points gained in game, competition 2 group of 20 3 (esp. pl) a lot 4 musical notation 5 mark or notch, esp. to keep tally 6 reason, account 7 grievance ▷ v 8 gain points in game 9 mark 10 cross out 11 arrange music (for) 12 keep tally of points
scorn ❶ n 1 contempt, derision ▷ v 2 despise **scornful** adj
scorpion n small lobster-shaped animal with sting at end of jointed tail
scotch v put an end to
scot-free adj without harm or loss
scoundrel n villain, blackguard
scour¹ ❶ v 1 clean, polish by rubbing 2 clean or flush out

THESAURUS

= group, set, circle, faction, followers ▷ v = train, coach, discipline, educate, drill
science n = discipline, body of knowledge, branch of knowledge
scoff¹ v = scorn, mock, laugh at, ridicule, knock (Inf)
scoff² v = gobble (up), wolf, devour, bolt, guzzle
scope n = opportunity, room, freedom, space, liberty; = range, capacity, reach, area, outlook
scorch v = burn, sear, roast, wither, shrivel

score v = gain, win, achieve, make, get; (Mus) = arrange, set, orchestrate, adapt; = cut, scratch, mark, slash, scrape ▷ n = rating, mark, grade, percentage; = points, result, total, outcome;
= composition, soundtrack, arrangement, orchestration
scorn n = contempt, disdain, mockery, derision, sarcasm ≠ respect ▷ v = despise, reject, disdain, slight, be above ≠ respect
scour¹ v = scrub, clean, polish, rub, buff

S

scourer n rough pad for cleaning pots and pans

scour² ❶ v move rapidly along or over (territory) in search of something

scourge n 1 whip, lash 2 severe affliction ▷ v 3 flog 4 punish severely

scout ❶ n 1 one sent out to reconnoitre ▷ v 2 act as scout

scowl v/n (make) gloomy or sullen frown

scrabble v scrape at with hands, claws in disorderly manner

scrag n 1 lean person or animal 2 lean end of a neck of mutton **scraggy** adj 1 thin, bony

scram v **scramming, scrammed** (Inf) go away hastily

scramble ❶ v 1 move along or up by crawling, climbing etc. 2 struggle with others (for) 3 mix up 4 cook (eggs) beaten up with milk ▷ n 5 scrambling 6 rough climb 7 disorderly proceeding

scrap ❶ n scrapping, scrapped

1 small piece or fragment 2 leftover material 3 (Inf) fight ▷ pl 4 leftover food ▷ v 5 break up, discard as useless 6 (Inf) fight **scrappy** adj 1 unequal in quality 2 badly finished **scrapbook** n book in which newspaper cuttings or pictures are stuck

scrape ❶ v 1 rub with something sharp 2 clean, smooth thus 3 grate 4 scratch 5 rub with harsh noise ▷ n 6 act, sound of scraping **scraper** n instrument for scraping

scratch ❶ v 1 score, make narrow surface mark or wound with something sharp 2 scrape (skin) with nails to relieve itching 3 remove, withdraw from list, race etc. ▷ n 4 wound, mark or sound made by scratching

scrawl v 1 write, draw untidily ▷ n 2 thing scrawled

scrawny adj **scrawnier, scrawniest** thin, bony

scream ❶ v 1 utter piercing cry, esp. of fear, pain etc. 2 utter in a

scour² v = **search**, hunt, comb, ransack

scout n = **vanguard**, lookout, precursor, outrider, reconnoiterer ▷ v = **reconnoitre**, investigate, watch, survey, observe

scramble v = **struggle**, climb, crawl, swarm, scrabble; = **strive**, rush, contend, vie, run ▷ n = **clamber**, ascent; = **race**, competition, struggle, rush, confusion

scrap n = **piece**, fragment, bit, grain, particle; = **waste**, junk, off

cuts ▷ v = **get rid of**, drop, abandon, ditch (Sl), discard ≠ **bring back**

scrape v = **rake**, sweep, drag, brush; = **grate**, grind, scratch, squeak, rasp; = **graze**, skin, scratch, bark, scuff; = **clean**, remove, scour ▷ n (Inf) = **predicament**, difficulty, fix (Inf), mess, dilemma

scratch v = **rub**, scrape, claw at; = **mark**, cut, score, damage, grate ▷ n = **mark**, scrape, graze, blemish, gash

scream v = **cry**, yell, shriek,

S

scream ▷ n **3** shrill, piercing cry

screech v/n scream

screed n long (tedious) letter, passage or speech

screen ❶ n **1** device to shelter from heat, light, draught, observation etc. **2** blank surface on which photographic images are projected **3** windscreen ▷ v **4** shelter, hide **5** show (film) **6** examine (group of people) for political motives or for presence of disease, weapons etc.

screw ❶ n **1** metal pin with spiral thread, twisted into materials to pin or fasten **2** anything resembling a screw in shape ▷ v **3** fasten with screw **4** twist around **screwdriver** n tool for turning screws

scribble ❶ v **1** write, draw carelessly **2** make meaningless marks with pen or pencil ▷ n **3** something scribbled

scribe n **1** writer **2** copyist ▷ v **3** scratch a line with pointed instrument

scrimp v **1** make too small or short **2** treat meanly

script ❶ n **1** (system or style of) handwriting **2** written text of film, play, radio or television programme

scripture n **1** sacred writings **2** the Bible

scroll n **1** roll of parchment or paper **2** ornament shaped thus

scrotum n, pl **-ta, -tums** pouch of skin containing testicles

scrounge v (Inf) get without cost, by begging **scrounger** n

scrub¹ ❶ v scrubbing, scrubbed **1** clean with hard brush and water **2** scour **3** (Inf) delete, cancel

scrub² n scrubbing, scrubbed **1** stunted trees **2** brushwood

scruff n nape of neck

scrum, scrummage n (Rugby) **1** restarting of play in which opposing packs of forwards push against each other to gain possession of the ball **2** disorderly struggle

scruple n **1** doubt or hesitation about what is morally right ▷ v **2** hesitate **scrupulous** adj **1** extremely conscientious **2** thorough

scrutiny ❶ n, pl **-nies 1** close examination **2** critical

screech, bawl ▷ n = **cry**, yell, howl, shriek, screech

screen n = **cover**, guard, shade, shelter, shield ▷ v = **broadcast**, show, put on, present, air; = **cover**, hide, conceal, shade, mask; = **investigate**, test, check, examine, scan; = **process**, sort, examine, filter, scan

screw v = **fasten**, fix, attach, bolt, clamp; = **turn**, twist, tighten; (Inf)

= **cheat**, do (Sl), rip (someone) off (Sl), skin (Sl), trick (Inf)

scribble v = **scrawl**, write, jot, dash off

script n = **text**, lines, words, book, copy; = **handwriting**, writing, calligraphy, penmanship

scrub¹ v = **scour**, clean, polish, rub, wash; (Inf) = **cancel**, drop, give up, abolish, forget about

scrutiny n = **examination**, study,

investigation **scrutinize** v
examine closely

scuba diving sport of swimming
under water using self-contained
breathing apparatus

scud v **scudding, scudded 1** run
fast **2** run before wind

scuff v **1** drag, scrape with feet in
walking **2** graze ▷ n **3** act, sound
of scuffing

scuffle v **1** fight in disorderly
manner **2** shuffle ▷ n **3** scuffling

scull n **1** oar used in stern of boat
2 short oar used in pairs ▷ v
3 propel, move by means of sculls

scullery n, pl **-leries** place for
washing dishes etc.

sculpture ❶ n **1** art of forming
solid figures **2** product of this art
▷ v **3** represent by sculpture
sculptor n

scum n **1** froth or other floating
matter on liquid **2** waste part of
anything **3** vile people **scummy**
adj

scungy adj **-ier, -iest** (Aust & NZ,
Inf) sordid or dirty

scurrilous adj coarse, indecently
abusive

scurry v **-rying, -ried 1** run hastily
▷ n **2** bustling haste **3** flurry

scurvy n disease caused by lack of
vitamin C

scuttle¹ n fireside container for coal

scuttle² v **1** rush away **2** run

hurriedly ▷ n **3** hurried run

scuttle³ v make hole in ship to sink
it

scythe n **1** manual implement
with long curved blade for cutting
grass ▷ v **2** cut with scythe

sea ❶ n **1** mass of salt water
covering greater part of earth
2 broad tract of this **3** waves
4 vast expanse ▷ adj **5** of the sea
seagull n gull **sea horse** fish
with bony-plated body and
horselike head **sea lion** kind of
large seal **seaman** n sailor
seasick adj **seasickness** n
nausea caused by motion of ship
seaweed n plant growing in sea
seaworthy adj in fit condition to
put to sea

seal¹ ❶ n **1** piece of metal or stone
engraved with device for
impression on wax etc.
2 impression thus made (on letters
etc.) **3** device, material preventing
passage of water, air, oil etc. ▷ v
4 affix seal to ratify, authorize
5 mark with stamp as evidence of
some quality **6** keep close or secret
7 settle **8** make watertight,
airtight etc.

seal² n amphibious furred
carnivorous mammal with flippers
as limbs

seam ❶ n **1** line of junction of two
edges, e.g. of two pieces of cloth

THESAURUS

investigation, search, analysis

sculpture v = carve, form, model,
fashion, shape

sea n = ocean, the deep, the waves,
main; = mass, army, host, crowd,

mob

seal¹ v = settle, clinch, conclude,
consummate, finalize ▷ n
= sealant, sealer, adhesive

seam n = joint, closure; = layer,

2 thin layer, stratum ▷ v **3** mark with furrows or wrinkles **seamless** adj **seamy** adj sordid

seance n meeting at which people attempt to communicate with the dead

sear ❶ v scorch

search ❶ v **1** look over or through to find something ▷ n **2** act of searching **3** quest **searching** adj thorough

season ❶ n **1** one of four divisions of year **2** period during which thing happens etc. **3** flavour with salt, herbs etc. **4** make reliable or ready for use **5** make experienced **seasonable** adj **1** appropriate for the season **2** opportune **seasonal** adj varying with seasons **seasoning** n flavouring

seat ❶ n **1** thing for sitting on **2** buttocks **3** base **4** right to sit (e.g. in council etc.) **5** place where something is located, centred **6** locality of disease, trouble etc. **7** country house ▷ v **8** make to sit

9 provide sitting accommodation for **seat belt** belt worn in vehicle to prevent injury in crash

secateurs pl n small pruning shears

secede v withdraw formally from federation, Church etc. **secession** n

seclude v guard from, remove from sight, view, contact with others **secluded** adj **1** remote **2** private **seclusion** n

second¹ ❶ adj **1** next after first **2** alternate, additional **3** of lower quality ▷ n **4** person or thing coming second **5** attendant **6** sixtieth part of minute ▷ v **7** support **second-class** adj inferior **second-hand** adj **1** bought after use by another **2** not original **second sight** supposed ability to predict events

second² v transfer (employee, officer) temporarily

secondary ❶ adj **1** of less importance **2** developed from

—— THESAURUS ——

vein, stratum, lode

sear v = **wither**, burn, scorch, sizzle

search v = **examine**, investigate, explore, inspect, comb ▷ n = **hunt**, look, investigation, examination, pursuit

season n = **period**, time, term, spell ▷ v = **flavour**, salt, spice, enliven, pep up

seat n = **chair**, bench, stall, stool, pew; = **membership**, place, constituency, chair, incumbency; = **centre**, place, site, heart, capital; = **mansion**, house, residence,

abode, ancestral hall ▷ v = **sit**, place, settle, set, fix; = **hold**, take, accommodate, sit, contain

second¹ adj = **next**, following, succeeding, subsequent; = **additional**, other, further, extra, alternative; = **inferior**, secondary, subordinate, lower, lesser ▷ n = **supporter**, assistant, aide, colleague, backer ▷ v = **support**, back, endorse, approve, go along with

secondary adj = **subordinate**, minor, lesser, lower, inferior

S

something else **3** (*Education*) after primary stage

secret ❶ *adj* **1** kept, meant to be kept from knowledge of others **2** hidden ▷ *n* **3** thing kept secret **secrecy** *n* keeping or being kept secret **secretive** *adj* given to having secrets

secretary *n, pl* **-ries 1** one employed to deal with papers and correspondence, keep records etc. **2** head of a state department **secretariat** *n* body of secretaries

secrete *v* **1** hide **2** conceal **3** (of gland etc.) collect and supply particular substance in body **secretion** *n*

sect ❶ *n* **1** group of people (within religious body etc.) with common interest **2** faction **sectarian** *adj*

section ❶ *n* **1** division **2** portion **3** distinct part **4** cutting **5** drawing of anything as if cut through

sector ❶ *n* part or subdivision

secular ❶ *adj* **1** worldly **2** lay, not religious

secure ❶ *adj* **1** safe **2** firmly fixed **3** certain ▷ *v* **4** gain possession of **5** make safe **6** make firm **security** *n, pl* **-ties 1** state of safety **2** protection **3** anything given as bond or pledge

sedate¹ *adj* calm, serious

sedate² *v* make calm by sedative **sedation** *n* **sedative** *adj* **1** having soothing or calming effect ▷ *n* **2** sedative drug

sediment ❶ *n* matter which settles to the bottom of liquid

sedition *n* stirring up of rebellion

seduce ❶ *v* persuade to commit some (wrong) deed, esp. sexual intercourse **seducer** *n* **seduction** *n* **seductive** *adj* alluring

see¹ ❶ *v* seeing, saw, seen **1** perceive with eyes or mentally **2** watch **3** find out **4** interview

≠ **main**; = **resultant**, contingent, derived, indirect ≠ **original**

secret *adj* = **undisclosed**, unknown, confidential, underground, undercover; = **concealed**, hidden, disguised ≠ **unconcealed**

sect *n* = **group**, division, faction, party, camp

section *n* = **part**, piece, portion, division, slice; = **district**, area, region, sector, zone

sector *n* = **part**, division; = **area**, part, region, district, zone

secular *adj* = **worldly**, lay, earthly, civil, temporal ≠ **religious**

secure *v* = **obtain**, get, acquire, score (*SI*), gain ≠ **lose**; = **attach**, stick, fix, bind, fasten ≠ **detach** ▷ *adj* = **safe**, protected, immune, unassailable ≠ **unprotected**; = **fast**, firm, fixed, stable, steady ≠ **insecure**; = **confident**, sure, easy, certain, assured ≠ **uneasy**

sediment *n* = **dregs**, grounds, residue, lees, deposit

seduce *v* = **tempt**, lure, entice, mislead, deceive; = **corrupt**, deprave, dishonour, debauch, deflower

see¹ *v* = **perceive**, spot, notice, sight, witness; = **understand**, get,

5 make sure **6** accompany
7 consider **seeing** *conj* in view of
the fact that

see² *n* diocese, office of bishop

seed 𝟏 *n* **1** reproductive germs of
plants **2** one grain of this **3** such
grains saved or used for sowing
4 sperm **5** origin ▷ *v* **6** sow with
seed **7** produce seed **seedling** *n*
young plant raised from seed
seedy *adj* **1** shabby **2** full of seed

seek 𝟏 *v* seeking, sought make
search or enquiry (for)

seem 𝟏 *v* appear (to be or to do)
seemly *adj* becoming and proper

seep 𝟏 *v* trickle through slowly

seesaw *n* **1** plank on which
children sit at opposite ends and
swing up and down ▷ *v* **2** move up
and down

seethe 𝟏 *v* seething, seethed
1 boil, foam **2** be very agitated
3 be in constant movement (as
large crowd sits)

segment 𝟏 *n* **1** piece cut off
2 section ▷ *v* **3** divide into
segments

segregate 𝟏 *v* set apart from rest
segregation *n*

seize 𝟏 *v* **1** grasp **2** lay hold of
3 capture **4** (of machine part) stick
tightly through overheating
seizure *n* **1** act of taking
2 sudden onset of disease

seldom 𝟏 *adv* not often, rarely

select 𝟏 *v* **1** pick out, choose ▷ *adj*
2 choice, picked **3** exclusive
selection *n* **1** option

follow, realize, appreciate; = **find
out**, learn, discover, determine,
verify; = **consider**, decide, reflect,
deliberate, think over; = **make
sure**, ensure, guarantee, make
certain, see to it; = **accompany**,
show, escort, lead, walk; = **speak
to**, receive, interview, consult,
confer with; = **meet**, come across,
happen on, bump into, run across;
= **go out with**, court, date *(Inf,
chiefly US)*, go steady with *(Inf)*

seed *n* = **grain**, pip, germ, kernel,
egg; = **beginning**, start, germ;
= **origin**, source, nucleus; *(chiefly
Bible)* = **offspring**, children,
descendants, issue, progeny

seek *v* = **look for**, pursue, search
for, be after, hunt; = **try**, attempt,
aim, strive, endeavour

seem *v* = **appear**, give the

impression of being, look

seep *v* = **ooze**, well, leak, soak,
trickle

seethe *v* = **be furious**, rage, fume,
simmer, see red *(Inf)*; = **boil**, bubble,
foam, fizz, froth

segment *n* = **section**, part, piece,
division, slice

segregate *v* = **set apart**, divide,
separate, isolate, discriminate
against ≠ **unite**

seize *v* = **grab**, grip, grasp, take,
snatch ≠ **let go**; = **take by storm**,
take over, annex, occupy, conquer

seldom *adv* = **rarely**, not often,
infrequently, hardly ever ≠ **often**

select *v* = **choose**, take, pick, opt
for, decide on ≠ **reject** ▷ *adj*
= **choice**, special, excellent,
superior, first-class ≠ **ordinary**;
= **exclusive**, elite, privileged,

S

2 assortment **selective** adj
selector n

self n, pl **selves** one's own person
or individuality **selfie** n (Inf)
photograph taken by pointing
camera at oneself **selfish** adj
1 unduly concerned with personal
profit or pleasure **2** greedy
selfless adj unselfish

self- comb. form of oneself or itself

sell ① v **selling, sold 1** hand over
for a price **2** stock, have for sale
3 make someone accept **4** (Inf)
betray, cheat **5** find purchasers
seller n

Sellotape n **1** type of adhesive
tape ▷ v **2** (without cap.) stick with
Sellotape

semaphore n **1** system of signalling
by human or mechanical arms

semblance n **1** (false) appearance
2 image, likeness

semen n **1** fluid carrying sperm of
male animals **2** sperm

semi- comb. form half, partly, not
completely, as in semicircle

semibreve n musical note equal
to four crotchets

semicolon n punctuation mark (;)

semiconductor n substance
whose electrical conductivity
increases with temperature, used in

transistors, circuits etc.

semidetached adj (of house)
joined to another by one side only

semifinal n match, round etc.
before final

seminal adj **1** capable of developing
2 influential **3** of semen or seed

seminar n meeting of group (of
students) for discussion

semiprecious adj (of gemstones)
having less value than precious
stones

semolina n hard grains left after
sifting of flour, used for puddings etc.

send ① v **sending, sent 1** cause
to go or be conveyed **2** despatch
3 transmit (by radio)

senile adj showing weakness of old
age **senility** n

senior ① adj **1** superior in rank or
standing **2** older ▷ n **3** superior
4 elder person **seniority** n

sensation ① n **1** operation of
sense, feeling, awareness **2** excited
feeling, state of excitement
3 exciting event **sensational** adj
producing great excitement
sensationalism n deliberate use
of sensational material

sense ① n **1** any of bodily faculties
of perception or feeling **2** ability to
perceive **3** consciousness

cliquish ≠ **indiscriminate**

sell v = **trade**, exchange, barter
≠ **buy**; = **deal in**, market, trade in,
stock, handle ≠ **buy**

send v = **dispatch**, forward, direct,
convey, remit = **transmit**,
broadcast, communicate

senior adj = **higher ranking**,

superior ≠ **subordinate**; = **the
elder**, major (Brit) ≠ **junior**

sensation n = **feeling**, sense,
impression, perception, awareness;
= **excitement**, thrill, stir, furore,
commotion

sense n = **feeling**, impression,
perception, awareness,

4 meaning 5 coherence 6 sound practical judgment ▷ v 7 perceive **senseless** adj

sensible ❶ adj 1 reasonable, wise 2 aware **sensibility** n ability to feel, esp. emotional or moral feelings

sensitive ❶ adj 1 open to, acutely affected by, external impressions 2 easily affected or altered 3 easily upset by criticism 4 responsive to slight changes **sensitivity**, **sensitiveness** n **sensitize** v make sensitive

sensor n device that detects or measures the presence of something

sensory adj relating to senses

sensual ❶ adj 1 of senses only and not of mind 2 given to pursuit of pleasures of sense

sensuous adj stimulating, or

apprehended by, senses, esp. in aesthetic manner

sentence ❶ n 1 combination of words expressing a thought 2 judgment passed on criminal by court or judge ▷ v 3 pass sentence on, condemn

sentient adj capable of feeling

sentiment ❶ n 1 tendency to be moved by feeling rather than reason 2 mental feeling 3 opinion **sentimental** adj given to indulgence in sentiment and in its expression **sentimentality** n

sentinel n sentry

sentry n, pl **-tries** soldier on watch

separate ❶ v 1 part 2 divide ▷ adj 3 disconnected, distinct, individual **separable** adj **separation** n 1 disconnection 2 living apart of married couple

— THESAURUS —

consciousness; = **understanding**, awareness; *sometimes plural* = **intelligence**, reason, understanding, brains (*Inf*), judgment ≠ **foolishness**; = **meaning**, significance, import, implication, drift ▷ v = **perceive**, feel, understand, pick up, realize ≠ **be unaware of**

sensible adj = **wise**, practical, prudent, shrewd, judicious ≠ **foolish**; = **intelligent**, practical, rational, sound, realistic ≠ **senseless**

sensitive adj = **thoughtful**, kindly, concerned, patient, attentive; = **susceptible to**, responsive to, easily affected by; = **touchy**, oversensitive, easily upset, easily

offended, easily hurt ≠ **insensitive**

sensual adj = **sexual**, erotic, raunchy (*Sl*), lewd, lascivious; = **physical**, bodily, voluptuous, animal, luxurious

sentence n = **punishment**, condemnation ▷ v = **condemn**, doom

sentiment n = **feeling**, idea, view, opinion, attitude; = **sentimentality**, emotion, tenderness, romanticism, sensibility

separate adj = **unconnected**, individual, particular, divided, divorced ≠ **connected**; = **individual**, independent, apart, distinct ≠ **joined** ▷ v = **divide**, detach, disconnect, disjoin

S

sepia n 1 reddish-brown pigment ▷ adj 2 of this colour

Sept. September

September n ninth month

septet n (music for) group of seven musicians

septic adj 1 (of wound) infected 2 of, caused by pus-forming bacteria

septicaemia n blood poisoning

sepulchre n 1 tomb 2 burial vault

sequel ❶ n 1 consequence 2 continuation, e.g. of story

sequence ❶ n arrangement of things in successive order

sequin n small ornamental metal disc on dresses etc.

seraph n, pl -aphs, -aphim angel

serenade n 1 sentimental song addressed to woman by lover, esp. at evening ▷ v 2 sing serenade (to someone)

serendipity n gift of making fortunate discoveries by accident

serene adj 1 calm, tranquil 2 unclouded **serenity** n

serf n one of class of medieval labourers bound to, and transferred with, land

sergeant n 1 noncommissioned officer in army 2 police officer above constable **sergeant major** highest noncommissioned officer in regiment

series ❶ n, pl -ries 1 sequence 2 succession, set (e.g. of radio, TV programmes) **serial** n story or play produced in successive episodes **serialize** v

serious ❶ adj 1 thoughtful, solemn 2 earnest, sincere 3 of importance 4 giving cause for concern

sermon ❶ n 1 discourse of religious instruction or exhortation 2 any similar discourse

serpent n snake **serpentine** adj twisting, winding like a snake

serrated adj having notched, sawlike edge

serum n watery animal fluid, esp. thin part of blood as used for inoculation or vaccination

serve ❶ v 1 work for, under

THESAURUS

≠ combine; = come apart, split, come away ≠ connect; = sever, break apart, split in two, divide in two ≠ join; = split up, part, divorce, break up, part company

sequel n = follow-up, continuation, development; = consequence, result, outcome, conclusion, end

sequence n = succession, course, series, order, chain

series n = sequence, course, chain, succession, run, soapie (Aust Sl)

serious adj = grave, bad, critical, dangerous, acute; = important, crucial, urgent, pressing, worrying ≠ unimportant; = thoughtful, detailed, careful, deep, profound; = deep, sophisticated

sermon n = homily, address

serve v = work for, help, aid, assist, be in the service of; = perform, do, complete, fulfil, discharge; = be adequate, do, suffice, suit, satisfy; = present, provide, supply, deliver, set out another **2** attend (to customers) in shop etc. **3** provide **4** help to (food etc.) **5** present (food etc.) in particular way **6** be member of military unit **7** spend time doing **8** be useful, suitable enough **servant** n personal or domestic attendant **service** n **1** act of serving **2** system organized to provide for needs of public **3** maintenance of vehicle **4** use **5** department of State employment **6** set of dishes etc. **7** form, session of public worship ▷ pl **8** armed forces ▷ v **9** overhaul **serviceable** adj **1** in working order, usable **2** durable **serviceman** n member of armed forced **service station** place supplying fuel, oil, maintenance for motor vehicles **serviette** n table napkin **servile** adj **1** slavish, without independence **2** fawning **servitude** n in bondage, slavery **sesame** n plant whose seeds and oil are used in cooking

session ❶ n **1** meeting of court etc. **2** continuous series of such meetings **3** any period devoted to an activity **set** ❶ v setting, set **1** put or place in specified position or condition **2** make ready **3** become firm or fixed **4** establish **5** prescribe, allot **6** put to music **7** (of sun) go down ▷ adj **8** fixed, established **9** deliberate **10** unvarying ▷ n **11** act or state of being set **12** bearing, posture **13** (Radio, TV) complete apparatus for reception or transmission **14** (Theatre, Cinema) organized settings and equipment to form ensemble of scene **15** number of associated things, persons **setback** n anything that hinders or impedes **set up** establish **sett, set** n badger's burrow **settee** n couch **setting** ❶ n **1** background **2** surroundings **3** scenery and other stage accessories

service n = **facility**, system, resource, utility, amenity; = **ceremony**, worship, rite, observance; = **work**, labour, employment, business, office; = **check**, maintenance check ▷ v = **overhaul**, check, maintain, tune (up), go over **session** n = **meeting**, hearing, sitting, period, conference **set** v = **put**, place, lay, position, rest; = **arrange**, decide (upon), settle, establish, determine; = **assign**, give, allot, prescribe; = **harden**,

stiffen, solidify, cake, thicken; = **go down**, sink, dip, decline, disappear; = **prepare**, lay, spread, arrange, make ready ▷ adj = **established**, planned, decided, agreed, arranged; = **strict**, rigid, stubborn, inflexible ≠ **flexible**; = **conventional**, traditional, stereotyped, unspontaneous ▷ n = **scenery**, setting, scene, stage set; = **position**, bearing, attitude, carriage, posture **setting** n = **surroundings**, site, location, set, scene

S

4 decorative metalwork holding precious stone etc. in position 5 tableware and cutlery for (single place at) table 6 music for song

settle ❶ v 1 arrange 2 establish 3 decide upon 4 end (®dispute etc.) 5 pay 6 make calm or stable 7 come to rest 8 subside 9 become clear 10 take up residence **settlement** n 1 act of settling 2 place newly inhabited 3 money bestowed legally **settler** n colonist

seven adj/n cardinal number next after six **seventh** adj ordinal number **seventeen** adj/n ten plus seven **seventeenth** adj **seventieth** adj **seventy** adj/n ten times seven

sever ❶ v 1 separate, divide 2 cut off **severance** n

several ❶ adj 1 some, a few 2 separate 3 individual ▷ pron 4 indefinite small number

severe ❶ adj 1 strict 2 harsh

3 austere 4 extreme **severity** n

sew v sewing, sewed, sewn 1 join with needle and thread 2 make by sewing **sewing** n

sewage n refuse, waste matter, excrement conveyed in sewer

sewer n underground drain

sex ❶ n 1 state of being male or female 2 males or females collectively 3 sexual intercourse ▷ adj 4 concerning sex ▷ v 5 ascertain sex of **sexism** n discrimination on basis of sex **sexist** n/adj **sexual** adj **sexy** adj **sexual intercourse** act of procreation in which male's penis is inserted into female's vagina

sextet n (composition for) six musicians

shabby ❶ adj -bier, -biest 1 faded, worn 2 poorly dressed 3 mean, dishonourable

shack ❶ n rough hut

shackle n 1 metal ring or fastening for prisoner's wrist or

————— THESAURUS —————

settle v = **resolve**, work out, put an end to, straighten out; = **pay**, clear, square (up), discharge; = **move to**, take up residence in, live in, dwell in, inhabit; = **colonize**, populate, people, pioneer; = **land**, alight, descend, light, come to rest; = **calm**, quiet, relax, relieve, reassure ≠ **disturb**

sever v = **cut**, separate, split, part, divide ≠ **join**; = **discontinue**, terminate, break off, put an end to, dissociate ≠ **continue**

several adj = **some**, a few, a number of, a handful of

severe adj = **serious**, critical, terrible, desperate, extreme; = **acute**, intense, violent, piercing, harrowing; = **strict**, hard, harsh, cruel, rigid ≠ **lenient**; = **grim**, serious, grave, forbidding, stern ≠ **genial**

sex n (Inf) = **lovemaking**, sexual relations, copulation, fornication, coitus

shabby adj = **tatty**, worn, ragged, scruffy, tattered ≠ **smart**; = **run-down**, seedy, mean, dilapidated

shack n = **hut**, cabin, shanty

DICTIONARY

shade ❶ n 1 partial darkness
2 shelter, place sheltered from light,
heat etc. 3 darker part of anything
4 depth of colour 5 screen 6 (US)
window blind ▷ v 7 screen from
light, darken 8 represent shades in
drawing **shady** adj 1 shielded
from sun 2 (Inf) dishonest

shadow ❶ n 1 dark figure
projected by anything that
intercepts rays of light 2 patch of
shade 3 slight trace ▷ v 4 cast
shadow over 5 follow and watch
closely **shadowy** adj

shaft ❶ n 1 straight rod, stem,
handle 2 arrow 3 ray, beam (of
light) 4 revolving rod for
transmitting power

shag n 1 long-napped cloth
2 coarse shredded tobacco
shaggy adj 1 covered with rough
hair 2 unkempt

shake ❶ v shaking, shook,
shaken 1 (cause to) move with
quick vibrations 2 tremble 3 grasp
the hand (of another) in greeting
4 upset 5 wave, brandish ▷ n
6 act of shaking 7 vibration 8 jolt
9 (Inf) short period of time **shaky**
adj 1 unsteady, insecure
2 questionable

shale n flaky fine-grained rock

shall v, past tense **should** makes
compound tenses or moods to
express obligation, command,
condition or intention

shallow ❶ adj 1 not deep
2 superficial ▷ n 3 shallow place

sham ❶ adj/n 1 imitation,
counterfeit ▷ v 2 pretend, feign

shamble v walk in shuffling,
awkward way

shambles ❶ pl n messy, disorderly
thing or place

shame ❶ n 1 emotion caused by
consciousness of guilt or dishonour

THESAURUS

shade n = **hue**, tone, colour, tint;
= **dash**, trace, hint, suggestion;
= **screen**, covering, cover, blind,
curtain; (Lit:) = **ghost**, spirit,
phantom, spectre, apparition ▷ v
= **darken**, shadow, cloud, dim;
= **cover**, protect, screen, hide,
shield

shadow n = **silhouette**, shape,
outline, profile; = **shade**, dimness,
darkness, gloom, cover ▷ v
= **shade**, screen, shield, darken,
overhang; = **follow**, tail (Inf), trail,
stalk

shaft n = **tunnel**, hole, passage,
burrow, passageway; = **handle**,

staff, pole, rod, stem

shake v = **jiggle**, agitate;
= **tremble**, shiver, quake, quiver;
= **rock**, totter; = **wave**, wield,
flourish, brandish ▷ n = **vibration**,
trembling, quaking, jerk, shiver

shallow adj = **superficial**, surface,
empty, slight, foolish ≠ **deep**

sham n = **fraud**, imitation, hoax,
pretence, forgery ≠ **the real thing**
▷ adj = **false**, artificial, bogus,
pretended, mock ≠ **real**

shambles n = **chaos**, mess,
disorder, confusion, muddle

shame n = **embarrassment**,
humiliation, ignominy,

in one's conduct or state **2** cause of
disgrace **3** pity, hard luck ▷ *v*
4 cause to feel shame **5** disgrace
6 force by shame (into) **shameful**
adj **shameless** *adj* **1** with no
sense of shame **2** indecent
shamefaced *adj* ashamed
shampoo *n* **1** preparation of liquid
soap for washing hair, carpets etc.
2 this process ▷ *v* **3** use shampoo
to wash
shamrock *n* clover leaf, esp. as
Irish emblem
shandy *n, pl* **-dies** drink of beer
and lemonade
shanty[1] *n* **1** temporary wooden
building **2** crude dwelling
shanty[2] *n* sailor's song
shape ❶ *n* **1** external form or
appearance **2** mould, pattern
3 (*Inf*) condition ▷ *v* **4** form, mould
5 develop **shapeless** *adj* **shapely**

adj well-proportioned
shard *n* broken piece of pottery
share ❶ *n* **1** portion **2** quota **3** lot
4 unit of ownership in public
company ▷ *v* **5** give, take a share
6 join with others in doing, using,
something **shareholder** *n*
shark *n* **1** large usu. predatory
sea fish **2** person who cheats
others
sharp ❶ *adj* **1** having keen cutting
edge or fine point **2** not gradual or
gentle **3** brisk **4** clever **5** harsh
6 dealing cleverly but unfairly
7 shrill **8** strongly marked, esp. in
outline **9** sour ▷ *adv* **10** promptly
sharpen *v* make sharp
sharpshooter *n* marksman
shatter ❶ *v* **1** break in pieces
2 ruin (plans etc.) **3** disturb
(person) greatly **shattered** *adj*
(*Inf*) completely exhausted

mortification, abashment
≠ **shamelessness**; = **disgrace**,
scandal, discredit, smear,
disrepute ≠ **honour** ▷ *v*
= **embarrass**, disgrace,
humiliate, humble, mortify
≠ **make proud**; = **dishonour**,
degrade, stain, smear, blot
≠ **honour**
shape *n* = **appearance**, form,
aspect, guise, likeness; = **form**,
profile, outline, lines, build;
= **pattern**, model, frame, mould;
= **condition**, state, health, trim,
fettle ▷ *v* = **form**, make, produce,
create, model; = **mould**, form,
make, fashion, model
share *n* = **part**, portion, quota,

ration, lot ▷ *v* = **divide**, split,
distribute, assign; = **go halves on**,
go fifty-fifty on (*Inf*)
sharp *adj* = **keen**, jagged, serrated
≠ **blunt**; = **quick-witted**, clever,
astute, knowing, quick ≠ **dim**;
= **cutting**, biting, bitter, harsh,
barbed ≠ **gentle**; = **sudden**,
marked, abrupt, extreme, distinct
≠ **gradual**; = **clear**, distinct,
well-defined, crisp ≠ **indistinct**;
= **sour**, tart, pungent, hot, acid
≠ **bland** ▷ *adv* = **promptly**,
precisely, exactly, on time, on the
dot ≠ **approximately**
shatter *v* = **smash**, break, burst,
crack, crush; = **destroy**, ruin,
wreck, demolish, torpedo

shave ❶ v shaving, shaved
1 cut close, esp. hair of face or
head 2 pare away 3 graze
4 reduce ▷ n 5 shaving shavings
pl n parings

shawl n piece of fabric to cover
woman's shoulders or wrap baby

she pron 1 female person, animal
already referred to ▷ comb. form
2 female, as in she-wolf

sheaf n, pl sheaves 1 bundle, esp.
of corn 2 loose leaves of paper

shear v shearing, sheared 1 clip
hair, wool from 2 cut through
3 fracture shears pl n large pair of
scissors

sheath n close-fitting cover, esp.
for knife or sword sheathe v put
into sheath

shebeen n (Irish, S Afr & Scot) place
where alcohol is sold illegally

shed¹ ❶ n shedding, shed roofed
shelter used as store or workshop

shed² ❶ v shedding, shed
1 (cause to) pour forth (e.g. tears,
blood) 2 cast off

sheen ❶ n gloss

sheep n, pl sheep ruminant
animal bred for wool or meat

sheepish adj embarrassed, shy

sheepdog n dog used for herding
sheep

sheer ❶ adj 1 perpendicular 2 (of
material) very fine, transparent
3 absolute, unmitigated

sheet ❶ n 1 large piece of cotton
etc. to cover bed 2 broad piece of
any thin material 3 large expanse

sheikh, sheik n Arab chief

shelf n, pl shelves 1 board fixed
horizontally (on wall etc.) for
holding things 2 ledge

shell ❶ n 1 hard outer case (esp. of
egg, nut etc.) 2 explosive projectile
3 outer part of structure left when
interior is removed ▷ v 4 take from
5 take out of shell 6 fire at
with shells shellfish n 1 mollusc
2 crustacean

shelter ❶ n 1 place, structure
giving protection 2 refuge ▷ v
3 give protection to 4 take shelter

shelve ❶ v 1 put on a shelf 2 put
off 3 slope gradually

shave v = trim, crop

shed¹ n = hut, shack, outhouse

shed² v = drop, spill, scatter; = cast
off, discard, moult, slough off;
= give out, cast, emit, give, radiate

sheen n = shine, gleam, gloss,
polish, brightness

sheer adj = total, complete,
absolute, utter, pure ≠ moderate;
= steep, abrupt, precipitous
≠ gradual; = fine, thin,
transparent, see-through,
gossamer ≠ thick

sheet n = page, leaf, folio, piece of
paper; = plate, piece, panel, slab

shell n = husk, case, pod ▷ v
= bomb, bombard, attack, blitz,
strafe

shelter n = cover, screen;
= protection, safety, refuge, cover
▷ v = take shelter, hide, seek
refuge, take cover; = protect,
shield, harbour, safeguard, cover
≠ endanger

shelve v = postpone, defer, freeze,
suspend, put aside

S

shepherd ❶ n 1 one who tends sheep ▷ v 2 guide, watch over
shepherd's pie dish of minced meat and potato
sherbet n fruit-flavoured effervescent powder
sheriff n (US) 1 law enforcement officer 2 in England and Wales, chief executive officer of the crown in a county 3 in Scotland, chief judge of a district 4 (Canad) municipal officer who enforces court judgements
sherry n, pl **-ries** fortified wine
shield ❶ n 1 piece of armour carried on arm 2 any protection used to stop blows, missiles etc. ▷ v 3 cover, protect
shift ❶ v 1 (cause to) move, change position ▷ n 2 move, change of position 3 relay of workers 4 time of their working 5 woman's underskirt or dress **shiftless** adj lacking in resource or character **shifty** adj evasive, of dubious character
shilling n former Brit. coin, now 5p
shimmer ❶ v 1 shine with quivering light ▷ n 2 such light

shin n 1 front of lower leg ▷ v 2 climb with arms and legs
shine ❶ v **shining, shone** 1 give out, reflect light 2 excel 3 polish ▷ n 4 brightness, lustre 5 polishing **shiny** adj
shingle n mass of pebbles
shingles n disease causing rash of small blisters
ship ❶ n 1 large seagoing vessel ▷ v 2 put on or send (esp. by ship) **shipment** n 1 act of shipping 2 goods shipped **shipping** n 1 freight transport business 2 ships collectively **shipshape** adj orderly, neat **shipwreck** n 1 destruction of ship ▷ v 2 cause shipwreck of **shipyard** n place for building and repair of ships
shire n county **shire horse** large powerful breed of horse
shirk v evade, try to avoid (duty etc.)
shirt n garment with sleeves and collar for upper part of body **shirty** adj **-tier, -tiest** (Inf) annoyed
shiver¹ ❶ v 1 tremble, usu. with cold or fear ▷ n 2 act, state of shivering

— THESAURUS —

shepherd n = drover, stockman, herdsman, grazier ▷ v = guide, conduct, steer, herd, usher
shield n = protection, cover, defence, screen, guard ▷ v = protect, cover, screen, guard, defend
shift v = move, move around, budge ▷ n = change, shifting, displacement
shimmer v = gleam, twinkle,

glisten, scintillate ▷ n = gleam, iridescence
shine v = gleam, flash, beam, glow, sparkle; = polish, buff, burnish, brush; = be outstanding, stand out, excel, be conspicuous ▷ n = polish, gloss, sheen
ship n = vessel, boat, craft
shiver¹ v = shudder, shake, tremble, quake, quiver ▷ n = tremble, shudder, quiver,

shiver² v/n splinter

shoal¹ n large number of fish swimming together

shoal² n 1 stretch of shallow water 2 sandbank

shock¹ ❶ v 1 horrify, scandalize ▷ n 2 violent or damaging blow 3 emotional disturbance 4 state of weakness, illness, caused by physical or mental shock 5 paralytic stroke 6 collision 7 effect on sensory nerves of electric discharge **shocking** adj 1 causing horror, disgust or astonishment 2 (Inf) very bad

shock² n mass of hair

shoddy adj -dier, -diest worthless, trashy

shoe n 1 covering for foot, not enclosing ankle 2 metal rim put on horse's hoof 3 various protective plates or undercoverings ▷ v 4 protect, furnish with shoe(s)

shonky adj -kier, -kiest (Aust & NZ, Inf) unreliable or unsound

shoo interj go away!

shoot ❶ v shooting, shot 1 wound, kill with missile fired from weapon 2 discharge weapon 3 send, slide, push rapidly 4 photograph, film 5 hunt 6 sprout ▷ n 7 young branch, sprout 8 hunting expedition

shop ❶ n 1 place for retail sale of goods and services 2 workshop, works building ▷ v 3 visit shops to buy **shoplifter** n one who steals from shop **shopsoiled** adj damaged from being displayed in shop

shore¹ ❶ n edge of sea or lake

shore² v prop (up)

short ❶ adj 1 not long 2 not tall 3 brief 4 not enough 5 lacking 6 abrupt ▷ adv 7 abruptly 8 without reaching end ▷ n 9 drink of spirits 10 short film ▷ pl 11 short trousers **shortage** n deficiency **shorten** v **shortly** adv 1 soon 2 briefly **shortbread, shortcake** n crumbly biscuit made with butter

trembling, flutter

shock¹ n = **upset**, blow, trauma, bombshell, turn (Inf); = **impact**, blow, clash, collision ▷ v = **shake**, stun, stagger, jolt, stupefy; = **horrify**, appal, disgust, revolt, sicken

shoot v = **open fire on**, blast (Sl), hit, kill, plug (Sl); = **fire**, launch, discharge, propel, hurl; = **speed**, race, rush, charge, fly ▷ n = **sprout**, branch, bud, sprig, offshoot

shop n = **store**, supermarket,

boutique, emporium, hypermarket

shore¹ n = **beach**, coast, sands, strand (Poet), seashore

short adj = **brief**, fleeting, momentary ≠ **long**; = **concise**, brief, succinct, summary, compressed ≠ **lengthy**; = **small**, little, squat, diminutive, petite ≠ **tall**; = **abrupt**, sharp, terse, curt, brusque ≠ **polite**; = **scarce**, wanting, low, limited, lacking ≠ **plentiful** ▷ adv = **abruptly**, suddenly, without warning ≠ **gradually**

short circuit (*Electricity*) connection, often accidental, of low resistance between two parts of circuit **shortcoming** n failing **short cut** quicker route or method **shorthand** n method of rapid writing

short list list of candidates from which final choice will be made **short-sighted** adj 1 unable to see faraway things clearly 2 lacking in foresight

shot ❶ n 1 act of shooting 2 small lead pellets 3 marksman 4 (*Inf*) attempt 5 photograph 6 dose 7 (*Inf*) injection **shotgun** n gun for firing shot at short range **shot put** contest in which athletes throw heavy metal ball

should past tense of SHALL

shoulder ❶ n 1 part of body to which arm or foreleg is attached 2 anything resembling shoulder 3 side of road ▷ v 4 undertake 5 put on one's shoulder 6 make way by pushing

shout ❶ n/v (utter) loud cry
shove ❶ v/n push
shovel ❶ n 1 instrument for scooping earth etc. ▷ v 2 lift, move (as) with shovel

show ❶ v **showing, showed, shown** 1 expose to view 2 point out 3 explain 4 prove 5 guide 6 appear 7 be noticeable ▷ n 8 display 9 entertainment 10 ostentation 11 pretence **showy** adj 1 gaudy 2 ostentatious **show business** the entertainment industry

showcase n 1 glass case to display objects 2 situation in which thing is displayed to best advantage **showdown** n confrontation **showman** n one skilled at presenting anything effectively **show off** 1 exhibit to invite admiration 2 behave in this way **show-off** n **showroom** n room in which goods for sale are displayed

shower ❶ n 1 short fall of rain 2 anything falling like rain 3 kind of

shot n = **discharge**, gunfire, crack, blast, explosion; = **ammunition**, bullet, slug, pellet, projectile; = **marksman**, shooter, markswoman; (*Inf*) = **strike**, throw, lob

shoulder v = **bear**, carry, take on, accept, assume; = **push**, elbow, shove, jostle, press

shout v = **cry (out)**, call (out), yell, scream, roar ▷ n = **cry**, call, yell, scream, roar

shove v = **push**, thrust, elbow, drive, press

shovel v = **move**, scoop, dredge, load, heap

show v = **indicate**, demonstrate, prove, reveal, display ≠ **disprove**; = **display**, exhibit; = **guide**, lead, conduct, accompany, direct; = **demonstrate**, describe, explain, teach, illustrate; = **express**, display, reveal, indicate, register ≠ **hide** ▷ n = **display**, sight, spectacle, array; = **exhibition**, fair, display, parade, pageant; = **appearance**, display, pose, parade

shower v = **cover**, dust, spray,

bath in which person stands under water spray ▷ v **4** bestow liberally **5** take bath in shower

shrapnel n shell splinters

shred ❶ n **1** fragment, torn strip ▷ v **2** cut, tear to shreds

shrew n **1** animal like mouse **2** bad-tempered woman

shrewd ❷ adj **1** astute **2** crafty

shriek ❸ n/v (utter) piercing cry

shrill adj piercing, sharp in tone

shrimp n **1** small edible crustacean **2** (Inf) undersized person

shrine n place of worship, usu. associated with saint

shrink ❹ v shrinking, shrank **1** become smaller **2** recoil **3** make smaller **shrinkage** n

shrivel v -elling, -elled shrink and wither

shroud ❺ n **1** wrapping for corpse **2** anything which envelops like a shroud ▷ v **3** put shroud on **4** veil

shrub n bush, woody plant

shrubbery n/pl -beries

shrug v shrugging, shrugged **1** raise (shoulders) as sign of indifference, ignorance etc. ▷ v **2** shrugging

shudder ❶ v **1** shake, tremble violently ▷ n **2** shuddering

shuffle ❶ v **1** move feet without lifting them **2** mix (cards) ▷ n **3** shuffling **4** rearrangement

shun ❶ v shunning, shunned keep away from

shunt v **1** push aside **2** move (train) from one line to another

shut ❶ v shutting, shut **1** close **2** forbid entrance to **shutter** n **1** movable window screen **2** device in camera admitting light as required

shuttle ❶ n **1** bobbin-like device to hold thread in weaving, sewing etc. **2** plane, bus etc. travelling to and fro

shuttlecock n cone with feathers, struck to and fro in badminton

--- THESAURUS ---

sprinkle

shred n = **strip**, bit, piece, scrap, fragment; = **particle**, trace, scrap, grain, atom

shrewd adj = **astute**, clever, sharp, keen, smart ≠ **naive**

shriek n = **scream**, cry, yell, screech, squeal

shrink v = **decrease**, dwindle, lessen, grow or get smaller, contract ≠ **grow**

shroud n = **winding sheet**, grave clothes; = **covering**, veil, mantle, screen, pall ▷ v = **conceal**, cover, screen, hide, blanket

shudder v = **shiver**, shake, tremble, quake, quiver ▷ n = **shiver**, tremor, quiver, spasm

shuffle v = **shamble**, stagger, stumble, dodder; = **scuffle**, drag, scrape; = **rearrange**, jumble, mix, disorder, disarrange

shun v = **avoid**, steer clear of, keep away from

shut v = **close**, secure, fasten, seal, slam ≠ **open**

shuttle v = **go back and forth**, commute, go to and fro, alternate

shy¹ ❶ adj **1** timid, bashful
2 lacking ▷ v **3** start back in fear
4 show sudden reluctance ▷ n
5 start of fear by horse
shy² n/v throw
sibilant adj/n hissing (sound)
sibling n brother or sister
sick ❶ adj **1** inclined to vomit
2 not well or healthy **3** (Inf)
macabre **4** (Inf) bored **5** (Inf)
disgusted **sicken** v **1** make,
become sick **2** disgust **sickly** adj
1 unhealthy **2** inducing nausea
sickness n
sickle n reaping hook
side ❶ n **1** one of the surfaces of
object that is to right or left
2 aspect **3** faction ▷ adj **4** at, in
the side **5** subordinate ▷ v **6** (usu.
with with) take up cause of **siding**
n short line of rails from main line
sideboard n piece of dining room
furniture **sideburns** pl n man's
side whiskers **side effect**

additional undesirable effect
sidekick n (Inf) close associate
sidelong adj **1** not directly
forward ▷ adv **2** obliquely
sidestep v avoid **sidetrack** v
divert from main topic **sideways**
adv to or from the side
sidewalk n (US & Canad) paved
path for pedestrians
sidle v **1** move in furtive or stealthy
manner **2** move sideways
siege n besieging of town
siesta n rest, sleep in afternoon
sieve n **1** device with perforated
bottom ▷ v **2** sift **3** strain
sift ❶ v separate coarser portion
from finer
sigh v/n (utter) long audible
breath
sight ❶ n **1** faculty of seeing
2 thing seen **3** glimpse **4** device
for guiding eye **5** spectacle ▷ v
6 catch sight of **7** adjust sights on
gun etc. **sightseeing** n visiting

shy¹ adj **= timid**, self-conscious,
bashful, retiring, shrinking
≠ confident; = cautious, wary,
hesitant, suspicious, distrustful
≠ reckless ▷ v sometimes with **off**
or **away = recoil**, flinch, draw back,
start, balk
sick adj **= unwell**, ill, poorly (Inf),
diseased, ailing **≠ well**;
= nauseous, ill, queasy, nauseated;
= tired, bored, fed up, weary, jaded;
(Inf) **= morbid**, sadistic, black,
macabre, ghoulish
side n **= border**, margin, boundary,
verge, flank **≠ middle; = face**,
surface, facet; **= party**, camp,

faction, cause; **= point of view**,
viewpoint, position, opinion,
angle; **= team**, squad, line-up
▷ adj **= subordinate**, minor,
secondary, subsidiary, lesser
≠ main
sift v **= part**, filter, strain, separate,
sieve; **= examine**, investigate, go
through, research, analyse
sight n **= vision**, eyes, eyesight,
seeing, eye; **= spectacle**, show,
scene, display, exhibition; **= view**,
range of vision, visibility; (Inf)
= eyesore, mess, monstrosity ▷ v
= spot, see, observe, distinguish,
perceive

S

places of interest

sign ❶ n 1 mark, gesture etc. to convey some meaning 2 (board bearing) notice etc. 3 symbol 4 omen ▷ v 5 put one's signature to 6 make sign or gesture

signal ❶ n 1 sign to convey order or information 2 (Radio) sequence of electrical impulses transmitted or received ▷ adj 3 remarkable ▷ v 4 make signals to 5 give orders etc. by signals

signatory n, pl **-ries** one of those who signs agreements, treaties

signature n person's name written by himself **signature tune** tune used to introduce television or radio programme

signet n small seal

significant ❶ adj 1 revealing 2 designed to make something known 3 important **significance** n

signify ❶ v **-fying, -fied** 1 mean 2 indicate 3 imply 4 be of importance

silage n fodder crop stored in state

of partial fermentation

silence ❶ n 1 absence of noise 2 refraining from speech ▷ v 3 make silent 4 put a stop to

silencer n device to reduce noise of engine exhaust, gun etc. **silent** adj

silhouette ❶ n 1 outline of object seen against light ▷ v 2 show in silhouette

silica n naturally occurring dioxide of silicon

silicon n brittle metal-like element found in sand, clay, stone **silicon chip** tiny wafer of silicon used in electronics

silk n 1 fibre made by silkworms 2 thread, fabric made from this **silky** adj **silkworm** n larva of certain moth

sill n ledge beneath window

silly ❶ adj **-lier, -liest** 1 foolish 2 trivial

silo n, pl **-los** pit, tower for storing fodder

silt n 1 mud deposited by water ▷ v 2 fill, be choked with silt

—— THESAURUS ——

sign n = **symbol**, mark, device, logo, badge; = **notice**, board, warning, placard; = **indication**, evidence, mark, signal, symptom ▷ v = **gesture**, indicate, signal, beckon, gesticulate; = **autograph**, initial, inscribe

signal n = **flare**, beam, beacon ▷ v = **gesture**, sign, wave, indicate, motion

significant adj = **important**, serious, material, vital, critical ≠ **insignificant**; = **meaningful**,

expressive, eloquent, indicative, suggestive ≠ **meaningless**

signify v = **indicate**, mean, suggest, imply, intimate

silence n = **quiet**, peace, calm, hush, lull ≠ **noise**; = **reticence**, dumbness, taciturnity, muteness ≠ **speech** ▷ v = **quieten**, still, quiet, cut off, stifle ≠ **make louder**

silhouette n = **outline**, form, shape, profile ▷ v = **outline**, etch

silly adj = **stupid**, ridiculous, absurd, daft, inane ≠ **clever**

S

silver n **1** white precious metal
2 silver coins **3** cutlery ▷ adj
4 made of or resembling silver
or its colour **silvery** adj

similar 𝗶 adj resembling, like
similarity n likeness

simile n comparison of one thing
with another

simmer 𝗶 v **1** keep or be just
below boiling point **2** be in state of
suppressed rage

simper v smile, utter in silly or
affected way

simple 𝗶 adj not complicated
2 plain **3** not complex **4** ordinary
5 stupid **simpleton** n foolish
person **simplicity** n **simplify** v
make simple, plain or easy **simply**
adv

simulate 𝗶 v **1** make pretence of
2 reproduce **simulation** n

simultaneous 𝗶 adj occurring at
the same time

sin 𝗶 n **1** breaking of divine or
moral law or principle ▷ v

2 commit sin **sinful** adj **sinner** n

since prep **1** during period of time
after ▷ conj **2** from time when
3 because ▷ adv **4** from that time

sincere 𝗶 adj **1** not hypocritical
2 genuine **sincerity** n

sine n in a right-angled triangle,
ratio of opposite side to hypotenuse

sinew n tough, fibrous cord joining
muscle to bone

sing 𝗶 v **singing, sang, sung**
1 utter (sounds, words) with
musical modulation **2** hum, ring
3 celebrate in song **singer** n

singe v **singeing, singed** burn
surface of

single 𝗶 adj **1** one only
2 unmarried **3** for one **4** denoting
ticket for outward journey only ▷ n
5 single thing ▷ v **6** pick (out)
single file persons in one line
single-handed adj without
assistance **single-minded** adj
having one aim only

singlet n sleeveless undervest

──────────── THESAURUS ────────────

similar adj = **alike**, resembling,
comparable ≠ **different**

simmer v = **fume**, seethe,
smoulder, rage, be angry

simple adj = **uncomplicated**,
clear, plain, understandable, lucid
≠ **complicated**; = **easy**,
straightforward, not difficult,
effortless, painless; = **plain**,
natural, classic, unfussy,
unembellished ≠ **elaborate**;
= **pure**, mere, sheer, unalloyed;
= **artless**, innocent, naive, natural,
sincere ≠ **sophisticated**

simulate v = **pretend**, act, feign,

affect, put on

simultaneous adj = **coinciding**,
concurrent, contemporaneous,
coincident, synchronous

sin n = **wickedness**, evil, crime,
error, transgression ▷ v
= **transgress**, offend, lapse, err, go
astray

sincere adj = **honest**, genuine,
real, true, serious ≠ **false**

sing v = **croon**, carol, chant,
warble, yodel; = **trill**, chirp, warble

single adj = **one**, sole, lone,
solitary, only; = **individual**,
separate, distinct; = **unmarried**,

DICTIONARY

singular ❶ *adj* **1** remarkable **2** unique **3** denoting one person or thing

sinister ❶ *adj* **1** threatening **2** evil-looking **3** wicked

sink ❶ *v* **sinking, sank, sunk 1** become submerged **2** drop **3** decline **4** penetrate (into) **5** cause to sink **6** make by digging out **7** invest ▷ *n* **8** fixed basin with waste pipe

sinuous *adj* curving

sinus *n* cavity in bone, esp. of skull

sip ❶ *v* **sipping, sipped 1** drink in very small portions ▷ *n* **2** amount sipped

siphon *n/v* (device to) draw liquid from container

sir *n* polite term of address for man

sire *n* **1** male parent, esp. of horse or domestic animal ▷ *v* **2** father

siren *n* device making loud wailing noise

sirloin *n* prime cut of beef

sis *interj* (*S Afr, Inf*) exclamation of disgust

sissy *adj/n, pl* **-sies** weak, cowardly (person)

sister *n* **1** daughter of same parents **2** woman fellow-member **3** senior nurse **sister-in-law** *n/pl* **sisters-in-law 1** sister of husband or wife **2** sibling's wife

sit ❶ *v* **sitting, sat 1** rest on buttocks, thighs **2** perch **3** pose for portrait **4** hold session **5** remain **6** take examination **7** keep watch over baby etc.

sitar *n* stringed musical instrument of India

site ❶ *n* **1** place, space for building ▷ *v* **2** provide with site

situate *v* place **situation** *n* **1** position **2** state of affairs **3** employment

six *adj/n* cardinal number one more than five **sixth** *adj* ordinal number **sixteen** *n/adj* six and ten **sixteenth** *adj* **sixtieth** *adj* **sixty** *n/adj* six times ten

size ❶ *n* **1** dimensions **2** one of series of standard measurements

THESAURUS

free, unattached, unwed; = **separate**, individual, exclusive, undivided, unshared

singular *adj* = **single**, individual; = **remarkable**, outstanding, exceptional, notable, eminent ≠ **ordinary**; = **unusual**, odd, strange, extraordinary, curious ≠ **conventional**

sinister *adj* = **threatening**, evil, menacing, dire, ominous ≠ **reassuring**

sink *v* = **go down**, founder, go under, submerge, capsize;

= **slump**, drop; = **fall**, drop, slip, plunge, subside; = **drop**, fall; = **stoop**, be reduced to, lower yourself

sip *v* = **drink**, taste, sample, sup ▷ *n* = **swallow**, drop, taste, thimbleful

sit *v* = **take a seat**, perch, settle down; = **place**, set, put, position, rest; = **be a member of**, serve on, have a seat on, preside on

site *n* = **area**, plot ▷ *v* = **locate**, put, place, set, position

size *n* = **dimensions**, extent, range, amount, mass

S

▷ v **3** arrange according to size
sizable adj quite large **size up** v (Inf) assess
sizzle 🟊 v/n (make) hissing, spluttering sound as of frying
skate¹ n **1** steel blade attached to boot ▷ v **2** glide as on skates **skateboard** n small board mounted on roller-skate wheels
skate² n large marine ray
skein n quantity of yarn, wool etc. in loose knot
skeleton 🟊 n **1** bones of animal **2** framework ▷ adj **3** reduced to a minimum
sketch 🟊 n **1** rough drawing **2** short humorous play ▷ v **3** make sketch (of) **sketchy** adj
skew adj/v (make) slanting or crooked
skewer n pin to fasten meat
ski n **1** long runner fastened to foot for sliding over snow or water ▷ v **2** slide on skis
skid v skidding, skidded **1** slide (sideways) ▷ n **2** instance of this
skill 🟊 n practical ability, cleverness, dexterity **skilful** adj **skilled** adj

skim 🟊 v skimming, skimmed **1** remove floating matter from surface of liquid **2** glide over lightly and rapidly **3** read quickly
skimp v **1** give short measure **2** do imperfectly **skimpy** adj scanty
skin 🟊 n **1** outer covering of body **2** animal hide **3** fruit rind ▷ v **4** remove skin of **skinless** adj **skinny** adj thin **skinflint** n miser
skint adj (Sl) having no money
skip¹ 🟊 v skipping, skipped **1** leap lightly **2** jump over rope **3** pass over, omit ▷ n **4** act of skipping
skip² n skipping, skipped large open container for builders' rubbish etc.
skipper n captain of ship
skirmish 🟊 n **1** small battle ▷ v **2** fight briefly
skirt 🟊 n **1** woman's garment hanging from waist **2** lower part of dress, coat etc. ▷ v **3** border **4** go round **skirting board** narrow board round bottom of wall
skit n satire, esp. theatrical
skite v/n (Aust & NZ) boast
skittish adj frisky, frivolous
skive v evade work

THESAURUS

sizzle v = **hiss**, spit, crackle, fry, frizzle
skeleton n = **bones**, bare bones
sketch n = **drawing**, design, draft, delineation ▷ v = **draw**, outline, represent, draft, depict
skill n = **expertise**, ability, proficiency, art, technique ≠ **clumsiness**
skim v = **remove**, separate, cream;

= **glide**, fly, coast, sail, float; usually with **over** or **through** = **scan**, glance, run your eye over
skin n = **hide**, pelt, fell; = **peel**, rind, husk, casing, outside
skip¹ v = **hop**, dance, bob, trip, bounce; = **miss out**, omit, leave out, overlook, pass over
skirt v = **border**, edge, flank; often with **around** or **round** = **go round**, circumvent

S

skivvy n, pl **-vies** servant who does menial work

skookum adj (Canad) powerful or big

skulduggery n (Inf) trickery

skulk v sneak out of the way

skull n bony case enclosing brain

skunk n small N Amer. animal which emits evil-smelling fluid

sky ❶ n, pl **skies** 1 expanse extending upwards from the horizon 2 outer space **skylark** n bird that sings while soaring at great height **skylight** n window in roof or ceiling **skyscraper** n very tall building

slab ❶ n thick, broad piece

slack ❶ adj 1 loose 2 careless 3 not busy ▷ n 4 loose part ▷ v 5 be idle or lazy **slacken** n 1 become looser 2 become slower

slag n refuse of smelted metal

slake v satisfy (thirst)

slalom n skiing race over winding course

slam ❶ v **slamming, slammed** 1 shut noisily 2 bang ▷ n 3 (noise of) this action

slang n colloquial language

slant ❶ v 1 slope 2 write, present (news etc.) with bias ▷ n 3 slope 4 point of view **slanting** adj

slap ❶ n 1 blow with open hand or flat instrument ▷ v 2 strike thus 3 (Inf) put down carelessly **slapdash** adj careless, hasty **slapstick** n boisterous knockabout comedy

slash v/n 1 gash 2 cut

slat n narrow strip

slate ❶ n 1 stone which splits easily in flat sheets 2 piece of this for covering roof ▷ v 3 cover with slates 4 abuse

slaughter ❶ n 1 killing ▷ v 2 kill **slaughterhouse** n place where animals are killed for food

sky n = **heavens**, firmament

slab n = **piece**, slice, lump, chunk, wedge

slack adj = **limp**, relaxed, loose, lax; = **loose**, baggy ≠ **taut**; = **slow**, quiet, inactive, dull, sluggish ≠ **busy**; = **negligent**, lazy, lax, idle, inactive ≠ **strict** ▷ v = **shirk**, idle, dodge, skive (Brit Sl) ▷ n = **surplus**, excess, glut, surfeit, superabundance

slam v = **bang**, crash, smash; = **throw**, dash, hurl, fling

slant v = **slope**, incline, tilt, list, bend; = **bias**, colour, twist, angle, distort ▷ n = **slope**, incline, tilt,

gradient, camber; = **bias**, emphasis, prejudice, angle, point of view

slap v = **smack**, beat, clap, cuff, swipe ▷ n = **smack**, blow, cuff, swipe, spank

slash v = **cut**, slit, gash, lacerate, score; = **reduce**, cut, decrease, drop, lower ▷ n = **cut**, slit, gash, rent, rip

slate v (Inf, chiefly Brit) = **criticize**, censure, rebuke, scold, tear into (Inf)

slaughter v = **kill**, murder, massacre, destroy, execute ▷ n = **slaying**, killing, murder, massacre, bloodshed

S

slave ❶ n 1 captive, person without freedom or personal rights ▷ v 2 work like slave **slavery** n **slavish** adj servile

slaver v/n (dribble) saliva from mouth

slay ❶ v slaying, slew, slain kill

sleazy adj -zier, -ziest sordid

sledge¹ n 1 carriage on runners for sliding on snow 2 toboggan ▷ v 3 move on sledge

sledge² n heavy hammer with long handle

sleek ❶ adj glossy, smooth, shiny

sleep ❶ n 1 unconscious state regularly occurring in man and animals 2 slumber, repose ▷ v 3 take rest in sleep **sleeper** n 1 one who sleeps 2 beam supporting rails 3 railway sleeping car **sleepless** adj **sleepy** adj

sleet n rain and snow falling together

sleeve n part of garment which covers arm

sleigh n sledge

slender ❶ adj 1 slim, slight 2 small in amount

sleuth n detective

slice ❶ n 1 thin flat piece cut off 2 share ▷ v 3 cut into slices

slick ❶ adj 1 smooth 2 glib 3 skilful ▷ v 4 make glossy, smooth ▷ n 5 slippery area 6 patch of oil on water

slide ❶ v sliding, slid 1 slip smoothly along 2 glide 3 pass ▷ n 4 sliding 5 track for sliding 6 glass mount for object to be viewed under microscope 7 photographic transparency

slight ❶ adj 1 small, trifling 2 slim ▷ v 3 disregard ▷ n 4 act of discourtesy **slightly** adv

slim ❶ adj slimmer, slimmest 1 thin 2 slight ▷ v 3 reduce weight

THESAURUS

slave n = **servant**, serf, vassal; = **drudge**, skivvy (chiefly Brit) ▷ v = **toil**, drudge, slog

slay v (Archaic or Lit) = **kill**, slaughter, massacre, butcher

sleek adj = **glossy**, shiny, lustrous, smooth ≠ **shaggy**

sleep n = **slumber(s)**, nap, doze, snooze (Inf), hibernation ▷ v = **slumber**, doze, snooze (Inf), hibernate, take a nap

slender adj = **slim**, narrow, slight, lean, willowy ≠ **chubby**; = **faint**, slight, remote, slim, thin ≠ **strong**

slice n = **piece**, segment, portion, wedge, sliver ▷ v = **cut**, divide, carve, sever, dissect

slick adj = **skilful**, deft, adroit, dexterous, professional ≠ **clumsy**; = **glib**, smooth, plausible, polished, specious ▷ v = **smooth**, sleek, plaster down

slide v = **slip**, slither, glide, skim, coast

slight adj = **small**, minor, insignificant, trivial, feeble ≠ **large**; = **slim**, small, delicate, spare, fragile ≠ **sturdy** ▷ n = **insult**, snub, affront, rebuff, slap in the face (Inf) ≠ **compliment**

slim adj = **slender**, slight, trim, thin, narrow ≠ **chubby**; = **slight**, remote, faint, slender ≠ **strong** ▷ v = **lose weight**, diet ≠ **put on**

slime n thick, liquid mud **slimy** adj 1 of, like, covered in slime 2 insincerely pleasant

sling ❶ n 1 loop for hurling stone 2 bandage for supporting wounded limb 3 rope for hoisting weights ▷ v 4 throw

slink v **slinking, slunk** move stealthily, sneak

slip ❶ v **slipping, slipped** 1 (cause to) move smoothly 2 pass out of (mind etc.) 3 lose balance by sliding 4 fall from person's grasp 5 (usu. with up) make mistake 6 put on or take off easily, quickly ▷ n 7 act or occasion of slipping 8 mistake 9 petticoat 10 small piece of paper **slipshod** adj slovenly, careless **slipstream** n stream of air forced backwards by fast-moving object

slipper n light shoe for indoors

slippery ❶ adj 1 so smooth as to cause slipping or to be difficult to hold 2 unreliable

slit ❶ v 1 make long straight cut in ▷ n 2 long straight cut

slither v slide unsteadily (down slope etc.)

sliver n splinter

slob n (Inf) lazy, untidy person

slobber v/n slaver

slog v **slogging, slogged** 1 hit vigorously 2 work doggedly ▷ n 3 struggle

slogan ❶ n distinctive phrase

slop v **slopping, slopped** 1 spill, splash ▷ n 2 liquid spilt 3 liquid food ▷ pl 4 liquid refuse **sloppy** adj careless, untidy

slope ❶ v 1 be, place at slant ▷ n 2 slant

slot ❶ n 1 narrow hole 2 slit for coins 3 place in series ▷ v 4 put in slot 5 (Inf) place in series

sloth n 1 S Amer. animal 2 sluggishness **slothful** adj

slouch v 1 walk, sit etc. in drooping manner ▷ n 2 drooping posture

slovenly adj dirty, untidy

slow ❶ adj 1 lasting a long time

weight

sling v (Inf) = **throw**, cast, toss, hurl, fling; = **hang**, suspend

slip v = **fall**, skid; = **slide**, slither; = **sneak**, creep, steal ▷ n = **mistake**, failure, error, blunder, lapse

slippery adj = **smooth**, icy, greasy, glassy, slippy (Inf or dialect); = **untrustworthy**, tricky, cunning, dishonest, devious

slit v = **cut (open)**, rip, slash, knife, pierce ▷ n = **cut**, gash, incision, tear, rent

slogan n = **catch phrase**, motto, tag-line, catchword

slope n = **inclination**, rise, incline, tilt, slant ▷ v = **slant**, incline, drop away, fall, rise

slot n = **opening**, hole, groove, vent, slit; (Inf) = **place**, time, space, opening, position ▷ v = **fit**, insert

slow adj = **unhurried**, sluggish, leisurely, lazy, ponderous ≠ **quick**; = **prolonged**, protracted, long-drawn-out, lingering, gradual; = **late**, behind, tardy ▷ v often with **down** = **decelerate**,

2 moving at low speed **3** dull ▷ *v* **4** slacken speed (of) **slowly** *adv*

sludge *n* thick mud

slug¹ *n* **1** land snail with no shell **2** bullet **sluggish** *adj* **1** slow, inert **2** not functioning well

slug² *v* **1** hit, slog ▷ *n* **2** heavy blow **3** portion of spirits

sluice *n* gate, door to control flow of water

slum ① *n* squalid street or neighbourhood

slumber *v/n* sleep

slump ① *v* **1** fall heavily **2** relax ungracefully **3** decline suddenly ▷ *n* **4** sudden decline

slur ① *v* **1** slurring, slurred **1** pass over lightly **2** run together (words) **3** disparage ▷ *n* **4** slight

slurp (*Inf*) ▷ *v* **1** eat or drink noisily ▷ *n* **2** slurping sound

slurry *n*, *pl* **-ries** muddy liquid

mixture, as in cement

slush *n* watery, muddy substance

slut *n* dirty (immoral) woman

sly ① *adj* **slyer, slyest 1** cunning **2** deceitful

smack¹ ① *v* **1** slap **2** open and close (lips) loudly ▷ *n* **3** slap **4** such sound **5** loud kiss ▷ *adv* **6** (*Inf*) squarely

smack² *n* **1** taste, flavour ▷ *v* **2** taste (of) **3** suggest

small ① *adj* **1** little, unimportant **2** short ▷ *n* **3** small slender part, esp. of the back **smallholding** *n* small area of farmland **smallpox** *n* contagious disease

smart ① *adj* **1** astute **2** clever **3** well-dressed ▷ *v* **4** feel, cause pain ▷ *n* **5** sharp pain **smarten** *v* make or become smart

smash ① *v* **1** break **2** ruin **3** destroy ▷ *n* **4** heavy blow

brake

slum *n* = **hovel**, ghetto, shanty

slump *v* = **fall**, sink, plunge, crash, collapse ≠ **increase**; = **sag**, hunch, droop, slouch, loll ▷ *n* = **fall**, drop, decline, crash, collapse ≠ **increase**; = **recession**, depression, stagnation, inactivity, hard *or* bad times

slur *n* = **insult**, stain, smear, affront, innuendo

sly *adj* = **roguish**, knowing, arch, mischievous, impish; = **cunning**, scheming, devious, secret, clever ≠ **open** = **secret**, furtive, stealthy, covert

smack¹ *v* = **slap**, hit, strike, clap, cuff ▷ *n* = **slap**, blow, cuff, swipe,

spank ▷ *adv* (*Inf*) = **directly**, right, straight, squarely, precisely

small *adj* = **little**, minute, tiny, mini, miniature ≠ **big**; = **unimportant**, minor, trivial, insignificant, little ≠ **important**; = **modest**, humble, unpretentious ≠ **grand**

smart *adj* = **chic**, trim, neat, stylish, elegant ≠ **scruffy**; = **clever**, bright, intelligent, quick, sharp ≠ **stupid**; = **brisk**, quick, lively, vigorous ≠ **sting**, burn, hurt

smash *v* = **break**, crush, shatter, crack, demolish; ≠ **shatter**, break, disintegrate, crack, splinter; = **collide**, crash, meet head-on, clash, come into collision ▷ *n*

5 collision **smashing** *adj* (*Inf*) excellent

smattering *n* slight superficial knowledge

smear ❶ *v* **1** rub with grease etc. **2** smudge **3** slander ▷ *n* **4** greasy mark **5** slander

smell ❶ *v* **smelling, smelt** **1** perceive by nose **2** give out odour ▷ *n* **3** faculty of perceiving odours **4** anything detected by sense of smell **smelly** *adj* having nasty smell

smelt *v* extract metal from ore

smile *n* **1** curving or parting of lips in pleased or amused expression ▷ *v* **2** give smile

smirk *n* **1** smile expressing scorn, smugness ▷ *v* **2** give smirk

smite *v* **smiting, smote, smitten** **1** strike **2** afflict

smith *n* worker in iron, gold etc. **smithy** *n* blacksmith's workshop

smithereens *pl n* shattered fragments

smock *n* loose, outer garment

smog *n* mixture of smoke and fog

smoke ❶ *n* **1** cloudy mass that rises from fire etc. ▷ *v* **2** give off smoke **3** inhale and expel tobacco smoke **4** expose to smoke **smoker** *n* **smoky** *adj* **smoke screen** thing intended to hide truth

smooth ❶ *adj* **1** not rough, even **2** calm **3** unctuous ▷ *v* **4** make smooth

smother ❶ *v* suffocate

smoulder *v* **1** burn slowly **2** (of feelings) be suppressed

smudge *v/n* (make) smear, stain (on)

smug ❶ *adj* **smugger, smuggest** self-satisfied, complacent

smuggle *v* import, export without paying customs duties **smuggler** *n*

smut *n* **1** piece of soot **2** obscene talk etc. **smutty** *adj*

snack ❶ *n* light, hasty meal

snag ❶ *n* **1** difficulty **2** sharp

= **collision**, crash, accident

smear *v* = **spread over**, daub, rub on, cover, coat; = **slander**, malign, blacken, besmirch; = **smudge**, soil, dirty, stain, sully ▷ *n* = **smudge**, daub, streak, blot, blotch; = **slander**, libel, defamation, calumny

smell *n* = **odour**, scent, fragrance, perfume, bouquet ▷ *v* = **stink**, reek, pong (*Brit Inf*); = **sniff**, scent

smooth *adj* = **even**, level, flat, plane, flush ≠ **uneven**; = **sleek**, polished, shiny, glossy, silky ≠ **rough**; = **mellow**, pleasant, mild, agreeable; = **flowing**, steady,

regular, uniform, rhythmic; = **easy**, effortless, well-ordered ▷ *v* = **flatten**, level, press, plane, iron; = **ease**, facilitate ≠ **hinder**

smother *v* = **extinguish**, put out, stifle, snuff; = **suffocate**, choke, strangle, stifle; = **suppress**, stifle, repress, hide, conceal

smug *adj* = **self-satisfied**, superior, complacent, conceited

snack *n* = **light meal**, bite, refreshment(s)

snag *n* = **difficulty**, hitch, problem, obstacle, catch ▷ *v* = **catch**, tear, rip protuberance **3** hole, loop in fabric ▷ v **4** catch, damage on snag

snail n v **1** slow-moving mollusc with shell

snake n **1** long scaly limbless reptile ▷ v **2** move like snake

snap ❶ v **snapping, snapped** **1** break suddenly **2** make cracking sound **3** bite (at) suddenly **4** speak suddenly, angrily ▷ n **5** act of snapping **6** fastener **7** card game **8** (Inf) snapshot ▷ adj **9** sudden, unplanned **snappy** adj **1** irritable **2** (Sl) quick **3** (Sl) fashionable **snapshot** n photograph

snare ❶ n/v trap

snarl n **1** growl of angry dog **2** tangle ▷ v **3** utter snarl

snatch ❶ v **1** make quick grab (at) **2** seize, catch ▷ n **3** grab **4** fragment

sneak ❶ v **1** move about furtively **2** act in underhand manner ▷ n **3** petty informer **sneaking** adj **1** secret **2** slight but persistent

sneakers pl n (US & Canad) canvas shoes with rubber soles

sneer ❶ n **1** scornful, contemptuous expression or

remark ▷ v **2** give sneer

sneeze v **1** emit breath through nose with sudden involuntary spasm and noise ▷ n **2** act of sneezing

snide adj malicious, supercilious

sniff ❶ v **1** inhale through nose with sharp hiss **2** smell **3** (with at) express disapproval etc. ▷ n **4** act of sniffing **sniffle** v sniff noisily, esp. when suffering from a cold

snigger n **1** sly, disrespectful laugh, esp. partly stifled ▷ v **2** produce snigger

snip v **1** snipping, snipped **1** cut with quick stroke ▷ n **2** quick cut **3** (Inf) bargain **snippet** n small piece

snipe n **1** wading bird ▷ v **2** shoot at enemy from cover **3** (with at) criticize **sniper** n

snivel v -elling, -elled **1** sniffle to show distress **2** whine

snob n one who pretentiously judges others by social rank etc. **snobbery** n **snobbish** adj

snooker n game played on table with balls and cues

snoop v **1** pry, meddle **2** peer into

snap v = **break**, crack, separate; = **pop**, click, crackle; = **speak sharply**, bark, lash out at, jump down (someone's) throat (Inf); = **bite at**, bite, nip ▷ adj = **instant**, immediate, sudden, spur-of-the-moment

snare n = **trap**, net, wire, gin, noose ▷ v = **trap**, catch, net, wire, seize

snatch v = **grab**, grip, grasp,

clutch; = **steal**, take, nick (Sl, chiefly Brit), pinch (Inf), lift (Inf) ▷ n = **bit**, part, fragment, piece, snippet

sneak v = **slink**, slip, steal, pad, skulk; = **slip**, smuggle, spirit ▷ n = **informer**, betrayer, telltale, Judas, accuser

sneer v = **scorn**, mock, ridicule, laugh, jeer ▷ n = **scorn**, ridicule, mockery, derision, jeer

sniff v = **breathe in**, inhale

snooty adj **snootier, snootiest** (Sl) haughty

snooze v/n (take) nap

snore v 1 breathe noisily when asleep ▷ n 2 sound of snoring

snorkel n tube for breathing underwater

snort v 1 make (contemptuous) noise by driving breath through nostrils ▷ n 2 act of snorting

snout n animal's nose

snow n 1 frozen vapour which falls in flakes ▷ v 2 fall, sprinkle as snow **snowy** adj **snowball** n 1 snow pressed into hard ball for throwing ▷ v 2 increase rapidly **snowdrift** n bank of deep snow **snowdrop** n small, white, bell-shaped spring flower **snowman** n figure shaped out of snow **snowplough** n vehicle for clearing away snow **snowshoes** pl n racket-shaped shoes for travelling on snow

snub ❶ v **snubbing, snubbed** 1 insult (esp. by ignoring) intentionally ▷ n 2 snubbing ▷ adj 3 short and blunt **snub-nosed** adj

snuff¹ n powdered tobacco

snuff² v extinguish (esp. candle)

snuffle v breathe noisily

snug adj **snugger, snuggest** warm, comfortable

snuggle v lie close to, nestle

so adv 1 to such an extent 2 in such a manner 3 very ▷ conj 4 therefore 5 in order that 6 with the result that ▷ interj 7 well! **so-and-so** n 1 (Inf) person whose name is not specified 2 unpleasant person **so-called** adj called by but doubtfully deserving that name

soak ❶ v 1 steep 2 absorb 3 drench **soaking** n/adj

soap n 1 compound of alkali and oil used in washing ▷ v 2 apply soap to **soapy** adj **soap opera** television, radio serial dealing with domestic themes

soar ❶ v 1 fly high 2 increase rapidly

sob ❶ v **sobbing, sobbed** 1 catch breath, esp. in weeping ▷ n 2 sobbing

sober ❶ adj 1 not drunk 2 temperate 3 subdued 4 dull 5 solemn ▷ v 6 make, become sober **sobriety** n

soccer n game of football, with spherical ball

sociable adj 1 friendly 2 convivial

social ❶ adj 1 living in communities 2 relating to society 3 sociable ▷ n 4 informal gathering **socialize** v **social**

snub v = insult, slight, put down, humiliate, cut (Inf) ▷ n = insult, put-down, affront, slap in the face

soak v = wet, damp, saturate, drench, moisten; = penetrate, permeate, seep

soar v = rise, increase, grow, mount, climb; = fly, wing, climb,

ascend ≠ plunge

sob v = cry, weep, howl, shed tears

sober adj = abstinent, temperate, abstemious, moderate ≠ drunk; = serious, cool, grave, reasonable, steady ≠ frivolous; = plain, dark, sombre, quiet, subdued ≠ bright

social adj = communal,

networking site website that allows subscribers to interact, esp. by forming online communities based around shared interests, experiences, etc.

socialism n political system which advocates public ownership of means of production **socialist** n/adj

society ❶ n, pl **-ties** 1 living associated with others 2 those so living 3 companionship 4 association 5 fashionable people collectively

sociology n study of societies **sociological** adj

sock¹ n cloth covering for foot

sock² (Sl) ▷ v 1 hit ▷ n 2 blow

socket n hole or recess for something to fit into

sod n lump of earth with grass

soda n 1 compound of sodium 2 soda water **soda water** water charged with carbon dioxide

sodden adj soaked

sodium n metallic alkaline element **sodium bicarbonate** compound

used in baking powder

sodomy n anal intercourse

sofa ❶ n upholstered seat with back and arms

soft ❶ adj 1 yielding easily to pressure 2 not hard 3 mild 4 easy 5 subdued 6 quiet 7 gentle 8 (too) lenient **soften** v make, become soft or softer **softly** adv

soft drink nonalcoholic drink

software n computer programs

soggy adj **-gier, -giest** damp and heavy

soil¹ ❶ n earth, ground

soil² v make, become dirty

solace n/v comfort in distress

solar adj of the sun

solarium n, pl **-lariums, -laria** place with beds and ultraviolet lights for acquiring artificial suntan

solder n 1 easily-melted alloy used for joining metal ▷ v 2 join with it

soldier ❶ n 1 one serving in army ▷ v 2 serve in army 3 (with on) persist doggedly

sole¹ ❶ adj one and only **solely** adv

community, collective, group, public ▷ n = **get-together** (Inf), party, gathering, function, reception

society n = **the community**, people, the public, humanity, civilization; = **culture**, community, population; = **organization**, group, club, union, league; = **upper classes**, gentry, elite, high society, beau monde

sofa n = **couch**, settee, divan, chaise longue

soft adj = **velvety**, smooth, silky,

feathery, downy ≠ **rough**; = **yielding**, elastic ≠ **hard**; = **soggy**, swampy, marshy, boggy; = **squashy**, sloppy, mushy, spongy, gelatinous; = **pliable**, flexible, supple, malleable, plastic

soil¹ n = **earth**, ground, clay, dust, dirt; = **territory**, country, land

soil² v = **dirty**, foul, stain, pollute, tarnish ≠ **clean**

soldier n = **fighter**, serviceman, trooper, warrior, man-at-arms

sole¹ adj = **only**, one, single, individual, alone

1 alone **2** only **3** entirely

sole² n **1** underside of foot **2** underpart of boot etc. ▷ v **3** fit with sole

sole³ n small edible flatfish

solemn ❶ adj **1** serious **2** formal **solemnity** n **solemnize** v celebrate, perform

solicit v **-iting, -ited 1** request **2** accost **solicitor** n lawyer who prepares documents, advises clients **solicitous** adj **1** anxious **2** eager **solicitude** n

solid ❶ adj **1** not hollow **2** composed of one substance **3** firm **4** reliable ▷ n **5** body of three dimensions **6** substance not liquid or gas **solidarity** n unity **solidify** v harden

soliloquy n, pl **-quies** (esp. in drama) thoughts spoken by person while alone

solitary ❶ adj alone, single **solitaire** n **1** game for one person **2** single precious stone set by itself **solitude** n state of being alone

solo n, pl **-los 1** music for one performer ▷ adj **2** unaccompanied, alone **soloist** n

solstice n shortest (winter) or longest (summer) day

solve ❶ v **1** work out **2** find answer to **soluble** adj **1** capable of being dissolved in liquid **2** able to be solved **solution** n **1** answer **2** dissolving **3** liquid with something dissolved in it **solvable** adj **solvency** n **solvent** adj **1** able to meet financial obligations ▷ n **2** liquid with power of dissolving

sombre ❶ adj dark, gloomy

sombrero n, pl **-ros** wide-brimmed hat

some adj **1** denoting an indefinite number, amount or extent **2** one or another **3** certain ▷ pron **4** portion, quantity **somebody** pron **1** some person ▷ n **2** important person **somehow** adv by some means **someone** pron somebody **something** pron thing not clearly defined **sometime** adv **1** at some unspecified time ▷ adj **2** former **sometimes** adv occasionally **somewhat** adv rather **somewhere** adv at some unspecified place **somersault** n tumbling head over heels

son n male child **son-in-law** n, pl

THESAURUS

solemn adj = **serious**, earnest, grave, sober, sedate ≠ **cheerful**; = **formal**, grand, grave, dignified, ceremonial ≠ **informal**

solid adj = **firm**, hard, compact, dense, concrete ≠ **unsubstantial**; = **strong**, stable, sturdy, substantial, unshakable ≠ **unstable**; = **reliable**,

dependable, upstanding, worthy, upright ≠ **unreliable**

solitary adj = **unsociable**, reclusive, unsocial, isolated, lonely ≠ **sociable**; = **lone**, alone

solve v = **answer**, work out, resolve, crack, clear up

sombre adj = **gloomy**, sad, sober, grave, dismal ≠ **cheerful**

sons-in-law child's husband

sonar *n* device for detecting underwater objects

sonata *n* piece of music in several movements

song ❶ *n* 1 singing 2 poem etc. for singing

sonic *adj* pert. to sound waves

sonnet *n* fourteen-line poem with definite rhyme scheme

sonorous *adj* giving out (deep) sound, resonant

soon ❶ *adv* 1 in a short time 2 before long 3 early, quickly

soot *n* black powdery substance formed from burning of coal etc. **sooty** *adj*

soothe ❶ *v* 1 make calm, tranquil 2 relieve (pain etc.)

sop *n* 1 piece of bread etc. soaked in liquid 2 bribe ▷ *v* 3 steep in water etc. 4 soak (up) **soppy** *adj* (*Inf*) oversentimental

soporific *adj* causing sleep

soprano *n, pl* **-pranos** highest voice in women and boys

sorbet *n* (fruit-flavoured) water ice

sorcerer *n* magician **sorcery** *n*

sordid *adj* 1 mean, squalid 2 base

sore ❶ *adj* 1 painful 2 causing annoyance ▷ *n* 3 sore place **sorely** *adv* greatly

sorrow ❶ *n/v* (feel) grief, sadness **sorrowful** *adj*

sorry ❶ *adj* **-rier, -riest** 1 feeling pity or regret 2 miserable, wretched

sort ❶ *n* 1 kind, class ▷ *v* 2 classify

sortie *n* sally by besieged forces

SOS *n* 1 international code signal of distress 2 call for help

so-so *adj* (*Inf*) mediocre

soufflé *n* dish of eggs beaten to froth, flavoured and baked

soul ❶ *n* 1 spiritual and immortal part of human being 2 person 3 sensitivity 4 type of Black music **soulful** *adj*

────── THESAURUS ──────

song *n* = **ballad**, air, tune, carol, chant

soon *adv* = **before long**, shortly, in the near future

soothe *v* = **calm**, still, quiet, hush, appease ≠ **upset**; = **relieve**, ease, alleviate, assuage ≠ **irritate**

sore *adj* = **painful**, smarting, raw, tender, burning; = **annoyed**, cross, angry, pained, hurt; = **annoying**, troublesome; (*Lit*) = **urgent**, desperate, extreme, dire, pressing

sorrow *n* = **grief**, sadness, woe, regret, distress ≠ **joy**; = **hardship**, trial, tribulation, affliction, trouble ≠ **good fortune** ▷ *v* = **grieve**,

mourn, lament, be sad, bemoan ≠ **rejoice**

sorry *adj* = **regretful**, apologetic, contrite, repentant, remorseful ≠ **unapologetic**; = **sympathetic**, moved, full of pity, compassionate, commiserative ≠ **unsympathetic**; = **wretched**, miserable, pathetic, mean, poor

sort *n* = **kind**, type, class, make, order ▷ *v* = **arrange**, group, order, rank, divide

soul *n* = **spirit**, essence, life, vital force; = **embodiment**, essence, epitome, personification, quintessence; = **person**, being,

sound¹ ❶ n 1 what is heard
2 noise ▷ v 3 make sound 4 give
impression of 5 utter **soundproof**
adj

sound² ❶ adj 1 in good condition
2 solid 3 of good judgment
4 thorough 5 deep **soundly** adv
thoroughly

sound³ v 1 find depth of, as water
2 ascertain views of 3 probe

sound⁴ ❶ n 1 channel 2 strait

soup n liquid food made by boiling
meat, vegetables etc.

sour ❶ adj 1 acid 2 gone bad
3 peevish 4 disagreeable ▷ v
5 make, become sour

source ❶ n 1 origin, starting point
2 spring

south n 1 point opposite north
2 region, part of country etc. lying
to that side ▷ adj/adv 3 from,
towards or in the south **southerly**
adj/n wind from the south

southern adj **southward** adj
southwards adv

souvenir ❶ n keepsake, memento

sou'wester n seaman's
waterproof headgear

sovereign ❶ n 1 king, queen
2 former gold coin worth 20
shillings ▷ adj 3 supreme
4 efficacious **sovereignty** n

SOW¹ ❶ v sowing, sowed, sown
scatter, plant seed

sow² n female adult pig

soya n plant yielding edible
beans **soya bean** edible bean
used for food and oil **soy sauce**
sauce made from fermented soya
beans

spa n 1 medicinal spring 2 place,
resort with one

space ❶ n 1 extent 2 room
3 period 4 empty places 5 area
6 expanse 7 region beyond earth's
atmosphere ▷ v 8 place at

— THESAURUS —

individual, body, creature

sound¹ n = **noise**, din, report, tone,
reverberation; = **idea**, impression,
drift ▷ v = **toll**, set off; = **resound**,
echo, go off, toll, set off; = **seem**,
seem to be, appear to be

sound² adj = **fit**, healthy, perfect,
intact, unhurt ≠ **frail**; = **sturdy**,
strong, solid, stable; = **sensible**,
wise, reasonable, right, correct
≠ **irresponsible**

sour adj = **sharp**, acid, tart, bitter,
pungent ≠ **sweet**; = **rancid**,
turned, gone off, curdled, gone bad
≠ **fresh**; = **bitter**, tart,
acrimonious, embittered,
disagreeable ≠ **good-natured**

source n = **cause**, origin,
derivation, beginning, author;
= **informant**, authority

souvenir n = **keepsake**, reminder,
memento

sovereign adj = **supreme**, ruling,
absolute, royal, principal;
= **excellent**, efficient, effectual ▷ n
= **monarch**, ruler, king or queen,
chief, potentate

sow¹ v = **scatter**, plant, seed,
implant

space n = **room**, capacity, extent,
margin, scope; = **period**, interval,
time, while, span; = **outer space**,
the universe, the galaxy, the solar
system, the cosmos

S

intervals **spacious** adj roomy, extensive **spacecraft, spaceship** n vehicle for travel beyond earth's atmosphere **spaceman** n astronaut

spade[1] n tool for digging

spade[2] n suit at cards

spaghetti n pasta in long strings

span ① n 1 extent, space 2 stretch of arch etc. 3 space from thumb to little finger ▷ v 4 stretch over 5 measure with hand

spangle n 1 small shiny metallic ornament ▷ v 2 decorate with spangles

spaniel n breed of dog with long ears and silky hair

spank v 1 slap with flat of hand, esp. on buttocks ▷ n 2 spanking

spanner n tool for gripping nut or bolt head

spar ① v **sparring, sparred** 1 box 2 dispute, esp. in fun ▷ n 3 sparring

spare ① v 1 leave unhurt 2 show mercy 3 do without 4 give away ▷ adj 5 additional 6 in reserve

7 thin 8 lean ▷ n 9 reserve copy **sparing** adj economical, careful

spark ① n 1 small glowing or burning particle 2 flash of light produced by electrical discharge 3 trace ▷ v 4 emit sparks 5 kindle

sparkle ① v 1 glitter 2 effervesce ▷ n 3 glitter 4 vitality **sparkling** adj 1 glittering 2 (of wines) effervescent

sparrow n small brownish bird **sparrowhawk** n hawk that hunts small birds

sparse adj thinly scattered

spartan adj strict, austere

spasm n 1 sudden convulsive (muscular) contraction 2 sudden burst of activity etc. **spasmodic** adj

spastic adj 1 affected by spasms 2 (Offens) suffering cerebral palsy

spate ① n 1 rush, outpouring 2 flood

spatial adj of, in space

spatter v 1 splash, cast drops over 2 be scattered in drops

━━━━━━━━━━━━ THESAURUS ━━━━━━━━━━━━

spacious adj = **roomy**, large, huge, broad, extensive ≠ **limited**

span n = **period**, term, duration, spell; = **extent**, reach, spread, length, distance ▷ v = **extend across**, cross, bridge, cover, link

spar v = **argue**, row, squabble, scrap (Inf), wrangle

spare adj = **back-up**, reserve, second, extra, additional; = **extra**, surplus, leftover, over, free ≠ **necessary** ▷ v = **afford**, give, grant, do without, part with;

= **have mercy on**, pardon, leave, let off (Inf), go easy on (Inf) ≠ **show no mercy to**

spark n = **flicker**, flash, gleam, glint, flare; = **trace**, hint, scrap, atom, jot ▷ v often with **off** = **start**, stimulate, provoke, inspire, trigger (off)

sparkle v = **glitter**, flash, shine, gleam, shimmer ▷ n = **glitter**, flash, gleam, flicker, brilliance; = **vivacity**, life, spirit, dash, vitality

spate n = **flood**, flow, torrent, rush, deluge

▷ n 3 spattering

spatula n utensil with broad, flat blade for various purposes

spawn n 1 eggs of fish or frog ▷ v 2 (of fish or frog) cast eggs

spay v remove ovaries from (female animal)

speak ❶ v speaking, spoke, spoken 1 utter words 2 converse 3 express 4 communicate in 5 give speech **speaker** n 1 one who speaks 2 speech maker 3 loudspeaker

spear n 1 long pointed weapon ▷ v 2 pierce with spear **spearhead** n 1 leading force in attack ▷ v 2 lead attack

spearmint n type of mint

special ❶ adj 1 beyond the usual 2 particular **specialist** n one who devotes himself to special subject **speciality** n special product, skill, characteristic etc. **specialization** n **specialize** v 1 be specialist 2 make special

species ❶ n, pl -cies group of plants or animals that are closely related

specific ❶ adj 1 exact in detail 2 characteristic **specification** n detailed description of something **specify** v state definitely or in detail

specimen ❶ n 1 part typifying whole 2 individual example

specious adj deceptively plausible, but false

speck n 1 small spot, particle ▷ v 2 mark with spots **speckle** n/v speck

spectacle ❶ n 1 show 2 thing exhibited 3 strange, interesting, or ridiculous sight ▷ pl 4 pair of lenses for correcting defective sight **spectacular** adj 1 impressive 2 showy **spectate** v **spectator** n one who looks on

spectre ❶ n 1 ghost 2 image of something unpleasant

spectrum n, pl -tra band of colours into which light can be decomposed, e.g. by prism

speculate ❶ v 1 guess, conjecture 2 engage in (risky) commercial transactions **speculation** n **speculative** adj

S

speak v = **talk**, say something; = **articulate**, say, pronounce, utter, tell

special adj = **exceptional**, important, significant, particular, unique ≠ ordinary; = **specific**, particular, distinctive, individual, appropriate ≠ general

species n = **kind**, sort, type, group, class

specific adj = **particular**, special, characteristic, distinguishing

≠ general

specimen n = **sample**, example, model, type, pattern; = **example**, model, type

spectacle n = **show**, display, exhibition, event, performance; = **sight**, wonder, scene, phenomenon, curiosity

spectre n = **ghost**, spirit, phantom, vision, apparition

speculate v = **conjecture**, consider, wonder, guess, surmise;

speculator n

speech ❶ n 1 act, faculty of speaking 2 words, language 3 (formal) talk given before audience **speechless** adj 1 dumb 2 at a loss for words

speed ❶ n 1 swiftness 2 rate of progress ▷ v 3 move quickly 4 drive vehicle at high speed 5 further **speeding** n driving at high speed, esp. over legal limit **speedy** adj **speedometer** n instrument to show speed of vehicle **speedwell** n plant with small blue flowers

spell¹ ❶ v spelling, spelt 1 give letters of in order 2 indicate, result in **spelling** n

spell² ❶ n 1 magic formula 2 enchantment **spellbound** adj 1 enchanted 2 entranced

spell³ ❶ n (short) period of time, work

spend ❶ v spending, spent 1 pay out 2 pass (time) 3 use up

completely **spendthrift** n wasteful person

sperm n sperms 1 male reproductive cell 2 semen

spew v vomit

sphere ❶ n 1 ball, globe 2 field of action **spherical** adj

spice ❶ n 1 aromatic or pungent vegetable substance 2 spices collectively 3 anything that adds relish, interest etc. ▷ v 4 season with spices **spicy** adj

spick-and-span adj neat, smart, new-looking

spider ❶ n small eight-legged creature which spins web to catch prey **spidery** adj thin and angular

spike ❶ n 1 sharp point 2 long cluster with flowers attached directly to stalk ▷ v 3 pierce, fasten with spike 4 render ineffective **spiky** adj

spill ❶ v spilling, spilt 1 (cause to) pour from, flow over, fall out, esp. unintentionally ▷ n 2 fall

= **gamble**, risk, venture, hazard

speech n = **communication**, talk, conversation, discussion, dialogue; = **diction**, pronunciation, articulation, delivery, fluency; = **language**, tongue, jargon, dialect, idiom

speed n = **rate**, pace ▷ v = **race**, rush, hurry, zoom, career ≠ **crawl**

spell¹ v = **indicate**, mean, signify, point to, imply

spell² n = **incantation**, charm; = **enchantment**, magic, fascination, glamour, allure

spell³ n = **period**, time, term,

stretch, course

spend v = **pay out**, fork out (SI), expend, disburse ≠ **save**; = **pass**, fill, occupy, while away; = **use up**, waste, squander, empty, drain ≠ **save**

sphere n = **ball**, globe, orb, globule, circle; = **field**, department, function, territory, capacity

spice n = **excitement**, zest, colour, pep, zing (Inf)

spike n = **point**, stake, spine, barb, prong ▷ v = **impale**, spit, spear, stick

spill v = **tip over**, overturn, capsize,

3 amount spilt **spillage** n

spin ⊕ v spinning, spun **1** (cause to) revolve rapidly **2** twist into thread **3** prolong ▷ n **4** spinning
spinning n act, process of drawing out and twisting into threads
spin-dryer n machine in which clothes are spun to remove excess water **spin-off** n incidental benefit

spinach n dark green leafy vegetable

spindle n rod, axis for spinning
spindly adj long and slender

spine ⊕ n **1** backbone **2** thin spike, esp. on fish etc. **3** ridge **4** back of book **spinal** adj
spineless adj **1** lacking in spine **2** cowardly

spinster n unmarried woman

spiral ⊕ n **1** continuous curve drawn at ever increasing distance from fixed point **2** anything resembling this ▷ adj **3** shaped like spiral

spire n pointed part of steeple

spirit ⊕ n **1** life principle animating body **2** disposition **3** liveliness **4** courage **5** essential character or meaning **6** soul **7** ghost ▷ pl **8** emotional state **9** strong alcoholic drink ▷ v **10** carry away mysteriously **spirited** adj lively

spiritual adj **1** given to, interested in things of the spirit ▷ n **2** sacred song orig. sung by Black slaves in America **spiritualism** n belief that spirits of the dead communicate with the living
spiritualist n **spirituality** n

spit¹ ⊕ v spitting, spat **1** eject saliva (from mouth) ▷ n **2** spitting, saliva **spittle** n saliva

spit² n **1** sharp rod to put through meat for roasting **2** sandy point projecting into the sea ▷ v **3** thrust through

spite ⊕ n **1** malice ▷ v **2** thwart spitefully **spiteful** adj **in spite of** prep **1** regardless of **2** notwithstanding

splash ⊕ v **1** scatter liquid about or

knock over, discharge

spin v = **revolve**, turn, rotate, reel, whirl; = **reel**, swim, whirl ▷ n (Inf) = **drive**, ride, joy ride (Inf); = **revolution**, roll, whirl, gyration

spine n = **backbone**, vertebrae, spinal column, vertebral column; = **barb**, spur, needle, spike, ray

spiral adj = **coiled**, winding, whorled, helical ▷ n = **coil**, helix, corkscrew, whorl

spirit n = **soul**, life; = **life force**, vital spark; = **ghost**, phantom, spectre, apparition; = **courage**,

guts (Inf), grit, backbone, spunk (Inf); = **liveliness**, energy, vigour, life force; = **attitude**, character, temper, outlook, temperament; = **heart**, sense, nature, soul, core

spit¹ v = **eject**, throw out ▷ n = **saliva**, dribble, spittle, drool, slaver

spite n = **malice**, malevolence, ill will, hatred, animosity ≠ **kindness** ▷ v = **annoy**, hurt, injure, harm, vex ≠ **benefit**

splash v = **paddle**, plunge, bathe, dabble, wade; = **scatter**, shower,

S

on, over something **2** print (story, photo) prominently in newspaper ▷ *n* **3** sound of splashing liquid **4** patch, esp. of colour **5** (effect of) extravagant display

splatter *v/n* spatter

splay *adj* **1** spread out **2** turned outwards ▷ *v* **3** spread out **4** twist outwards

spleen *n* organ in the abdomen **splenetic** *adj* spiteful, irritable

splendid ❶ *adj* magnificent, excellent **splendour** *n*

splice *v* **1** join by interweaving strands ▷ *n* **2** spliced joint

splint *n* rigid support for broken limb etc.

splinter ❶ *n* **1** thin fragment ▷ *v* **2** break into fragments

split ❶ *v* **splitting, split** **1** break asunder **2** separate **3** divide ▷ *n* **4** crack **5** division **split second** very short period of time

splutter *v* **1** make hissing, spitting sounds **2** utter incoherently with

spitting sounds ▷ *n* **3** spluttering

spoil ❶ *v* **spoiling, spoilt** **1** damage, injure **2** damage manners or behaviour of (esp. child) by indulgence **3** go bad **spoils** *pl n* booty **spoilsport** *n* person who spoils others' enjoyment

spoke *n* radial bar of a wheel

spokesman, spokeswoman, spokesperson *n* one deputed to speak for others

sponge *n* **1** marine animal **2** its skeleton, or a synthetic substance like it, used to absorb liquids **3** type of light cake ▷ *v* **4** wipe with sponge **5** live at the expense of others **spongy** *adj* **1** spongelike **2** wet and soft

sponsor ❶ *n* **1** one promoting something **2** one who agrees to give money to charity on completion of a specified activity by another **3** godparent ▷ *v* **4** act as sponsor **sponsorship** *n*

spontaneous ❶ *adj* **1** voluntary

━━━━━━━━━━━ THESAURUS ━━━━━━━━━━━

spray, sprinkle, wet ▷ *n* = **dash**, touch, spattering; = **spot**, burst, patch, spurt

splendid *adj* = **excellent**, wonderful, marvellous, great (*Inf*), cracking (*Brit Inf*) ≠ **poor**; = **magnificent**, grand, impressive, rich, superb ≠ **squalid**

splinter *n* = **sliver**, fragment, chip, flake ▷ *v* = **shatter**, split, fracture, disintegrate

split *v* = **break**, crack, burst, open, give way; = **cut**, break, crack, snap, chop; = **divide**, separate, disunite, disband, cleave; ≠ **diverge**

separate, branch, fork, part ▷ *n* = **division**, breach, rift, rupture, discord; = **separation**, break-up, split-up

spoil *v* = **ruin**, destroy, wreck, damage, injure ≠ **improve**; = **overindulge**, indulge, pamper, cosset, coddle ≠ **deprive**; = **indulge**, pamper, satisfy, gratify, pander to

sponsor *v* = **back**, fund, finance, promote, subsidize ▷ *n* = **backer**, patron, promoter

spontaneous *adj* = **unplanned**, impromptu, unprompted, willing,

S

2 natural **spontaneity** n

spoof n mildly satirical parody

spook n (Inf) ghost **spooky** adj

spool n reel, bobbin

spoon n 1 implement with shallow bowl at end of handle for carrying food to mouth etc. ▷ v 2 lift with spoon **spoonful** n **spoon-feed** v give (someone) too much help

sporadic adj 1 intermittent 2 scattered

spore n minute reproductive body of some plants

sporran n pouch worn in front of kilt

sport ❶ n 1 game, activity for pleasure, competition, exercise 2 enjoyment 3 cheerful person, good loser ▷ v 4 wear (esp. ostentatiously) 5 frolic 6 play (sport) **sporting** adj 1 of sport 2 behaving with fairness, generosity **sports car** fast low-built car **sportsman** n 1 one who engages in sport 2 good loser

spot ❶ n 1 small mark, stain 2 blemish 3 pimple 4 place

5 (difficult) situation 6 (Inf) small quantity ▷ v 7 mark with spots 8 detect 9 observe **spotless** adj 1 unblemished 2 pure **spotty** adj 1 with spots 2 uneven **spotlight** n 1 powerful light illuminating small area 2 centre of attention

spouse ❶ n husband or wife

spout v 1 pour out ▷ n 2 projecting tube or lip for pouring liquids 3 copious discharge

sprain v/n wrench, twist

sprat n small sea fish

sprawl ❶ v 1 lie or sit about awkwardly 2 spread in rambling, unplanned way ▷ n 3 sprawling

spray¹ ❶ n 1 (device for producing) fine drops of liquid ▷ v 2 sprinkle with shower of fine drops

spray² ❶ n 1 branch, twig with buds, flowers etc. 2 ornament like this

spread ❶ v spreading, spread 1 extend 2 stretch out 3 open out 4 scatter 5 distribute 6 unfold 7 cover ▷ n 8 extent 9 increase 10 ample meal 11 food which can

natural ≠ planned

sport n = **game**, exercise, recreation, play, amusement; = **fun**, joking, teasing, banter, jest ▷ v (Inf) = **wear**, display, flaunt, exhibit, flourish

spot n = **mark**, stain, speck, scar, blot; = **pimple**, pustule, zit (Sl); = **place**, site, point, position, scene; (Inf) = **predicament**, trouble, difficulty, mess, plight ▷ v = **see**, observe, catch sight of, sight, recognize; = **mark**, stain, soil, dirty,

fleck

spouse n = **partner**, mate, husband or wife, consort, significant other (US Inf)

sprawl v = **loll**, slump, lounge, flop, slouch

spray¹ n = **droplets**, fine mist, drizzle; = **aerosol**, sprinkler, atomizer ▷ v = **scatter**, shower, sprinkle, diffuse

spray² n = **sprig**, floral arrangement, branch, corsage

spread v = **open (out)**, extend,

S

be spread on bread etc.
spread-eagled adj with arms and legs outstretched
spree ❶ n 1 session of overindulgence 2 romp
sprig n small twig
sprightly adj -lier, -liest lively, brisk
spring ❶ v springing, sprang
1 leap 2 shoot up or forth 3 come into being 4 appear 5 grow 6 become bent or spilt 7 produce unexpectedly 8 set off (trap) ▷ n 9 leap 10 recoil 11 piece of coiled or bent metal with much resilience 12 flow of water from earth 13 first season of year **springy** adj elastic
spring-clean v clean (house) thoroughly
springbok n S.Afr. antelope
sprinkle ❶ v scatter small drops on, strew **sprinkler** n **sprinkling** n small quantity or number
sprint ❶ v 1 run short distance at great speed ▷ n 2 such run, race **sprinter** n

sprite n elf
sprocket n toothed wheel, attached to chain
sprout ❶ v 1 put forth shoots, spring up ▷ n 2 shoot
spruce¹ n variety of fir
spruce² adj neat in dress
spruce up make neat and smart
spry adj spryer, spryest nimble, vigorous
spur ❶ n 1 pricking instrument attached to horseman's heel 2 incitement 3 stimulus ▷ v 4 urge on
spurious adj not genuine
spurn ❶ v reject with scorn
spurt v 1 send, come out in jet 2 rush suddenly ▷ n 3 jet 4 short sudden effort
spy ❶ n, pl **spies** 1 one who watches (esp. in rival countries, companies etc.) and reports secretly ▷ v 2 act as spy 3 catch sight of
squabble ❶ v/n (engage in) petty,

stretch, unfold, sprawl; = **extend**, open, stretch ▷ n = **increase**, development, advance, expansion, proliferation; = **extent**, span, stretch, sweep
spree n = **fling**, binge (Inf), orgy
spring n = **flexibility**, bounce, resilience, elasticity, buoyancy ▷ v = **jump**, bound, leap, bounce, vault; often with **from** = **originate**, come, derive, start, issue
sprinkle v = **scatter**, dust, strew, pepper, shower
sprint v = **run**, race, shoot, tear, dash

sprout v = **germinate**, bud, shoot, spring
spur v = **incite**, drive, prompt, urge, stimulate ▷ n = **stimulus**, incentive, impetus, motive, impulse
spurn v = **reject**, slight, scorn, rebuff, snub ≠ **accept**
spy n = **undercover agent**, mole, nark (Brit, Aust, & NZ Sl) ▷ v = **catch sight of**, spot, notice, observe, glimpse
squabble v = **quarrel**, fight, argue, row, dispute ▷ n = **quarrel**, fight, row, argument, dispute

S

noisy quarrel

squad ❶ n small party, esp. of soldiers **squadron** n division of cavalry regiment, fleet or air force

squalid adj mean and dirty **squalor** n

squall n 1 harsh cry 2 sudden gust of wind 3 short storm ▷ v 4 yell

squander ❶ v spend wastefully

square ❶ n 1 equilateral rectangle 2 area of this shape 3 town, open space (of this shape) 4 product of a number multiplied by itself 5 instrument for drawing right angles ▷ adj 6 square in form 7 honest 8 straight, even 9 level, equal ▷ v 10 make square 11 find square of 12 pay 13 fit, suit

squash ❶ v 1 crush flat 2 pulp 3 suppress ▷ n 4 juice of crushed fruit 5 crowd 6 game played with rackets and ball in walled court

squat v **squatting, squatted** 1 sit on heels 2 occupy unused premises illegally ▷ adj 3 short and thick **squatter** n

squawk n 1 short harsh cry, esp. of bird ▷ v 2 utter this

squeak v/n (make) short shrill

sound or cry

squeal n 1 long piercing squeak ▷ v 2 make one

squeamish adj 1 easily made sick 2 easily shocked

squeeze ❶ v 1 press 2 wring 3 force 4 hug ▷ n 5 act of squeezing

squelch v/n (make) wet sucking sound

squid n type of cuttlefish

squiggle n wavy line

squint v 1 have the eyes turn in different directions 2 glance sideways ▷ n 3 this eye disorder 4 glance

squire n country gentleman

squirm v 1 wriggle 2 be embarrassed ▷ n 3 squirming

squirrel n small graceful bushy-tailed tree animal

squirt v 1 (of liquid) force, be forced through narrow opening ▷ n 2 jet of liquid

st. stone (weight)

stab ❶ v **stabbing, stabbed** 1 pierce, strike (at) with pointed weapon ▷ n 2 blow, wound so inflicted 3 sudden sensation, e.g.

S

squad n = **team**, group, band, company, force

squander v = **waste**, spend, fritter away, blow (Sl), misuse **≠ save**

square adj = **fair**, straight, genuine, ethical, honest ▷ v often with **with** = **agree**, match, fit, correspond, tally

squash v = **crush**, press, flatten, mash, smash; = **suppress**, quell, silence, annihilate

squeeze v = **press**, crush, squash, pinch; = **clutch**, press, grip, crush, pinch; = **cram**, press, crowd, force, stuff; = **hug**, embrace, cuddle, clasp, enfold ▷ n = **press**, grip, clasp, crush, pinch; = **crush**, jam, squash, press, crowd

stab v = **pierce**, stick, wound, knife, thrust ▷ n (Inf) = **attempt**, go, try, endeavour; = **twinge**, prick, pang, ache

of fear **4** attempt
stabilize v make or become stable
  stabilizer n device to maintain
  stability of ship, aircraft etc.
stable¹ n **1** building for horses
  2 racehorses of particular owner,
  establishment **3** such
  establishment ▷ v **4** put into
  stable
stable² ❶ adj **1** firmly fixed
  2 steadfast, resolute **stability** n
  1 steadiness **2** ability to resist
  change
staccato adj/adv (Mus) with the
  notes sharply separated
stack ❶ n **1** ordered pile, heap
  2 chimney ▷ v **3** pile in stack
stadium n, pl **-diums, -dia**
  open-air arena for athletics etc.
staff ❶ n **1** body of officers or
  workers **2** pole ▷ v **3** supply with
  personnel
stag n male deer
stage ❶ n **1** period, division of
  development **2** (platform of)
  theatre **3** stopping-place on road,
  distance between two of them ▷ v

4 put (play) on stage **5** arrange,
  bring about
stagger ❶ v **1** walk unsteadily
  2 astound **3** arrange in overlapping
  or alternating positions, times
  4 distribute over a period
staid adj of sober and quiet
  character, sedate
stain ❶ v **1** spot, mark **2** apply
  liquid colouring to (wood etc.) ▷ n
  3 discoloration or mark **4** moral
  blemish **stainless** adj **stainless
  steel** rustless steel alloy
stairs pl n set of steps, esp. as part
  of house **staircase, stairway** n
  1 structure enclosing stairs **2** stairs
stake ❶ n **1** sharpened stick or
  post **2** bet **3** investment ▷ v
  4 secure, mark out with stakes
  5 wager, risk
stalactite n lime deposit hanging
  from roof of cave
stalagmite n lime deposit
  sticking up from floor of cave
stale ❶ adj **1** old, lacking freshness
  2 lacking energy, interest through
  monotony **stalemate** n deadlock

stable² adj = **secure**, lasting,
  strong, sound, fast ≠ **insecure**;
  = **well-balanced**, balanced,
  sensible, reasonable,
  rational
stack n = **pile**, heap, mountain,
  mass, load ▷ v = **pile**, heap up,
  load, assemble, accumulate
staff n = **workers**, employees,
  personnel, workforce, team;
  = **stick**, pole, rod, crook, cane
stage n = **step**, leg, phase, point,
  level

stagger v = **totter**, reel, sway,
  lurch, wobble; = **astound**, amaze,
  stun, shock, shake
stain n = **mark**, spot, blot, blemish,
  discoloration; = **stigma**, shame,
  disgrace, slur, dishonour; = **dye**,
  colour, tint ▷ v = **mark**, soil,
  discolour, dirty, tinge; = **dye**, colour,
  tint
stake n = **pole**, post, stick, pale,
  paling
stale adj = **old**, hard, dry, decayed
  ≠ **fresh**; = **musty**, fusty

stalk¹ ❶ v 1 follow stealthily
2 walk in stiff and stately manner

stalk² n 1 plant's stem 2 anything like this

stall ❶ n 1 compartment in stable etc. 2 erection for display and sale of goods 3 front seat in theatre etc.
▷ v 4 (of motor engine) unintentionally stop 5 delay

stallion n uncastrated male horse, esp. for breeding

stalwart ❶ adj 1 strong, brave
2 staunch ▷ n 3 stalwart person

stamina ❶ n power of endurance

stammer ❶ v 1 speak, say with repetition of syllables ▷ n 2 habit of so speaking

stamp ❶ v 1 put down foot with force 2 impress mark on 3 affix postage stamp ▷ n 4 stamping with foot 5 imprinted mark
6 appliance for marking 7 piece of gummed paper printed with device as evidence of postage etc.

stampede n 1 sudden frightened rush, esp. of herd of cattle, crowd
▷ v 2 rush

stance ❶ n 1 manner, position of standing 2 attitude

stanch see STAUNCH

stanchion n upright bar used as support

stand ❶ v **standing, stood**
1 have, take, set in upright position
2 be situated 3 remain firm or stationary 4 endure 5 offer oneself as a candidate 6 be symbol etc. of 7 (Inf) provide free, treat to
▷ n 8 holding firm 9 position
10 something on which thing may be placed 11 structure from which spectators can watch sport etc.

standing n 1 reputation, status
2 duration ▷ adj 3 erect 4 lasting
5 stagnant **standoffish** adj reserved or haughty

standard ❶ n 1 accepted example of something against

<hr>

THESAURUS

stalk¹ v = **pursue**, follow, track, hunt, shadow

stall v = **play for time**, delay, hedge, temporize

stalwart adj = **loyal**, faithful, firm, true, dependable; = **strong**, strapping, sturdy, stout ≠ **puny**

stamina n = **staying power**, endurance, resilience, force, power

stammer v = **stutter**, falter, pause, hesitate, stumble over your words

stamp n = **imprint**, mark, brand, signature, earmark ▷ v = **print**, mark, impress; = **trample**, step, tread, crush; = **identify**, mark,

brand, label, reveal

stance n = **attitude**, stand, position, viewpoint, standpoint; = **posture**, carriage, bearing, deportment

stand v = **be upright**, be erect, be vertical; = **get to your feet**, rise, stand up, straighten up; = **be located**, be, sit, be positioned, be situated or located; = **be valid**, continue, exist, prevail, remain valid
▷ n = **position**, attitude, stance, opinion, determination; = **stall**, booth, kiosk, table = **support**, base, platform, stage, rack

standard n = **level**, grade;

S

which others are judged **2** degree, quality **3** flag ▷ *adj* **4** usual **5** of recognized authority, accepted as correct **standardize** *v* regulate by a standard

standpipe *n* tap attached to water main to provide public water supply

standpoint *n* point of view

standstill *n* complete halt

stanza *n* group of lines of verse

staple *n* **1** U-shaped piece of metal used to fasten **2** main product ▷ *adj* **3** principal ▷ *v* **4** fasten with staple **stapler** *n*

star ❶ *n* **1** celestial body, seen as twinkling point of light **2** asterisk (°) **3** celebrated player, actor ▷ *v* **4** adorn with stars **5** mark (with asterisk) **6** feature as star performer ▷ *adj* **7** most important **stardom** *n* **starry** *adj* covered with stars

starfish *n* small star-shaped sea creature

starboard *n* right-hand side of

ship or aeroplane

starch *n* **1** substance forming the main food element in bread, potatoes etc., and used mixed with water, for stiffening linen etc. ▷ *v* **2** stiffen thus **starchy** *adj* **1** containing starch **2** stiff

stare ❶ *v* **1** look fixedly (at) ▷ *n* **2** staring gaze

stark ❶ *adj* **1** blunt, bare **2** desolate **3** absolute ▷ *adv* **4** completely

starling *n* glossy black speckled songbird

start ❶ *v* **1** begin **2** set going **3** make sudden movement ▷ *n* **4** beginning **5** abrupt movement **6** advantage of a lead in a race **starter** *n* **1** first course of meal **2** electric motor starting car engine **3** competitor in race **4** supervisor of start of race

startle ❶ *v* give a fright to

starve *v* (cause to) suffer or die from hunger **starvation** *n*

stash *v* (*Inf*) store in secret place

= **criterion**, measure, guideline, example, model; *often plural*
= **principles**, ideals, morals, ethics;
= **flag**, banner, ensign ▷ *adj*
= **usual**, normal, customary, average, basic ≠ **unusual**
= **accepted**, official, established, approved, recognized ≠ **unofficial**

star *n* = **heavenly body**, celestial body; = **celebrity**, big name, megastar (*Inf*), name, luminary ▷ *adj* = **leading**, major, celebrated, brilliant, well-known

stare *v* = **gaze**, look, goggle,

watch, gape

stark *adj* = **plain**, harsh, basic, grim, straightforward; = **sharp**, clear, striking, distinct, clear-cut ▷ *adv* = **absolutely**, quite, completely, entirely, altogether

start *v* = **set about**, begin, proceed, embark upon, take the first step ≠ **stop**; = **begin**, arise, originate, appear ≠ **end**; = **set in motion**, initiate, instigate, open, trigger ≠ **stop**; = **establish**, begin, found, create, launch ≠ **terminate** ▷ *n* = **beginning**,

DICTIONARY

state ❶ n 1 condition 2 politically organized people 3 government 4 pomp ▷ v 5 express in words **stately** adj dignified, lofty **statement** n 1 expression in words 2 account **statesman** n respected political leader **statesmanship** n

static ❶ adj 1 motionless, inactive ▷ n 2 electrical interference in radio reception

station ❶ n 1 place where thing stops or is placed 2 stopping place for railway trains 3 local office for police force, fire brigade etc. 4 place equipped for radio or television transmission 5 bus garage 6 post 7 position in life ▷ v 8 put in position **stationary** adj 1 not moving 2 not changing

station wagon n (US & Canad) automobile with a rear door and luggage space behind the rear seats

statue n solid carved or cast image **statuesque** adj 1 like statue 2 dignified **statuette** n small statue

stature ❶ n 1 bodily height 2 greatness

status ❶ n 1 position, rank 2 prestige 3 relation to others **status quo** existing state of affairs **statute** n law **statutory** adj

staunch, stanch ❶ adj trustworthy, loyal

stave n 1 strip of wood in barrel ▷ v 2 break hole in 3 ward (off)

stay¹ ❶ v 1 remain 2 reside 3 endure 4 stop 5 postpone ▷ n 6 remaining, residing 7 postponement

stay² n support, prop

stead n place **in stead** in place (of)

steady ❶ adj **steadier, steadiest** 1 firm 2 regular 3 temperate ▷ v

THESAURUS

outset, opening, birth, foundation ≠ **end**; = **jump**, spasm, convulsion

startle v = **surprise**, shock, frighten, scare, make (someone) jump

state n = **country**, nation, land, republic, territory; = **government**, ministry, administration, executive, regime; = **condition**, shape ▷ v = **say**, declare, specify, present, voice

static adj = **stationary**, still, motionless, fixed, immobile ≠ **moving**

station n = **railway station**, stop, stage, halt, terminal;

= **headquarters**, base, depot; = **position**, rank, status, standing, post ▷ v = **assign**, post, locate, set, establish

stature n = **height**, build, size

status n = **position**, rank, grade

staunch adj = **loyal**, faithful, stalwart, firm, sound

stay¹ v = **remain**, continue to be, linger, stop, wait ≠ **go** ▷ n = **visit**, stop, holiday, stopover, sojourn; = **postponement**, delay, suspension, stopping, halt

steady adj = **continuous**, regular, constant, consistent, persistent ≠ **irregular**; = **stable**, fixed, secure,

S

4 make steady **steadily** adv
steadfast adj firm, unyielding
steak n thick slice of meat
steal ❶ v **stealing, stole, stolen**
1 take without right or permission
2 move silently
stealth ❶ n secret or underhand
procedure, behaviour **stealthy** adj
steam n 1 vapour of boiling water
▷ v 2 give off steam 3 move by
steam power 4 cook or treat with
steam **steamer** n steam-
propelled ship **steam engine**
engine worked by steam
steamroller n steam-powered
vehicle with heavy rollers, used to
level road surfaces
steed n (Lit) horse
steel n 1 hard and malleable metal
made by mixing carbon in iron ▷ v
2 harden
steep¹ ❶ adj 1 sloping abruptly
2 (of prices) very high
steep² ❶ v soak, saturate
steeple n church tower with spire
steeplechase n race with obstacles
to jump **steeplejack** n one who
builds, repairs chimneys etc.
steer¹ ❶ v 1 guide, direct course of

vessel, motor vehicle etc. 2 direct
one's course
steer² n castrated male ox
stellar adj of stars
stem¹ ❶ n 1 stalk, trunk 2 part of
word to which inflections are added
stem² ❶ v **stemming, stemmed**
check, dam up
stench n foul smell
stencil n 1 thin sheet pierced with
pattern which is brushed over with
paint or ink, leaving pattern on
surface under it 2 the pattern ▷ v
3 make pattern thus
step ❶ v **stepping, stepped**
1 move and set down foot
2 proceed (in this way) 3 measure
in paces ▷ n 4 stepping 5 series of
foot movements forming part of
dance 6 measure, act, stage in
proceeding 7 board, rung etc. to
put foot on 8 degree in scale
stepladder n folding portable
ladder with supporting frame
stereophonic adj (of sound)
giving effect of coming from many
directions **stereo** n
1 stereophonic sound, record player
etc. ▷ adj 2 stereophonic

firm, safe ≠ **unstable**; = **regular**,
established
steal v = **take**, nick (Sl, chiefly Brit),
pinch (Inf), lift (Inf), embezzle;
= **copy**, take, appropriate, pinch
(Inf)
stealth n = **secrecy**, furtiveness,
slyness, sneakiness,
unobtrusiveness
steep¹ adj = **sheer**, precipitous,
abrupt, vertical ≠ **gradual**;

= **sharp**, sudden, abrupt, marked,
extreme
steer¹ v = **drive**, control, direct,
handle, pilot
stem¹ n = **stalk**, branch, trunk,
shoot, axis
stem² v = **stop**, hold back, staunch,
check, dam
step n = **pace**, stride, footstep;
= **move**, measure, action, means,
act ▷ v = **walk**, pace, tread, move

S

stereotype ❶ n 1 something (monotonously) familiar, conventional ▷ v 2 form stereotype

sterile ❶ adj 1 unable to produce fruit, crops, young etc. 2 free from (harmful) germs **sterility** n **sterilize** v render sterile

sterling ❶ adj 1 genuine, true 2 of solid worth 3 in British money ▷ n 4 British money

stern¹ adj severe, strict

stern² adj rear part of ship

sternum n, pl **-na, -nums** breast bone

steroid n organic compound, oft. used to increase body strength

stethoscope n instrument for listening to action of heart, lungs etc.

stew n 1 food cooked slowly in closed vessel ▷ v 2 cook slowly

steward n 1 one who manages another's property 2 official managing race meeting, assembly etc. 3 attendant on ship or aircraft

stick ❶ n sticking, **stuck** 1 long, thin piece of wood 2 anything shaped like a stick ▷ v 3 pierce, stab 4 place, fasten, as by pins, glue 5 protrude 6 adhere 7 come to stop 8 jam 9 remain **sticker** n adhesive label, poster **sticky** adj 1 covered with, like adhesive substance 2 (of weather) warm, humid 3 (Inf) awkward, tricky

stickleback n small fish with sharp spines on back

stickler n person who insists on something

stiff ❶ adj 1 not easily bent or moved 2 difficult 3 thick, not fluid 4 formal 5 strong or fresh, as breeze **stiffen** v **stiffness** n

stifle ❶ v smother, suppress

stigma ❶ n, pl **-mas, -mata** mark of disgrace **stigmatize** v

stile n arrangement of steps for climbing a fence

still¹ ❶ adj 1 motionless, noiseless

stereotype n = **formula**, pattern ▷ v = **categorize**, typecast, pigeonhole, standardize

sterile adj = **germ-free**, sterilized, disinfected, aseptic ≠ **unhygienic**; = **barren**, infertile, unproductive, childless ≠ **fertile**

sterling adj = **excellent**, sound, fine, superlative

stick n = **twig**, branch; = **cane**, staff, pole, rod, crook ▷ v (Inf) = **put**, place, set, lay, deposit; = **poke**, dig, stab, thrust, pierce; = **fasten**, fix, bind, hold, bond; = **adhere**, cling, become joined, become welded; = **stay**, remain, linger, persist; (Sl) = **tolerate**, take, stand, stomach, abide

stiff adj = **inflexible**, rigid, unyielding, hard, firm ≠ **flexible**; = **formal**, constrained, forced, unnatural, stilted ≠ **informal**; = **vigorous**, great, strong; = **severe**, strict, harsh, hard, heavy

stifle v = **suppress**, repress, stop, check, silence; = **restrain**, suppress, repress, smother

stigma n = **disgrace**, shame, dishonour, stain, slur

still¹ adj = **motionless**, stationary,

S

▷ v **2** quiet ▷ adv **3** to this time **4** yet **5** even ▷ n **6** photograph, esp. of film scene **stillness** n **stillborn** adj born dead

still² n apparatus for distilling

stimulus ❶ n, pl **-li 1** something that rouses to activity **2** incentive **stimulant** n drug etc. acting as stimulus **stimulate** v rouse up, spur **stimulation** n

sting ❶ v **stinging, stung 1** thrust sting into **2** cause sharp pain to **3** feel sharp pain ▷ n **4** (wound, pain, caused by) sharp pointed organ, often poisonous, of certain creatures

stingy adj **-gier, -giest 1** mean **2** niggardly

stink ❶ v **1** give out strongly offensive smell **2** (Sl) be abhorrent

stint ❶ v **1** be frugal, miserly ▷ n **2** allotted amount of work or time **3** limitation, restriction

stipulate ❶ v specify in making a

bargain **stipulation** n **1** proviso **2** condition

stir ❶ v **stirring, stirred 1** (begin to) move **2** rouse **3** excite ▷ n **4** commotion, disturbance

stirrup n loop for supporting foot of rider on horse

stitch n **1** movement of needle in sewing etc. **2** its result in the work **3** sharp pain in side **4** least fragment (of clothing) ▷ v **5** sew

stoat n small mammal with brown coat and black-tipped tail

stock ❶ n **1** goods, material stored, esp. for sale or later use **2** financial shares in, or capital of, company etc. **3** standing, reputation **4** farm animals, livestock **5** plant, stem from which cuttings are taken **6** handle of gun, tool etc. **7** liquid broth produced by boiling meat etc. **8** flowering plant **9** lineage ▷ adj **10** kept in stock **11** standard **12** hackneyed ▷ v

calm, peaceful, serene ≠ **moving**; = **silent**, quiet, hushed ≠ **noisy** ▷ v = **quieten**, calm, settle, quiet, silence ≠ **get louder**

stimulus n = **incentive**, spur, encouragement, impetus, inducement

sting v = **hurt**, burn, wound; = **smart**, burn, pain, hurt, tingle

stink v = **reek**, pong (Brit Inf) ▷ n = **stench**, pong (Brit Inf), foul smell, fetor

stint n = **term**, time, turn, period, share ▷ v = **be mean**, hold back, be sparing, skimp on, be frugal

stipulate v = **specify**, agree,

require, contract, settle

stir v = **mix**, beat, agitate; = **stimulate**, move, excite, spur, provoke ≠ **inhibit** ▷ n = **commotion**, excitement, activity, disorder, fuss

stock n = **shares**, holdings, securities, investments, bonds; = **property**, capital, assets, funds; = **goods**, merchandise, wares, range, choice; = **supply**, store, reserve, fund, stockpile ▷ v = **sell**, supply, handle, keep, trade in; = **fill**, supply, provide with, equip, furnish ▷ adj = **hackneyed**, routine, banal, trite, overused; = **regular**, usual,

S

13 keep, store 14 supply with livestock, fish etc. **stockist** n dealer who stocks a particular product **stocky** adj thickset
stockbroker n agent for buying, selling shares in companies **stock exchange** institution for buying and selling shares **stockpile** v acquire and store large quantity of (something) **stocktaking** n examination, counting and valuing of goods in a shop etc.
stockade n enclosure of stakes, barrier
stocking n close-fitting covering for leg and foot
stodgy adj stodgier, stodgiest heavy, dull
stoep [stoop] n (S Afr) verandah
stoic adj 1 capable of much self-control, great endurance without complaint ▷ n 2 stoical person **stoical** adj **stoicism** n
stoke v feed, tend fire or furnace **stoker** n
stole n long scarf or shawl
stolid adj hard to excite
stomach ❶ n 1 sac forming chief digestive organ in any animal 2 appetite ▷ v 3 put up with

stomp v tread heavily
stone n 1 (piece of) rock 2 gem 3 hard seed of fruit 4 hard deposit formed in kidneys, bladder 5 unit of weight, 14 pounds ▷ v 6 throw stones at 7 free (fruit) from stones **stony** adj 1 of, like stone 2 hard 3 cold **stone-deaf** adj completely deaf
stooge n person taken advantage of
stool n backless chair
stoop ❶ v 1 lean forward or down 2 abase, degrade oneself ▷ n 3 stooping posture
stop ❶ v 1 bring, come to halt 2 prevent 3 desist from 4 fill up an opening 5 cease 6 stay ▷ n 7 place where something stops 8 stopping or becoming stopped 9 punctuation mark, esp. full stop 10 set of pipes in organ having tones of a distinct quality **stoppage** n **stopper** n plug for closing bottle etc.
stopcock n valve to control flow of fluid in pipe **stopwatch** n watch which can be stopped for exact timing of race
store ❶ v 1 stock, keep ▷ n

S

ordinary, conventional, customary
stomach n = belly, gut (Inf), abdomen, tummy (Inf), puku (NZ); = **tummy**, pot ▷ v = **bear**, take, tolerate, endure, swallow
stoop v = bend, bow, duck, crouch ▷ n = slouch, bad posture, round-shoulderedness, sink to, descend to
stop v = quit, cease, refrain, put an

end to, discontinue ≠ start; = **prevent**, cut short, arrest, restrain, hold back ≠ facilitate; = **end**, conclude, finish, terminate ≠ continue; = cease, shut down, discontinue, desist ≠ continue ▷ n = **halt**, standstill; = **station**, stage, depot, terminus
store n = shop, outlet, market, mart; = **supply**, stock, reserve,

2 shop **3** abundance **4** stock **5** place for keeping goods **6** warehouse ▷ *pl* **7** stocks of goods, provisions **storage** *n*

storey *n* horizontal division of a building

stork *n* large wading bird

storm ❶ *n* **1** violent weather with wind, rain etc. **2** assault on fortress **3** violent outbreak ▷ *v* **4** assault **5** take by storm **6** rage **stormy** *adj* like storm

story ❶ *n, pl* **-ries 1** account, tale **2** newspaper report

stout ❶ *adj* **1** fat **2** sturdy, resolute ▷ *n* **3** strong dark beer

stove *n* apparatus for cooking, heating etc.

stow *v* pack away **stowaway** *n* person who hides in ship to obtain free passage

straddle *v* **1** bestride **2** spread legs wide

straggle *v* stray, get dispersed, linger **straggler** *n*

straight ❶ *adj* **1** without bend **2** honest **3** level **4** in order **5** in continuous succession **6** (of spirits) undiluted **7** (of face) expressionless ▷ *n* **8** straight state or part ▷ *adv* **9** direct **straighten** *v* **straightaway** *adv* immediately **straightforward** *adj* **1** open, frank **2** simple

strain¹ ❶ *v* **1** stretch tightly **2** stretch to excess **3** filter **4** make great effort ▷ *n* **5** stretching force **6** violent effort **7** injury from being strained **8** great demand **9** (condition caused by) overwork, worry etc. **strained** *adj* **strainer** *n* filter, sieve

fund, quantity; = **repository**, warehouse, depository, storeroom ▷ *v* often with *away* or *up* = **put by**, save, hoard, keep, reserve

storm *n* = **tempest**, hurricane, gale, blizzard, squall; = **outburst**, row, outcry, furore, outbreak ▷ *v* = **rush**, stamp, flounce, fly; = **rage**, rant, thunder, rave, bluster; = **attack**, charge, rush, assault, assail

story *n* = **tale**, romance, narrative, history, legend; = **anecdote**, account, tale, report

stout *adj* = **fat**, big, heavy, overweight, plump ≠ **slim**; = **strong**, strapping, muscular, robust, sturdy ≠ **puny**; = **brave**, bold, courageous, fearless, resolute

≠ **timid**

straight *adj* = **level**, even, right, square, true ≠ **crooked**; = **frank**, plain, straightforward, blunt, outright ≠ **evasive**; = **successive**, consecutive, continuous, running, solid ≠ **discontinuous**; *(Sl)* = **conventional**, conservative, bourgeois ≠ **fashionable**; = **honest**, just, fair, reliable, respectable ≠ **dishonest**; = **undiluted**, pure, neat, unadulterated, unmixed; = **in order**, organized, arranged, neat, tidy ≠ **untidy** ▷ *adv* = **directly**, precisely, exactly, unswervingly, by the shortest route

strain¹ *v* = **stretch**, tax, overtax; = **strive**, struggle, endeavour,

strain² n 1 breed or race 2 trace

strait ❶ n 1 channel of water connecting two larger areas of water ▷ pl 2 position of difficulty or distress **straitjacket** n jacket to confine arms of violent person **strait-laced** adj prudish

strand¹ v 1 run aground 2 leave, be left in difficulties

strand² ❶ n single thread of string, wire etc.

strange ❶ adj 1 odd 2 unaccustomed 3 foreign **strangeness** n **stranger** n 1 unknown person 2 foreigner 3 one unaccustomed (to)

strangle ❶ v 1 kill by squeezing windpipe 2 suppress **strangulation** n strangling **stranglehold** n

strap ❶ n 1 strip, esp. of leather ▷ v 2 fasten, beat with strap **strapping** adj tall and well-made

strategy ❶ n, pl -gies 1 overall plan 2 art of war **stratagem** n plan, trick **strategic** adj **strategist** n

stratosphere n layer of atmosphere high above the earth

stratum n, pl **strata** 1 layer, esp. of rock 2 class in society **stratification** or **stratify** v form, deposit in layers

straw n 1 stalks of grain 2 long, narrow tube used to suck up liquid **strawberry** n 1 creeping plant producing red, juicy fruit 2 the fruit

stray ❶ v 1 wander 2 digress 3 get lost ▷ adj 4 strayed 5 occasional 6 scattered ▷ n 7 stray animal

streak ❶ n 1 long line or band 2 element ▷ v 3 mark with streaks 4 move fast 5 run naked in public **streaker** n **streaky** adj

stream ❶ n 1 flowing body of

THESAURUS

labour, go for it (Inf) ≠ relax; = sieve, filter, sift, purify ▷ n = pressure, stress, demands, burden; = stress, anxiety; = worry, effort, struggle ≠ ease; = burden, tension; = injury, wrench, sprain, pull

strait n often plural = channel, sound, narrows

strand² n = filament, fibre, thread, string

strange adj = odd, curious, weird, wonderful, extraordinary ≠ ordinary; = unfamiliar, new, unknown, foreign, novel ≠ familiar

strangle v = throttle, choke,

asphyxiate, strangulate; = suppress, inhibit, subdue, stifle, repress

strap n = tie, thong, belt ▷ v = fasten, tie, secure, bind, lash

strategy n = policy, procedure, approach, scheme

stray v = wander, go astray, drift; = drift, wander, roam, meander, rove ▷ adj = lost, abandoned, homeless, roaming, vagrant; = random, chance, accidental

streak n = band, line, strip, stroke, layer; = trace, touch, element, strain, dash ▷ v = speed, fly, tear, flash, sprint

stream n = river, brook, burn

water or other liquid **2** steady flow
▷ v **3** flow **4** run with liquid **5** (*Comp*) send video or audio material over the internet so that the receiving system can play it almost simultaneously **streamer** n (paper) ribbon, narrow flag **streaming** n

street ⊕ n **1** road in town or village, usu. lined with houses **streetwise** adj adept at surviving in dangerous environment

streetcar n (*US & Canad*) public transport vehicle powered by an overhead wire and running on rails laid in the road

strength ⊕ n **1** quality of being strong **2** power **strengthen** v

strenuous adj **1** energetic **2** earnest

stress ⊕ n **1** emphasis **2** tension ▷ v **3** emphasize

stretch ⊕ v **1** extend **2** exert to utmost **3** tighten, pull out **4** reach **5** have elasticity ▷ n **6** stretching,

being stretched **7** expanse **8** spell

stretcher n **1** person, thing that stretches **2** appliance on which disabled person is carried

strew v **strewing, strewed** scatter over surface, spread

stricken adj seriously affected by disease, grief etc.

strict adj **1** stern, not lax or indulgent **2** precisely defined

stricture n critical remark

stride v **striding, strode, stridden 1** walk with long steps ▷ n **2** single step **3** length of step

strident adj harsh, loud **stridently** adv **stridency** n

strife n **1** conflict **2** quarrelling

strike ⊕ v **striking, struck 1** hit (against) **2** ignite **3** attack **4** sound (time), as bell in clock etc. **5** affect **6** enter mind of **7** cease work as protest or to make demands ▷ n **8** act of striking **striker** n **striking** adj noteworthy, impressive

(*Scot*), beck, tributary; **= flow**, current, rush, run, course ▷ v **= flow**, run, pour, issue, flood

street n **= road**, lane, avenue, terrace, row

strength n **= might**, muscle, brawn ≠ **weakness**; **= will**, resolution, courage, character, nerve; **= health**, fitness, vigour

stress v **= emphasize**, underline, dwell on ▷ n **= emphasis**, significance, force, weight; **= strain**, pressure, worry, tension, burden; **= accent**, beat, emphasis, accentuation

stretch v **= extend**, cover, spread, reach, put forth; **= last**, continue, go on, carry on, reach; **= pull**, distend, strain, tighten, draw out ▷ n **= expanse**, area, tract, spread, distance; **= period**, time, spell, stint, term

strife n **= conflict**, battle, clash, quarrel, friction

strike v **= walk out**, down tools, revolt, mutiny; **= hit**, smack, thump, beat, knock; **= drive**, hit, smack, wallop (*Inf*); **= collide with**, hit, run into, bump into; **= knock**, smack, thump, beat

string ❶ n **1** (length of) thin cord or other material **2** series **3** fibre in plants ▷ pl **4** conditions ▷ v **5** provide with, thread on string **6** form in line, series **stringed** adj (of musical instruments) furnished with strings **stringy** adj **1** like string **2** fibrous

stringent ❶ adj strict, binding **stringency** n

strip ❶ v **stripping, stripped 1** lay bare, take covering off **2** undress ▷ n **3** long, narrow piece **stripper** n **striptease** n cabaret or theatre in which person undresses

stripe n narrow mark, band **striped, stripy** adj marked with stripes

strive ❶ v **striving, strove, striven** try hard, struggle

stroke ❶ n **1** blow **2** sudden action, occurrence **3** apoplexy

4 chime of clock **5** mark made by pen, brush etc. **6** style, method of swimming **7** act of stroking ▷ v **8** pass hand lightly over

stroll ❶ v **1** walk in leisurely or idle manner ▷ n **2** leisurely walk

stroller n (US & Canad) chair-shaped carriage for a baby

strong ❶ adj **1** powerful, robust, healthy **2** difficult to break **3** noticeable **4** intense **5** emphatic **6** not diluted **7** having a certain number **strongly** adv

stronghold n fortress

strongroom n room for keeping valuables

stroppy adj **-pier, -piest** (Sl) angry or awkward

structure ❶ n **1** (arrangement of parts in) construction, building etc. **2** form ▷ v **3** give structure to **structural** adj

struggle ❶ v **1** contend **2** fight

string n = **cord**, twine, fibre; = **series**, line, row, file, sequence

stringent adj = **strict**, tough, rigorous, tight, severe ≠ **lax**

strip v = **undress**, disrobe, unclothe; = **plunder**, rob, loot, empty, sack

strive v = **try**, labour, struggle, attempt, toil

stroke v = **caress**, rub, fondle, pet ▷ n = **apoplexy**, fit, seizure, attack, collapse; = **blow**, hit, knock, pat, rap

stroll v = **walk**, ramble, amble, promenade, saunter ▷ n = **walk**, promenade, constitutional, ramble, breath of air

strong adj = **powerful**, muscular, tough, athletic, strapping ≠ **weak**; = **fit**, robust, lusty; = **durable**, substantial, sturdy, heavy-duty, well-built ≠ **flimsy**; = **extreme**, radical, drastic, strict, harsh; = **decisive**, firm, forceful, decided, determined

structure n = **arrangement**, form, make-up, design, organization; = **building**, construction, erection, edifice ▷ v = **arrange**, organize, design, shape, build up

struggle v = **strive**, labour, toil, work, strain; = **fight**, battle, wrestle, grapple, compete ▷ n

S

3 proceed, work, move with difficulty and effort ▷ *n* **4** struggling

strum *v* strumming, strummed strike notes of guitar etc.

strut ❶ *v* strutting, strutted **1** walk affectedly or pompously ▷ *n* **2** rigid support **3** strutting walk

strychnine *n* poisonous drug

stub *n* **1** remnant of anything, e.g. pencil **2** counterfoil ▷ *v* **3** strike (toes) against fixed object **4** extinguish by pressing against surface **stubby** *adj* short, broad

stubble *n* **1** stumps of cut grain after reaping **2** short growth of beard

stubborn ❶ *adj* unyielding, obstinate

stucco *n* plaster

stud¹ *n* **1** nail with large head **2** removable double-headed button ▷ *v* **3** set with studs

stud² *n* set of horses kept for breeding

studio ❶ *n, pl* -dios **1** workroom of artist, photographer etc.

2 building, room where film, television or radio shows are made, broadcast

study ❶ *v* studying, studied **1** be engaged in learning **2** make study of **3** scrutinize ▷ *n* **4** effort to acquire knowledge **5** subject of this **6** room to study in **7** book, report etc. produced as result of study **8** sketch **student** *n* one who studies **studied** *adj* carefully designed, premeditated **studious** *adj* **1** fond of study **2** painstaking **3** deliberate

stuff ❶ *v* **1** pack, cram, fill (completely) **2** eat large amount **3** fill with seasoned mixture **4** fill (animal's skin) with material to preserve lifelike form ▷ *n* **5** material **6** any substance **7** belongings **stuffing** *n* material for stuffing **stuffy** *adj* **1** lacking fresh air **2** (*Inf*) dull, conventional

stumble ❶ *v* **1** trip and nearly fall **2** falter ▷ *n* **3** stumbling

stump ❶ *n* **1** remnant of tree,

THESAURUS

= **effort**, labour, toil, work, pains; = **fight**, battle, conflict, clash, contest

strut *v* = **swagger**, parade, peacock, prance

stubborn *adj* = **obstinate**, dogged, inflexible, persistent, intractable ≠ compliant

studio *n* = **workshop**, workroom, atelier

study *v* = **learn**, cram (*Inf*), swot (up) (*Brit Inf*), read up, mug up (*Brit Sl*); = **examine**, survey, look at, scrutinize; = **contemplate**, read,

examine, consider, go into ▷ *n* = **examination**, investigation, analysis, consideration, inspection; = **piece of research**, survey, report, paper, review

stuff *n* = **things**, gear, possessions, effects, equipment; = **substance**, material, essence, matter ▷ *v* = **shove**, force, push, squeeze, jam

stumble *v* = **trip**, fall, slip, reel, stagger; = **totter**, reel, lurch, wobble

stump *v* = **baffle**, confuse, puzzle, bewilder, perplex tooth etc., when main part has been cut away **2** one of uprights of wicket in cricket ▷ v **3** confuse, puzzle **4** walk heavily, noisily

stumpy adj short and thickset

stun ❶ v **stunning, stunned** **1** knock senseless **2** amaze **stunning** adj

stunt[1] n feat of dexterity or daring

stunt[2] v stop growth of

stupefy v **-fying, -fied 1** make insensitive, lethargic **2** astound **stupefaction** n

stupendous adj **1** astonishing **2** amazing **3** huge

stupid ❶ adj **1** slow-witted **2** silly **stupidity** n

stupor n dazed state

sturdy ❶ adj **-dier, -diest** **1** robust, strongly built **2** vigorous

sturgeon n fish yielding caviare

stutter v **1** speak with difficulty **2** stammer ▷ n **3** tendency to stutter

sty n, pl **sties** place to keep pigs in

stye, sty n, pl **styes, sties** inflammation on eyelid

style ❶ n **1** design **2** manner of writing, doing etc. **3** fashion **4** elegance ▷ v **5** design **stylish** adj fashionable **stylist** n **1** one cultivating style **2** designer

stylus n (in record player) tiny point running in groove of record

suave adj smoothly polite

sub n short for SUBMARINE, SUBSCRIPTION, SUBSTITUTE

subconscious adj **1** acting, existing without one's awareness ▷ n **2** (Psychology) part of human mind unknown, or only partly known, to possessor

subdivide v divide again **subdivision** n

subdue ❶ v **-duing, -dued** overcome **subdued** adj **1** cowed, quiet **2** not bright

subject ❶ n **1** person or thing being dealt with or studied **2** person

stun v = **overcome**, shock, confuse, astonish, stagger; = **daze**, knock out, stupefy, numb, benumb

stunt[1] n = **feat**, act, trick, exploit, deed

stupid adj = **unintelligent**, thick, simple, slow, dim ≠ **intelligent**; = **silly**, foolish, daft (Inf), rash, pointless ≠ **sensible**; = **senseless**, dazed, groggy, insensate, semiconscious

sturdy adj = **robust**, hardy, powerful, athletic, muscular ≠ **puny**; = **substantial**, solid, durable, well-made, well-built

≠ **flimsy**

style n = **manner**, way, method, approach, technique; = **elegance**, taste, chic, flair, polish; = **design**, form, cut; = **type**, sort, kind, variety, category ▷ v = **design**, cut, tailor, fashion, shape; = **call**, name, term, label, entitle

subdue v = **overcome**, defeat, master, break, control; = **moderate**, suppress, soften, mellow, tone down ≠ **arouse**

subject n = **topic**, question, issue, matter, point; = **citizen**, resident, native, inhabitant, national ▷ adj

S

under rule of government or
monarch ▷ adj **3** owing allegiance
4 dependent **5** liable (to) ▷ v
6 cause to undergo **7** subdue
subjection n act of bringing, or
state of being, under control
subjective adj **1** based on personal
feelings, not impartial **2** existing in
the mind **subjectivity** n
subjugate v **1** force to submit
2 conquer **subjugation** n
sublet v **-letting, -let** rent out
property rented from someone else
sublime ❶ adj **1** elevated
2 inspiring awe **3** exalted
subliminal adj relating to mental
processes of which the individual is
not aware
submarine n **1** craft which can
travel below surface of sea and
remain submerged for long periods
▷ adj **2** below surface of sea
submerge ❶ v place, go under
water **submersion** n
subordinate ❶ n/adj **1** (one) of
lower rank or less importance ▷ v

2 make, treat as subordinate
subordination n
subprime adj **1** (of a loan) made to
a borrower with a poor credit rating
subprime mortgage ▷ n **2** such a loan
subscribe ❶ v **1** pay, promise to
pay (contribution) **2** give support,
approval **subscription** n money
paid
subsequent ❶ adj later,
following or coming after in time
subservient adj submissive,
servile
subside ❶ v **1** abate **2** sink
subsidence n
subsidiary ❶ adj/n secondary
(person or thing)
subsidize v **1** help financially
2 pay grant to **subsidy** n, pl **-dies**
money granted
subsist v exist, sustain life
subsistence n the means by
which one supports life
substance ❶ n **1** (particular kind
of) matter **2** essence **3** wealth
substantial adj considerable

——————————— THESAURUS ———————————

= **subordinate**, dependent,
satellite, inferior, obedient ▷ v
= **put through**, expose, submit, lay
open
sublime adj = **noble**, glorious,
high, great, grand ≠ **lowly**
submerge ❶ v = **flood**, swamp,
engulf, overflow, inundate
subordinate n = **inferior**, junior,
assistant, aide, second ≠ **superior**
▷ adj = **inferior**, lesser, lower,
junior, subject ≠ **superior**
subscribe v = **support**, advocate,
endorse; = **contribute**, give,

donate
subsequent adj = **following**,
later, succeeding, after, successive
≠ **previous**
subside v = **decrease**, diminish,
lessen, ease, wane ≠ **increase**;
= **collapse**, sink, cave in, drop,
lower
subsidiary adj = **secondary**,
lesser, subordinate, minor,
supplementary ≠ **main**
substance n = **material**, body,
stuff, fabric; = **importance**,
significance, concreteness;

S

2 of real value **3** really existing

substantiate v bring evidence for, prove

substitute ❶ v **1** put, serve in place of ▷ n **2** thing, person put in place of another ▷ adj **3** serving as a substitute **substitution** n

subsume v incorporate in larger group

subterfuge n trick, lying excuse used to evade something

subterranean adj underground

subtitle n **1** secondary title of book ▷ pl **2** translation superimposed on foreign film ▷ v **3** provide with subtitle or subtitles

subtle ❶ adj **1** not immediately obvious **2** ingenious **3** crafty **4** making fine distinctions **subtlety** n **subtly** adv

subtract v take away, deduct **subtraction** n

suburb n residential area on outskirts of city **suburban** adj **suburbia** n suburbs and their inhabitants

subvert v **1** overthrow **2** corrupt **subversion** n **subversive** adj

subway n **1** underground passage

2 (US & Canad) underground railway

succeed ❶ v **1** accomplish purpose **2** turn out satisfactorily **3** follow **4** take place of **success** n **1** favourable accomplishment, attainment, issue or outcome **2** successful person or thing **successful** adj **succession** n **1** following **2** series **3** succeeding **successive** adj **1** following in order **2** consecutive **successor** n

succinct adj brief and clear

succour v/n help in distress

succulent adj **1** juicy **2** (of plant) having thick, fleshy leaves ▷ n **3** such plant **succulence** n

succumb ❶ v give way

such adj **1** of the kind or degree mentioned **2** so great, so much

suck v **1** draw into mouth **2** hold in mouth **3** draw in ▷ n **4** sucking **sucker** n **1** person, thing that sucks **2** shoot coming from root or base of stem of plant **3** (Inf) one who is easily deceived

suckle v feed from the breast **suckling** n unweaned infant

suction n **1** drawing or sucking of air or fluid **2** force produced by

= **meaning**, main point, gist, import, significance; = **wealth**, means, property, assets, resources

substitute v = **replace**, exchange, swap, change, switch ▷ n = **replacement**, reserve, surrogate, deputy, sub

subtle adj = **faint**, slight, implied, delicate, understated ≠ **obvious**; = **crafty**, cunning, sly, shrewd, ingenious ≠ **straightforward**;

= **muted**, soft, subdued, low-key, toned down

succeed v = **triumph**, win, prevail; = **work out**, work, be successful; = **make it** (Inf), do well, be successful, triumph, thrive ≠ **fail**

succumb v often with **to** = **surrender**, yield, submit, give in, cave in (Inf) ≠ **beat**; **with to** = **catch**, fall ill with

S

difference in pressure

sudden ❶ adj 1 done, occurring unexpectedly 2 abrupt **suddenly** adv

suds pl n froth of soap and water

sue ❶ v suing, sued 1 prosecute 2 seek justice from 3 make application or entreaty

suede n leather with soft, velvety finish

suet n hard animal fat

suffer ❶ v 1 undergo 2 tolerate **suffering** n

suffice ❶ v be adequate, satisfactory (for) **sufficiency** n adequate amount **sufficient** adj enough, adequate

suffix n group of letters added to end of word

suffocate v 1 kill, be killed by deprivation of oxygen 2 smother **suffocation** n

suffrage n vote or right of voting

suffuse v well up and spread over

sugar n 1 sweet crystalline substance ▷ v 2 sweeten, make pleasant (with sugar) **sugary** adj

suggest ❶ v 1 propose 2 call up the idea of **suggestible** adj easily

influenced **suggestion** n 1 hint 2 proposal 3 insinuation of impression, belief etc. into mind

suggestive adj containing suggestions, esp. of something indecent

suicide n 1 act of killing oneself 2 one who does this **suicidal** adj

suit ❶ n 1 set of clothing 2 garment worn for particular event, purpose 3 one of four sets in pack of cards 4 action at law ▷ v 5 make, be fit or appropriate for 6 be acceptable to (someone) **suitability** n **suitable** adj fitting, convenient **suitcase** n flat rectangular travelling case

suite ❶ n 1 matched set of furniture 2 set of rooms 3 retinue

suitor n 1 wooer 2 one who sues

sulk v 1 be silent, resentful ▷ n 2 this mood **sulky** adj

sullen adj unwilling to talk or be sociable, morose

sully v -lying, -lied stain, tarnish

sulphur n pale yellow nonmetallic element **sulphuric** adj **sulphurous** adj

_____ THESAURUS _____

sudden adj = **quick**, rapid, unexpected, swift, hurried ≠ **gradual**

sue v (Law) = **take (someone) to court**, prosecute, charge, summon, indict

suffer v = **be in pain**, hurt, ache; = **be affected**, have trouble with, be afflicted, be troubled with

suffice v = **be enough**, do, be sufficient, be adequate, serve

suggest v = **recommend**, propose, advise, advocate, prescribe; = **hint at**, imply, intimate

suit n = **outfit**, costume, ensemble, dress, clothing; = **lawsuit**, case, trial, proceeding, cause ▷ v = **be acceptable to**, please, satisfy, do, gratify; = **agree with**, become, match, go with, harmonize with

suite n = **rooms**, apartment

sultan n ruler of Muslim country

sultry adj **-trier, -triest 1** (of weather) hot, humid **2** (of person) looking sensual

sum ❶ n **1** amount, total **2** problem in arithmetic ▷ v **3** add up **4** make summary of main parts

summary ❶ n, pl **-ries 1** brief statement of chief points of something ▷ adj **2** done quickly **summarily** adv **1** speedily **2** abruptly **summarize** v make summary of

summer n second, warmest season

summit ❶ n top, peak

summon ❶ v **1** demand attendance of **2** bid witness appear in court **3** gather up (energies etc.) **summons** n **1** call **2** authoritative demand

sumo n Japanese style of wrestling

sumptuous ❶ adj lavish, magnificent **sumptuousness** n

sun n **1** luminous body round which earth and other planets revolve **2** its rays ▷ v **3** expose to sun's rays **sunless** adj **sunny** adj **1** like the sun **2** warm **3** cheerful **sunbathe** n lie in sunshine **sunbeam** n ray of sun **sunburn** n inflammation of skin due to excessive exposure to

sun sundown n sunset **sunflower** n plant with large golden flowers **sunrise** n appearance of sun above the horizon **sunset** n disappearance of sun below the horizon **sunshine** n light and warmth from sun **sunstroke** n illness caused by prolonged exposure to sun **sundae** n ice cream topped with fruit etc.

Sunday n first day of the week **Sunday school** school for religious instruction of children

sundry adj several, various **sundries** pl n odd items, not mentioned in detail

sup v **supping, supped 1** take by sips **2** take supper ▷ n **3** mouthful of liquid

super adj (Inf) very good

super- comb. form above, greater, exceedingly, as in superhuman; supertanker

superannuation n **1** pension given on retirement **2** contribution by employee to pension

superb ❶ adj extremely good or impressive

supercilious adj displaying arrogant pride, scorn

superficial ❶ adj **1** of or on

— THESAURUS —

sum n = **amount**, quantity, volume

summary n = **synopsis**, résumé, précis, review, outline

summit n = **peak**, top, tip, pinnacle, apex ≠ **base**

summon v = **send for**, call, bid, invite; often with **up** = **gather**, muster, draw on

sumptuous adj = **luxurious**, grand, superb, splendid, gorgeous ≠ **plain**

superb adj = **splendid**, excellent, magnificent, fine, grand ≠ **inferior**

superficial adj = **shallow**, frivolous, empty-headed, silly, trivial ≠ **serious**; = **hasty**, cursory, surface **2** not careful or thorough **3** without depth, shallow

superfluous adj extra, unnecessary **superfluity** n

superhuman adj beyond normal human ability or experience

superimpose v place on or over something else

superintend v **1** have charge of **2** overlook **3** supervise **superintendent** n senior police officer

superior ⊙ adj **1** greater in quality or quantity **2** upper, higher in position, rank or quality **3** showing consciousness of being so ▷ n **4** supervisor, manager **superiority** n

superlative adj **1** of, in highest degree or quality **2** surpassing **3** (Grammar) denoting form of adjective, adverb meaning most

supermarket n large self-service store

supernatural ⊙ adj **1** being beyond the powers or laws of nature **2** miraculous

supernumerary adj exceeding

the required or regular number

superpower n extremely powerful nation

supersede v take the place of

supersonic adj denoting speed greater than that of sound

superstition n religion, opinion or practice based on belief in luck or magic **superstitious** adj

superstructure n **1** structure above foundations **2** part of ship above deck

supervise ⊙ v **1** oversee **2** direct **3** inspect and control **supervision** n **supervisor** n **supervisory** adj

supine adj lying on back with face upwards

supper n (light) evening meal

supplant v take the place of

supple adj **1** pliable **2** flexible **supply** adv

supplement ⊙ n **1** thing added to fill up, supply deficiency, esp. extra part added to book etc. ▷ v **2** add to **3** supply deficiency **supplementary** adj

supply ⊙ v **-plying, -plied** **1** furnish **2** make available

S

perfunctory, hurried, casual ≠ **thorough**; = **slight**, surface, external, on the surface, exterior ≠ **profound**

superior adj = **better**, higher, greater, grander, surpassing ≠ **inferior**; = **first-class**, excellent, first-rate, choice, exclusive ≠ **average**; = **supercilious**, patronizing, condescending, haughty, disdainful ▷ n = **boss**, senior, director, manager, chief (Inf)

≠ **subordinate**

supernatural adj = **paranormal**, unearthly, uncanny, ghostly, psychic

supervise v = **observe**, guide, monitor, oversee, keep an eye on

supplement v = **add to**, reinforce, augment, extend ▷ n = **pull-out**, insert; = **appendix**, add-on, postscript; = **addition**, extra

supply v = **provide**, give, furnish, produce, stock ▷ n = **store**, fund, stock, source, reserve

DICTIONARY

3 provide ▷ n **4** stock, store **5** food, materials needed for journey etc.

support ❶ v **1** hold up **2** sustain **3** assist ▷ n **4** supporting, being supported **5** means of support **supporter** n adherent **supporting** adj (of role in film etc.) less important **supportive** adj

suppose ❶ v **1** assume as theory **2** take for granted **3** accept as likely **supposed** adj **1** assumed **2** expected, obliged **3** permitted **supposedly** adv according to what is **supposed supposition** n **1** assumption **2** belief without proof **3** conjecture

suppress ❶ v **1** put down, restrain **2** keep or withdraw from publication **suppression** n

suppurate v fester, form pus

supreme adj **1** highest in authority or rank **2** utmost **supremacy** n position of being supreme **supremo** n person in overall authority

surcharge v/n (make) additional charge

sure ❶ adj **1** certain **2** trustworthy **3** without doubt ▷ adv **4** (Inf) certainly **surely** adv **surety** n person, thing acting as guarantee for another's obligations

surf n **1** waves breaking on shore ▷ v **2** ride surf **surfer** n **surfing** n sport of riding over surf **surfboard** n board used in surfing

surface ❶ n **1** outside face of object **2** plane **3** top **4** superficial appearance ▷ adj **5** involving the surface only ▷ v **6** come to surface

surfeit n **1** excess **2** disgust caused by excess ▷ v **3** feed to excess

surge ❶ n **1** wave **2** sudden increase ▷ v **3** move in large waves **4** swell

surgeon n medical expert who performs operations **surgery** n

THESAURUS

support v = **help**, back, champion, second, aid ≠ **oppose**; = **provide for**, maintain, look after, keep, fund ≠ **live off**; = **bear out**, confirm, verify, substantiate, corroborate ≠ **refute**; = **bear**, carry, sustain, prop (up), reinforce ▷ n = **furtherance**, backing, promotion, assistance, encouragement; = **help**, loyalty ≠ **opposition**

suppose v = **imagine**, consider, conjecture, postulate, hypothesize; = **think**, imagine, expect, assume, guess (Inf, chiefly US & Canad)

suppress v = **stamp out**, stop,

check, crush, conquer ≠ **encourage**; = **check**, inhibit, subdue, stop, quell

sure adj = **certain**, positive, decided, convinced, confident ≠ **uncertain**; = **inevitable**, guaranteed, bound, assured, inescapable ≠ **unsure**; = **reliable**, accurate, dependable, undoubted, undeniable ≠ **unreliable**

surface n = **covering**, face, exterior, side, top ▷ v = **emerge**, come up, come to the surface

surge n = **rush**, flood; = **flow**, wave, rush, roller, gush ▷ v = **rush**, pour, rise, gush; = **roll**, rush, heave

1 medical treatment by operation **2** doctor's, dentist's consulting room **surgical** *adj*

surly *adj* **-lier, -liest** cross and rude

surmise *v/n* guess, conjecture

surmount *v* get over, overcome

surname *n* family name

surpass ❶ *v* **1** go beyond **2** excel **3** outstrip **surpassing** *adj* excellent

surplus ❶ *n* **1** what remains over in excess ▷ *adj* **2** spare, superfluous

surprise ❶ *n* **1** something unexpected **2** emotion aroused by being taken unawares ▷ *v* **3** cause surprise to **4** astonish **5** take, come upon unexpectedly

surrealism *n* incongruous combination of images **surreal** *adj*

surrender ❶ *v* **1** hand over, give up **2** yield **3** cease resistance ▷ *n* **4** act of surrendering

surreptitious *adj* **1** done secretly or stealthily **2** furtive

surrogate *n* substitute **surrogate mother** woman who bears child on behalf of childless couple

surround ❶ *v* **1** be, come all round, encompass **2** encircle ▷ *n* **3** border, edging **surroundings** *pl n* conditions, scenery etc. around a person, place, environment

surveillance ❶ *n* close watch, supervision

survey ❶ *v* **1** view, scrutinize **2** inspect, examine **3** measure, map (land) ▷ *n* **4** act of surveying **5** inspection **6** report incorporating results of survey **surveyor** *n*

survive ❶ *v* **1** continue to live or exist **2** outlive **survival** *n* continuation of existence **survivor** *n* one who survives

surpass *v* = **outdo**, beat, exceed, eclipse, excel

surplus *n* = **excess**, surfeit ≠ **shortage** ▷ *adj* = **extra**, spare, excess, remaining, odd ≠ **insufficient**

surprise *n* = **shock**, revelation, jolt, bombshell, eye-opener (*Inf*); = **amazement**, astonishment, wonder, incredulity ▷ *v* = **amaze**, astonish, stun, startle, stagger; = **catch unawares** or **off-guard**, spring upon

surrender *v* = **give in**, yield, submit, give way, succumb ≠ **resist**; = **give up**, abandon, relinquish, yield, concede ▷ *n* = **submission**,

cave-in (*Inf*), capitulation, resignation, renunciation

surround *v* = **enclose**, ring, encircle, encompass, envelop

surveillance *n* = **observation**, watch, scrutiny, supervision, inspection

survey *n* = **poll**, study, research, review, inquiry; = **examination**, inspection, scrutiny ▷ *v* = **interview**, question, poll, research, investigate; = **look over**, view, examine, observe, contemplate; = **measure**, estimate, assess, appraise

survive *v* = **remain alive**, last, live on, endure

S

susceptible ❶ adj **1** yielding readily (to) **2** capable (of) **3** impressionable **susceptibility** n

suspect ❶ v **1** doubt innocence of **2** have impression of existence or presence of **3** be inclined to believe that ▷ adj **4** of suspicious character ▷ n **5** suspected person

suspend ❶ v **1** hang up **2** cause to cease for a time **3** keep inoperative **4** sustain in fluid **suspenders** pl n straps for supporting stockings

suspense n **1** state of uncertainty, esp. while awaiting news, an event etc. **2** anxiety, worry **suspension** n **1** state of being suspended **2** springs on axle of body of vehicle

suspicion ❶ n **1** suspecting, being suspected **2** slight trace **suspicious** adj

sustain ❶ v **1** keep, hold up **2** endure **3** keep alive **4** confirm **sustenance** n food

SUV sport (or sports) utility vehicle: a powerful car with four-wheel drive, designed for road and off-road use

svelte adj gracefully slim

swab n **1** mop **2** pad of surgical wool etc. for cleaning **3** taking specimen etc. ▷ v **4** clean with swab

swag n (Sl) stolen property

swagger v **1** strut **2** boast ▷ n **3** strutting gait **4** boastful manner

swallow¹ ❶ v **1** cause, allow to pass down gullet **2** suppress ▷ n **3** act of swallowing

swallow² n migratory bird with forked tail

swamp ❶ n **1** bog ▷ v **2** entangle in swamp **3** overwhelm **4** flood

swan n large, web-footed water bird with curved neck

swap, swop ❶ v **swapping, swapped 1** exchange **2** barter ▷ n **3** exchange

susceptible adj = **responsive**, sensitive, receptive, impressionable, suggestible ≠ **unresponsive**

suspect v = **believe**, feel, guess, consider, suppose ≠ **know**; = **distrust**, doubt, mistrust ≠ **trust** ▷ adj = **dubious**, doubtful, questionable, iffy (Inf) ≠ **innocent**

suspend v = **postpone**, put off, cease, interrupt, shelve ≠ **continue**; = **hang**, attach, dangle

suspicion n = **distrust**, scepticism, mistrust, doubt, misgiving; = **idea**, notion, hunch,

guess, impression; = **trace**, touch, hint, suggestion, shade

sustain v = **maintain**, continue, keep up, prolong, protract; = **suffer**, experience, undergo, feel, bear; = **help**, aid, assist; = **keep alive**, nourish, provide for

swallow¹ v = **eat**, consume, devour, swig (Inf)

swamp n = **bog**, marsh, quagmire, slough, fen ▷ v = **flood**, engulf, submerge, inundate; = **overload**, overwhelm, inundate

swap, swop v = **exchange**, trade, switch, interchange, barter

swarm ❶ n 1 large cluster of insects 2 vast crowd ▷ v 3 (of bees) be on the move in swarm 4 gather in large numbers

swarthy adj -thier, -thiest dark-complexioned

swastika n symbol of cross with arms bent at right angles

swat v swatting, swatted 1 hit smartly 2 kill, esp. insects

swathe ❶ v cover with wraps or bandages

sway ❶ v 1 swing unsteadily 2 (cause to) vacillate in opinion etc. ▷ n 3 control 4 power 5 swaying motion

swear ❶ v swearing, swore, sworn 1 promise on oath 2 cause to take an oath 3 declare 4 curse **swearword** n word considered obscene or blasphemous

sweat ❶ n 1 moisture oozing from, forming on skin 2 (Inf) state of anxiety ▷ v 3 (cause to) exude sweat 4 toil **sweaty** adj

sweatshirt n long-sleeved cotton jersey

sweater n woollen jersey

swede n variety of turnip

sweep ❶ v sweeping, swept 1 clean with broom 2 pass quickly or magnificently 3 extend in continuous curve 4 carry away suddenly ▷ n 5 act of cleaning with broom 6 sweeping motion 7 wide curve 8 one who cleans chimneys **sweeping** adj 1 wide-ranging 2 without limitations **sweepstake** n lottery with stakes of participants as prize

sweet ❶ adj 1 tasting like sugar 2 agreeable 3 kind, charming 4 fragrant 5 tuneful 6 dear, beloved ▷ n 7 small piece of sweet food 8 sweet course served at end of meal **sweeten** v **sweetener** n 1 sweetening agent 2 (Sl) bribe **sweetness** n **sweet corn** type of maize with sweet yellow kernels **sweetheart** n lover **sweet pea**

━━━━━━━━━━━━━━━━━━━━━━━━━ THESAURUS ━━━━━━━━━━━━━━━━━━━━━━━━━

swarm n = **multitude**, crowd, mass, army, host ▷ v = **crowd**, flock, throng, mass, stream; = **teem**, crawl, abound, bristle

swathe v = **wrap**, drape, envelop, cloak, shroud

sway v = **move from side to side**, rock, roll, swing; = **influence**, affect, guide, persuade, induce ▷ n = **power**, control, influence, authority, clout (Inf)

swear v = **curse**, blaspheme, be foul-mouthed; = **vow**, promise, testify, attest; = **declare**, assert, affirm

sweat n (Inf) = **panic**, anxiety, worry, distress, agitation ▷ v = **perspire**, glow; (Inf) = **worry**, fret, agonize, torture yourself

sweep v = **brush**, clean; = **clear**, remove, brush, clean ▷ n = **movement**, move, swing, stroke; = **extent**, range, stretch, scope

sweet adj = **sugary**, cloying, saccharine, icky (Inf) ≠ **sour**; = **fragrant**, aromatic ≠ **stinking**; = **fresh**, clean, pure ▷ n usually plural = **confectionery**, candy (US), lolly (Aust & NZ), bonbon; (Brit) = **dessert**, pudding

S

...lant of pea family with bright
...lowers **sweet-talk** v (Inf) coax,
...latter

**... well ❶ v swelling, swelled,
...swollen 1** expand **2** be greatly
...illed with pride, emotion ▷ n **3** act
...of swelling or being swollen
4 wave of sea **swelling** n
...enlargement of part of body, caused
...by injury or infection

...verve v **1** swing round, change
...direction during motion **2** turn aside
...from duty etc.) ▷ n **3** swerving

...wift ❶ adj 1 rapid, quick ▷ n
2 bird like a swallow

...wig n **1** large swallow of drink ▷ v
2 drink thus

...will v **1** drink greedily **2** pour
...water over or through ▷ n **3** liquid
...pig food **4** rinsing

**...wim v swimming, swam, swum
1** support and move oneself in
...water **2** float **3** be flooded **4** have
...feeling of dizziness ▷ n **5** spell of
...swimming **swimmer** n
swimmingly adv successfully

...windle n/v cheat **swindler** n

...wine n **1** pig **2** contemptible
...person

**swing ❶ v swinging, swung
1** (cause to) move to and fro
2 (cause to) pivot, turn **3** hang
4 be hanged **5** hit out (at) ▷ n
6 act, instance of swinging **7** seat
hung to swing on **8** fluctuation
(esp. in voting pattern)

swingeing adj punishing, severe

swipe v strike with wide, sweeping
or glancing blow

swirl ❶ v 1 (cause to) move with
eddying motion ▷ n **2** such motion

swish v 1 (cause to) move with
hissing sound ▷ n **2** the sound

switch ❶ n 1 mechanism to
complete or interrupt electric
circuit etc. **2** abrupt change
3 flexible stick or twig **4** tress of
false hair ▷ v **5** change abruptly
6 exchange **7** affect (current etc.)
with switch **switchboard** n
installation for connecting
telephone calls

swivel n **-elling, -elled
1** mechanism of two parts which
can revolve the one on the other ▷ v
2 turn (on swivel)

swoop ❶ v 1 dive, as hawk ▷ n
2 act of swooping

S

---

well v = **increase**, rise, grow,
mount, expand ≠ **decrease**;
= **expand**, increase, grow, rise,
balloon ≠ **shrink** ▷ n = **wave**,
surge, billow

...wift adj = **quick**, prompt, rapid

...wing v = **brandish**, wave,
shake, flourish, wield; = **sway**,
rock, wave, veer, oscillate; usually
with **round** = **turn**, swivel, curve,
rotate, pivot; = **hit out**, strike,

swipe, lash out at, slap ▷ n
= **swaying**, sway

swirl v = **whirl**, churn, spin, twist,
eddy

switch n = **control**, button, lever,
on/off device; = **change**, shift,
reversal ▷ v = **change**, shift,
divert, deviate; = **exchange**, swap,
substitute

swoop v = **pounce**, attack, charge,
rush, descend

sword n weapon with long blade
swordfish n fish with elongated sharp upper jaw

swot (Inf) ▷ v **1** study hard ▷ n **2** one who works hard at lessons

sycamore n tree related to maple

sycophant n one using flattery to gain favours **sycophantic** adj

syllable n division of word as unit for pronunciation

syllabus n, pl **-buses, -bi** outline of course of study

syllogism n form of logical reasoning consisting of two premises and conclusion

symbol ❶ n **1** sign **2** thing representing or typifying something **symbolic** adj **symbolism** n **symbolize** v

symmetry n proportion between parts **symmetrical** adj

sympathy ❶ n, pl **-thies** **1** feeling for another in pain etc. **2** compassion, pity **3** sharing of emotion etc. **sympathetic** adj **sympathize** v

symphony n, pl **-nies** composition for full orchestra

symposium n, pl **-siums, -sia** conference

symptom ❶ n **1** change in body indicating disease **2** sign **symptomatic** adj

synagogue n Jewish place of worship

sync, synch n (Inf) synchronization

synchromesh adj (of gearbox) having device that synchronizes speeds of gears before they engag

synchronize v **1** make agree in time **2** happen at same time **synchronization** n

syncopate v accentuate weak be in bar of music **syncopation** n

syndicate n **1** body of persons associated for some enterprise ▷ **2** form syndicate **3** publish in ma newspapers at the same time

syndrome n combination of several symptoms in disease

synod n church council

synonym n word with same meaning as another **synonymou** adj

synopsis n, pl **-ses** summary, outline

syntax n arrangement of words in sentence

synthesis n, pl **-ses** putting together, combination **synthesiz** v make artificially **synthesizer** n electronic keyboard instrument reproducing wide range of musica sounds **synthetic** adj **1** artificial **2** of synthesis

syphilis n contagious venereal disease

syringe n **1** instrument for drawing in liquid and forcing it out

symbol n = **metaphor**, image, sign, representation, token

sympathy n = **compassion**, understanding, pity,

commiseration ≠ **indifference**; = **affinity**, agreement, rapport, fellow feeling ≠ **opposition**

symptom n = **sign**, mark, indication, warning

S

in fine spray ▷ v **2** spray, cleanse
with syringe
syrup n **1** thick solution obtained
in process of refining sugar **2** any

liquid like this
system ❶ n **1** complex whole
2 method **3** classification
systematic adj methodical

THESAURUS

---

system n = **arrangement**,
structure, organization, scheme,

classification; = **method**, practice,
technique, procedure, routine

t

ta *interj* (*Inf*) thank you

tab *n* tag, label, short strap

Tabasco® *n* hot red pepper sauce

tabby *adj/n, pl* **-bies** (cat) with stripes on lighter background

table ❶ *n* **1** flat board supported by legs **2** facts, figures arranged in lines or columns ▷ *v* **3** submit (motion etc.) for discussion

tablespoon *n* spoon for serving food

tableau *n, pl* **-leaux** group of persons representing some scene

tablet *n* **1** pill of compressed powdered medicine **2** cake of soap etc. **3** inscribed slab of stone, wood etc. **4** hand-held computer

tabloid *n* small-sized newspaper

with many photographs and usu. sensational style

taboo ❶ *adj, pl* **-boos 1** forbidden ▷ *n* **2** prohibition resulting from social conventions etc.

tacit *adj* implied but not spoken

taciturn *adj* habitually silent

tack¹ ❶ *n* **1** small nail **2** long loose stitch **3** (*Naut*) course of ship obliquely to windward **4** approach, method ▷ *v* **5** nail with tacks **6** stitch lightly **7** append **8** sail to windward

tack² *n* riding harness for horses

tackies, takkies *pl n, sing* **tacky** (*S Afr, Inf*) tennis shoes or plimsolls

tackle ❶ *n* **1** equipment, esp. for lifting **2** (*Sport*) physical challenge of opponent ▷ *v* **3** undertake **4** challenge

tacky¹ *adj* **tackier, tackiest 1** sticky **2** not quite dry

tacky² *adj* **tackier, tackiest** vulgar, tasteless

tact *n* skill in dealing with people or situations **tactful** *adj* **tactless** *adj*

tactics *pl n* **1** art of handling troops, ships in battle **2** methods, plans **tactical** *adj* **tactician** *n*

tactile *adj* of sense of touch

———————————— THESAURUS ————————————

table *n* = **counter**, bench, stand, board, surface; = **list**, chart, tabulation, record, roll ▷ *v* (*Brit*) = **submit**, propose, put forward, move, suggest

taboo *n* = **prohibition**, ban, restriction, anathema, interdict ▷ *adj* = **forbidden**, banned, prohibited, unacceptable, outlawed

≠ permitted

tack¹ *n* = **nail**, pin, drawing pin ▷ *v* = **fasten**, fix, attach, pin, nail; (*Brit*) = **stitch**, sew, hem, bind, baste

tackle *v* = **deal with**, set about, get stuck into (*Inf*), come or get to grips with; = **undertake**, attempt, embark upon, get stuck into (*Inf*), have a go or stab at (*Inf*) ▷ *n* tadpole n immature frog

taffeta n stiff silk fabric

tag¹ n 1 label identifying or showing price of (something) 2 hanging end ▷ v 3 add (on)

tag² n 1 children's game where one chased becomes the chaser upon being touched ▷ v 2 touch

tail ❶ n 1 flexible appendage at animal's rear 2 hindmost, lower or inferior part of anything ▷ pl 3 reverse side of coin ▷ v 4 remove tail of 5 (Inf) follow closely **tailback** n queue of traffic stretching back from obstruction **tailboard** n hinged rear board on lorry etc. **tail coat** man's evening dress jacket **tail off** diminish gradually **tailspin** n spinning fall of aircraft **tailwind** n wind coming from rear

tailor ❶ n maker of clothing, esp. for men **tailor-made** adj well-fitting

taint ❶ v 1 affect or be affected by pollution etc. ▷ n 2 defect 3 contamination

take ❶ v taking, took, taken 1 grasp 2 get 3 receive 4 understand 5 consider 6 use 7 capture 8 steal 9 accept 10 bear 11 consume 12 assume 13 carry 14 accompany 15 subtract 16 require 17 contain, hold 18 be effective 19 please ▷ n 20 (recording of) scene filmed without break **takings** pl n earnings, receipts **take after** resemble in face or character **takeaway** n 1 shop, restaurant selling meals for eating elsewhere 2 meal bought at this place **take in** 1 understand 2 include 3 make (garment etc.) smaller 4 deceive **take off** 1 remove 2 (of aircraft) leave ground 3 (Inf) go away 4 (Inf) mimic **take-off** n **takeover** n act of taking control of company by buying large number of its shares

talc, talcum powder n powder, usu. scented, to absorb body moisture

tale ❶ n story, narrative

= **block**, challenge, apparatus

tag¹ n = **label**, tab, note, ticket, slip ▷ v = **label**, mark

tail n = **extremity**, appendage, brush, rear end, hindquarters ▷ v (Inf) = **follow**, track, shadow, trail, stalk

tailor n = **outfitter**, couturier, dressmaker, seamstress, clothier ▷ v = **adapt**, adjust, modify, style, fashion

taint v = **spoil**, ruin, contaminate, damage, stain ≠ **purify**

take v = **grip**, grab, seize, catch, grasp; = **carry**, bring, bear, transport, ferry ≠ **send**; = **accompany**, lead, bring, guide, conduct; = **remove**, draw, pull, fish, withdraw; = **steal**, appropriate, pocket, pinch (Inf), misappropriate ≠ **return**; = **capture**, seize, take into custody, lay hold of ≠ **release**; = **tolerate**, stand, bear, stomach, endure ≠ **avoid**

tale n = **story**, narrative, anecdote, account, legend

t

talent ❶ n natural ability **talented** adj gifted

talisman n, pl **-mans** object supposed to have magic power

talk ❶ v 1 express, exchange ideas etc. in words 2 discuss ▷ n 3 lecture 4 conversation 5 rumour 6 discussion **talkative** adj

tall ❶ adj 1 high 2 of great stature

tally ❶ v **-lying, -lied** 1 correspond one with the other 2 count ▷ n 3 record, account

talon n claw

tambourine n flat half-drum with jingling discs of metal attached

tame ❶ adj 1 not wild, domesticated 2 uninteresting ▷ v 3 make tame

tamper v interfere (with)

tampon n plug of cotton wool inserted into vagina during menstruation

tan adj/n 1 (of) brown colour of skin after exposure to sun etc. ▷ v 2 (cause to) go brown 3 (of animal hide) convert to leather **tannin** n vegetable substance used as tanning agent

tandem n bicycle for two

tandoori adj (of Indian food) cooked in a clay oven

tang n strong pungent taste or smell **tangy** adj

tangent n line that touches a curve **tangential** adj

tangerine n (fruit of) Asian citrus tree

tangible ❶ adj 1 that can be touched 2 real **tangibility** n

tangle ❶ n 1 confused mass or situation ▷ v 2 confuse

tango n, pl **-gos** dance of S Amer. origin

tank n 1 storage vessel for liquids or gases 2 armoured motor vehicle

     THESAURUS

talent n = **ability**, gift, aptitude, capacity, genius

talk v = **speak**, chat, chatter, converse, communicate; = **discuss**, confer, negotiate, parley, confabulate; = **inform**, grass (Brit SI), tell all, give the game away, blab ▷ n = **speech**, lecture, presentation, report, address

tall adj = **lofty**, big, great, long-legged, lanky; = **high**, towering, soaring, steep, elevated ≠ **short**; (Inf) = **implausible**, incredible, far-fetched, exaggerated, absurd ≠ **plausible**

tally n = **record**, score, total, count, reckoning ▷ v = **agree**, match, accord, fit, square ≠ **disagree**

tame adj = **domesticated**, docile, broken, gentle, obedient ≠ **wild**; = **submissive**, meek, compliant, subdued, manageable ≠ **stubborn**; = **unexciting**, boring, dull, bland, uninspiring ≠ **exciting** ▷ v = **domesticate**, train, break in, house-train ≠ **make fiercer**; = **subdue**, suppress, master, discipline, humble ≠ **arouse**

tangible adj = **definite**, real, positive, material, actual ≠ **intangible**

tangle n = **knot**, twist, web, jungle, coil; = **mess**, jam, fix (Inf), confusion, complication ▷ v on tracks **tanker** n ship, lorry for carrying liquid

tankard n large drinking cup

Tannoy® n type of public-address system

tantalize v torment by appearing to offer something

tantamount adj **tantamount to** equivalent in effect to

tantrum ❶ n outburst of temper

tap¹ ❶ v **tapping, tapped** 1 strike lightly but with some noise ▷ n 2 tapping **tap dance** dance in which the feet beat out elaborate rhythms

tap² ❶ n 1 valve with handle, plug etc. to regulate or stop flow of fluid ▷ v 2 draw off with tap 3 use, draw on 4 make secret connection to telephone wire to overhear conversation on it

tape ❶ n 1 narrow strip of fabric, paper etc. 2 magnetic recording ▷ v 3 record (speech, music etc.) **tape measure** tape marked off in centimetres, inches etc. **tape recorder** apparatus for recording sound on magnetized tape

tapeworm n long flat parasitic worm

taper v 1 become gradually thinner ▷ n 2 thin candle

tapestry n, pl **-tries** fabric decorated with woven designs

tapioca n beadlike starch made from cassava root

tar n 1 thick black liquid distilled from coal etc. ▷ v 2 coat, treat with tar

tarantula n large (poisonous) hairy spider

tardy adj **tardier, tardiest** slow, late

target ❶ n 1 thing aimed at 2 victim

tariff ❶ n 1 tax levied on imports etc. 2 list of charges

Tarmac n mixture of tar etc. giving hard, smooth surface to road

tarn n small mountain lake

tarnish ❶ v 1 (cause to) become stained or sullied ▷ n 2 discoloration, blemish

tarot n pack of cards used in fortune-telling

tarpaulin n (sheet of) heavy

= **twist**, knot, mat, coil, mesh ≠ **disentangle**

tantrum n = **outburst**, temper, hysterics, fit, flare-up

tap¹ v = **knock**, strike, pat, rap, beat ▷ n = **knock**, pat, rap, touch, drumming

tap² n = **valve**, stopcock ▷ v = **listen in on**, monitor, bug (Inf), spy on, eavesdrop on

tape n = **binding**, strip, band, string, ribbon ▷ v = **record**, video,

tape-record, make a recording of; sometimes with **up** = **bind**, secure, stick, seal, wrap

target n = **mark**, goal; = **goal**, aim, objective, end, mark

tariff n = **tax**, duty, toll, levy, excise; = **price list**, schedule

tarnish v = **damage**, taint, blacken, sully, smirch ≠ **enhance**; = **stain**, discolour, darken, blot, blemish ≠ **brighten** ▷ n = **stain**, taint, discoloration, spot, blot

t

hard-wearing waterproof fabric

tarragon n aromatic herb

tarry v **-rying, -ried 1** linger, delay **2** stay behind

tart¹ ❶ n **1** small pie or flan filled with fruit, jam etc. **2** loose woman

tart² ❶ adj **1** sour **2** sharp **3** bitter

tartan n woollen cloth woven in pattern of coloured checks

tartar n crust deposited on teeth

task ❶ n **1** piece of work (esp. unpleasant or difficult) set or undertaken **taskmaster** n overseer

tassel n **1** ornament of fringed knot of threads etc. **2** tuft

taste ❶ n **1** sense by which flavour, quality of substance is detected by the tongue **2** (brief) experience of something **3** small amount **4** liking **5** power of discerning, judging ▷ v **6** observe or distinguish the taste of a substance **7** take small amount into mouth **8** experience **9** have specific flavour **tasteful** adj with, showing good taste **tasteless** adj

1 bland, insipid **2** showing bad taste **tasty** adj pleasantly flavoured **taste bud** small organ of taste on tongue

tattered adj ragged **tatters** pl n ragged pieces

tattle v/n gossip, chatter

tattletale (chiefly US and Canad) n a scandalmonger or gossip

tattoo¹ n **1** beat of drum and bugle call **2** military spectacle

tattoo² v **1** mark skin in coloured patterns etc. by pricking ▷ n **2** pattern made thus

tatty adj **-tier, -tiest** shabby, worn out

taunt ❶ v **1** provoke with insults etc. ▷ n **2** scornful remark

taupe adj brownish-grey

taut adj **1** drawn tight **2** under strain

tavern ❶ n inn, public house

tawdry adj **-drier, -driest** showy, but cheap

tawny n/adj **-nier, -niest** (of) light yellowish-brown colour

tax ❶ n **1** compulsory payments

tart¹ n = **pie**, pastry, pasty, tartlet, patty

tart² adj = **sharp**, acid, sour, bitter, pungent ≠ **sweet**

task n = **job**, duty, assignment, exercise, mission

taste n = **flavour**, savour, relish, smack, tang ≠ **blandness**; = **bit**, bite, mouthful, sample, dash; = **liking**, preference, penchant, fondness, partiality ≠ **dislike**; = **refinement**, style, judgment, discrimination, appreciation

≠ lack of judgment ▷ v = **have a flavour**, smack of, savour of; = **sample**, try, test, sip, savour; = **distinguish**, perceive, discern, differentiate; = **experience**, know, undergo, partake of, encounter ≠ **miss**

taunt v = **jeer**, mock, tease, ridicule, provoke ▷ n = **jeer**, dig, insult, ridicule, teasing

tavern n = **inn**, bar, pub (Inf, chiefly Brit), public house, hostelry

tax n = **charge**, duty, toll, levy, tariff

DICTIONARY

imposed by government to raise revenue **2** heavy demand on something ▷ v **3** impose tax on **4** strain **taxation** n levying of taxes **tax return** statement of income for tax purposes

taxi, taxicab n **1** motor vehicle for hire with driver ▷ v **2** (of aircraft) run along ground

taxidermy n art of stuffing animal skins **taxidermist** n

TB tuberculosis

tbc to be confirmed

tea n **1** dried leaves of plant cultivated esp. in Asia **2** infusion of it as beverage **3** meal eaten in afternoon or early evening **tea bag** small porous bag of tea leaves **teapot** n container for making and serving tea **teaspoon** n small spoon for stirring tea etc. **tea towel** towel for drying dishes

teach ● v **teaching, taught 1** instruct **2** educate **3** train **teacher** n

teak n (hard wood from) E Indian tree

team ● n **1** set of animals, players of game etc. ▷ v **2** (usu. with up) (cause to) make a team **teamwork** n cooperative work by team

tear¹ ● v **tearing, tore, torn 1** pull apart **2** become torn **3** rush ▷ n **4** hole or split **tearaway** n wild or unruly person

tear² n drop of fluid falling from eye **tearful** adj **1** inclined to weep **2** involving tears **teardrop** n **tear gas** irritant gas causing temporary blindness

tease ● v **1** tantalize, torment, irritate ▷ n **2** one who teases

teat n **1** nipple of breast **2** rubber nipple of baby's bottle

technical ● adj **1** of, specializing in industrial, practical or mechanical arts **2** belonging to particular science **3** according to letter of the law **technicality** n point of procedure **technician** n one skilled in technique of an art **technique** n **1** method of performance in an art **2** skill required for mastery of subject

Technicolor® n colour photography, esp. in cinema

technology n **1** application of practical, mechanical sciences **2** technical skills, knowledge **technological** adj

tedious ● adj causing fatigue or boredom **tedium** n monotony

THESAURUS

▷ v = **charge**, rate, assess; = **strain**, stretch, try, test, load

teach v = **instruct**, train, coach, inform, educate

team n = **side**, squad; = **group**, company, set, body, band

tear¹ v = **rip**, split, rend, shred, rupture; = **scratch**, cut (open), gash, lacerate, injure; = **pull**

apart, claw, lacerate, mutilate, mangle ▷ n = **hole**, split, rip, rent, snag

tease v = **mock**, provoke, torment, taunt, goad

technical adj = **scientific**, technological, skilled, specialist, specialized

tedious adj = **boring**, dull, dreary,

tee n (Golf) **1** place from which first stroke of hole is made **2** small peg supporting ball for first stroke

teem v **1** abound with **2** swarm **3** rain heavily

teens pl n years of life from 13 to 19 **teenage** adj **teenager** n young person between 13 and 19

teeter v seesaw, wobble

teeth n pl of TOOTH

teethe v (of baby) grow first teeth **teething troubles** problems, difficulties at first stage of something

teetotal adj pledged to abstain from alcohol **teetotaller** n

Teflon® n substance used for nonstick coatings on saucepans etc.

telecommunications pl n communications by telephone, television etc.

telegram n formerly, message sent by telegraph

telegraph n **1** formerly, electrical apparatus for transmitting messages over distance ▷ v **2** send by telegraph

telepathy n action of one mind on another at a distance **telepathic** adj

telephone ❶ n **1** apparatus for communicating sound to hearer at a distance ▷ v **2** communicate, speak by telephone **telephonist** n person operating telephone switchboard

teleprinter n apparatus for sending and receiving typed messages by wire

telescope ❶ n **1** optical instrument for magnifying distant objects ▷ v **2** slide together **telescopic** adj

television ❶ n **1** system of producing on screen images of distant objects, events etc. by electromagnetic radiation **2** device for receiving this **3** programmes etc. viewed on television set **televise** v **1** transmit by television **2** make, produce as television programme

telex n **1** international communication service ▷ v **2** send by telex

tell ❶ v telling, told **1** let know **2** order **3** narrate, make known **4** discern **5** distinguish **6** give account **7** be of weight, importance **teller** n **1** narrator

monotonous, drab ≠ **exciting**

telephone n = **phone**, mobile (phone), handset, landline, phone and bone (Sl) ▷ v = **call**, phone, ring (chiefly Brit), dial

telescope n = **glass**, scope (Inf), spyglass ▷ v = **shorten**, contract, compress, shrink, condense ≠ **lengthen**

television n = **TV**, telly (Brit Inf),

small screen (Inf), the box (Brit Inf), the tube (Sl)

tell v = **inform**, notify, state to, reveal to, express to; = **describe**, relate, recount, report, portray; = **instruct**, order, command, direct, bid; = **distinguish**, discriminate, discern, differentiate, identify; = **have** or **take effect**, register, weigh, count, take its toll

2 bank cashier **telling** adj effective, striking **tell off** reprimand **telltale** n **1** sneak ▷ adj **2** revealing

telly n, pl **-lies** (Inf) television (set)

temerity n boldness, audacity

temp n (Inf) one employed on temporary basis

temper ❶ n **1** frame of mind **2** angry state **3** calmness, composure ▷ v **4** restrain, moderate **5** harden (metal)

temperament ❶ n **1** natural disposition **2** emotional mood **temperamental** adj **1** moody **2** erratic

temperate adj **1** (of climate) mild **2** not extreme **3** showing moderation **temperance** n **1** moderation **2** abstinence, esp. from alcohol

temperature n **1** degree of heat or coldness **2** (Inf) high body temperature

tempest n violent storm **tempestuous** adj **1** stormy **2** violent

template n pattern used to cut out shapes accurately

temple ❶ n building for worship

tempo n, pl **-pi, -pos** rate, rhythm

temporal adj **1** of time **2** of this life or world

temporary ❶ adj lasting only a short time

tempt ❶ v try to persuade, entice, esp. to something wrong or unwise **temptation** n **tempter** n **tempting** adj attractive, inviting

ten n/adj cardinal number after nine **tenth** adj ordinal number

tenable adj able to be held, defended, maintained

tenacious adj **1** holding fast **2** retentive **3** stubborn **tenacity** n

tenant ❶ n one who holds lands, house etc. on rent or lease **tenancy** n

tench n, pl **tench** freshwater fish

tend¹ ❶ v **1** be inclined **2** be conducive **3** make in direction of **tendency** n inclination **tendentious** adj controversial

temper n = **irritability**, irascibility, passion, resentment, petulance ≠ **good humour**; = **frame of mind**, nature, mind, mood, constitution; = **rage**, fury, bad mood, passion, tantrum; = **self-control**, composure, cool (Sl), calmness, equanimity ≠ **anger** ▷ v = **moderate**, restrain, tone down, soften, soothe ≠ **intensify**; = **strengthen**, harden, toughen, anneal ≠ **soften**

temperament n = **nature**, character, personality, make-up, constitution

temple n = **shrine**, church, sanctuary, house of God

temporary adj = **impermanent**, transitory, brief, fleeting, interim ≠ **permanent**

tempt v = **attract**, allure

tenant n = **leaseholder**, resident, renter, occupant, inhabitant

tend¹ v = **be inclined**, be liable, have a tendency, be apt, be prone

t

tend² ❶ v take care of

tender¹ ❶ adj 1 not tough 2 easily injured 3 gentle, loving 4 delicate

tender² ❶ v 1 offer 2 make offer or estimate ▷ n 3 offer or estimate for contract to undertake specific work **legal tender** currency that must, by law, be accepted as payment

tendon n sinew attaching muscle to bone etc.

tendril n slender curling stem by which climbing plant clings

tenement n building divided into separate flats

tenet n belief

tennis n game in which ball is struck with racket by players on opposite sides of net

tenor n 1 male voice between alto and bass 2 general course, meaning

tenpin bowling game in which players try to knock over ten skittles with ball

tense ❶ adj 1 stretched tight 2 taut 3 emotionally strained ▷ v

4 make, become tense **tensile** adj of, relating to tension **tension** n 1 stretching 2 strain when stretched 3 emotional strain 4 suspense 5 (Electricity) voltage

tent n portable shelter of canvas

tentacle n flexible organ of some animals (e.g. octopus) used for grasping, feeding etc.

tentative ❶ adj 1 experimental 2 cautious

tenterhooks pl n on tenterhooks in anxious suspense

tenuous adj 1 flimsy 2 thin

tenure n (length of time of) possession of office etc.

tepee n N Amer. Indian cone-shaped tent

tepid adj moderately warm

tequila n Mexican alcoholic drink

term ❶ n 1 word, expression 2 limited period of time 3 period during which schools are open ▷ pl 4 conditions 5 relationship ▷ v 6 name

terminal ❶ adj 1 at, forming an end 2 (of disease) ending in death

---

THESAURUS

---

tend² v = **take care of**, look after, keep, attend, nurture ≠ **neglect**; = **maintain**, take care of, nurture, cultivate, manage ≠ **neglect**

tender¹ adj = **gentle**, loving, kind, caring, sympathetic ≠ **harsh**; = **vulnerable**, young, sensitive, raw, youthful ≠ **experienced**

tender² n = **offer**, bid, estimate, proposal, submission ▷ v = **offer**, present, submit, give, propose

tense adj = **strained**, uneasy, stressful, fraught, charged;

= **nervous**, edgy, strained, anxious, apprehensive ≠ **calm** ▷ v

= **tighten**, strain, brace, stretch, flex ≠ **relax**

tentative adj = **unconfirmed**, provisional, indefinite, test, trial ≠ **confirmed**; = **hesitant**, cautious, uncertain, doubtful, faltering ≠ **confident**

term n = **word**, name, expression, title, label; = **period**, time, spell, while, season ▷ v = **call**, name, label, style, entitle

t

▷ *n* **3** terminal part or structure **4** point where current enters, leaves battery etc. **5** device permitting operation of computer at distance

terminate ❶ *v* bring, come to an end **termination** *n*

terminology *n* set of technical terms or vocabulary

terminus *n, pl* **-ni, -nuses 1** finishing point **2** railway station etc. at end of line

termite *n* wood-eating insect

tern *n* sea bird like gull

terrace *n* **1** raised level place **2** row of houses built as one block **3** (*oft. pl*) unroofed tiers for spectators at sports stadium ▷ *v* **4** form into terrace

terracotta *n/adj* **1** (made of) hard unglazed pottery **2** (of) brownish-red colour

terrain ❶ *n* area of ground, esp. with reference to its physical character

terrapin *n* type of aquatic tortoise

terrestrial ❶ *adj* **1** of the earth **2** of, living on land

terrible ❶ *adj* **1** serious **2** (*Inf*) very bad **3** causing fear **terribly** *adv*

terrier *n* small dog of various breeds

terrific ❶ *adj* **1** very great **2** (*Inf*) good **3** awe-inspiring

terrify ❶ *v* **-fying, -fied** frighten greatly **terrifying** *adj*

territory ❶ *n, pl* **-ries 1** region **2** geographical area, esp. a sovereign state **territorial** *adj* **Territorial Army** reserve army

terror ❶ *n* **1** great fear **2** (*Inf*) troublesome person or thing **terrorism** *n* use of violence to achieve ends **terrorist** *n/adj* **terrorize** *v* **1** oppress by violence **2** terrify

terse *adj* **1** concise **2** abrupt

tertiary *adj* third in degree, order etc.

Terylene® ❶ *n* **1** synthetic yarn **2** fabric made of it

terminal *adj* = **fatal**, deadly, lethal, killing, mortal; = **final**, last, closing, finishing, concluding ≠ **initial** ▷ *n* = **terminus**, station, depot, end of the line

terminate *v* = **end**, stop, conclude, finish, complete ≠ **begin**

terrain *n* = **ground**, country, land, landscape, topography

terrestrial *adj* = **earthly**, worldly, global

terrible *adj* = **awful**, shocking, terrifying, horrible, dreadful; (*Inf*) = **bad**, awful, dreadful, dire,

abysmal ≠ **wonderful**; = **serious**, desperate, severe, extreme, dangerous ≠ **mild**

terrific *adj* (*Inf*) = **excellent**, wonderful, brilliant, amazing, outstanding ≠ **awful**; = **intense**, great, huge, enormous, tremendous

terrify *v* = **frighten**, scare, alarm, terrorize, make your hair stand on end

territory *n* = **district**, area, land, region, country

terror *n* = **fear**, alarm, dread,

t

test ❶ v **1** try, put to the proof **2** carry out examination on ▷ n **3** examination **4** means of trial **testing** adj difficult **test case** lawsuit viewed as means of establishing precedent **test match** international sports contest, esp. one of series **test tube** tubelike glass vessel

testament ❶ n (Law) **1** will **2** (with cap.) one of the two main divisions of the Bible

testate adj (of dead person) having left a valid will

testicle, testis n either of two male reproductive glands

testify ❶ v -fying, -fied **1** declare **2** bear witness (to)

testimony ❶ n, pl -nies **1** affirmation **2** evidence

testimonial n **1** certificate of character etc. **2** gift expressing regard for recipient

testy adj -tier, -tiest irritable

tetanus n (also called **lockjaw**) acute infectious disease

tête-à-tête n, pl -têtes, -tête private conversation

tether n **1** rope for fastening

(grazing) animal ▷ v **2** tie up with rope

tetrahedron n, pl -drons, -dra solid contained by four plane faces

text ❶ n **1** (actual words of) book, passage etc. **2** passage of Bible **textual** adj **textbook** n book of instruction on particular subject

textile n any fabric or cloth, esp. woven

texture ❶ n **1** structure, appearance **2** consistency

than conj introduces second part of comparison

thank ❶ v **1** express gratitude to **2** say thanks **thankful** adj grateful **thankless** adj unrewarding or unappreciated **thanks** pl n words of gratitude

that adj **1** refers to thing already mentioned **2** refers to thing further away ▷ pron **3** refers to particular thing **4** introduces relative clause ▷ conj **5** introduces noun or adverbial clause

thatch n **1** reeds, straw etc. used as roofing material ▷ v **2** build roof with this

— THESAURUS —

fright, panic; = **nightmare**, monster, bogeyman, devil, fiend

test v = **check**, investigate, assess, research, analyse; = **examine**, put someone to the test ▷ n = **trial**, research, check, investigation, analysis

testament n = **proof**, evidence, testimony, witness, demonstration; = **will**, last wishes

testify v = **bear witness**, state, swear, certify, assert ≠ **disprove**

testimony n = **evidence**, statement, submission, affidavit, deposition; = **proof**, evidence, demonstration, indication, support

text n = **contents**, words, content, wording, body; = **words**, wording

texture n = **feel**, consistency, structure, surface, tissue

thank v = **say thank you to**, show your appreciation to

thaw ❶ v 1 melt 2 (cause to) unfreeze ▷ n 3 melting (of frost etc.)

the adj the definite article

theatre n 1 place where plays etc. are performed 2 dramatic works generally 3 hospital operating room **theatrical** adj 1 of, for the theatre 2 exaggerated

thee pron (Obs) object of THOU

theft ❶ n stealing

their adj of, belonging to them **theirs** pron belonging to them

them pron object of THEY **themselves** pron emphatic or reflexive form of THEY

theme ❶ n 1 main topic of book etc. 2 subject of composition 3 recurring melody **thematic** adj **theme park** leisure area designed round one subject

then adv 1 at that time 2 next 3 that being so

thence adv (Obs) from that place or time

theology n, pl -**gies** systematic study of religion and religious beliefs **theologian** n **theological** adj

theorem n proposition which can be demonstrated

theory ❶ n, pl -**ries** 1 supposition

to account for something 2 system of rules and principles, esp. distinguished from practice **theoretical** adj 1 based on theory 2 speculative

therapy ❶ n, pl -**pies** healing treatment **therapeutic** adj 1 of healing 2 serving to improve health **therapist** n

there adv 1 in that place 2 to that point **thereby** adv by that means **therefore** adv that being so **thereupon** adv immediately

therm n unit of measurement of heat **thermal** adj

thermodynamics pl n science that deals with interrelationship of different forms of energy

thermometer n instrument to measure temperature

Thermos® n vacuum flask

thermostat n apparatus for regulating temperature

thesaurus n, pl -**ruses** book containing lists of synonyms

these pron pl of THIS

thesis ❶ n, pl **theses** 1 written work submitted for degree, diploma 2 theory maintained in argument

thespian adj 1 of the theatre ▷ n 2 actor, actress

t

thaw v = melt, dissolve, soften, defrost, warm ≠ freeze

theft n = stealing, robbery, thieving, fraud, embezzlement

theme n = motif, leitmotif; = subject, idea, topic, essence, subject matter

theory n = belief, feeling,

speculation, assumption, hunch

therapy n = remedy, treatment, cure, healing, method of healing

thesis n = proposition, theory, hypothesis, idea, view; = dissertation, paper, treatise, essay, monograph

they *pron* pronoun of the third person plural

thick ❶ *adj* **1** fat, broad, not thin **2** dense **3** crowded **4** viscous **5** (of voice) throaty **6** (*Inf*) stupid ▷ *n* **7** busiest part **thicken** *v* **1** make, become thick **2** become complicated **thickness** *n* **1** dimension through an object **2** layer **thickset** *adj* sturdy, stocky

thicket *n* thick growth of trees

thief ❶ *n, pl* **thieves** one who steals **thieve** *v* steal

thigh *n* upper part of leg

thimble *n* cap protecting end of finger when sewing

thin ❶ *adj* **thinner, thinnest** 1 of little thickness **2** slim **3** of little density **4** sparse **5** fine **6** not close-packed ▷ *v* **7** make, become thin

thing ❶ *n* **1** (material) object **2** fact, idea

think ❶ *v* **thinking, thought** **1** have one's mind at work **2** reflect, meditate **3** reason **4** deliberate **5** believe

third *adj* **1** of number three in a series ▷ *n* **2** third part **third degree** violent interrogation **third party** (*Law*) person involved by chance in legal proceedings etc.

thirst ❶ *n* **1** desire to drink **2** feeling caused by lack of drink **3** craving ▷ *v* **4** have thirst **thirsty** *adj*

thirteen *adj/n* three plus ten **thirteenth** *adj/n*

thirty *adj/n* three times ten **thirtieth** *adj/n*

this *adj/pron* denotes thing, person near or just mentioned

thistle *n* prickly plant

thither *adv* (*Obs*) to or towards that place

thong *n* narrow strip of leather, strap

thorax *n, pl* **thoraxes, thoraces** part of body between neck and belly

thorn ❶ *n* **1** prickle on plant **2** bush noted for its thorns **thorny** *adj*

thick *adj* = **bulky**, broad, big, large, fat ≠ **thin**; = **wide**, across, deep, broad, in extent *or* diameter; = **dense**, close, heavy, compact, impenetrable; = **heavy**, heavyweight, dense, chunky, bulky; = **opaque**, heavy, dense, impenetrable

thief *n* = **robber**, burglar, stealer, plunderer, shoplifter

thin *adj* = **narrow**, fine, attenuated ≠ **thick**; = **slim**, spare, lean, slight, slender ≠ **fat**; = **meagre**, sparse, scanty, poor, scattered ≠ **plentiful**; = **fine**, delicate, flimsy, sheer,

skimpy ≠ **thick**; = **unconvincing**, inadequate, feeble, poor, weak ≠ **convincing**

thing *n* = **substance**, stuff, being, body, material ▷ *pl n* = **possessions**, stuff, gear, belongings, effects

think *v* = **believe**, be of the opinion, be of the view; = **judge**, consider, estimate, reckon, deem

thirst *n* = **dryness**, thirstiness, drought; = **craving**, appetite, longing, desire, passion ≠ **aversion**

thorn *n* = **prickle**, spike, spine, barb

thorough ❶ adj **1** careful, methodical **2** complete
thoroughly adv **thoroughbred** n pure-bred animal, esp. horse
thoroughfare n **1** road or passage **2** right of way

those pron pl of THAT

thou pron (Obs) the second person singular pronoun

though ❶ conj **1** even if ▷ adv **2** nevertheless

thought ❶ n **1** process, product of thinking **2** what one thinks **3** meditation **thoughtful** adj **1** considerate **2** showing careful thought **3** reflective **thoughtless** adj **1** inconsiderate **2** careless

thousand n/adj ten hundred **thousandth** adj

thrash ❶ v **1** beat **2** defeat soundly **3** move in wild manner

thread ❶ n **1** yarn **2** ridge cut on screw **3** theme ▷ v **4** put thread into **5** fit film etc. into machine **6** put on thread **7** pick (one's way etc.) **threadbare** adj **1** worn, shabby **2** hackneyed

threat ❶ n **1** declaration of intention to harm, injure etc. **2** dangerous person or thing **threaten** v make or be threat to

three adj/n one more than two **three-dimensional** adj having height, width and depth **three-ply** adj having three layers or strands **threesome** n group of three

thresh v **1** beat to separate grain from husks **2** thrash

threshold ❶ n **1** bar of stone forming bottom of doorway **2** entrance **3** starting point

thrice adv three times

---

thorough adj = **comprehensive**, full, complete, sweeping, intensive ≠ **cursory**; = **careful**, conscientious, painstaking, efficient, meticulous ≠ **careless**

though conj = **although**, while, even if, even though, notwithstanding ▷ adv = **nevertheless**, still, however, yet, nonetheless

thought n = **thinking**, consideration, reflection, deliberation, musing; = **opinion**, view, idea, concept, notion; = **consideration**, study, attention, care, regard; = **intention**, plan, idea, design, aim; = **hope**, expectation, prospect, aspiration,
anticipation

thrash v = **defeat**, beat, crush, slaughter (Inf), rout; = **beat**, wallop, whip, belt (Inf), cane; = **thresh**, flail, jerk, writhe, toss and turn

thread n = **strand**, fibre, yarn, filament, line; = **theme**, train of thought, direction, plot, drift ▷ v = **move**, pass, ease, thrust, squeeze through

threat n = **danger**, risk, hazard, menace, peril; = **threatening remark**, menace; = **warning**, foreshadowing, foreboding

threshold n = **entrance**, doorway, door, doorstep; = **start**, beginning, opening, dawn, verge ≠ **end**; = **limit**, margin, starting point, minimum

thrift ❶ n saving, economy
  thrifty adj economical

thrill ❶ n 1 sudden sensation of
  excitement and pleasure ▷ v
  2 (cause to) feel a thrill 3 tremble
  thriller n suspenseful book, film
  etc. **thrilling** adj

thrive v thriving, thrived
  1 grow well 2 prosper

throat n 1 front of neck 2 passage
  from mouth to stomach **throaty**
  adj 1 hoarse 2 deep, guttural

throb ❶ v throbbing, throbbed
  1 quiver strongly, pulsate ▷ n
  2 pulsation

throes pl n violent pangs, pain etc.
  in the throes of in the process of

thrombosis n, pl **-ses** clot in
  blood vessel or heart

throne n 1 ceremonial seat
  2 power of sovereign

throng ❶ n/v crowd

throttle ❶ n 1 device controlling

amount of fuel entering engine ▷ v
2 strangle 3 restrict

through ❶ prep 1 from end to end
2 in consequence of 3 by means of
▷ adv 4 from end to end 5 to the
end ▷ adj 6 completed 7 (Inf)
finished 8 continuous 9 (of
transport, traffic) not stopping

throughout adv/prep in every part
(of) **throughput** n quantity of
material processed

throw ❶ v throwing, threw,
thrown 1 fling, cast 2 move, put
abruptly, carelessly 3 cause to fall
▷ n 4 act or distance of throwing
throwaway adj 1 designed to be
discarded after use 2 done, said
casually **throwback** n person,
thing that reverts to earlier type

thrush n songbird

thrust ❶ v thrusting, thrust
1 push, drive 2 stab ▷ n 3 lunge,
stab 4 propulsive force or power

————————————— THESAURUS

thrift n = **economy**, prudence,
  frugality, saving, parsimony
  ≠ **extravagance**

thrill n = **pleasure**, kick (Inf), buzz
  (Sl), high, stimulation ≠ **tedium**
  ▷ v = **excite**, stimulate, arouse,
  move, stir

thrive v = **prosper**, do well,
  flourish, increase, grow
  ≠ **decline**

throb v = **pulsate**, pound, beat,
  pulse, thump; = **vibrate**, pulsate,
  reverberate, shake, judder (Inf) ▷ n
  = **pulse**, pounding, beat, thump,
  thumping

throng v = **crowd**, flock,
  congregate, converge, mill around

≠ **disperse**

throttle v = **strangle**, choke,
  garrotte, strangulate

through prep = **via**, by way of, by,
  between, past; = **because of**, by
  way of, by means of; = **using**, via, by
  way of, by means of, by virtue of
  ▷ adj = **completed**, done, finished,
  ended

throw v = **hurl**, toss, fling, send,
  launch; = **toss**, fling, chuck (Inf),
  cast, hurl ▷ n = **toss**, pitch, fling,
  sling, lob (Inf)

thrust v = **push**, force, shove,
  drive, plunge ▷ n = **stab**, pierce,
  lunge; = **push**, shove, poke,
  prod

DICTIONARY

thud n **1** dull heavy sound ▷ v **2** make thud

thug ① n violent person

thumb n **1** shortest, thickest finger of hand ▷ v **2** handle with thumb **3** signal for lift in vehicle

thumbtack n the US and Canadian name for DRAWING PIN

thump ① n **1** (sound of) dull heavy blow ▷ v **2** strike heavily

thunder ① n **1** loud noise accompanying lightning ▷ v **2** make noise of or like thunder **thunderbolt, thunderclap** n **1** lightning followed by thunder **2** anything unexpected

Thursday n fifth day of the week

thus ① adv **1** in this way **2** therefore

thwart ① v foil, frustrate

thy adj (Obs) of or associated with you **thyself** pron emphatic or reflexive form of THOU

thyme n aromatic herb

tiara n coronet

tibia n, pl **tibiae, tibias** shinbone

tic n spasmodic twitch in muscles,

tick¹ ① n **1** slight tapping sound, as of watch movement **2** small mark (✓) **3** (Inf) moment ▷ v **4** mark with tick **5** make slight tapping sound

tick² n small insect-like parasite living on blood

ticket ① n **1** card, paper entitling holder to admission, travel etc. **2** label ▷ v **3** attach label to

tickle v **1** touch, stroke (person etc.) to produce laughter etc. **2** amuse **3** itch ▷ n **4** act, instance of this **ticklish** adj **1** sensitive to tickling **2** requiring care

tiddlywinks pl n game of trying to flip small plastic discs into cup

tide ① n rise and fall of sea happening twice each day **tidal** adj **tidal wave** great wave, esp. produced by earthquake **tide over** help someone for a while

tidings pl n news

tidy ① adj **-dier, -diest 1** orderly, neat ▷ v **2** put in order

THESAURUS

thug n = **ruffian**, hooligan, tough, heavy (Sl), gangster

thump v = **strike**, hit, punch, pound, beat ▷ n = **blow**, knock, punch, rap, smack; = **thud**, crash, bang, clunk, thwack

thunder n = **rumble**, crash, boom, explosion ▷ v = **rumble**, crash, boom, roar, resound; = **shout**, roar, yell, bark, bellow

thus adv = **therefore**, so, hence, consequently, accordingly; = **in this way**, so, like this, as follows

thwart v = **frustrate**, foil, prevent,

snooker, hinder ≠ **assist**

tick¹ n = **check mark**, mark, line, stroke, dash; (Brit Inf) = **moment**, second, minute, flash, instant ▷ v = **mark**, indicate, check off; = **click**, tap, ticktock

ticket n = **voucher**, pass, coupon, card, slip; = **label**, tag, marker, sticker, card

tide n = **current**, flow, stream, ebb, undertow

tidy adj = **neat**, orderly, clean, spruce, well-kept ≠ **untidy**; (Inf) = **considerable**, large, substantial,

tie ❶ v **tying, tied 1** fasten, bind **2** restrict **3** equal (score of) ▷ n **4** that with which anything is bound **5** restraint **6** piece of material worn knotted round neck **7** connecting link **8** contest with equal scores **tied** adj **1** (of public house) selling beer etc. of only one brewer **2** (of cottage etc.) rented to tenant employed by owner

tier ❶ n row, rank, layer

tiff n petty quarrel

tiger n large carnivorous feline animal

tight ❶ adj **1** taut, tense **2** closely fitting **3** secure, firm **4** not allowing passage of water etc. **5** cramped **6** (Inf) mean **7** (Inf) drunk **tighten** v **tights** pl n one-piece clinging garment

covering body from waist to feet

tightrope n taut rope on which acrobats perform

tile n **1** flat piece of ceramic, plastic etc. used for roofs, floors etc. ▷ v **2** cover with tiles

till¹ ❶ v cultivate

till² ❶ n **1** drawer for money in shop counter **2** cash register

tiller n lever to move rudder of boat

tilt ❶ v **1** slope, slant **2** take part in medieval combat with lances **3** thrust (at) ▷ n **4** slope **5** (Hist) combat for mounted men with lances

timber ❶ n **1** wood for building etc. **2** trees

timbre n distinctive quality of voice or sound

time ❶ n **1** past, present and future as continuous whole **2** hour

━━━━━━━━━━━━━━━━━ THESAURUS ━━━━━━━━━━━━━━━━━

goodly, healthy ≠ **small** ▷ v = **neaten**, straighten, order, clean, groom ≠ **disorder**

tie v = **fasten**, bind, join, link, connect ≠ **unfasten**; = **tether**, secure; = **restrict**, limit, confine, bind, restrain ≠ **free** ▷ n = **fastening**, binding, link, bond, knot; = **bond**, relationship, connection, commitment, liaison; = **draw**, dead heat, deadlock, stalemate

tier n = **row**, bank, layer, line, level

tight adj = **close-fitting**, narrow, cramped, snug, constricted ≠ **loose**; = **secure**, firm, fast, fixed; = **taut**, stretched, rigid ≠ **slack**; = **close**, even, well-matched,

hard-fought, evenly-balanced ≠ **uneven**; (Inf) = **miserly**, mean, stingy, grasping, parsimonious ≠ **generous**; (Inf) = **drunk**, intoxicated, plastered (Sl), under the influence (Inf), tipsy ≠ **sober**

till¹ v = **cultivate**, dig, plough, work

till² n = **cash register**, cash box

tilt v = **slant**, tip, slope, list, lean ▷ n = **slope**, angle, inclination, list, pitch; (Medieval history) = **joust**, fight, tournament, lists, combat

timber n = **beams**, boards, planks; = **wood**, logs

time n = **period**, term, space, stretch, spell; = **occasion**, point, moment, stage, instance; = **tempo**,

3 duration **4** period **5** point in duration **6** duration **7** occasion **8** leisure ▷ v **9** choose time for **10** note time taken by **timeless** adj changeless, everlasting **timely** adj at appropriate time **timer** n person, device for recording or indicating time **time bomb** bomb designed to explode at prearranged time **time-lag** n period between cause and effect **timetable** n plan showing times of arrival and departure etc.

timid adj **1** easily frightened **2** shy **timorous** adj **1** timid **2** indicating fear

timpani pl n set of kettledrums

tin n **1** malleable metal **2** container made of tin ▷ v **3** put in tin, esp. for preserving **tinny** adj (of sound) thin, metallic **tinpot** adj (Inf) worthless

tinder n dry easily-burning material used to start fire

tinge ❶ v n **1** slight trace ▷ v **2** colour, flavour slightly

tingle v/n (feel) thrill or pricking sensation

tinker ❶ v n **1** formerly, travelling mender of pots and pans ▷ v **2** fiddle, meddle (with)

tinkle v **1** (cause to) give out sounds like small bell ▷ n **2** this sound or action

tinsel n glittering decorative metallic substance

tint ❶ n **1** (shade of) colour **2** tinge ▷ v **3** give tint to

tiny ❶ adj **tinier, tiniest** very small, minute

tip¹ ❶ n **1** slender or pointed end of anything **2** small piece forming an extremity ▷ v **3** put a tip on

tip² ❶ n **1** small present of money given for service rendered **2** helpful piece of information **tip-off 3** warning, hint ▷ v **4** reward with money **tip off 5** give tip to

tip³ ❶ v **1** tipping, tipped **1** tilt, upset **2** touch lightly **3** topple over ▷ n **4** place where rubbish is dumped

tipple v **1** drink (alcohol) habitually

beat, rhythm, measure ▷ v = **schedule**, set, plan, book, programme

tinge n = **tint**, colour, shade; = **trace**, bit, drop, touch, suggestion ▷ v = **tint**, colour

tinker v = **meddle**, play, potter, fiddle (Inf), dabble

tint n = **shade**, colour, tone, hue; = **dye**, wash, rinse, tinge, tincture ▷ v = **dye**, colour

tiny adj = **small**, little, minute, slight, miniature ≠ **huge**

tip¹ n = **end**, point, head, extremity, sharp end; = **peak**, top, summit, pinnacle, zenith ▷ v = **cap**, top, crown, surmount, finish

tip² v = **reward**, remunerate, give a tip to, sweeten (Inf); = **predict**, back, recommend, think of ▷ n = **gratuity**, gift, reward, present, sweetener (Inf); = **hint**, suggestion, piece of advice, pointer

tip³ v = **pour**, drop, empty, dump, drain; (Brit) = **dump**, empty, unload, pour out

▷ n **2** drink

tipsy adj **-sier, -siest** (slightly) drunk

tiptoe v **-toeing, -toed 1** walk on ball of foot and toes **2** walk softly

tiptop adj of the best quality or condition

tirade n long angry speech or denunciation

tire ❶ v **1** reduce energy of, weary **2** bore **3** become tired, bored **tired** adj **1** weary **2** hackneyed **tireless** adj not tiring easily **tiresome** adj irritating, tedious **tiring** adj

tissue n **1** substance of animal body, plant **2** soft paper handkerchief

tit n small bird

titanic adj huge, epic

titanium n light metallic element

titbit n **1** tasty morsel of food **2** scrap (of scandal etc.)

tithe n **1** (esp. formerly) tenth part of income, paid to church as tax ▷ v **2** exact tithes from

titillate v stimulate agreeably

title ❶ n **1** name of book **2** heading **3** name, esp. denoting rank **4** legal right or document proving it **5** (Sport) championship

titter v/n snigger, giggle

titular adj **1** pert. to title **2** nominal

TNT see TRINITROTOLUENE

to prep **1** denoting direction, destination **2** introducing comparison, indirect object, infinitive etc. ▷ adv **3** to fixed position **to and fro** back and forth

toad n animal like large frog **toady** n **1** servile flatterer ▷ v **2** be ingratiating **toadstool** n fungus like mushroom

toast ❶ n **1** slice of bread browned on both sides by heat **2** tribute, proposal of health etc. marked by people drinking together **3** person or thing so toasted ▷ v **4** make (bread etc.) crisp and brown **5** drink toast to **6** warm at fire **toaster** n electrical device for toasting bread

tobacco n, pl **-cos, -coes** plant with leaves used for smoking **tobacconist** n one who sells tobacco products

toboggan n sledge for sliding down slope of snow

today n **1** this day ▷ adv **2** on this day **3** nowadays

toddle v walk with unsteady short steps **toddler** n young child beginning to walk

━━━━━━━━━━━━━━━━━━━━━━━ THESAURUS ━━━━━━━━━━━━━━━━━━━━━━━

tire v = **exhaust**, drain, fatigue, weary, wear out ≠ **refresh**; = **flag**, become tired, fail

title n = **name**, designation, term, handle (SI), moniker or monicker (SI); (Sport); = **championship**, trophy, bays, crown, honour; (Law) = **ownership**, right, claim, privilege, entitlement

toast v = **brown**, grill, crisp, roast; = **warm (up)**, heat (up), thaw, bring back to life ▷ n = **tribute**, compliment, salute, health, pledge; = **favourite**, celebrity, darling, talk, pet ▷ v = **drink to**, honour, salute, drink (to) the health of

to-do n, pl **-dos** (Inf) fuss, commotion

toe n 1 digit of foot 2 anything resembling this **toe the line** conform

toffee n chewy sweet made of boiled sugar etc.

toga n garment worn in ancient Rome

together ⓘ adv 1 in company 2 simultaneously

toggle n small peg fixed crosswise on cord etc. and used for fastening

toil ⓘ n 1 heavy work or task ▷ v 2 labour

toilet ⓘ n 1 lavatory 2 process of washing, dressing 3 articles used for this **toiletries** pl n objects, cosmetics used for cleaning or grooming

token ⓘ n 1 sign, symbol 2 disc used as money 3 gift card, voucher exchangeable for goods ▷ adj 4 nominal

tolerate ⓘ v 1 put up with

2 permit **tolerable** adj 1 bearable 2 fair **tolerance** n **tolerant** adj 1 forbearing 2 broad-minded **toleration** n

toll[1] ⓘ v 1 ring (bell) slowly at regular intervals ▷ n 2 ringing

toll[2] ⓘ n 1 tax, esp. for use of bridge or road 2 loss, damage

tom n male cat

tomahawk n fighting axe of N Amer. Indians

tomato n, pl **-toes** 1 plant with red fruit 2 the fruit

tomb ⓘ n 1 grave 2 monument over one **tombstone** n

tombola n lottery with tickets drawn from revolving drum

tomboy n girl who acts, dresses like boy

tome n large book

tomfoolery n foolish behaviour

tomorrow adv/n (on) the day after today

tom-tom n drum beaten with hands

together adv = **collectively**, jointly, as one, with each other, in conjunction ≠ **separately**; = **at the same time**, simultaneously, concurrently, at one fell swoop ▷ adj (Inf) = **self-possessed**, composed, well-balanced, well-adjusted

toil v = **labour**, work, struggle, strive, sweat (Inf) ▷ n = **hard work**, effort, application, sweat, graft (Inf) ≠ **idleness**

toilet n = **lavatory**, bathroom, loo (Brit Inf), privy, cloakroom (Brit)

token n = **symbol**, mark, sign,

note, expression ▷ adj = **nominal**, symbolic, minimal, hollow, superficial

tolerate v = **endure**, stand, take, stomach, put up with (Inf); = **allow**, accept, permit, take, brook ≠ **forbid**

toll[1] v = **ring**, sound, strike, chime, knell ▷ n = **ringing**, chime, knell, clang, peal

toll[2] n = **charge**, tax, fee, duty, payment; = **damage**, cost, loss, roll, penalty

tomb n = **grave**, vault, crypt, mausoleum, sarcophagus

ton n **1** measure of weight, 1016 kg (2240 lbs.) (US) **2** measure of weight, 907 kg (2000 lbs.) **tonnage** n carrying capacity of ship

tone ❶ n **1** quality of musical sound, voice, colour etc. **2** general character ▷ v **3** blend, harmonize (with) **tone-deaf** adj unable to perceive subtle differences in pitch

tongs pl n apparatus for handling coal, sugar etc.

tongue ❶ n **1** organ inside mouth, used for speech, taste etc. **2** language, speech

tonic ❶ n **1** medicine etc. with invigorating effect **2** (Mus) first note of scale ▷ adj **3** invigorating, restorative **tonic water** mineral water oft. containing quinine

tonight n **1** this (coming) night ▷ adv **2** on this night

tonne n metric ton, 1000 kg

tonsil n gland in throat **tonsillitis** n inflammation of tonsils

tonsure n **1** shaving of part of head as religious practice **2** part shaved

too ❶ adv **1** also, in addition

2 overmuch

tool ❶ n **1** implement or appliance for mechanical operations **2** means to an end ▷ v **3** work on with tool **toolbar** n (Comp) row or column of selectable buttons on a computer screen, each allowing the user to access a particular function

toonie, twonie n (Inf) Canadian two-dollar coin

toot n short sound of horn, trumpet etc.

tooth n, pl **teeth 1** bonelike projection in gums of upper and lower jaws of vertebrates **2** prong, cog **toothless** adj **toothpaste** n paste used to clean teeth **toothpick** n small stick for removing food from between teeth

top ❶ n **1** highest part, summit **2** highest rank **3** first in merit **4** garment for upper part of body **5** lid, stopper of bottle etc. ▷ adj **6** highest in position, rank ▷ v **7** cut off, pass, reach, surpass top **8** provide top for **topmost** adj highest **topping** n sauce or garnish for food **top brass**

tone n = **pitch**, inflection, intonation, timbre, modulation; = **volume**, timbre; = **character**, style, feel, air, spirit ▷ v = **harmonize**, match, blend, suit, go well with

tongue n = **language**, speech, dialect, parlance

tonic n = **stimulant**, boost, pick-me-up (Inf), fillip, shot in the arm (Inf)

too adv = **also**, as well, further, in

addition, moreover; = **excessively**, very, extremely, overly, unduly

tool n = **implement**, device, appliance, machine, instrument; = **puppet**, creature, pawn, stooge (Sl), minion

top n = **peak**, summit, head, crown, height ≠ **bottom**; = **lid**, cove r, cap, plug, stopper; = **first place**, head, peak, lead, high point ▷ adj = **highest**, loftiest, furthest up, uppermost ▷ v

DICTIONARY

important officials **top hat** man's tall cylindrical hat **top-heavy** adj unbalanced **top-notch** adj excellent, first-class **topsoil** n surface layer of soil

topaz n precious stone of various colours

topiary n trimming trees, bushes into decorative shapes

topic ❶ n subject of discourse, conversation etc. **topical** adj up-to-date, having news value

topography n, pl **-phies** (description of) surface features of a place **topographic** adj

topple ❶ v (cause to) fall over

topsy-turvy adj in confusion

tor n high rocky hill

torch n **1** portable hand light containing electric battery **2** burning wooden shaft **3** any apparatus burning with hot flame

toreador n bullfighter

torment ❶ v **1** torture in body or mind **2** afflict **3** tease ▷ n **4** suffering, agony of body or mind **5** pest **tormentor, -er** n

tornado ❶ n, pl **-dos, -does** **1** whirlwind **2** violent storm

torpedo n, pl **-does** **1** self-propelled underwater missile with explosive warhead ▷ v **2** strike with torpedo

torpid adj sluggish, apathetic **torpor** n torpid state

torrent n **1** rushing stream **2** downpour **torrential** adj

torrid adj **1** parched **2** highly emotional

torsion n twist, twisting

torso n, pl **-sos** (statue of) body without head or limbs

tortilla n thin Mexican pancake

tortoise n four-footed reptile covered with shell of horny plates **tortoiseshell** n mottled brown shell of turtle

tortuous adj **1** winding, twisting **2** involved, not straightforward

torture ❶ n **1** infliction of severe pain ▷ v **2** inflict severe pain

Tory n, pl **Tories** member of conservative political party

toss ❶ v **1** throw up, about **2** be thrown, fling oneself about

THESAURUS

= **lead**, head, be at the top of, be first in; **= cover**, garnish, finish, crown, cap; **= surpass**, better, beat, improve on, cap **≠ not be as good as**

topic n **= subject**, point, question, issue, matter

topple v **= fall over**, fall, collapse, tumble, overturn

torment n **= suffering**, distress, misery, pain, hell **≠ bliss** ▷ v **= torture**, distress, rack, crucify

≠ comfort; **= tease**, annoy, bother, irritate, harass

tornado n **= whirlwind**, storm, hurricane, gale, cyclone

torture v **= torment**, abuse, persecute, afflict, scourge **≠ comfort** ▷ n **= ill-treatment**, abuse, torment, persecution, maltreatment

toss v **= throw**, pitch, hurl, fling, launch, rock ▷ n **= throw**, pitch, lob (Inf)

▷ n 3 the act of tossing

tot¹ ❶ n 1 very small child 2 small quantity, esp. of drink

tot² v **totting, totted** 1 add (up) 2 amount to

total ❶ n 1 whole amount 2 sum ▷ adj 3 complete, absolute ▷ v 4 amount to 5 add up **totality** n **totally** adv

totalitarian adj of dictatorial, one-party government

totem n tribal badge or emblem **totem pole** carved post of Amer. Indians

totter v 1 walk unsteadily 2 begin to fall

toucan n large-billed tropical Amer. bird

touch ❶ v 1 come into contact with 2 put hand on 3 reach 4 affect emotions of 5 deal with 6 (with or) refer to ▷ n 7 sense by which qualities of object etc. are

perceived by touching 8 touching 9 characteristic manner or ability 10 slight contact, amount etc. **touching** adj 1 emotionally moving ▷ prep 2 concerning **touchy** adj easily offended **touch down** (of aircraft) land **touchline** n side line of pitch in some games **touchstone** n criterion **touché** interj acknowledgment that remark or blow has struck target **tough** ❶ adj 1 strong 2 able to bear hardship, strain 3 strict 4 difficult 5 needing effort to chew 6 violent ▷ n 7 (Inf) rough, violent person **toughen** v **toupee** n wig **tour** ❶ n 1 travelling round 2 journey to one place after another ▷ v 3 make tour **tourism** n **tourist** n **tournament** ❶ n competition,

— THESAURUS —

tot¹ n = **infant**, child, baby, toddler, mite; = **measure**, shot (Inf), finger, nip, slug

total n = **sum**, entirety, grand total, whole, aggregate ≠ **part** ▷ adj = **complete**, absolute, utter, whole, entire ≠ **partial** ▷ v = **amount to**, make, come to, reach, equal; = **add up**, work out, compute, reckon, tot up ≠ **subtract**

touch v = **feel**, handle, finger, stroke, brush; = **come into contact**, meet, contact, border, graze; = **affect**, influence, inspire, impress; = **consume**, take, drink, eat, partake of; = **move**, stir, disturb ▷ n = **contact**, push,

stroke, brush, press; = **feeling**, handling, physical contact; = **bit**, spot, trace, drop, dash; = **style**, method, technique, way, manner

tough adj = **hardy**, strong, seasoned, strapping, vigorous; = **violent**, rough, ruthless, pugnacious, hard-bitten; = **strict**, severe, stern, hard, firm ≠ **lenient**; = **hard**, difficult, troublesome, uphill, strenuous ▷ n = **ruffian**, bully, thug, hooligan, bruiser (Inf)

tour n = **journey**, expedition, excursion, trip, outing ▷ v = **visit**, explore, go round, inspect, walk round

tournament n = **competition**,

contest usu. with several stages

tourniquet n bandage, surgical instrument to stop bleeding

tousled adj ruffled

tout v 1 solicit custom ▷ n 2 person who sells tickets at inflated prices

tow v 1 drag along behind, esp. at end of rope ▷ n 2 towing or being towed **towpath** n path beside canal or river

towards, toward ❶ prep 1 in direction of 2 with regard to 3 as contribution to

towel n cloth for wiping off moisture after washing

tower ❶ n 1 tall strong structure, esp. part of church etc. 2 fortress ▷ v 3 stand very high 4 loom (over)

town n collection of dwellings etc. larger than village and smaller than city **township** n small town

toxic ❶ adj 1 poisonous 2 due to poison **toxicity** n strength of a poison **toxin** n poison

toy ❶ n 1 something designed to be played with ▷ adj 2 very small ▷ v 3 trifle **toy boy** much younger lover of older woman

toy-toy (SAfr) n 1 dance of political protest ▷ v 2 perform this dance

trace ❶ n 1 track left by anything 2 indication 3 minute quantity ▷ v 4 follow course of 5 find out 6 make plan of 7 draw or copy exactly **tracing paper** transparent paper placed over drawing, map etc. to enable exact copy to be taken

trachea n, pl **tracheae** windpipe

track ❶ n 1 mark left by passage of anything 2 path 3 rough road 4 course 5 railway line 6 jointed metal band as on tank etc. 7 separate song, piece on record ▷ v 8 follow trail or path of **track events** athletic sports held on running track **track record** past accomplishments **tracksuit** n loose-fitting suit worn by athletes etc.

— THESAURUS —

meeting, event, series, contest

tow v = **drag**, draw, pull, haul, tug

towards prep = **in the direction of**, to, for, on the way to, en route for; = **regarding**, about, concerning, respecting, in relation to

tower n = **column**, pillar, turret, belfry, steeple

toxic adj = **poisonous**, deadly, lethal, harmful, pernicious ≠ **harmless**

toy n = **plaything**, game, doll

trace v = **find**, track (down), discover, detect, unearth; = **outline**, sketch, draw; = **copy**, map, draft, outline, sketch ▷ n = **bit**, drop, touch, shadow, suggestion; = **remnant**, sign, record, mark, evidence; = **track**, trail, footstep, path, footprint

track n = **path**, way, road, route, trail; = **course**, line, path, orbit, trajectory; = **line**, tramline, marks, traces ▷ v = **follow**, pursue, chase, trace, tail (Inf)

t

tract¹ **①** *n* wide expanse, area

tract² **①** *n* pamphlet, esp. religious one

traction *n* action of pulling

tractor *n* motor vehicle for hauling, pulling etc.

trade ① *n* **1** commerce, business **2** skilled craft **3** exchange ▷ *v* **4** engage in trade **trader** *n* **trade-in** *n* used article given in part payment for new **trademark, trade name** *n* distinctive legal mark on maker's goods **trade-off** *n* exchange made as compromise **tradesman** *n* **1** dealer **2** skilled worker **trade union** society of workers for protection of their interests

tradition ① *n* **1** unwritten body of beliefs, facts etc. handed down from generation to generation **2** custom, practice of long standing **traditional** *adj*

traffic ① *n* **1** vehicles passing to

and fro in street, town etc. **2** (illicit) trade ▷ *v* **3** trade **traffic lights** set of coloured lights at road junctions etc.

tragedy ① *n, pl* **-dies 1** sad event **2** dramatic, literary work dealing with serious, sad topic **tragedian** *n* actor in, writer of tragedies **tragic** *adj* **1** of, in manner of tragedy **2** disastrous **3** appalling

trail ① *v* **1** drag behind one **2** lag behind **3** track, pursue ▷ *n* **4** track or trace **5** rough path **trailer** *n* vehicle towed by another vehicle

train ① *v* **1** educate, instruct, cause to grow in particular way **2** follow course of training **3** aim (gun etc.) ▷ *n* **4** line of railway vehicles joined to locomotive **5** succession, esp. of thoughts etc. **6** procession **7** trailing part of dress **trainee** *n* one training to be skilled worker **trainer** *n* **training** *n*

━━━━━━━━━━━━━━ THESAURUS ━━━━━━━━━━━━━━

tract¹ *n* = **area**, region, district, stretch, territory

tract² *n* = **treatise**, essay, booklet, pamphlet, dissertation

trade *n* = **commerce**, business, transactions, dealing, exchange; = **job**, employment, business, craft, profession ▷ *v* = **deal**, do business, traffic, truck, bargain; = **exchange**, switch, swap, barter

tradition institution ▷ *n* = **established practice**, custom, convention, habit, ritual

traffic *n* = **transport**, vehicles, transportation, freight; = **trade**, commerce, business, exchange,

truck ▷ *v* = **trade**, deal, exchange, bargain, do business

tragedy *n* = **disaster**, catastrophe, misfortune, adversity, calamity ≠ fortune

trail *n* = **path**, track, route, way, course; = **tracks**, path, marks, wake, trace ▷ *v* = **follow**, track, chase, pursue, dog; = **drag**, draw, pull, sweep, haul; = **lag**, follow, drift, wander, linger

train *v* = **instruct**, school, prepare, coach, teach; = **exercise**, prepare, work out, practise, do exercise; = **aim**, point, level, position, direct ▷ *n* = **sequence**, series, chain,

traipse v walk wearily

trait ❶ n characteristic feature

traitor ❶ n one who is guilty of treason **traitorous** adj

trajectory n, pl **-ries** line of flight

tram n vehicle running on rails laid on roadway

tramp ❶ v 1 travel on foot 2 walk heavily ▷ n 3 (homeless) person who travels about on foot 4 walk 5 cargo ship without fixed route

trample ❶ v tread on and crush under foot

trampoline n tough canvas sheet stretched horizontally with elastic cords etc. to frame

trance ❶ n 1 unconscious or dazed state 2 state of ecstasy or total absorption

tranche n portion

tranquil adj 1 calm, quiet 2 serene **tranquillity** n **tranquillize** v make calm **tranquillizer** n drug which induces calm state

trans- comb. form across, through, beyond

transact v 1 carry through 2 negotiate **transaction** n 1 performing of business 2 single sale or purchase ▷ pl 3 proceedings

transcend ❶ v 1 rise above 2 surpass **transcendence** n **transcendent** adj **transcendental** adj 1 surpassing experience 2 supernatural 3 abstruse **transcendentalism** n

transcribe v 1 copy out 2 record for later broadcast **transcript** n copy

transfer ❶ v **-ferring, -ferred** 1 move, send from one person, place etc. to another ▷ n 2 removal of person or thing from one place to another **transference** n transfer

transfigure v alter appearance of

transfix v 1 astound, stun 2 pierce through

transform ❶ v change shape, character of **transformation** n **transformer** n (Electricity) apparatus for changing voltage

transgress v 1 break (law) 2 sin

—————— THESAURUS ——————

string, set

trait n = **characteristic**, feature, quality, attribute, quirk

traitor n = **betrayer**, deserter, turncoat, renegade, defector ≠ loyalist

tramp v = **trudge**, stump, toil, plod, traipse (Inf.); = **hike**, walk, trek, roam, march ▷ n = **vagrant**, derelict, drifter, down-and-out; = **tread**, stamp, footstep, footfall; = **hike**, march, trek, ramble, slog

trample v often with **on** = **stamp**, crush, squash, tread, flatten

trance n = **daze**, dream, abstraction, rapture, reverie

transcend v = **surpass**, exceed, go beyond, rise above, eclipse

transfer v = **move**, transport, shift, relocate, transpose ▷ n = **transference**, move, handover, change, shift

transform v = **change**, convert, alter, transmute, remodel

t

transgression n

transient adj fleeting, not permanent

transistor n (Electronics) **1** small, semiconducting device used to amplify electric currents **2** portable radio using transistors

transit ❶ n passage, crossing **transition** n change from one state to another **transitive** adj (of verb) requiring direct object **transitory** adj not lasting long

translate ❶ v **1** turn from one language into another **2** interpret **translation** n **translator** n

translucent adj letting light pass through, semitransparent

transmit ❶ v **-mitting, -mitted 1** send, cause to pass to another place, person etc. **2** send out (signals) by means of radio waves **transmission** n **1** transmitting **2** gears by which power is communicated from engine to road wheels

transmute v change in form, properties or nature

transparent ❶ adj **1** letting light pass without distortion **2** that can be seen through **transparency** n **1** quality of being transparent **2** photographic slide

transpire v **1** become known **2** (Inf) happen **3** (of plants) give off water vapour through leaves

transplant ❶ v **1** move and plant again in another place **2** transfer organ surgically ▷ n **3** surgical transplanting of organ

transport ❶ v **1** convey from one place to another **2** deport ▷ n **3** system of conveyance **4** vehicle used for this **transportation** n **1** transporting **2** (Hist) deportation to penal colony

transpose v **1** change order of **2** put music into different key

transverse adj **1** lying across **2** at right angles

transvestite n person who wears clothes of opposite sex

trap ❶ n **1** device for catching game etc. **2** anything planned to deceive, betray etc. **3** arrangement

——————— THESAURUS ———————

transit n = **movement**, transfer, transport, passage, crossing

translate v = **render**, put, change, convert, interpret

transmit v = **broadcast**, televise, relay, air, radio, stream; = **pass on**, carry, spread, send, bear

transparent adj = **clear**, sheer, see-through, lucid, translucent ≠ **opaque**; = **obvious**, plain, patent, evident, explicit ≠ **uncertain**

transplant v = **implant**, transfer,

graft

transport n = **vehicle**, transportation, conveyance; = **transference**, carrying, delivery, distribution, transportation; often plural = **ecstasy**, delight, heaven, bliss, euphoria ≠ **despondency** ▷ v = **convey**, take, move, bring, send; = **enrapture**, move, delight, entrance, enchant; (Hist) = **exile**, banish, deport

trap n = **snare**, net, gin, pitfall, noose; = **ambush**, set-up (Inf) ▷ v

of pipes to prevent escape of gas
4 movable opening ▷ v **5** catch
6 trick **trapper** n one who traps
animals for their fur **trapdoor** n
door in floor or roof

trapeze n horizontal bar
suspended from two ropes for
acrobatics etc.

trapezium n, pl **-ziums, -zia**
four-sided figure with two parallel
sides of unequal length

trappings pl n equipment,
ornaments

trash ❶ n **1** rubbish **2** nonsense
3 (US & Canad) anything worthless

trauma ❶ n **1** emotional shock
2 injury, wound **traumatic** adj
traumatize v

travail v/n labour, toil

travel ❶ v **-elling, -elled 1** go,
move from one place to another
▷ v **2** act of travelling ▷ pl
3 (account of) travelling **traveller**
n one who travels **travelogue** n
film etc. about travels

traverse v **1** cross, go through or
over ▷ n **2** traversing **3** path
across

travesty n, pl **-ties 1** grotesque
imitation ▷ v **2** make, be a travesty

of

trawl v fish at deep levels with net
dragged behind boat **trawler** n
trawling boat

tray n flat board, usu. with rim, for
carrying things

treachery n, pl **-eries** deceit,
betrayal **treacherous** adj
1 disloyal **2** unsafe

treacle n thick syrup produced
when sugar is refined

tread ❶ v treading, trod,
trodden **1** walk **2** trample (on)
▷ n **3** treading **4** fashion of
walking **5** upper surface of step
6 part of tyre which makes contact
with ground **treadmill** n dreary
routine

treadle n lever worked by foot to
turn wheel

treason ❶ n **1** violation by subject
of allegiance to sovereign or state
2 treachery

treasure ❶ n **1** riches **2** valued
person or thing ▷ v **3** prize, cherish
treasurer n official in charge of
funds **treasury** n **1** place for
treasure **2** government
department in charge of finance
treasure-trove n treasure found

t

= catch, snare, ensnare, entrap,
take; **= trick**, fool, cheat, lure, seduce

trash n = **nonsense**, rubbish, rot,
drivel, twaddle ≠ **sense**; (chiefly US
& Canad) = **litter**, refuse, waste,
rubbish, junk (Inf)

trauma n = **shock**, suffering, pain,
torture, ordeal; = **injury**, damage,
hurt, wound, agony

travel v = **go**, journey, move, tour,

progress

tread v = **step**, walk, march, pace,
stamp ▷ n = **step**, walk, pace,
stride, footstep

treason n = **disloyalty**, mutiny,
treachery, duplicity, sedition
≠ **loyalty**

treasure n = **riches**, money, gold,
fortune, wealth; (Inf) = **angel**,
darling, jewel, gem, paragon ▷ v

with no evidence of ownership

treat ❶ n **1** pleasure, entertainment given ▷ v **2** deal with, act towards **3** give medical treatment to **4** provide with treat **treatment** n **1** method of counteracting disease **2** act or mode of treating

treatise n formal essay

treaty ❶ n, pl **-ties** signed contract between states etc.

treble adj **1** threefold **2** (Mus) high-pitched ▷ n **3** soprano voice ▷ v **4** increase threefold

tree n large perennial plant with woody trunk

trek ❶ n **1** long difficult journey ▷ v **2** make trek

trellis n lattice or grating of light bars

tremble ❶ v **1** quiver, shake **2** feel fear ▷ n **3** involuntary shaking

tremendous ❶ adj **1** vast, immense **2** (Inf) exciting **3** (Inf) excellent

tremor n **1** quiver **2** shaking

tremulous adj quivering slightly

trench ❶ n long narrow ditch **trench coat** double-breasted waterproof coat

trenchant adj cutting, incisive

trend ❶ n **1** direction, tendency **2** fashion **trendy** adj (Inf) consciously fashionable

trepidation n fear, anxiety

trespass v **1** intrude on property etc. of another ▷ n **2** wrongful entering on another's land **3** wrongdoing **trespasser** n

trestle n board fixed on pairs of spreading legs

trevally n, pl **-lies** (Aust & NZ) any of various food and game fishes

trews pl n close-fitting tartan trousers

tri- comb. form three

trial ❶ n **1** test, examination **2** (Law) investigation of case before judge **3** thing, person that strains endurance or patience

— THESAURUS —

= **prize**, value, esteem, adore, cherish

treat v = **behave towards**, deal with, handle, act towards, use; = **take care of**, minister to, attend to, give medical treatment to, doctor (Inf); = **provide**, stand (Inf), entertain, lay on, regale ▷ n = **entertainment**, party, surprise, gift, celebration; = **pleasure**, delight, joy, thrill, satisfaction

treaty n = **agreement**, pact, contract, alliance, convention

trek v = **journey**, march, hike, tramp, rove ▷ n = **slog**, tramp

tremble v = **shake**, shiver, quake, shudder, quiver ▷ n = **shake**, shiver, quake, shudder, wobble

tremendous adj = **huge**, great, enormous, terrific, formidable ≠ **tiny**; = **excellent**, great, wonderful, brilliant, amazing ≠ **terrible**

trench n = **ditch**, channel, drain, gutter, trough

trend n = **tendency**, swing, drift, inclination, current; = **fashion**, craze, fad (Inf), mode, thing

trial n (Law) = **hearing**, case, court case, inquiry, tribunal; = **test**,

DICTIONARY

triangle n figure with three angles **triangular** adj

tribe ❶ n **1** race **2** subdivision of race of people **tribal** adj

tribulation n trouble, affliction

tribunal ❶ n **1** lawcourt **2** body appointed to inquire into specific matter

tributary n, pl **-taries** stream flowing into another

tribute ❶ v **1** sign of honour **2** tax paid by one state to another

trice n moment, instant

trick ❶ n **1** deception **2** prank **3** feat of skill or cunning **4** knack **5** cards played in one round ▷ v **6** deceive, cheat **trickery** n **trickster** n **tricky** adj difficult

trickle ❶ v **1** (cause to) run, flow, move in thin stream or drops ▷ n **2** trickling flow

tricolour n three-coloured striped flag

tricycle n three-wheeled cycle

trident n three-pronged spear

trifle ❶ n **1** insignificant thing or matter **2** small amount **3** pudding of sponge cake, whipped cream etc. ▷ v **4** toy (with)

trigger ❶ n **1** catch which releases spring, esp. to fire gun ▷ v **2** (oft. with *off*) set in action etc.
trigger-happy adj tending to be irresponsible

trigonometry n branch of mathematics dealing with relations of sides and angles of triangles

trilby n, pl **-bies** man's soft felt hat

trill v/n (sing, play with) rapid alternation between two close notes

trillion n **1** one million million, 10^{12} **2** (*Obs*) one million million million, 10^{18}

trilogy n, pl **-gies** series of three related (literary) works

trim ❶ adj trimmer, trimmest **1** neat, smart **2** slender **3** in good order ▷ v **4** shorten slightly by cutting **5** prune **6** decorate **7** adjust ▷ n **8** decoration **9** order,

THESAURUS

experiment, evaluation, audition, dry run (*Inf*)

tribe n = **race**, people, family, clan

tribunal n = **hearing**, court, trial

tribute n = **accolade**, testimonial, eulogy, recognition, compliment ≠ **criticism**

trick n = **joke**, stunt, spoof (*Inf*), prank, practical joke; = **deception**, trap, fraud, manoeuvre, ploy; = **sleight of hand**, stunt, legerdemain; = **secret**, skill, knack, hang (*Inf*), technique;

= **mannerism**, habit, characteristic, trait, quirk ▷ v = **deceive**, trap, take someone in (*Inf*), fool, cheat

trickle v = **dribble**, run, drop, stream, drip ▷ n = **dribble**, drip, seepage, thin stream

trifle n = **knick-knack**, toy, plaything, bauble, bagatelle

trigger v = **bring about**, start, cause, produce, generate ≠ **prevent**

trim adj = **neat**, smart, tidy, spruce, dapper ≠ **untidy**; = **slender**, fit,

state of being trim **trimming** n
(oft. pl) decoration, addition

trinitrotoluene n powerful
explosive

trinity n, pl **-ties** 1 the state of
being threefold 2 (with cap.) state
of God as three persons, Father, Son
and Holy Spirit

trinket n small ornament

trio ❶ n, pl **trios** 1 group of three
2 music for three parts

trip ❶ n 1 (short) journey for
pleasure 2 stumble 3 (Inf)
hallucinatory experience caused by
drug ▷ v 4 (cause to) stumble
5 (cause to) make mistake 6 run
lightly

tripe n 1 stomach of cow as food
2 (Inf) nonsense

triple ❶ adj 1 threefold ▷ v
2 treble **triplet** n one of three
offspring born at one birth

triplicate adj 1 threefold ▷ n
2 state of being triplicate 3 one of
set of three copies

tripod n stool, stand etc. with
three feet

trite adj hackneyed, banal

triumph ❶ n 1 great success
2 victory 3 exultation ▷ v
4 achieve great success or victory
5 rejoice over victory **triumphal**
adj **triumphant** adj

troll n giant or dwarf in
Scandinavian mythology and
folklore

trolley n 1 small wheeled table for
food and drink 2 wheeled cart for
moving goods etc. 3 (US) tram

trollop n promiscuous woman

trombone n deep-toned brass
instrument **trombonist** n

troop ❶ n 1 group of persons ▷ pl
2 soldiers ▷ v 3 move in troop
trooper n cavalry soldier

trophy ❶ n, pl **-phies** prize,
award

tropic n 1 either of two lines of
latitude N and S of equator ▷ pl
2 area of earth's surface between

THESAURUS

slim, sleek, streamlined ▷ v = **cut**,
crop, clip, shave, tidy; = **decorate**,
dress, array, adorn, ornament ▷ n
= **decoration**, edging, border,
piping, trimming; = **condition**,
health, shape (Inf), fitness,
wellness; = **cut**, crop, clipping,
shave, pruning

trio n = **threesome**, trinity, trilogy,
triad, triumvirate

trip n = **journey**, outing, excursion,
day out, run; = **stumble**, fall, slip,
misstep ▷ v = **stumble**, fall, fall
over, slip, tumble; = **skip**, dance,
hop, gambol

triple adj = **treble**, three times ▷ v
= **treble**, increase threefold

triumph n = **success**, victory,
accomplishment, achievement,
coup ≠ **failure**; = **joy**, pride,
happiness, rejoicing, elation ▷ v
often with **over** = **succeed**, win,
overcome, prevail, prosper ≠ **fail**;
= **rejoice**, celebrate, glory, revel,
gloat

troop n ≠ **group**, company, team,
body, unit ▷ v = **flock**, march,
stream, swarm, throng

trophy n = **prize**, cup, award,
laurels; = **souvenir**, spoils, relic,

these lines **tropical** adj **1** pert. to, within tropics **2** (of climate) very hot

trot ❶ v trotting, trotted **1** (of horse) move at medium pace **2** (of person) run easily with short strides ▷ n **3** trotting, jog **trotter** n **1** horse trained to trot in race **2** foot of pig etc.

troubadour n medieval travelling poet and singer

trouble ❶ n **1** state or cause of mental distress, pain, inconvenience etc. **2** care ▷ v **3** be trouble to **4** be inconvenienced, be agitated **5** cause distress **troublesome** adj **troubleshooter** n person employed to deal with problems

trough ❶ n **1** long open vessel, esp. for animals' food or water **2** hollow between waves

trounce v beat thoroughly, thrash

troupe ❶ n company of performers **trouper** n

trousers pl n garment covering legs

trousseau n, pl **-seaux, -seaus**

bride's outfit of clothing

trout n freshwater fish

trowel n small tool like spade

truant n one absent without leave **truancy** n

truce ❶ n temporary cessation of fighting

truck[1] n wheeled (motor) vehicle for moving goods

truck[2] n dealing, esp. in have no truck with

trucker n (US & Canad) truck driver

truculent adj aggressive, defiant

trudge v **1** walk laboriously ▷ n **2** tiring walk

true ❶ adj truer, truest **1** in accordance with facts **2** faithful **3** correct **4** genuine **truism** n self-evident truth **truly** adv **truth** n **1** state of being true **2** something that is true **truthful** adj **1** accustomed to speak the truth **2** accurate

truffle n **1** edible underground fungus **2** sweet flavoured with chocolate

trump n **1** card of suit ranking above others ▷ v **2** play trump

memento, booty

trot v = **run**, jog, scamper, lope, canter ▷ n = **run**, jog, lope, canter

trouble n = **bother**, problems, concern, worry, stress; usually plural = **distress**, problem, worry, pain, anxiety ≠ **pleasure**; = **ailment**, disease, failure, complaint, illness; = **disorder**, fighting, conflict, bother, unrest ≠ **peace** ▷ v = **bother**, worry, upset, disturb, distress ≠ **please**; = **afflict**, hurt,

bother, cause discomfort to, pain; = **inconvenience**, disturb, burden, put out, impose upon ≠ **relieve**

trough n = **manger**, water trough

truce n = **ceasefire**, peace, moratorium, respite, lull

true adj = **correct**, right, accurate, precise, factual ≠ **false**; = **faithful**, loyal, devoted, dedicated, steady ≠ **unfaithful**; = **exact**, perfect, accurate, precise, spot-on (Brit Inf) ≠ **inaccurate**

t

trump up invent, concoct

trumpet n 1 metal wind instrument like horn ▷ v 2 blow trumpet 3 make sound like one 4 proclaim **trumpeter** n

truncate v cut short

truncheon n short thick club

trundle v move heavily, as on small wheels

trunk ❶ n 1 main stem of tree 2 person's body excluding head and limbs 3 box for clothes etc. 4 elephant's snout ▷ pl 5 man's swimming costume **trunk call** long-distance telephone call **trunk road** main road

truss v 1 fasten up, tie up ▷ n 2 support 3 medical supporting device

trust ❶ n 1 confidence 2 firm belief 3 reliance 4 combination of business firms 5 care 6 property held for another ▷ v 7 rely on 8 believe in 9 expect, hope 10 consign for care **trustee** n one legally holding property for another **trustful, trusting** adj **trustworthy** adj **trusty** adj

try ❶ v **trying, tried** 1 attempt 2 test, sample 3 afflict 4 examine

in court of law ▷ n 5 attempt, effort 6 (Rugby) score gained by touching ball down over opponent's goal line **tried** adj proved **trying** adj troublesome

tryst n arrangement to meet, esp. secretly

T-shirt n informal (short-sleeved) sweater

tub n 1 open wooden vessel like bottom half of barrel 2 small round container 3 bath **tubby** adj short and fat

tuba n valved brass wind instrument of low pitch

tube n 1 long, narrow hollow cylinder 2 flexible cylinder with cap to hold pastes 3 underground electric railway **tubular** adj

tuber n fleshy underground stem of some plants

tuberculosis n communicable disease, esp. of lung **tubercular** adj **tuberculin** n bacillus used to treat tuberculosis

tuck ❶ v 1 push, fold into small space 2 gather, stitch in folds ▷ n 3 stitched fold 4 (Inf) food

tucker n (Aust & NZ, Inf) food

Tuesday n third day of the week

————— THESAURUS —————

trunk n = **stem**, stalk, bole; = **chest**, case, box, crate, coffer; = **body**, torso

trust v = **believe in**, have faith in, depend on, count on, bank on ≠ **distrust**; = **entrust**, commit, assign, confide, consign; = **expect**, hope, suppose, assume, presume ▷ n = **confidence**, credit, belief, faith, expectation

≠ **distrust**

try v = **attempt**, seek, aim, strive, struggle; = **experiment with**, try out, put to the test, test, taste ▷ n = **attempt**, go (Inf), shot (Inf), effort, crack (Inf)

tuck v = **push**, stick, stuff, slip, ease ▷ n = **food**, grub (Sl), nosh (Sl); = **fold**, gather, pleat, pinch

tuft n bunch of feathers etc.

tug ❶ v **tugging, tugged 1** pull hard or violently ▷ n **2** violent pull **3** ship used to tow other vessels

tug-of-war n contest in which two teams pull against one another on rope

tuition ❶ n teaching, esp. private

tulip n plant with bright cup-shaped flowers

tumble ❶ v **1** (cause to) fall or roll, twist etc. **2** rumple ▷ n **3** fall **tumbler** n **1** stemless drinking glass **2** acrobat **tumbledown** adj dilapidated **tumble dryer** machine that dries laundry by rotating it in warm air

tummy n, pl **-mies** (Inf) stomach

tumour ❶ n abnormal growth in or on body

tumult n violent uproar, commotion **tumultuous** adj

tuna n large marine food and game fish

tundra n vast treeless zone between ice cap and timber line

tune ❶ n **1** melody **2** quality of being in pitch **3** adjustment of musical instrument ▷ v **4** put in tune **5** adjust machine to obtain efficient running **6** adjust radio to

receive broadcast **tuneful** adj

tuner n

tungsten n greyish-white metal

tunic n **1** close-fitting jacket forming part of uniform **2** loose hip-length garment

tunnel ❶ n **1** underground passage, esp. as track for railway line ▷ v **2** make tunnel (through)

tupik, tupek n (Canad) (esp. in the Arctic) a tent of animal skins, a traditional type of Inuit dwelling

turban n headdress made by coiling length of cloth round head

turbine n rotary engine driven by steam, gas, water or air playing on blades

turbot n large flatfish

tureen n serving dish for soup

turf ❶ n, pl **turfs, turves 1** short grass with earth bound to it by matted roots ▷ v **2** lay with turf **turf accountant** bookmaker **turf out** (Inf) throw out

turgid adj **1** swollen, inflated **2** bombastic

turkey n large bird reared for food

Turkish adj of Turkey **Turkish bath** steam bath **Turkish delight** jelly-like sweet coated with icing sugar

— THESAURUS —

tug v = **pull**, pluck, jerk, yank, wrench ▷ n = **pull**, jerk, yank

tuition n = **training**, schooling, education, teaching, lessons

tumble v = **fall**, drop, topple, plummet, stumble ▷ n = **fall**, drop, trip, plunge, spill

tumour n = **growth**, cancer, swelling, lump, carcinoma

(Pathology)

tune n = **melody**, air, song, theme, strain(s); = **harmony**, pitch, euphony ▷ v = **tune up**, adjust

tunnel n = **passage**, underpass, passageway, subway, channel ▷ v = **dig**, burrow, mine, bore, drill

turf n = **grass**, sward

t

turmoil ❶ n confusion, commotion

turn ❶ v 1 move around, rotate 2 change, alter position or direction (of) 3 (oft. with *into*) change in nature 4 make, shape on lathe ▷ n 5 turning 6 inclination etc. 7 period 8 short walk 9 (part of) rotation 10 performance **turning** n road, path leading off main route **turncoat** n person who deserts party, cause etc. to join another **turn down** 1 reduce volume or brightness of 2 refuse **turnout** n number of people appearing for some purpose **turnover** n 1 total sales made by business 2 rate at which staff leave and are replaced **turnstile** n revolving gate for controlling admission of people **turntable** n revolving platform **turn up** v appear

turnip n plant with edible root **turpentine** n oil from certain trees used in paints etc. **turps** n (*Inf*) turpentine **turquoise** n 1 bluish-green precious stone 2 this colour **turret** n 1 small tower 2 revolving armoured tower on tank etc. **turtle** n sea tortoise

tusk n long pointed side tooth of elephant etc.

tussle n/v fight, wrestle, struggle

tutor ❶ n 1 one teaching individuals or small groups ▷ v 2 teach **tutorial** n period of instruction

tutu n skirt worn by ballerinas

tuxedo n (*US & Canad*) dinner jacket

TV television

twang n 1 vibrating metallic sound 2 nasal speech ▷ v 3 (cause to) make such sounds

tweak v 1 pinch and twist or pull ▷ n 2 tweaking

twee adj (*Inf*) oversentimental

tweed n rough-surfaced cloth used for clothing

tweet n 1 chirp 2 message on Twitter website ▷ v 3 chirp 4 post message on Twitter website

tweezers pl n small forceps or tongs

twelve adj/n two more than ten **twelfth** adj ordinal number

twenty adj/n twice ten **twentieth** adj ordinal number

twerp n (*Inf*) stupid person

twice adv two times

twiddle v 1 fiddle 2 twist

THESAURUS

turmoil n = confusion, disorder, chaos, upheaval, disarray ≠ **peace**

turn v = change course, swing round, wheel round, veer, move; = **rotate**, spin, go round (and round), revolve, roll; = **change**, transform, shape, convert, alter; = **shape**, form, fashion, cast, frame; = **go bad**, go off (*Brit Inf*),

curdle, spoil, sour ▷ n = **rotation**, cycle, circle, revolution, spin; = **change of direction**, shift, departure, deviation; = **direction**, course, tack, tendency, drift

tutor n = **teacher**, coach, instructor, educator, guide ▷ v = **teach**, educate, school, train, coach

DICTIONARY

twig ❶ n small branch, shoot
twilight ❶ n soft light after sunset
twill n fabric with surface of parallel ridges
twin ❶ n 1 one of two children born together ▷ v 2 pair, be paired
twine v 1 twist, coil round ▷ n 2 string, cord
twinge n 1 momentary sharp pain 2 qualm
twinkle ❶ v 1 shine with dancing light, sparkle ▷ n 2 twinkling 3 flash
twirl v 1 turn or twist round quickly 2 whirl 3 twiddle
twist ❶ v 1 make, become spiral, by turning with one end fast 2 distort, change 3 wind ▷ n 4 twisting
twit n twitting, twitted (Inf) 1 foolish person ▷ v 2 taunt
twitch ❶ v 1 give momentary sharp pull or jerk (to) ▷ n 2 such pull 3 spasmodic jerk
twitter v 1 (of birds) utter

tremulous sounds 2 with capital T website where people can post short messages about their current activities ▷ n 3 tremulous sound 4 sometimes with capital T write a short message on the Twitter website
two n/adj one more than one
two-faced adj deceitful
tycoon ❶ n powerful, influential businessman
type ❶ n 1 class 2 sort 3 model 4 pattern 5 characteristic build 6 specimen 7 block bearing letter used for printing ▷ v 8 print with typewriter **typecast** v repeatedly cast (actor, actress) in similar roles
typescript n typewritten document **typewriter** n keyed writing machine **typist** n one who operates typewriter
typhoid fever acute infectious disease, esp. of intestines
typhoon n violent tropical storm
typhus n infectious feverish disease

THESAURUS

twig n = **branch**, stick, sprig, shoot, spray
twilight n = **dusk**, evening, sunset, early evening, nightfall ≠ **dawn**
twin n = **double**, counterpart, mate, match, fellow ▷ v = **pair**, match, join, couple, link
twinkle v = **sparkle**, flash, shine, glitter, gleam ▷ n = **sparkle**, flash, spark, gleam, flicker
twist v = **coil**, curl, wind, wrap, screw; = **distort**, screw up, contort, mangle ≠ **straighten** ▷ n

= **surprise**, change, turn, development, revelation;
= **development**, emphasis, variation, slant; = **wind**, turn, spin, swivel, twirl; = **curve**, turn, bend, loop, arc
twitch v = **jerk**, flutter, jump, squirm; = **pull (at)**, tug (at), pluck (at), yank (at) ▷ n = **jerk**, tic, spasm, jump, flutter
tycoon n = **magnate**, capitalist, baron, industrialist, financier
type n = **kind**, sort, class, variety, group

typical ❶ *adj* **1** true to type
2 characteristic **typically** *adv*
typography *n* **1** art of printing
2 style of printing
tyrant *n* oppressive or cruel ruler
tyrannical *adj* **1** despotic

2 ruthless **tyrannize** *v* exert
ruthless or tyrannical authority
(over) **tyrannous** *adj* **tyranny** *n*
despotism

tyre *n* (inflated) rubber ring over
rim of wheel of road vehicle

─────────────── THESAURUS ───────

typical *adj* = **archetypal**,
standard, model, normal, stock

≠ unusual

t

u

ubiquitous ❶ adj everywhere at once

udder n milk-secreting organ of cow etc.

UFO unidentified flying object

ugly ❶ adj **uglier, ugliest**
1 unpleasant to see, hideous
2 threatening

ukulele, ukelele n small four-stringed guitar

ulcer ❶ n open sore on skin

ulterior adj lying beneath, beyond what is revealed

ultimate ❶ adj 1 last, conclusive
2 highest 3 fundamental

ultimatum n final terms

ultra- comb. form beyond, excessively, as in ultramodern

ultraviolet adj (of electromagnetic radiation) beyond limit of visibility at violet end of spectrum

umbrage n offence, resentment

umbrella n folding circular cover of nylon etc. on stick, carried in hand to protect against rain

umpire ❶ n 1 person chosen to decide question, or to enforce rules in game ▷ v 2 act as umpire

umpteen adj (Inf) very many

un- comb. form indicating not, reversal of an action

unaccountable adj that cannot be explained

unanimous ❶ adj in complete agreement **unanimity** n

unassuming adj modest

unaware ❶ adj not aware
unawares adv unexpectedly

uncanny adj weird, mysterious

unceremonious adj 1 without ceremony 2 abrupt, rude

THESAURUS

---

ubiquitous adj = **ever-present**, pervasive, omnipresent, everywhere, universal

ugly adj = **unattractive**, homely (chiefly US), plain, unsightly, unlovely ≠ **beautiful**;
= **unpleasant**, shocking, terrible, nasty, distasteful ≠ **pleasant**

ulcer n = **sore**, abscess, peptic ulcer, gumboil

ultimate adj = **final**, last, end;

= **supreme**, highest, greatest, paramount, superlative

umpire n = **referee**, judge, arbiter, arbitrator ▷ v = **referee**, judge, adjudicate, arbitrate

unanimous adj = **agreed**, united, in agreement, harmonious, like-minded ≠ **divided**

unaware adj = **ignorant**, unconscious, oblivious, uninformed, unknowing ≠ **aware**

uncertain ❶ *adj* **1** not able to be known **2** changeable **uncertainty** *n*

uncle *n* **1** brother of father or mother **2** husband of parent's sibling

unconscious ❶ *adj* **1** insensible **2** not aware ▷ *n* **3** set of thoughts, memories etc. of which one is not normally aware

uncouth *adj* clumsy, boorish

unction *n* anointing **unctuous** *adj* excessively polite

under ❶ *prep* **1** below, beneath **2** included in **3** less than **4** subjected to ▷ *adv* **5** in lower place or condition ▷ *adj* **6** lower

under- *comb. form* beneath, below, lower, as in *underground*

underarm *adj* **1** from armpit to wrist **2** (*Sport*) with hand swung below shoulder level

undercarriage *n* **1** aircraft's landing gear **2** framework supporting body of vehicle

undercurrent *n* **1** current that is not apparent at surface

2 underlying opinion, emotion

undercut *v* charge less than (another trader)

underdog ❶ *n* person, team unlikely to win

undergo ❶ *v* experience, endure, sustain

undergraduate *n* student member of university

underground ❶ *adj* **1** under the ground **2** secret ▷ *adv* **3** secretly ▷ *n* **4** secret but organized resistance to government in power **5** railway system under the ground

undergrowth *n* small trees, bushes growing beneath taller trees

underhand *adj* secret, sly

underlie *v* **1** lie, be placed under **2** be the foundation, cause, or basis of

underline ❶ *v* **1** put line under **2** emphasize

underling *n* subordinate

————— THESAURUS —————

uncertain *adj* = **unsure**, undecided, vague, unclear, dubious ≠ **sure** = **doubtful**, questionable, indefinite, unconfirmed, conjectural ≠ **decided**

unconscious *adj* = **senseless**, knocked out, out cold (*Inf*), out, stunned ≠ **awake**; = **unaware**, ignorant, oblivious, unknowing ≠ **aware**; = **unintentional**, unwitting, inadvertent, accidental ≠ **intentional**

under *prep* = **below**, beneath, underneath ≠ **over**; = **subordinate**

to, subject to, governed by, secondary to ▷ *adv* = **below**, down, beneath ≠ **up**

underdog *n* = **weaker party**, little fellow (*Inf*), outsider

undergo *v* = **experience**, go through, stand, suffer, bear

underground *adj* = **subterranean**, basement, lower-level, sunken, covered; = **secret**, covert, hidden, guerrilla, revolutionary

underline *v* = **emphasize**, stress, highlight, accentuate ≠ **minimize**

u

undermine ① v **1** wear away base, support of **2** weaken insidiously

underneath adv **1** below ▷ prep **2** under ▷ adj **3** lower ▷ n **4** lower surface

underpants pl n man's underwear for lower part of body

underpass n road that passes under another road or railway line

underpin v give strength, support to

understand ① v **1** know and comprehend **2** realize **3** infer **4** take for granted

understudy n **1** one prepared to take over theatrical part ▷ v **2** act as understudy

undertake ① v **1** make oneself responsible for **2** enter upon **3** promise **undertaker** n one who arranges funerals **undertaking** n

undertone n **1** dropped tone of

voice **2** underlying suggestion

underwear ① n garments worn next to skin

underworld ① n **1** criminals and their associates **2** (Myth) abode of the dead

underwrite ① v **1** agree to pay **2** accept liability in insurance policy **underwriter** n

undo ① v **1** untie, unfasten **2** reverse **3** cause downfall of

undulate v move up and down like waves

unearth ① v **1** dig up **2** discover

uneasy ① adj **1** anxious **2** uncomfortable

unemployed ① adj having no paid employment, out of work **unemployment** n

unexceptionable adj beyond criticism

unfold ① v **1** open, spread out **2** reveal

—— THESAURUS ——

= **underscore**, mark

undermine v = **weaken**, sabotage, subvert, compromise, disable ≠ **reinforce**

understand v = **comprehend**, get, take in, perceive, grasp (Inf); = **believe**, gather, think, see, suppose

undertake v = **agree**, promise, contract, guarantee, engage

underwear n = **underclothes**, lingerie, undies (Inf), undergarments, underthings

underworld n = **criminals**, gangsters, organized crime, gangland (Inf); = **nether world**, Hades, nether regions

underwrite v = **finance**, back, fund, guarantee, sponsor

undo v = **open**, unfasten, loose, untie, unbutton; = **reverse**, cancel, offset, neutralize, invalidate; = **ruin**, defeat, destroy, wreck, shatter

unearth v = **discover**, find, reveal, expose, uncover; = **dig up**, excavate, exhume, dredge up

uneasy adj = **anxious**, worried, troubled, nervous, disturbed ≠ **relaxed**; = **precarious**, strained, uncomfortable, tense, awkward

unemployed adj = **out of work**, redundant, laid off, jobless, idle ≠ **working**

unfold v = **reveal**, tell, present,

u

ungainly adj **-lier, -liest** awkward, clumsy

uni- comb. form one, as in unicycle

unicorn n mythical horselike animal with single long horn

uniform ❶ n **1** identifying clothes worn by members of same group, e.g. soldiers, nurses etc. ▷ adj **2** not changing **3** regular **uniformity** n

unify ❶ v **-fying, -fied** make or become one **unification** n

unilateral adj **1** one-sided **2** (of contract) binding one party only

union ❶ n **1** joining into one **2** state, result of being joined **3** federation **4** trade union **unionize** v organize (workers) into trade union

unique ❶ adj **1** being only one of its kind **2** unparalleled

unison n (Mus) **1** singing etc. of same notes as others **2** agreement

unit ❶ n **1** single thing or person **2** group or individual being part of larger whole **3** standard quantity

unite ❶ v **1** join into one **2** associate **3** become one **4** combine **unity 1** state of being one **2** harmony **3** agreement

universe ❶ n **1** all existing things considered as constituting systematic whole **2** the world **universal** adj relating to all things or all people

university n, pl **-ties** educational institution that awards degrees

unkempt adj untidy

unless conj if not, except

unlike adj **1** dissimilar, different ▷ prep **2** not typical of **unlikely** adj improbable

unravel ❶ v **-elling, -elled** undo, untangle

unrest ❶ n discontent

unruly adj **-lier, -liest** badly

— THESAURUS —

show, disclose; = **open**, spread out, undo, expand, unfurl

uniform n = **regalia**, suit, livery, colours, habit ▷ adj = **consistent**, unvarying, similar, even, same ≠ **varying**; = **alike**, similar, like, same, equal

unify v = **unite**, join, combine, merge, consolidate ≠ **divide**

union n = **joining**, uniting, unification, combination, coalition; = **alliance**, league, association, coalition, federation

unique adj = **distinct**, special, exclusive, peculiar, only; = **unparalleled**, unmatched, unequalled, matchless, without

equal

unit n = **entity**, whole, item, feature; = **section**, company, group, force, detail; = **measure**, quantity, measurement

unite v = **join**, link, combine, couple, blend ≠ **separate**; = **cooperate**, ally, join forces, band, pool ≠ **split**

universe n = **cosmos**, space, creation, nature, heavens

unravel v = **solve**, explain, work out, resolve, figure out (Inf); = **undo**, separate, disentangle, free, unwind

unrest n = **discontent**, rebellion, protest, strife, agitation ≠ **peace**

u

behaved, disorderly
unsavoury adj distasteful
unscathed adj not harmed
unsightly adj ugly
unthinkable ❶ adj 1 out of the question 2 inconceivable 3 unreasonable
until conj 1 to the time that 2 (with a negative) before ▷ prep 3 up to the time of
unto prep (Obs)
untoward adj awkward, inconvenient
unwieldy adj 1 awkward 2 bulky
unwind v 1 slacken, undo, unravel 2 become relaxed
unwitting adj 1 not knowing 2 not intentional
up prep 1 from lower to higher position 2 along ▷ adv 3 in or to higher position, source, activity etc. 4 indicating completion **upward** adj/adv **upwards** adv **upbeat** adj (Inf) cheerful **up-to-date** adj modern, fashionable
upbringing ❶ n rearing and education of children

update ❶ v bring up to date
upfront adj (Inf) open, frank
upgrade ❶ v 1 promote to higher position 2 improve
upheaval ❶ n sudden or violent disturbance
uphold ❶ v maintain, support etc.
upholster v fit springs, coverings on chairs etc. **upholstery** n
upkeep n act, cost of keeping something in good repair
upon prep on
uptown (US & Canad) adj/adv towards, in, or relating to some part of a town that is away from the centre ▷ n such a part of a town, esp. a residential part
upper ❶ adj 1 situated above 2 of superior quality, status etc. ▷ n 3 upper part of boot or shoe **upper case** capital letters **upper hand** position of control
upright ❶ adj 1 erect 2 honest, just ▷ adv 3 vertically ▷ n 4 thing standing upright, e.g. post in framework
uprising ❶ n rebellion, revolt

THESAURUS

unthinkable adj = impossible, out of the question, inconceivable, absurd, unreasonable; = **inconceivable**, incredible, unimaginable
upbringing n = education, training, breeding, rearing, raising
update v = bring up to date, improve, correct, renew, revise
upgrade v = improve, better, update, reform, add to
upheaval n = disturbance,

revolution, disorder, turmoil, disruption
uphold v = support, back, defend, aid, champion
upper adj = topmost, top ≠ bottom; = higher, high ≠ lower
upright adj = vertical, straight, standing up, erect, perpendicular ≠ horizontal; = honest, good, principled, just, ethical ≠ dishonourable
uprising n = rebellion, rising,

u

uproar ❶ n tumult, disturbance
uproot v 1 pull up, as by roots
2 displace from usual surroundings
upset ❶ v 1 overturn 2 distress
3 disrupt ▷ n 4 unexpected defeat
5 confusion ▷ adj 6 disturbed
7 emotionally troubled
upshot n outcome, end
upside down, upside-down ❶
1 turned over completely 2 (Inf)
confused
upstage v overshadow
upstart n one suddenly raised to
wealth, power etc.
uptight adj (Inf) 1 tense
2 repressed
uranium n white radioactive
metallic element
urban ❶ adj relating to town or
city
urbane adj elegant, sophisticated
urchin n mischievous, unkempt
child
urge ❶ v 1 exhort earnestly

2 entreat 3 drive on ▷ n 4 strong
desire **urgency** n **urgent** adj
needing attention at once
urine n fluid excreted by kidneys to
bladder and passed as waste from
body **urinal** n place for urinating
urinate v discharge urine
urn v 1 vessel like vase 2 large
container with tap
us pron object of we
USB Universal Serial Bus: standard
for connecting sockets on
computers **USB drive** n (Comp)
small portable data storage device
with a USB connection
use ❶ v 1 employ 2 exercise
3 exploit 4 consume ▷ n
5 employment 6 need to employ
7 serviceableness 8 profit 9 habit
usable adj fit for use **usage** n
1 act of using 2 custom **used** adj
1 second-hand 2 accustomed
useful adj **useless** adj 1 having
no practical use 2 (Inf) inept

— THESAURUS —

revolution, revolt, disturbance
uproar n = **commotion**, noise,
racket, riot, turmoil
upset adj = **distressed**, shaken,
disturbed, worried, troubled;
= **sick**, queasy, bad, ill ▷ v
= **distress**, trouble, disturb, worry,
alarm; = **tip over**, overturn,
capsize, knock over, spill; = **mess
up**, spoil, disturb, change, confuse
▷ n = **distress**, worry, trouble,
shock, bother; = **reversal**, shake-up
(Inf), defeat; = **illness**, complaint,
disorder, bug (Inf), sickness
upside down, upside-down
adj = **inverted**, overturned,

upturned; (Inf) = **confused**,
disordered, chaotic, muddled,
topsy-turvy
urban adj = **civic**, city, town,
metropolitan, municipal
urge v = **beg**, exhort, plead,
implore, beseech; = **advocate**,
recommend, advise, support,
counsel ≠ **discourage** ▷ n
= **impulse**, longing, wish, desire,
drive ≠ **reluctance**
use v = **employ**, utilize, work, apply,
operate; sometimes with up
= **consume**, exhaust, spend, run
through, expend; = **take
advantage of**, exploit, manipulate

usher ❶ n 1 doorkeeper, one showing people to seats etc. ▷ v 2 introduce, announce
usual ❶ adj habitual, ordinary **usually** adv as a rule
usurp v seize wrongfully
utensil n vessel, implement, esp. in domestic use
uterus n womb
utility ❶ n 1 usefulness 2 benefit 3 useful thing ▷ adj 4 made for practical purposes **utilitarian** adj useful rather than beautiful **utilize** v
utmost ❶ adj 1 to the highest degree 2 extreme, furthest ▷ n 3 greatest possible amount
Utopia n imaginary ideal state
utter¹ ❶ v express, say **utterance** n
utter² ❶ adj complete, total **utterly** adv

—— THESAURUS ——

▷ n = **usage**, employment, operation, application = **service**, handling, practice, exercise; = **purpose**, end, reason, object
usher v = **escort**, lead, direct, guide, conduct ▷ n = **attendant**, guide, doorman, escort, doorkeeper
usual adj = **normal**, customary, regular, general, common ≠ **unusual**

utility n = **usefulness**, benefit, convenience, practicality, efficacy
utmost adj = **greatest**, highest, maximum, supreme, paramount; = **farthest**, extreme, last, final ▷ n = **best**, greatest, maximum, highest, hardest
utter¹ v = **say**, state, speak, voice, express
utter² adj = **absolute**, complete, total, sheer, outright

u

V

vacant ❶ adj empty, unoccupied
vacancy n, pl **-cies** untaken job, room etc.
vacate v quit, leave empty
vacation n **1** time when universities and law courts are closed **2** (US & Canad) holidays
vaccinate v inoculate with vaccine **vaccination** n **vaccine** n any substance used for inoculation against disease
vacillate v **1** waver **2** move to and fro **vacillation** n
vacuous adj not expressing intelligent thought
vacuum ❶ n, pl **vacuums, vacua** place, region containing no matter and from which all or most

air, gas has been removed
vacuum cleaner apparatus for removing dust by suction
vacuum flask double-walled flask with vacuum between walls, for keeping contents hot or cold
vagabond n **1** person with no fixed home **2** wandering beggar or thief
vagina n passage from womb to exterior
vagrant n vagabond, tramp **vagrancy** n
vague ❶ adj **1** indefinite or uncertain **2** indistinct **3** not clearly expressed
vain ❶ adj **1** conceited **2** worthless **3** unavailing
vale n (Poet) valley
valentine n (one receiving) card, gift, expressing affection, on Saint Valentine's day
valet n gentleman's personal servant
valiant adj brave, courageous
valid ❶ adj **1** sound **2** of binding force in law **validate** v make valid **validity** n
Valium® n drug used as tranquillizer

THESAURUS

vacant adj = **empty**, free, available, abandoned, deserted ≠ occupied; = **unfilled**, unoccupied ≠ taken
vacuum n = **gap**, lack, absence, space, deficiency
vague adj = **unclear**, indefinite, hazy, confused, loose ≠ clear; = **imprecise**, unspecified,

generalized, rough, loose
vain adj = **futile**, useless, pointless, unsuccessful, idle ≠ successful; = **conceited**, narcissistic, proud, arrogant, swaggering ≠ modest
valid adj = **sound**, good, reasonable, telling, convincing ≠ unfounded; = **legal**, official,

valley ❶ n 1 low area between hills 2 river basin

valour n bravery

value ❶ n 1 cost 2 worth 3 usefulness 4 importance ▷ pl 5 principles, standards ▷ v 6 estimate value of 7 prize

valuable adj 1 precious 2 worthy ▷ n 3 (usu. pl) valuable thing

valuation n estimated worth

value-added tax tax on difference between cost of basic materials and cost of article made from them

valve n 1 device to control passage of fluid etc. through pipe 2 (Anat) part of body allowing one-way passage of fluids

vampire n (in folklore) corpse that rises from dead to drink blood of the living **vampire bat** bat that sucks blood of animals

van¹ n 1 covered vehicle, esp. for goods 2 railway carriage for goods and use of guard

van² n short for VANGUARD

vandal n one who wantonly and deliberately damages or destroys

vandalism n **vandalize** v

vane n 1 weathercock 2 blade of propeller

vanguard n leading, foremost group, position etc.

vanilla n 1 tropical climbing orchid 2 its seed pod 3 essence of this for flavouring

vanish ❶ v disappear

vanity ❶ n, pl **-ties** excessive pride or conceit

vanquish v conquer, overcome

vantage n advantage **vantage point** position that gives overall view

vapid adj flat, dull, insipid

vapour n 1 gaseous form of a substance 2 steam, mist **vaporize** v convert into, pass off in, vapour **vaporizer** n

variable ❶ see VARY

variegated adj having patches of different colours

variety ❶ n, pl **-ties** 1 state of being varied or various 2 diversity 3 varied assortment 4 sort or kind

legitimate, genuine, authentic ≠ **invalid**

valley n = **hollow**, dale, glen, vale, depression

value n = **importance**, benefit, worth, merit, point ≠ **worthlessness**; = **cost**, price, worth, rate, market price ▷ v = **appreciate**, rate, prize, regard highly, respect ≠ **undervalue**; = **evaluate**, price, estimate, rate, cost

vanish v = **disappear**, dissolve,

evaporate, fade away, melt away ≠ **appear**

vanity n = **pride**, arrogance, conceit, narcissism, egotism ≠ **modesty**

variable adj = **changeable**, unstable, fluctuating, shifting, flexible ≠ **constant**

variety n = **diversity**, change, variation, difference, diversification ≠ **uniformity**; = **range**, selection, assortment, mix, collection; = **type**, sort, kind, class, brand

various ❶ adj diverse, of several kinds

varnish ❶ n 1 resinous solution put on surface to make it hard and shiny ▷ v 2 apply varnish to

vary ❶ v varying, varied (cause to) change, diversify, differ **variability** n **variable** adj 1 changeable 2 unsteady or fickle ▷ n 3 something subject to variation **variance** n state of discord, discrepancy **variant** adj 1 different ▷ n 2 alternative form **variation** n 1 alteration 2 extent to which thing varies 3 modification **varied** adj 1 diverse 2 modified

vase n vessel, jar as ornament or for holding flowers

Vaseline® n jelly-like petroleum product

vast ❶ adj very large

VAT value-added tax

vat n large tub, tank

vault¹ ❶ n 1 arched roof 2 cellar 3 burial chamber 4 secure room for storing valuables

vault² ❶ v 1 spring, jump over with the hands resting on something ▷ n 2 such jump

veal n calf flesh as food

vector n (Maths) quantity that has size and direction

veer ❶ v 1 change direction 2 change one's mind

vegan n one who eats no meat, eggs, or dairy products

vegetable n 1 plant, esp. edible one ▷ adj 2 of, from, concerned with plants

vegetarian n 1 one who does not eat meat or fish ▷ adj 2 suitable for vegetarians

vegetate v 1 (of plants) grow, develop 2 (of people) live dull, unproductive life **vegetation** n plants collectively

vehement adj marked by intensity of feeling

vehicle ❶ n means of conveying

veil ❶ n 1 light material to cover face or head ▷ v 2 cover with, as with, veil

vein ❶ n 1 tube in body taking

       THESAURUS

various adj = **different**, assorted, miscellaneous, varied, distinct ≠ **similar**

varnish v = **lacquer**, polish, glaze, gloss

vary v = **differ**, be different, be dissimilar, disagree, diverge; = **change**, shift, swing, alter, fluctuate

vast adj = **huge**, massive, enormous, great, wide ≠ **tiny**

vault¹ n = **strongroom**, repository, depository; = **crypt**, tomb,

catacomb, cellar, mausoleum

vault² v = **jump**, spring, leap, clear, bound

veer v = **change direction**, turn, swerve, shift, sheer

vehicle n = **conveyance**, machine, motor vehicle

veil n = **mask**, cover, shroud, film, curtain ▷ v = **cover**, screen, hide, mask, shield ≠ **reveal**

vein n = **mood**, style, note, tone, mode; = **seam**, layer, stratum, course, current blood to heart **2** fissure in rock filled with ore **veined** adj

Velcro® n fabric with tiny hooked threads that adheres to coarse surface

velocity ❶ n, pl **-ties 1** rate of motion in given direction **2** speed

velvet n silk or cotton fabric with thick, short pile **velvety** adj **1** of, like velvet **2** soft and smooth

vend v sell **vendor** n **vending machine** machine that dispenses goods automatically

vendetta n prolonged quarrel

veneer n **1** thin layer of fine wood **2** superficial appearance ▷ v **3** cover with veneer

venerable adj worthy of reverence **venerate** v look up to, respect, revere **veneration** n

vengeance ❶ n revenge **vengeful** adj

venison n flesh of deer as food

venom n **1** poison **2** spite **venomous** adj

vent ❶ n **1** small hole or outlet ▷ v **2** give outlet to **3** utter

ventilate v supply with fresh air **ventilation** n **ventilator** n

ventricle n cavity of heart or brain

ventriloquist n one who can so

speak that the sounds seem to come from some other person or place **ventriloquism** n

venture ❶ v **1** expose to hazard **2** risk **3** dare **4** have courage to do something or go somewhere ▷ n **5** risky undertaking

venture capitalist provider of capital for new commercial enterprises

venue n **1** meeting place **2** location

veracious adj truthful **veracity** n

verandah, veranda n open or partly enclosed porch on outside of house

verb n part of speech used to express action or being **verbal** adj of, by, or relating to words spoken rather than written **verbatim** adj/adv word for word

verbose adj long-winded

verdant adj green and fresh

verdict ❶ n **1** decision of jury **2** opinion reached after examination of facts

verge ❶ n **1** edge **2** brink **3** grass border along road ▷ v **4** come close to **5** be on the border of

verger n church caretaker

THESAURUS

velocity n = **speed**, pace, rapidity, quickness, swiftness

vengeance n = **revenge**, retaliation, reprisal, retribution, requital ≠ forgiveness

vent n = **outlet**, opening, aperture, duct, orifice ▷ v = **express**, release, voice, air, discharge ≠ hold back

venture n = **undertaking**, project,

enterprise, campaign, risk ▷ v = **go**, travel, journey, set out, wander; = **dare**, presume, have the courage to, be brave enough, hazard; = **put forward**, volunteer

verdict n = **decision**, finding, judgment, opinion, sentence

verge n = **brink**, point, edge, threshold

V

verify ❶ v -ifying, -ified 1 prove, confirm truth of 2 test accuracy of **verification** n

veritable adj actual, true

vermilion adj/n (of) bright red colour

vermin pl n harmful animals, parasites etc.

vernacular n 1 commonly spoken language or dialect of particular country or place ▷ adj 2 of vernacular 3 native

verruca n wart, esp. on the foot

versatile ❶ adj capable of, adapted to many different uses, skills etc. **versatility** n

verse n 1 stanza or short subdivision of poem or the Bible 2 poetry **versed in** skilled in

version ❶ n 1 description from certain point of view 2 translation 3 adaptation

versus prep against

vertebra n, pl **vertebrae** single section of backbone **vertebrate** n/adj (animal) with backbone

vertical ❶ adj 1 at right angles to

the horizon 2 upright 3 overhead

vertigo n giddiness

verve n 1 enthusiasm 2 vigour

very ❶ adv 1 extremely, to great extent ▷ adj 2 exact, ideal 3 absolute

vespers pl n evening church service

vessel ❶ n 1 any object used as a container, esp. for liquids 2 ship, large boat 3 tubular structure conveying liquids (e.g. blood) in body

vest n 1 undergarment for upper body ▷ v 2 place 3 confer

vestment n robe or official garment

vestibule n entrance hall, lobby

vestige n small trace, amount

vestry n, pl -tries room in church for keeping vestments, holding meetings etc.

vet ❶ n short for VETERINARY SURGEON v check suitability of

veteran ❶ n 1 one who has served a long time, esp. in fighting services ▷ adj 2 long-serving

————————— THESAURUS —————————

verify v = **check**, make sure, examine, monitor, inspect

versatile adj = **adaptable**, flexible, all-round, resourceful, multifaceted ≠ **unadaptable**

version n = **form**, variety, variant, sort, class; = **adaptation**, edition, interpretation, form, copy; = **account**, report, description, record, reading

vertical adj sheer, perpendicular, straight (up and down), erect ≠ **horizontal**

very adv = **extremely**, highly, greatly, really, deeply ▷ adj = **exact**, precise, selfsame

vessel n = **ship**, boat, craft; = **container**, receptacle, can, bowl, tank

vet v = **check**, examine, investigate, review, appraise

veteran n = **old hand**, past master, warhorse (Inf), old stager ≠ **novice** ▷ adj = **long-serving**, seasoned, experienced, old, established

veterinary adj of, concerning the health of animals **veterinary surgeon** one qualified to treat animal ailments

veto ❶ n, pl **-toes 1** power of rejecting piece of legislation **2** any prohibition ▷ v **3** enforce veto against

vex v **1** annoy **2** distress **vexation** n **1** cause of irritation **2** state of distress

VHF very high frequency

VI Vancouver Island

via prep by way of

viable ❶ adj **1** practicable **2** able to live and grow independently

viaduct n bridge over valley for road or railway

vibrate v **1** (cause to) move to and fro rapidly and continuously **2** give off (light or sound) by vibration **3** oscillate **4** quiver **vibrant** adj **1** throbbing **2** vibrating **3** appearing vigorous **vibration** n

VIC Victoria (Australian state)

vicar n clergyman in charge of parish **vicarage** n vicar's house

vicarious adj obtained, enjoyed or undergone by imagining another's experiences

vice¹ ❶ n **1** evil or immoral habit or practice **2** criminal immorality, esp. prostitution **3** fault, imperfection

vice² n appliance with screw mechanism for holding things while working on them

vice³ adj serving in place of

viceroy n ruler acting for king in province or dependency

vice versa ❶ (Lat) conversely, the other way round

vicinity n neighbourhood

vicious ❶ adj **1** wicked, cruel **2** ferocious, dangerous **vicious circle** sequence of problems and solutions which always leads back to original problem

victim ❶ n **1** person or thing killed, injured etc. as result of another's deed, or accident, circumstances etc. **2** person cheated **3** sacrifice **victimization** n **victimize** v **1** punish unfairly **2** make victim of

victor ❶ n **1** conqueror **2** winner

veto v = **ban**, block, reject, rule out, turn down ≠ **pass** ▷ n = **ban**, dismissal, rejection, vetoing, boycott ≠ **ratification**

viable adj = **workable**, practical, feasible, suitable, realistic ≠ **unworkable**

vice¹ n = **fault**, failing, weakness, limitation, defect ≠ **good point**; = **wickedness**, evil, corruption, sin, depravity ≠ **virtue**

vice versa adv = **the other way round**, conversely, in reverse, contrariwise

vicious adj = **savage**, brutal, violent, cruel, ferocious ≠ **gentle**; = **malicious**, vindictive, spiteful, mean, cruel

victim n = **casualty**, sufferer, fatality ≠ **survivor**; = **scapegoat**, sacrifice, martyr

victor n = **winner**, champion, conqueror, vanquisher, prizewinner ≠ **loser**

victorious adj 1 winning 2 triumphant **victory** n winning of battle etc.

video adj, pl -**os** 1 relating to or used in transmission or production of television image ▷ n 2 video cassette recorder 3 cassette containing video tape ▷ v 4 record on video **video cassette recorder** tape recorder for recording and playing back TV programmes and films on cassette **video tape** magnetic tape used to record TV programmes

vie v **vying**, **vied** (with with) contend, compete against or for someone, something

view n 1 survey by eyes or mind 2 range of vision 3 picture 4 scene 5 opinion 6 purpose ▷ v 7 look at 8 survey 9 consider **viewer** n 1 one who views 2 one who watches television 3 optical device to assist viewing of photographic slides **viewfinder** n window on camera showing what will appear in photograph **viewpoint** n 1 way of regarding subject 2 position commanding view of landscape

vigil n keeping awake, watch **vigilance** n **vigilant** adj watchful, alert

vigilante n person who takes it upon himself or herself to enforce the law

vignette n concise description of typical features

vigour, US **vigor** ❶ n 1 force, strength 2 energy, activity **vigorous** adj 1 strong 2 energetic 3 flourishing

vile ❶ adj 1 very wicked, shameful 2 disgusting 3 despicable

vilify v **-ifying, -ified** unjustly attack the character of

villa n 1 large, luxurious country house 2 detached or semidetached suburban house

village n small group of houses in country area

villain ❶ n wicked person **villainous** adj

vindicate ❶ v 1 clear of charges 2 justify **vindication** n

vindictive adj 1 revengeful 2 inspired by resentment

vine n long-stemmed climbing plant bearing grapes **vineyard** n

vie v = **compete**, struggle, contend, strive

view n sometimes plural = **opinion**, belief, feeling, attitude, impression; = **scene**, picture, sight, prospect, perspective; = **vision**, sight, visibility, perspective, eyeshot ▷ v = **regard**, see, consider, perceive, treat

vigour, US **vigor** n = **energy**, vitality, power, spirit, strength ≠ **weakness**

vile adj = **wicked**, evil, corrupt, perverted, degenerate ≠ **honourable**; = **disgusting**, foul, revolting, offensive, nasty ≠ **pleasant**

villain n = **evildoer**, criminal, rogue, scoundrel, wretch; = **baddy** (Inf), antihero ≠ **hero**

vindicate v = **clear**, acquit, exonerate, absolve, let off the hook ≠ **condemn**

v

plantation of vines

vinegar n acid liquid obtained from wine and other alcoholic liquors

vintage ❶ n 1 gathering of the grapes 2 the yield 3 wine of particular year 4 time of origin ▷ adj 5 best and most typical

vintner n dealer in wine

vinyl n 1 plastic material with variety of domestic and industrial uses 2 record made of vinyl

viola n see VIOLIN

violate ❶ v 1 break (law, agreement etc.) 2 rape 3 outrage, desecrate **violation** n

violence ❶ n 1 use of physical force, usu. intended to cause injury or destruction 2 great force or strength in action, feeling or expression **violent** adj

violet n 1 plant with small bluish-mauve or white flowers 2 bluish-purple colour ▷ adj 3 of this colour

violin n small four-stringed musical instrument **viola** n large violin with lower range **violinist** n

VIP ❶ very important person

viper n poisonous snake

viral adj 1 pert. to a virus 2 spreading rapidly via the internet

virgin ❶ n 1 one who has not had sexual intercourse ▷ adj 2 without experience of sexual intercourse 3 uncorrupted 4 (of land) untilled **virginal** adj **virginity** n

virile adj 1 (of male) capable of copulation or procreation 2 strong, forceful **virility** n

virtual adj so in effect, though not in appearance or name

virtue ❶ n 1 moral goodness 2 good quality 3 merit **virtuous** adj morally good

virtuoso n, pl -sos, -si 1 one with special skill, esp. in music ▷ adj 2 showing great skill **virtuosity** n

virulent adj 1 very infectious, poisonous etc. 2 malicious

virus n infecting agent that causes disease

visa n endorsement on passport permitting bearer to travel into country of issuing government

visage n face

vis-à-vis prep in relation to, regarding

viscount n Brit. nobleman ranking

vintage adj = high-quality, best, prime, quality, choice

violate v = break, infringe, disobey, transgress, ignore ≠ obey; = invade, infringe on, disturb, upset, shatter; = desecrate, profane, defile, abuse, pollute ≠ honour; = rape, molest, sexually assault, ravish, abuse

violence n = brutality, bloodshed, savagery, fighting, terrorism; = force, power, strength, might, ferocity

VIP n = celebrity, big name, star, somebody, luminary

virgin n = maiden, girl (Archaic) ▷ adj = pure, chaste, immaculate, virginal, vestal ≠ corrupted

virtue n = goodness, integrity, worth, morality, righteousness ≠ vice; = merit, strength, asset, plus (Inf), attribute ≠ failing

V

below earl and above baron

viscous adj thick and sticky

visible ❶ adj that can be seen
  visibility n degree of clarity of vision

vision ❶ n 1 sight 2 insight
  3 dream 4 hallucination
  visionary adj 1 marked by vision
  2 impractical ▷ n 3 mystic
  4 impractical person

visit ❶ v -iting, -ited 1 go, come
  and see 2 stay temporarily with
  (someone) ▷ n 3 stay 4 call at
  person's home etc. **visitation** n
  1 formal visit or inspection
  2 affliction or plague **visitor** n

visor n 1 movable front part of
  helmet 2 eyeshade, esp. on car
  3 peak on cap

vista ❶ n extensive view

visual ❶ adj 1 of sight 2 visible
  visualize v form mental image of

vital ❶ adj 1 necessary to,

affecting life 2 lively 3 animated
  4 essential **vitality** n life, vigour

vitamin n any of group of
  substances occurring in foodstuffs
  and essential to health

viva interj long live

vivacious adj lively, sprightly
  vivacity n

vivid ❶ adj 1 bright, intense
  2 true to life

vivisection n dissection of, or
  operating on, living animals

vixen n female fox

vizor see VISOR

vocabulary ❶ n, pl -aries 1 list
  of words, usu. in alphabetical order
  2 stock of words used in particular
  language or subject

vocal ❶ adj 1 of, with, or giving
  out voice 2 outspoken, articulate
  vocalist n singer **vocals** pl n
  singing part

vocation ❶ n (urge, inclination,

visible adj = **perceptible**,
observable, clear, apparent, evident
≠ **invisible**

vision n = **image**, idea, dream,
plans, hopes; = **hallucination**,
illusion, apparition, revelation,
delusion; = **sight**, seeing, eyesight,
view, perception; = **foresight**,
imagination, perception, insight,
awareness

visit v = **call on**, drop in on (Inf),
stay at, stay with, stop by ▷ n
= **call**, social call

vista n = **view**, scene, prospect,
landscape, panorama

visual adj = **optical**, optic, ocular;
= **observable**, visible, perceptible,

discernible ≠ **imperceptible**

vital adj = **essential**, important,
necessary, key, basic
≠ **unnecessary**; = **lively**, vigorous,
energetic, spirited, dynamic
≠ **lethargic**

vivid adj = **clear**, detailed, realistic,
telling, moving ≠ **vague**; = **bright**,
brilliant, intense, clear, rich ≠ **dull**

vocabulary n = **language**, words,
lexicon

vocal adj = **outspoken**, frank,
forthright, strident, vociferous
≠ **quiet**; = **spoken**, voiced, uttered,
oral, said

vocation n = **profession**, calling,
job, trade, career

predisposition to) particular career, profession etc. **vocational adj

vociferous adj shouting, noisy

vodka n spirit distilled from potatoes or grain

vogue ❶ n 1 fashion, style 2 popularity

voice ❶ n 1 sound given out by person in speaking, singing etc. 2 quality of the sound 3 expressed opinion 4 (right to) share in discussion ▷ v 5 give utterance to, express

void ❶ adj 1 empty 2 destitute 3 not legally binding ▷ n 4 empty space ▷ v 5 make ineffectual or invalid 6 empty out

vol. volume

volatile ❶ adj 1 evaporating quickly 2 lively 3 changeable

volcano n, pl **-noes, -nos** 1 hole in earth's crust through which lava, ashes, smoke etc. are discharged 2 mountain so formed **volcanic** adj

vole n small rodent

volition n exercise of will

volley ❶ n 1 simultaneous discharge of weapons or missiles 2 rush of oaths, questions etc. 3 (Sport) kick, stroke etc. at moving ball before it touches ground ▷ v 4 discharge 5 kick, strike etc. in volley **volleyball** n game where ball is hit over high net

volt n unit of electric potential **voltage** n electric potential difference expressed in volts

voluble adj talking easily and at length

volume ❶ n 1 space occupied 2 mass 3 amount 4 power, fullness of voice or sound 5 book 6 part of book bound in one cover **voluminous** adj bulky, copious

voluntary ❶ adj 1 having, done by free will 2 done without payment 3 supported by free-will contributions **volunteer** n 1 one who offers service, joins force etc. of his or her own free will ▷ v 2 offer oneself or one's services

— THESAURUS —

vogue n = **fashion**, trend, craze, style, mode

voice n = **tone**, sound, articulation ▷ v = **express**, declare, air, raise, reveal

void n = **emptiness**, space, vacuum, oblivion, blankness ▷ adj = **invalid**, null and void, inoperative, useless, ineffective ▷ v = **invalidate**, nullify, cancel, withdraw, reverse

volatile adj = **changeable**, shifting, variable, unsettled, unstable ≠ **stable**;

= **temperamental**, erratic, mercurial, up and down (Inf), fickle ≠ **calm**

volley n = **barrage**, blast, burst, shower, hail

volume n = **amount**, quantity, level, body, total; = **capacity**, size, mass, extent, proportions; = **book**, work, title, opus, publication

voluntary adj = **intentional**, deliberate, planned, calculated, wilful ≠ **unintentional**; = **optional**, discretionary, up to the individual, open, unforced

V

DICTIONARY

voluptuous adj 1 of, contributing to pleasures of the senses 2 sexually alluring because of full, shapely figure

vomit 0 v **-iting, -ited** 1 eject (contents of stomach) through mouth ▷ n 2 matter vomited

voodoo n religion involving ancestor worship and witchcraft

voracious adj greedy, ravenous **voracity** n

vortex n, pl **-texes, -tices** 1 whirlpool 2 whirling motion

vote 0 n 1 formal expression of choice 2 individual pronouncement 3 right to give it 4 result of voting ▷ v 5 express, declare opinion, choice, preference etc. by vote

vouch v (usu. with for) guarantee **voucher** n 1 document to establish facts 2 ticket as substitute for cash

vow 0 n 1 solemn promise, esp. religious one ▷ v 2 promise, threaten by vow

vowel n 1 any speech sound pronounced without stoppage or friction of the breath 2 letter standing for such sound, as a, e, i, o, u

voyage 0 n 1 journey, esp. long one, by sea or air ▷ v 2 make voyage

vulcanize v treat (rubber) with sulphur at high temperature to increase its durability **vulcanization** n

vulgar 0 adj 1 offending against good taste 2 common **vulgarity** n

vulnerable 0 adj 1 capable of being physically or emotionally wounded or hurt 2 exposed, open to attack, persuasion etc. **vulnerability** n

vulture n large bird which feeds on carrion

THESAURUS

≠ **obligatory**

vomit v = **be sick**, throw up (Inf), spew, heave, retch

vote n = **poll**, election, ballot, referendum, popular vote

vow v = **promise**, pledge, swear, commit, engage ▷ n = **promise**, commitment, pledge, oath, profession

voyage n = **journey**, trip, passage, expedition, crossing

vulgar adj = **tasteless**, common ≠ **tasteful**

vulnerable adj = **susceptible**, helpless, unprotected, defenceless, exposed ≠ **immune**; = **exposed**, open, unprotected, defenceless, accessible ≠ **well-protected**

WA **1 2** Washington **3 4** Western Australia

wacky *adj* **wackier, wackiest** (*Inf*) eccentric, funny

wad *n* **1** small pad of fibrous material **2** thick roll of banknotes ▷ *v* **3** pad, stuff etc. with wad

waddle *v* **1** walk like duck ▷ *n* **2** this gait

wade ❶ *v* walk through something that hampers movement, esp. water **wader** *n* person or bird that wades

wafer *n* thin, crisp biscuit

waffle¹ *n/v* (*Inf*) (use) long-winded and meaningless language

waffle² *n* kind of pancake

waft *v* **1** convey smoothly through air or water ▷ *n* **2** breath of wind **3** odour, whiff

wag ❶ *v* **wagging, wagged** **1** (cause to) move rapidly from side to side ▷ *n* **2** instance of wagging **3** (*Inf*) witty person **wagtail** *n* small bird with long tail

wage ❶ *n* **1** (*oft. pl*) payment for work done ▷ *v* **2** carry on

wager *n/v* bet

waggle *v/n* wag

wagon, waggon *n* **1** four-wheeled vehicle for heavy loads **2** railway freight truck

waif *n* homeless person, esp. child

wail ❶ *v/n* cry, lament

waist *n* **1** part of body between hips and ribs **2** various narrow central parts **waistcoat** *n* sleeveless garment worn under jacket or coat

wait ❶ *v* **1** stay in one place, remain inactive in expectation (of something) **2** be prepared (for something) **3** delay **4** serve in restaurant etc. ▷ *n* **5** act or period of waiting **waiter** *n* attendant on guests at hotel, restaurant etc.

waive ❶ *v* **1** forgo **2** not insist on

THESAURUS

waddle *v* = **shuffle**, totter, toddle, sway, wobble

wade *v* = **paddle**, splash, splash about, slop; = **walk through**, cross, ford, travel across, pitch in

wag *v* = **wave**, shake, waggle, stir, quiver ▷ *n* = **wave**, shake, quiver, vibration, wiggle; = **nod**, bob, shake

wage *n often plural* = **payment**, pay, remuneration, fee, reward ▷ *v* = **engage in**, conduct, pursue, carry on, undertake

wail *v* = **cry**, weep, grieve, lament, howl ▷ *n* = **cry**, moan, howl, lament, yowl

wait *v* = **stay**, remain, stop, pause, rest ≠ **go** ▷ *n* = **delay**, gap, pause, interval, stay

waive *v* = **give up**, relinquish, renounce, forsake, drop ≠ **claim**

W

waiver n (written statement of) this act

wake[1] **⊙** v **waking, woke, woken** **1** rouse from sleep **2** stir up ▷ n **3** vigil **4** watch beside corpse **waken** v wake

wake[2] n track or path left by anything that has passed

walk **⊙** v **1** (cause, assist to) move, travel on foot at ordinary pace **2** cross, pass through by walking **3** escort, conduct by walking ▷ n **4** act, instance of walking **5** path or other place or route for walking **walking stick** stick used as support when walking **Walkman**® n small portable cassette player with headphones **walkover** n (Inf) easy victory

wall **⊙** n **1** structure of brick, stone etc. serving as fence, side of building etc. **2** surface of one **3** anything resembling this ▷ v **4** enclose with wall **5** block up with wall **wallflower** n garden plant **wallpaper** n paper, usu. patterned, to cover interior walls

wallaby n, pl **-bies** Aust.

marsupial similar to and smaller than kangaroo

wallet **⊙** n small folding case, esp. for paper money, documents etc.

wallop (Inf) ▷ v **1** beat soundly **2** strike hard ▷ n **3** stroke or blow

wallow v **1** roll (in liquid or mud) **2** revel (in) ▷ n **3** wallowing

walnut n **1** large nut with crinkled shell **2** tree it grows on **3** its wood

walrus n, pl **-ruses, -rus** large sea mammal with long tusks

waltz n **1** ballroom dance **2** music for it ▷ v **3** perform waltz

wampum n (US & Canad) shells woven together, formerly used by N American Indians for money and ornament

wan adj **wanner, wannest** pale, pallid

wand n stick, esp. as carried by magician etc.

wander **⊙** v **1** roam, ramble **2** go astray, deviate ▷ n **3** wandering

wane **⊙** v/n **1** decline **2** (of moon) decrease in size

wangle v (Inf) get by devious methods

wake[1] v = **awake**, stir, awaken, come to, arise ≠ **fall asleep**; = **awaken**, arouse, rouse, waken ▷ n = **vigil**, watch, funeral, deathwatch

walk v = **stride**, stroll, go, move, step; = **escort**, take, see, show, partner ▷ n = **stroll**, hike, ramble, march, trek; = **gait**, step, bearing, carriage, tread; = **path**, footpath, track, way, road

wall n = **partition**, screen, barrier,

enclosure, blockade; = **barrier**, obstacle, barricade, obstruction, check

wallet n = **purse**, pocketbook, pouch, case, holder

wander v = **roam**, walk, drift, stroll, range ▷ n = **excursion**, walk, stroll, cruise, ramble

wane v = **decline**, weaken, diminish, fail, fade ≠ **grow**; = **diminish**, decrease, dwindle ≠ **wax**

W

want ❶ v 1 desire 2 lack ▷ n
3 desire 4 need 5 deficiency
wanted adj being sought, esp. by
police **wanting** adj 1 lacking
2 below standard

wanton adj 1 dissolute 2 without
motive 3 unrestrained

war ❶ n 1 fighting between
nations 2 state of hostility
3 conflict, contest ▷ v 4 make war
warlike adj 1 of, for war 2 fond of
war **warrior** n fighter **warfare** n
hostilities **warhead** n part of
missile etc. containing explosives

warble v sing with trills **warbler**
n any of various kinds of small
songbirds

ward ❶ n 1 division of city, hospital
etc. 2 minor under care of guardian
warder n jailer **ward off** avert,
repel

warden ❶ n person in charge of

building, college etc.

wardrobe ❶ n 1 piece of furniture
for hanging clothes in 2 person's
supply of clothes

ware n 1 goods 2 articles
collectively ▷ pl 3 goods for sale
warehouse n storehouse for
goods

warm ❶ adj 1 moderately hot
2 serving to maintain heat
3 affectionate 4 enthusiastic ▷ v
5 make, become warm **warmth** n
1 mild heat 2 cordiality 3 intensity
of emotion **warm up** v 1 make or
become warmer 2 do preliminary
exercises

warn ❶ v 1 put on guard
2 caution 3 give advance
information to **warning** n

warp ❶ v 1 (cause to) twist (out of
shape) 2 pervert or be perverted

warrant ❶ n 1 authority

—————— THESAURUS ——————

want v = **wish for**, desire, long for,
crave, covet ≠ **have**; = **need**,
demand, require, call for ▷ n
= **lack**, need, absence, shortage,
deficiency ≠ **abundance**;
= **poverty**, hardship, privation,
penury, destitution ≠ **wealth**;
= **wish**, will, need, desire,
requirement

war n = **conflict**, drive, attack,
fighting, fight ≠ **peace** ▷ v = **fight**,
battle, clash, wage war, campaign
≠ **make peace**

ward n = **room**, department, unit,
quarter, division; = **district**,
constituency, area, division, zone;
= **dependant**, charge, pupil, minor,
protégé

warden = **jailer**, prison officer,
guard, screw (Sl)

wardrobe n = **clothes cupboard**,
cupboard, closet, cabinet;
= **clothes**, apparel, attire

warm adj = **balmy**, mild,
temperate, pleasant, fine ≠ **cool**;
= **cosy**, snug, toasty (Inf),
comfortable, homely ▷ v = **warm
up**, heat, thaw (out), heat up
≠ **cool down**

warn v = **notify**, tell, remind,
inform, alert; = **advise**, urge,
recommend, counsel, caution

warp v = **distort**, bend, twist,
buckle, deform ▷ n = **twist**, bend,
defect, flaw, distortion

warrant v = **call for**, demand,

W

2 document giving authority ▷ *v*
3 guarantee **4** authorize, justify
warranty *n, pl* **-ties 1** guarantee
of quality of goods **2** security
warren *n* (burrows inhabited by)
colony of rabbits
warrigal *(Aust) n* **1 2** dingo ▷ *adj*
3 4 wild
warrior ❶ *n* see WAR
wart *n* small hard growth on skin
wart hog kind of Afr. wild pig
wary ❶ *adj* **warier, wariest**
watchful, cautious, alert
was past tense, first and third
person sing. of BE
wash ❶ *v* **1** clean (oneself, clothes
etc.) with water, soap etc. **2** be
washable **3** move, be moved by
water **4** flow, sweep over, against
▷ *n* **5** act of washing **6** clothes
washed at one time **7** sweep of
water, esp. set up by moving ship
washable *adj* capable of being

washed without damage **washer**
n **1** one who, that which, washes
2 ring put under nut **washing** *n*
clothes to be washed **washout** *n*
(*Inf*) complete failure **wash up**
wash dishes and cutlery after meal
wasp *n* striped stinging insect
resembling bee
waste ❶ *v* **1** expend uselessly
2 fail to take advantage **3** dwindle
4 pine away ▷ *n* **5** act of wasting
6 rubbish **7** desert ▷ *adj*
8 worthless, useless **9** desert
10 wasted **wasteful** *adj*
extravagant
watch ❶ *v* **1** observe closely
2 guard **3** wait expectantly (for)
4 be on watch ▷ *n* **5** portable
timepiece for wrist, pocket etc.
6 state of being on the lookout
7 spell of duty **watchful** *adj*
watchdog *n* **1** dog kept to guard
property **2** person or group

require, merit, rate; **= guarantee**,
declare, pledge, promise,
ensure ▷ *n* **= authorization**,
permit, licence, permission,
authority
warrior *n* **= soldier**, combatant,
fighter, gladiator, trooper
wary *adj* **= suspicious**, sceptical,
guarded, distrustful, chary
wash *v* **= clean**, scrub, sponge,
rinse, scour; **= launder**, clean, rinse,
dry-clean; **= rinse**, clean, scrub,
lather ▷ *n* **= laundering**, cleaning,
clean, cleansing, dip; **= backwash**,
slipstream, path, trail, train;
= splash, surge, swell, rise and fall,
undulation

waste *v* **= squander**, throw away,
blow (*Sl*), lavish, misuse **≠ save** ▷ *n*
= squandering, misuse,
extravagance, frittering away,
dissipation **≠ saving**; **= rubbish**,
refuse, debris, scrap, litter ▷ *adj*
= unwanted, useless, worthless,
unused, leftover **≠ necessary**;
= uncultivated, wild, bare, barren,
empty **≠ cultivated**
watch *v* **= look at**, observe, regard,
eye, see; **= spy on**, follow, track,
monitor, keep an eye on ▷ *n*
= wristwatch, timepiece,
chronometer; **= guard**,
surveillance, observation, vigil,
lookout

DICTIONARY

guarding against inefficiency or illegality **watchman** n man guarding building etc., esp. at night
watchword n 1 password
2 rallying cry

water ❶ n 1 transparent, colourless, odourless, tasteless liquid, substance of rain, river etc.
2 body of water 3 urine ▷ v 4 put water on or into 5 irrigate or provide with water 6 salivate 7 (of eyes) fill with tears **watery** adj 1 wet 2 weak **water closet** sanitary convenience flushed with water **watercolour** n 1 paint thinned with water 2 painting in this **watercress** n plant growing in clear ponds and streams **waterfall** n vertical descent of waters of river **water lily** plant that floats on surface of fresh water **waterlogged** adj saturated, filled with water **watermark** n faint translucent design in sheet of paper **watermelon** n melon with green skin and red flesh **water polo** team game played by swimmers with ball **waterproof** adj 1 not letting water through ▷ v 2 make waterproof ▷ n 3 waterproof garment **watershed** n 1 line

separating two river systems
2 divide **water-skiing** n sport of riding over water on skis towed by speedboat **watertight** adj
1 preventing water from entering or escaping 2 with no weak points

watt n unit of electric power

wave ❶ v 1 move to and fro, as hand in greeting or farewell
2 signal by waving 3 give, take shape of waves (as hair etc.) ▷ n
4 ridge and trough on water etc.
5 act, gesture of waving
6 vibration, as in radio waves
7 prolonged spell 8 upsurge
9 wavelike shapes in hair etc.
wavy adj **wavelength** n distance between the same points of two successive waves

waver ❶ v 1 hesitate, be irresolute
2 be, become unsteady

wax¹ ❶ v grow, increase

wax² n 1 yellow, soft, pliable material made by bees 2 this or similar substance used for sealing, making candles etc. 3 waxy secretion of ear ▷ v 4 put wax on **waxy** adj like wax

way ❶ n 1 manner 2 method
3 direction 4 path 5 passage
6 progress 7 state or condition

THESAURUS

water n = **liquid**, H_2O; = **get wet**, cry, weep, become wet, exude water

wave v = **signal**, sign, gesture, gesticulate; = **guide**, point, direct, indicate, signal; = **brandish**, swing, flourish, wag, shake ▷ n
= **gesture**, sign, signal, indication, gesticulation; = **ripple**, breaker,

swell, ridge, roller

waver v = **hesitate**, dither (chiefly Brit), vacillate, falter, fluctuate ≠ be **decisive**; = **flicker**, shake, tremble, wobble, quiver

wax¹ v = **increase**, grow, develop, expand, swell ≠ **wane**

way n = **method**, means, system, process, technique; = **manner**,

W

8 room for activity **wayfarer** n traveller, esp. on foot **waylay** v lie in wait for and accost, attack **wayside** n/adj (by) side or edge of road **wayward** adj capricious, perverse, wilful

WC water closet

we pron first person plural pronoun

weak ❶ adj 1 lacking strength 2 irresolute 3 (of sound) faint 4 (of argument) unconvincing 5 unprotected, vulnerable 6 lacking flavour **weaken** v **weakling** n feeble creature **weakly** adj 1 weak 2 sickly ▷ adv 3 in weak manner **weakness** n

weal n streak left on flesh by blow of stick or whip

wealth ❶ n 1 riches 2 abundance **wealthy** adj

wean v 1 accustom to food other than mother's milk 2 win over,

coax away from

weapon n implement to fight with

wear ❶ v wearing, wore, worn 1 have on the body 2 show 3 (cause to) become impaired by use 4 harass or weaken 5 last ▷ n 6 act of wearing 7 things to wear 8 damage caused by use 9 ability to resist effect of constant use

weary ❶ adj -rier, -riest 1 tired, exhausted, jaded 2 tiring 3 tedious ▷ v 4 make, become weary **weariness** n

weasel n small carnivorous mammal with long body and short legs

weather ❶ n 1 day-to-day meteorological conditions, esp. temperature etc. of a place ▷ v 2 affect by weather 3 endure 4 resist 5 come safely through **weathercock** n revolving object

THESAURUS

style, fashion, mode; often plural = **custom**, manner, habit, style, practice; = **route**, direction, course, road, path; = **journey**, approach, passage; = **distance**, length, stretch

weak adj = **feeble**, frail, debilitated, fragile, sickly ≠ **strong**; = **slight**, faint, feeble, pathetic, hollow; = **fragile**, brittle, flimsy, fine, delicate; = **unsafe**, exposed, vulnerable, helpless, unprotected ≠ **secure**

wealth n = **riches**, fortune, prosperity, affluence, money ≠ **poverty**; = **property**, capital, fortune

wear v = **be dressed in**, have on,

sport (Inf), put on; = **show**, present, bear, display, assume; = **deteriorate**, fray, wear thin ▷ n = **clothes**, things, dress, gear (Inf); attire; = **damage**, wear and tear, erosion, deterioration, attrition ≠ **repair**

weary adj = **tired**, exhausted, drained, worn out, done in (Inf) ≠ **energetic**; = **tiring**, arduous, tiresome, laborious, wearisome ≠ **refreshing** ▷ v = **grow tired**, tire, become bored

weather n = **climate**, conditions, temperature, forecast, outlook ▷ v = **withstand**, stand, survive, overcome, resist ≠ **surrender to**

DICTIONARY

to show which way wind blows

weave ❶ v **weaving, wove, woven 1** form into texture or fabric by interlacing, esp. on loom **2** construct **3** make one's way, esp. with side to side motion

web n **1** woven fabric **2** net spun by spider **3** membrane between toes of waterfowl, frogs etc.

wed ❶ v **wedding, wedded 1** marry **2** unite closely **wedding** n marriage ceremony **wedlock** n marriage

wedge ❶ n **1** piece of wood, metal etc. tapering to a thin edge ▷ v **2** fasten, split with wedge **3** stick by compression or crowding

Wednesday n fourth day of the week

wee adj **1** small **2** little

weed n **1** plant growing where undesired ▷ v **2** clear of weeds **weedy** adj **1** full of weeds **2** weak

week n period of seven days

weekly adj/adv happening, done, published etc. once a week

weekday n any day of the week except Saturday or Sunday

weekend n Saturday and Sunday

weep ❶ v **weeping, wept 1** shed tears (for) **2** grieve

weigh ❶ v **1** find weight of **2** consider **3** have weight **4** be burdensome **weight** n **1** measure of the heaviness of an object **2** quality of heaviness **3** heavy mass **4** object of known mass for weighing **5** importance, influence ▷ v **6** add weight to **weighting** n extra allowance paid in special circumstances

weir n river dam

weird ❶ adj **1** unearthly, uncanny **2** strange, bizarre

welcome ❶ adj **-coming, -comed 1** received gladly **2** freely permitted ▷ n **3** kindly greeting ▷ v **4** greet with pleasure **5** receive gladly

THESAURUS

weave v = **knit**, intertwine, plait, braid, entwine; = **zigzag**, wind, crisscross; = **create**, tell, recount, narrate, build

web n = **cobweb**, spider's web; = **mesh**, lattice

wed v = **get married to**, be united to ≠ **divorce**; = **get married**, marry, be united, tie the knot (Inf), take the plunge (Inf) ≠ **divorce**

wedge v = **squeeze**, force, lodge, jam, crowd ▷ n = **block**, lump, chunk

weep v = **cry**, shed tears, sob, whimper, mourn ≠ **rejoice**

weigh v = **have a weight of**, tip the scales at (Inf); often with **up** = **consider**, examine, contemplate, evaluate, ponder; = **compare**, balance, contrast, juxtapose, place side by side

weird adj = **strange**, odd, unusual, bizarre, mysterious ≠ **normal**; = **bizarre**, odd, strange, unusual, queer ≠ **ordinary**

welcome v = **greet**, meet, receive, embrace, hail ≠ **reject**; = **accept gladly**, appreciate, embrace, approve of, be pleased by ▷ n = **greeting**, welcoming, reception,

W

weld ❶ v 1 unite metal by softening with heat 2 unite closely ▷ n 3 welded joint **welder** n

welfare ❶ n wellbeing **welfare state** system in which government takes responsibility for wellbeing of citizens

well¹ ❶ adv **better, best** 1 in good manner or degree 2 suitably 3 intimately 4 fully 5 favourably 6 kindly 7 to a considerable degree ▷ adj 8 in good health 9 satisfactory ▷ interj 10 exclamation of surprise, interrogation etc. **wellbeing** n state of being well, happy, or prosperous **well-disposed** adj inclined to be friendly **well-mannered** adj having good manners **well-off** adj fairly rich **well-read** adj having read much **well²** ❶ n 1 hole sunk into the earth to reach water, gas, oil etc. 2 spring ▷ v 3 spring, gush

wellies pl n (Inf) wellingtons **wellingtons** pl n high waterproof boots

welter v 1 roll or tumble ▷ n 2 turmoil, disorder

wench n young woman

wend v go, travel

went past tense of GO

were past tense of BE

werewolf n in folklore, person who can turn into a wolf

west n 1 part of sky where sun sets 2 part of country etc. lying to this side ▷ adj 3 that is toward or in this region ▷ adv 4 to the west **westerly** adj/adv **western** adj **westernize** v adapt to customs and culture of the West **westward** adj/adv **westwards** adv

wet ❶ adj **wetter, wettest** 1 having water or other liquid on a surface or being soaked in it 2 rainy 3 (of paint, ink etc.) not yet dry ▷ v 4 make wet ▷ n 5 moisture, rain

---

THESAURUS

acceptance, hail ≠ **rejection**

weld v = **join**, link, bond, bind, connect; = **unite**, combine, blend, unify, fuse

welfare n = **wellbeing**, good, interest, health, security

well¹ adv = **skilfully**, expertly, adeptly, professionally, correctly ≠ **badly**; = **satisfactorily**, nicely, smoothly, successfully, pleasantly ≠ **badly**; = **thoroughly**, completely, fully, carefully, effectively; = **intimately**, deeply, fully, profoundly ≠ **slightly**; = **favourably**, highly, kindly, warmly,

enthusiastically ≠ **unfavourably**; = **considerably**, easily, very much, significantly, substantially; = **fully**, highly, greatly, amply, very much; = **possibly**, probably, certainly, reasonably, conceivably ▷ adj = **healthy**, sound, fit, blooming, in fine fettle ≠ **ill**; = **satisfactory**, right, fine, pleasing, proper ≠ **unsatisfactory**

well² n = **hole**, bore, pit, shaft ▷ v = **flow**, spring, pour, jet, surge

wet adj = **damp**, soaking, saturated, moist, watery ≠ **dry**;

wet suit close-fitting rubber suit worn by divers etc.

whack ❶ v 1 strike with sharp resounding sound ▷ n 2 such blow

wharf ❷ n, pl **wharves, wharfs** platform at harbour, on river etc. for loading and unloading ships

what pron 1 which thing 2 that which 3 request for statement to be repeated ▷ adj 4 which 5 as much as 6 how great, surprising etc. ▷ adv 7 in which way

whatever pron 1 anything which 2 of what kind it may be

whatsoever adj at all

wheat n cereal plant yielding grain from which bread is chiefly made

wheedle v coax, cajole

wheel ❶ n 1 circular frame or disc revolving on axle 2 anything like a wheel in shape or function 3 act of turning ▷ v 4 (cause to) turn as if on axis 5 (cause to) move on or as if on wheels 6 (cause to) change course, esp. in opposite direction

wheelbarrow n barrow with one wheel **wheelchair** n chair mounted on large wheels, used by invalids

wheeze v 1 breathe with whistling

noise ▷ n 2 this sound

whelk n edible shellfish

when adv 1 at what time ▷ conj 2 at the time that 3 although 4 since ▷ pron 5 at which time

whenever adj/conj at whatever time

where adv/conj 1 at what place 2 at or to the place in which

whereabouts adv/conj 1 in what, which place ▷ n 2 present position

whereas conj 1 considering that 2 while, on the contrary **whereby** conj by which **whereupon** conj at which point **wherever** adv at whatever place **wherewithal** n necessary funds, resources etc.

whet v **whetting, whetted** 1 sharpen 2 stimulate

whether conj introduces the first of two alternatives

whey n watery part of milk left after cheese making

which adj 1 used in requests for a selection from alternatives ▷ pron 2 person or thing referred to

whichever pron

whiff ❶ n 1 brief smell or suggestion of 2 puff of air

while conj 1 in the time that 2 in

───── THESAURUS ─────

= **rainy**, damp, drizzly, showery, raining ≠ **sunny**; (Inf) = **feeble**, soft, weak, ineffectual, weedy (Inf) ▷ v = **moisten**, spray, dampen, water, soak ≠ **dry** ▷ n = **rain**, drizzle ≠ **fine weather**;
= **moisture**, water, liquid, damp, humidity ≠ **dryness**

whack (Inf) v = **strike**, hit, belt (Inf), bang, smack ▷ n = **blow**, hit,

stroke, belt (Inf); bang; (Inf) = **share**, part, cut (Inf), bit, portion; (Inf) = **attempt**, go (Inf), try, turn, shot (Inf)

wharf n = **dock**, pier, berth, quay, jetty

wheel n = **disc**, ring, hoop ▷ v = **push**, trundle, roll

whiff n = **smell**, hint, scent, sniff, aroma

W

spite of the fact that, although **3** whereas ▷ v **4** pass (time) idly ▷ n **5** period of time

whim ① n sudden, passing fancy **whimsy, whimsey** n fanciful mood **whimsical** adj **1** fanciful **2** full of whims

whimper v **1** cry or whine softly **2** complain in this way ▷ n **3** such cry or complaint

whine ① n **1** high-pitched plaintive cry **2** peevish complaint ▷ v **3** utter this

whinge v **1** complain ▷ n **1** complain

whinny v **-nying, -nied 1** neigh softly ▷ n **2** soft neigh

whip ① n **1** lash attached to handle for urging or punishing ▷ v **2** strike with whip **3** beat (cream, eggs) to a froth **4** pull, move quickly

whippet n dog like small greyhound

whirl ① v **1** swing rapidly round **2** move rapidly in a circular course

3 drive at high speed ▷ n **4** whirling movement **5** confusion, bustle, giddiness **whirlpool** n circular current, eddy **whirlwind** n **1** wind whirling round while moving forwards ▷ adj **2** very quick

whirr, whir v **1** (cause to) fly, spin etc. with buzzing sound ▷ n **2** this sound

whisk ① v **1** brush, sweep, beat lightly **2** move, remove quickly **3** beat to a froth ▷ n **4** light brush **5** egg-beating implement

whisker n **1** any of the long stiff hairs at side of mouth of cat or other animal ▷ pl **2** hair on a man's face

whisky n, pl **-kies** (Irish, Canad, US **whiskey**) spirit distilled from fermented cereals

whisper ① v **1** speak in soft, hushed tones, without vibration of vocal cords **2** rustle ▷ n **3** such speech **4** trace or suspicion **5** rustle

whim n = **impulse**, caprice, fancy, urge, notion

whine v = **cry**, sob, wail, whimper, sniffle ▷ n = **cry**, moan, sob, wail, whimper; = **drone**, note, hum

whip n = **lash**, cane, birch, crop, scourge ▷ v = **lash**, cane, flog, beat, strap; (Inf) = **dash**, shoot, fly, tear, rush; = **whisk**, beat, mix vigorously, stir vigorously; = **incite**, drive, stir, spur, work up

whirl v = **spin**, turn, twist, rotate, twirl; = **rotate**, roll, twist, revolve,

swirl ▷ n = **revolution**, turn, roll, spin, twist; = **bustle**, round, series, succession, flurry; = **confusion**, daze, dither (chiefly Brit), giddiness, spin

whisk v = **flick**, whip, sweep, brush; = **beat**, whip vigorously, stir vigorously, whip, fluff up ▷ n = **flick**, sweep, brush, whip; = **beater**, mixer, blender

whisper v = **murmur**, breathe ≠ **shout**; = **rustle**, sigh, hiss, swish ▷ n = **murmur**, mutter, mumble, undertone; (Inf) = **rumour**, report,

whist *n* card game

whistle *v* 1 produce shrill sound by forcing breath through rounded, nearly closed lips 2 make similar sound 3 utter, summon etc. by whistle ▷ *n* 4 such sound 5 any similar sound 6 instrument to make it

white ❶ *adj* 1 of the colour of snow 2 pale 3 light in colour 4 having a light-coloured skin ▷ *n* 5 colour of snow 6 white pigment 7 white part 8 clear fluid round yolk of egg 9 (*with cap.*) white person **whiten** *v* **whitewash** *n* 1 substance for whitening walls etc. ▷ *v* 2 apply this 3 cover up, gloss over

whither *adv* (*Obs*) 1 to what place 2 to which

whittle ❶ *v* 1 cut, carve with knife 2 pare away

whizz, whiz *n* **whizzing, whizzed** 1 loud hissing sound ▷ *v* 2 move with such sound, or make it

who *pron* 1 what or which person or persons 2 that **whoever** *pron* who, any one or every one that

whodunnit, whodunit *n* (*Inf*) detective story

whole ❶ *adj* 1 containing all elements or parts 2 not defective or imperfect 3 healthy ▷ *n* 4 complete thing or system

wholly *adv* **wholehearted** *adj* 1 sincere 2 enthusiastic

wholesale *n* 1 sale of goods in large quantities to retailers ▷ *adj* 2 dealing by wholesale 3 extensive

wholesome *adj* producing good effect, physically or morally

whom *pron* objective form of WHO

whoop *n/v* (make) shout or cry expressing excitement etc.

whooping cough infectious disease marked by convulsive coughing with loud whoop or drawing in of breath

whopper *n* (*Inf*) unusually large thing **whopping** *adj*

whore ❶ *n* prostitute

whose *pron* of whom or which

why *adv* for what cause or reason

wick *n* strip of thread feeding flame of lamp of candle with oil, grease etc.

wicked *adj* 1 evil, sinful 2 very bad

wicker *adj* made of woven cane

wicket *n* 1 set of cricket stumps 2 small gate

wide ❶ *adj* 1 having a great extent from side to side, broad 2 having

---

THESAURUS

gossip, innuendo, insinuation; = **rustle**, sigh, hiss, swish

white *adj* = **pale**, wan, pasty, pallid, ashen

whittle *v* = **carve**, cut, hew, shape, trim

whole *adj* = **complete**, full, total, entire, uncut ≠ **partial**; = **undamaged**, intact, unscathed, unbroken, untouched ≠ **damaged**

whore *n* = **prostitute**, tart (*Inf*), streetwalker, call girl

wide *adj* = **spacious**, broad, extensive, roomy, commodious ≠ **confined**; = **baggy**, full, loose, ample, billowing; = **expanded**, dilated, distended ≠ **shut**; = **broad**, extensive, wide-ranging, large,

considerable distance between
3 spacious **4** vast **5** far from the
mark **6** opened fully ▷ *adv* **7** to the
full extent **8** far from the intended
target **widen** *v* **width** *n* breadth
widespread *adj* extending over a
wide area

widow *n* **1** woman whose spouse
is dead and who has not married
again ▷ *v* **2** make a widow of
widower *n* man whose spouse is
dead and who has not married
again

wield ❶ *v* hold and use

wife *n, pl* **wives** female partner
in marriage

wig *n* artificial hair for the head

wiggle *v* **1** (cause to) move jerkily
from side to side ▷ *n* **2** wiggling

wild ❶ *adj* **1** not tamed or
domesticated **2** not cultivated
3 savage **4** stormy **5** uncontrolled
6 random **7** excited **8** rash
wildcat *n* any of various
undomesticated feline animals
wild-goose chase search that has

little chance of success **wildlife** *n*
wild animals and plants collectively

wildebeest *n* gnu

wilderness ❶ *n* desert, waste
place

wildfire *n* **1** raging, uncontrollable
fire **2** anything spreading, moving
fast

wilful *adj* **1** obstinate **2** self-willed
3 intentional

will ❶ *n, past* **would 1** faculty of
deciding what one will do
2 purpose **3** volition
4 determination **5** wish
6 directions written for disposal of
property after death ▷ *v* **7** wish
8 intend **9** leave as legacy **willing**
adj **1** ready **2** given cheerfully
willingly *adv* **willingness** *n*
willpower *n* ability to control
oneself, one's actions, impulses

will² *v, past* **would** forms future
tense and indicates intention or
conditional result

will-o'-the-wisp *n* elusive
person or thing

THESAURUS

sweeping ≠ **restricted** ▷ *adv*
= **fully**, completely ≠ **partly**; = **off
target**, astray, off course, off the
mark

wield *v* = **brandish**, flourish,
manipulate, swing, use; = **exert**,
maintain, exercise, have, possess

wife *n* = **spouse**, partner, mate,
bride, better half (*humorous*)

wild *adj* = **untamed**, fierce,
savage, ferocious, unbroken
≠ **tame**; = **uncultivated**,
natural ≠ **cultivated**; = **stormy**,
violent, rough, raging, choppy;

= **excited**, crazy (*Inf*), enthusiastic,
raving, hysterical
≠ **unenthusiastic**;
= **uncontrolled**, disorderly,
turbulent, wayward, unruly
≠ **calm**; = **mad** (*Inf*), furious,
fuming, infuriated, incensed

wilderness *n* = **wilds**, desert,
wasteland, uncultivated region

will¹ *n* = **determination**, drive,
purpose, commitment, resolution;
= **wish**, mind, desire, intention,
fancy; = **choice**, prerogative,
volition ▷ *v* = **wish**, want, prefer,

DICTIONARY

willow n 1 tree with long thin flexible branches 2 its wood
willowy adj slender, supple
willy-nilly adv/adj (occurring) whether desired or not
wilt ❷ v (cause to) become limp, lose strength etc.
wimp n (Inf) feeble person
wimple n garment framing face, worn by nuns
win ❸ v winning, won 1 be successful, victorious 2 get by labour or effort ▷ n 3 victory, esp. in games **winner** n **winning** adj charming **winnings** pl n sum won in game, betting etc. **win-win** adj guaranteeing a favourable outcome for all involved **a win-win situation**
wince ❶ v 1 flinch, draw back, as from pain etc. ▷ n 2 this act
winch n 1 machine for hoisting or hauling using cable wound round drum ▷ v 2 move (something) by using a winch
wind ❶ n 1 air in motion 2 breath 3 flatulence ▷ v 4 render short of breath, esp. by blow etc. **windward** n side against which wind is blowing **windy** adj 1 exposed to wind 2 flatulent **windfall** n

1 unexpected good luck 2 fallen fruit **wind farm** collection of wind-driven turbines for generating electricity **wind instrument** musical instrument played by blowing or air pressure **windmill** n wind-driven apparatus with fanlike sails for raising water, crushing grain etc. **windpipe** n passage from throat to lungs **windscreen** n protective sheet of glass etc. in front of driver or pilot **windsurfing** n sport of sailing standing up on board with single sail
wind² ❷ v 1 twine 2 meander 3 twist round, coil 4 wrap 5 make ready for working by tightening spring ▷ n 6 act of winding 7 single turn of something wound
window n 1 hole in wall (with glass) to admit light, air etc. 2 anything similar in appearance or function 3 area for display of goods behind glass of shop front **window-shopping** n looking at goods without intending to buy **windshield** n the US and Canadian name for WINDSCREEN
wine n 1 fermented juice of grape etc. 2 purplish-red colour

THESAURUS

desire, see fit; = **bequeath**, give, leave, transfer, gift
wilt v = **droop**, wither, sag, shrivel; = **weaken**, languish, droop
win v = **be victorious in**, succeed in, prevail in, come first in, be the victor in ≠ **lose**; = **be victorious**, succeed, triumph, overcome, prevail ≠ **lose** ▷ n = **victory**, success, triumph, conquest

≠ **defeat**
wince v = **flinch**, start, shrink, cringe, quail ▷ n = **flinch**, start, cringe
wind¹ n = **air**, blast, hurricane, breeze, draught; = **flatulence**, gas; = **breath**, puff, respiration;
wind² v = **meander**, turn, bend, twist, curve; = **wrap**, twist, reel, curl, loop

W

—————— DICTIONARY ——————

wing ❶ n 1 feathered limb used by bird in flying 2 organ of flight of insect or some animals 3 main lifting surface of aircraft 4 side area of building, stage etc. 5 group within political party etc. ▷ v 6 fly 7 move, go very fast 8 disable, wound slightly **winger** n (Sport) player positioned at side of pitch

wink ❶ v 1 close and open (one eye) rapidly, esp. to indicate friendliness or as signal 2 twinkle ▷ n 3 act of winking

winkle n edible sea snail **winkle out** extract, prise out

winsome adj charming

winter n 1 coldest season ▷ v 2 pass, spend the winter **wintry** adj 1 of, like winter 2 cold

wipe ❶ v 1 rub so as to clean ▷ n 2 wiping **wiper** n 1 one that wipes 2 automatic wiping apparatus **wipe out** erase 2 annihilate 3 (Sl) kill

wire n 1 metal drawn into thin, flexible strand 2 something made of wire, e.g. fence 3 telegram ▷ v 4 provide, fasten with wire 5 send by telegraph **wiring** n system of wires **wiry** adj 1 like wire 2 lean and tough **wire-haired** adj (of various breeds of dog) with short stiff hair

wise adj 1 having intelligence and knowledge 2 sensible **wisdom** n (accumulated) knowledge, learning **wisdom tooth** large tooth cut usu. after age of twenty

wish ❶ v 1 desire ▷ n 2 expression of desire 3 thing desired **wishful** adj too optimistic

wishy-washy adj (Inf) insipid, bland

wisp n 1 light, delicate streak, as of smoke 2 twisted handful, usu. of straw etc. 3 stray lock of hair **wispy** adj

wistful adj 1 longing, yearning 2 sadly pensive

wit ❶ n 1 ability to use words, ideas in clever, amusing way 2 person with this ability 3 intellect 4 understanding 5 humour **witticism** n witty remark **wittingly** adv 1 on purpose 2 knowingly **witty** adj

witch ❶ n 1 person, usu. female, who practises magic 2 ugly,

—————— THESAURUS ——————

wing n = **faction**, group, arm, section, branch ▷ v = **fly**, soar, glide, take wing; = **wound**, hit, clip

wink v = **blink**, bat, flutter; = **twinkle**, flash, shine, sparkle, gleam ▷ n = **blink**, flutter, blink, glimmer

wipe v = **clean**, polish, brush, rub, sponge; = **erase**, remove ▷ n = **rub**, brush

wish n = **desire**, want, hope, urge, intention ≠ **aversion** ▷ v = **want**, feel, choose, please, desire

wit n = **humour**, quips, banter, puns, repartee ≠ **seriousness**; = **humorist**, card (Inf), comedian, wag, joker; often plural = **cleverness**, sense, brains, wisdom, common sense ≠ **stupidity**

witch n = **enchantress**, magician, hag, crone, sorceress wicked woman **3** fascinating woman **witchcraft** n **witch doctor** in certain societies, man appearing to cure or cause injury, disease by magic

with prep **1** in company or possession of **2** against **3** in relation to **4** through **5** by means of **within** prep/adv in, inside

without prep **1** lacking **2** (Obs) outside

withdraw ① v -drawing, -drew, -drawn draw back or out **withdrawal** n **withdrawn** adj reserved, unsociable

wither ① v (cause to) wilt, dry up, decline **withering** adj (of glance etc.) scornful

withhold ① v -holding, -held **1** restrain **2** refrain from giving

withstand ① v -standing, -stood oppose, resist, esp. successfully

witness ① n **1** one who sees something **2** testimony **3** one who gives testimony ▷ v **4** give testimony **5** see **6** attest **7** sign

(document) as genuine

wizard ① n **1** sorcerer, magician **2** (Inf) virtuoso **wizardry** n

wizened adj shrivelled, wrinkled

wobble ① v **1** move unsteadily **2** sway ▷ n **3** unsteady movement **wobbly** adj

woe ① n grief **woebegone** adj looking sorrowful **woeful** adj **1** sorrowful **2** pitiful **3** wretched

wok n bowl-shaped Chinese cooking pan

wolf n, pl **wolves 1** wild predatory doglike animal ▷ v **2** eat ravenously

wolverine n carnivorous mammal inhabiting Arctic regions

woman ① n, pl **women 1** adult human female **2** women collectively **womanish** adj effeminate **womanize** v (of man) indulge in many casual affairs **womanly** adj of, proper to woman

womb n female organ in which young develop before birth

wombat n Aust. burrowing marsupial with heavy body, short

— THESAURUS —

withdraw v = **remove**, take off, pull out, extract, take away

wither v = **wilt**, decline, decay, disintegrate, perish ≠ **flourish**; = **waste**, decline, shrink

withhold v = **keep secret**, refuse, hide, reserve, retain ≠ **reveal**

withstand v = **resist**, suffer, bear, oppose, cope with ≠ **give into**

witness n = **observer**, viewer, spectator, looker-on, watcher ▷ v = **see**, view, watch, note, notice;

= **countersign**, sign, endorse, validate

wizard n = **magician**, witch, shaman, sorcerer, occultist

wobble v = **shake**, rock, sway, tremble, teeter; = **tremble**, shake ▷ n = **unsteadiness**, shake, tremble

woe n = **misery**, distress, grief, agony, gloom ≠ **happiness**

woman n = **lady**, girl, female, sheila (Aust & NZ Inf), vrou (S Afr) ≠ **man**

W

legs and dense fur

won past tense and past participle of WIN

wonder ❶ n 1 emotion excited by amazing or unusual thing 2 marvel, miracle ▷ v 3 be curious about 4 feel amazement **wonderful** adj 1 remarkable 2 very fine **wondrous** adj 1 inspiring wonder 2 strange

wont n 1 custom ▷ adj 2 accustomed

woo ❶ v court, seek to marry

wood ❶ n substance of trees, timber **firewood** tract of land with growing trees **wooded** adj having many trees **wooden** adj 1 made of wood 2 without expression **woody** adj **woodland** n woods, forest **woodpecker** n bird which searches tree trunks for insects **wood pigeon** large pigeon of Europe and Asia **woodwind** adj/n (of) wind instruments of orchestra **woodworm** n insect larva that bores into wood

woof n barking noise

wool ❶ n 1 soft hair of sheep, goat etc. 2 yarn spun from this **woollen** adj **woolly** adj 1 of wool 2 vague, muddled ▷ n 3 woollen garment

wop-wops pl n (NZ, Inf) remote rural areas

word ❶ n 1 smallest separate meaningful unit of speech or writing 2 term 3 message 4 brief remark 5 information 6 promise 7 command ▷ v 8 express in words, esp. in particular way **wordy** adj using too many words **word processor** keyboard, computer and VDU for electronic organization and storage of text

wore past tense of WEAR

work ❶ n 1 labour 2 employment 3 occupation 4 something made or accomplished 5 production of art or science ▷ pl 6 factory 7 total of person's deeds, writings etc. 8 mechanism of clock etc. ▷ v 9 (cause to)

wonder v = **think**, question, puzzle, speculate, query; = **be amazed**, stare, marvel, be astonished, gape ▷ n = **amazement**, surprise, admiration, awe, fascination; = **phenomenon**, sight, miracle, spectacle, curiosity

woo cultivate; = **court**, pursue

wood n = **timber**, planks, planking, lumber (US); **woods** = **woodland**, forest, grove, thicket, copse

wool n = **fleece**, hair, coat

word n = **term**, name, expression;

= **chat**, tête-à-tête, talk, discussion, consultation; = **comment**, remark, utterance; = **message**, news, report, information, notice; = **promise**, guarantee, pledge, vow, assurance; = **command**, order, decree, bidding, mandate ▷ v = **express**, say, state, put, phrase

work v = **be employed**, be in work; = **labour**, sweat, slave, toil, slog (away) ▷ = **relax**; = **function**, go, run, operate, be in working order ≠ **be out of order**; = **succeed**, operate **10** make, shape **11** apply effort **12** labour **13** be employed **14** turn out successfully **15** ferment **workable** adj **worker** n **workaholic** n person addicted to work **working class** social class consisting of wage earners, esp. manual **working-class** adj **workman** n **manual worker workmanship** n **1** skill of workman **2** way thing is finished **workshop** n place where things are made

world ❶ n **1** the universe **2** the planet earth **3** sphere of existence **4** mankind **5** any planet **6** society **worldly** adj **1** earthly **2** absorbed in pursuit of material gain

worm n **1** small limbless creeping snakelike creature **2** anything resembling worm in shape or movement ▷ pl **3** (disorder caused by) infestation of worms, esp. in intestines ▷ v **4** crawl **5** insinuate (oneself) **6** extract (secret) craftily **7** rid of worms

worn ❶ past participle of WEAR

worry ❶ v **-rying, -ried 1** be (unduly) concerned **2** trouble, pester, harass **3** (of dog) seize, shake with teeth ▷ n **4** (cause of) anxiety, concern **worried** adj

worse adj/adv comparative of BAD or BADLY **worsen** v make, grow worse **worst** adj/adv superlative of BAD or BADLY

worship ❶ v **-shipping, -shipped 1** show religious devotion to **2** adore **3** love and admire ▷ n **4** act of worshipping **worshipful** adj **worshipper** n

worsted n **1** woollen yarn ▷ adj **2** made of woollen cloth

worth ❶ adj **1** having or deserving to have value specified **2** meriting ▷ n **3** excellence **4** merit, value **5** usefulness **6** quantity to be had for given sum **worthless** adj **worthwhile** adj worth the time, effort etc. involved **worthy** adj

work out, pay off (Inf), be successful, be effective; = **handle**, move, excite, manipulate, rouse ▷ n = **employment**, business, job, trade, duty ≠ **play** ; = **effort**, industry, labour, sweat, toil ≠ **leisure** ; = **task**, jobs, projects, commissions, duties; = **handiwork**, doing, act, feat, deed

world n = **earth**, planet, globe; = **mankind**, man, everyone, the public, everybody; = **sphere**, area, field, environment, realm

worn adj = **ragged**, frayed, shabby, tattered, tatty

worry v = **be anxious**, be concerned, be worried, obsess, brood ≠ **be unconcerned** ; = **trouble**, upset, bother, disturb, annoy ≠ **soothe** ▷ n = **anxiety**, concern, fear, trouble, unease ≠ **peace of mind** ; = **problem**, care, trouble, bother, hassle (Inf)

worship v = **revere**, praise, honour, adore, glorify ≠ **dishonour** ; = **love**, adore, idolize, put on a pedestal ≠ **despise** ▷ n = **reverence**, praise, regard, respect, honour

worth n = **value**, price, rate, cost,

W

DICTIONARY

1 virtuous **2** meriting

would v expressing wish, intention, probability: past tense of WILL **would-be** adj wishing, pretending to be

wound¹ ◍ n **1** injury, hurt from cut, stab etc. ▷ v **2** inflict wound on, injure **3** pain

wound² past tense and past participle of WIND²

wove past tense of WEAVE **woven** past participle of WEAVE

wow interj exclamation of astonishment

wowser n (Aust & NZ, Sl)
1 puritanical person
2 teetotaller

wraith n apparition

wrangle ◍ v **1** quarrel (noisily) **2** dispute ▷ n **3** noisy quarrel **4** dispute

wrap ◍ v **wrapping, wrapped** **1** cover, esp. by putting something round **2** put round ▷ n **3** loose garment **wrapper** n covering **wrapping** n material used to wrap

wrath ◍ n anger

wreak v **1** inflict (vengeance) **2** cause

wreath n something twisted into ring form, esp. band of flowers etc. as memorial or tribute on grave etc. **wreathe** v **1** form into wreath **2** surround **3** wind round

wreck ◍ n **1** destruction of ship **2** wrecked ship **3** ruin ▷ v **4** cause wreck of **wreckage** n

wren n kind of small songbird

wrench ◍ v **1** twist **2** distort **3** seize forcibly **4** sprain ▷ n **5** violent twist **6** tool for twisting or screwing **7** spanner

wrest v **1** take by force **2** twist violently

wrestle ◍ v **1** fight (esp. as sport) by grappling and trying to throw down **2** strive (with) **3** struggle ▷ n **4** wrestling **wrestler** n **wrestling** n

wretch n **1** despicable person **2** miserable creature **wretched** adj **1** miserable, unhappy

---

THESAURUS

estimate ≠ **worthlessness**; = **merit**, value, quality, importance, excellence ≠ **unworthiness**

wound¹ n = **injury**, cut, hurt, trauma (Pathology), gash ▷ v = **injure**, cut, wing, hurt, pierce; = **offend**, hurt, annoy, sting, mortify

wrangle v = **argue**, fight, row, dispute, disagree ▷ n = **argument**, row, dispute, quarrel, squabble

wrap v = **cover**, enclose, shroud, swathe, encase ▷ n = **cloak**, cape, stole, mantle, shawl

wrath n = **anger**, rage, temper, fury, resentment ≠ **satisfaction**

wreck v = **destroy**, break, smash, ruin, devastate ▷ **build** ▷ n = **shipwreck**, hulk

wrench v = **twist**, force, pull, tear, rip; = **sprain**, strain, rick ▷ n = **twist**, pull, rip, tug, jerk; = **sprain**, strain, twist; = **blow**, shock, upheaval, pang; = **spanner**, adjustable spanner

wrestle v = **fight**, battle, struggle, combat, grapple

DICTIONARY

2 worthless
wriggle v **1** move with twisting action, squirm ▷ n **2** this action
wring v **wringing, wrung 1** twist **2** extort **3** squeeze out
wrinkle ❶ n **1** slight ridge or furrow on skin etc. ▷ v **2** make, become wrinkled **wrinkly** adj
wrist n joint between wrist and arm
writ ❶ n written command from law court or other authority
write ❶ v **writing, wrote, written 1** mark paper etc. with symbols or words **2** compose **3** send a letter **4** set down in words **5** communicate in writing **writer** n **1** one who writes **2** author

writing n **write-off** n (Inf) something damaged beyond repair
writhe v twist, squirm in or as in pain etc.
wrong ❶ adj **1** not right or good **2** not suitable **3** incorrect **4** mistaken **5** not functioning properly ▷ n **6** that which is wrong **7** harm ▷ v **8** do wrong to **9** think badly of without justification
wrongful adj **wrongly** adv
wrote past tense of WRITE
wrought adj (of metals) shaped by hammering or beating
wrung past tense and past participle of WRING
wry adj **wrier, wriest** turned to one side, contorted dryly humorous

THESAURUS

wrinkle n = **line**, fold, crease, furrow, crow's-foot ▷ v = **crease**, gather, fold, crumple, furrow ≠ **smooth**
writ n = **summons**, document, decree, indictment, court order
write v = **record**, scribble, inscribe, set down, jot down
wrong adj = **amiss**, faulty, unsatisfactory, not right, defective; = **incorrect**, mistaken, false,

inaccurate, untrue; = **inappropriate**, incorrect, unsuitable, unacceptable, undesirable ≠ **correct**; = **bad**, criminal, illegal, evil, unlawful ≠ **moral** ▷ adv = **incorrectly**, badly, wrongly, mistakenly, erroneously ≠ **correctly** ▷ n = **offence**, injury, crime, error, sin ≠ **good deed** ▷ v = **mistreat**, abuse, hurt, harm, cheat ≠ **treat well**

xenophobia *n* hatred, fear, of strangers or aliens

Xerox *n* **1** machine for copying printed material ▷ *v* **2** copy with Xerox

Xmas *n* short for CHRISTMAS

X-ray, x-ray *n* **1** stream of radiation capable of penetrating solid bodies ▷ *v* **2** photograph by X-rays

xylophone *n* musical instrument of wooden bars which sound when struck

y

ya *interj* (S Afr) yes

yacht *n* vessel propelled by sail or power

yak *n* ox of Central Asia

yakka *n* (Aust & NZ, Inf) work

yam *n* sweet potato

yank **❶** *v* **1** jerk, tug **2** pull quickly ▷ *n* **3** quick tug

yap *v* **yapping, yapped 1** bark (as small dog) **2** talk idly

yard¹ *n* unit of length, .915 metre
yardstick *n* standard of measurement or comparison

yard² *n* piece of enclosed ground, oft. adjoining building and used for some specific purpose

yarn **❶** *n* **1** spun thread **2** tale

yawn *v* **1** open mouth wide, esp. in sleepiness **2** gape ▷ *n* **3** act of yawning

ye *pron* (Obs) you

year *n* **1** time taken by one revolution of earth round sun, about 365 days **2** twelve months
yearling *n* animal one year old
yearly *adv* **1** every year, once a year ▷ *adj* **2** happening once a year

yearn **❶** *v* feel longing, desire

yeast *n* substance used as fermenting agent, esp. in raising bread

yebo *interj* (S Afr, Inf) yes

yell **❶** *v/n* **1** shout **2** scream

yellow *adj* **1** of the colour of lemons, gold etc. **2** cowardly ▷ *n* **3** this colour **yellow fever** acute infectious tropical disease

yelp *v/n* (produce) quick, shrill cry

yen **❶** *n* (Inf) longing, craving

yeoman *n, pl* **-men** (Hist) farmer cultivating his own land

yes *interj* expresses consent, agreement, or approval

yesterday *n, adv* **1** (on) day before today **2** (in) recent past

yet **❶** *adv* **1** now **2** still **3** besides **4** hitherto ▷ *conj* **5** but, at the

---

THESAURUS

---

yank *n* = **pull**, tug, jerk, snatch, hitch

yarn *n* = **thread**, fibre, cotton, wool; (Inf) = **story**, tale, anecdote, account, narrative

yearn *v* often with **for** = **long**, desire, hunger, ache, crave

yell *v* = **scream**, shout, cry out, howl, call out ≠ **whisper** ▷ *n* = **scream**, cry, shout, roar, howl

≠ **whisper**

yen *n* = **longing**, desire, craving, yearning, passion

yet *adv* = **so far**, until now, up to now, still, as yet; = **now**, right now, just now, so soon; = **still**, in addition, besides, to boot, into the bargain ▷ *conj* = **nevertheless**, still, however, for all that, notwithstanding

y

same time, nevertheless

yeti n apelike creature said to inhabit Himalayas

yew n **1** evergreen tree with dark leaves **2** its wood

yield ❶ v 1 give or return **2** produce **3** give up, surrender ▷ n **4** amount produced

yob, yobbo, yobbo ❶ n (Inf) bad-mannered aggressive youth

yodel v **-delling, -delled** warble in falsetto tone

yoga n Hindu system of certain physical and mental exercises

yogurt, yoghurt n thick, custard-like preparation of curdled milk

yoke n **1** wooden bar put across the necks of two animals to hold them together **2** various objects like a yoke in shape or use **3** fitted part of garment, esp. round neck, shoulders **4** bond or tie **5** domination ▷ v **6** put yoke on **7** couple, unite

yokel n (old-fashioned) country dweller

yolk n yellow central part of egg

Yorkshire pudding baked batter made from flour, milk and eggs

you pron **1** refers to person or persons addressed **2** refers to unspecified person or persons

young ❶ adj **1** not far advanced in growth, life or existence **2** not yet old ▷ n **3** offspring **youngster** n child

your adj of, belonging to you **yours** pron **yourself** pron emphatic or reflexive form of you

youth ❶ n **1** state or time of being young **2** young man **3** young people **youthful** adj

YT Yukon Territory

Yule n Christmas season

yuppie n young highly-paid professional person ▷ adj of, like yuppies

---

yield v = **bow**, submit, give in, surrender, succumb; = **relinquish**, resign, hand over, surrender, turn over ≠ **retain** ▷ n = **produce**, crop, harvest, output

yob, yobbo n = **thug**, hooligan, lout, hoon (Aust & NZ Sl), ruffian

young adj = **immature**, juvenile, youthful, little, green ≠ **old** ▷ pl n = **offspring**, babies, litter, family, issue ≠ **parents**

youth n = **immaturity**, adolescence, boyhood or girlhood, salad days ≠ **old age**; = **boy**, lad, youngster, kid (Inf), teenager ≠ **adult**

Z

zany *adj* **zanier, zaniest** comical, funny in unusual way

zap *v* **zapping, zapped** (*Sl*) attack, kill or destroy

zeal ❶ *n* **1** fervour **2** keenness, enthusiasm **zealot** *n* **1** fanatic **2** enthusiast **zealous** *adj*

zebra *n* striped Afr. animal like a horse

zenith *n* **1** point of the heavens directly above an observer **2** summit **3** climax

zephyr *n* soft, gentle breeze

zero ❶ *n, pl* **-ros, -roes 1** nothing **2** figure 0 **3** point on graduated instrument from which positive and negative quantities are reckoned **4** the lowest point

zest *n* **1** enjoyment **2** excitement, interest, flavour **3** peel of orange or lemon

zigzag *n* **1** line or course with sharp turns in alternating directions ▷ *v* **2** move along in zigzag course

zinc *n* bluish-white metallic element

zip, zipper ❶ *n* **1** fastener with two rows of teeth that are closed and opened by a sliding clip **2** short whizzing sound **3** (*Inf*) energy, vigour ▷ *v* **4** fasten with zip **5** move with zip

zither *n* flat stringed instrument

zodiac *n* imaginary belt of the heavens along which the sun, moon and chief planets appear to move

zombie, zombi *n* person appearing lifeless

zone ❶ *n* region with particular characteristics or use

zoo *n, pl* **zoos** place where live animals are kept for show

zoology *n* study of animals **zoological** *adj* **zoologist** *n*

zoom ❶ *v* move, rise very rapidly move with buzzing or humming sound

zucchini *n* the US and Canadian name for COURGETTE

THESAURUS

zeal *n* = **enthusiasm**, passion, zest, spirit, verve ≠ **apathy**

zero *n* = **nought**, nothing, nil; = **rock bottom**, the bottom, an all-time low, a nadir, as low as you can get

zip *n* (*Inf*) = **energy**, drive, vigour, verve, zest ≠ **lethargy**

zone *n* = **area**, region, section, sector, district

zoom *v* = **speed**, shoot, fly, rush, flash